LIKE DREAMERS

ALSO BY YOSSI KLEIN HALEVI

At the Entrance to the Garden of Eden: A Jew's Search for God with Christians and Muslims in the Holy Land

Memoirs of a Jewish Extremist: An American Story

THE OLD CITY OF JERUSALEM

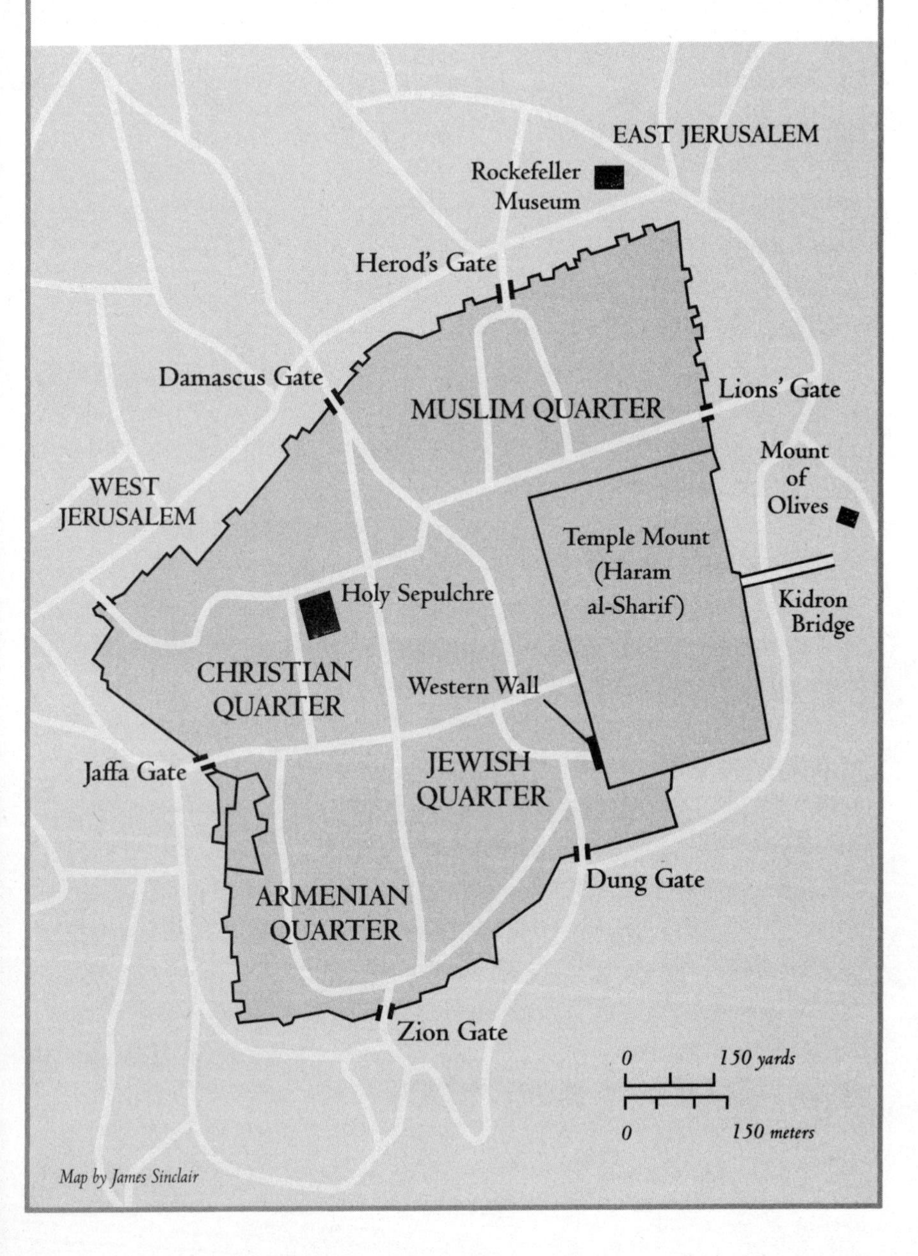
EAST JERUSALEM
Rockefeller Museum
Herod's Gate
Damascus Gate
MUSLIM QUARTER
Lions' Gate
Mount of Olives
WEST JERUSALEM
Temple Mount (Haram al-Sharif)
Holy Sepulchre
Kidron Bridge
CHRISTIAN QUARTER
Western Wall
Jaffa Gate
JEWISH QUARTER
Dung Gate
ARMENIAN QUARTER
Zion Gate
0
150 yards
0
150 meters
Map by James Sinclair

LIKE DREAMERS

THE STORY OF THE ISRAELI PARATROOPERS WHO REUNITED JERUSALEM AND DIVIDED A NATION

YOSSI KLEIN HALEVI

HARPER
www.harpercollins.com

HarperCollins books may be purchased for educational, business, or sales promotional use. For information, please e-mail the Special Markets Department at SPsales@harpercollins.com.

FIRST EDITION

Library of Congress Cataloging-in-Publication Data

Klein Halevi, Yossi.
Like dreamers : the story of the Israeli paratroopers who reunited Jerusalem and divided a nation / Yossi Klein Halevi.—First edition.
p. cm
Includes bibliographical references.
ISBN 978-0-06-054576-5
1. Israel. Tseva haganah le-Yisra'el. Hel-ha-tsanhanim—History—20th century. 2. Israel. Tseva haganah le-Yisra'el—Parachute troops—History—20th century. 3. Israel—Parachute troops—Biography. 4. Arab-Israeli conflict—1967–1973. 5. Arab-Israeli conflict—1973–1993. I. Title.
UD485.I8K54 2013
356'.16609569409045—dc23 2013018850

13 14 15 16 17 OV/RRD 10 9 8 7 6

For Moriah, Gavriel, and Shachar—

the next chapter is yours.

A SONG OF ASCENTS

When the Lord returned the exiles of Zion,
we were like dreamers.
Then our mouths filled with laughter,
And our tongues with songs of joy.
Then they said among the nations:
"The Lord has done great things for them."
The Lord has done great things for us.

—Psalm 126

We are writing the next chapter of the Bible.

—Hanan Porat, June 7, 1967

Sky-diving without a parachute,
Open to all directions,
And the longing for each direction
Is destroying me.

—Meir Ariel, "The Snake's Shed Skin," 1988

CONTENTS

PART THREE: ATONEMENT (1973–1982)

PART FOUR: MIDDLE AGE (1982–1992)

PART FIVE: END OF THE SIX-DAY WAR (1992–2004)

WHO'S WHO

THE KIBBUTZNIK PARATROOPERS

ARIK ACHMON Born on Kibbutz Givat Brenner and moved to Kibbutz Netzer Sereni after the split over Stalinism. Served as the 55th Brigade's chief intelligence officer in the Six-Day War and helped lead the crossing of the Suez Canal during the Yom Kippur War. Went on to help establish Israel's domestic aviation industry and shift the statist economy toward capitalism.

UDI ADIV Born on Kibbutz Gan Shmuel. In 1972 traveled to Damascus to help create an anti-Zionist terrorist underground. Served twelve years in an Israeli prison.

MEIR ARIEL The greatest Hebrew poet-singer of his generation. First came to public attention after the Six-Day War, with his song "Jerusalem of Iron." Member Kibbutz Mishmarot. Died in 1999.

AVITAL GEVA Born on Kibbutz Ein Shemer. Wounded in the battle for Jerusalem, went on to become a leading conceptual artist. In 1977 founded an educational greenhouse to teach young people ecological principles and kibbutz values. Represented the state of Israel in the 1993 Venice Biennale. Active in the antioccupation movement Peace Now.

THE RELIGIOUS ZIONIST PARATROOPERS

YOEL BIN-NUN A founder of the Gush Emunim (Bloc of the Faithful) settlement movement. Led a generation of religious Zionists to study the Bible as a way of understanding contemporary Israel. Broke with the settlement movement following the assassination of prime minister Yitzhak Rabin in 1995. A founder of the settlements of Alon Shvut and Ofra.

YISRAEL HAREL (FORMERLY HASENFRATZ) A child survivor of the Holocaust, and a leader in the Bnei Akiva religious Zionist youth movement. Founded the West Bank settlements' umbrella organization, the Yesha Council, and its magazine, *Nekudah*, and served for many years as settler spokesman. A veteran settler in Ofra.

HANAN PORAT Founder of the first West Bank settlement, Kfar Etzion. Wounded in the Yom Kippur War, then helped found Gush Emunim. First settler elected to the Israeli parliament. Died in 2011.

FAMILY MEMBERS

YEHUDIT ACHMON Psychologist, married to Arik Achmon. Grew up on Kibbutz Mishmar Ha'Emek. Daughter of Yaakov Hazan, leader of the socialist Zionist movement Hashomer Hatzair.

TOVA AND URI ADIV Udi's parents. Led campaign for his release from prison.

TIRZA ARIEL Businesswoman, married to Meir Ariel. Grew up on Kibbutz Kfar Szold, moved to Kibbutz Mishmarot after marrying Meir.

ESTHER BIN-NUN Dietitian, married to Yoel Bin-Nun. A member of the Ofra settlement before leaving with Yoel after the Rabin assassination.

ADA GEVA Bible teacher and high school principal, married to Avital Geva. Member of Kibbutz Ein Shemer. Daughter of Ein Shemer's fallen hero, Anatole Shtarkman.

KUBA GEVA Avital's father. Kibbutz Ein Shemer's architect.

SARAH HAREL Social worker, married to Yisrael Harel. Grew up in an ultra-Orthodox family. Member of the Ofra settlement. Died in 2006.

SYLVIA KLINGBERG Far-left Matzpen activist, Udi Adiv's first wife. Daughter of Soviet spy Marcus Klingberg.

LEAH LESHEM Led campaign to free Udi Adiv. Married Udi when he was released from prison.

OTHER PARATROOPERS

YISRAEL ARIEL (FORMERLY SHTIGLITZ) Rabbi of the Sinai settlement of Yamit, helped lead the struggle to prevent Israel's withdrawal from the Sinai Desert in 1982.

EMIL GRUENSWEIG Peace Now activist killed by a grenade in an attack on a demonstration against Ariel Sharon in 1983.

MOTTA GUR Commander of the 55th Brigade in the battle for Jerusalem, later chief of staff of the Israel Defense Forces (IDF). Died in 1995.

AMNON HARODI Member of Kibbutz Ein Shemer, killed in the battle for Jerusalem.

YOSEF "YOSKE BALAGAN" SCHWARTZ Arik Achmon's ex-brother-in-law and paratrooper jester.

MOSHE "MOISHELEH" STEMPEL-PELES Deputy commander of the 55th Brigade in June 1967. Killed in action in 1968.

OTHER RELIGIOUS ZIONISTS

YEHUDAH AMITAL Rabbi of the Mount Etzion yeshiva. A Holocaust survivor and leading opponent of religious extremism.

AVINOAM "ABU" AMICHAI A founder of Kfar Etzion; killed in the Yom Kippur War.

SANDY AMICHAI Kfar Etzion's first American; married Avinoam "Abu" Amichai.

YEHUDAH ETZION Student and study partner of Yoel Bin-Nun. Imprisoned for leading a plot to blow up the Dome of the Rock on the Temple Mount.

SHLOMO GOREN Longtime chief rabbi of the IDF. Became chief rabbi of Israel in 1973.

ABRAHAM ISAAC KOOK First chief rabbi of the pre-state Jewish community in the land of Israel. One of the great Jewish mystics and thinkers of the modern era. Died in 1935.

ZVI YEHUDAH KOOK Son of Rabbi Abraham Isaac Kook, rabbinic head of the Mercaz Harav yeshiva and spiritual father of the Gush Emunim settlement movement. Died in 1982.

MOSHE LEVINGER Founder of the Jewish community in the West Bank city of Hebron, and of the adjacent Jewish town, Kiryat Arba. Helped found the Gush Emunim settlement movement.

OTHERS

MOTTI ASHKENAZI Commanded the only Israeli outpost along the Suez Canal that didn't fall to the Egyptians during the Yom Kippur War. Initiated the protest movement that toppled the government of prime minister Golda Meir in 1974.

SHALOM HANOCH A founding father of Israeli rock music. Grew up on Kibbutz Mishmarot. Childhood friend of Meir Ariel.

URI ILAN Israeli soldier from Kibbutz Gan Shmuel who committed suicide in a Syrian prison.

ENZO SERENI Italian-born Zionist pioneer, a founder of Kibbutz Givat Brenner. Killed on a parachuting mission to Nazi-occupied Europe. Kibbutz Netzer Sereni is named in his memory.

DAOUD TURKI Arab Israeli leader of an anti-Israel terrorist underground. Charged with treason along with Udi Adiv and sentenced to seventeen years.

INTRODUCTION: JUNE 6, 1967

THE LONG LINES of silent young men moved single-file through the blacked-out streets, illumined only by flashes exploding in the approaching distance. Not even the outlines of houses were visible, as if the city of white stone had been reabsorbed by the hills. It was a cool June night in Jerusalem, but many of the men were sweating. Their uniforms were olive green or camouflage-patterned, US Army surplus more suitable for the jungles of Vietnam than for urban warfare. Most of the men were in their twenties, reservists abruptly extracted from university or from farms. For most this would be their first war. They were entering battle already exhausted: many had stayed awake through the night before, too anxious for sleep.

It was just past midnight, and the men of the 55th Paratroopers Reserve Brigade were heading toward no-man's-land, the swath of barbed wire and minefields and trenches dividing Jordanian-held East Jerusalem from Israeli-held West Jerusalem. That morning the Israeli air force had launched a preemptive strike against Egypt, whose leader, Gamal Abdel Nasser, had moved his army to the Israeli border, blockaded Israel's southern shipping route, and threatened the imminent destruction of the Jewish state. The Jordanian army had opened a second front in Jerusalem, shelling Jewish neighborhoods and hitting hundreds of apartments. Most residents were in shelters, all lights extinguished. Every so often a jeep or ambulance raced, without headlights, through the empty streets.

Lieutenant Avital Geva, twenty-six-year-old deputy commander of Company D, 28th Battalion, walked at the head of his men. He squinted into the darkness and saw nothing, not even shadows. Avital left the front of the line and walked alongside the men. "Spread out, guys," he urged quietly, "spread out."

Nearby, on a fourth-floor rooftop, Major Arik Achmon, chief intelligence officer of the 55th Brigade, was on the radio with the central front command near Tel Aviv, seeking information on the Jordanian troops barely a kilometer away. Headquarters didn't seem to know much more than he did. Until the night before, the brigade's battle plans had focused on a parachute jump into the Sinai Desert, and Arik had organized the necessary intelligence. But then, when the Jordanians began shelling Israel's capital, the men of the 55th were hastily dispatched onto requisitioned tourist buses and driven to Jerusalem.

A shell crashed into the facade of the building. Arik was covered with the dust of shattered bricks. "Helmets!" shouted Colonel Motta Gur, commander of the 55th Brigade. Arik checked himself: steady, as always.

The paratroopers filled the side streets that ended in no-man's-land. Sandbags were piled before little stone houses with corrugated roofs. Flares formed red-and-white arcs, exposing the paratroopers, flashes of silhouettes.

Pavement erupted.

"Medic!" Dozens lay bleeding. Avital Geva rushed through the darkness, shouting people's names.

A flash. Avital fell. "My face!" he screamed. "My face!" Someone laid him on a car, pointed a flashlight at his face. Covered with blood. Gasping, conscious, he was carried into a jeep, which sped through the exploding streets.

Corporal Yoel Bin-Nun, bearing on his back his unit's communications box, ran through the blacked-out streets. In civilian life he was a yeshiva student and knew these Orthodox streets; now, though, he was totally disoriented. He was trying to find the men of the 71st Battalion, who were scheduled to be the first of the brigade's three battalions to cross into no-man's-land. They would be followed by the men of Yoel's battalion, the 28th. And it was Yoel's assignment to follow the 71st to the crossing area, radio his battalion, and then point a flashlight, guiding his fellow soldiers into East Jerusalem. But where was the 71st?

02:15. Israeli sappers cut an opening in the first line of barbed wire. Bangalores—long metal tubes filled with explosives—were extended through the opening and detonated, creating a narrow scorched path in the minefield.

Yoel Bin-Nun found the crossing point. Crouching, he aimed his flashlight toward the men behind him and repeated, *"Pirtza pirtza pirtza"*—breach breach breach.

THE PARATROOPERS WHO reunited Jerusalem in 1967 and restored Jewish sovereignty to the Holy City fulfilled a dream of two millennia. They changed the history of Israel and of the Middle East. They also changed my life.

In late June 1967, a few weeks after the end of the Six-Day War, I flew to Israel with my father. I was a fourteen-year-old boy from Brooklyn, and my father, a Holocaust survivor, had decided that he couldn't keep away any longer.

Every evening, in the weeks leading up to the war, we would watch the news together. As Arab armies massed along Israel's borders, demonstrators in the streets of Cairo and Damascus chanted "Death to Israel." Yet the international community seemed indifferent. Even the United States, caught in an increasingly hopeless war in Vietnam, offered little more than sympathy. My father and I shared the same unspoken thought: again. Barely two decades after the Holocaust, the Jews were facing destruction again. Once again, we were alone.

And then, in six days, Israel reversed threat into unimagined victory. The Israeli army destroyed the Egyptian army and conquered the Sinai Desert, three times the size of the state of Israel, seized the Golan Heights from Syria, and routed the Jordanian army in the West Bank—the biblical Judea and Samaria, birthplace of the Jewish people. And the paratroopers reunited a divided Jerusalem.

A photograph taken of paratroopers at the Western Wall became the instant symbol of the war. In the photograph three young men stand, with the wall behind them, gazing into the distance. One holds his helmet in his hands. Their expressions are a combination of exhaustion, tenderness, and awe. At their moment of triumph they seem not like conquerors but like pilgrims at the end of a long journey.

The Israel I encountered that summer belonged to the paratroopers. The photograph of the three paratroopers at the wall was everywhere. The radio played a song sung by a paratrooper named Meir Ariel, about "Jerusalem of iron, of lead and of blackness," an attempt to remind a euphoric nation of the price of victory.

At the Wall I watched my father become a believing Jew. He had lost his faith in the Holocaust; but now, he said, he forgave God. The Protector of Israel had regained His will. It was possible for Jews to pray again.

I met my father's two brothers who had survived the Holocaust, along with distant relatives whose relationship to us was too complicated to follow, post-Holocaust approximations of family. That summer everyone in Israel felt like family. Cars would stop and offer lifts to hikers who weren't hitching. In a farming community on the shores of the Sea of Galilee, which had suffered for years under Syrian guns and whose children had grown up in air raid shelters, my father hugged and kissed a teenage girl walking by, and no one thought it untoward.

Israel celebrated its existence, life itself. We had done it: survived the twentieth century. Not merely survived but reversed annihilation into a kind of redemption, awakened from our worst nightmare into our most extravagant dream.

That summer Israel was possessed by messianic dreams of wholeness. There were those who believed that peace had finally come, and with it the end of the Jews' exile from humanity. (Perhaps only Jews could conceive of a normal national life in messianic terms.) There were those whose longing for wholeness was soothed by the reunification of the divided land and the divided city, which some saw as precursor of the imminence of the messianic era, ending the fragmentation of humanity itself.

For my father the dream of wholeness was fulfilled by Jewish unity. Perhaps not since the revelation at Mount Sinai—when the people of Israel were camped "as one body with one heart," as a famous rabbinic commentary put it—had the Jews been as united as we were in those terrible, exhilarating weeks of late spring 1967. The great weakness of the Jews, my father believed, was the temptation of schism, even in the face of catastrophe. But when we were united, he reassured me, no enemy could destroy us.

The ultimate expression of the Israeli dream of wholeness was the kibbutz, or agrarian commune. Several hundred were spread throughout the country, especially along the old borders. The kibbutz was an attempt to transcend human nature, replace selfishness with cooperation. Decisions were voted on by members, positions of authority rotated. Children were raised in communal homes away from parents and encouraged to run their own affairs. Many of Israel's political leaders, and many of its leading soldiers, had been kibbutzniks. The Jewish state was the first democratic country to have been founded in large part by egalitarian collectives, and whose key institutions—trade unions, health clinics, bus cooperatives, even the army—were created by radical socialists.

Though the secular kibbutzim had no use for religion, they claimed its messianic vision of restoring the Jews to the land and creating a just society, a light to the nations. The kibbutz was the symbol of Israel in the world, and that seemed natural. The very existence of a sovereign Jewish state after two thousand years of homelessness defied the natural order, and so did the kibbutz. One utopian dream symbolized the other.

That summer I resolved to return one day and become an Israeli. Perhaps I would move to a kibbutz. The great Jewish adventure was happening in my lifetime; how could I keep away?

IN THE SUMMER of 1982, at age twenty-nine, I moved to Israel as an immigrant. Israel had just invaded Lebanon, to end the threat of terrorist attacks on the Galilee (and, more grandiosely, to create a "new Middle East"). Instead of uniting Israelis, as it had in 1967, war now divided them. For the first time there were antigovernment demonstrations, even as soldiers were fighting at the front. The euphoria of the summer of '67, the delusion of a happy ending to Jewish history, had been replaced by an awareness of the agonizing complexity of Israel's dilemmas.

I was now a journalist, writing for American publications, including the New York City newspaper the *Village Voice*, and so I set about trying to understand my new home. Most urgently, that meant understanding Israel's schisms. On the streets people were shouting at each other about Lebanon. I covered the founding of West Bank settlements and followed the antisettlement movement Peace Now. I tried to listen to the conflicting certainties that divided those who saw the results of 1967 as blessing from those who saw them as curse. Israel was losing the feeling of family that had drawn me there in the first place. Much of my career became focused on explaining the unraveling of the Israeli consensus.

From time to time I thought about interviewing veterans of the battle of Jerusalem. In a sense they were responsible for bringing me to Israel. How had the war changed their lives? What role did they play in trying to influence the political outcome of their military victory?

Those questions were partly answered in a newspaper article I came across about a reunion of the paratroopers, which noted that some of the most prominent leaders of the settlement movement, as well as prominent activists in the peace movement, had emerged from the 55th Brigade. The men who as civilians were dividing Israel would meet every year on reserve duty, sharing tents and periodically going to war together. Did their ideological antipathies undermine their cohesion as soldiers? Or did their shared army experience temper the ferocity of their political differences? Perhaps someday, I thought, I'll write an article about them.

IN THE FALL of 2002, I began to seek them out. The Israeli-Palestinian peace process of the 1990s had collapsed, and suicide bombers were blowing up buses and cafés in my city, Jerusalem. The Israeli home front was now the battlefield. How, Israelis wondered, could it have come to this? Most Israelis believed that their country had tried to make peace, only to be rejected by the Palestinian leadership. Yet Israel was widely faulted around the world. Even many Israelis on the left were now wondering whether any amount of territorial concessions would gain Israel peace and legitimacy, whether the Jewish state would ever find its place in the Middle East and be accepted by the international community as a normal nation.

At that low point in Israel's history, I turned to the men who had brought Israel its most transcendent moment. In recounting their lives, I intended to tell the story of how we had gone from the hope of those days to the shattering now, and how we might reclaim something of the optimism on which Israel had been built.

By the time I encountered them in 2002, the veterans of the 55th Brigade were middle-aged and older, no longer part of the reserves. I learned that in the 1973 Yom Kippur War, they had led the nighttime crossing of the Suez Canal onto the Egyptian mainland that turned the war in Israel's favor, one of the most daring military initiatives in the country's history. (They called their veterans' group the Association of Paratroopers Who Liberated Jerusalem and Crossed the Canal.) The 55th, then, had been in those years the Israeli army's elite combat force. I decided to write a narrative history of the post-'67 left-right schism, as experienced by leading personalities who had been paratroopers.

Probing deeper, I discovered an even more compelling aspect to this story. In 1967 perhaps half the soldiers of the 55th Brigade, and up to 70 percent of its officers, had been kibbutzniks. There was a second, if much smaller and militarily marginal, group within the brigade: religious Zionists, Orthodox Jews who celebrated the secular Jewish state as a divine miracle. After the Six-Day War religious Zionists, many of them convinced that redemption was imminent, initiated the West Bank settlement movement. In response, kibbutzniks helped found the peace movement that opposed the settlements.

Secular kibbutzniks and religious Zionists disagreed about God and faith and the place of religion in Jewish identity and in the life of the state. Yet for all their differences, religious Zionism and the secular kibbutz movement agreed that the goal of Jewish statehood must be more than the mere creation of a safe refuge for the Jewish people. Both movements saw the Jewish return home as an event of such shattering force that something grand—world transformative—must result. The founders of the kibbutz movement in the early years of the twentieth century envisioned the future Jewish state as a laboratory for democratic egalitarianism. Many religious Zionists believed that the creation of a Jewish state would be the catalyst for the messianic era.

Here, then, was a much bigger story about Israel than merely its left-right divide. It was a story about the fate of Israel's utopian dreams, the vast hopes imposed on this besieged, embattled strip of land crowded with traumatized Jewish refugees.

The meeting between religious Zionists and secular kibbutzniks in the 55th Brigade occurred at the most mythic moment in Israel's history. The return to the Wall, to the Old City of Jerusalem and the biblical lands just beyond, brought Judaism to the center of Israeli identity, from which it had been largely marginalized by Israel's secular founders.

THIS IS NOT a book about the Israeli paratroopers, though that is a story well worth telling.

Instead, this book tells the story, through the lives of seven paratroopers, of Israel's competing utopian dreams—and how the Israel symbolized by the kibbutz became the Israel symbolized by the settlement.

Even though about half of Israel's Jewish population is of Middle Eastern origin, the main characters here are all Ashkenazim, of European Jewish descent. That is because the great ideological struggles that defined Israel in its formative years were fought primarily among the state's founders and their children, most of whom were Ashkenazim. Israeli elites, especially in politics and the military, have in recent years become more reflective of the country's Jewish diversity. But that was not the case for most of the decades covered by this book.

Among the religious Zionists portrayed here, one founded the first West Bank settlement, while another became the settlement movement's great heretic. Among the kibbutzniks, one helped found Peace Now and then abandoned the movement, convinced that peace with the Palestinians was impossible anytime soon.

These men not only helped define the political debate of post-'67 Israel but also its social and cultural transformations. Improbably, one former kibbutznik became a pioneer in the transition from a state-run economy to free-enterprise Israel. Another emerged as Israel's leading poet-singer, a bohemian symbol who then became an observant Jew.

Born and raised with the reborn Jewish state, they were the first sovereign Jews in two thousand years. Their lives were the fulfillment of Jewish longing to return to Zion. Their burden was to carry those expectations.

The paratrooper ethos demands initiative and responsibility, and as soldiers and as civilians, they internalized that code. To a large extent, Israel today lives in the partial fulfillment and partial failure of their contradictory dreams.

Often these seven men argued vehemently within me. At times I have agreed with each of them—and passionately disagreed with each of them. But even then—perhaps especially then—I remained moved by their courage, their faith in human initiative and contempt for self-pity, their dauntless quest for solutions to unbearable dilemmas that would intimidate others into paralysis. In the ten years I spent among the veterans of the 55th Brigade, I was often reminded why I decided, in the summer of 1967, to tie my future with theirs.

PART ONE

THE LIONS' GATE (MAY–JUNE 1967)

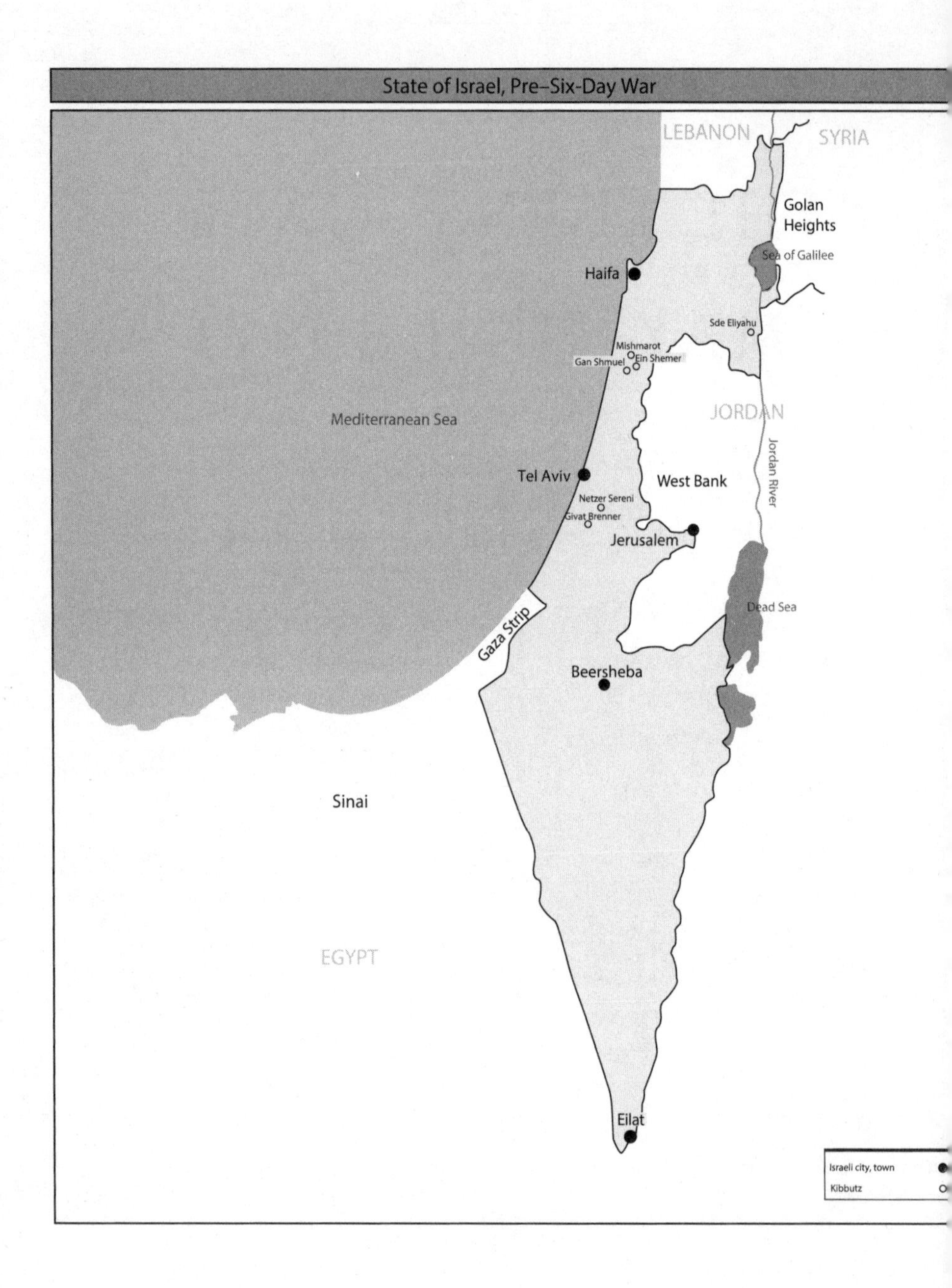
State of Israel, Pre–Six-Day War
LEBANON
SYRIA
Golan Heights
Sea of Galilee
Haifa
Sde Eliyahu
Mishmarot
Ein Shemer
Gan Shmuel
JORDAN
Mediterranean Sea
Jordan River
Tel Aviv
West Bank
Netzer Sereni
Givat Brenner
Jerusalem
Dead Sea
Gaza Strip
Beersheba
Sinai
EGYPT
Eilat
Israeli city, town
Kibbutz

CHAPTER 1

MAY DAY

THE SOCIALISM OF "THE GANG"

IN THE ORANGE orchards of Kibbutz Ein Shemer, Avital Geva, barefoot and shirtless in the early-morning sun, was frying eggs in a blackened pan. Turkish coffee was boiling in the aluminum pot, and his friends were laying out plates of tomatoes and cucumbers and olives, white cheese and jam. "*Ya Allah*, what a feast!" exclaimed Avital, as if encountering for the first time the food he had eaten for breakfast every day since childhood.

It was mid-May 1967. Avital and his crew had been working since dawn, to outwit the heat of the day. Rather than return to the communal dining room for breakfast, the young men allowed themselves the privilege of eating together beneath the corrugated roof they'd erected for just that purpose. Could there be greater joy, thought Avital, than working the fields with one's closest friends and sharing food grown by their kibbutz?

One could almost forget about the crisis on the Egyptian border.

Late spring was Avital's favorite time in the orchards. The air was heavy with trees in flower. The last of the Valencia oranges had just been harvested, and the first swellings appeared of what would be the autumn harvest. Meanwhile the orchards had to be prepared for the long, dry summer. Every morning the crew dragged two dozen irrigation pipes, each six meters long, from row to row. Though only twenty-six years old, Avital had been appointed head of the orchards, one of the kibbutz's main sources of income. Ein Shemer's orchards were among the country's most productive. Avital experimented with new machinery that would increase the harvest without entirely mechanizing the process, preserving a tactile encounter with the fruit. If you don't say good morning to the tree, he had learned from the old-timers, the tree won't say happy new year to you. Avital could spend an entire morning pruning a single tree, satisfying his artistic longings. "Michelangelo," his friends called him, and half meant it.

Work in the orchards, Avital insisted, should be fun. When the kibbutz's high school students were sent to help with the harvest, Avital dispatched tractors to retrieve them from their dormitories and gave them the wheel. Awaiting them in the orchards were bins of biscuits; during breaks, he made French fries, an extravagance in a kibbutz whose diet was determined by austere Polish cooks. He divided the young people into teams, and the one that filled the most bins won chocolate.

Avital's close-cropped hair exposed an expression at once tender and resolute. The lower lip protruded, and a sturdy chin rose to uphold it. His blue eyes seemed translucent.

"Hevreh?" he called out. "The eggs are ready!" Avital turned ordinary words into superlatives. And for Avital no word was more urgently joyful than *hevreh*—the gang—which he sang and elongated with new syllables. For Avital, *hevreh* was a kind of miracle, transforming separated beings into a single organism bound by common purpose, by love. The essence of kibbutz: a society of *hevreh*, in which no one was extraneous. Like poor Meir, heavy and sluggish, an Egyptian Jew lost among the Polish Jews of Ein Shemer, who'd been shunted from one part of the kibbutz workforce to the other until Avital insisted he join the *hevreh* in the orchards. And when they went on a bicycle trip up the steep hills to Nazareth, they brought Meir along, installing him like a peasant king on a couch mounted on a tractor-drawn wagon.

Banter around the breakfast table turned to the situation in the south. The crisis had begun a few days earlier, on Israel's Independence Day, when Egyptian president Nasser announced that he was dispatching troops toward the Egyptian-Israeli border. Then he ordered UN peacekeeping forces to quit the border, and incredibly, the UN complied. Now Egyptian troops and tanks were taking their place. Radio Cairo and Radio Damascus were broadcasting speeches by Arab leaders promising the imminent destruction of Israel.

"Why aren't they calling us up?" demanded Avital, a lieutenant in the 55th Brigade, the reservist unit of the elite paratroopers. How could he be sitting here while the country faced a threat to its life?

"Maybe there will be a diplomatic solution," someone suggested.

"Not with the Russians pushing the Arabs to war," someone else added. "When my two friends were killed by the Syrians, the Russian ambassador in the UN said that Israelis killed Israelis to blame the Syrians. That's when I finished with Mother Russia."

"Mother Russia," Avital repeated with contempt.

AS A CHILD, Avital had been confused about Marxism and the Soviet Union, and on Kibbutz Ein Shemer, that was a pedagogical problem. Ein Shemer belonged to the Marxist Zionist movement Hashomer Hatzair (the Young Watchman). Avital and his friends had been raised to revere the Soviet Union as the "second homeland," as movement leader Yaakov Hazan once put it. Beginning in second grade they were taught Marxist principles by rote. "An avant-garde alone cannot create a revolution!" they chanted. But what exactly was an avant-garde, wondered Avital, and what was its relationship to the children of Ein Shemer? The words seemed too big for him; he could hardly pronounce them. Other children seemed to readily grasp the difference between deceptive socialism and true communism; why couldn't he?

He was twelve years old in 1953 when Stalin died. Ein Shemer went into mourning. The annual satirical play performed on the spring holiday of Purim was canceled. The movement's newspaper, *Al Hamishmar* (On Vigilant Watch)—whose logo read, "For Zionism—For Socialism—For the Fraternity of Nations"—spread across the front page a heroic image of Stalin, his stern gaze focused on a distant vision. "The Progressive World Mourns the Death of J. V. Stalin," read the banner headline.

Of course Stalin's death saddened Avital, but however terrible to admit, it seemed abstract to him. What did he really have to do with this man with the big mustache and row of medals on his chest? At Ein Shemer's memorial, they played a recording of Stalin's speech marking the victory over Nazism, but it was in Russian, and Avital couldn't understand the words.

A few years later, when a new Soviet leader, Nikita Khrushchev, came to power and repudiated Stalinism, Hashomer Hatzair acknowledged that Stalin had made mistakes, even committed crimes. But lest we forget, insisted the ideological guides of the movement, it was not easy transforming a country of peasants into a communal society. The kibbutz and the Soviet Union were different aspects of the same historical march: the kibbutz an experiment in pure communism, the Soviet Union an experiment in mass communism. Both were necessary to prove the practicality of radical equality. And lest we forget: Stalin defeated Hitler, and the Red Army liberated Auschwitz. And in 1948 the Soviets had supported Jewish statehood and shipped Czech weapons to the IDF.

Avital was not indifferent to the Soviet romance: just as Europe had produced the ultimate evil, how right that it should produce the ultimate good. The weekly films screened on the kibbutz included Soviet-made features about the Red Army's struggle against Nazism. Though the Hebrew subtitles were often out of sync with the images, watching those films was thrilling. In one, a Soviet soldier threw himself against a German machine-gun post, allowing his comrades to conquer the position.

Sometimes Hazan—as everyone in the movement called Yaakov Hazan, revered leader of Hashomer Hatzair—would visit Avital's parents, old friends from Warsaw. Avital would eavesdrop on their conversation about the latest "important and fateful matter," as Hazan put it, before slipping away in boredom. Afterward, what he'd recall wasn't Hazan's analysis but the warmth with which Hazan and his parents interacted, without any sense of distance. Just like the two Ein Shemer comrades who happened to be members of the Knesset but who took their turn like everyone else serving in the dining room.

Avital loved Ein Shemer, with its modest members riding rusty bicycles in their work clothes and *kova tembel*, the brimless, floppy "fools' hat" whose very name was self-deprecating. Almost everything here had been planted or built by their own hands. Everyone was valued for who they were, not only for what they did.

For the founders of Ein Shemer, physical labor was an act of devotion, virtually a religious ritual. Working the land of Israel became a substitute faith for the Jewish tradition they abandoned; the socialist Zionist poet Avraham Shlonsky compared the roads being built by pioneers to straps of phylacteries, and the houses to its black boxes. The kibbutz transformed holidays from religious events into celebrations of the agricultural cycle, just as they were in ancient Israel, except without God. Yom Kippur, the holiest day of the Jewish year but which lacked agricultural symbolism, was just another workday on Ein Shemer.

SONG OF THE FOREST

WITH SEVERAL HUNDRED members and no industry, Ein Shemer, located near the coast between Tel Aviv and Haifa, wasn't one of the larger or more prosperous kibbutzim. But nothing here felt provincial to Avital. Big issues informed daily conversation. Ein Shemer's members included high-ranking officers, pilots, paratroopers. No kibbutz, they boasted here, produced more writers.

And none, thought Avital, was more beautiful. The entrance to Ein Shemer was lined on either side with ficus trees whose branches reached toward each other and formed a canopy. Nearby was the old courtyard, a remnant of the kibbutz's early years, a long stone house protected by a stone wall. No one lived there anymore, but it was preserved as a memory of Ein Shemer's heroic origins, when the kibbutz was condensed to a single building surrounded by parched fields, a place so forlorn the comrades joked that their clocks lagged behind real time but no one noticed. The kibbutz had since evolved into rows of red-roofed houses, some with verandas; tomato and cotton fields, orange orchards, cowshed and chicken coops. The smell of cow dung mingled with orange blossoms and fresh-cut hay. A contiguous lawn spread across the sloping terrain, linking the parents' area and the children's area in a single public space.

Ein Shemer's neighbors were Arab Israeli villages in the area known as the Triangle, and the Jordanian border was only a few kilometers away; but Avital grew up with a sense of safety. As soon as the last rains ended around Passover, the children went barefoot and didn't put on shoes again until the first rains of autumn. In winter they ate oranges and grapefruits off the trees; in summer they roasted fresh-picked corn on campfires. Work and play were interchangeable: the children would be placed atop a pen filled with just-picked cotton and jump up and down until it flattened, while a comrade played the accordion. They learned to cherish the hard beauty of the land of Israel, wildflowers growing in porous stone, meager forests of thin pines clinging to rocky slopes. One day, during school hours, a teacher rushed from class to class and summoned the children outside: an oriole had been spotted. Everyone quietly filed out and watched until the bird flew away.

AT AGE FOURTEEN, Avital was chosen by Hashomer Hatzair to become a counselor, leading a group of the kibbutz's eleven-year-olds. Other counselors told their scouts about the Rosenbergs, the accused atomic spies executed by the American government, but Avital felt incompetent to lead a political discussion.

Instead Avital emphasized the movement's other values, love of land and *hevreh*. He led his scouts on hikes, singing all the way. *"El hama'ayan!"* he called out: To the spring! "To the spring!" his scouts repeated. "Came a little lamb," Avital sang. "Came a little lamb," voices echoed. When one of the children wearied, Avital carried him on his back.

"Listen, *hevreh*," he told his twenty scouts one evening. "I'm going to set up camp in the forest, and you're going to have to find me." The forest was three kilometers away from the kibbutz. But how will we find you? the children protested. "There's a full moon," Avital said, smiling. "Just follow the music of the forest."

He went ahead and, when he came to a clearing, retrieved from his knapsack a cordless phonograph and a recording of Mendelssohn's *Fingal's Cave*. As the music played, he began a campfire. Soon the scouts appeared, drawn by the music and the fire.

AYN RAND IN EIN SHEMER

THERE WAS ONE threat to Avital's harmonious world: his father, Kuba, Ein Shemer's architect. Kuba had taught himself the basics of architecture and had planned almost every structure in Ein Shemer from its founding in 1927; later the kibbutz sent him for two years of formal study abroad. Even among the driven pioneers of Ein Shemer, Kuba was relentless. He crammed a drafting table into the tiny room he shared with his wife, Franka, and which was barely large enough to contain bed, table, and dresser. When Avital would visit from the young people's communal house, he would find Kuba bent over the latest plans.

Kuba longed to build grandly. But his opponents denounced his work as impractical, accused him of preferring aesthetics over need. He designed buildings that seemed to them whimsical, like the Bauhaus-style rounded balcony of the "pink house," so called because Kuba insisted on painting it pink. They ridiculed his experiments, like placing a kitchenette in the bathroom. When he designed the kibbutz movement's first two-story apartments, the comrades complained: Why had he put the bathroom on the first floor and the bedroom on the second? And why were the ceilings so low, and where were they supposed to put a broom?

Kuba fought back, turning the weekly kibbutz meetings into shouting matches. His favorite book was Ayn Rand's *The Fountainhead*. Kuba revered its main character, architect Howard Roark, who champions a classical vision against the crass tastes of society, which ultimately destroys him. Kuba insisted that Avital read the book too. "This is me," he said, referring to Roark. There was something astonishing in the passion of Kuba, committed Marxist, for Ayn Rand, ideologue of selfishness. But he shared with Rand an identification with the brilliant outsider, the radical individualist misunderstood by conformists.

Avital feared his father's artistic ego. To a kibbutznik, the word *I* sounded vaguely immoral. All that was great and worthy in Israel had been achieved by transmuting *I* into *we*. When Avital spoke of the work in the orchards, it wasn't about him as manager but about the team.

Kuba threatened to quit the kibbutz, and Avital worried that one day the comrades would oblige him by throwing him out.

Avital showed artistic talent and loved to paint. But he tried to compensate for Kuba's assault on the collective with commitment to its harmony. He offered his creativity to the commune, painting holiday stage sets and drawing sketches for Ein Shemer's mimeographed newsletter.

Most of all he tried to be a peacemaker. Kuba felt himself surrounded by enemies? Avital turned the kibbutz into one extended *hevreh*. The son of Kuba's worst enemy, Benek, who supervised Ein Shemer's building projects and resented the extravagant architect, was Rafi, whom Avital had "adopted" in kindergarten and protected against bullies. The two became best friends, and never spoke about their fathers.

AVITAL IN LOVE

TOWARD EVENING, the work in the cotton fields and orange orchards done, the men and women and young people of Ein Shemer walked in silent procession to the cemetery. It was late November 1958, cold and raining. Of course, thought Avital; it always rained on the anniversary of Anatole's death. The kibbutzniks, wearing US Army surplus coats and shapeless plastic raincoats, walked beneath the limp wet branches of the eucalyptus trees that shadowed the little cemetery. They passed the rows of flat white stones and came to a stone from which rose a modest pillar and on which was chiseled a single word, Anatole's Hebrew name, "Elimelech."

Though Avital had only been five years old at the time, he vividly recalled that terrible day in 1946, just before Hanukkah, when Anatole was killed. It began with a rumor. Word reached Ein Shemer that British soldiers were surrounding Kibbutz Givat Haim, searching for "illegal immigrants," as the British referred to Holocaust survivors trying to reach the land of Israel. Jews from around the area, including forty young men from Ein Shemer, rushed toward the besieged kibbutz.

In fact there were no survivors hiding there, and the British were instead searching for members of the Haganah Zionist militia who had destroyed a radar station monitoring the sea for refugee boats. An overwhelming British force—ten thousand soldiers, backed by tanks—seized the kibbutz.

Several hundred Jews began walking toward a line of British troops positioned near the gate. A British officer ordered them to stop. The unarmed Jews continued to move forward. The British raised their bayoneted rifles. "Onward, for the homeland!" someone called out. No one broke ranks. The soldiers opened fire. Eight Jews, including Anatole, fell.

The crowd gathered around Anatole's grave. He was Ein Shemer's martyr, the only member of the kibbutz to have died that day. Even now, twelve years later, the wound felt open. No one recited Kaddish, the traditional prayer for the dead: Ein Shemer had divorced the God of Israel. But there were passionate eulogies, religious in their invocation of sacrifice.

Avital was watching Ada, Anatole's daughter. She was standing beside her mother and older sister, revealing only an intense seriousness. Ada, with high cheekbones and slender eyes, was fourteen, and Avital, barely three years older, had decided she was the love of his life.

Avital had observed her qualities. Unusual in someone so young, she seemed indifferent to what others thought of her. She took care of the weaker children, just as Avital did. He noted how she would take responsibility without being asked, like washing the cups and the coffeepot after a campfire. He noted her modesty.

Avital didn't tell Ada that he intended one day to marry her. For all his exuberance, Avital was shy. He didn't join the other teenage boys in peeking into the girls' shower; his friends laughed at how he blushed when they told an off-color joke. But long before Avital dared approach, Ada had felt his luminous eyes on her. In the young people's dining room, in the forest on overnights, there was Avital, keeping his distance, watching. Peering into me, Ada thought. To her surprise, she didn't feel invaded but caressed. She wasn't interested in a boyfriend. *But he does have beautiful eyes—*

Avital's moment came in the orchards. During winter, Ein Shemer's young people worked for three hours after school, helping with the orange harvest. Avital, in charge of the teenagers, put Ada in his group. He taught her how to clip an orange, leaving a bit of stem for beauty, how to grasp the fruit even when one's hand seemed to freeze in the wind. When he saw that she was afraid to climb the ladder, he leaped up and held his hand out, and continued to hold her hand even after she ascended. *"Pitzit,"* he said tenderly; little one.

They met furtively, away from the prying collective. Their rendezvous point was a row of cypress trees that protected the orchards from the wind. Ada confided to Avital emotions she couldn't share with anyone else, her longing for the father whose absence defined her life. She had been barely two years old when he died. Who was this man who had disappeared into history and whom the collective could recall only through its own most cherished ideals?

"I saw them get off the truck," Avital said to her, recalling the day of Anatole's death. "Completely quiet, as if they were afraid to speak. You felt the silence for days afterward."

"I'm angry at him for leaving me. Why didn't he think of his children before making his heroic gesture?"

They were chaste. But that wasn't unusual. Despite titillating stories in the city about kibbutz life, Hashomer Hatzair discouraged sex between its scouts. A *shomer* (guardian or watchman) must be pure in thought, speech, and action, proclaimed the movement's "ten commandments," and Avital and Ada took those injunctions as seriously as religious Jews took the Ten Commandments. Aside from mixed showers until sixth grade—an experience Avital recalled with embarrassment—there was little intimate encounter between the sexes. The young kibbutzniks regarded each other more as siblings than as potential partners.

Sensing Ada's need for freedom, Avital was careful not to call her his girlfriend. He resolved to be patient.

"What would you think if I became a combat pilot?" he asked one evening as they strolled on the quiet road outside the kibbutz.

"That doesn't seem like a good idea to me," she said carefully. "I don't want more risks."

No more risks, that is, among those I love.

"So I'll go to the paratroopers," Avital offered.

"That makes me happy," Ada said.

THE SOLDIER'S SONG

THROUGH THE SUMMER of 1959, Avital, nearly eighteen, had prepared for imminent induction, running and climbing and leaping off the kibbutz's two-story buildings to simulate a parachute jump.

Avital was drafted into the paratroopers at the beginning of the rainy season. The IDF bus dropped the new recruits off several kilometers from the base. Carrying a kit bag weighted with helmet, ammunition clips, pouches, and canteens, they began running. They entered the base and continued running—and, it seemed to Avital, they didn't stop running for the next eighteen months. At night they collapsed in muddy boots and rain-soaked clothes for a few hours of fitful rest, often interrupted for moving camp or yet another jog up a hilltop, backpack filled with rocks. Some nights they got no sleep at all, continuing without rest through the next day's regimen of target practice and grenade throwing and wall scaling and shooting their way through abandoned buildings to simulate urban warfare. Half the recruits dropped out, but Avital persisted.

After basic training, they jumped. Often at night: the door opens to blackness, fierce wind. A soldier stands on either side of the opening to shove out the hesitant. Avital needs no prodding. He leaps, inhaled by the universe. Then the chute opens and the work begins. Check that the strings aren't tangled, shift the reserve chute from chest to armpit to avoid landing against it and breaking ribs. Approaching earth, release the sack containing gun and ammunition belt and let it drop. Then press legs together, bend knees slightly, and prepare to push back against the rising earth.

Friday evening, after a near-sleepless week of climbing and crawling and navigating in moonless nights, they sat around a campfire and sang. Songs extolling the fellowship of fighters and remembering the fallen, "the beautiful and pure young men."

Yet even here there was discord. For the first time in his life, Avital encountered hostility for his beloved Hashomer Hatzair. Its acronym, Shmutz, also happened to mean "filth" in Yiddish, and some of the soldiers delighted in that coincidence. Avital laughed when they threw rocks at his tent to rouse him in the morning and shouted, "Wake up, Communist!" *No problem,* hevreh, *I can take a joke—*

"You Shmutzniks care about saving the whole world," a friend said to him. "Why don't you worry about your own people?"

"We care about the Jewish people and the world," said Avital. *Where's the contradiction?*

Avital graduated officer training school with the rank of lieutenant and was given command of a course for squad commanders. He adopted the same methods of inspiration with his soldiers that he had applied as a youth movement counselor. When a soldier fell asleep during guard duty, Avital sent the offender not to jail but on leave. "Take a break," Avital said. "And when you understand what you've done, come back." For Avital, rank was merely a technical function: he befriended his soldiers and his superiors. Once, during a training exercise, his fellow junior officers were astonished to see a general hug him.

AVITAL AND ADA wrote each other regularly, sometimes every day. His soldiers joked about his fidelity: he refused to join them on forays into town to pick up girls—easy for the boys in red boots and berets. On leave, he assisted Ada, who was now a counselor in Hashomer Hatzair. Avital helped her scouts build a bridge across a small wadi. They found abandoned logs, and he taught the children how to bind them without resorting to nails—for Hashomer Hatzair, a violation of nature. Avital confided to Ada his vision of married life: "A home has to be a safe place. Without gossip, without bitterness. No mud, only pure water. Like a flowing stream."

Toward the end of Avital's service, the paratroopers prepared an air show for twelfth-graders from around the country, to entice them to volunteer for the corps. Ada's senior class was invited. Avital was excited that Ada would glimpse something of his life. In these last three years she had refused to ask him about the army, refused to be enchanted by his military persona. She loved the boy of the orchards, not the hero in training. But now, hoped Avital, the two most important parts of his life would converge.

The students assembled on a beach and watched paratroopers jumping from propeller planes. Avital was assigned to security on the beach.

Something was wrong: one of the parachutes wasn't opening. He's falling! people shouted. Ada turned away in shock. The soldier fell into the sea. The students were dispatched to their buses before the body was retrieved.

On his next leave home, Avital braced himself for Ada's reaction. Surely the incident had only intensified her fear of losing a loved one to the all-devouring needs of the nation. But Ada never mentioned it, and neither did Avital.

A COLLECTIVE WEDDING

AVITAL RETURNED TO Ein Shemer and was placed in charge of the orchards. The veterans knew he could be trusted with the future of the kibbutz, because he understood that without constant watering and pruning, this miracle conjured from the void would wither. They saw in Avital and his friends their own vindication. In a single generation—from Poland to Ein Shemer—the kibbutz had created young people who seemed to lack even a genetic memory of exile. The astonishing rapidity with which the rerootedness of the Jews had occurred was proof of its rightness, its harmony with the laws of the universe.

Avital loved the founders. They had come to the land of Israel as teenagers, without family; and when their communities were destroyed in Europe, they became an extended family of orphans. Here they reinvented themselves from children of the bourgeoisie into farmers and welders. One veteran taught himself farming from a Russian textbook, using a dictionary to explain the technical terms. Ada's stepfather, a self-trained agronomist, invented a new strain of apple. When the veterans went on a hike to the ancient desert fortress of Masada, Avital and Ada volunteered to join them, helping the old people up the steep slope, carrying packs and preparing meals.

They were, friends said, the ultimate couple. No emotional scenes, no raised voices. The opposite of an "agricultural couple," so estranged from each other you could drive a tractor between them.

IN THE WINTER of 1965, they married.

Avital and Ada would have preferred a civil marriage, but that wasn't an option in Israel. And so they endured a curt religious ceremony in the office of the "red rabbi," so called for specializing in weddings of kibbutzniks and not imposing stringent religious demands.

At night the entire kibbutz came out to celebrate—three marriages at once, to cut expenses. Ada wore a light blue dress and held flowers. Avital wore his best khakis. A band sang satirical songs about the kibbutz. The founders marveled at the bounty of chicken and cake and fruit. Ein Shemer's secretary general, the elected official charged with running the kibbutz, blessed the new couple with happiness and fertility, recalled Ada's martyred father, and noted the generous buffet. Who would have believed, she said, that we would ever achieve such abundance? "I believed it," called out Hazan, leader of Hashomer Hatzair, who'd been invited as a family friend. "I never doubted we would reach this day."

A kibbutznik took snapshots of the wedding couples, but when he tried to photograph Avital and Ada, Avital waved him away. Ada would have liked a photograph of the two of them alone, but she too was uncomfortable being the center of attention, even on her wedding night.

A CRISIS OF FAITH

KUBA'S FEUD WITH the kibbutz worsened.

"Why can't you compromise, Kuba?" Avital demanded of his father. "Why is everything a struggle?"

"You too?" shouted Kuba.

"You fight over every project as if it's house-to-house combat."

"You're a coward," Kuba taunted. "You're afraid to stand up to them."

"This is Ein Shemer," said Avital. "We're not in Stalingrad."

IN 1967, EIN SHEMER turned forty. There was much to celebrate. Nearly six hundred people lived on the kibbutz. Every apartment now had its own separate bathroom. While members continued to eat together in the dining room, they could buy modest supplies in the kibbutz's new grocery, housed in a former stable. Even the communal kitchen, thanks to cooking classes sponsored by the movement, was improving. A seltzer dispenser was installed in the dining room, and for the founders, who had hauled water from a distant well in the early years, there was no greater luxury than cold seltzer on tap.

But the young people were beginning to question the egalitarian premises of the kibbutz. Why should a lazy member get the same salary as a devoted worker? Why should the collective decide a young person's professional future? And just how special was the kibbutz? Clearly it hadn't created a new man: kibbutzniks could be as petty and envious as people anywhere. And even if the kibbutz really was the most evolved human community, was communal life suitable for everyone?

Avital's lack of interest in Marxist ideology, which he had once regarded as a flaw, had become the norm among Ein Shemer's youth. Still, he felt that his friends were going too far in their disaffection. No, Ein Shemer hadn't created the perfect society. But had any group of human beings ever come closer?

THE SHOWDOWN BETWEEN the generations happened on May Day 1967. For years, Ein Shemer's veterans had bemoaned the decline of ideological fervor among their children. The forms of May Day observance remained—the roll call of comrades, the gymnastic displays like forming a human pyramid, the festive meal featuring borscht. But the passion was gone.

For Ein Shemer's founders, the day celebrating the workers of the world was sacred, joining their loyalties to the Zionist revolution and to the Communist revolution. May Day transformed them from a footnote to a harbinger: they weren't merely a private experiment in altruism in a tiny country in the Middle East fighting for survival but a model that would no doubt be adopted one day, in one form or another, throughout the world.

In the weeks leading up to the May Day march in Tel Aviv, the Ein Shemer newsletter tried to rouse the comrades with guilt: "Once people were ready to sacrifice for the ideal, and all that's being asked of us today is to board a bus and march for two or three kilometers like on a hike, and suddenly that's too difficult."

The newsletter published an informal poll about attitudes toward the march among Ein Shemer's young people. The responses among "tomorrow's political fighters," as the newsletter called them, were not encouraging. Ada was acerbic: "I'm not a monkey on display in a zoo. There at least they feed him peanuts, but [on the march] you don't even get that much." Avital, blunt but conciliatory, said, "My attitude toward the demonstration is negative. [But] I'll go out of a sense of obligation."

Barely two dozen comrades from Ein Shemer attended the march. But a worse blow came at the May Day symposium held in the kibbutz dining room. Amnon Harodi, one of Avital's closest friends and a fellow paratrooper reservist from the 55th, declared that Hashomer Hatzair should end its infatuation with the Soviet Union. The red flag meant nothing to him: "It's their flag, not mine."

The response came in the following week's newsletter. How was it possible, wrote one veteran, for comrades to feel no connection to the working class? "Comrades should know what the fate of the kibbutz movement will be if the government falls to the right."

TWO WEEKS AFTER MAY DAY, Nasser began moving troops and Soviet-supplied tanks toward the border. Nasser's threats to destroy Israel, encouraged by the Kremlin, ended the debate over the Soviet Union in Ein Shemer. The young people openly cursed the Second Homeland, and the old-timers were silent.

Messengers appeared, calling up reservist pilots and tankists. One by one, Avital's friends in the orchards were disappearing. But the dozen reservists of the 55th Brigade who lived in Ein Shemer had not yet been drafted. The commander of Avital's unit, Company D, happened to be a fellow Ein Shemer member, Haggai Erlichman. "Any word?" Avital asked him. "Don't worry," Haggai replied dryly, "if they need us they'll know how to find us."

On May 22 Nasser shut the Straits of Tiran, Israel's southern shipping route to the east. That same night, a messenger from the 55th Brigade arrived at Ein Shemer.

"I know you, Avital," said Ada, helping him pack. "If someone needs help, you'll do everything you can. All I ask is that you don't throw your life away on a heroic gesture. Or at least not a heroic gesture that has no chance of succeeding."

"I'll do my best," Avital promised.

CHAPTER 2

THE CENTER

THE TORAH OF REDEMPTION

WHEN YOEL BIN-NUN was twelve years old, he confided to a girl his deepest longing. "I want the Temple to be rebuilt," he said. The year was 1958, and they were walking home from a meeting of Bnei Akiva, the religious Zionist youth movement. "With animal sacrifices and blood and all of that?" she asked, incredulous. "That's what is written in the Torah," he replied.

Yoel, named for a grandfather killed in the Holocaust, sensed that his life's purpose was linked to understanding the mystery of Israel's resurrection. What was the meaning of the juxtaposition of destruction and rebirth, either of which would have been sufficient to define Jewish history for centuries to come? And what role was he, a part of the first generation of sovereign Jews since the destruction of the Temple, meant to play in his people's destiny?

Yoel offered his passion to Bnei Akiva, the Children of Akiva, named for the rabbi martyred by the Romans and whose emblem was the Ten Commandments, a sickle, and a sheaf of wheat—religious and socialist. The symbol of a Bnei Akiva boy was the knitted *kippah*, or skullcap. Unlike the traditional black skullcap, the knitted *kippah* wove two colors together, a relative vivacity.

Wearing a *kippah* on the streets of Haifa, where Yoel grew up, was not self-evident for a religious boy. "Red Haifa" was Israel's most secular city. City hall fought the creation of religious schools and buses ran on the Sabbath; it was the only city with a Jewish majority to officially desecrate the holy day. Most Bnei Akiva boys wore berets in public—an ineffective disguise, since only religious boys wore them. Secular children taunted them with a nonsense rhyme, *"Aduk fistuk"*—pious pistachios.

But Yoel and his friends insisted on wearing *kippot* in the streets.

Surprisingly, they were not harassed. If you respect yourself, Yoel discovered, others would respect you too.

Still, young religious Zionists suffered from an inferiority complex. Israel's pioneers and military heroes were almost all secular. The secular youth movements dismissed Bnei Akivaniks as Zionism's rear guard, more suited to becoming accountants than farmers and fighters. As members of the Haifa Bnei Akiva branch hiked up to the desert fortress of Masada, they were taunted by secular youth: "When Bnei Akiva go up Masada, they say Shema Yisrael"—the prayer recited by religious Jews at the moment of death. Even worse than being wimps, religious Zionists were a threat: their political leaders forced government coalitions to adopt religious laws, like ensuring rabbinic control over marriage and divorce.

And yet ultra-Orthodox Jews resented religious Zionists for validating heretical Zionism. In ninth grade, Yoel's Talmud teacher, an ultra-Orthodox rabbi named Moshe Rebhun, told his students he wouldn't be celebrating Independence Day. Zionism, he explained, had inverted the meaning of return to Zion, which was supposed to bring the Jewish people closer to God. Instead, the secular Zionists had uprooted Torah from the people. "You Zionists should ask yourselves why the holiest parts of Jerusalem aren't under the control of the Zionist state," taunted Rabbi Rebhun. "We have to go up to Mount Zion just to get a glimpse of the Temple Mount. And why? Because the Zionists don't deserve it." The Torah, he concluded triumphantly, was given in the Sinai Desert, outside the land of Israel, to teach Jews that the law was more important than the land.

Yoel entertained his friends by mimicking the rabbi's German-accented Hebrew: "Why was the *Taurah* given in Sinai?" But Rabbi Rebhun's challenge weighed on him.

AT BNEI AKIVA meetings they were debating whether to separate the sexes during folk dancing. Bnei Akiva hardly encouraged promiscuity: when members went on overnight hikes, they strung blankets across trees between the boys' and girls' areas. But "mixed dancing" was a Bnei Akiva tradition, a link with secular Zionist youth movements. Proponents warned that a total separation of the sexes would shift Bnei Akiva closer to ultra-Orthodoxy.

Yoel sided with the opponents. Just as we are scrupulous about kosher food, he argued, we should be scrupulous about the laws of sexual modesty.

Yoel's friends gave him a nickname, at once mocking and respectful of his longing for purity: Tasbin. It was the name of a laundry detergent.

YOEL MIGHT HAVE become even more deeply drawn to religious stringencies were it not for his parents. His mother, Shoshana, was studying the ancient Hittites while raising four children. His father, Yechiel, was founder and principal of a religious girls' high school and teachers' seminary, an innovator in bringing advanced religious education to women.

Tough and resourceful, Shoshana had immigrated to the land of Israel in 1938, but then volunteered to return to Nazi Germany and lead a group of Bnei Akiva girls across the border. On the train, a suspicious Nazi officer pointed a gun at one of the girls; Shoshana, blond and able to pass as Aryan, indignantly exclaimed, "Is that the German education you received?" The confused officer let them go. Shoshana and her girls arrived in the Port of Haifa two days before the start of World War II.

Yechiel had come, destitute, to the land of Israel, and intended to send for his parents and sister once he settled in; but the war intervened, and it was too late. A pedant about the Hebrew language, he would glare at an unlucky student who happened to make a mistake in diction and force her to repeat the sentence until she corrected herself. That insistence on Hebraic precision was, for Yechiel, a spiritual mission. Language, he lectured his students, was the most sacred value, the mother of all values. And how much more so the Hebrew language, in which God and men had once conversed and which the exiled Jews had preserved in a cordon of study and prayer.

Yechiel constantly corrected Yoel's Hebrew, and even that of his friends; he refused to return the cap of a boy visiting the Bin-Nun home until he corrected a grammatical mistake.

Yoel wanted to be a hero like his mother, a rescuer of Israel; but also an educator like his father, a refiner of his people. Yoel too began correcting the linguistic mistakes of his friends, but quietly, almost to himself.

IT WAS IN his parents' home that Yoel discovered Rabbi Abraham Isaac Kook—one of the great Jewish mystics, the first Ashkenazi chief rabbi of pre-state Israel. An Orthodox weekly to which the Bin-Nuns subscribed was serializing a biography of Rabbi Kook, called *The Man against the Stream.* As soon as the newspaper arrived on Friday, Yoel would turn to the latest installment, captivated by Rabbi Kook's personality. Ultra-Orthodox in his observance, he anguished about the Holy Land being built by secularists. Yet he celebrated Zionism as a harbinger of the messianic era and once danced with secular pioneers for hours, exchanging his black clothes for pioneering khaki.

Rabbi Kook, Yoel read, insisted on defining his own way. He was denounced in street posters as a heretic; ultra-Orthodox Jews snatched a body at a funeral to prevent him from delivering the eulogy.

In his mother's library, Yoel found a booklet with excerpts of Rabbi Kook's writings. She had considered the booklet precious enough to include among the few belongings she took on her flight out of Nazi Germany. Yoel read Rabbi Kook the way other young people read poetry, sensing himself expanding into language he didn't yet fully understand.

Rabbi Kook was offering not just a more mystical version of religious Zionism but a unique philosophy. All of existence, he wrote, was in a state of divine becoming, and the enemy of the good was constriction, smallness, *exile*—of the Jews from the land of Israel, of humanity from God. He strained against the limits of conventional religion: false piety and conformism impeded human growth and freedom, diminished God's grandeur. He so celebrated progress as the deepest expression of divinity that he saw the Creator Himself as "evolving" toward ever greater states of perfection, through the moral and intellectual progression of His creatures. And he embraced Darwinian evolution as the closest scientific analogue to the kabbalistic worldview. By enhancing the human, we enhance the divine. Asked to sum up his teaching, he replied, "Everything is rising."

For Rabbi Kook, Zionism was far more than a political movement, an attempt to provide mere safe haven for a persecuted people. The Jews had been chosen as catalysts of human evolution; but only by ending the exile would their spiritual genius be freed, and world redemption begin.

Encountering Rabbi Kook, Yoel felt exhilaration but above all relief. Here at last was a rabbi who fearlessly confronted the spiritual meaning of this time. And in his embrace of paradox—Darwinian and pietist, Zionist and ultra-Orthodox, universalist and Jewish particularist—he offered Yoel a model for embracing his own conflicting longings between religious stringency and openness to the world.

YOEL GRADUATED FROM high school in 1963 at age seventeen, skipping a grade. With a year to go before the army, he decided to study in the Jerusalem yeshiva founded by Rabbi Kook and which now bore his name: Mercaz Harav, known to its students simply as Mercaz—the Center. And that is how they perceived its role: as the spiritual center of the Jewish people, and so of the world.

Yet even within the religious Zionist community—which numbered about 10 percent of Israeli society—Mercaz and its messianic theology were hardly central. The elder Rabbi Kook's memory was revered, but few religious Zionists were actively awaiting the Messiah's arrival. They dutifully recited the religious Zionist prayer asking God to bless the state of Israel as "the first flowering of our redemption," but they were hardly preoccupied with the redemption process. For most religious Zionists, the creation of a refuge for the Jewish people was redemption enough.

Yoel's parents wanted him to become an academic. But after encountering Rabbi Kook, academia seemed small. Instead, Yoel would become a rabbi, a teacher. What could be more vital than helping Jews understand the spiritual significance of this time, when their wildest fears and dreams had been fulfilled?

In the fall of 1963, just before Rosh Hashanah, Yoel left his parents' home and went off to Mercaz, in search of the Torah of redemption.

THE STUBBORN DISCIPLE

THE MERCAZ HARAV yeshiva was located in an alley near Jaffa Road, West Jerusalem's main street, a stone building with arched windows and high-ceilinged halls. The entrance was a crenellated stone gate that recalled the wall around Jerusalem's Old City—barely a ten-minute walk from the yeshiva but inaccessible, blocked by barbed wire and Jordanian soldiers. The building had been the home of Rabbi Kook, and its meager furnishings reflected his modesty. In the rabbi's den, his desk was preserved exactly as he had left it, with fraying volumes of Talmud open to the pages he had last studied. The kitchen was a drop-in center for Jerusalem's beggars.

Yoel spent his days in the combined study hall and synagogue. Two rows of dark brown pews faced a Torah ark, beside which a sign urged students, "Know before Whom you stand." A marble plaque commemorating a donor ended with the prayer for rebuilding the Temple, "on the holy mountain in Jerusalem, in our day."

Walking into the study hall where Rabbi Kook had taught, Yoel felt haunted by holiness. Students were encouraged to devise their own curriculum, and Yoel decided to focus on Talmud and on Rabbi Kook's writings. That combination would provide him with the grounding in Jewish law necessary to become a rabbi, and with the vision to transcend the conventional rabbinate. Often he found himself in the study hall until late at night, oblivious to time, lost in the talmudic past and Rabbi Kook's messianic future. His two chosen areas of study struggled within him. It was like trying to define reality simultaneously through a microscope and a telescope. The talmudic sensibility cautioned patience, its leisurely arguments unfolding through the centuries: If you are planting a tree and you hear that the Messiah has come, said the rabbis, continue planting. But the Kookian sensibility was restless with anticipation, straining against limits. If this wasn't the time, then when would it ever be?

The focus of holiness in Mercaz, the living embodiment of Rabbi Kook's teachings, was his son, Rabbi Zvi Yehudah Kook. His deeply lined face was at once kindly and fierce, committed to protecting what he loved. Rabbi Zvi Yehudah didn't allow students to call him Rabbi Kook. That title, he said, belonged to his father alone. I am a fellow student of the rabbi, he insisted. Though he met with students in his father's study, he sat not in the armchair but on a footstool.

Rabbi Zvi Yehudah, as disciples called him with an intimate reverence, seemed typically ultra-Orthodox—wide-brimmed black fedora, long white beard, long black jacket. But this appearance was deceptive. Rabbi Zvi Yehudah's soul despised the quietism of the ghetto, longed for the God of split waters and revelation.

Childless, he regarded his students as surrogate sons. He personally delivered the mail to them every morning, savoring the chance to bring them joy. They were his sabras, his native Israelis; some of them had already served in the holy army of Israel, warrior-scholars combining physical and religious vigor. One day, the rabbi believed, his students would help lead Israel back to holiness, to wholeness.

Like his father, Rabbi Zvi Yehudah was convinced of the divine impetus behind Zionism. How could the Jewish state possibly be a mere political entity devoid of spiritual significance? Was the fulfillment of the ancient prophecy of return to Zion—under apocalyptic circumstances no sane person would have believed possible—intended to merely create another Belgium?

This state was not just a miracle: it was, in its essence, sacred. Flag, government, army: holy holy holy. The Jewish state was the instrument for the restoration of Israel's glory, and so of God's glory. The Mercaz sensibility was summed up by the prayer that students sang on Friday evening with particular devotion: "Arise, shake off the dust / wear your glorious garments, my people . . . Rouse yourself, rouse yourself, for your light has come."

Rabbi Zvi Yehudah practiced his father's unconditional love for all Jews, especially the secular, who had a key role to play in the messianic process. Judaism and religion generally, Rabbi Kook the elder had taught, had become corrupted by small-minded religionists; and so, however painful, a rebellion was necessary to purify the faith. The return to Zion had to be led by the secular because religious Jews lacked the spiritual vitality to implement Judaism's great dream. The Kookian dialectic: the spiritual failure of the religious provoked the rebellion of the secular who, however inadvertently, were preparing the way for the next, higher stage of religious evolution by restoring the holy people to the holy land.

Rabbi Zvi Yehudah, keenly aware of their redemptive role, treated secularists not only with the love due to fellow Jews but with respect. He insisted that secular men visiting his home feel comfortable and remove the head covering they wore in his honor. He rebuked one visiting kibbutznik: Do you expect me to remove my *kippah* if I visit your kibbutz? Leaders of the League against Religious Coercion, who campaigned for separation of religion and state, sought him out, intrigued by the rabbi who respected their longing for freedom—even for freedom from religion—as a sign of spiritual vitality.

Rabbi Zvi Yehudah especially loved the kibbutzniks. When a secular kibbutznik appeared at Mercaz, seeking to study Talmud, the rabbi treated him with the honor reserved in other yeshivas for a scholar; students vied for the privilege of being his study partner. Beneath their pork-eating, Yom Kippur–violating veneer, Rabbi Zvi Yehudah discerned in kibbutzniks holy Jews. They were working the land of Israel, defending the people of Israel. The kibbutz's very utopianism negated its professed commitment to "normalizing" the Jewish people. What other nation had been founded by voluntary communes seeking to purify human nature of selfishness? The kibbutz confirmed Mercaz's essential insight on secular Zionism: that the return to Zion was a utopian venture, masquerading as a mundane political movement.

To support his radical Jewish ecumenism, Rabbi Zvi Yehudah cited the rabbinic comparison of the Jewish people to the "four species," four plants that Jews bless on Sukkoth, the harvest-time Festival of Booths. Each of those four plants—citron, palm branch, myrtle, willow—is said to represent another kind of Jew: on one end of the spectrum the citron's pleasing scent and taste represents the saint, whose inner life and deeds are equally pure; on the other end, the willow, without odor and inedible, represents the Jew bereft of redeeming qualities. But the blessing can only be recited if all four plants are bound together, the willow along with the citron. So too the Jewish people, said the rabbi, each of whose components has a unique role in redemption.

Rabbi Zvi Yehudah could perhaps afford such magnanimity because he was, like his father, convinced that secular Zionism was a temporary aberration. Secularism was necessary to revitalize the nation after centuries of disembodied exile, but eventually it must yield to the longings of the Jewish soul for God. Rabbi Kook the father had compared secular pioneers to the workmen who built the ancient Temple: during the period of construction, they were permitted to enter the Holy of Holies at will; once the Temple was completed, though, only the high priest could enter that consecrated space, and then only on Yom Kippur. Secular Zionism was preparing the way for the rebuilt Temple, and for its own disappearance.

UNLIKE THE OTHER students, who gathered around Rabbi Zvi Yehudah after morning prayers on their way to breakfast, Yoel observed him from a distance. How far should he go in entrusting himself to the rabbi's guidance? Was he really a worthy successor to his father?

Yoel was skeptical about the rabbi's uncritical embrace of every Jew, no matter how far removed from the faith. Yes, Rabbi Zvi Yehudah's father loved all Jews, but he'd also anguished over their religious violations. Yet Rabbi Zvi Yehudah seemed far more upset by the anti-Zionism of the ultra-Orthodox than by the heresies of the secular.

Yoel attended a weekly class on the Torah reading in Rabbi Zvi Yehudah's apartment, which was so modest it lacked a telephone. Yoel was troubled to see, hanging on the wall of the rabbi's study, a photograph of Theodor Herzl, founder of political Zionism, beside photographs of venerable rabbis. It was one thing to appreciate Herzl's contribution to Jewish national renewal, but to venerate him as a holy man?

"K'vod harav"—honored rabbi—Yoel said after class, "I don't understand what Herzl's picture is doing there."

Rabbi Zvi Yehudah appeared bemused. He appreciated his clever student who challenged him in class and whom he affectionately called *ha'akshan*, the stubborn one.

"Herzl was God's emissary to save the Jewish people," the rabbi replied.

But why, persisted Yoel, did God allow antireligious leaders to preside over the Jewish state? Why had God allowed the central religious vision of the Jews, the return to Zion, to be co-opted by those who rejected religion?

The rabbi responded with a question. "Is Ben-Gurion as evil as Ahab?" he asked, referring to the idolatrous king of ancient Israel.

"No, Ben-Gurion is not as evil as Ahab," replied Yoel.

"Elijah ran before Ahab's chariot," the rabbi concluded.

The prophet Elijah had honored Ahab because he was king of Israel, representative, however flawed, of God's will on earth. Surely, then, Rabbi Zvi Yehudah could honor Herzl, who had initiated the restoration of Jewish sovereignty.

Yoel wasn't convinced. How could Rabbi Zvi Yehudah gloss over the secular assault on religion, the state's history of secular coercion? Yoel's father had had to fight the Mapai-led Haifa municipality for the right to establish a religious girls' high school. As a Bnei Akiva activist, Yoel had gone into the immigrant camps around Haifa to convince parents to send their children to religious schools. One father told Yoel that he'd been warned by bureaucrats of the all-powerful Histadrut trade union that if he didn't send his children to a secular school, he wouldn't find work in the centralized economy. Yoel couldn't forget the fear in the man's eyes; what, then, was redemptive about secular rule?

One day Yoel got up the courage to knock on the door of Rabbi Zvi Yehudah's home. "May I walk the rabbi to the yeshiva?" Yoel asked. Rabbi Zvi Yehudah, delighted to see "the stubborn one," took Yoel by the arm and walked the streets of his ultra-Orthodox neighborhood, appropriately named Geulah, "Redemption." Yoel walked slowly, in time with Rabbi Zvi Yehudah's heavy steps.

They came across a campaign rally for an ultra-Orthodox party. An activist was addressing a crowd of black-hatted men, whom he referred to as "the community of holy citrons." By comparing the ultra-Orthodox to the citron among the "four species," the speaker was in effect calling them the saints of the Jewish people. Rabbi Zvi Yehudah tightened his grip on Yoel's arm. "The altar is not wrapped in citrons!" he said vehemently.

"What?" said Yoel, uncomprehending. He bent closer to hear the rabbi's words. Yoel had difficulty understanding Rabbi Zvi Yehudah, who often spoke in a hurried mumble as though to himself, and whose Yiddish-accented Hebrew was filled with fragments of biblical and rabbinic phrases that formed a private theological language.

The rabbi's pace quickened, energized by anger. He pulled at Yoel, as if to remove him from a place of sin. Yoel was surprised by the strength of the old man's grip. "The altar is not wrapped in citrons," he repeated to himself. "The altar is wrapped in willows!"

Finally the rabbi explained: in the Jerusalem Temple, the altar on which sacrifices were offered was wreathed with willows, because Israel's sacrifices would be acceptable to God only if all parts of the Jewish people—and not just the saints, the citrons—were included. "There is no holy community of citrons!" Rabbi Zvi Yehudah repeated, outraged. "Only the holy community of Israel!"

Yoel understood: there is no holiness for Israel without its flawed souls, the willows. Jewish unity wasn't merely a political but a spiritual imperative: a holy people bringing the message of God's oneness to the world must be in harmony with itself, must be whole.

Yoel felt a love for Rabbi Zvi Yehudah that he had never felt, perhaps, for anyone before, and sensed that he had found his spiritual father.

ROMANCE ON MOUNT GILBOA

YOEL'S YEAR IN MERCAZ ended. Reluctantly he left the study hall, and in January 1965 he put on the khaki uniform of Nahal, which combined military service with agricultural work, and which settled remote areas, intending to found kibbutzim. Because it trained recruits in parachuting, Nahal was considered a paratrooper unit—though hardly as elite as the "real" paratroopers.

Yoel did well enough in basic training. He had stamina for running up hills and marching long kilometers while carrying soldiers on stretchers. But he had discovered the point where Jewish history and cosmic intentionality intersect, and army life bored him. Sometimes on leave he went straight to Mercaz, rather than to his parents' home.

Following basic training, Yoel's Nahal group—fifty male and female recruits from Bnei Akiva—was assigned to an outpost on Mount Gilboa, bordering the northern West Bank. They arrived just before the late spring festival of Shavuot. Five prefab buildings—including a synagogue and a library—clustered high above the valley, white boxes on a stony slope. There were no adults to supervise the recruits; the commanding officer, hardly older than his nineteen-year-old soldiers, had been sent to jail after his jeep overturned and military police discovered he had no driver's license. Still, this was Bnei Akiva: even the couples that quickly formed maintained their modest ways.

At night, Yoel and his friends sat around a campfire and gazed at the sporadic lights beyond the border. Samaria, the biblical northern kingdom, was so close. There wasn't even a fence, only a stone marker placed by the Jordanian authorities. Members of a previous Nahal group had sometimes driven to the nearest Arab village on the Jordanian side. But such casual violation of the border was no longer possible: Yasser Arafat's Al Fatah group had begun attacking Israeli targets from Jordan and the soldiers were now on permanent alert.

The Nahal outpost was intended to eventually become part of a small network of religious kibbutzim, and so the soldiers not only guarded and patrolled but worked in chicken coops and fishponds. They woke with dawn and worked until the heat of midday.

Manual labor bored Yoel. Friends considered him lazy. In an evaluation of group members prepared by an official of the religious kibbutz movement, this curt note appeared beside Yoel's name: "A serious boy, but not for kibbutz." Yoel would serve the Jewish people in his own way.

In the absence of an army chaplain, Yoel volunteered to organize religious life on the mountain. He assembled prayer quorums three times a day and read from the Torah in his deep, melodic voice. But when he tried to insert Kookian ideas into his weekly Torah class, friends said to each other, There he goes again, drifting off into the clouds.

The group was assigned the task of planting pine trees along the Gilboa, to mark the border and prevent encroachment by Jordanian villagers. The saplings required constant attention; only shrubs grew easily here. The ancient curse, group members said. King Saul and his son Jonathan had fallen in battle on Mount Gilboa; and David, in his eulogy, had damned the land: "Mountains of Gilboa, let there be no dew, neither let there be rain, upon you."

Yoel didn't think they should be planting at all, but not because of David's curse. This is a *shmitta* year, he noted, the last year of the seven-year cycle during which the land of Israel must remain fallow. How, he asked, can we violate *shmitta*, a commandment from the Torah? Friends cited Rabbi Kook: Didn't he permit planting during the *shmitta* year to prevent Zionist agriculture from collapsing? That lenient rule, countered Yoel, was meant for farmers, not for soldiers planting trees.

Yoel took his argument to the government official in charge of the area's forestation, a religious Jew whose daughter happened to be a member of the Nahal group. "There is no justification for planting trees during *shmitta*," insisted Yoel.

"We're at war to protect our borders," the forester retorted, annoyed. "Just as it is permitted to fight on Shabbat when necessary, it is permitted to plant here during the seventh year."

WHAT FIRST ATTRACTED Yoel to the forester's daughter was that she wasn't like the other girls in the group, didn't laugh recklessly or gossip. Esther Raab was inward but not aloof. Warm, generous, above all serious: the qualities Yoel was hoping for in a wife. Esther, for her part, had become intrigued by Yoel when she heard about the Mercaz student who had come to the army with a suitcase filled with books. Yoel, like Esther, seemed incapable of frivolity.

Yoel also happened to be deeply handsome. Beneath light brown curls was a face of gravitas. He spoke with quiet confidence, and Esther was drawn to his precocious capacity for wisdom.

Esther had grown up in a town near Haifa. In the 1948 war, her father had been one of the defenders of religious Zionist settlements known as the Etzion Bloc in the Judean Hills outside of Jerusalem, and was taken prisoner by the Jordanians when the bloc fell, just before the state of Israel was declared.

When the Nahal group gathered in the evening for folk dancing, Yoel and Esther slipped away. They walked for hours on the mountain, their footsteps the only sounds against the wind. They didn't hold hands.

Yoel told Esther he intended to devote his life to *tikkun olam b'malchut Shaddai*, repairing the world through the kingdom of God. I'm going to become an educator, he said, help to bring young Israelis closer to Judaism. Esther said she wanted to live in a kibbutz, but was concerned about collective child-rearing. Children belong with their parents, she said; it's no wonder that so many kibbutz children run away from the children's house.

"How many children do you want?" Yoel asked.

"Twelve," she answered.

Yoel laughed.

IN MARCH 1967, on the eve of the holiday of Purim, Yoel's Nahal service ended. Having participated in Nahal's parachuting course, Yoel was assigned for future reserve duty to the 55th Paratroopers Brigade.

But reserve duty was the last thing on his mind. After a brief stop at his parents' home, he returned to Mercaz, where he was honored with the role of chanting the book of Esther—the ultimate Mercaz story, destruction reversed into redemption.

The yeshiva was thriving. While Yoel was away, it had moved to a new building, and the student population had grown from barely forty students to nearly two hundred. Yoel noted that Rabbi Zvi Yehudah had begun to speak more clearly, his mumble replaced by an emphatic tone. Some said that the rabbi's clarity, along with the yeshiva's expansion, were portents:

history was quickening, the messianic dénouement approaching, the Kookian worldview about to emerge from obscurity.

Yoel settled into Mercaz's new study hall, several times larger than the old one. He chose a new area of study: the talmudic tractate that deals with the priestly service in the Jerusalem Temple. Yoel craved knowledge of the ancient time when Jews had been intimate with God's presence—when the purpose of the Jews, to bring heaven to earth, was manifest. Since the destruction of the Temple, Jews had studied its service in the hope for its eventual restoration. If Jewish sovereignty had been restored and the ingathering of the exiles begun, then even a rebuilt temple no longer seemed beyond the reach of dreams.

"THEY DIVIDED MY LAND!"

THE EVE OF Israel's nineteenth Independence Day, May 14, 1967. In the Mercaz dining room, several hundred young men wearing white shirts and knitted skullcaps and black polyester pants and sandals with socks were crowded around long tables. Before them lay the remnants of a festive meal, half-eaten challah rolls, empty bottles of malt beer.

"This is the day that God made, we will rejoice in it," read a banner on the wall, quoting Psalms. Independence Day was claimed by the secular and rejected by the ultra-Orthodox for the same reason: as a celebration of human effort rather than divine intervention. For Mercaz, though, this was one of the most sacred moments of the year: the founding of the state against impossible odds, immediately after the Holocaust, meant that the God of Israel could no longer bear the humiliation of His people.

Rabbi Zvi Yehudah rose to speak. The young men stood, an honor guard. Though seventy-six years old, the rabbi moved with vigor.

"We must make more of an effort and become accustomed to opening our eyes to discover the endless wonders of God's deeds," he said, his voice strong even without a microphone. Students crowded toward the front of the room, eager to hear every word.

"There were times," he continued, "in the early years of the state, when the celebration [of Independence Day] in the yeshiva had not yet been established, and I would wander for one, two, or three hours in the streets of Jerusalem. Needless to say we don't want to encourage promiscuity in

Jerusalem, but I felt obliged and commanded to be at one with the joy of our people, with the masses, with the boys and the girls."

Students looked at each other appreciatively: What other venerable Orthodox rabbi would celebrate with boys and girls together?

The rabbi continued: "One matter, which borders on the desecration of God's name, caused me deep sorrow. Where are the elders, the guides of the community, the great [ultra-Orthodox] rabbis, when our people are celebrating in the streets of Jerusalem?"

And yet, he confessed, there was one occasion when he too couldn't join in the dancing, and kept aloof from the people's celebration. It happened on the night in 1947 when the UN voted for partition of the land of Israel into two states, one Jewish, one Arab. "The whole nation flowed into the streets to celebrate its feelings of joy," he said. "[But] I couldn't go out and join in the rejoicing. I sat alone, and burdened. In those first hours I couldn't make my peace with what had happened, with the terrible news that the word of God in the book of the Prophets had now been fulfilled: 'They divided my land!'"

And now he suddenly cried out: "Where is our Hebron? Have we forgotten it? And where is our Shechem—have we forgotten it? And where is our Jericho—have we forgotten it? And where is the other bank of the Jordan River? Where is every clod of earth? Every piece of God's land? Do we have the right to cede even a centimeter of it? God forbid! . . .

"In that state, my whole body was stunned, wounded and severed into pieces. I couldn't celebrate. 'They divided my land!' They divided the land of God! . . . I couldn't go outside to dance and rejoice. That is how the situation was nineteen years ago."

Total silence. The students had never heard such grief, such outrage, from their rabbi.

"A day or two later the sage Rabbi Yaakov Moshe Harlap came to my house. . . . We sat together . . . stunned and silent. We communed for a few moments. We recovered and we said together as one, 'It is God Who did this, it is wondrous in our eyes.'"

Yoel sat toward the back of the room, pulling at his short brown beard. What, he wondered, was the meaning of Rabbi Zvi Yehudah's outburst? For nineteen years, the rabbi had encouraged his students to celebrate God's generosity to His people without equivocation, had suppressed his pain over the brokenness of the land. Why the sudden cry now? And what a cry! As if the wound had just been inflicted. For Rabbi Zvi Yehudah, nothing was random. What was he trying to tell them?

THE NEXT EVENING, as Israel was concluding its Independence Day celebrations of family barbeques and the annual Hebrew song contest and military parade and Bible quiz, the radio reported that Egypt's president, Nasser, had begun mobilizing troops. The Israeli government responded with a partial mobilization of the reserves.

Yoel went to see Esther. She was working as house mother in a school for blind children, practically next door to Mercaz. Esther had rarely seen Yoel so agitated. What did the news portend? Were we heading for war? And was Rabbi Zvi Yehudah's outburst the night before somehow connected to today's news? "Esther, you should have heard him: 'Where is our Hebron? Where is our Jericho?' I've never heard such a cry in my life. Rabbi Zvi Yehudah wasn't speaking. He was roaring."

CHAPTER 3

BORN TO SERVE

AN EXEMPLARY KIBBUTZNIK

ARIK ACHMON, chief intelligence officer of the 55th Brigade, was at work in the accounting department of the newspaper *Yediot Aharonot* when the call came from Motta Gur, commander of the brigade: I need to see you now.

The IDF, Motta explained when they met, was planning a preemptive strike in the Sinai Desert. The 55th would be parachuting behind Egyptian lines and taking the coastal town of El Arish, the most fortified position on the way to the Suez Canal. Arik's job was to write a preliminary assessment of Egyptian strength in El Arish. For now, continued Motta, the plan was to be kept secret, even from Arik's own intelligence staff. Motta gave him two days to produce a report. "Get to work," said Motta.

Arik had just experienced the most intense year of his life. He had divorced, assumed care of his two children on weekends, quit his kibbutz for the city, begun full-time studies at Tel Aviv University, and was working half-time. And he was learning how to function as chief intelligence officer of the 55th Brigade, devoting most of the free time he didn't have to what he called "on-the-job training." He'd begun studying for final exams in his economics classes, but now that would have to wait.

Arik found a temporary replacement for his job at the newspaper, told his professors he couldn't take finals—"army matters," he said, without explaining—and began knocking on doors at IDF intelligence headquarters in Tel Aviv. Even an experienced intelligence officer would have had difficulty coping with Motta's deadline. Though Arik assumed he was as competent as anyone and better than most, he was not experienced. Until ten months ago he'd been a company commander, with no background in intelligence. And now he was about to help Motta plan a war in a matter of days.

ARIK ACHMON HAD been waiting for this moment all his life.

Growing up in the years before statehood on Givat Brenner, a kibbutz south of Tel Aviv, Arik had longed to take his place among the heroes of Israel. Arik and his friends would eavesdrop on the meetings of the commanders of the Palmach, the Jewish community's elite commando force, young men with careless hair and kaffiyehs around their necks who regularly convened in Givat Brenner (which was named for a Hebrew writer killed in an Arab pogrom). The kibbutz boys would listen to the Palmachniks sing, in Hebrew, the rousing and melancholy songs of the Red Army's war against Hitler: "Cossack horsemen galloping to battle! Hey hey hey!" "A fire is burning in our land, the enemy is at the gates." Arik knew their names—Yigal Allon, Yitzhak Rabin—the way teenagers elsewhere followed sports heroes. Afterward, when seven Arab armies attacked the newborn Jewish state, it was largely the Palmachniks who had beaten them back. Many of those young men whom Arik saw in Givat Brenner didn't return from the front.

Above all, there was Sereni. Enzo Sereni, an Italian-born Jew with a doctorate in philosophy, had left behind a family fortune to become a kibbutznik. It was even rumored that he was an aristocrat, and the soft-spoken Sereni certainly seemed like one among the blunt pioneers from Poland and Lithuania. He had once considered converting to Christianity and becoming a monk; instead he chose to serve his despised people, satisfying his monastic tendencies in the austerity of Givat Brenner. Sereni and his wife, Ada, were the unofficial house parents in Givat Brenner's children's home. Arik loved Sereni's bedtime stories about his travels through prewar Nazi Germany to help young Jews escape and to Iraq to help Jews organize against pogroms. At night in the children's home—bare walls, bare floor, four iron cots to a room—Sereni would sing, in a rousing voice, the Italian Communist anthem "Avanti Popolo!" (Onward, Masses!), and the children would shout along, leaping on their cots. "Bolsheviks," he called them tenderly. A pacifist, Sereni refused to carry a weapon or even a stick on guard duty. He walked the neighboring Arab villages, befriending *mukhtars* and peasants. As a boy Arik had feared the Arabs: one of his earliest memories was of hiding under a bed while Arabs fired at the kibbutz. But, walking with Sereni, he learned that if you looked people in the eye and respected them as neighbors or as adversaries, there was no reason to be afraid.

With World War II, Sereni conceded defeat: it was no longer possible to be a pacifist. At age forty, he volunteered for commando duty with the British army. In 1943, when Arik was ten, Sereni disappeared on his last journey—part of a small group of Zionist pioneers who parachuted into Nazi-occupied Europe in a forlorn attempt to rescue Jews. Sereni and seven of his friends, including the poet Hannah Szenes, were captured. Sereni was sent to Dachau and died there, among the Jews he had tried to save—but of course not quite one of them, thought Arik, because Sereni had chosen his fate, had died a soldier.

With the founding of the state in 1948, Arik, age fifteen, began training to defend his home. As the Egyptian army advanced on Givat Brenner, its teenagers were taught hand-to-hand combat, how to crawl through rugged terrain at night and slip behind enemy lines; at the shooting range, Arik attained sniper level. The young people dug trenches and served as runners between the watchtowers. The barely equipped Israeli army brought three World War I–era cannons on wheels to defend Givat Brenner; the cannons were nicknamed "Napoleonchiks," little Napoleons, because they were small but bombastic, creating more noise than damage. Tel Nof, the base for the tiny Israeli air force, was near Givat Brenner, and every day Arik would watch the skies as the entire fleet of four Messerschmitts took off, then count them as they returned. Egyptian Spitfires attacked Tel Nof; Israeli soldiers fired back with rifles.

For all of Arik's intimacy with the military, he'd remained a spectator. The Egyptian army was stopped several kilometers before reaching Givat Brenner, and the war passed him by. A friend of Arik's, only two years older than him, joined a rescue patrol setting out from the kibbutz and was killed in battle. Arik wished that he were two years older and able to prove himself too.

MEANWHILE, ARIK TRIED to be an exemplary kibbutznik. As a boy in the children's house, the parallel communal society where Givat Brenner's young people were encouraged to run their own lives without adult interference, he had volunteered for every position—the work committee that assigned after-school tasks, the culture committee that planned hikes, the social committee that resolved disputes among children and between children and teachers. At age eleven, Arik had been chosen to work after school in the cowshed, the "commando unit" of the kibbutz workforce, as he proudly called it. While his friends tended the vegetable garden around the children's house, Arik worked long and unpredictable hours, milking the cows by hand and hauling fifteen-liter buckets of milk, just like an adult. The boy knows how to work, they said of him, the ultimate kibbutz compliment. Arik relished that moment when, straight from the cowshed, still in his dirty khaki work clothes, he made his entry into the children's dining room in the middle of dinner.

He thinks he's better than anyone else, some complained. It was true: Arik sensed he was more analytical, less emotional, and calmer under pressure than the others. For all his communal devotion, friends perceived in him an aloofness, the emotional equivalent of ideological heresy. Arik exasperated his friends. He could be so helpful, so dependable. But so damn inconsiderate of others' feelings! And that look: all he had to do was stare at you with a slight tilt of his head, a corner of his mouth considering a smirk, to leave you feeling worthless. He seemed to gaze at the world from a distance, a wary observer. Friends knew better than to expect sympathy from him. Sympathy, he felt, only nurtured weakness.

Arik's arrogance was encouraged by his mother. Hannah Achmon was the ultimate kibbutznik, so devoted to the commune's nursery that she had deferred having her own children until the first of Givat Brenner's children reached first grade. But she compensated for that selflessness with a fierce possessiveness toward Arik. There has never been, and will never be, a child born who is more successful than my Arik, she announced to the other mothers. When there was a family problem, Hannah turned to her teenage son rather than to her husband, Yekutiel, whom she dismissed as ineffectual. And she encouraged Arik's three younger siblings to turn to Arik too.

Arik was the most diligent worker among the young people, the best debater in class. Arik sensed he was destined for greatness—not the self-centered fame of the capitalist world, of course, but a greatness drawn from proximity to epic events.

WHEN ARIK TURNED seventeen, the perfect world of his childhood began to devour itself. It was 1951, and Givat Brenner was torn over whether the new state of Israel should align with the Soviet Union or the West. Givat Brenner's Marxists declared the Soviet Union under Stalin as the hope for world redemption, and demanded that progressive, egalitarian Israel choose the right side of history. The Red Army, some predicted, would soon be marching triumphantly into the Middle East.

Opposing the Marxists was Mapai, the pro-Western social democratic party headed by prime minister David Ben-Gurion. Like his parents, Arik was a Mapainik—a besieged minority in Givat Brenner. At the kibbutz's weekly meetings, Stalinists denounced them as enemies of socialism, poisoners of the youth. Three years earlier the comrades had been prepared to die together defending their commune from the Egyptian army; now Mapainiks and Stalinists couldn't even share a table in the communal dining room.

Arik's class was about to graduate from high school and be inducted, in a public ceremony, into kibbutz membership. No young person had ever refused to participate. But for Arik, Givat Brenner was no longer home. The Mapainiks, including his parents, were openly talking about seceding, a process that was happening on other kibbutzim too.

"So what if it's a farce?" a friend argued. "Take the membership and leave. That's what I'm doing. Just don't break ranks, don't embarrass the *hevreh* [the gang]."

"I'm not going to lie to myself and to the whole kibbutz and pretend that everything is fine," Arik said. "End of discussion."

ON A FRIDAY EVENING in the summer of 1951, members gathered on the kibbutz's highest hill for the induction ceremony of the graduates. Past ceremonies were accompanied by an orchestra and choir, a stage covered with blue-and-white Zionist flags and revolutionary red flags. Now, though, with the impending split, the stage was bare, and a lone accordionist tried to rouse the listless comrades seated on folding chairs on the grass.

The graduates mounted the stage, girls in white blouses and blue skirts, boys in embroidered collarless shirts. Barefoot, paired, boys holding girls by the waist, they leaped to the songs of the pioneers, rousing songs of determination and hope, subverted by a melancholy minor key.

Arms folded, Arik stood to one side. From here he could see the kibbutz spread below, receding in the darkness. Spread on the slopes were the houses of the veterans, long concrete buildings with four doors leading to four identical one-room apartments. And beside them, outhouses and public showers.

Farther down the hill, the children's houses with red-shingled roofs. And the wheat fields and orange groves. And the cowshed, whose odor permeated the kibbutz, carried even now by the night's cool breeze. And just behind where Arik stood, Sereni House, holding the hero's archives.

A kibbutz veteran addressed the graduates. "You now face the challenge of continuing our path," he said, "of ensuring the very existence of the collective." He read out the names of the new members, pausing after each to allow the audience to affirm the young person's candidacy. Arms that in previous induction ceremonies had been raised like flagpoles were now limp. "There remains a shadow of doubt concerning . . . Arie Achmon," he continued, invoking Arik's formal name. "I hope the situation will be clarified soon."

Arik felt all eyes against him. Mapainik, secessionist. Was he imagining it, or was there hatred in their stares? He told himself he didn't care. And, no, there was no "shadow of doubt," no situation awaiting clarification. For the first time in his life, Arik Achmon had stepped out of line.

ON THE BORDER

TWO MONTHS LATER, Arik was drafted. He returned to Givat Brenner during leaves, but that arrangement was temporary. Givat Brenner was heading for a split, and Arik's parents would soon be leaving.

Like most kibbutz recruits, Arik assumed he would join Nahal, the unit that combined military training with agricultural work on the border. But the kibbutz movement had other plans for him. In every draft, the movement chose three of its most promising young people to help infuse the kibbutz spirit among the new immigrants in the Golani infantry brigade. The movement chose Arik. He was mortified: What did he care about immigrant absorption? *I'm a soldier, not a social worker.* Still, he didn't challenge the order: He had been raised to serve. Humiliated, he went to Golani.

In Golani, Arik encountered the new Israel that was rising in the immigrant camps, Jews from Yemen and North Africa who had never heard of a kibbutz and who couldn't understand what Arik meant by communal property. How could everyone own everything and no one own anything?

And then there were the other refugees, Holocaust survivors. *Sabon*, "soap," Arik and his friends called them, after the rumor that the Nazis had made soap out of Jewish flesh. Arik felt little connection to what had happened to Jews in Europe. Almost all of his family had come to the land of Israel before the war; they had intuited the flood, built their ark. As for those who had drowned: well, they too could have saved themselves. There had to be something wrong, he thought, with so many people who allowed themselves to be killed so easily.

IT WAS A time of crisis. The new state was overwhelmed with Jewish refugees from Europe and from the endangered diasporas of the Arab world, crowding into tent camps and shantytowns. Meanwhile Palestinian refugees slipped across the open border, killing and wounding. We promised the Jews a safe refuge, Prime Minister Ben-Gurion declared, and we must keep that promise.

But the IDF, which hadn't recovered from its devastating losses in the 1948 war, wasn't coping. In one border skirmish, seven Israeli soldiers were killed and one Jordanian soldier wounded, a disastrous ratio for a vastly outnumbered nation; as an added humiliation, the Israeli bodies were seized and dismembered. Hundreds of Palestinian infiltrators—many unarmed, who came to steal, not kill—were shot by IDF soldiers and by farmers, but that too failed as deterrence.

Desperate, the army tried to impose a nightly curfew on Palestinian villages across the border in Jordan from which infiltrators had emerged; anyone leaving their homes would be shot.

On a moonless winter night in 1952, Arik and six other soldiers, under the command of a corporal with no combat experience, set out from their base in central Israel and crossed the unmarked border into the West Bank.

After four kilometers they came to a village. They took cover on a hill overlooking the dirt road and lay there in the cold. After perhaps an hour they heard men's voices, loud and joking. "Fire!" said the commander. Prematurely: the targets were out of range. A soldier threw a grenade; it didn't explode. "Move out!" shouted the commander.

Why weren't they charging? But the order was given, and Arik joined the others in humiliating retreat. As they entered the gate of their base, the soldiers sang an improvised ditty, "We went out to fight, we ran in flight."

"You should be thrown out of the army," the base commander said to the squad leader at the debriefing. Turning to Arik and his friends, he continued, "It's a shame that this is the example you've gotten of an IDF commander. Your mission was to kill anyone who broke curfew. Instead, you fled."

Two nights later, Arik's unit hiked up Mount Gilboa, on the Israeli side of the northernmost border with the West Bank. They waited through the night. Just before dawn, they heard sheep. Then a shepherd's voice. Perhaps five hundred meters away, within range. Arik pointed his light machine gun down the slope and emptied four cartridges. It was still too dark to see whether he had hit the shepherd, but Arik was a good shot, and he assumed that he did.

THE CURFEW POLICY wasn't working. A young couple was shot dead in a farming community, a girl was murdered by seven terrorists in her home in Jerusalem.

Arik was sent for officers' training. His commanders noted his steadiness under pressure, his insistence on accurate reporting, even when that reflected poorly on his performance. He was named an outstanding graduate, pinned in a ceremony by the IDF chief of staff. A natural soldier: as if Arik, born in the portentious year of 1933, had intuited his responsibility to undo Jewish helplessness.

In the fall of 1953, toward the end of Arik's service, Commando Unit 101 was formed by a twenty-five-year-old major named Ariel Sharon. At a time when three out of four of the army's retaliatory missions were failing, Unit 101 intended to operate with a spirit of mad daring. Sharon drove across the country handpicking 101's members from kibbutzim and private farms, as if only men who worked the land were able to defend it. The new unit's missions almost always succeeded. On incursions into the West Bank and Gaza, its members ambushed Palestinian raiding parties and blew up houses in villages that assisted terrorists. One night, three 101 commandos slipped into a Gaza refugee camp, dynamited a terrorist headquarters, and shot their way out against hundreds of armed opponents. Take the war into enemy territory, insisted Sharon: the border was permeable in both directions. One unit member took friends on hikes into Jordan and Syria, a native son's revolt against siege. For the Jewish immigrants crowding into Israel's uncertain refuge, 101 confirmed Zionism's instinct: if you realigned the people of Israel with the land of Israel, the ancient archetypes would reemerge.

Arik, now an instructor at officers' school, watched 101's war with longing. It wasn't only the glory he was missing but a chance to prove his worth as a soldier. What was he doing training cadets when the guys were out on nightly raids, establishing Israel's deterrence? Joining 101 was by invitation only; unit members voted on each candidate. Many of the unit's members were Arik's friends. They sent word to him: What are you waiting for?

But when Arik asked the kibbutz movement for permission to extend his army service and join 101, he was told to demobilize. Kibbutz Givat Brenner had formally split, and its several hundred Mapainiks, including Arik's parents and three siblings, had found a new home in a kibbutz called Netzer Sereni—literally, "Sereni's young shoot"—named for Arik's childhood hero. The kibbutz had been founded by Holocaust survivors in their twenties, and the survivors and the Givat Brenner expatriates were struggling to create a coherent society. The movement needed Arik.

Demobilized with the rank of lieutenant, Arik reluctantly returned his gun and kitbag, packed all his belongings into a small knapsack, and hitched to Netzer Sereni.

KIBBUTZ BUCHENWALD

WITH ITS PALM TREES and sand dunes and red-colored earth, Netzer Sereni, just south of Tel Aviv and not far from Givat Brenner, was a familiar landscape for Arik. Netzer, as members called it, was sparser and poorer than Givat Brenner. But Arik relished the challenge of building a new community. He was appointed manager of the cowshed, and introduced an automated milking system that boosted Netzer's output to among the highest in the kibbutz movement.

Netzer's founders had planned their kibbutz while still inmates in the Buchenwald concentration camp. Collectivized for death, they dreamed of starting a commune in the land of Israel. Weeks after liberation, they formed "Kibbutz Buchenwald" and set up a training farm in Germany.

Arik heard their stories late at night in the cowshed, where he was the only native Israeli among survivors. The details were conveyed matter-of-factly, with black humor, like the way they identified themselves as "graduates" of a particular camp. Young people exchanging stories: Arik told them about Givat Brenner, they told him about Buchenwald.

Arik had never shown the slightest interest in the Holocaust. But now, among his new friends, he needed to know every detail of the destruction: How did the system work? How had the Germans managed to deceive the Jews? At what point had the victims realized what was happening? How many guards were there at the entrance to the ghetto, in the camp? The questions weren't emotive but technical, the probings of a one-man commission of inquiry. He was curious, fascinated. He imagined himself there, at every stage, calmly assessing his options, how to slip out, save his family, hit back.

The guys in the cowshed, Arik discovered, were the opposite of the cowardly survivor stereotype. They'd survived through not passivity but constant alertness. Even in Buchenwald they had functioned as a collective, sharing what food they could and hiding sick friends from "selections" to the gas. And then, barely a month after liberation, they were already functioning as a kibbutz. *Sabon: what jerks we were—*

ARIK MARRIED HIS GIRLFRIEND, Rina, daughter of a writer whose realistic novels about kibbutz life scandalized his fellow kibbutzniks. Arik and Rina celebrated in the Netzer dining room. The entire kibbutz, some three hundred people, danced the hora into the night. It was Netzer's first wedding, a sign of hope.

Netzer was beginning to thrive. Its metal shop produced the spring cots the government distributed to new immigrants, and its factory for flatbed trucks was the only one in Israel. Lawns spread against the sand dunes. The former Brennerites, with their work experience, and the survivors, with their determination to prove themselves, made a formidable team.

Yet the more Arik got to know survivors, the more he despaired of creating a common society with them. The survivors had their own codes, and Arik could never be sure what they were really saying. They were either not speaking to each other because of some obscure insult or else ready to die for each other. A kibbutz was supposed to be a place of trust; who could build a commune with such people?

One survivor sifted through the garbage for food. Another stole bread from the dining room. When bottles of wine intended for a kibbutz party went missing, Arik suspected one of the survivors. He searched the young man's room as the suspect hugged himself and whimpered. Finally the real culprit was found. Afterward, whenever he passed the young man he'd falsely accused, Arik averted his eyes.

When tensions emerged between the survivors and the veterans of Givat Brenner, Arik tried to mediate. But the differences in mentality were too vast. Brennerites tended to be relaxed about egalitarian infringements, like receiving outside gifts, while survivors regarded infractions as a threat to the kibbutz. As kibbutz veterans, Brennerites dismissed the socialist passion of survivors as exaggerated. What do they know about kibbutz life? Brennerites complained. Among survivors, the "experience" of the Brennerites became a bitter joke: *Nu*, really, what do we know about life? We don't have their *experience*.

Survivors noted with resentment that when Brennerites visited Tel Aviv, they were entertained by relatives and even taken out to restaurants, while the survivors wandered Tel Aviv's streets. Some survivors demanded a stipend for outings to the city. But no compensation could redress the gap that separated those who had come to the land of Israel before the Holocaust and those who had come afterward.

With the best intentions, survivors and Brennerites had tried to form a kibbutz together. But each group retreated into itself. The founders of Kibbutz Buchenwald had survived apocalypse and aspired to utopia; now they were being defeated by ordinary life.

ARIK DIVIDED HIS LIFE into what he called "missions." There was the kibbutz mission, the army mission, the family mission. In precisely that order.

Arik and Rina were drifting apart. Arik never put his arm around Rina, one friend noted; Rina would hug Arik's friends, but not Arik. When they weren't making arrangements, they didn't know what to talk about.

Arik sought respite in reserve duty. As an officer, deputy commander of an infantry company, he was frequently called up for maneuvers and planning sessions. But reserve duty too wasn't satisfying: his unit was mediocre, and in time of war unlikely to see frontline duty.

In those rare moments when Arik looked at himself objectively, he saw a cowhand, without prospects for real intellectual growth, caught in an emotionally dysfunctional marriage and kibbutz. He would quickly dispel that image. How many young people were given his responsibilities? So Netzer had problems; true service meant doing your best in whatever conditions fate had placed you. Arik intensified his commitment to the kibbutz. At age twenty-four, he was elected Netzer's work coordinator, a position usually reserved for a veteran comrade.

In his annual report to the Netzer community, Arik wrote that the cowshed had yielded a good profit and that its cows continued to produce beyond the national average. We have much to be proud of, he noted. But then he warned: those achievements, "won at great effort, can be squandered if, heaven forbid, we allow our striving to flag." It was, perhaps, a warning to himself.

IN AUGUST 1956 Arik received a note from Aharon Davidi, commander of the IDF's lone paratrooper battalion, and Arik's former commander in officers' school. "Achmonchik," the note affectionately began, "we're starting a reservists' battalion. Come."

Unit 101 had been absorbed into the paratroopers, now the army's elite combat force. The merger happened after 101 was implicated in a massacre. A Palestinian had thrown a grenade into a home in Yehud, near Tel Aviv, killing an immigrant mother from Turkey and her two young children. Unit 101 retaliated by blowing up dozens of houses in the West Bank village of Qibye, killing some sixty civilians hiding in their homes who had either ignored warnings to flee, not heard the warnings, or not received them at all.

The purpose of the merger was to rein in 101 while infusing the paratroopers, until then a lackluster unit, with its fighting spirit. Paratroopers so thoroughly internalized the 101 ethos that one recruit escaped a hospital bed to join his friends on a mission.

Arik went to see Davidi, whose interests included Chinese philosophy and playing mental chess against himself. They met at paratrooper headquarters in the Tel Nof air force base near Givat Brenner. The paratroopers, explained Davidi, were being expanded into a brigade: two battalions of draftees and a third battalion of reservists, to be known as the 28th. Arik was being appointed a platoon commander in Company A, 28th Battalion.

"Davidi," said Arik, "I'm a deputy commander in another unit."

"A technicality."

He sent Arik to a paratrooper officer named Motta Gur. Arik recognized him: Motta had once come to Givat Brenner to instruct its teenagers in hand-to-hand combat. "Davidi says you're one of us," said Motta, "so you're one of us. We're starting a three-week parachuting course next week. Can you come?" Of course he couldn't come: he had responsibilities on the kibbutz and at home. But Motta wasn't really asking. Of course he would come.

He jumped from a Dakota propeller plane, without a reserve parachute. For a few precious moments, he soared above his life, exhilarated by weightlessness. Landing, he felt the earth rise up to greet him.

TERRORISTS DISPATCHED BY the Egyptian government strafed an Israeli wedding. Three children were murdered in an attack on a synagogue. Other atrocities followed. The IDF prepared its response: an invasion of Egyptian-controlled Gaza and the Sinai Desert, the second Arab-Israeli war.

Arik received two draft calls, one from his infantry unit, one from the 28th Paratroopers' Battalion. He ignored the first and showed up for the second; technically, he was now AWOL.

The 1956 Suez War confirmed the paratroopers' preeminence within the IDF. In the war's most famous battle, paratroopers led by Motta Gur were caught in an ambush in the Mitla Pass near the Suez Canal, and shot their way past Egyptian forces positioned on the hills above.

Yet, maddeningly, Arik wasn't at Mitla. Instead, his unit had been dispatched to deal with Egyptian POWs. One of Arik's soldiers, manning a roadblock, radioed him that Egyptians were descending from the hills to surrender, "but I'm going to finish them off." Arik replied, "If you do that, I'll finish *you* off." The Egyptians were taken prisoner.

Arik couldn't believe his bad luck. He'd been too young for the Palmach, too obedient a kibbutznik for Unit 101. And now, finally, in the right place at the right time, he'd been cheated again of the chance to prove himself.

THE MILITARY POLICE are looking for you, Arik was told when he returned home to Netzer.

Arik reported to the commander of his former unit. "The only reason I'm not putting you on trial is because you ran off to the paratroopers," the officer said. "But those adventures are over."

Arik explained his dilemma to Ariel Sharon. "You're staying with us," said Sharon, laughing. For Sharon, Arik Achmon's willingness to risk prison for the paratroopers was proof enough he belonged.

A week later, a plain IDF envelope arrived in Netzer Sereni: Arik Achmon was officially a paratrooper.

THE PARATROOPERS SURRENDER

ARIK WAS APPOINTED commander of Company A, 28th Battalion.

The eighty reservists of Company A included veterans of the paratroopers' retaliation raids of the mid-1950s, like Arik's brother-in-law Yosef Schwartz, known informally as Yoske Balagan ("Yoske the mayhem maker"), who was married to Rina's sister. The veterans loved to tell Yoske stories, like the time he responded to cancellation of weekend leave by setting fire to a field near the base, forcing the army to send the men home.

Yoske's buddy in Company A was Aryeh Weiner, a neighbor of Arik's from Netzer Sereni. Weiner, whose family survived the war in Romania, had come to pre-state Israel alone at age twelve on an illegal immigrant boat running the British blockade. He claimed he'd gotten his father's agreement to leave, thanks to a card game: If I win this hand, his father had said, you have my blessings. His father won, and Weiner set off for the Holy Land.

Weiner and Yoske wouldn't let Arik forget that he wasn't a veteran like them. Who does he think he is, they demanded, this guy who's never experienced real combat? Who is he to tell us how to be paratroopers?

One day during reserve duty, when Arik was lecturing his men on battle tactics, Weiner called out, "And what do you know about that? Did you ever hear the sound of bullets over your head?"

"I've been with the battalion from the beginning," Arik said.

"And I'm one of its founders," countered Weiner.

They're right, thought Arik. He hadn't paid his dues.

Arik tried to win them over by proving his analytical prowess. But he came across as arrogant. "Arik knows everything," Yoske said. "An ignoramus like me, what do I know? I barely finished second grade and grew up on the streets before the Irgun gave me a gun and the British put a bullet in my stomach. But Arik? No matter what the subject, he knows."

For all its small torments, reserve duty provided respite from the growing silence between Arik and Rina and the growing estrangement among Netzer's comrades. He looked forward to the nighttime jumps and sea landings and coordinated infantry and tank assaults in the desert. Often Arik would spend Shabbat, his day off on the kibbutz, touring the border with fellow officers to check the army's state of alertness. No one asked them to do it. They simply trusted only themselves with Israel's defense.

IN THE SUMMER OF 1963, the 28th Battalion set up a tent camp in the Carmel mountains near Haifa for a monthlong training exercise. On the first day of mobilization reservists lined up before tables set up in a forest clearing and signed for equipment: Belgian surplus FN rifles, British surplus ammunition belts, American surplus sleeping bags (woolen in the Israeli summer), two-man pup tents, some with missing stakes.

There was a new addition to the battalion: a dozen religious young men in knitted *kippot*. Graduates of Nahal, they had received some parachuting training. But the paratrooper veterans regarded them as pretend soldiers, better suited for picking tomatoes than commando missions.

"Look at those Nahlawim," said Yoske Balagan, using a mocking term for Nahal recruits.

"Pathetic," agreed Weiner.

"They don't even know how to put up a tent," continued Yoske. "Imagine going out on a mission with these guys. They'd be more dangerous to us than to the enemy."

Worst of all were the religious Nahlawim. What, demanded Yoske, were these *dosim*, these religious nerds, doing in the paratroopers?

When it came to the IDF's religious regulations, the overwhelmingly secular paratroopers were a law unto themselves. The army insisted that all its kitchens be kosher, so that religious and secular soldiers could eat together; but the paratroopers roasted nonkosher porcupines at their campfires and routinely mixed dairy and meat.

Arik saw the religious reservists swaying together in a tight cluster of prayer and wondered, How were these *dosim* supposed to become paratroopers?

But the *dosim* surprised him. He watched them charge and crawl and parachute, and they were as good as any of the other men. If anything, they seemed even more keen on proving themselves. He watched them, too, when they wrapped themselves in phylacteries for dawn prayers, rising a half hour earlier than the others rather than ask for time off from the morning routine—the opposite of ultra-Orthodox Jews, who hid behind their faith to avoid military service altogether.

One Friday afternoon, when soldiers were sent home on leave close to sundown, Arik's religious soldiers preferred to stay in camp rather than risk traveling on the Sabbath. They didn't ask to be let out early, Arik noted approvingly.

Arik called together the veterans of Company A. "There are standing orders about keeping kosher in the army," he said. "From now on those orders are going to be obeyed. No mixing milk and meat utensils. No nonkosher meat in the kitchen."

"Have you gone totally crazy?" said Yoske. "This is the paratroopers!"

"Yoske, I know you don't like the way I think or do things generally. But this is how it's going to be."

"Since when did Arik Achmon become a friend of the *dosim*?"

"I'm not going to allow any soldiers under my command to feel uncomfortable. There's going to be basic respect. You can set up a burner near my tent and do what you want there."

Arik stopped referring to religious soldiers as *dosim*. They were people of values. *Underneath the* kippah*, they're just like us—*

ARIK THE KIBBUTZNIK: THE END

ARIK WAS APPOINTED manager of Netzer's agricultural sector. Unlike previous managers, Arik continued to wear his work clothes, ready to fix a tractor. Once a week he worked in the fields; a manager, he said, should know his organization from within.

When that two-year position ended, Arik was assigned to the cotton fields. What a waste, he thought. How was it possible to advance professionally on the kibbutz when you were removed from a position in which you proved yourself, just because of some ideological principle of rotation? How would the kibbutz be able to hold its most talented people when they felt stifled at every turn? And how much longer could he bear those endless weekly meetings—an ocean of words and a desert of ideas, as he put it, where the decisions of his life were subjected to majority vote, and every nudnik got his democratic say about whether and what Arik should study at university? *If I had an honorable way out of here, I would grab it—*

And then his marriage to Rina collapsed.

Belatedly, Arik had tried to consider her needs. They divided domestic tasks, and he cleaned the house. When Rina got permission from the kibbutz to study at university, Arik assumed responsibility for their daughter, Tsafra.

Rumors began reaching Arik that Rina had been spotted on campus with a young man. Arik didn't confront her, hoping it would pass. When they finally talked, he persuaded her to give their marriage another try. In 1964 their son, Ori, was born. But that only created the need for more arrangements.

Arik had tried to change, become a good husband and father. At the beginning, he was sure, there had been love. They still respected each other. But distance had become habit. He had tried too late to salvage the "family mission."

ARIK WAS CALLED up for reserve duty on the Syrian border. It was early summer 1966. There had been shooting attacks against Israeli farmers, and the IDF had retaliated against Syrian positions. There were fears too that Syria would renew attempts to dry up Israel's main water reservoir, the Sea of Galilee, whose sources were in the Syrian-controlled Golan Heights. The Middle East seemed to be drifting again toward war.

At night, looking into the blackness where the hills of Syria and Jordan converged, he realized: It's over. His marriage, and also his life on the kibbutz. He had given his best to Givat Brenner, and then to Netzer. But in the end the problem wasn't the Stalinists of Givat Brenner or the survivors of Netzer, but Arik himself—the ultimate kibbutznik, who never missed a weekly meeting, who was always on call for the movement, who always had a rational solution for increasing efficiency in the cowshed and the cotton fields. Yet he had forcibly collectivized himself against his nature. *The truth? Communal life was never for me—*

Divorce was the one reason for leaving the collective that kibbutzniks accepted. Arik asked for a leave of absence—he would need to keep a room in Netzer to see his two children on weekends—and enrolled in the economics department of Tel Aviv University.

In August 1966, at age thirty-three, with two suitcases containing all his possessions, he headed for the sand dunes of North Tel Aviv, the near-deserted extremity of the city where a new university was rising. He waived the kibbutz's offer to pay his tuition, which would have obligated him to return to Netzer after his studies. Instead, he received a grant of 1,500 lira for ten years of work, enough to cover a semester's tuition and two months' rent for a room near campus.

PREPARING FOR WAR

THE 28TH BATTALION was absorbed into a new brigade of paratrooper reservists, the 55th. It included another two newly formed battalions, in addition to auxiliary units of medics and non-combat logistical staff, some two thousand men altogether. Motta Gur was appointed commander. In the 1950s Motta had formed a unit of new immigrants into one of the IDF's best fighting forces, proving that not only native-born Israelis could fight. He'd led a raid on a terrorist base in Gaza, and then, with Egyptian soldiers in pursuit, ran several kilometers toward the Israeli border, carrying a dead soldier on his back. He was soft-spoken, calm under pressure, willing to be corrected by his men, ambitious—precisely the qualities Arik valued in himself.

"Arik," said Motta, "I want an intelligence officer who doesn't play by the book. Someone capable of creative thinking. I sifted through all the available candidates," he added dryly, "and you won by default."

Motta was offering him the position of chief intelligence officer of the 55th Brigade, a leap from company commander to the brigade's fourth highest position. Arik had no experience in intelligence. And he was trying to start a new life. He had signed up for a full load of courses and was working part-time in the *Yediot Aharonot* advertising department, spending weekends with his children in Netzer. Motta was asking him to risk stretching beyond his breaking point, to abandon any pretense of a normal life and be on constant call.

"I'm about to begin university studies," Arik protested feebly.

"With me you won't do much studying," said Motta.

Of course Arik could say no: this was the reserves, and he was a civilian. But Motta wasn't asking for Arik's consent; he knew Arik wouldn't refuse.

Arik went to see an old friend who now headed the IDF course for intelligence officers. "How do I do this?" asked Arik. His friend handed him three books on intelligence gathering. "Read these," he said. "Next week we have a three-day drill in the desert for the graduates of our latest course. Come." Arik read, then went to the drill. When it ended, his friend said, "Now you are an intelligence officer."

NASSER'S TROOP BUILDUP along the border intensifed; war seemed inevitable. Motta asked Arik to gather available intelligence for the area around El Arish, the coastal town in Sinai where the paratroopers would land in the event of war. Arik collected maps, aerial photographs, and reports of Egyptian troop movements. Two days after being given the assignment, Arik presented Motta with a ten-page handwritten paper summing up the available data.

Arik said nothing about his war preparations to Yehudit Hazan, the psychology student he was dating. He had met Yehudit at officers' school in the early 1950s. Fellow kibbutzniks, they'd been part of the same circle. Now they were both in their early thirties, divorced with children. After only a few months together, they were discussing marriage.

Yehudit, who'd been granted study leave by her kibbutz, was the daughter of Yaakov Hazan, the leader of Hashomer Hatzair. She bore that distinction uneasily; Arik recalled how in the army she had tried not to divulge her last name, to avoid the taint of privilege. She was smart, empathic, tough. And she wasn't intimidated by Arik's high opinion of his own capabilities. *I'm not easily impressed*, thought Arik, *but with Yehudit I've met my match. She's actually as intelligent and disciplined as I am. My equal in every way, except that she's a better person—*

Nearly thirty-four, Arik was older than most of the reservists of the 55th Brigade. A receding hairline emphasized the proportioned momentum of his face: forehead sloping toward upturned nose, chin repeating that same confident thrust. Sometimes, though, his lower lip would recede behind his upper lip and reveal a boyish hesitation.

There was one complication in the marriage plans of Arik and Yehudit: she didn't want to leave her kibbutz, Mishmar Ha'Emek, which her parents had helped found. Yehudit was the only one of her siblings who still lived there. "It will devastate my father if I leave," she said.

"Everything will work out," Arik reassured her.

He didn't tell her that there was no way he was returning to the farm.

CHAPTER 4

A TIME OF WAITING

"JERUSALEM OF GOLD"

MAY 1967. ON the streets of Cairo, demonstrators waved banners of skulls and crossbones and chanted, "We want war!" Caricatures in the Arab world's government newspapers fantasized about the coming victory. An Egyptian cartoon showed a hook-nosed Jew being strangled by a Star of David; a Syrian cartoon showed a pile of skulls in the smoking ruins of Tel Aviv. One ad in an Egyptian newspaper depicted a hand plunging a knife into a Star of David, and was signed, "Nile Oils and Soaps Company."

Barely twenty kilometers wide at its narrowest point, which happened to be around the coastal area containing most of its population, Israel could be severed in minutes. The claustrophobia that Israelis had tried to ignore—extending kibbutz fields and housing projects to the very edge of the border—was now unavoidable. The nation could field an impressive force in war—300,000 soldiers and reservists—but only at the cost of wholly mobilizing its barely three million people. The combined Arab armies confronting Israel had nearly twice as many soldiers, four times as many planes, and nearly five times as many tanks.

As young men began disappearing from Israel's streets and fields, high school students and pensioners volunteered to take their place, working as mailmen and harvesters. The army requisitioned tour buses, taxis, private cars. Gradually, civilian Israel was absorbed into military Israel.

Shelters in apartment buildings were swept clean, trenches dug around houses, windows taped against shattering. Pits were dug in parks, in preparation for mass graves.

Aside from emptying grocery shelves—a resurgence of the refugee instinct—Israelis responded without panic. Hitching soldiers barely had to extend their hand before drivers would stop. So many high school students and pensioners volunteered for the postal service that mail was often delivered two or three times a day. Even thieves contributed to the national effort: as war approached, apartment break-ins stopped.

On May 22, a week after the crisis began, Nasser blockaded the Straits of Tiran, Israel's southern shipping route to the east. The 55th Brigade began calling up its men.

YOEL BIN-NUN WAS haunted by his rabbi's lament on Independence Day: "They divided my land!" Something like a heavenly voice, Yoel was convinced, had exploded in Rabbi Zvi Yehudah. At night, in a restless half-sleep, Yoel imagined Israeli soldiers entering Jericho and Hebron.

The Mercaz study hall was emptying. And then an emissary from the army appeared for Yoel. He packed a knapsack with phylacteries, a pocket Bible, a book by Rabbi Kook. Before heading out to his meeting point, he went to the school for the blind near Mercaz, to say good-bye to Esther. She wasn't there, so he left a note: "To Esther, *shlomot*, peace upon you! I'm off to my unit. Don't leave Jerusalem. Great things are going to happen here. Until we meet again, Yoel."

THE RESERVISTS OF the 55th Brigade left young wives and girlfriends and boarded buses covered with the dust of back roads. They were brought to citrus orchards near Lod Airport, on the Jordanian border, below the hills of the West Bank. Pup tents lined the dirt paths between the trees in even rows, divided and subdivided into battalions and companies, each company with its own field kitchen.

The orchard was young, and its low-hanging branches provided thin shade against the strong sun. In the humidity of the coastal plain, men stripped to undershirts and spent the midday hours burrowed in tents, so small one could barely sit upright inside them. The only relief was provided by makeshift showers, cold water pouring from pipes. There were no outhouses: white tape marked areas where soldiers relieved themselves. The orchards filled with clouds of gnats, so bold that the men had to cover their mouths when they yawned.

Of the brigade's 2,000 men, only one requested sick leave. Far more typically, reservists whom doctors determined weren't fit to jump refused to be sent home. One officer appeared for duty in a cast. Young men studying abroad flew back to Lod Airport and, without stopping at home, hitched directly to the orchards.

Despite rumors of an imminent Israeli offensive in Sinai, the reservists stayed put. They dug trenches around the encampment, stood guard duty, took refresher courses in first aid and explosives, cleaned and recleaned their Uzis and Belgian FN rifles, whose long steel barrels rusted easily and required constant attention. They played backgammon and chess and amused themselves by listening to Radio Cairo's Hebrew broadcasts, which warned the Jews to flee. They laughed at the bad Hebrew and laughed, too, at the threats. Of course we'll win, they reassured each other; the only question is the cost.

They argued constantly, Israeli style—not to convince an opponent but to bolster one's certainties. Was prime minister Levi Eshkol right to try to exhaust the diplomatic option, or was he showing weakness? Should we listen to the Americans and show restraint? Can we go to war without American backing?

Whatever the differences among them, they shared a growing sense of aloneness, of Jewish isolation. Israel's foreign minister, Abba Eban, sought help in Western capitals, but no nation was prepared to stand with Israel. France, Israel's closest ally, turned against the Jewish state. The United States, which had promised to defend Israel's access to the Straits of Tiran when Israel withdrew from the Sinai Desert after the 1956 war, was preoccupied with Vietnam. And the UN was the UN. We can only depend on ourselves, said the young reservists, and on our fellow Jews in the Diaspora. Angry and anxious, the young Israelis increasingly sounded like the old Jews of exile they were meant to replace.

WHEN THEY TIRED of talking politics, they argued religion.

"How can you believe in God after the Holocaust?" a kibbutznik demanded of Yoel Bin-Nun.

"How can you not believe in God when He returned us to the land of Israel after the Holocaust?" said Yoel.

"Prove to me that God exists," the kibbutznik challenged.

"Prove to me that He doesn't," Yoel countered.

ARIK ACHMON SPENT his days shuttling between central headquarters in Tel Aviv and southern command headquarters in the desert city of Beersheba. When the updates he sought on Egyptian troop movements weren't forthcoming, he turned to an acquaintance in intelligence who provided the information. For Arik, there was always a friend in the right place. At night he returned to the big tent in the orchards, where his staff of ten reservists would incorporate the new material into their scenarios. They were soon able to identify every minefield, tent camp, and even sandbag position in El Arish.

Arik couldn't bear the endless speculations among the men and the anxious huddling around transistor radios for news updates. One of his soldiers evoked the possibility of another Holocaust, and Arik waved his hand dismissively. "Of course they would destroy us if they could," he said. "But we won't give them the pleasure."

Regretfully Arik acknowledged the likelihood that he wouldn't experience frontline combat in the imminent war. Arik was now part of Motta's inner circle. Arik would help direct the battle from behind the lines, at Motta's side.

In the nine months since being appointed Motta's intelligence officer, he had come to respect Motta more than any commander. Like Arik, Motta combined absolute confidence in his own judgment—he intended to one day become chief of staff—with a readiness to admit when proven wrong. During strategy sessions, even Motta's driver felt free to question him. And Motta knew how to reassure his men: when a young reservist in the orchards admitted he was terrified of being dropped behind enemy lines, Motta recounted his own fears as a young soldier during a nighttime jump and how relieved he was when the jump was canceled.

Arik's respect for Motta was reciprocated. Motta wrote in his diary: "What's good about Arik: He understands the importance of precision in presenting facts, and doesn't draw hasty conclusions." In matters of life and death, Motta could depend on Arik.

ONE NIGHT, AFTER reviewing the latest invasion plans, Arik went for a walk through the orchards with Moisheleh Stempel-Peles, Motta's deputy commander. They passed men sitting beside campfires, drinking Turkish coffee, arguing about the government, singing softly.

Squat, thick-necked, Moisheleh had spent the Holocaust years as a child wandering with his family through the Soviet Union. In the paratroopers, he had won a medal for valor during a retaliatory raid against a Gaza police station: under fire, he rushed to the building's entrance to replace a defective explosive.

When Motta first told Arik that he'd chosen Moisheleh as his deputy, Arik was unimpressed. "That blockhead?" said Arik. Moisheleh's opinion of Arik had been no better: a *shvitzer*, thinks he's smarter than everyone else, and meanwhile he's never experienced real combat. But in their nights together, each had learned to respect the other. Moisheleh was smarter, and Arik tougher, than either had realized.

They walked together in silence. "Arik, I want to tell you something," Moisheleh said. During the 1956 Sinai campaign, he continued quietly, he had ordered his men to beat bound Egyptian POWs. "I wanted to toughen them, teach them how to be real soldiers. Now I look at myself and can't believe what an animal I was."

Arik nodded, grateful for Moisheleh's trust in him.

PRESIDENT NASSER PROMISED the imminent end of the Jewish state. Radio Cairo's Hebrew announcer urged Jews to start packing.

Israel counterattacked with song. The new hits playing from the tinny transistor radios in the orchards were rousing, defiant. One song promised that, just as the people of Israel had emerged from all the "narrow straits" of their history, so too would they emerge from the crisis over the Straits of Tiran. Another song ridiculed Nasser's boast that he was waiting for the IDF's chief of staff, Yitzhak Rabin: "Nasser is waiting for Rabin ayayay!" The tune was so upbeat, the anticipated victory so tangible, that just hearing that song was enough to cheer the paratroopers.

In fact, no one but Rabin's closest confidants knew that the chief of staff had suffered a brief nervous breakdown—acute anxiety, his doctor called it. Israel was facing not just a war but a war of survival, the end of the Jewish dream of sovereignty, and the responsibility had overwhelmed Rabin. Tranquilized, rested, he returned to active duty.

THE RADIO CONSTANTLY played the newest hit, "Jerusalem of Gold." Written by Naomi Shemer, the country's greatest songwriter, it had been first sung at the annual Hebrew song festival on Independence Day by an unknown nineteen-year-old soldier named Shuli Natan. Her harplike voice was at once quivering and strong, and a shiver seemed to go through the whole country. Israelis had suppressed their longing for the missing parts of Jerusalem, but now they were singing along with Shuli Natan, mourning their divided capital: "The city that sits in solitude / and in its heart a wall."

The paratroopers in the orchards sang the refrain over and over: "Jerusalem of gold, and of copper and of light / I am a harp for all your songs."

Something is happening, thought Yoel Bin-Nun. On the very day that Rabbi Zvi Yehudah had cried out for the missing places of Judea and Samaria, Shuli Natan awakened the nation's suppressed anguish for the Old City of Jerusalem. *What is God preparing us for?*

THE MORALE PROBLEM OF CORPORAL UDI ADIV

IN THE HUMID, INSOMNIAC EVENING, Avital Geva joined his men quietly singing around a campfire. Avital found the singing far preferable to the endless arguments about war strategies and government policy. He didn't believe the country faced destruction, but he feared that the coming war would be Israel's hardest since 1948, and he expected the fighting to last for months. At best, he thought, the IDF would fight the Arabs to a draw.

Avital noted with concern that one corporal in Company D refused to join the campfire. His name was Udi Adiv, and he was from Gan Shmuel, a kibbutz just down the road from Ein Shemer. Udi seemed to have a morale problem. Some of the soldiers complained to Avital that Udi was denouncing what he called "Israel's plans for an imperialist war against Nasser."

Avital was wary of provoking a fight with someone from Gan Shmuel. Though Gan Shmuel and Ein Shemer were both part of the Hashomer Hatzair movement, and were located mere minutes apart, the two kibbutzim shunned each other. The rift had begun decades earlier, when several dozen members of Ein Shemer were expelled over some now-obscure ideological argument and moved a few kilometers away to Gan Shmuel. The grudge had never been forgiven. In Gan Shmuel, they referred to their garbage bins as Ein Shemers. In Ein Shemer, they mockingly called the members of Gan Shmuel —a far more prosperous kibbutz than theirs—Boazites, after the wealthy farmer of the book of Ruth. Even now, the two kibbutzim maintained separate schools. That's all I need, thought Avital, to reopen this stupid feud between Ein Shemer and Gan Shmuel.

Udi Adiv sat in his tent, wondering what he was doing here. He tried to warn his fellow reservists: We're being led to the slaughter for the glory of the generals! There is no "threat to Jewish survival," Israel is in no danger from the Arab world. Nasser is a revolutionary whom progressive Israelis should embrace.

Fellow kibbutzniks berated him: Did "the generals" invent Nasser's threats and the Arab crowds marching with genocidal banners? What was missing in Udi's DNA that he'd lost his most basic Jewish instincts for survival? Only Udi's tentmate, Rami, an aspiring actor, reacted to his politics with equanimity. Udi had brought with him a book of Greek tragedies, and Rami tried to distract him by discussing the plays.

"NEXT WEEK IN JERUSALEM"

ON SHABBAT AFTERNOON, in the waning light, Yoel Bin-Nun and his fellow religious soldiers sat outside the large tent that functioned as a synagogue. They ate cold canned goulash and sang songs of longing for a redeemed world.

With evening, the end of Shabbat merged into the holiday of Lag Ba'Omer and melancholy gave way to rousing song. "Bar Yochai, you are annointed, you are blessed," the young men sang, celebrating the ancient mystic who according to legend hid in a cave from the Romans, subsisting on water and carob pods, and who died on Lag Ba'Omer.

They formed a line. Yoel Bin-Nun held the shoulder of the man before him. They danced through the tent area and came to a clearing, a makeshift parking lot. Secular soldiers stood on the hoods of jeeps and clapped along. "Next year in Jerusalem," the religious soldiers sang. "Next *week* in Jerusalem!" a Mercaz student called out, and the dancers adopted the new lyric. "Next week in Jerusalem—in rebuilt Jerusalem!"

Though ordinarily not an enthusiastic dancer, Yoel was deeply moved by this outbreak of defiant joy. Finally, he thought, a moment of inspiration.

Avital Geva watched the dancers and wondered: How do they manage to go so quickly from anxiety to ecstasy? There was something forced about it, he felt. Untrustworthy.

BOOSTING MORALE

MOTTA GUR STOOD on the hood of a truck, illumined by a spotlight. It was night, and otherwise totally dark in the orchards. Motta had assembled the reservists for a talk, and after a week here, with Arab threats intensifying and no clear government policy in sight, they were restless and demoralized.

"It's clear to me," said Motta, "that no matter what I say, you'll continue to complain.... So go ahead and slander—the government, the army, the commanders, everything."

Laughter.

"Eisenhower writes that a soldier who doesn't complain isn't a soldier. So be soldiers, and complain.... Argue, analyze, curse, [bemoan] the home and the fields and the studies you've left behind. Hit as hard as you like. Just keep smiling...

"If we will be summoned to battle, we will go. If we will be sent home, we will go too. We are, after all, disciplined paratroopers."

OVER THE WEEKEND, parents and wives and girlfriends appeared at the orchards. Guards halfheartedly tried to prevent them from entering, then gave up. The paths through the citrus groves filled with picnickers.

THE PLAGUE OF GNATS drawn by piles of excrement was making life in the orchards unbearable. On May 31, the tent camp was moved to a clearing in a forest of cypresses and pines. The paratroopers began to train in house-to-house combat in an abandoned British army base. But they didn't fire their guns: the hard-pressed IDF was saving its bullets for the war.

Avital, singing, led his men on all-day hikes across sand dunes and at night on navigation exercises in the hills. They passed untended wheat fields ripe for harvest, casualties of the reservist mobilization. Avital felt the pain of those abandoned fields, of farmers who had sown but not reaped.

JORDAN JOINED THE Egyptian-Syrian military alliance. Israel was now facing a three-front war.

In Jerusalem, a national unity government formed. For the first time, an Israeli coalition included the right-wing party Herut (Freedom), headed by Menachem Begin, whom former prime minister David Ben-Gurion had refused to even refer to by name. The bitter feud between Zionism's left and right was suspended.

Yoel Bin-Nun was ecstatic. "This is the first national unity government since the days of the kingdom of David and Solomon," he said. Why had the Temple been destroyed? Not because of a failure of military or political strategy, argued Yoel, but because of a failure of brotherly love. Even as the Romans tightened their siege around Jerusalem, the Jews had turned against each other, burned the granaries of rival camps, and murdered rival leaders. And how will the Temple be rebuilt? concluded Yoel. By the merit of unconditional love of Jew for Jew.

On guard duty, around the campfire, Yoel spoke to secular soldiers about Israel's spiritual destiny. Some shunned him as a "missionary," others argued about why a secular state needed religious laws. One kibbutznik asked Yoel to teach him the writings of Rabbi Kook. They studied a passage about the rise and fall of religion, which begins with a vital insight, then decays in institutional constriction—a necessary stage, wrote Rabbi Kook, to purify and renew faith. "Just like dialectical materialism," the kibbutznik enthused. "Dialectical *idealism*," Yoel corrected.

When a friend spoke about "religious paratroopers," Yoel interrupted him. "There are no religious paratroopers or secular paratroopers," he said. "Only Israeli paratroopers."

JERUSALEM, JUST IN CASE

THE BRIGADE'S BATTLE PLANS were nearly complete. "I can do a doctorate on El Arish," said Arik Achmon.

But Motta was uneasy. Now that King Hussein had signed a military pact with Nasser, a Jordanian attack on Jewish Jerusalem couldn't be ruled out. At the general staff there was concern the Jordanians would attack Mount Scopus, the only outpost in East Jerusalem that Israel had managed to retain after the 1948 war. Every two weeks a convoy of Israeli soldiers was escorted by the UN through Jordanian lines to Mount Scopus. The soldiers were disguised as police, because the armistice agreement forbade an Israeli military presence there. Motta feared that the Jordanians might try to attack the convoy—the next one was scheduled for the coming week—and then overrun the outpost.

"I don't want to be caught with my pants down," Motta said.

Motta and Arik drove to Jerusalem in Motta's "Kaiser," a big cranky car temporarily requisitioned by the IDF. On the road leading up from the coastal plain, the Kaiser repeatedly stalled.

Not even the brightness of a late spring day could dispel the sadness of the divided city. West Jerusalem's main street, Jaffa Road, ended abruptly in barbed wire, just before the Old City walls. The housing projects along the border had little windows and sliding metal shutters to protect against snipers.

Motta and Arik drove into an ultra-Orthodox neighborhood. A sign, posted beside a line of laundry, read, Danger! Frontier Ahead. They stopped on the edge of a slope leading down into no-man's-land, a tangle of barbed wire and minefields several hundred meters long. On the Jordanian side were trenches and concrete bunkers; on the Israeli side, sandbag emplacements.

Crouching behind sandbags, Motta devised a plan for defending the IDF convoy to Mount Scopus. He pointed in the direction of a bend in the road sloping up toward the mount: that's where the convoy is likely to be attacked. It was precisely the point where a convoy heading toward Hadassah Hospital on Mount Scopus had been ambushed by Arab fighters in the 1948 war; seventy-nine people, mostly doctors and nurses, had been massacred. One battalion, said Motta, would head straight for the bend, while the brigade's other two battalions would seize the high ground overlooking the area, warding off Jordanian reinforcements. "A quick operation," he said.

Motta instructed Arik to present him with a preliminary intelligence report on Jerusalem. "It's a full night's work," Arik noted, a distraction from El Arish.

"Just do it," said Motta.

Arik drove to the command headquarters in charge of the central front, which included Jerusalem, and asked for intelligence assessments, maps, aerial photographs of Mount Scopus. You're too late, he was told;

intelligence officers from other brigades have taken the best material. Arik, of course, knew someone at headquarters, an intelligence officer who confided that there was other material. "It's forbidden to remove this from here," the officer said, handing him two massive folders bound by straps and containing the originals of the most sensitive documents on Jerusalem. "*Dir balak*"—Be careful—he warned in Arabic, "I can go to jail for this. Have it back here first thing tomorrow morning, before anyone notices it's missing." "*Al a'rasi*," Arik reassured him, responding in Arabic—"On my head."

That evening, Arik and his staff sifted through the folders. The material was first-rate: there were street maps, aerial photographs revealing Jordanian bunkers and sandbag positions. By midnight Arik had completed a preliminary intelligence summary. If we have to fight in Jerusalem, he told his men, at least we won't be going in entirely cold. To himself he added, The difference between what I know about El Arish and what I know about Jerusalem is on a scale of a hundred to one.

SHABBAT MORNING, JUNE 3. In the tent synagogue there was celebration: a medic named Yossi Yochai was to be married in the coming week. Yossi was summoned to bless the Torah. Reciting the blessing—"Who has chosen us from all the nations and given us His Torah"—the groom's voice caught.

The soldiers showered Yossi with candies and peanuts and sunflower seeds, gathered from gift packages sent by schoolchildren. One big young man named Yisrael Diamant lifted Yossi onto his shoulders and carried him outside. The others followed, dancing and singing: "The rejoicing of bride and groom will be heard in the Judean hills and in the outskirts of Jerusalem."

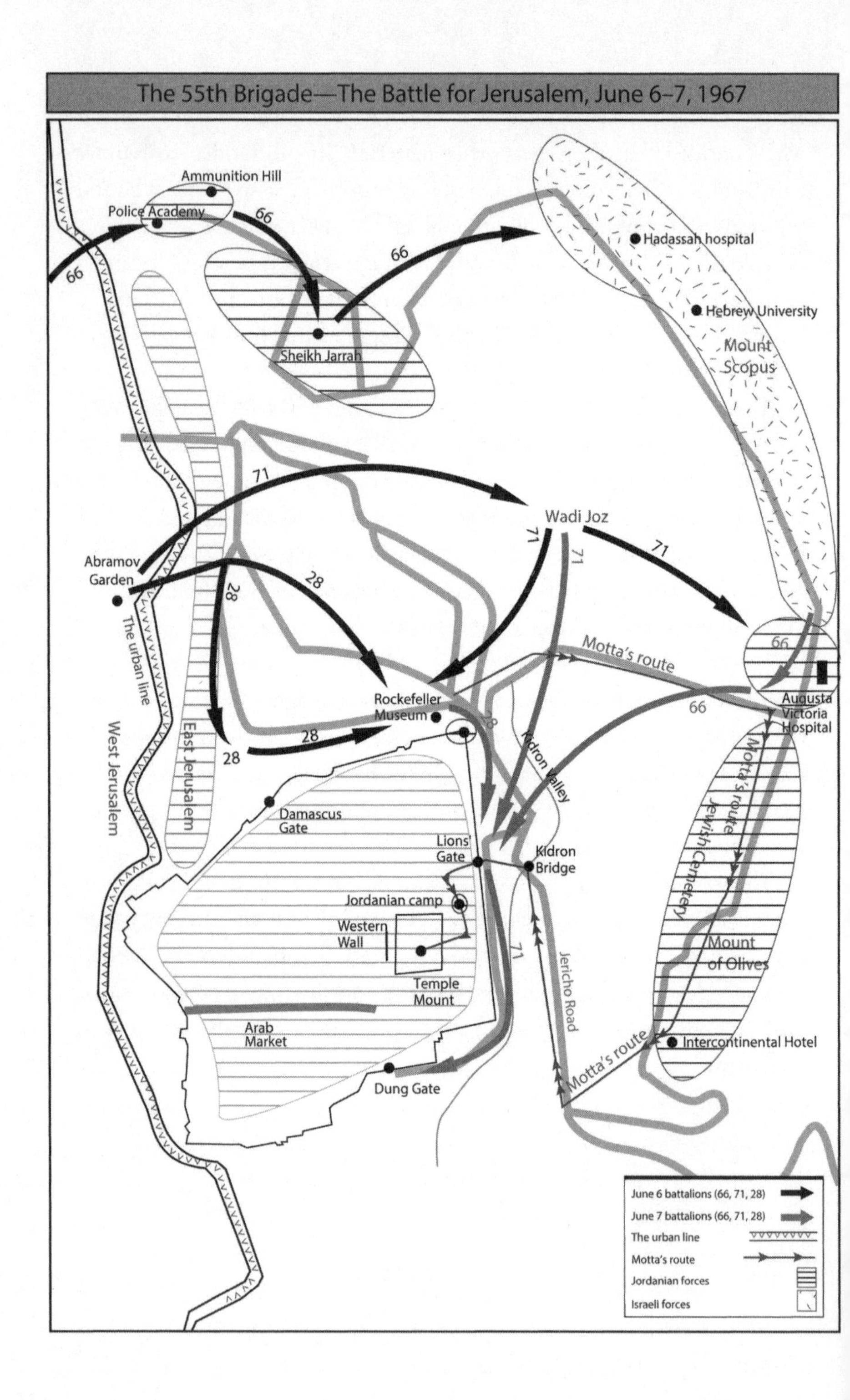

The 55th Brigade—The Battle for Jerusalem, June 6–7, 1967
Ammunition Hill
Police Academy
66
Sheikh Jarrah
Hadassah hospital
Hebrew University
Mount Scopus
71
Wadi Joz
Abramov Garden
28
Rockefeller Museum
Motta's route
Augusta Victoria Hospital
The urban line
West Jerusalem
East Jerusalem
Kidron Valley
Damascus Gate
Lions' Gate
Kidron Bridge
Jordanian camp
Western Wall
Temple Mount
Jewish Cemetery
Mount of Olives
Jericho Road
Arab Market
Intercontinental Hotel
Dung Gate
June 6 battalions (66, 71, 28)
June 7 battalions (66, 71, 28)
The urban line
Motta's route
Jordanian forces
Israeli forces

CHAPTER 5

NO-MAN'S-LAND

A CHANGE IN PLAN

"THE WAR IS about to begin," Motta said to Arik.

It was Sunday morning, June 4. "Run over to southern command," Motta instructed, "for a final update on El Arish."

Arik drove two hours south to Beersheba. The IDF, he learned, was about to launch a preemptive strike against Egypt, and the paratroopers were being sent to Tel Nof, the air force base from where they would be flown to Sinai. Busy with briefings, Arik forgot about the intelligence material on Jerusalem he'd promised to return.

For the third time in less than two weeks, the 55th moved camp. The men loaded mortars and machine guns and crates of bullets and C-rations onto buses. They relocated to a grove of eucalyptus trees located between Tel Nof and Givat Brenner, Arik Achmon's childhood kibbutz. Arik couldn't see the kibbutz, whose lights were blacked out. All these years he'd tried to wipe Givat Brenner from his memory. But the loss of his childhood home remained his deepest grief.

The men were told to dig foxholes, but many found the earth too hard and so simply lay on the ground for a few hours of restless sleep. Some smoked and paced. One young man broke out laughing for no apparent reason.

"Moisheleh," Arik said to Stempel-Peles with a touch of envy, "how do you feel about being in the first helicopter?"

Moisheleh was scheduled to lead the team that would land near El Arish and mark the area for the parachute drop.

"Here's how I see it," said Moisheleh. "The helicopter lands, I step out, take a piss, and then the war begins."

The brigade's officers were told to lecture their men about gas warfare. Just in case: the Egyptian army had used poison gas in its war in Yemen. Arik didn't bother; who had time for such nonsense?

07:10, MONDAY, JUNE 5. Dozens of Mirages and Mystères began taking off from Tel Nof and heading south. The planes were flying so low over the trees that Yoel Bin-Nun thought he could lift his hand and touch their wings.

For the next ninety minutes, planes took off and returned and took off again.

Exhausted, energized, paratroopers gathered around transistor radios and heard the laconic announcement by the IDF spokesman: Hostilities have broken out on the southern front. There was no hint that Israeli planes had almost entirely destroyed the Egyptian air force on the ground, and that the war in the south had just been decided.

Some paratroopers tuned into Radio Cairo's Hebrew broadcast. It urged Israelis to raise white flags before the conquering Egyptian army, which in a few hours would reach Tel Aviv.

On Israel Radio, the military commentator noted that all Israelis, whether or not they normally prayed, were united in the prayer that the "Guardian of Israel shall neither slumber nor sleep."

Motta and Arik were summoned to a briefing in Tel Nof. Ground forces were advancing into Gaza and Sinai faster than expected, they were told. El Arish might well be conquered before the paratroopers even got there. The 55th was no longer needed in Sinai. Instead, the brigade's three battalions would be separated: one would be dispatched to protect Lod Airport, while the other two would await a new assignment.

Arik was devastated. *Nineteen fifty-six all over again, only worse—*

As they left the briefing, Motta said quietly, "Arik, I won't let them do it to us."

14:00. General Uzi Narkiss, commander of the central front, summoned Motta, along with Arik, to his headquarters near Tel Aviv. The paratroopers, said Narkiss, were being sent to Jerusalem.

A few hours earlier, Narkiss explained, the Jordanian army had opened indiscriminate fire on the Jewish neighborhoods of West Jerusalem. Hundreds of apartments had been hit; dozens were wounded. The Israeli government had sent a message to Jordan's King Hussein: Stay out of the war, and we won't attack. Hussein ignored the offer.

Narkiss had fought in the failed battle for the Old City of Jerusalem in

1948. Then, the poorly equipped and outnumbered defenders of the Jewish Quarter had been overwhelmed by the Jordanian Legion, which expelled the Jewish residents and destroyed the centuries-old quarter, turning synagogues into stables and latrines. Since then, Jordan had barred Israelis from praying at the Western Wall. Now, though, the Old City might be within reach again.

Your mission, Narkiss said to Motta, is to break through the formidable barriers of minefields and trenches separating East and West Jerusalem and reach the Israeli enclave on Mount Scopus. But, he added, "Be prepared to take the Old City. I hope you will erase the shame of 1948."

Arik wasn't interested in historical calculations. His only concern was to thwart the enemy, not to regain a stone wall where the pious once prayed. Until explicitly stated otherwise, their mission was to protect the garrison on Mount Scopus, nothing more.

Arik's new assignment was to fine-tune the rough plan that Motta had devised two days earlier during their impulsive trip to the Jerusalem front. Within the next few hours, the 55th Brigade would be moving to Jerusalem; by early morning, they would be crossing the no-man's-land that cut across the city. In assembling the data for an attack on El Arish, Arik had had nearly two weeks and access to the most detailed intelligence. To help formulate a battle plan for Jerusalem, he had twelve hours.

AND THEN ARIK remembered: the two intelligence files on Jerusalem. What a stroke of luck that he hadn't returned them. He would keep those now to distribute among the officers. Still, the several hundred street maps and aerial photographs contained in those files were hardly adequate. The brigade would need several thousand maps and photos to distribute among the units.

Arik instructed two staff members to drive to central command headquarters. There should be enough intelligence material there, he said, to amply equip the brigade. "Take an empty van," he added. "You'll need it for all the boxes."

But when Arik's men arrived at headquarters, they were told: Other units got here first. There's nothing left.

INTO BLACKNESS

DEEPLY TANNED FROM nearly two weeks in the sun, the men of the 55th boarded requisitioned tour buses and headed toward Jerusalem.

The convoy took a back route, partly on dirt roads, to avoid Jordanian shelling of the Jerusalem–Tel Aviv highway. The bus aisles were crowded with guns and ammunition belts. Dust penetrated the windows and mingled with the haze of cigarette smoke. Some men tried to nap. One soldier held up a grenade pin, which he'd been saving for a practical joke, and called out, "Anyone lose this?"

Some sang along with the radio, which was playing only Hebrew songs, many about the desert, in solidarity with the soldiers fighting in Sinai. Then the play list shifted to songs about Jerusalem.

"Maybe we'll liberate the Western Wall," someone said.

"Hey, Yoske, why don't you build us a wall?" someone else called out to Yoske Balagan, whose latest job had been working as a building contractor.

A religious soldier read aloud psalms extolling Jerusalem. When he paused, secular soldiers urged him to continue.

Around the Harel intersection, named for the Palmach brigade that had helped break the 1948 siege around Jerusalem, the convoy turned onto the highway—a three-lane road whose middle lane was intended for those daring to pass from either side. Explosions were audible. Traffic was slowed by tanks and trucks heading toward the besieged city. The bus convoy barely moved. Soldiers shouted at the drivers to step on the gas. Some pounded on the seats before them, as if prodding a horse.

Yoel watched the landscape and recalled his first trip to Jerusalem, with his third-grade class. As they approached, the teacher had pointed out a minaret on a hill and said, "That is Nebi Samuel, burial place of Samuel the Prophet. From there Jordanian cannons bombarded Jerusalem in 1948."

"Can they bomb us again?" a child asked.

Approaching Jerusalem now, Yoel looked across the valley at Nebi Samuel and saw smoke rising from artillery positions. The Jordanians were firing on Jerusalem.

MOTTA AND ARIK and Amos Yaron, the brigade's operations officer, were driven to Jerusalem in a requisitioned Oldsmobile, hardly better than the Kaiser: it too overheated on the steep incline to the capital.

Together they fine-tuned Motta's plan. One battalion would cut through Wadi Joz, a valley on the Jordanian side of the line, and head toward Mount Scopus. A second battalion would seize Ammunition Hill, a Jordanian stronghold overlooking the main road to Mount Scopus. Meanwhile a third battalion would conquer the Rockefeller Museum just outside the Old City, and there await the government's decision about whether to enter its walls.

The Oldsmobile sped through Jerusalem's empty streets and came to an army base close to no-man's-land. A concrete wall separated the brick barracks from the stone apartment buildings of the ultra-Orthodox streets. As if sensing Motta's arrival, Jordanian mortars began exploding around the barracks.

Arik ran to the office of the intelligence officer. "Give me whatever you have," Arik said. "Nothing's left," replied the officer; "the other units took everything." With all the calm he could summon, Arik told himself, We could be facing a catastrophe.

THE BUSES, SLOW AND WEIGHTED, entered Jerusalem toward evening. They were met by the sound of explosives. Instinctively men reached for their guns. Avital Geva noted that he'd never heard such loud explosions in training exercises. Though the shells were falling on the other side of town, they seemed to be crashing into the next street.

Aside from ambulances, the streets of Western Jerusalem were entirely still. The paratroopers tried to rouse the silenced city with song: "Jerusalem of gold, and of copper and of light!"

They disembarked on Herzl Boulevard, flanked with low, stone-faced apartment buildings. Word spread: The paratroopers are here. Residents emerged from shelters, invited the young men into their homes for sandwiches and coffee and seltzer with raspberry syrup. A dentist offered to check their teeth. Why do Jews need to be hit on the head, wondered Yoske Balagan, in order to be nice to each other?

An elderly woman handed an Israeli flag to Yoram Zamosh, a twenty-five-year-old captain and one of the brigade's few religious officers. Hang this over the liberated wall, she said. Zamosh happened to be the right address for that request: a student at Mercaz, he'd often climbed the rooftops overlooking no-man's-land with a telescope, seeking glimpses of the Western Wall. "I'll do it," promised Zamosh.

JUST BEFORE NIGHTFALL, Arik Achmon took the commanders of the 66th and 71st Battalions on a tour of the border. The commander of the 28th Battalion, a Galilee farmer, got lost in the maze of ultra-Orthodox streets and missed the briefing. For the two other battalion commanders, this was their first glimpse of the imminent battlefield. They stood on the roof of an apartment house mere meters from the barbed wire fence. Arik told them what he knew, which wasn't much: Over there is Ammunition Hill; farther south, Abramov Garden. The goal of the 66th and 71st was Mount Scopus; the goal of the 28th was the Rockefeller Museum. Arik didn't mention the Old City; it wasn't on his mind.

Then he joined Motta and Uzi Narkiss, commander of the front, on another rooftop. Narkiss offered Motta two options: either cross at midnight—less than four hours away—or wait until morning, when air cover could be provided. Motta opted for the cover of night: there was, he argued, only limited use for air power in urban warfare. But, he added, midnight was too soon to prepare the brigade for crossing; give us another two hours. Narkiss agreed.

ON HERZL BOULEVARD, the company commanders briefed their men. One group met in the apartment of an officer's cousin; others gathered around the dimmed headlights of a bus. The officers used the maps and aerial photographs from Arik's two files, stretched thin among the companies. If not for those two files, the brigade would be entering battle entirely blind.

Even so, the briefings were barely intelligible: a flash of light on a map of strange streets, a photograph almost invisible in the darkness.

For the four hundred men of the 28th Battalion, only a handful of maps and aerial photographs were available of their destination, the area around the Rockefeller Museum. Avital Geva shined a flashlight onto one of the photographs, covered with red arrows pointing in directions that only confused him, and tried to explain their mission to the men of Company D. He knew that the crossing point was a place called Abramov Garden that wasn't a garden but a hill overlooking no-man's-land, and that the destination was the Rockefeller. But he didn't know anything more than that, not even the names of the streets that led to the museum. "We start here—" He pointed to no-man's land. "And then we go there—" He pointed toward the Rockefeller. Where were the enemy positions? What was the strength of their numbers? Avital couldn't say.

An officer looking for someone to take him on a reconnaissance mission to the front called out, "Is there anyone here from Jerusalem who knows the way?"

GRENADES FASTENED TO ammunition belts. Bullet clips in shirt pockets for rapid reloading. Canteens. Bandages.

23:00. The men boarded the buses. A slow-moving convoy, without headlights. A soldier who knew the city walked in front, guiding the buses toward no-man's-land. Yet even native Jerusalemites could scarcely find their way in the near-total darkness. One bus, transporting the sappers of the 71st Battalion, who were supposed to lead the breakthrough at Abramov Garden, couldn't be located. The driver had panicked and turned back.

It took nearly two hours for the convoy to reach the ultra-Orthodox neighborhoods near the front, ordinarily a brief drive from Herzl Boulevard.

The men of the 28th disembarked near the Bikur Cholim hospital, ten minutes' walk from the border.

They walked in two slow lines, on either side of the street, each man trusting the footsteps of the man before him. The blacked-out streets were illuminated only by exploding flashes.

They came to Beit Yisrael, an ultra-Orthodox neighborhood with gray stone houses. Several houses seemed dropped randomly at the edge of no-man's-land.

Avital Geva, together with his commander and friend from Ein Shemer, Haggai Erlichman, led the line of Company D. With Haggai beside him, Avital felt more secure. Haggai had fought in the retaliation raids of the 1950s, but unlike some others never told stories of his heroism. Avital respected his reticence.

Udi Adiv, the antiwar kibbutznik, found himself behind a veteran of the unit who had fought in the 1956 war. "What's it like to be in combat?"

Udi asked, seeking the reassurance of experience. "You feel your whole body exposed," the veteran replied quietly. "You wonder which part will be hurt." "Don't you get used to it?" Udi asked. "You never get used to it," the other man said.

THE COMPANIES SPREAD into the side streets and alleys around Abramov Garden, overlooking no-man's-land. In about an hour, at 02:00, the men of the 71st Battalion were scheduled to blow open a path through the minefield, to be followed by the men of the 28th.

Yoel Bin-Nun of the 28th Battalion was told by his officer to strap a radio on his back and follow him. Their mission was to find the 71st, attach themselves to its tail end, and then point flashlights to help the men of the 28th cross into no-man's-land.

The two men ran through the streets. But in the darkness they could see almost nothing.

They came to an ultra-Orthodox yeshiva. There in the courtyard, several dozen men from the 71st were gathered, preparing to move out. Paratroopers in an ultra-Orthodox yeshiva! marveled Yoel. The Jewish people is being gathered together.

"MY FACE! MY FACE!"

02:15. THE SAPPERS from the 71st—their wayward bus had turned up at the last moment—approached no-man's-land. They encountered their first surprise: a line of Israeli barbed wire that hadn't appeared in the aerial photos. They flattened the wire with their boots and reached the border fifty meters away. There they laid bangalores, long metal tubes filled with dynamite, under a row of barbed wire. They blew the beginnings of a scorched path, fifty centimeters wide and free of mines. Then they entered the breach, blew holes through the next three layers of barbed wire, stretched the bangalores farther, and extended the safe passageway through no-man's-land, which they marked with white tape.

One by one, paratroopers from the 71st descended the slope into a valley of thistles. A tank offered cover. The sky turned red and white with arcing flares. Over no-man's-land rose clouds of smoke, providing cover for the men running single file along the scorched path.

Jordanian soldiers, in bunkers and in houses, returned fire. Burning buildings lit the night. Yet the Jordanians failed to notice the paratroopers moving toward them and aimed over their heads. Mortar shells fell into side streets around Abramov Garden. Directly into the men of the 28th Battalion, Company D.

Pavement exploded. Houses blew open. Soldiers crouched behind cars and stone walls. Some lay down, exposed, gripping the ground.

A flash of light: Avital Geva fell backward, bleeding from his shoulders and knees. Someone rushed to help, but another mortar exploded and he fell too. Haggai appraised the wounds of both men: not critical. Avital was propped against a stone wall. His helmet was removed, to help him breathe more easily.

An explosion. "My face!" screamed Avital. "My face!" Blood covered his eyes. "I can't see!" He steadied himself. Haggai noted Avital's self-control.

Someone jump-started a car, and Avital was driven a few blocks away to the Bikur Cholim hospital. He dimly discerned a corridor crowded with wounded men, some lying on cots and stretchers, others leaning against the wall. Then he passed out.

BLINDING FLASHES, DISTORTIONS of light.

Udi Adiv hid in a doorway, terrified. "Medic!" came anguished cries from the street.

This wasn't Udi's war; he had mentally opted out before it began. Still, he couldn't refuse a call for help. He ran into the street and joined one of the teams ferrying stretchers to a first aid station. They laid the wounded man beside several others; in the dim light of a kerosene lamp he thought he saw an eyeball hanging from its socket. He turned away and went to retrieve another wounded soldier, feeling every part of his body exposed.

THE BATTLE HADN'T even been engaged, and the paratroopers were being decimated. They'd been taught to charge when ambushed, but the enemy was invisible and beyond reach. In Company D alone, fully one-third of its ninety-two men were wounded before they even crossed the line. Stretchers ran out; men with severed limbs lay in the street. The less injured tried to lift those more seriously wounded. Some could only moan; some couldn't even moan.

A basement shelter crowded with ultra-Orthodox families became a first aid station. Old people brought blankets and water; modest women who never exposed their knees and elbows in public tore their dresses for bandages.

A medic, hearing the whistle of an incoming mortar shell, leaped onto the man he was treating; the medic was killed, the patient saved. Another medic died in an explosion at a first aid station. He was Yossi Yochai, whose imminent wedding had been celebrated in the tent synagogue of the 28th Battalion.

THE JORDANIANS CONTINUED to fire on the streets behind Abramov Garden, still unaware that the paratroopers were heading toward them.

A waning crescent moon rose. The last men of the 71st passed through the barbed wire. Yoel's officer radioed the commander of the 28th, and its men began appearing from the alleys. Some had lost connection with their companies and joined other units. Yoel and his officer crouched at either side of the opening and aimed their flashlights at the men gathering behind them. *"Pirtzah pirtzah pirtzah"*—Breach breach breach—Yoel repeated like a chant.

ARIK ACHMON STOOD on the rooftop of a four-story building overlooking no-man's-land, where Motta had established his operational headquarters, and wished he were down below, leading his former unit, Company A, across the line.

"Sit on the radio," Motta told Arik. "I need to think."

This was Arik's second sleepless night. If he was exhausted, he didn't notice. He suddenly remembered that tonight, according to the Hebrew lunar calendar, was his birthday. Though he preferred the English date, his parents, passionate Hebraists, had always celebrated the Hebrew date. He was pleased by the confluence of his birthday with this moment.

HOW DO YOU GET TO THE ROCKEFELLER?

04:30. WITH THE first light, most of the men of the 28th Battalion had crossed no-man's-land. The men of Company D remained behind, evacuating their wounded.

The Rockefeller Museum, a fortresslike building with an octagonal tower, was no more than a fifteen-minute walk from the breakthrough point. Two companies turned right, past the now-deserted American Colony, a gracious hotel with arched passageways and courtyard fountain and Armenian-tiled hallways.

Jordanian soldiers hiding in houses and in the minaret of a mosque fired on the advancing line. One Israeli officer was shot in the thigh and lay in the road, blood spurting from an open vein. "Keep going," he told his men.

The paratroopers came to a fork in the road, beneath the bell tower of St. George's Cathedral. The battalion commander detected shooting to his right and directed the line of paratroopers there, onto Nablus Road.

In fact, they were supposed to turn left, onto Salah a-Din Street. The mistake was disastrous. Almost all the Jordanian positions were concentrated on Nablus Road, facing no-man's-land. Had the paratroopers turned onto Salah a-Din Street, they would have encountered little resistance and arrived at the Rockefeller within minutes. But when the Jordanians realized that the paratroopers were advancing directly behind them, they simply turned their machine guns around and transformed Nablus Road into a battleground.

The battalion commander radioed for help. Motta dispatched Moisheleh. Arik asked Motta to allow him to go too, but Motta insisted Arik remain with him. Maybe we should move the command post closer to the line, Arik suggested. Motta rejected that idea, too; this was a good vantage point from which to manage the three battalions.

AS PARATROOPERS MOVED along Nablus Road, shooting came from side streets and rooftops, from every direction and no direction. A machine gun inside the YMCA building on Nablus Road fired on the street. An Israeli tank silenced the position.

A paratrooper entered a courtyard, came face-to-face with a Jordanian soldier. The Israeli emptied his Uzi into the Jordanian, then threw up.

From the back of an alley, a machine gun fired on the slowly advancing line. A paratrooper tried to take out the position with a grenade, but was wounded. Another paratrooper entered to retrieve him, but he too was shot. A third, a fourth: the alley filled with the dead and dying. Among the dead was Yehoshua Diamant, the big man who had carried the groom, Yossi Yochai, on his shoulders during the Sabbath celebration in the tent camp.

SHELLS EXPLODED AROUND Motta's rooftop headquarters. Three shells hit the building's facade, blowing off the roof's railing. A journalist from the IDF newspaper went into shock and couldn't move. Arik put his arm around him and said, "From now on, you stay close to me."

IN THE CHAOS of the night, Yoel Bin-Nun had found himself crossing no-man's-land with only a part of his company. As dawn rose, the men ran, zigzag, across the narrow scorched path. They reached a clearing on the other side and took cover behind boulders.

Their commander, Michael Odem, had no map of the area. He pointed in what he thought was the general direction of the Rockefeller Museum, the 28th Battalion's destination, and led his men through an alley alongside the American Colony Hotel. They climbed over walls and fences, cut through gardens of bougainvillea and jasmine, and came to Wadi Joz, the valley between Mount Scopus and the Old City.

They found an old man wandering alone. Where is the Rockefeller? Odem asked in Arabic. The old man claimed he didn't know. Odem slapped him. The old man insisted: I don't know. The unit moved on, and saw, just up the road, the octagonal white tower of the Rockefeller.

They came across two men from the 71st Battalion. One was wounded. Odem told Yoel and three others to grab a stretcher and take the wounded man to the first aid station, back up the hill near the American Colony.

They reached the station without incident. Yoel took the opportunity to say his morning prayers. He began to recite from memory: "Blessed are You, Lord of the World, Who girds Israel with strength. . . ." Yoel had no phylacteries; they couldn't fit in his ammunition pouches. He missed the strength of binding himself in the black straps, missed fastening the boxes filled with prayers on forehead and forearm, opposite the heart, joining thought, emotion, and action in the service of God. But he was wearing other straps—attached to his gun, holding up his pouches. He looked out onto no-man's-land, but now from the east. "Blessed are You, Lord of the World, Who crowns Israel in glory. . . ."

ODEM'S UNIT APPROACHED the Rockefeller. The walled compound was a white fortress of modernity facing the ancient walls of the Old City. The road along the Rockefeller led to the Lions' Gate, one of the Old City's seven entrances.

Odem divided his men into two groups. One ran toward the courtyard behind the museum and found a back entrance. The men shot open the lock on the door. Inside, several Jordanian soldiers tried to escape but were taken prisoner.

The second group ran around the corner toward the front entrance, directly across from the ten-meter-high wall of the Old City. Snipers fired from slits intended for bowmen, wounding a paratrooper. His friends threw grenades toward the wall but missed. They tried to shoot open the museum's front door, but it was bolted shut and they had no explosives. The firing from the wall intensified. They found a side door and smashed their way through.

The Jordanian flag flying from the tower was replaced with an Israeli flag. The paratroopers cheered. Jordanian soldiers on the wall fired toward the flag, but failed to bring it down.

THE SURVIVORS OF Company D reached the Rockefeller. By the time they had crossed no-man's-land, Jordanian positions had been destroyed, and they arrived at the museum without firing a shot.

Udi Adiv and several others were dispatched to positions behind a concrete wall facing the much higher wall surrounding the Old City. It was a senseless order: the paratroopers were exposed to Jordanian soldiers firing down at them from the Old City wall, barely twenty meters away. Udi returned fire, but without aiming, hoping not to hurt anyone.

The soldier beside him slumped over. Udi didn't know his name, only the name of his kibbutz. Udi held him. Then he saw the bullet hole through his forehead. Something was oozing. Udi, in horror, thought it might be brains.

MOTTA AND HIS staff left their rooftop post, boarded three half-tracks, and drove toward the Rockefeller. The entourage included three archaeologists who had found their way to Motta's rooftop and asked to be taken along if he conquered the museum, where they hoped to find Dead Sea scrolls, writings of the ancient Jewish sect the Essenes.

Another commander might have dismissed the request as a distraction. But Motta was keenly aware that the battle for Jerusalem was different from other battles. He kept a detailed diary, recording not only military details but also poetic moments, like the anti-Zionist Hasid who helped evacuate wounded "Zionist" soldiers. For Motta, archaeologists, no less than paratroopers, belonged to this war, which was about not only survival but also retrieval: what had been taken from the Jewish people was about to be returned.

The half-tracks missed the turn into the rear courtyard of the museum and arrived at the Old City wall. Arik looked up and saw Jordanian soldiers just above them. "Turn around!" he shouted at the driver. The half-track U-turned before the Jordanians noticed its presence. The two other half-tracks followed. "We were almost killed back there," Arik told Motta, as they pulled into the rear courtyard of the Rockefeller.

BY LATE MORNING, the Arab areas outside the Old City, including Nablus Road, were under the control of the 55th Brigade. Soldiers from the 28th Battalion found their way to the Rockefeller, awaiting a government decision on a final assault on the Old City.

From inside the Rockefeller's thick walls, one could almost imagine that the war was over. For the first time since arriving in Jerusalem the evening before, the men removed their helmets and ammunition belts. Exhausted, they curled up in the hallways, on the cool stone floor.

After searching in vain for scrolls, the three archaeologists organized a tour of the museum for the paratroopers.

"HISTORY WILL NEVER FORGIVE YOU"

A JEEP ENTERED the rear courtyard of the Rockefeller, and out leaped Rabbi Shlomo Goren, chief chaplain of the Israeli army. Just what we need, thought Arik: the nudnik.

Hawk-faced, with a graying beard, Rabbi Goren had spent the first day of the war in Sinai. His jeep had been hit, a soldier beside him killed. Then the rabbi heard that the paratroopers were on their way to Jerusalem, and he rushed up to the bombarded city. He had appeared the night before at

Motta's command post, demanding to be included in the breakthrough into the Old City. For the last twelve hours he'd crisscrossed the battle zone, oblivious to shelling.

In truth, Arik respected Goren. The rabbi had courage. After the 1948 war, he had won permission from the Jordanians to search a battlefield for the remains of Israeli soldiers; entering a minefield, Goren leaped from one boulder to another, collecting body parts for burial.

Arik appreciated the rabbi for transforming the army into a place where religious Jews could feel at home. Goren brought synagogues to every base and made army kitchens kosher. He created a corpus of religious rulings on military issues, which *halacha*, or Jewish law, had neglected during two thousand years of Jewish powerlessness. For Goren, participation in the army, defending the Jewish people in its land, was a supreme religious value, superseding other sacred principles, like Sabbath observance. Goren not just permitted but obligated a soldier to violate the Sabbath and ride in a jeep on patrol.

Goren was the son-in-law of one of Mercaz's most beloved figures, Rabbi David Cohen, known as a *nazir*, an ascetic who, in anticipation of the return of prophecy to Israel, had assumed the biblical stringencies of the holy man who didn't drink wine or cut his hair. He may well have been the first *nazir* since biblical times. The *nazir* had added a new austerity: in 1948, when the Old City fell, he took a vow not to leave his home until Jewish sovereignty was restored to all of Jerusalem. Except on a few occasions, he had kept his vow.

Goren was one of the generation's leading authorities on religious law, and he made sure that no one forgot it. He fought constantly with fellow rabbis over status and honor. And now here he was, exactly where he was meant to be—chief chaplain with the rank of general in the first Jewish army in twenty centuries, camped outside the walls of the Old City.

Motta greeted Goren as an old friend.

"*Nu*, Motta, are we moving?" asked Goren.

"I'm sorry, Rabbi. Maybe you'll manage to get [government] permission to enter."

"What? There's no permission? . . . I don't understand. . . . Maybe anyway, Motta—"

"Rabbi, we paratroopers are disciplined—"

"History will never forgive you. To be here and not enter!"

"I take my orders from my commanders," said Motta.

THE ISRAELI CABINET was divided about whether to take the Old City. Menachem Begin, leader of the right, along with hawkish Labor ministers, insisted that Israel couldn't forfeit the historic opportunity. Leaders of the religious Zionist faction, the National Religious Party, elderly and cautious men, were opposed; the world wouldn't let Israel rule Jerusalem, they feared. Moshe Dayan wondered aloud whether Israel needed "this Vatican," the religiously charged ancient part of Jerusalem. Prime Minister Eshkol was ambivalent.

THE VETERANS FROM Unit 101, now members of an elite scouts' unit, showed up at the Rockefeller. Like Rabbi Goren, they had begun the war in Sinai, but when it became clear they were no longer needed there they'd come in a convoy of jeeps and offered themselves to Motta's service. "Nu, vaiter?"—So, what's next?—the scouts' commander, Micha Kapusta, asked in Yiddish.

"I'll put you to good use," said Motta. "Just don't go running around on your own."

The immediate plan was to conquer a Jordanian army camp next to Augusta Victoria Hospital on the Mount of Olives. Augusta Victoria was the highest point overlooking the Old City from the east. If the government did approve an invasion of the Old City, the paratroopers would be prepared to attack simultaneously from the Rockefeller and from the Mount of Olives.

With nightfall, Motta dispatched a tank column to Augusta Victoria. The tank commanders were instructed to turn sharply left at an intersection about a hundred meters past the museum, leading east, up to the Mount of Olives.

Five World War II–era Sherman tanks without night-vision equipment moved out in single column. In the blackout covering the city it was nearly impossible to see. The tanks missed the turn and continued straight ahead, south, under the wall of the Old City.

A bazooka shell hit the third tank in the column, igniting its camouflage netting. The commander tried to put out the flames and was hit by gunfire. The four other tanks continued past the Lions' Gate and stopped on a small bridge over the Valley of Kidron, between the Old City and the church at Gethsemane, where Jesus prayed before the Crucifixion.

Where are you? Motta radioed the tank column commander. I don't know, the commander replied. Motta decided to continue the mission and instructed the scouts' unit to head toward Augusta Victoria in place of the missing tanks.

Arik stood outside the Rockefeller with Yishai Zimmerman, who was to lead the scouts to Augusta Victoria. Arik pointed toward the elusive intersection . "There's a sharp left turn going up to the Mount of Olives," he said. "You can't see it from here, and it's very easy to miss. *Dir balak* [be careful], don't miss that turn. Otherwise, you'll find yourselves exposed directly under the Old City wall."

"Trust me," Zimmerman reassured him. "Everything will be okay."

But Zimmerman too missed the turn. Jordanian soldiers were waiting for the scouts as their six jeeps approached the Kidron bridge. Arik heard shooting. A jeep sped back into the Rockefeller courtyard, bearing Zimmerman, bleeding profusely.

Jordanian flares exposed the small Israeli convoy. A machine gun positioned below the Old City wall opened fire. The jeeps reached the Kidron bridge. A scout was killed, and others leaped over the bridge, a seven-meter fall. One man held on to the edge with burned hands. A jeep tried to turn around and crashed into the jeep just behind it. The lead tank too tried to turn around and toppled into the valley below.

A soldier was on fire. Another rushed over, tearing off the wounded man's clothes. Shoot me, the burning man pleaded. His rescuer hoisted him over his shoulders. A Jordanian bullet hit the wounded man in the head.

The main part of the scouts' column hadn't yet left the area near the Rockefeller. Arik ran toward the jeeps. "Stop!" he shouted at Kapusta, the commander.

Motta ordered tanks from another unit to prepare to move out, toward Augusta Victoria. "Arik," said Motta, "take Kapusta and make order in the *balagan*"—the chaos.

Arik and Kapusta headed on foot toward the bridge to help extricate the jeeps trapped near Gethsemane; they had no idea that the tanks were there too. As they approached the corner of the Old City wall, a Jordanian soldier aimed a bazooka. The shell exploded two meters from where they stood. They flew in the air. Stumbled up: intact.

They ran across the road, away from the wall, descending onto the slope just below the road and leading into the valley. Out of sight of the snipers, they began walking toward the bridge.

The air smelled of explosives; Arik's lungs burned. But the shooting had stopped, and it seemed safe now to retrieve the wounded. "I'll take it from here," said Kapusta.

Meanwhile Motta had received an order from central command: Suspend the attack on Augusta Victoria. A column of Jordanian tanks was believed to be heading toward Jerusalem from the Jericho road. The paratroopers were to organize the city's defense.

SERGEANT MEIR ARIEL collapsed in the arched hallway of the Rockefeller, near a glass case displaying Canaanite figurines. How was he supposed to sleep? He had seen dead bodies. He had seen a friend wounded in the leg by machine gun fire. He had almost been killed. A bullet meant for his gut had been absorbed by his canteen; when the water trickled down his leg, he wondered if he'd wet himself.

Meir had distinguished himself in the paratroopers as a misfit. As a draftee he would show up for roll call unshaven, shoelaces dangling; once, before jumping out of a plane, he threw up. He was often caught in the female barracks, and his punishment was to dig holes, one meter wide and one meter deep. Those punishments became so routine that Meir would anticipate them by watering the ground to soften it for the next round of digging. Yet somehow Meir had persevered, invariably forgiven by his officers, who were charmed by this young man with long black curls who played guitar around the campfire to his own compositions.

After seizing the Rockefeller, some of the guys in Meir's unit had posed for a photograph holding a Jordanian flag, and they'd insisted Meir join them. Reluctantly, he stood at the edge of the group; when the camera flashed, he turned away. The look on his face said, What am I doing in this victory pose?

Meir wanted to be a singer, or maybe a filmmaker. Something other than what he was: a tractor driver in the cotton fields of Kibbutz Mishmarot. Meir observed himself with the perplexed distance of an outsider. What was this collection of random personas—human, male, kibbutznik, Israeli—cobbled together and demanding coherence? And now he might be about to die. He didn't object to dying if that meant protecting his family, his father, who had survived exile in Siberia for Zionist activities, his kibbutz, which made place for every misfit, including him. The Jews deserved their safe corner in this world. His objection was that he might die without discovering who he was.

Meir was thinking now of Naomi Shemer's song. "Jerusalem of gold, and of copper and of light . . ." Its sweetness tormented him.

He retrieved a pen that he always kept, just in case a line to a song appeared, and wrote on the back of an envelope: "In your darkness Jerusalem . . ."

The words conformed to Shemer's melody. Meir was writing a parody, nothing more, a song for a future campfire. "Jerusalem of iron and of lead and of blackness . . ."

"Meir," a friend interrupted, "no one is going to pick up your mail here."

"I'm just doodling," said Meir.

CHAPTER 6

"THE TEMPLE MOUNT IS IN OUR HANDS"

FRIENDLY FIRE

"GET SOME SLEEP, that's an order," Motta said to Arik, who hadn't slept in two nights. "But first check on the readiness of the Seventy-First Battalion."

Of all the battalions, the 71st had emerged most intact from the battle for Jerusalem. In less than twenty-four hours, the brigade had suffered nearly a hundred dead and four hundred wounded. The most devastated battalion was the 66th, whose men had fought the toughest battle, hand-to-hand combat with elite Jordanian troops in the trenches of Ammunition Hill. With the conquest of Ammunition Hill, the road to the besieged Israeli enclave on Mount Scopus lay open, and the survivors of the 66th were heading there now.

Arik left the Rockefeller, where the 28th Battalion was camped, and began making the rounds of the 71st, whose men were spread through the Arab neighborhoods outside the Old City walls, in hotels and in the houses of families who had fled the fighting.

Arik briefed the commanders about plans to stop the Jordanian tanks said to be heading toward Jerusalem.

02:00. Red-eyed, unwashed, Arik returned to the Rockefeller, lay on the stone floor, rolled his jacket into a pillow, and slept.

Two hours later, Motta woke him. An order had come from central command to resume the attack on Augusta Victoria. In securing the eastern ridge, the paratroopers would be the first line of defense against the Jordanian tanks.

06:00. ISRAELI ARTILLERY began shelling the Muslim Quarter inside the Old City, where Jordanian units had been concentrated. "Avoid the Temple Mount," Motta ordered, though the Jordanians had established a military position there too.

Motta and Arik stood on the roof of a house just above the Rockefeller, where the brigade command had set up a field headquarters. Several soldiers were smoking in the museum courtyard. Jordanian POWs sat with bound hands beneath a corrugated roof.

A shell fell just outside the walled courtyard. Motta ran downstairs. "Get inside!" he shouted to the soldiers. Motta's communications officer phoned central command, to determine whether the shell was Jordanian or Israeli. No one knew.

It was Israeli. And then, before the soldiers and the POWs could move inside, another two errant shells fell.

Motta rushed into the courtyard. Bodies missing limbs, wounded lying in blood. "All of you inside!" Motta shouted. "More shells are about to fall!" The medics ignored him.

"BEN-TZUR, DRIVE!"

08:30. MOTTA AND HIS STAFF left the Rockefeller in a half-track and a four-wheel-drive command car, accompanied by a column of tanks and the survivors of the reconnaissance unit. Arik had mapped out an alternative route to Augusta Victoria: through the valley known as Wadi Joz, away from the Old City and toward Mount Scopus, and then a right turn up to the Mount of Olives.

Meanwhile, the 71st and the 66th were converging on Augusta Victoria. The puzzled commanders radioed Motta's portable headquarters: We're encountering no resistance.

Where were the Jordanians?

"Motta," said Arik, "my estimation is that the Jordanians have stopped fighting."

In fact most of the Jordanian soldiers—including the units based inside the Old City—had retreated in the middle of the night toward Jericho. The failure of the Israeli commandos to take the ridge overlooking the Old City had, ironically, kept the road to Jericho open, allowing the Jordanians inside the walls to join the retreat. Only a few remained behind, apparently unaware that the Jordanian army was no longer functioning. Though Arik didn't know it, the Old City lay open.

Nor were there any Jordanian tanks. The intelligence had been wrong: There would be no Jordanian counterattack.

09:15. STANDING INSIDE Motta's half-track, Arik received this message from central command: "Go into the Old City immediately and capture it." The government had given its approval.

Arik, his tone deliberately understated, passed on the message to Motta. "Confirm receipt of the order," replied Motta, "and tell them we'll execute it right away."

Motta's half-track drove along the ridge of the Mount of Olives.

Arik radioed central command: What is the strength of the Jordanians inside the walls? On the Temple Mount? As usual, there was no specific intelligence.

The half-track parked near the multi-arched entrance of the Intercontinental Hotel, overlooking the Lions' Gate.

Motta sat on the ground and gazed at the walled city. It was a bright, cool morning, and the sun was on his back. The gold and silver domes of the Temple Mount glowed before him. He closed his eyes, as if in prayer. He was about to enter the Jewish pantheon, along with King David, who'd conquered Jerusalem and turned it into his capital; Judah the Maccabee, who'd purified the Temple after its desecration by the Hellenists; Bar Kochba, who'd thrown himself against Rome and lost the Jews' last desperate battle for Jerusalem. Then came the centuries of enforced separation, landscape transformed into memory. And now landscape was reemerging from dream, shimmering back into tangible reach.

Until this moment, Arik had felt no historical resonance in the battle for Jerusalem. They had come to the city to protect its Jews, nothing more. But now his thoughts too drifted into history. The paratroopers were about to become the first soldiers of a sovereign Jewish state in eighteen centuries to enter the capital of the Jewish people. Even for Arik Achmon, that was a disorienting thought.

Arik forced his attention back to practicalities. He aimed his binoculars at the Temple Mount. No sign of movement. Were they walking into an ambush?

Motta took the radio and addressed his three battalion commanders. "Fifty-Fifth Paratrooper Brigade," he began, deliberately violating army regulations against identifying a unit over the radio during combat, recording the moment for history, "we are sitting on the ridge overlooking the Old City, and soon we shall enter it—the Old City of Jerusalem, which generations have dreamed of and longed for. We will be the first to enter . . . Twenty-Eighth and Seventy-First Battalions—move toward the Lions' Gate! Sixty-Sixth Battalion—follow them. Move, move toward the gate."

The men of the 28th left the Rockefeller in two columns and headed toward the Lions' Gate. A shot from the wall hit a soldier in the neck. Yoel Bin-Nun rushed toward him. Someone else reached the wounded man first and stanched the spurting blood. Meanwhile, a kibbutznik jump-started a parked car. Yoel helped lift the wounded man inside, and the car sped off to the hospital.

Rabbi Goren appeared on foot, holding a shofar and a small Torah scroll. Goren seemed oblivious to the sporadic shooting from the wall; he hadn't bothered to put on a helmet. He seemed to Yoel to embody Jewish history, which couldn't wait any longer for this moment.

"Where's Yossi Fradkin?" Goren shouted to no one in particular, seeking out the commander of the 28th. "They told me he is going to the Temple Mount!"

The Temple Mount, Yoel repeated to himself. *Soon we will be standing on the Temple Mount—* What did it mean? The Temple Mount had been so inaccessible that Jews could only imagine reclaiming it in the time of the Messiah.

And yet here was Yoel, heading toward the holiest place on earth in the boots of war, in the company not of prophets but of pork-eating kibbutzniks. "Like dreamers," the Psalmist wrote of the Jews returning to Zion. Perhaps he was suggesting not only joy but dislocation.

MOTTA'S HALF-TRACK DROVE slowly down the hill, on a narrow road paved through the Mount of Olives' ancient Jewish cemetery. Many of the tombstones were broken, vandalized. Arik's grandfather was buried here.

They passed the arched facade of the Church of All Nations, onto the bridge over the Valley of Kidron. The bodies of four Israeli scouts killed the night before lay beside a charred jeep. Arik turned away.

"Sa, Ben-Tzur!" Motta shouted to his driver. Ben-Tzur, drive!

A steep, narrow road led up to two massive, bronze-plated wooden doors; on either side was a relief of two lions.

10:12. An Israeli tank shell blew open the left door, which collapsed backward. The right door, still standing, was splintered. A bus parked nearby caught fire, filling the half-opened entrance with smoke. "Ben-Tzur, *sa*!" Motta shouted. Drive!

Ben-Tzur went into first gear, drove around the smoking bus, then crashed through the right door. A pile of stones dislodged from the arch lay just beyond the gate; they drove over it onto a narrow cobblestone road. The Via Dolorosa.

Total silence. For the first time since they'd come to Jerusalem, Arik felt afraid. They were alone in the Old City, entirely exposed. Snipers could aim from any of the stone buildings hemming them in.

Arik held a map of the Old City. "Turn left!" he called.

"Ben-Tzur, sa!" Motta repeated. Drive!

They rode onto a strip of asphalt. Past a Jordanian tent encampment: abandoned.

A motorcycle lay before them. Ben-Tzur stopped. Motta turned toward Arik: "Booby-trapped?"

Motta didn't wait for an answer. "Ben-Tzur, *sa*!" Over the motorcycle. The half-track shook, but continued intact.

To their right was a wide outdoor staircase, leading up to the Dome of the Rock.

Motta and Arik ran up the stairs.

They came to the gold-domed building. Its facade was covered with blue-and-green-patterned tiles, conveying the movement of the sea. To Arik, Motta appeared in a trance. *You are now his bodyguard—*

Arik circled the perimeter of the plaza: No Jordanians. Silence.

Motta leaned against a wall, as if to steady himself. He took the radio: "Cease fire," he ordered the battalion commanders. "All units, cease firing." Then, radioing Uzi Narkiss, commander of the central front, Motta Gur said, "The Temple Mount is in our hands."

He was not only reporting. He was restating a claim.

Motta's communications officer, Orni, produced an Israeli flag from his pouch. "Should we hang it on top of the Dome?" Arik asked Motta.

"Yallah," Motta replied—Go on.

Arik and Orni approached the copper doors, intending to hoist the flag onto the crescent moon atop the dome. The entrance was bolted; Arik shot it open with his Uzi.

The men entered the domed silence, boots on thick patterned carpets. Somewhere in here, some Jewish authorities believed, had been the Holy of Holies, the inner sanctum of the Temple where the Divine Presence was concentrated. The rabbis had forbidden Jews from ascending the Mount after the destruction of the Temple, for fear of trespassing on the ultimate sacred ground. Arik knew none of this, and it wouldn't have mattered to him if he did. Nor was Arik thinking about how the image of an Israeli flag flying over an Islamic holy place would affect Muslims. He thought only about raising the flag, a cry of victory.

Orni and Arik ascended a staircase to the balcony overlooking the sanctuary. A door opened onto a fenced-off ledge; they were now outside the dome. A hatch protruded from one of the gold plates. Lifting the plate and climbing through, they found themselves in an empty space, barely a meter wide, between the gold dome and a dome made of stone. A ladder embedded in the stone led upward to another hatch in the gold dome. They opened that second hatch and found themselves once again outside, but this time on top of the gold dome. Standing on Arik's shoulders, Orni reached up and fastened the Israeli flag to the Islamic crescent.

Arik looked out at the city of white stone, and the Judean Desert just beyond. For a few moments there were no plans to finalize, no areas to secure, only an overwhelming sense of vindication.

THE MESSIAH AND ELIJAH COME TO THE WALL

CAPTAIN YORAM ZAMOSH reached the Mount. Zamosh was the Mercaz student who had been given an Israeli flag by an elderly woman just before the battle and who had promised to hang it on the Wall.

Motta's deputy, Moisheleh Stempel-Peles, along with several other paratroopers, was searching for a way down to the Wall, and Zamosh joined them. They came upon an old Arab man in a white robe, an official of the

Waqf, the Islamic trust in charge of the Mount. He pointed them toward a fenced-off ledge.

The paratroopers stepped onto the ledge. Below them—the Wall. From his ammunition belt Zamosh extracted the flag and fastened it onto the fence. Then the men sang "Hatikvah," the national anthem.

Zamosh recalled a legend he'd learned as a child: when the Roman legion commanded by Titus burned the Temple, priests threw its keys toward heaven, and a hand reached out and retrieved them for safekeeping. Now, Zamosh thought, the keys had been returned.

RABBI GOREN HURRIED toward the Lions' Gate. There were shots; Goren ignored them. Yossi Fradkin, commander of the 28th Battalion, told Goren to move close to a wall. Goren ignored him too. "Rabbi," Fradkin said, "you're in the way."

"No one moves me," said Goren.

THE THREE BATTALIONS converged on the Lions' Gate, turning into a single mass.

A lone sniper fired from a minaret; a paratrooper silenced him.

Rabbi Goren reached the Temple Mount. "You handle him," Motta said to Arik.

Arik escorted Goren and his assistant into the Dome of the Rock. "What do you say, Major"—Goren turned to Arik—"to blow or not to blow?"

Goren's assistant, standing behind the rabbi, shook his head vehemently at Arik: No! If Goren blew the shofar inside the Dome of the Rock, he would be staking a religious claim that could create a holy war with Islam. Arik didn't understand the implications of blowing the shofar here, but he yielded to the assistant's opposition.

"I don't think it's a good idea," said Arik, and Goren relented.

DEFENSE MINISTER MOSHE DAYAN stood on Mount Scopus and, raising binoculars to his single eye, watched the Temple Mount across the valley.

Dayan had lost an eye on a commando raid in 1941 against French Vichy forces in Lebanon. He had been looking through binoculars when a bullet hit the lens, splintering glass and metal casing into his left eye. He lay conscious without anesthetic for twelve hours before reaching a hospital. It felt, he later said, as if sledgehammers were pounding his head. The pounding, though eased, never stopped.

Now, seeing an Israeli flag flying over the Dome of the Rock, Dayan was appalled. He radioed Motta: You're going to set the whole Middle East on fire. Remove the flag immediately.

Motta relayed the order to Arik, who dispatched one of his men: he couldn't bear to do it himself.

RABBI GOREN SENT his assistant, Rabbi Menachem Hacohen, to retrieve Rabbi Zvi Yehudah and Goren's father-in-law, the *nazir*, the ascetic. The first civilians at the liberated wall, Goren insisted, must be the rabbis of Mercaz.

Hacohen borrowed a jeep mounted with a cannon and drove to the house of the *nazir*. The elderly man in long white hair and beard wasn't speaking: he had recently taken a vow of silence. Hacohen told him, "I've come to bring you to the Wall." Overwhelmed, the *nazir* followed him out the front door wearing only socks; his wife ran after him with shoes.

Next stop: Rabbi Zvi Yehudah. Hacohen found the rabbi in prayer. "I've come to take you to the Wall," Hacohen said. Rabbi Zvi Yehudah seemed stunned, uncomprehending. Hacohen removed the elderly man's prayer shawl and phylacteries, lifted him into his arms, and carried him to the jeep.

YOEL BIN-NUN APPROACHED the Lions' Gate. Spread before him was the landscape of messianic dream. Terraced into the Mount of Olives were thousands of flat tombstones, of Jews who had chosen to be buried directly across from the Temple Mount, to be resurrected when the Messiah came. In the Valley of Kidron rose the conical stone monument called the Pillar of Absalom, after the rebellious son of King David, founder of the messianic line. Nearby, embedded in the Old City wall, was the Gate of Mercy, through which, according to tradition, the Messiah would enter, and which had been sealed by Muslims to thwart the redeemer of Israel.

Yoel ran up the steep road leading to the Lions' Gate, past the still-smoking bus, and through the crowded gate.

When he reached the steps leading to the Dome of the Rock, he abruptly stopped: beyond lay the region of the Holy of Holies.

He felt lightheaded, as if on a mountain peak. *To move from battle to this—*

He couldn't pray: prayer seemed inadequate. What was left to ask for? He felt himself to be an answered prayer to all those who had believed this day would come, that Jewish history would vindicate Jewish faith.

He studied the topography. "This was the women's area of the Temple," he told a friend. "How do you know, Yoel?" his friend asked, surprised. Yoel explained that he happened to be studying the laws of the Temple just before the war, and he could plainly see the Talmud's description of the layout of the Mount.

Young men on their way up the stairs stopped to ask Yoel directions to the Western Wall. Yoel shrugged; the Wall didn't interest him. The Jews had prayed there only because they'd been barred from the Mount. Why descend to the place of lamenting God's absence from the place that celebrated His glory?

Yoel thought of his high school rabbi, who had claimed that Israel's failure to control the Temple Mount was proof that God had rejected Zionism. What was the rabbi thinking now?

"So, Yoel, what do you say?" his kibbutznik officer asked.

"Two thousand years of exile are over," replied Yoel.

HANAN PORAT, a student of the Mercaz yeshiva who was part of the 66th Battalion, walked along the Mount of Olives, overlooking the Old City.

Hanan had been spared the trench fighting on Ammunition Hill; instead, his company had veered toward the Jordanian-held building on the border known as the Police School, which fell after a brief battle, and then proceeded toward Mount Scopus.

But this morning, only minutes earlier, Hanan's beloved officer had been killed just beside him, by an unknown attacker. Hanan had stood over the body, unable to move, until pried away by a friend.

He was still in shock when he saw a jeep, with two elderly bearded men in the back seat, pass between the two columns of paratroopers moving along either side of the road. Was he hallucinating? *Impossible*—there was Rabbi Zvi Yehudah and the *nazir*, both in helmets, fedoras held on their laps. Hanan ran out of the line. "Rabbi Zvi Yehudah!" he shouted. "Rabbi

Zvi Yehudah!" The old men couldn't hear him. Hanan continued shouting, waving his arms, running after the vision of holiness long after the jeep had sped away.

AVITAL GEVA AWOKE in the Bikur Cholim hospital, head covered with bandages. He didn't know what day it was. He tried to remember when he had last been conscious. He assumed he was in a hospital.

He had already undergone several operations to remove shrapnel from his forehead. Fragments had lodged two millimeters above one eye; shrapnel remained in his legs and shoulders.

He heard shouts. "Reunited Jerusalem!" "The heroic paratroopers!" "The wall!" Jerusalem reunited? The paratroopers at the Wall? His last memory had been of slaughter in blacked-out streets. All had seemed lost then, the battle over before it began. Too medicated to speak, Avital felt desperate with questions. How many of his men had survived? Who among them had reached the Wall? And how could he not be with them?

YISRAEL SHTIGLITZ, a Mercaz student, reached the Temple Mount. Unlike his friend, Yoel, he didn't linger but headed for the Western Wall. For Shtiglitz, the Wall was home: he had been there often as a child, before the establishment of the state. He recalled how Arabs had forbidden Jews to bring chairs to the Wall or read there from the Torah. One Shabbat, as Shtiglitz stood beside his father in prayer, an Arab man on a donkey rode into the worshippers, scattering them with his stick. The humiliation of a powerless people. But now Shtiglitz had returned to the Wall as a liberator.

A soldier told Shtiglitz that two bearded old Jews had been seen on the Mount, heading down toward the Wall. What are you talking about? Shtiglitz demanded. How could elderly Jews be wandering around a war zone? Then he understood: They've come. The Messiah, accompanied by Elijah the Prophet. If Jewish soldiers were on the Temple Mount, why not that?

Shtiglitz ran down the stone steps leading from the Temple Mount to the narrow space that separated a row of houses from the Wall—a foundation of boulders, rising in gradually smaller layers of stone, caper bushes growing in the cracks.

Then he saw them. Not quite the Messiah and Elijah, but almost as awesome. Rabbi Zvi Yehudah and the *nazir*, surrounded by paratroopers. Rabbi Zvi Yehudah stood, erect, as if emulating the uprightness of the young men around him. Eyes closed, hands clasped together, steadying himself.

The rabbi embraced Shtiglitz. Then they stood together, stroking each other's shoulder in silence.

Jewish history's most sealed gate had opened. Anything could happen now.

EXHAUSTED, GRIEVING, EXULTANT, paratroopers crossed the Temple Mount and rushed down to the Western Wall.

Hanan Porat too was looking for a way to get to the Wall. The Temple Mount may have been the locus of holiness, center of the universe, but Hanan craved the Wall, where Jews had prayed for this moment. As he ran down the steps, he told a friend, "We are writing the next chapter of the Bible."

The narrow space before the Wall—barely five meters wide and twenty meters long—filled with soldiers. Rabbi Goren was lifted onto shoulders. He tried to blow the shofar but was too overcome. "Rabbi," said an officer, a kibbutznik, "give me the shofar. I play the trumpet." Goren complied. The sound that emerged resembled the blast of a bugle.

A kibbutznik asked Hanan Porat to teach him an appropriate prayer. Hanan replied, "Just say the Shema"—the basic Jewish prayer that begins, "Hear O Israel, the Lord our God the Lord is one," and which any Orthodox child can recite. But the kibbutznik had never heard of the Shema. "Repeat after me," said Hanan, and they said the prayer together.

MOTTA AND ARIK came down to the Western Wall. Arik was unmoved. What did he have to do with this outbreak of piety among the paratroopers, of all people? Arik heard some of the soldiers speaking about a "miracle" and felt uneasy. What miracle? The Jews had won because they stopped waiting for miracles and learned to protect themselves.

Motta watched the *nazir*. The old man in long brown jacket and fedora was standing before the Wall, rigid with awe. Not even his lips moved in prayer. He seemed to merge with the stones, thought Motta, an implacable presence, just like the Jews. Motta didn't approach the Wall, didn't know the gestures of devotion. But watching the *nazir*, he felt himself touching the stones vicariously. He took out his diary and wrote, "I was bound to [the *nazir*] from a distance. . . . Through his body, which seemed paralyzed, I felt the Jewish heartbeat."

UDI ADIV WATCHED Rabbi Goren hoisted above a circle of dancing soldiers and felt repelled. *People died so that Goren can prance before his holy stones—*

Despite himself, though, something about this place moved him. He leaned against the row of Arab houses in the narrow lane and, for the first time in his life, confronted antiquity. The kibbutz celebrated youth, the future, not nostalgia. This stone alley, with its gray light: he felt a longing that disoriented him. He was an Israeli, a new creature; if he thought about his Jewish identity at all, it is the way a human being relates to the fetus he once was, as mere unconscious prelude. In Udi's vocabulary, *Jewish* was equated with the ills of exile: rootless, parasitic, superstitious. Yet here, in the Western Wall's solitary dignity, was beauty. In this world of stone, he felt softness; in this quarry of memory, peace.

Udi looked on as soldiers caressed the Wall and buried their heads in its crevices. He felt no need to unburden himself to these stones, no urge even to touch them. He was grateful to be alive and intact, grateful that the murderous flashes of light had stopped. The confinement of this small space felt soothing. Once, exiled Jews had unburdened themselves to the Wall in defeat; now an Israeli soldier received comfort here in his unwanted victory.

YOEL BIN-NUN HAD no idea how long he had been on the Temple Mount—an hour? a day?—before his unit was dispatched to secure the Old City market.

The men walked along the Via Dolorosa, then turned right toward the Damascus Gate. On the stone walls were posters of Nasser and of Ahmed Shukeiry, the Palestinian leader who had vowed to throw the Jews into the sea.

Suddenly a young man emerged from a narrow metal door. Running. Straight toward them.

Yoel and several others fired. The young man fell.

"What are you doing!" shouted a soldier.

"He could have had a grenade," replied Yoel.

The wounded man writhed on the stone pavement. People appeared and dragged him inside a doorway.

"*HEVREH*, HAVE YOU completely lost it?" Yoske Balagan said when he arrived at the Western Wall. "Whoever heard of such a thing, paratroopers weeping?"

Even at military funerals, the paratrooper ethos was to remain stoic. Yoske had fought on Nablus Road, retrieving a wounded soldier under machine gun fire. But he hadn't lost his self-control. And yet here were some of his friends, weeping.

"Yoske," one said, "we just heard the numbers." Nearly a hundred dead, a third of the brigade wounded.

Yoske approached the Wall and stood in silence, for once at a loss for words. The guardian of the paratroopers' secular ethos felt emotions he couldn't explain.

He approached Rabbi Goren. "Do you remember me, Rabbi?" asked Yoske. "I stole your wife's pajamas at the seder you conducted for the paratroopers in 1957."

"What I remember," replied Goren genially, "was you lunatics responding to my blessings with '*Sachtein*' [To your health, in Arabic]."

Pointing to Goren's shofar, Yoske pleaded, "Rabbi, don't shoot me with that." Goren laughed. Yoske felt reconciled with the faith of his fathers.

NAOMI SHEMER WAS in a date grove in Sinai, waiting to sing for the troops, when she heard a radio broadcast of the paratroopers at the Western Wall. They were singing her song, "Jerusalem of Gold." But the words of lament for the inaccessible parts of the city had become outdated; the song needed a new stanza.

Borrowing a soldier's back, she wrote: "We've returned to the wells / the market and the square / A ram's horn calls out on the Temple Mount in the Old City."

MEIR ARIEL RAN down the steps leading to the Western Wall. Any moment, he thought, it's going to hit me: here I am, fulfillment of two thousand years of longing.

He paused at the final step. The narrow space before the Wall was packed with soldiers. Some were writing notes and placing them between the stones. Some were praying. Meir checked himself: No longing, no exultation. Nothing. What's wrong with me? he wondered. What kind of Jew am I?

CHAPTER 7

"JERUSALEM OF IRON"

THE MORNING AFTER

SPORADIC GUNFIRE CEASED. The Jordanian soldiers who remained in the Old City surrendered or else slipped into civilian clothes. Paratroopers patrolled the empty market and the Arab neighborhoods outside the walls. Arab men were randomly detained, but most were soon released. A doctor from the 55th Brigade helped an Arab woman give birth.

The Arab population—close to 70,000 people, 25 percent of the population of reunited Jerusalem—was under curfew, at the mercy of an unknown enemy. From many windows hung pieces of white cloth, improvised flags of surrender.

What would they have done to us and our families, paratroopers said to each other, if they had won the war?

IN DAZED JOY, thousands of Jews headed for the Western Wall. Simply walking several hundred meters across the city's border seemed to defy a law of nature. Not all the mines had been cleared, and one man lost a leg; but nothing could stop the crowds.

Meir Ariel watched them moving toward the Wall. "People of Israel!" he called out to no one in particular. "Now you can enter the Old City. But before you came here, a hail of lead entered the bodies of my friends."

An ultra-Orthodox Jew at the Wall told Yoske Balagan, "We prayed the whole time for you."

"Thank you very much," replied Yoske. "But I'm more grateful to the IDF, which equipped me with an Uzi."

A REPORTER FOR the Yiddish radio station circulated among the paratroopers, asking if anyone spoke *mama loshen*, the mother tongue. Yoske directed him to Aryeh Weiner, the kibbutznik from Netzer Sereni who had come alone to Israel on a refugee boat at age twelve. Weiner had just placed a note in a crack between the stones, which contained this prayer: "I hope I win the lottery."

"How did you get here?" the reporter asked him.

"We parachuted into the Old City," Weiner lied, unable to speak straight-faced in Yiddish.

Weiner's version was transmitted to the Yiddish-speaking world: The paratroopers had descended onto the Holy City like angels.

SOME ISRAELIS CAME TO LOOT. They smashed windows and pried open the shutters of shops on Salah a-Din Street, just outside the Old City walls, filling their cars with groceries and clothes. Paratroopers found themselves patrolling to thwart not only Arab attacks but Israeli plundering. "Jerusalem of gold?" one paratrooper shouted at looters. "Jerusalem of shit!"

Among themselves, paratroopers argued the moral gradations of looting. Was it permitted to take food from a grocery if you intended to eat it immediately, but not permitted to hoard? Could one take cheap tourist memorabilia, like postcards, but not electronic goods? One paratrooper argued: Why should civilians loot when we who fought get nothing? Another paratrooper, who had helped himself to food in a shuttered Arab grocery, searched for the owner to pay him.

Yoel Bin-Nun's unit was patrolling in East Jerusalem when they noticed an Israeli walking with a big radio on his shoulder. Yoel's officer, a kibbutznik, grabbed the radio, threw it to the ground, and smashed it with his boot. Yoel caught his eye and offered a grateful smile.

MOTTA SENT ARIK to escort David Ben-Gurion to the Western Wall. The country's first prime minister and his wife, Paula, had been brought to the old border by Ezer Weizman, the former air force commander and now IDF's chief of operations. Weizman said that the Ben-Gurions would ride with him, and that Arik should follow. "I represent the paratroopers," Arik said. "I want to be with Ben-Gurion." Weizman wasn't used to taking orders, let alone from a major, but he wasn't about to argue with one of Motta's men the day after the reunification of Jerusalem. Arik and Ezer exchanged jeeps, and Arik sat beside Ben-Gurion.

Ben-Gurion, kibbutznik's floppy hat atop his white winged hair, was silent. To Arik, he seemed in shock. Arik too preferred silence: he had just learned the names of the fallen from his old unit, Company A. Paula, though, didn't stop talking. She asked Arik about a relative of hers whom she thought was in the 55th Brigade, and Arik assured her he wasn't. She insisted he was.

Arik had always seemed to just miss his moment. But now he was exactly where he was meant to be. Whatever failures he had experienced and whatever disappointments still awaited him, he had had the privilege of being among the liberators of Jerusalem.

ADA GEVA FOUND a note in her cubby in the dining room: "A friend of Avital's called to say he's been lightly wounded." Of course "lightly wounded," thought Ada; what else would Avital say?

Without visible reaction, as if she'd expected this news all along, she returned to her room and packed a bag. Then she went to tell Avital's parents. "I'm going to see him," she said. "In the middle of a war?" asked Kuba. "How will you get there?" "Hitching," she replied.

She began walking toward the road. Kuba borrowed a kibbutz car and drove her to Jerusalem.

In the Bikur Cholim hospital, the halls were crowded with wounded men on mattresses. Some were screaming; most were still. Ada was impressed with the calmness of the staff. *The way it's supposed to be—*

She approached the nurses' station. There was no list of the wounded, and no one could tell her where Avital was. And so Ada and Kuba went from room to room. Ada, nearsighted, peered at the wounded. *Which one is mine? They're all mine—*

She saw a head entirely bandaged, except for lips, nostrils, and a single eye. She squeezed between the beds, bent down, and kissed the luminous blue eye of the boy of the orchards.

TO THE SYRIAN FRONT

THE EGYPTIAN AND JORDANIAN ARMIES were routed. The IDF had reached the Suez Canal and the Jordan River—conquering the West

Bank, ancient Judea and Samaria. Hebron, Nablus, Bethlehem—biblical geography had suddenly converged with the borders of modern Israel.

There was fighting on the Syrian front. The Syrians were shelling kibbutzim in the Galilee, and after initial hesitation, Defense Minister Dayan ordered the IDF to take the Golan Heights.

Motta and Arik went to IDF headquarters in Tel Aviv to get their next assignment. Stay in Jerusalem and keep the peace, they were told; other units will take over from here. Motta insisted on joining the Golan battle. When Israel is at war, he argued, the paratroopers don't patrol the home front.

And so the men of the 55th boarded buses again, this time heading north. Some joked: now they want us to take Damascus. Most sat or smoked in silence.

Meir Ariel wrote. He was completing the takeoff on "Jerusalem of Gold" that he'd begun in the Rockefeller. His Hebrew was elegant, eccentric: "In your darkness, Jerusalem," the song began. The complicated word he chose for "in your darkness," *b'machshakayich*, was hardly part of daily speech. Meir borrowed it from the Psalms: "The dark places of the land are full of the habitations of violence." Had Meir the kibbutznik been reading Psalms during the war, seeking divine protection?

He invented words—like the verb *ragum*, literally "mortared," by which he meant, under mortar attack: "The battalion, mortared, pushed onward / all blood and smoke / and mother after mother entered / into the community of the bereaved."

Meir had intended to rebuke Naomi Shemer's naïveté; but he too couldn't help celebrating Jerusalem: "In your darkness Jerusalem / we found a loving heart / when we came to expand your borders / and disperse a foe." The refrain couldn't sustain its bleakness: "Jerusalem of iron / and of lead and of blackness / to your walls we summoned freedom."

THE CONVOY OF BUSES stopped along the Boulevard of the Kibbutzim, a two-lane road of palm trees behind which spread some of the country's leading kibbutzim. Just ahead was the Sea of Galilee, and beyond it, the Golan Heights.

Many of the paratroopers were from kibbutzim in the area. Word instantly spread, and hundreds of mothers and fathers and wives appeared.

There were relieved embraces with husbands and sons. And there were hushed conversations about the wounded and the dead.

Quietly, the bereaved walked slowly back toward the gates of their kibbutzim, to share their grief with the collective.

THE LAST WAR

THE IDF CONQUERED the Golan Heights before the 55th Brigade managed to reach the front. By Saturday, June 10, the Six-Day War was over.

On Sunday morning, June 11, after a Shabbat rest in kibbutzim in the north, the paratroopers rode back to Jerusalem, to be discharged. On Meir's bus they sang the song he had taught them over Shabbat: "Jerusalem of iron / and of lead and of blackness." This is our song, friends told him. Perhaps because it was written by one of them; perhaps because it protested sentimentality, but affirmed the war's justness.

The buses took a shortcut through the Jordan Valley, until a few days earlier Jordanian territory. On one side of the narrow road were the desert hills of the West Bank, on the other, the plains of Jordan and mountains beyond. The border was unmarked, the Middle East open.

Along the road were lines of refugees, barefoot children and women balancing all of their possessions in bundles on their heads. The buses stopped, and soldiers got off to offer water. Some refugees, suspicious, drank from the canteens only after the men drank first.

Arik rode back to Jerusalem with Motta. "The wars are over," said Arik.

Surely now the Arabs would understand the futility of trying to destroy Israel. "You've been retired, Motta," he added, smiling. "But don't worry, I'll help you find a civilian job."

THE ROW OF RAMSHACKLE HOUSES facing the Western Wall was bulldozed, and now a large plaza, white with dust, replaced the alley that had been able to accommodate at most a few dozen people. The several hundred residents of the Mughrabi Quarter, as the cluster of houses was known, were moved to a refugee camp on the northern edge of the city.

When Udi Adiv's unit passed the area near the Wall, he was stunned. The stone alley with its gray filtered light, the intimacy and the mystery—gone. In its place a plaza as flat and glaring as the cotton fields of his kibbutz.

Udi looked at the piles of rubble that had once been homes, and thought, Whatever the Zionists touch, they destroy—

THE NEW EXPANSE at the Wall disturbed Yoel Bin-Nun too. But Yoel saw it as an act of surrender. Clearly the government was trying to divert Jewish attachment to the Mount by creating a pilgrimage site below, so that each of the faiths would have its own ample area. How could the Western Wall—a mere retaining wall of the Temple, without intrinsic holiness—possibly replace the Mount? And how could a victorious Israel forfeit its claim to Judaism's holiest site?

Yoel devised a plan: the area around the Dome of the Rock would be cordoned off, while along the edge of the Mount, where pilgrims are permitted by Jewish law to step, a synagogue would be built.

Yoel would have happily shared his plan with the government. But no one was asking his opinion.

A HERO OF ISRAEL

IN THE AMPHITHEATER on Mount Scopus, weeds grew in the cracked stone benches, and thistles covered the sloping earth. Nearby were the empty buildings of the original Hebrew University campus, abandoned in 1948.

But now the amphitheater was getting an instant facelift. It was Monday, June 12, and tonight some of Israel's leading performers were to assemble on its stage for a victory concert in honor of the 55th Brigade. And so paratroopers were cleaning benches and clearing debris.

In a small grove near the amphitheater, Arik sat under a pine tree, dealing with arrangements for the discharge of the brigade. He was interrupted by an officer from the 28th Battalion. "Arik, listen, Meir Ariel has written an important song, something like 'Jerusalem of Gold' but from our point of view. I've asked him to sing it tonight but he refuses. I know he respects you; I need you to talk to him."

Arik felt an almost fatherly responsibility toward Meir. Arik believed he was at least partly responsible for Meir having joined the paratroopers in the first place.

They had met in 1959. Arik was twenty-six, Meir nearly eighteen. Arik had been given time off from his duties at Netzer Sereni to work as coordinator of the youth division of the Ichud (Unity) movement, the social democratic kibbutz federation to which Netzer Sereni belonged. His job was to organize seminars and hikes, and most of all to instill enthusiasm among kibbutz youth, many of whom were showing signs of ideological apathy.

One evening Arik drove to Mishmarot, a kibbutz on a back road behind the village of Pardes Hanna, south of Haifa and near the coast. Mishmarot, small and peripheral, was considered a problematic kibbutz, lacking ideological passion.

Arik entered the youth club, but the dozen teenagers playing backgammon and strumming guitars ignored him. "*Hevreh*," he called out, "my name is Arik, I'm from the Ichud, and I want to talk to you about some things that could be interesting for you."

Arik prodded them into a circle. One teenage boy with curly black hair remained sitting on a windowsill, blatantly disinterested.

"The movement can provide a range of activities for you," said Arik.

"It's all nonsense," said the teenager on the windowsill.

"Why nonsense?" asked Arik.

"The 'movement' "—he spoke the word with mockery—"is interested in itself, not in us."

"Of course the movement has its own interests," said Arik. "But that doesn't negate your interests."

"And what will happen if we don't get involved; will the movement throw us out?"

Arik detected not just contempt but a legitimate anger at the rigidity of the kibbutz.

"What's your name?" asked Arik.

"Meir," he said.

"Listen, Meir, no one is going to throw you out of the movement. But you'd be missing out on a chance to connect with young people from other kibbutzim in activities you would enjoy and that would help you grow."

"Look, Arik, we're a small kibbutz, nothing much happens here. It's a shame for you to waste your time with us."

Afterward Arik approached Meir.

"Tell me, Meir, you're in twelfth grade, right? What are your plans for next year?"

"Not sure," Meir said.

"A guy like you, kibbutznik, strong spirit, you belong among us in the paratroopers."

"I'll think about it."

ARIK WALKED OVER to the area where the men of the 28th Battalion had laid their sleeping bags and found Meir.

"The *hevreh* want you to sing the song you wrote about Jerusalem," said Arik.

"There's no way," Meir said. "It's just something I wrote, *stam*. I just want to forget the war and get out of here."

"Show me the song, Meir."

Meir retrieved a sheet from his shirt pocket. Arik read the lyrics, written in small script.

"Meir?" said Arik. "You *have* to do this. If you refuse, I'll order you to sing."

"Singing can't be ordered."

"Meir, with everything we've been through—you owe it to your friends."

Meir nodded.

TOWARD SUNSET, THE MEN of the 55th Brigade gathered in the amphitheater. In the distance rose the desert hills of the West Bank and the Dead Sea beyond: the new landscape of Israel.

The heroes of Jerusalem wanted nothing more than to go home. Not even performances by the country's leading singers could rouse them. One offered an old song of longing for Zion, "From the peak of Mount Scopus, I offer you peace, Jerusalem." Few sang along or even bothered to applaud. Arik nodded off.

The MC, an actress named Rivka Michaeli, announced, "There is a soldier here—" Someone whispered into her ear. "Meir Ariel, who is invited to come to the stage."

"Me-ir! Me-ir!" friends chanted, clapping rhythmically.

Meir ascended to the stage. One of the performers, Nehama Hendel, played on her guitar the opening chords of "Jerusalem of Gold." His voice surprisingly strong, enunciating each word, Meir began, "In your darkness, Jerusalem, we found a loving heart / when we came to expand your borders and disperse a foe / Dawn abruptly rose / not yet whitened and already red."

When he came to the refrain—"Jerusalem of iron, and of lead and of blackness / to your walls we summoned freedom"—some in the audience joined in.

By the next refrain, everyone seemed to be singing. When Meir ended—"Jerusalem of gold / and of lead and of dream / may peace dwell forever between your walls"—the audience continued to sing. Arik, deeply moved by the unexpected power of Meir's presence, sang too.

As the crowd began to disperse, Rivka Michaeli approached Meir and asked him to sing again for her tape recorder. Some of Meir's friends stayed behind and sang along on the refrain.

The recording was broadcast next morning on the radio. In those three minutes, Meir Ariel became a hero of Israel.

VICTORS, MOURNERS

THE THREE BATTALIONS of the 55th Brigade assembled on the Temple Mount for a victory lineup. Only a week earlier they had been boarding buses ascending in a slow convoy to Jerusalem.

They gathered in the area between the Dome of the Rock and the silver-domed Al-Aqsa Mosque. The ceremony was delayed for the wounded. Motta had given the order that those who could be moved from their hospital beds should be brought to the ceremony.

Yoel Bin-Nun stood at the foot of the steps leading up to the Dome of the Rock. Any farther, and he risked treading on the area of the Holy of Holies.

"Why aren't you going up?" a kibbutznik asked him.

"This is the area of the Temple," Yoel explained. "A victory lineup could have been done at the Wall. I see the bulldozers have already cleared the area," he added sarcastically.

"But Yoel, isn't the Temple Mount the essence?"

Yoel savored the irony: here was a kibbutznik from Hashomer Hatzair berating a Kookian for seemingly underplaying the centrality of the Temple Mount. Kibbutzniks and Kookniks together: that's what made the victory possible.

In two days, Israel would be celebrating the holiday of Shavuot, marking the giving of the Torah at Sinai. For Yoel, it was also the festival of Jewish unity: the Torah was received by the whole people of Israel, functioning like a single body with one heart. And not since Sinai had the Jews been as united as they were in these last weeks. The spiritual calculus was self-evident: disunity brings destruction; unity, redemption.

The midday sun was strong, and men began removing their helmets. One dropped to the stone ground, then another, until there was a volley of crashing helmets. To Hanan Porat, it seemed a spontaneous ceremony marking the end of the war, perhaps the end of all war.

Accompanied by nurses, the wounded arrived, in casts and on wheelchairs. Avital Geva wasn't among them: he was recovering from one operation and awaiting the next.

The intact rushed over to the wounded. There were hugs, anxious inquiries about missing friends.

Then the men lined up by battalion and faced the Dome of the Rock. Motta, Stempel, and Uzi Narkiss stood before the soldiers. Motta had asked Arik to join them, but he preferred to stand with his staff.

I would gladly have forgone this victory, thought Arik, had it not been forced on us.

Motta addressed his men: "Many Jews risked their lives, throughout our long history, to come to Jerusalem and live in it. Innumerable songs expressed the deep longing. . . . In the War of Independence, great efforts were made to return to the nation its heart—the Old City and the Western Wall.

"To you fell the great honor of completing the circle, to return to the nation its capital and the center of its holiness.

"Many paratroopers, including our closest friends, the most veteran and the best among us, fell in the difficult battle. It was a merciless battle, in which you functioned as a body that pushes aside everything in its way without noting its wounds. You didn't complain. . . . Instead, you aspired only forward. . . .

"Jerusalem is yours—forever."

THE BRIGADE WAS discharged, but the officers stayed on for debriefings and hospital visits. Motta asked Arik to remain in uniform for another three months, until the fall semester at university, to prepare the final report on the battle for Jerusalem. Arik had had other plans. He needed to make up exams. And he intended to marry Yehudit Hazan. But he couldn't say no to Motta.

That night, the two men shared a hotel room. After showering, they sat in their underwear, on the edge of their beds. "Tell me who," said Motta.

Until then, Motta hadn't had a complete list of the brigade's dead. Arik began reciting from memory the names of their fallen friends, over twenty of the brigade's veterans alone, with whom they'd served since the mid-1950s.

Motta broke out in loud sobs.

Arik couldn't remember the last time he had wept; that was a privilege denied him. He bowed his head, averting his gaze to give Motta an approximation of privacy, and waited until the weeping passed.

PART TWO

THE SEVENTH DAY

(1967–1973)

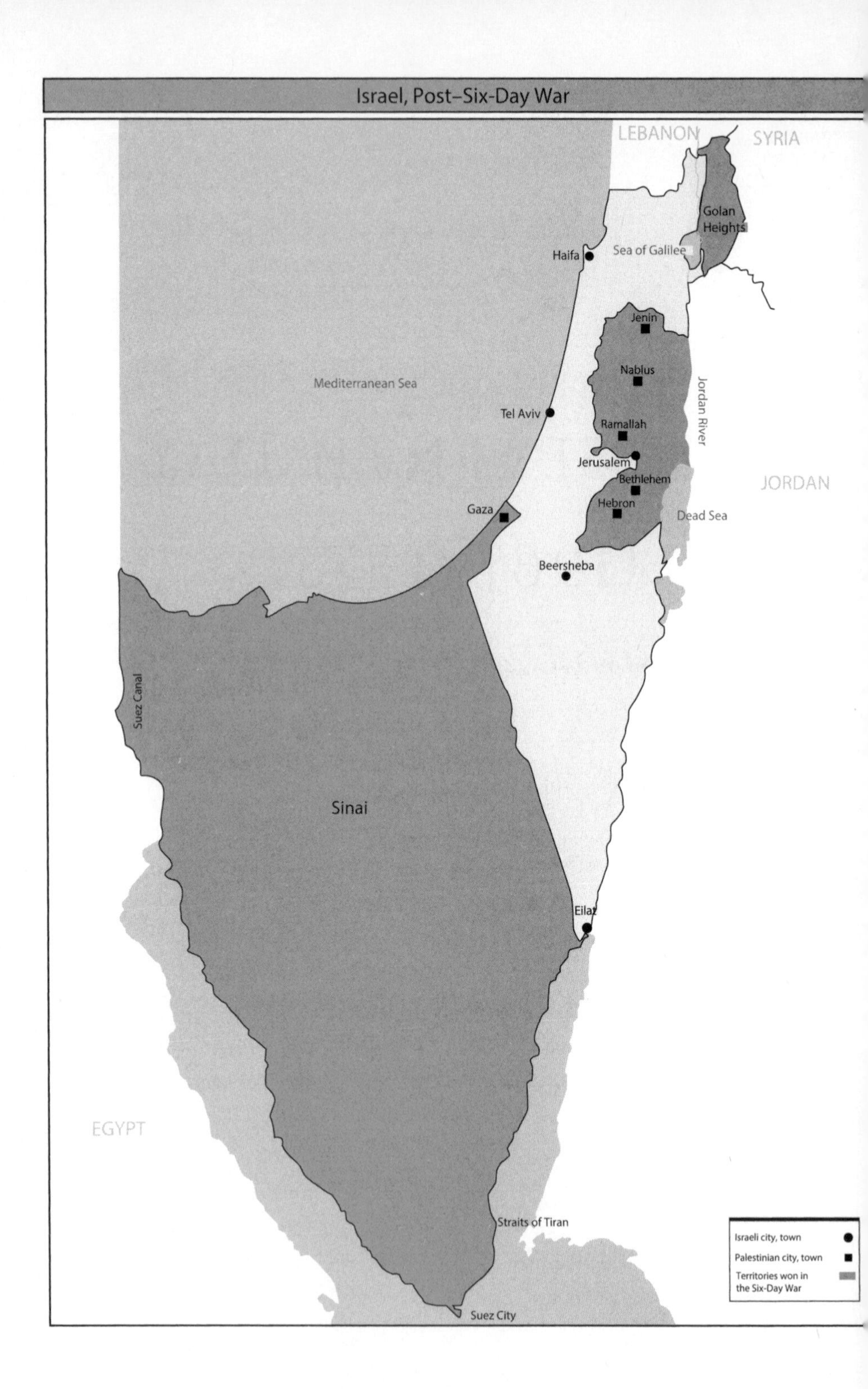
Israel, Post–Six-Day War
LEBANON
SYRIA
Golan Heights
Haifa
Sea of Galilee
Jenin
Nablus
Mediterranean Sea
Jordan River
Tel Aviv
Ramallah
Jerusalem
Bethlehem
JORDAN
Hebron
Gaza
Dead Sea
Beersheba
Suez Canal
Sinai
Eilat
EGYPT
Straits of Tiran
Suez City
Israeli city, town
Palestinian city, town
Territories won in the Six-Day War

CHAPTER 8

THE SUMMER OF MERCAZ

LIKE DREAMERS

THE PREDAWN STREETS of West Jerusalem filled with pilgrims. It was the holiday of Shavuot, Pentecost, celebrating revelation. The war had ended five days earlier, and all of Jewish Jerusalem seemed to be moving east. Many too had come from around the country, to be part of the first holiday at the Wall since its liberation—and the first mass pilgrimage of Jews to the area of the Temple Mount since Titus burned the Temple 1,900 years earlier. There were women wheeling baby carriages and grandmothers in kerchiefs and kibbutzniks in floppy hats and Orthodox men in prayer shawls and Hasidic fur hats and black fedoras and berets and knitted *kippot*. It was impossible, but here they were, sovereign again in Jerusalem, just as Jews had always prayed for and believed would happen. Strangers smiled at each other: We are the ones who made it to the end of the story.

Ada, on vigil in Avital's hospital room, heard movement from the street. Through the arched window she saw the vast crowds heading toward the Old City. "There are thousands of people outside," she told Avital.

"Go join them," he urged.

Everyone seemed to be moving in slow motion. Ada felt as if she were floating. An Israeli crowd could be as edgy as a food line in a refugee camp, yet here there was no pushing, no concern that someone was cutting ahead or not moving quickly enough. They are all my family, she thought; I love them just for being Jews.

As the crowds crossed what had been no-man's-land, soldiers urged pilgrims to remain on the road: not all the mines had been cleared. Passersby reached out to shake hands with soldiers or simply to touch them, as if they had personally liberated the Wall.

From behind the shutters of Arab houses, eyes silently followed the procession.

Jaffa Gate and the Arab market just beyond were closed by the army, precaution against terrorist attack. The crowds were directed onto the winding road around the Old City wall.

Despite intense pain in his feet, Rabbi Zvi Yehudah walked with determined steps. There was no traffic and people filled the streets, but the rabbi insisted on remaining on the sidewalk, deferring to the holy soldiers of Israel. Just in case a jeep needs to get through, he explained to the young men crowding around him.

Only a month earlier, they had heard him lament the loss of Judea and Samaria. On Independence Day, the precise moment when Nasser set in motion the Six-Day War, he had revealed his grief for the broken land. Since then, his students had served in units that had taken Hebron and Jericho and Nablus—the very places whose names he had cried out that night.

"How did our rabbi know?" asked a student.

"I didn't prepare a speech," Rabbi Zvi Yehudah replied. "I was spoken through."

THE SON RETURNS

HANAN PORAT HITCHED a ride on an army jeep heading south, into Judea, the West Bank. Since spotting Rabbi Zvi Yehudah riding by as the paratroopers moved toward the Old City, Hanan had been overwhelmed by wonder. He rode now through the deserted streets of Bethlehem, just past Jerusalem; torn white sheets of surrender hung from antennas and arched windows. The one-and-a-half-lane road curved upward. Then he spotted a strip of asphalt leading into terraced hills. "Here," Hanan called to the driver and leaped from the jeep.

He had been four years old when he last saw these hills. Then, on a rainy winter night, he and several dozen other children, stiff in layers of wool clothing, knitted caps covering their ears, had been lifted into an armored car and squeezed onto benches. The heat was stifling. The mothers boarded an open truck, packed with mattresses and pots. Through a crack in the roof of the armored car fathers peered into the darkness for one last glimpse of their children.

It was late 1947, and their kibbutz, Kfar Etzion, along with three other kibbutzim in the hills between Jerusalem and Hebron known as the Etzion Bloc, was under siege. The Jewish state was about to be established, and Arab villagers, backed by the Jordanian Legion, were intensifying their attacks. Removing the children and mothers from Kfar Etzion was a last-minute rescue mission. They were driven that night to a monastery in Jerusalem and moved into the basement. Each family's space was defined by a thin partition. Hanan's father, the kibbutz's military liaison, happened to be in Jerusalem, helping organize futile rescue operations for the Etzion Bloc.

On May 13, 1948, the mothers and children gathered around a shortwave radio, as they did every evening, to hear reports from Kfar Etzion—Malka, "queen," in military code. The voice of Kfar Etzion's commander addressed the wives and children: "Our spirits are strong. You too must be strong." Then they heard popping noises, followed by a long pause. And then another voice: "*Malka nafla*"—"Malka has fallen."

In the basement, total silence. Then wailing and screams. One woman tried to drink a jerry can filled with kerosene, but was stopped by others. Hanan and his friends were quickly dispatched to the courtyard.

Only afterward did the families learn what had happened that day. In the morning, armored cars of the Jordanian army had broken through the defenses of Kfar Etzion. Into the breach came hundreds of armed men from the surrounding villages. The eighty surviving defenders raised a white flag. And then a machine gun opened fire. The few who escaped into a bunker were killed by grenades.

In an instant, all the children in the basement had become fatherless. Except, that is, for Hanan and his younger twin siblings, and a few other lucky children whose fathers happened to be outside Kfar Etzion when the siege closed in.

The day after the massacre, David Ben-Gurion declared the establishment of the state. Meanwhile, the defenders of the three remaining kibbutzim in the Etzion Bloc surrendered to the Jordanian army, and were taken prisoner to Jordan. After the war, the eve of Independence Day was declared Memorial Day for Israel's fallen, partly in memory of the fallen of Kfar Etzion.

The refugees of Kfar Etzion created an urban kibbutz in exile. They moved to Jaffa—into Arab houses built around a courtyard and abandoned by their residents during the war. All earnings were shared. Grief too was managed communally: children with fathers were cautioned by their parents not to say the word *abba* in the presence of children without fathers. In school, the children of Kfar Etzion formed a pack, excluding outsiders from their games; on the school bus they acted so wildly that the other children didn't want to ride with them. The Etzion kids wore their own private uniform—khaki pants, work boots, and floppy hat—to school: kibbutzniks against the city.

Hanan assured his friends with a kind of mystical certainty that their exile from Kfar Etzion was temporary, that one day soon they would return. He led them on endurance tests as preparation for that day, leaping from roof to roof and walking barefoot on thorns.

The widows began to remarry; the Jaffa kibbutz was fraying. Finally, one night, after putting the children to bed in their communal rooms, the parents met to vote on dismantling the kibbutz. The children, expert at discovering the secrets of the grown-ups, sensed threat. Stepping quietly to evade the night watchman, they walked single file across the courtyard and slipped into a room adjacent to the dining room where the meeting was being held. There they eavesdropped on the discussion. This is no way to raise children, they heard one of the widows say. Unless we separate them, agreed another, they'll be beyond control. As the members voted to disband, Hanan and his friends, barefoot in pajamas, pressed together in the dark and wept.

The families went their separate ways. Some joined existing kibbutzim; some, like Hanan's family, became private farmers. But the children remained an emotional collective. Every summer they attended their own camp, where the bunks and play areas were named after places in Kfar Etzion—the Hill of Boulders, the Grove of the Song of Songs. One of their favorite games was to recapture Kfar Etzion, sons assuming the names of fallen fathers. "To guard the traditions of the fathers," they sang, "and not allow the flame to die / to prepare ourselves for the future / and keep together, bind our tie." Hanan took that as a personal vow.

On Memorial Day, they gathered with their families in the national military cemetery on Mount Herzl, at the mass grave of the defenders of Kfar Etzion—near the memorial for Enzo Sereni and his fellow parachutists who were killed in Europe during World War II and whose bodies were never retrieved. Then the mourners proceeded to the southern edge of Jerusalem, on the border of Bethlehem, and gazed toward the area of what had once been Kfar Etzion. All that was visible was a lone oak tree, said to be seven hundred years old, and that became their marker and symbol.

Among the children of Kfar Etzion, none took on its collective identity as fiercely, as totally, as did Hanan. Perhaps that was partly because his life was defined not only by the massacre but by his family's escape. Only by submerging his being into the identity of the group could he erase the shame of exclusion from its inner circle of mourning. He thought often of that moment in the monastery basement when the voice over the radio announced, "Malka has fallen," and his friends became fatherless. But Hanan's loss was, in its way, also acute: he had forfeited his right to a separate self.

Hanan assumed the role of organizing the "children," as they called themselves even now, in their early twenties. He ensured that they continued to meet socially, reinforcing the hope of return. On Independence Day, he had brought the Kfar Etzion children to Mercaz, where they heard Rabbi Zvi Yehudah's prophetic outburst and were received by the *nazir*, who blessed them with the hope of returning to the homes of their fathers.

IT WAS MIDDAY as Hanan began walking into the terraced hills, toward Kfar Etzion. A surprising breeze softened the strong sun. He had imagined this moment so often. And now, at age twenty-four, he was returning as a victor, a liberator of Jerusalem. He could almost see the houses and cowshed and synagogue just ahead. He wasn't sure whether those images came from his own childhood recollections, or whether they had been borrowed from stories; his consciousness had been so absorbed into the collective memory that it no longer mattered.

After about a mile he came to an abandoned Jordanian army camp: the site of Kfar Etzion. In the total silence he could hear his footsteps. He searched for the houses, but there were only army barracks, resembling long metal tubes. Even the orchards and vineyards were gone. *Nothing left, not even the memory of our presence—*

The wind scattered papers on the ground. There was no shade against the midday sun.

Hanan came to the oak tree. He stood beneath the powerful branches and felt small and helpless. He caressed the trunk, rested his head against it, his own Western Wall.

YOEL BIN-NUN'S PRIVATE GRIEF

THE PEOPLE OF Israel were on the move. They posed for photographs before burned Soviet tanks in Sinai, explored Syrian army bunkers on the Golan Heights, and marveled at how vulnerable Israeli farmers had been just below. Reverently they touched ancestral tombs, of Abraham and Sarah in Hebron, Rachel in Bethlehem. They were an uprooted generation, their parental graves left behind in a hundred exiles; Holocaust survivors lacked even parental graves. Now all that had been lost seemed somehow restored.

The symbol of that restoration was the paratroopers at the Wall. The iconic image, taken by photographer David Rubinger, showed three paratroopers standing before the Wall and looking into the distance, humbled by awe. They were men of the 66th Battalion, and they had fought on Ammunition Hill.

The IDF's newspaper published a poem by lyricist Haim Hefer: "This Wall has heard many prayers / This Wall has seen many walls crumble / But this Wall never saw paratroopers weep . . . / Perhaps it's because the boys of nineteen / who were born together with the state / carry on their backs—two thousand years."

In fact, the paratroopers weren't the only Israeli soldiers who deserved credit for reuniting Jerusalem. The Jerusalem Brigade—composed of reservists who lived in Jerusalem—had fought in the city's southern neighborhoods, while the tanks of the Harel Brigade had fought in northern Jerusalem. Half the Israeli casualties in the battle for Jerusalem were from those units. But their contribution was obscured by the mythic power of the paratroopers on the Temple Mount and at the Western Wall.

TO BE AN Israeli in the summer of 1967 was to be a hero. Everyone had a share in the victory: the high school students who had distributed mail, the pensioners who'd enforced the blackout, even the ultra-Orthodox who had violated the Sabbath to fill sandbags. An instant documentary film on the war played to packed theaters; when an ultra-Orthodox soldier appeared on-screen, secular Israelis cheered. With the magnanimity of victors, Israelis forgave each other their ideological flaws.

How did we do it? Israelis asked themselves, sharing the wonder expressed around the world. In six days, a country of less than three million had defeated three Arab armies, conquered mountains and ancient market labyrinths and desert expanse. Israel had more than tripled its size, from 8,000 to 26,000 square miles. And not just "territories," but Judea and Samaria: when Jews in exile had prayed to be restored to the land of Israel, they'd meant Jerusalem, Bethlehem, Hebron.

Bookstores displayed instant photo albums of the victory, as if Israelis needed some explanation of how the nation had moved in barely one month from fears of a second holocaust to military mastery of the Middle East. Kiosks sold necklaces with bullets and hung signs that read, "All Honor to the IDF." Moshe Dayan half smiled from falafel stands. The new slang for stepping on the gas was, "Ben-Tzur, drive!"—Motta's cry to his driver as they crashed through the Lions' Gate.

The war seemed to end Israelis' great unspoken question: Could a country under permanent siege by its neighbors, and whose wildly diverse population hadn't functioned together as a nation for two thousand years, overcome the odds and survive? The answer of June 1967 seemed unequivocal: Israel was here to stay.

In celebrating their military prowess, Israelis were celebrating existence. For Jews to have learned to fight so well, so soon after they had died in their helpless millions, was an affirmation of their life force. The world hadn't changed: not only was Auschwitz possible, but so was an assault on its survivors. No matter: the Jews had changed.

AFTER A MORNING of Talmud study, Yoel Bin-Nun walked up the road from Mercaz to the military cemetery on Mount Herzl. He entered the gate and joined the procession of the bereaved.

There were lone soldiers walking slowly with bowed heads, groups of kibbutzniks with firm steps, Holocaust survivors in straw fedoras, Moroccan women in kerchiefs, Iraqi men in berets. The uphill path was flanked by walls of porous rock. Stone stairs carved into the hill led to areas with newly planted pine trees, each area devoted to the fallen of another war. Rows of identical marble stones were engraved with name, date of birth, date of death, and, when appropriate, date of immigration to Israel. Instead of flower beds there were patches of ivy, muted colors in a garden of stone.

How could Yoel possibly make sense of his multiple shatterings? He had entered the heights and the depths, had emerged illumined and burned. He felt none of the euphoria of victory. The very tone of the national self-congratulation offended him. The crude jokes about Arab cowardice, the souvenirs Israelis bought in Arab markets like trophies: What was this vulgarity, this idolatrous cult of power? How dare Israelis say, "All honor to the IDF," as if this were a man-made miracle?

He ascended a long flight of stairs and found the newly cleared area for the fallen of the Six-Day War. Dozens of rectangular patches of earth were lined in even rows. Tombstones had not yet been laid; instead, each patch was marked by a sign with the name of a buried soldier. Yoel paused to read the signs: "Tobol," "Leibovitch," "Turgeman," names drawn from North Africa and Eastern Europe, ingathered in Jerusalem.

He lingered by the grave marked "Yosef Yechezkel Yochai"—Yossi, the medic who had been killed just before his wedding. Yoel recalled how they'd danced with him in the paratroopers' makeshift synagogue, how Yisrael Diamant, who fell on Nablus Road, had lifted Yossi on his shoulders. Swaying slowly, Yoel recited a psalm for their souls.

THIS IS THE TIME

"*NU*, DEAR FRIENDS," said Rabbi Zvi Yehudah, "what should we study now?"

Several dozen students, many sitting on the floor, crowded into the rabbi's small salon. Tape remained on the windows, a wartime precaution against blasts.

Hanan Porat broke the silence. "Rabbeinu"—Our rabbi and master—he said, "hasn't the time come to study the laws of the Temple?"

For a religious Jew who prayed three times a day for the Temple to be rebuilt, that was not an unexpected question in the summer of 1967.

"Hanan," replied the rabbi enigmatically, "we will be learning the laws of war for many years to come."

"But the Temple Mount is in our hands!" protested Hanan.

"Hanan," he repeated, "we will be learning the laws of war for many years to come."

But Hanan is right! thought Yoel. This is the time! Any generation of believing Jews would have known how to read the signs. Redemption was the heart of Judaism: a holy people consecrated to a holy land, at its center a holy city and a holy mountain—a tactile sanctity, because redemption must happen in this world. And now, in six days of re-creation, all that had been broken had been made whole. Surely even the most stubborn skeptics would now understand that God was in this story.

THE MERCAZ STUDY HALL filled with hundreds of celebrants. Rabbi Zvi Yehudah had summoned an "Assembly of Thanksgiving," and the yeshiva's dining room, which had accommodated the crowds for his Independence Day speech, was hardly adequate now. On the dais sat the president of Israel, Zalman Shazar. In the front row sat the novelist and Nobel laureate Shai Agnon.

Mercaz—"the center"—had finally fulfilled its ambitious name. From the beginning of the crisis, which Rabbi Zvi Yehudah had seemed to intuit in his Independence Day speech, to the war's astonishing culmination, when he and the *nazir* were the first civilians at the Western Wall, Mercaz had been central to the greatest moment in Israel's history. Mercaz felt vindicated in its most daring theological premise: that secular Zionism was a trustworthy repository of the redemptive process. The secular state that had tried to sever the people of Israel from the God of Israel had instead confirmed faith. For Mercaz, the kibbutznik paratroopers at the Wall were a revelation. Who could have imagined kibbutzniks praying at the symbol of piety and exile?

Rabbi Zvi Yehudah entered the study hall. Students held each other by the shoulders and danced before him. "Raise your heads, gates," they sang, "and admit the glorious King."

The rabbi spoke from a lectern draped with an Israeli flag. In covering a lectern that held holy books with the flag of secular Israel, Rabbi Zvi Yehudah was saying: This flag is no less holy than the velvet cloth covering the Torah ark behind me. On the wall hung a banner that read, "May the Temple be rebuilt, speedily in our time"—prayer turned into demand.

Voice strong, tone defiant, the rabbi warned the world not to interfere with God's plan and try to wrench the liberated lands from Israel's control. Not even the democratically elected government of Israel, he continued, had the right to withdraw from the territories—a warning aimed at the Labor-led national unity government, which declared its willingness to exchange territory for peace.

Hanan Porat approached the lectern. Broad-shouldered and powerfully handsome, with a wave of brown hair, he projected far beyond his short stature. Of the dozen paratroopers in Mercaz—who were holy, Rabbi Zvi Yehudah liked to say, only half joking, because they descended from heaven like the Torah at Sinai—the rabbi especially loved Hanan, heir of Kfar Etzion. Hanan embodied the Mercaz synthesis of yeshiva student and sabra, spirit and matter. And now Hanan carried the additional aura of the Six-Day War's most heroic battle, Ammunition Hill, where paratroopers had fought face-to-face with Jordanian soldiers in the trenches. Hanan happened not to have actually fought in the trenches and had seen little fighting during the war, all of which Hanan acknowledged. Still, for young religious Zionists, Hanan was a hero.

In his permanently hoarse voice, Hanan read a poetic account of a journey he'd recently taken to Kfar Etzion, this time in the company of friends. A middle-aged man, one of the few survivors of the massacre, ran atop the bunker where the last of Kfar Etzion's defenders had died and began pounding with a pickax. "It was as if he were trying to signal to someone down below. And a faint echo from the void seemed to respond: 'I am still alive, where are you, my friend? Respond, give me a sign!' "

The president of Israel stood and kissed Hanan on the forehead.

HANAN MAILED OUT a questionnaire to the children of Kfar Etzion: Are you prepared to return? And if so, what kind of settlement should we create? A kibbutz or a noncommunal village? A community only for the Orthodox, or open to everyone?

A dozen friends affirmed their readiness to "go up" and settle. "I don't care what will be established there," one wrote. "Even if it will be a yeshiva, you can assign me the job of janitor."

But when they gathered together for a planning session, tensions emerged.

"What if the government doesn't agree to our return?" a friend asked Hanan.

"We go up anyway," Hanan replied. "Let's see them removing us!"

"We're returning home in memory of our parents," his friend countered. "If we go up without authority, we will desecrate their memory."

The deeper tension within the group was about whether the return to Kfar Etzion was a personal act of restoration or, as Hanan insisted, a national act with messianic implications. The resurrected Kfar Etzion, he told his friends, would be the first of many settlements in Judea and Samaria. They were blessed to be the avant-garde. And in restoring the wholeness of the Holy Land, the world would be healed, redeemed.

Listening to Hanan, one of his friends thought: He can only see the return in abstract terms because he's not an orphan like us.

They argued about whether the new Kfar Etzion should be a kibbutz like its predecessor. Hanan wasn't sure: a kibbutz, with its limited size and screening committee for applicants, would absorb at best a few hundred people, when the goal should be to attract thousands. A kibbutz, he said sarcastically, isn't a mitzvah from the Torah.

His friends, though, insisted on a kibbutz, and Hanan relented. It was, after all, poetic for the first West Bank settlement to be a kibbutz, a link between the movement that had helped found the state of Israel with the movement that was about to complete it.

"I NEED YOUR HELP," Hanan said to Yoel over breakfast of white cheese and olives in the Mercaz dining room.

"When we return," he continued, "I want us to have a yeshiva. Kfar Etzion can't just be a place of physical renewal. There has to be a light emanating from it to the people of Israel."

"I'm with you, Hanan," said Yoel. "What do you need from me?"

"I want you to come and teach."

Yoel mentioned Hanan's offer to his fiancée. Esther Raab's father had been among those taken prisoner by the Jordanians in 1948 from a kibbutz near Kfar Etzion. "Returning to the Etzion Bloc," said Esther, "is the dream of my life."

A CONVERSATION AMONG SOLDIERS

A HALF DOZEN students from the Mercaz yeshiva sat around a reel-to-reel tape recorder, speaking about their experiences in the war. They were being interviewed by two editors of the kibbutz literary magazine, *Shdemot* (Fields). The magazine, whose editors included the young novelist Amos Oz, was dispatching teams of interviewers to kibbutzim around the country, to record the anguish and ambivalence of young kibbutzniks who had just fought their first war. The intention was to turn the interviews into a book.

Though kibbutzniks were barely 4 percent of the population, nearly two hundred of them had been killed in the war, a quarter of Israel's fatalities. Raised on reticence, young kibbutzniks suddenly felt a need to talk—about losing friends and about killing for the first time; about the shifting face of the enemy, from crowds chanting "Death to Israel" to lines of Arab refugees; about their identification with Jewish vulnerability before the war and their unease with Jewish power afterward. The victory they had helped bring had turned Israel into an occupier—true, history's most improbable occupier, having gone to battle not to conquer but survive. No one had intended this. But now kibbutzniks, the children of utopia, were suddenly occupiers.

The only nonkibbutzniks being interviewed for the project were students from Mercaz. Mercaz's infatuation with kibbutzniks was finally reciprocated. Through their shared experience of war, kibbutzniks had discovered in young religious Zionists a fellow elite, ethical and sacrificial. Kibbutzniks recalled how religious soldiers had danced in the orchards before the war, raising morale, and how they had opposed the looting in Jerusalem after the battle. Now the editors of *Shdemot* were reaching out to them. Surely the Mercaz students were as appalled as the kibbutzniks by the postwar coarsening of Israeli society—the gloating and the glorification of power. Surely the kibbutzniks and the Mercazniks would find comfort in a common alienation.

They met in the Jerusalem apartment of Yochanan Fried, a Mercaz student who had fought in the unit that conquered Bethlehem. An Arab watchman had given him the key to Rachel's Tomb. Our Mother Rachel, Jews lovingly called the biblical matriarch, who in the imagery of the prophet Jeremiah wept for the people of Israel as they were led into exile. Yochanan had borrowed a jeep, driven straight to the home of Rabbi Zvi Yehudah and presented him with the key—which the rabbi refused to accept, insisting that it be returned to the IDF.

The young people filled Yochanan's small living room. Two walls were covered with books—religious works with titles printed in gold letters, along with the prose and poetry of secular Israel. Rabbi Kook the father, in long gray beard and fur hat, gazed from a photograph, at once tender and austere.

There was no unease between the Mercazniks and the kibbutzniks, no sense of "us" and "them." Regardless of what they wore or didn't wear on their heads now, they had all worn the same helmets a few weeks earlier.

"Before we speak about the moral questions," one of the kibbutznik interviewers began, "it's important that each of us expresses his personal feelings."

"I feel like we're moving toward something big," said Dov, a former kibbutznik who had become Orthodox and was now studying at Mercaz. "I don't depend on reason anymore. I have a feeling that I'm being pushed, I'm already moving . . . together with the whole people of Israel I'm moving toward something . . . I don't know. . . . But I believe it is something good."

The interviewer had asked for a personal statement, and Dov had responded with the Messiah.

The interviewer tried again: Did faith help the Mercaz students cope with fear during the war? "It seems to me," the interviewer elaborated, "that the deeper one's [Jewish] roots are, and the deeper one's connection with the past—then fear has different dimensions than it does with us [secularists]. . . . And I'm also interested in hearing about something that was hard for me during the war—the whole matter of taking life. How is it for a person of faith?"

The Mercaz students didn't seem to understand the question. The kibbutznik was speaking as a human being facing life and death; the Mercazniks could only respond in national terms.

The second interviewer intervened. "My friends and I—we didn't hate the enemy. The opposite: We wanted to live with him. And we didn't rejoice when the enemy was destroyed. The opposite: His [humiliating] fall weighed on us. For example, to see the long convoys of burned vehicles in Sinai, the fleeing refugees . . ."

"We're so used to seeing two sides," a Mercaznik named Naftali sarcastically replied. "A normal nation says, If an army rises up against me, against a whole nation, a nation of Holocaust refugees, a nation that suffered throughout its history— If one Egyptian dares to stand on the border [to attack us], then he's a despicable murderer. He's a partner to an historical crime, and for me it's a commandment to kill him, and all the convoys should be scattered through the Sinai Desert. And those who escape—kill them before they reach the [Suez] Canal."

"What about Judaism's love for the human being?"

"I have love for human beings," said Naftali, "but not for someone who comes to kill me."

"You want us to be a normal people?" the kibbutznik asked.

Yochanan, the host, intervened: "Naftali said those things in a sharp way and formulated them in the wrong way. But at a time of [great developments for] the people, the details don't exist. They exist but in a different way."

"It seems to me there's a gap between us," an interviewer said. "I don't accept the whole notion of a chosen people."

But there was another, unspoken gap between them. Religious Zionists who proclaimed their belief in chosenness were, in effect, insisting on the right of the Jews to behave as any other nation, while secular Zionists who rejected chosenness were insisting that Jews be held to a higher standard.

An interviewer tried a different direction. "Can you obey orders against your moral principles? Did you find yourself in that situation?"

Yoel Bin-Nun, at age twenty-one the youngest participant, spoke up. "In a place where moral principles can contradict each other," he said slowly, "it's clear to me that no simple soldier is capable of weighing all the considerations. In that kind of situation I have no choice but to accept the order."

"Do you have to be practically blind?" demanded the interviewer.

"It's a necessary reality," replied Yoel.

But then Yoel conceded ambivalence. Hesitantly, he alluded to the shooting incident after the paratroopers had entered the Old City. "The truth is," he said, "that if I examine myself retroactively, when I had to carry out all of these 'beautiful' acts, I had very little strength to do it. I'm willing to say that to everyone. . . . It was hard for me. . . . I had doubts. . . ."

"In the middle of the war?" Dov the Mercaznik demanded.

"Yes, in the middle of the war," replied Yoel. "And it's impossible to avoid it."

CHAPTER 9

THE KIBBUTZNIKS COME HOME

A RECKONING WITH HISTORY

ARIK ACHMON MADE the rounds of the wounded, and sought out Avital Geva. Though they knew each other only cursorily from reserve duty, Avital was one of the junior officers whom Arik most appreciated—perhaps envied—for his spontaneity, his joy.

As Arik approached Avital's bed, Avital began to weep.

"Are your wounds so painful?" Arik asked awkwardly.

Avital didn't seem to hear the question. Still weeping, he said, "Mother Russia. The Second Homeland. How could this betrayal have happened to us?"

Crazy Shmutzniks, thought Arik, even now they still feel betrayed by the Soviet Union.

But Arik had misunderstood Avital's anguish. Avital wasn't mourning the betrayal of the Soviet Union, for which he cared nothing. He was, instead, grieving for Hashomer Hatzair's betrayal of itself. Hashomer Hatzair had prided itself on its ability to understand the inner meaning of history but had missed the most obvious truths, had mistaken enemies for friends, mass murderers for saviors. How would his beloved movement survive the shame?

AVITAL'S HOSPITAL ROOM filled with family and friends. "*Hevreh?* Not to worry," he reassured well-wishers. "It looks worse than it is."

The bandages over his face were removed, but mortar fragments remained in his shoulders and legs.

Avital transformed his ward into a kind of kibbutz where no one was a stranger. He introduced his visitors to his fellow patients and joked with the nurses and doctors. Relieved friends told each other that nothing had changed: Avital remained Avital. The Ein Shemer newsletter downplayed his wounds: "Luckily for all of us, Avital was only lightly wounded. He is receiving excellent care. The nurses constantly hover around him, and were it not for a little pain, he might even be enjoying himself."

But as Avital had revealed in a rare moment to Arik, he was quietly grieving. One of his closest friends from Ein Shemer, Amnon Harodi, had been killed in the battle for Jerusalem, his body blown in half by a mortar shell. Avital kept recalling the image of Amnon saying good-bye to his pregnant wife as he went off to war. With his goatee and ironic expression, Amnon had been a farmer intellectual, suspecting every dogma. It was Amnon who, in Ein Shemer's May Day symposium just before the war, had dared to publicly say what so many of the young people were thinking: that working-class solidarity and loyalty to the Soviet Union and even the red flag were illusions, an embarrassment.

And now the Soviets, having armed the Arabs and encouraged them to war, had helped kill Amnon. *How could we have been so stupid—*

THE SUMMER OF ARIK ACHMON

FOR ARIK, IT was a time of vindication. At a postmortem gathering of IDF intelligence officers, Arik was treated with special respect, recognition of his effectiveness during the war despite the handicap of poor intelligence. On a visit to Netzer Sereni, he ran into his paratrooper buddy Aryeh Weiner, who had mocked him for not being a war veteran. "Weiner," said Arik, dryly, "I've now heard bullets over my head." There were benefits, he discovered, to being part of an epic. Seeking a waiver for exams, he put on a dress uniform, red beret tucked under his epaulet, and drove in a confiscated Jordanian jeep to the campus of Tel Aviv University; when he happened to mention that he'd been among the liberators of Jerusalem, his request was readily granted.

Arik knew that Yehudit wasn't interested in his war stories, so he kept those to himself. Yehudit hadn't even known to what unit he belonged: when she heard on the radio that "Arik," the chief intelligence officer of Motta Gur's brigade, had raised the flag over the Temple Mount, she hadn't realized it was *her* Arik. Yehudit resented the paratroopers for competing for Arik's time. All the other reservists had been demobilized; why was Arik still in uniform? So what if he had an obligation to Motta, what about his obligation to her?

ARIK AND MOISHELEH Stempel-Peles, Motta's deputy commander, stood outside the little whitewashed house in Rishpon, a farming community near the sea. Naomi Mizrahi opened the door. When she saw the two men in uniform, she wept.

Naomi's husband, Yirmi, had headed the machine gun unit of Company A, which Arik had commanded before becoming the brigade's intelligence officer. Arik had felt close to the good-natured Yemenite, one of the first Sephardim to break into the paratroopers' club of kibbutzniks. Yirmi had been hit with shrapnel in his hand in the first hours of the battle for Jerusalem, but he'd refused to be evacuated and led his men across no-man's-land. He was killed by a sniper shortly afterward.

Naomi had been left with two young children and a patch of field. What was Arik supposed to say? What comfort could he offer that wouldn't sound perfunctory?

Moisheleh unbuckled his belt and sighed as his ample stomach expanded. "How are the children coping?" he asked Naomi. "What about your financial situation? Is there a will?"

Naomi stopped crying and started talking. Moisheleh retrieved a notebook and wrote. His tone remained matter-of-fact, businesslike. As if to say: This happened to you, but it could just as well be my wife sitting in your place. No awkward words of consolation, no false pieties, only offers of practical assistance. Arik watched with admiration. Here was a form of condolence he could manage.

"This isn't a one-time visit, it's a connection," Moisheleh said as they left. "You'll be hearing from us."

A SHATTERING IN GAN SHMUEL

IN THE HUMID JULY NIGHT, Udi Adiv paced the paved paths of Kibbutz Gan Shmuel, lined with little red-roofed houses shaded by cypresses and fig trees. Sprinklers rotated across the lawns, bright green even in summer. On a hill in the distance were the rooms of the children and the teenagers, a self-contained youth collective with its own dining room, responsible for its own rules. Paradise, thought Udi with contempt.

Udi had returned home a hero. Old-timers pressed his hand, slapped him on the back. "Glad you made it back safely," one said, offering a kibbutznik's version of effusiveness. The teenagers of Gan Shmuel regarded him with awe: not only a star of the kibbutz basketball team but a liberator of Jerusalem.

He looked the part: tall, broad-shouldered, square jaw, deep-set eyes. But the edges of his mouth were often downturned, so that even when he laughed he seemed to be grimacing.

In the dining room, Udi exhorted friends to confront the truth about "Zionist imperialism." He'd seen too much in the war, they told each other; one friend was convinced that Udi was suffering from shell shock. How, they wondered, had he so mistaken Israel's fears for arrogance? His body broke out in rashes, and no medication could ease the unbearable itching.

Yet several young people did gather around Udi. After work in the cotton fields, dragging pipes across the field while standing ankle-deep in brackish water, they smoked hashish and listened to Udi denounce Hashomer Hatzair and the fiction of "progressive Zionism." The Jews, he said, weren't a nation but a religion and so had no right to their own state. The occupation didn't begin in 1967 but in 1948, with the creation of Israel.

Suddenly the legitimacy of Zionism was being debated in Gan Shmuel, where everyone read the newspaper of Hashomer Hatzair and young men kept their hair hardly longer than army regulation. There were no more diligent workers than the kibbutzniks of Gan Shmuel. Members often waived their Shabbat rest to work a few hours in the fields or the canning factory. Comrades told the story of how, during the British Mandate, when soldiers searched the kibbutz for illegal weapons, a kibbutznik was asked to identify himself. Responding in precise English, he said, "I am a gentleman of potatoes."

But another, more restless Gan Shmuel was emerging from the war. The collapse of faith in the Soviet Union that had occurred on nearby Ein Shemer had happened here too. The few remaining true believers were taunted by their comrades as traitors—"You and your Soviet Union"—as if they hadn't been, until several weeks earlier, pro-Soviet too. In this breakdown of old certainties, everything was suddenly open to question.

Especially the fate of Cherkas. Near the cotton fields of Gan Shmuel were the ruins of an Arab village called Cherkas. As a child Udi and his friends had gone there to pick mulberries; Udi had feared being stranded among the abandoned stone houses without roofs, as though its ghosts would possess him. Cherkas had been destroyed in 1948 by the Israeli army, concerned that the village could become a hostile base overlooking the road to Nazareth. Cherkas's residents were resettled in Israeli Arab villages a few kilometers away. The army offered the fields bordering the road to Gan Shmuel; the kibbutzniks voted to accept the offer. They had just emerged from a war of survival; if the army said there was a threat to keeping that land in Arab hands, they weren't about to argue. And if Cherkas's residents were moved just up the road, well, worse things happened in war.

No one in Gan Shmuel talked about Cherkas. But now Udi found that silence unbearable. How had their parents simply watched Cherkas vanish without protest? For Udi, a direct line connected the destruction of Cherkas with the destruction of the Arab shantytown at the Western Wall.

FAME DISCOVERS MEIR ARIEL

IN MIDAFTERNOON, AFTER a day's work in the cotton fields of Kibbutz Mishmarot, Meir Ariel returned to his little apartment with its icebox, its thin-legged couch that opened into a bed, and its olive tree trunk that balanced a small table, and turned on the radio. The songs alternated between the Six-Day War and San Francisco's Summer of Love. And then suddenly there was Meir, singing through the static from the amphitheater on Mount Scopus: "Jerusalem of iron, of lead and of blackness . . ."

"They're making me out to be this big hero," Meir complained to his wife, Tirza.

"Why should you care how you become famous?" countered Tirza.

Yes, of course he wanted to be famous. But not like this, not with a takeoff of someone else's song. And since when did he represent the paratroopers? He had always been an ambivalent soldier, a civilian in uniform. Borrowed ethos, borrowed melody: a fraud.

Journalists appeared in Mishmarot. Meir dutifully played along, giving reporters quotable one-liners. I had to write an alternative to Naomi

Shemer's anthem, he explained in one interview, because "the metals got switched," from gold to iron. But the profiles about the sensitive paratrooper-farmer only deepened his unease. He tried to compensate with irony, telling a journalist that he experienced more fear onstage on Mount Scopus than he had during the entire war. But that only reinforced the endearing image of the shy, stoic paratrooper.

He had intended his song as a protest against sentimentality, myth; yet the song itself had become absorbed into the national mythos, one more reason for Israelis to celebrate themselves: Look how conflicted, how humane, our fighters are. A song meant to be shared with friends had somehow been let loose, and now the whole country was peering into his soul.

Shuli Natan, the female soldier with the quivering voice who had popularized "Jerusalem of Gold," went on pilgrimage to Mishmarot, accompanied by a reporter. Her conversation with Meir was recorded in the newspaper *Ha'aretz*:

MEIR: The words that gave me the push to sing were the words of Naomi Shemer.

SHULI: I don't think you can compare the words [of the two songs]. Naomi's song is a prayer of longing, a hymn. Your words are an exact description of the historic change that happened.

MEIR: Naomi Shemer's song is more than a passing phenomenon. The words I wrote are just a response to events.

Ha'aretz summed up the encounter with this headline: "Shuli Offered a Prayer—The Paratrooper Ariel Fulfilled It."

Naomi Shemer wasn't charmed. She wrote Meir, threatening to sue for plagiarism. The curse of "Jerusalem of Iron": now he'd made an enemy of Israel's greatest songwriter. "Why is she so upset?" Meir told Tirza. "I never intended this to get out." But then he reconsidered: "She's right. I hitched a ride on her song."

Shemer agreed to meet Meir. As the date of their meeting approached, Meir became increasingly anxious. Naomi Shemer was, at age thirty-seven, the most beloved composer of Hebrew song. She had written the sound track of the state in its exuberant youth—songs about a soldier returning home from war and a soldier who doesn't return, about cowboys in the desert and a couple in sandals on a little bridge in Tel Aviv; songs that were sung on school outings and army hikes and in kibbutz dining rooms and even in synagogues, where her melodies were attached to prayers. No song went more deep than "Jerusalem of Gold," which had been instantly adopted by Israelis, even before the war, as a second anthem. And Meir had violated that song.

Tirza accompanied Meir to the Tel Aviv restaurant where they met with Shemer. "I didn't intend to hurt you in any way," Meir said to her. "I'm not chasing headlines. I want to make this right, but I don't have much to offer. I work in the cotton fields of Kibbutz Mishmarot."

Shemer, herself a former kibbutznik, was gracious. She acknowledged being moved by "Jerusalem of Iron," praised its language. She paid for the meal.

They settled on splitting the royalties from any future income related to "Jerusalem of Iron." Meir would have given her all the royalties if she'd asked: as a kibbutznik, he wouldn't see the money anyway.

MISHMAROT REJOICED IN Meir's success. Meir had forever linked the little kibbutz with Israel's greatest moment. The mimeographed newsletter reported on his media triumphs. "We wish Meir success in writing songs in times of peace and tranquillity for our people and our land," the newsletter wrote. Even Meir's father, Sasha, the dour principal of the local school, was proud, though of course he didn't admit it.

At age twenty-five Meir remained a beautiful boy, with high cheekbones and long black curls. Only his almond-shaped eyes, which sometimes seemed to shift between green and blue and with a faraway look that was likewise imprecise, hinted at the torment in his soul.

Meir wanted to be a normal kibbutznik, unburdened by brooding thoughts about death and meaning. But normalcy eluded him. As a boy, he would sleepwalk out of the children's house, an unconscious protest against separation from his parents, until he was finally allowed to sleep in their apartment. Now he wandered in daydreams. His friends laughed about how he'd run over irrigation pipes while driving a tractor, caught up in a line to a new song or simply in the sound of the wind through the eucalyptus trees.

His struggle for stability left him tender and tolerant, not toward his own weaknesses but toward those of others. Meir, they said on Mishmarot, never got angry; when someone behaved poorly Meir smiled sadly, as if to say, *Nu, hevreh*, what do you expect, that's how we are, we human beings.

Meir—"Meirkeh"—was beloved in Mishmarot. He played accordion for the weekly folk dancing, confided his love poems to the Mishmarot newsletter. When there was a death in the kibbutz family, he wrote a rhymed eulogy for the funeral. Meir revered the old-timers who, though barely in their fifties, looked so much older, worn by austerity and labor. What amazing people they were, moving across continents, always just one step ahead of death, creating a new state and culture and way of life. Where did these Jews get the stamina to emerge as victors from the twentieth century?

Yet Mishmarot was different from its two bigger and more successful neighbors, Gan Shmuel, home of Udi Adiv, and Ein Shemer, home of Avital Geva. And not only because Mishmarot had always been anti-Marxist and social democratic. Here young women wore makeup and young men jeans. On Gan Shmuel, foreign volunteers with long hair were taken for haircuts the day they arrived; on Mishmarot, Meir had let his hair grow and no one seemed to mind.

Mishmarot was a small kibbutz, with barely one hundred members, off a back road near the regional cemetery. Little houses with verandas angled along sloping dirt paths. Mishmarot of course had its cotton fields and chicken coops, but its main source of income was the plywood factory, which had scandalized the neighboring kibbutzim by bringing in a capitalist partner.

"You call this a kibbutz?" mocked Meir's wife, Tirza, who'd grown up in a kibbutz on the Syrian border. "Everyone does what they want. You want to be on a committee? Fine. You don't want to be on a committee? Also fine. This isn't a kibbutz, it's anarchy." Mishmarot's anarchic spirit was especially evident in the summer of 1967. During the war, the children had been evacuated from their communal house to underground shelters. But now that the war was over, mothers simply kept their children home. The children's home, central to kibbutz life, was shut down, without so much as debate at the weekly meeting.

Mishmarot reserved its communal passion for song. Several of Meir's friends had written songs that made it to the radio; one, about a soldier returning home after battle and unable to readjust to normal life, was a hit that summer. On holidays and at weddings, the kibbutz's musical group, part choral group, part pop band, sang satirical songs written by Meir and his collaborator, Shalom Hanoch. Shalom was currently concluding his army service in the IDF's entertainment troupe, and when he finished he intended to become a rock singer.

As a child, lying forlorn at night in the communal children's house, wetting his bed and sucking his fingers, Meir would listen to the singing of the grown-ups. Only then, soothed by the hopeful songs of the pioneers, would he fall into restless sleep.

Later, as teenagers, Meir and his friends would sit on the grass with guitars and sing the songs of Elvis and the Beatles that had reached their remote corner, despite the best intentions of the socialist government to censor the 1960s. (The government had once prevented a Beatles concert in Israel, so as not to corrupt the youth.) Meir and his friend Shalom described that time in a wistful song called "Legend of the Lawn," an ode to teenage romance on the kibbutz, boy and girl awkwardly reaching out toward each other through a tangle of bodies: "There's a pile of *hevreh* on the grass / Those kinds of things—I like / girls-boys together, it's nice that / there's courage sometimes to mix . . . / Beneath my head lies a thigh / and on my stomach a burst of curls . . . / I can't tell whose hand is crawling over me / and turning my body into a piano."

Shalom had written the melancholy music as a parody of an old Zionist song. But the music was so lovely, and Meir's lyrics so evocative, that Mishmarot's young people adopted it as an anthem.

A RECORD PRODUCER appeared at Meir's door with a contract for an album, to be titled *Jerusalem of Iron*.

"I just wrote that as a parody," Meir protested feebly, and signed.

In a newspaper interview, he explained why. "After urgent consultations with my wife, I decided first of all to exploit the opportunity given to me; second, to prove to whomever I need to prove to that I can write better songs [than 'Jerusalem of Iron']. My own songs. I don't think that 'Jerusalem of Iron' is a good song. It simply belongs to those days. I hate pathos."

AVITAL GEVA BOYCOTTS THE WALL

AFTER A MONTH in the hospital, Avital returned to Kibbutz Ein Shemer. He gave Ada strict instructions: No welcome-home party.

Instead friends filled their apartment at all hours. They had recently moved from one room to a room and a half, with a private bathroom. The new apartment was on the edge of the orchards, beside two cypress trees with great branches, planted to protect the oranges from the wind. As teenagers, Avital and Ada would meet there secretly, trying to evade the watchful collective. Since Avital's injury, his relationship with Ada, always close, had become almost telepathic. It was, one friend noted, as if they had become a single being.

IN FLOPPY CONICAL CAPS and wide straw hats and work boots and sandals, with sleeping bags and knapsacks weighted with canned meat and corn and with East German cameras around their necks, the kibbutzniks of Ein Shemer piled into open-backed trucks to discover the restored homeland. After a day of hiking in the Golan Heights, in Hebron and Bethlehem, they would retire to youth hostels or monasteries, twenty to a room, and awaken at dawn for another day of hiking. During one trip they drove to the site, near Ammunition Hill, where Amnon Harodi had been blown apart.

Avital refused to join them. "I don't want to tour battlegrounds," he told Ada. And he especially did not want to go to the Western Wall. "Not interested," he said curtly. He was in no mood for rejoicing or gratitude. *I'd give up the whole pile of stones to get Amnon back—*

Ada returned from the West Bank disgusted. "You should see our people," she said, "gloating like conquerors and bargaining over trinkets."

IN EIN SHEMER there were no more arguments about the Soviet Union. The break with "that bitch," as Amnon Harodi had called it, suddenly seemed self-evident. The Ein Shemer newsletter even denounced the leaders of the Soviet Union as "red Czars"—a description that not long ago would likely have been condemned by kibbutzniks as fascist.

Avital wasn't mollified. The ideological shift had happened too abruptly, without introspection. Avital was struggling to understand how a community of decent, even noble human beings had been so blinded to evil and threat. They had behaved no differently from the religious fanatics they loved to despise. *Worse, comrades: we turned a mass murderer and anti-Semite into a saint!* They had walled themselves off from the rest of the nation, reading only the movement's newspaper and dismissing all criticism of their ideology as lies. Unless they tried to understand how they had gotten to that point, they could make a similar mistake again.

STEADIED BY A cane, Avital shuffled along the paths of his beloved kibbutz, beneath the canopy of ficus trees, through the children's area where he'd grown up, through the orchards now being irrigated in preparation for the autumn harvest. Then he wandered into Ein Shemer's greenhouses, which grew roses. Avital hated roses—too pretty, too tame—but the greenhouses intoxicated him. Everything rising, new life breaking through. In the moist density, he felt his own vitality stirring again.

THE SILENCE BETWEEN FATHER AND SON

URI AND TOVA Adiv were worried about their son, Udi. But they didn't know how to show their concern. As a boy Udi hadn't been hugged or kissed by Tova, who considered such gestures a form of spoiling. Udi's father, Uri, a big silent man, found speech almost painful; whatever he had to say he conveyed in practical ways. He had served as kibbutz secretary general and was sometimes dispatched by the movement to help organize a struggling kibbutz. He had little left for his children. Young Udi would fall asleep at night on the windowsill in the children's house, hoping to catch a glimpse of his father returning from the fields.

Uri had been attracted to Tova in part by her rhetorical eloquence. Tova, a famous beauty in her youth, had been ashamed of her good looks, which made her feel frivolous. Tova was respected and feared in the kibbutz for the same reason: her indiscriminate sense of outrage. At kibbutz meetings, she denounced with equal vehemence the kibbutz school's insensitivity in dealing with nonconformist children and the Labor government for aligning with the West. Tova remained loyal to Stalin long after Soviet premier Nikita Khrushchev's attack against Stalin's "cult of personality." True, she said, Stalin had his faults, but he inspired human beings to fight for justice, just like Moses. Though Uri had doubts about the Soviet Union—his cousin had been imprisoned by Stalin for spreading Yiddish culture—he kept those to himself, not daring to argue with Tova.

The stories Tova told to Udi as a child were about the struggle against oppression, like the three brothers in czarist Russia who led a peasant revolt, just like the Macabees. Udi learned from a young age that the deepest emotions should be trusted to ideology, that the way to win Tova's affection was by proving his ideological fervor. He adopted Tova's rhetorical skills, and could recite from memory whole passages of *The Communist Manifesto*.

Udi longed to ease human suffering. Once, on a bus during a class trip in third grade, Udi stood and offered his seat to an exhausted-looking Arab laborer. Later, in high school, having noticed a bus driver speaking rudely to an Arab passenger, Udi wrote a protest letter to the bus cooperative.

AFTER DINNER IN the kibbutz dining room, Udi went to his parents' apartment, one room with a wooden partition marking off the bedroom from the salon. As in other Gan Shmuel apartments, there were no mezuzahs on the doorposts, nothing to mark this a Jewish home. On the salon wall hung Pablo Picasso's *Don Quixote*.

Udi wanted his parents to understand the changes he was going through as a result of the war. But after a lifetime of silence between them, the best Udi could manage was mockery. "They told us that the state was in danger of destruction," Udi said. "That we're about to be thrown into the sea. It was all a lie—war hysteria encouraged by the fascist generals so that they could conquer Rabbi Goren's holy stones."

"What are you talking about?" his father shouted with sudden vehemence.

"You talk about the solidarity of workers," Udi pressed. "But when an Arab wanted to join Gan Shmuel, the kibbutz rejected him. And when the army offered the kibbutz the fields of Cherkas, what did the good socialists of Gan Shmuel do? You took a vote! How typical of Hashomer Hatzair to confiscate land democratically."

"I'm not saying everything is perfect here," said Uri, "but you're going too far."

"Listen to him," Tova pleaded with her husband, "he's speaking from his experience in the war." Uri glared at her; unaccustomed to his firmness, she demurred.

"There are no bigger hypocrites than Hashomer Hatzair," Udi taunted. "You wanted to have it all ways: to be anticolonialists and to collaborate with the British. And now the Americans are our big friends. Zionism couldn't succeed without colonialist support. And Hashomer Hatzair made it all progressive!"

Uri wanted to ask his son, Who are you turning into colonialists? The impoverished dreamers who created the most egalitarian society in history? Who faced destruction everywhere we turned? We offered our Arab neighbors a hand in friendship. And when we were attacked, we fought well and won. You want me to apologize for surviving? If they had won the war, not a Jew would have been left alive in this land. But all you know is that we took land from Cherkas. Maybe we were wrong. Things happen that one later regrets. But you—you have it all figured out. You want to turn Zionism itself into a crime—

But Uri, unused to argument, couldn't find those words. Instead, he pounded the table with his big fist and shouted words that formed no coherent argument. It wouldn't have mattered if they did: father and son weren't trying to convince but silence each other.

Only when neighbors complained did the shouting subside.

A MODEST WEDDING

MOTTA AND ARIK drove to the Suez Canal, to plan a brigade maneuver: a simulation of an Egyptian crossing of the canal. Before the war, they had routinely spent weekends driving along the country's narrow borders, and were never more than a few hours from home. But the drive to the canal took ten hours.

They passed lines of charred Egyptian tanks. Atop one tank, Israeli tourists posed for a picture.

Arik had a delicate issue he needed to raise with Motta. Since the war, Motta had initiated an aggressive campaign to commemorate the battle for Jerusalem. He all but ordered reluctant reservists to grant interviews to a journalist writing a book about the war; when Yoske Balagan balked, Motta threatened him with a call-up notice. Motta even organized a filmed re-creation of scenes from the battle, complete with exploding smoke grenades.

"Motta, listen," said Arik, "the guys are unhappy with all the glorification. It's not our style."

"Don't be such hypocrites," Motta retorted. "There were other battles in this war that were greater military achievements than ours. Raful [commander of the standing army's paratrooper brigade, which operated in Sinai] fought a battle that was more impressive. But in thirty years, no one will remember Raful's battle, and everyone will remember the battle for Jerusalem. And then, when you tell it to your grandchildren, you'll thank me."

SOME RESERVISTS WERE grumbling about the battle's failures. How was it possible, they asked, that we went to war with such little intelligence? And what recklessness for Motta to blindly charge into the Old City in his search for glory: a single sniper could have taken out the whole senior command! And what about the fight for Ammunition Hill, Jerusalem's bloodiest battle: Why send paratroopers into the trenches, when the position could simply have been circumvented?

Nonsense, said Arik: Ammunition Hill overlooked the road to Mount Scopus, where an Israeli unit was under siege, and the whole length of no-man's-land. As for Motta charging into the Old City, yes, that was reckless, but Motta was in the grip of history and had no choice.

By rational standards, argued Arik, preparing an urban assault in less than twelve hours and without adequate intelligence was impossible. "But we knew that it had to be done, and so we did it. We didn't make calculations about expected losses and argue whether the mission would be 'worth it.' All that mattered was achieving the objective. That's what it means to be a paratrooper."

JUST BEFORE THE holiday of Sukkoth, Arik and Yehudit married. They deferred the question of kibbutz versus city: until they finished their studies, they would live in Tel Aviv, close to the university.

The little wedding party—parents and a few friends—gathered in an office in Tel Aviv's official rabbinate. Yehudit wore a simple suit sewn by a friend, Arik an open-necked white shirt and khaki pants. No one thought to bring a camera.

The appearance in the Tel Aviv rabbinate of Yehudit's father, Yaakov Hazan, head of Zionism's most anticlerical movement, caused a stir. Officials peeked into the room to get a glimpse of the great heretic, dapper in a beret, who good-naturedly greeted the bearded men.

"Do what you have to do, and nothing more," Arik ordered the officiating rabbi, as though he were one of his soldiers. "No speeches, no circling the groom."

The rabbi rushed through the ceremony. Arik stepped on the glass, gave Yehudit a chaste kiss. The newlyweds went to lunch at Tel Aviv's most exclusive restaurant, with white tablecloths and a French menu. At a nearby table, Moshe Dayan was having lunch with his mistress. Then Arik went to be with his two children in Kibbutz Netzer Sereni, and Yehudit went to be with her two children in Kibbutz Mishmar Ha'Emek.

CHAPTER 10

THE CHILDREN RETURN TO THEIR BORDERS

COMFORTING MOTHER RACHEL

WRY AND SLOW-SPEAKING, mixing Yiddish with Hebrew, Prime Minister Eshkol, age seventy-two, eyed with bemused affection the fast-talking young man in the knitted *kippah* sloping on the side of his head, so absorbed in his vision that he showed little of the respect one would expect of a twenty-four-year-old meeting the leader of his country. Hanan Porat—shirt hanging from pants, uncombed hair permanently windblown—eyed Eshkol in return with impatience. Hanan had come on an historic mission, on behalf of the children of Kfar Etzion, and here was Eshkol, bantering.

In fact Hanan's contempt for Eshkol was widely shared among Israelis, who even in the aftermath of the Six-Day War couldn't forgive him for hesitating to attack during the agonizing weeks of the "waiting period." Eshkol should have been a hero: he had, after all, led Israel from its worst crisis to its greatest victory, launching a preemptive attack only once he had exhausted every diplomatic option, ensuring a united cabinet and American sympathy.

Now Hanan was challenging Eshkol to confront the consequences of victory. Though the cabinet had secretly voted to offer a withdrawal from the Sinai and the Golan Heights in exchange for peace, it was divided over the future of the West Bank. The government had annexed only East Jerusalem, pointedly leaving the status of the West Bank open for negotiation.

But negotiations seemed more remote than ever. The Arab League had just issued its three noes: no negotiations, no recognition, no peace. Eshkol shared the fear of his cabinet's doves of ruling a million Palestinians, the threat to the demographic intactness of a Jewish state. But even the doves agreed that there could be no return to the fragile prewar borders; the only debate was how much of the West Bank should eventually be returned.

Hanan's group of orphans seemed to be offering Eshkol a sensible compromise. The site of Kfar Etzion was near Jerusalem, not deep in the West Bank; even if Israel were to eventually annex Kfar Etzion, it wouldn't substantially change the borders. A modest return: a few children to the literal homes of their parents, not the return of the Jewish people to its ancestral home.

"What do you want, *kinderlach*?" Eshkol asked, using the Yiddish endearment for children.

"To go up," said Hanan.

"*Nu, kinderlach,* if you want to go up, then go."

"Listen," Hanan pressed, "in ten days it will be Rosh Hashanah," the Jewish new year. "We very much want to pray in the place where our parents prayed."

"*Nu, kinderlach,*" said the prime minister, "if you want to pray, then pray."

ON SEPTEMBER 27, 1967—two days after receiving Eshkol's blessing—a caravan equipped for an instant settlement proceeded slowly through Jerusalem. Two rented buses, cars, vans, and open-backed trucks were led by a 1948-era bus that had once traveled the route between Jerusalem and Kfar Etzion. Hanan and his friends left nothing to subtlety: the sides of the bus were covered with gray-painted wood sheets to simulate the armor that had covered buses then, and bore the words, "We Once Traveled Like This."

The procession stopped at the military cemetery on Mount Herzl, and several dozen people walked toward the mass grave of Kfar Etzion. They were young men in *kippot*, some in reservist uniforms, young women in long skirts and sandals, the few surviving fathers of Kfar Etzion in fedoras and peddler's caps, the widows in kerchiefs.

They approached a grassy slope beside a stone wall with marble plaques, each engraved with the name of one of the fallen. The crowd recited the mourners' prayer together: "May He Who brings peace above bring peace to us and all of Israel."

Next stop: Rachel's Tomb, a small, white-domed building at the entrance to Bethlehem. The group pressed around the stone sarcophagus. One of the Kfar Etzion "children" chanted the portion from Jeremiah that imagines Mother Rachel weeping for the exiled children of Israel: "So says God: Keep your voice from weeping and your eyes from tears, for your work shall be rewarded, says God, and they shall return again from the land of the enemy. And there is hope for your future, says God, and your children shall return to their borders."

Hanan Porat felt a shiver. Metaphor and reality converged: those verses had been written for him and his friends, for this moment.

They came to the site of Kfar Etzion. It was a bright, windy day. The stony hills, parched from the long summer, awaited the first rains. Hanan declared: "Today we have removed the disgrace of the term 'administered territories' and restored the appropriate term, 'redeemed territories.'" Psalms of thanksgiving were offered. An Israeli flag was raised on a flagpole left behind by the Jordanian army.

And then, to work. A survivor of Kfar Etzion, its former carpenter, built a table; another survivor watered a carob and a fig tree that had survived the Jordanian uprooting of the kibbutz's trees. The young people unloaded a generator and spring cots and boxes of canned food, drew up schedules for kitchen duty and for guard duty. An army truck brought water.

The settlers, all single, divided into male and female barracks. The barracks were rounded aluminum structures resembling long igloos, built by the British and inherited by the Jordanian army. In the male barracks they hung a photograph of Rabbi Kook.

Toward evening the well-wishers departed, leaving a dozen members of the original group of children evacuated from Kfar Etzion alone on the mountain: the first West Bank settlement, a kibbutz of orphans.

PARTING OF THE WAYS

SOLDIERS' TALK, A collection of interviews with kibbutznik veterans of the war, was self-published by the editors of the magazine *Shdemot*. Lacking funds, they'd posted notices in kibbutz dining rooms soliciting advance purchases, and on that basis printed an initial press run of 12,000 copies. To the shock of the young editors, the book sold nearly a hundred thousand copies, a massive best seller in a country of less than three million people.

The tone of *Soldiers' Talk* was more of anguish than protest. The soldiers interviewed didn't minimize the threat Israel had faced; there were no voices among them like Udi Adiv's. Instead, there were hesitant expressions of discovering a sense of responsibility to the Jewish people and its history, a love for Jerusalem that surprised them. One kibbutznik who fought in Sinai confessed to feeling envy when he heard that the paratroopers were fighting in Jerusalem. Another told of being on a bus with his unit in Sinai when they heard that the Old City was in Israeli hands. Everyone began to sing "Jerusalem of Gold."

There were expressions of horror. A kibbutznik who fought in East Jerusalem and who said he never wanted to see the city again recounted his first experience of killing a man. Here was a tone of self-doubt that the nation had rarely heard before from its soldiers. And anger—at the Arabs for trying to destroy the Jews, and at their fellow Israelis for exulting in victory, at having to fight for survival and having to conquer. One soldier recalled seeing young children—the age of his son—with their hands raised in surrender. Another recalled entering an Arab village as residents dutifully applauded. He felt, he said, sullied.

ONE GROUP OF interviewees was missing from *Soldiers' Talk*: the students of Mercaz. No mention of the five-hour discussion in Yochanan Fried's living room.

The omission was deliberate. When the editors of *Shdemot* read the Mercaz transcript, they had been horrified. Where was the soul-searching, the doubt? The Mercaz students, said one editor, seemed even willing to sacrifice the sacredness of human life, Judaism's main contribution to humanity.

Among Mercaz students too there was bewilderment and contempt. What was happening to the kibbutzniks, they asked, to our commanders? Were they losing their nerve? Yochanan Fried was stunned to read one kibbutznik admit he'd felt happy when his bullet missed its mark: *that* was a soldier protecting Israel? Instead of holy kibbutzniks, there was now talk in Mercaz of the children of the pioneers shaming the fathers. "Crybabies," said a Mercaz student.

Yoel Bin-Nun was conflicted. He shared his friends' incredulity at the lack of vision and self-confidence expressed in *Soldiers' Talk*. Yet he also shared its moral struggles. He had, after all, been the only one among the Mercaz students at the discussion who had conceded ambivalence. Most of all he regretted the lost opportunity to bring what he called Israel's two spiritual elites—the kibbutzniks and the Mercaz students—closer together.

BREZHNEV BOULEVARD

EVERY FEW MONTHS Avital Geva returned to a Jerusalem clinic for another operation to remove shrapnel from his shoulder and legs.

The elderly doctor, Yitzhak Kook, who had volunteered during the war and operated on dozens of soldiers, happened to be the nephew of the late chief rabbi Abraham Isaac Kook. Not that that meant anything to Avital: the religious world was a blur to him. But Avital was drawn to the doctor, who quoted the Bible and the Talmud in discussions about medicine and politics and who offered Avital a glimpse into a world of religious wisdom he wished he understood.

Dr. Kook took a special liking to the ebullient young man who spoke with such warmth about his kibbutz and with such bitterness about its ideological blindness. With the affection of a Kookian for kibbutzniks, the doctor wanted to know what Avital and his friends were thinking about collective life, whether they were as restless as the newspapers claimed.

Finally the doctor told Avital that there was nothing more he could do for him. Some fragments would remain. Not so bad, Avital concluded; only on cold days did he feel the metal pressing.

AVITAL RETURNED TO the orchards. But he wasn't quite the same Avital. The kibbutznik who'd delighted in the changes of the seasons, the appearance of the autumn squill and the late winter anemones, now felt an unfamiliar disaffection. Sleep eluded him. He'd been blown out of his life and couldn't find his way back in.

Ada suggested he study art. He'd enjoyed drawing sketches for the kibbutz newsletter, banners with holiday themes for the kibbutz dining room. And so twice a week, he went off to art school in Jaffa. There he discovered conceptual art. The notion of art as a carrier of ideas rather than mere aesthetics appealed to his kibbutznik soul.

One morning in the orchards, while eating breakfast with his friends Rafi and Manu, Avital said, "*Hevreh*, the anniversary of the Bolshevik revolution is approaching. We have to give it the honor it deserves."

Avital revealed a plan: to turn the orchards into a paean to Soviet bombast by hanging street signs along the dirt paths, each sign bearing the name of a Soviet hero.

"Roads should have names," agreed Rafi.

Avital drove to the plywood factory in nearby Kibbutz Mishmarot and bought thirty sheets of wood. In the orchard's packing shed, he painted on them the names of Soviet leaders. Rafi and Manu helped him hammer the signs to the cypress trees that circled the orchard.

The next Shabbat, when kibbutzniks strolled in the citrus groves, they saw big signs proclaiming: Karl Marx Avenue, Brezhnev Boulevard, Red Square.

Avital's father, Kuba, cautioned him: "Don't push too far." He meant: don't provoke the collective like I did.

Most of the kibbutzniks, though, seemed to delight in Avital's new style of political discourse. Humor instead of rhetoric to make a political point! One man, whose pilot son was a POW in Syria, silently pressed Avital's hand. The kibbutz movement's newspaper sent a photographer.

WINTER IN KFAR ETZION

THE FIRST RAINS of late autumn turned the dirt paths of Kfar Etzion into rivulets. The young people walked with clumps of mud on their work boots. The furious winds seemed intent on uprooting them from the exposed mountain. Every few days the generator broke down, leaving the community without electricity. Then, in the premature winter, the water pipe froze. Sometimes, when there were terrorism alerts, the army imposed a curfew on the winding road to Jerusalem.

But every day also seemed to bring another small sign of permanence. Sympathetic cabinet ministers dispatched a tractor, a new generator, turkey chicks, a greenhouse for growing carnations. Crates of fruit were sent by a kibbutz, Ha-Lamed Hey (the Thirty-Five), named in memory of a Palmach unit ambushed in 1948 on its way to a failed rescue mission for Kfar Etzion. A Tel Aviv dentist about to retire offered to sell his office equipment and donate the proceeds to Kfar Etzion. Hanan received dozens of letters with urgent requests to join the kibbutz, like one from a university student prepared to drop out if Kfar Etzion would accept him. A newlywed couple asked to spend their honeymoon there.

Letters of gratitude came from around the country. The rector of Tel Aviv University wrote a short note: "The pioneers of Kfar Etzion are showing the way." High school students sent a poem of praise on a picture postcard, a photograph of paratroopers dancing at the Western Wall.

A TAXI APPEARED on the mountain, and out hobbled a young American woman with a torn sandal, carrying a suitcase. Sandy Sussman, age twenty-one, former head of the Bnei Akiva branch of Los Angeles, had just moved to Israel. A friend had told her that Kfar Etzion was the place to be, and so here she was. Looking around, she was struck by the hard beauty of the surrounding hills and by the barrenness of the kibbutz itself, little more than a row of what looked like long igloos.

Hanan was skeptical. What did an American know about hardship? "It's not Bnei Akiva summer camp," he said to Sandy.

Finally he relented. "Welcome, my child," he said to the young woman, four years his junior.

Sandy accepted life on the mountain without complaint, determined to prove herself. There was no sink in the communal dining room, so they washed dishes under an outdoor faucet; communal bathrooms were a hole in the ground. Sandy loved the informality: boys and girls wandered in their pajamas, and she felt free to wear curlers to the dining room. The girls did guard duty along with the boys, learning how to shoot and dismantle an Uzi. When a boy wanted to get to know a girl, he would arrange for her to be his guarding partner. Which is how Sandy got to know Avinoam Amichai—Abu, as his friends called him.

Sandy and Avinoam became Kfar Etzion's first couple. Round-faced, generous, the comedian of the *hevreh,* Avinoam had left university studies to become a carpenter on the kibbutz. A reservist in the 55th Brigade, he had met Hanan at the Western Wall the morning of its liberation. "We're going home," he'd said then.

Late one night, the watchmen roused the sleeping kibbutz: It's snowing! When one young woman refused to get out of bed, they carried her cot outside and overturned her into the snow. Sandy, coming from Los Angeles, had never seen falling snow. It seemed as if the world were dissolving into its pure essence. Fog covered the hills. The silence was broken only by the delighted cries of young people throwing snowballs and pushing each other into the drifts.

Hanan watched his friends and thought, We are redeeming this place with our laughter. Just as the Psalmist had written, "Those who sow with tears will reap with joy."

HANAN WAS CONSTANTLY on the road, meeting officials and recruiting volunteers. He often returned to the kibbutz past midnight, dependent on infrequent buses and hitches. He performed his kibbutz responsibilities along with everyone else; the only privilege he allowed himself was to be chronically late for guard duty and kitchen shift.

Hanan was more than just the coordinator of Kfar Etzion; he was its *abba*, father of the orphans. In the absence of a rabbi he functioned as the community's spiritual leader, teaching Torah and inserting wherever possible the messianic vision of Rabbi Kook. We are not merely redeeming our parents' home, he reminded his friends, but preparing the way for redemption.

"How can you be so sure?" a friend challenged him one night as the two patrolled the barbed wire perimeter. In the near total blackness, the stars seemed closer than the next hill. "Rabbi Akiva believed that Bar Kochba was the Messiah," his friend pressed, referring to the leader of the fatal Jewish revolt against Rome. "But instead of redemption, Bar Kochba brought the destruction of a thousand Jewish communities and the beginning of exile. If a great sage like Rabbi Akiva could be wrong, then so can you."

"But we see it happening!" said Hanan.

"Rabbi Akiva also said, 'We see it happening.' And look what happened."

LATE ONE NIGHT Hanan sat alone in the area of the dining room designated as the synagogue. He opened a religious book but couldn't concentrate. He was so tired. Wrangling one more benefit for Kfar Etzion from government bureaucrats, mediating between the conflicting personalities and ideologies at home. He longed for the purity of the Mercaz study hall. Before the war had turned his life upside down, he had thought of remaining there for another ten years.

He paced the room and came to the small Torah ark, protected by a velvet curtain stitched with a drawing of fire emerging from the altar of the Temple.

There was so much to do. The return to Kfar Etzion was only the beginning. The next stage was to settle the area around Kfar Etzion, the old Etzion Bloc, where three other kibbutzim had existed before they too were destroyed in 1948. One day, Hanan was certain, these hills would be filled with Jewish homes and schools and workshops. And then the same would happen on hills throughout Judea and Samaria. There was no time for melancholy, self-doubt.

Hanan had always done what was necessary. And he was ready now to lay himself on the altar of Jewish rebirth, even if that meant suppressing his own needs.

He recalled a line by Hannah Szenes, the young poet who had joined Enzo Sereni's group of parachutists behind Nazi lines, and been captured and executed. The line was inscribed on the memorial to Israel's paratroopers at the Tel Nof air force base: "A voice summons and you begin to walk." She had sacrificed poetic ambitions, family, life in the land of Israel, life itself. *I will not disappoint the children of Kfar Etzion who depend on me, the public that looks toward this mountain as a beacon—*

He rested his head against the curtain and wept.

SANDY AND AVINOAM MARRIED. Hundreds of people—rabbis, politicians, strangers—came to celebrate the first wedding in Kfar Etzion in two decades. Sandy wore a wedding gown given to her by a member of the original kibbutz. Celebrants danced to taped Jewish music on the new grass outside the dining room, singing over and over the prophetic words whose fulfillment they were: "The rejoicing of bride and groom will be heard in the cities of Judea and in the streets of Jerusalem."

The couple's friends sang a song they'd written for the occasion. But unlike the usual practice, this song was in praise not of the couple but of the community. "History is returning," they sang. "Life again is thriving in

Etzion. . . . We'll take revenge upon our enemies / by building and planting and rejoicing."

The wedding was reported on the radio, an event of national importance.

RESTORING THE ROOT

THE PARK HOTEL IN HEBRON, a two-story building with bathrooms in the halls and holes for toilets, was fully booked for the holiday. It was April 12, 1968, the eve of Passover. Dozens of young couples with small children appeared, claiming to be Swiss tourists but speaking Hebrew. They said they had come only for the holiday, but one family arrived with a truck carrying a refrigerator and a washing machine.

The "Swiss tourists" had in fact come to settle in Hebron, city of Abraham and Sarah. Their intention was to celebrate Passover together and then, when the holiday ended, simply refuse to leave, declaring the renewal of Hebron's Jewish community, with or without government approval. A young man in a beret and carrying a cat approached the hotel and called out in French-accented Hebrew, "Is this where those crazy people came to set up a Jewish settlement in Hebron? I'm with you!"

Hebron was the most tense place in the territories. Just a few days earlier, an Israeli policeman had been killed patrolling the city's market. The Israeli public had almost universally supported the return to Kfar Etzion; but Israelis were deeply divided over settling inside Hebron.

For the Jews in the Park Hotel, though, the argument was self-evident. Hebron was the burial place of the biblical patriarchs and matriarchs. What other nation had preserved the tombs of its ancient founders, could point to its precise point of origin? Here David had established his kingdom before moving to Jerusalem; here, Ruth the Moabite, the prototype convert to Judaism and great-grandmother of King David, was said to be buried. The ruins of medieval synagogues proved an unbroken Jewish attachment. If Jews didn't belong in Hebron, what right did they have to Tel Aviv, barely sixty years old, an infant by the measure of the Middle East?

The only reason Jews were no longer living in Hebron was that in 1929 Arabs had destroyed its defenseless Orthodox Jewish community. Incited by false rumors that the Jews intended to take over the Temple Mount, the mob had massacred sixty-nine Jews, hacking limbs and gouging out eyes.

(Several hundred Jews had been saved by their Arab neighbors.) The survivors then fled to Jerusalem. Like the return to Kfar Etzion, there was nothing abstract about a return to Hebron.

The seder was held in the hotel's dining room. On the walls hung embroidered quotes from the Koran. Novelist Moshe Shamir, who had grown up in Hashomer Hatzair, offered commentary on "Dayenu," the Passover song expressing gratitude for whatever God in His mercy offered the Jewish people. Shamir attacked the intent of the song: Our fathers, he said, were ready to settle for too little. Last year, he continued, before the war, we accepted the state of Israel without reunified Jerusalem and without Hebron. And so we are forbidden to say "*dayenu*," forbidden to settle for less than total redemption of the land of Israel.

Afterward celebrants danced with the soldiers guarding the hotel. "Next year in Hebron," they sang.

SHORTLY AFTER PASSOVER, Arik Achmon visited Hebron. He was curious: several of his friends were on reserve duty there, and he wanted an insider's report about the Jews who had moved into the Park Hotel and then refused to leave. Prime Minister Eshkol had denounced the would-be settlers but then agreed to move the group into an army base in the city, pending a final decision on their fate.

Arik often spent Shabbat driving through the territories, exploring the new Israel he and his friends had helped create. He was concerned, though not acutely, about the future: retaining the territories, with their one million Arabs, seemed to him inconceivable; sooner or later Israel would find the right moment to withdraw. Driving to Hebron, he took an Uzi for precaution. Though an Israeli felt no danger in most of the territories, Hebron, with its religious passions and history of slaughter, was an exception.

"The Jews here are as bad as the Arabs," a friend told Arik. "For them, the Arabs are invisible. It's as if they don't exist."

The settlers' leader, Rabbi Moshe Levinger, constantly spoke of the humiliations Jews had endured in this city of their birth—how the Muslims hadn't even allowed Jews into the Tomb of the Patriarchs, confining them to the seventh outdoor step. In revenge he provocatively danced before Muslim worshippers sitting on prayer rugs in the Tomb of the Patriarchs, just to prove he could. Levinger was telling Hebron's Arabs: You murdered the most passive and helpless Jews; now you've gotten the Jews you deserve.

Despite himself, Arik was fascinated by this unexpected outbreak of defiant pioneering emerging from religious Zionists, of all communities. He had to admire their courage: kerchiefed women strolled babies through the market where soldiers patrolled warily.

But the image of a gaunt-faced Levinger avenging Jewish honor by taunting the conquered Arabs troubled Arik long after his visit to Hebron. Levinger liked to compare himself to the Zionist pioneers who had founded the state, but he was defying a sovereign Jewish government, not British occupiers. Levinger was invoking an alternative—religious—legitimacy to the secular state. A foreign spirit, antithetical to Zionism, was stirring.

THE BOOK OF JOSHUA

YOEL BIN-NUN MARRIED Esther Raab, his girlfriend from their Nahal days on Mount Gilboa. They were both twenty-two years old. The wedding, blessed with the presence of Rabbi Zvi Yehudah, was modest, plates of humus and canned corn and schnitzel; the couple didn't hire a photographer. Yoel's friends from Mercaz danced ecstatically, unaccompanied by music: according to Jerusalem's strict Orthodox custom, bands couldn't play at weddings as a sign of mourning for the destroyed Temple.

Just before Hanukkah 1967, the newlyweds moved to Kfar Etzion. Hanan had wanted Yoel and Esther to join the kibbutz. "Out of the question," said Yoel. There was no way he was going to subject his freedom to the will of a commune, waste his time on weekly meetings and kitchen duty.

Instead, Yoel and Esther came as staff members of Kfar Etzion's new *hesder* yeshiva—which combined military training with religious study for eighteen-year-old IDF recruits. Esther was the house mother, Yoel a teacher. Yoel was a rabbi in all but name: at some time of his own choosing he would take the state rabbinate's exam on the intracacies of Jewish law and become ordained, a formality.

The couple was given a single room, without bathroom or sink. They shared an outhouse with the yeshiva's thirty-five students.

One of the "igloos" was turned into the Mount Etzion Yeshiva. The small kerosene heaters were hardly adequate against that first bitter winter. Yoel and his students leaned on wooden lecterns wearing hooded coats.

Yoel taught Bible. That was unusual: a young man beginning his teaching career in the yeshiva world would not ordinarily choose Bible but Talmud, the truly "serious" subject. But Yoel had a spiritual intuition: the generation reclaiming the land would also be the generation to reclaim the Bible. Only Hebrew-speaking Jews living in the land of Israel could understand, as Jews in exile could not, the impact of topography and seasonal change and agricultural cycles on the Bible's imagery and narrative and even moral and legal commandments. The Bible, Yoel taught, had been written for a specific people in a specific place—for nomads transformed into farmers. Its agricultural laws, like leaving the land fallow every seven years and reserving the corners of a field for the poor, were intended to turn mere labor into divine service, bind a consecrated people to a holy land. In exile, Jews had been severed from that living connection. But now that they were back, they could rediscover the link between topography and text.

Yoel began with the book of Joshua: the tribes of Israel crossing the Jordan River and entering the land, a blueprint of conquest for the generation of conquest. Students didn't miss the point that their teacher, a paratrooper and liberator of Jerusalem, carried the same family name as Joshua Bin-Nun.

POCKET-SIZE BIBLE IN HAND, wearing sunglasses and the kibbutzniks' brimless hat, Yoel led his students through the biblical landscape. They searched for springs, ruins, the topography of biblical accounts that would reveal the sites of ancient battlegrounds. They traced the route where Abraham walked from Hebron to Jerusalem, and the route of the Palmach fighters of 1948 who tried to break the siege on Kfar Etzion—a seamless history as though uninterrupted by twenty centuries of exile.

In the intense light of the Judean Hills, time seemed to bend. In Yoel's telling, the battles of Joshua merged with the battles of Motta Gur; the walls collapsing in Jericho prefigured the Jordanian soldiers retreating before dawn from the Old City. Don't read Torah as untouchable scripture, Yoel urged: see yourselves in this story.

THE SINGING PARATROOPER PLANS HIS ESCAPE

THE ALBUM COVER of *Jerusalem of Iron* showed a smiling Meir Ariel in a camouflage uniform with a red beret in his epaulet—a false detail, since a beret was worn only with a dress uniform. For Meir, though, that was the least of the deception. How had he allowed them to turn him into a symbol of the paratroopers? "The singing paratrooper," they were calling him on the radio.

Meir tried to undermine the military image in his autobiographical liner notes: "Okay childhood, questionable teenhood, wet his bed until a late age, still sucking, joined the paratroopers as a last desperate attempt to get onto the straight and narrow. . . ." For Meir that was the jacket's only truthful content.

TIRZA WAS PREGNANT. It had happened during the war: after the battle for Jerusalem, just before the brigade was dispatched to the north, Meir had gotten a few hours' leave; Tirza, assuming he was about to return to battle, had insisted they make love. "I want to duplicate you, just in case," she'd said.

They had met, a year before the war, at a kibbutz seminar for aspiring actors.

"Don't get interested in me," she had warned. "I'm getting married next month."

"I pity the guy who will marry you," he said.

Twenty-four hours later, he proposed: "Let's get married tomorrow. We'll find some strangers to play our parents and we'll go to the rabbinate."

"What happened to 'I pity the guy who will marry you?' " she asked, bemused.

"I have the feeling," he said, "that with you I can go to places I'd never get to on my own."

After the seminar, she had tried to forget him and moved back to her fiancé's kibbutz. But Meir tracked her down. He phoned the kibbutz office and left a message: "Tell her the Mishmarot soccer team called."

It was late afternoon when she arrived in Mishmarot. She found Meir's room across from a cactus garden, in a row of rooms for the kibbutz's discharged soldiers. Meir's room was so filthy, she thought, you could grow a lawn on his bed. She lay down and fell asleep. Several hours later, Meir awakened her with a kiss. "Want to see a play?" he asked.

They ran to catch the open-backed truck crowded with Mishmarot members going to a play in nearby Kibbutz Gan Shmuel. Tirza felt all eyes on her, and the looks weren't welcoming. Only later did she discover that Meir had a serious girlfriend, a daughter of Mishmarot, and that Tirza had just announced herself as the spoiler.

They slept together for the first time that night. The next morning Meir went off to a month of reserve duty. "If you come back in one piece," said Tirza, "we'll marry." Two weeks after he returned, they married. Barely six weeks after their first meeting, four of those weeks spent apart.

"THEY HATE ME HERE," said Tirza.

"No one hates you," said Meir.

"I know what they all say behind my back: 'How can he fall in love with that hysterical girl?'"

Tirza was beautiful and funny and impulsive to the point of offense. She had too much ambition, too much craving for the wider world, to be content as a kibbutznik. Was this it? she wondered, living among too-intimate strangers, washing diapers in the day-care center? What am I doing in this kibbutz *botz*, this mud?

Tirza dared to argue about kibbutz ideology with Meir's father, Sasha, the feared family patriarch. Sasha, a small, austere man with winged hair, carried in his gaunt face the years of hunger he had endured in Siberia, to which he'd been exiled by the Communists for Zionist activity. Once a group of kibbutz children was playing soccer near Sasha's room and kicked a ball by mistake through his open door. Sasha emerged, holding the ball and a knife; smiling, he stabbed the ball.

Tirza loved the way Meir respected his parents. He addressed his father with a soft-spoken reverence, so un-Israeli, and didn't respond to Sasha's rebukes. ("When are you going to stop wasting your time writing songs for the radio and go to university?")

And Meir loved Tirza. Around Tirza he felt fully alive. In choosing her as his bride, he conceded the impossibility of a normal life.

WE HAVE TO GET AWAY, he told her. Just for a while, to a place where they never heard of the singing paratrooper, where I can clear my head and return to myself. Israel was too small; it would have to be abroad. Extracting Tirza from Mishmarot, even briefly, was also a good idea. A separation of forces, he called it.

Taking a trip abroad was no routine matter for a kibbutznik without an income and dependent on the collective for approval. But Meir had a plan. The kibbutz movement was looking for emissaries to American Jewish communities; the two-year stint involved teaching Zionism and socialism to Jewish teenagers.

Meir enrolled in a year-long preparatory course at his movement's educational center. There he studied conversational English and Jewish history and Judaism, including the basic blessings that he didn't know. Why, he wondered, had his kibbutz education denied him the tools to at least understand the Judaism he wasn't observing?

Meir was assigned to the Detroit branch of the Labor Zionist youth movement, Habonim (the Builders). "When we're there," he told Tirza, "I'm going to study filmmaking. I'm finished with music."

The Ariels' first child, a daughter, Shiraz, was born nine months after the war. Three months later, in June 1968, the Ariel family set off for America.

CHAPTER 11

ATTRITION

ON THE JORDAN RIVER

THE HAPPY ENDING of Jewish history barely lasted the summer of 1967. Arab attacks resumed on all fronts. The Egyptian army shelled Israeli troops along the Suez Canal. The PLO sent terrorists across the Jordan River and placed bombs in Israeli markets. Abroad, Israeli planes were hijacked. Arik Achmon was wrong, after all. The Six-Day War hadn't convinced the Arab world that Israel's existence was permanent.

Reserve duty resumed, even more intensively than before the war. The new borders required greater effort to protect. The IDF built camps and bunkers along the Suez Canal, on the Golan Heights, in the Jordan Valley. Still, for the first time the coastal plain, where most Israelis lived, was no longer directly threatened. The paratroopers' war in the streets of Jerusalem seemed to mark the end of the unbearable intimacy between the home front and the battlefront. A surprise attack could no longer sever the state in minutes; the IDF's doctrine of preemption, of taking the war into enemy territory, was replaced by a defensive strategy. In protecting Israel, the IDF finally had a reasonable margin for error.

The 28th Battalion was assigned a month's reserve duty in the Jordan Valley, the desert strip separating the West Bank and Jordan, Israel's new eastern border, stretching from the southern edge of the Sea of Galilee to the Dead Sea. The battalion set up headquarters in the former Jordanian police station in Jericho, a quiet town of palm trees and winter villas; just outside the town was a refugee camp of mud houses, dating from the 1948 war.

It was late winter. By day the reservists sat in huts abandoned by the Jordanian army, drinking coffee and arguing about the future of the newly won territories. In the freezing nights, they lay in ambush for terrorists wading across the Jordan River. It rained heavily, and the Jordan, in dry times a thin stream barely two meters wide, rushed with vigor. The limestone hills turned green.

Whatever divisions had once existed between the kibbutznik veterans of the paratroopers and the religious newcomers from Nahal disappeared. Now they were all veterans of the battle for Jerusalem. When religious soldiers needed a tenth man to complete a prayer quorum, Yoske Balagan volunteered. "At the Wall I discovered I'm a Jew," he said.

One Shabbat, Yoel Bin-Nun's officer announced a drill, a simulated terrorist attack from across the river. The officer called Yoel aside and said, "You don't have to participate." He intended to spare Yoel the choice between obeying orders and violating Shabbat. But Yoel was indignant. "No way," he said. "An exercise is also potentially a matter of life and death"—and so superseded Shabbat observance.

Even as Yoel rejected religious privilege, he insisted on religious strictures in the army's shared space. When soldiers caught a rabbit—a nonkosher animal—and cooked it in a pot in the field kitchen, Yoel complained to his commander. "Let them do whatever they want," said Yoel, "but not with army property." The IDF belongs to all of us, Yoel was saying; don't exclude me from the collective kitchen.

With his knowing gaze and reassuring smile, Yoel was, for his fellow soldiers, the beautiful face of Judaism. He spoke in a deep soft voice, imparting Torah wisdom on the issues of the day. Yoel wasn't trying to "convert" secularists but seeking a common language with them. In Yoel's vocabulary, there were no "religious" or "secular" Jews, only those who observed more and those who observed less. Every soldier was in some sense religious: Was there any greater *mitzvah* than protecting the people of Israel in its land?

A secular young man with whom Yoel shared a hut posted a pinup of a naked woman over his bed. Yoel averted his eyes but said nothing. The pinup disappeared.

UDI ADIV'S FELLOW RESERVISTS in Company D wanted to like the basketball player from Gan Shmuel who knew how to make Turkish coffee with just the right balance between bitter and sweet. But they couldn't bear Udi's politics. He thinks everything is our fault, they complained, that the Arabs only want to throw flowers at us.

"What are we doing here?" Udi said over a game of backgammon to a young man from Kibbutz Ein Shemer. "This is occupied territory."

"I agree," said his friend. "But we have to protect the country."

"You're no socialist," taunted Udi. "A real socialist, when he sees injustice—he doesn't just talk, he acts."

"If you mean protesting, by all means. But if you're talking about taking the law into your hands, then that's anarchy."

Manning a roadblock, Udi allowed Arabs to pass through without a security check. One night, while waiting with his unit in an ambush for terrorists crossing the river, Udi fell asleep. (No terrorists appeared.) He did it on purpose, the others accused.

Udi insisted it had been a mistake; he'd just drifted into sleep. But word in the unit was that Udi Adiv had committed a paratrooper's most unforgivable sin, turning his back on his friends.

AVITAL GEVA LIMPED into the Jericho police station. He wasn't supposed to be here; he was still on medical leave. But he couldn't keep away from the guys. He promised Ada he would be gone for a day, but he stayed a week.

The men of Company D told Avital about Udi's behavior during the ambush. "He's mocking us," one said, "I heard him snoring."

"*Sleeping* during an ambush?" said Avital, almost shouting. "Risking the lives of his friends?"

Avital pulled rank and summoned Udi to the police station. They met in the hallway.

"Look, Udi," Avital began hesitantly. "The guys say you're sabotaging things here. That you deliberately went to sleep on an ambush. What do you say?"

"I say it's not true," Udi replied.

"Look, Udi, politics is one thing, the army is another," said Avital. "Whatever your politics are, you have to keep them out of the army. Otherwise we'll tear each other apart."

Udi thought, Who is this Avital Geva? One more idiot hero—

Avital thought, What am I supposed to do with this fanatic? I swear, this guy reminds me of a Stalinist—

"I can arrange for you to stay in the brigade as a truck driver," Avital offered.

"I'm not interested in driving a truck," said Udi.

AVITAL WENT TO SEE Haggai Erlichman, commander of Company D and a member of Ein Shemer. "What are you going to do about Udi Adiv?" demanded Avital.

Haggai was hesitant. Avital understood: bad blood had existed for decades between Ein Shemer and Udi's kibbutz, Gan Shmuel. Only in the last years, with a new generation, had the enmity begun to ease. But what would happen if an Ein Shemer officer expelled a Gan Shmuel member from the paratroopers?

"There's going to be trouble in the neighborhood," warned Haggai.

"It's him or me," countered Avital.

Back home, Udi received a letter informing him that he was no longer a paratrooper.

TO THE FRINGE

THE TEL AVIV living room was crowded with long-haired young people arguing about how to hasten the imminent revolution. Arab and Jewish workers, someone said, were about to rise up together and destroy the Zionist state, along with reactionary Arab regimes. Revolution was spreading from Paris to Saigon; surely Tel Aviv wasn't far behind.

Udi Adiv listened, fascinated. With his short hair and sideburns and sandals, he was a conspicuous kibbutznik among the bohemians. The anti-Zionist group Matzpen (Compass) was the most detested political movement in the country. In all of Israel there were barely fifty Matzpen activists. The whole Tel Aviv chapter fit comfortably into this salon. Founded by dissidents from the Israel Communist Party, Matzpen was an uneasy coalition of Maoists and Trotskyites and anarchists, united only by antipathy to Zionism. Though Matzpen considered itself an Arab-Jewish movement, almost all of its members were Jews.

Udi became an activist. He spray-painted antioccupation slogans on the apartment of a right-wing editor, visited Arab Israeli villages in a vain attempt to recruit members. When he tried to sell the Matzpen newspaper on the streets of Tel Aviv, he was spat upon, the papers knocked from his hands.

Fired from jobs, sometimes shunned by their families, Matzpen members prided themselves on being a kind of esoteric elite, the Jews who knew the truth about Zionism. Yet even in their contempt, Udi and his friends proved Zionism's success. Only Zionist empowerment could have made young Jews feel safe enough, barely twenty-five years after the Holocaust, to despise Jewish power.

IN HER SILK scarf, heels, and beret, Sylvia Klingberg was incongruously elegant among the activists of Matzpen. Udi was drawn to Sylvia not only because of her dark beauty but because she was one of the most politically adept among the "Matzpen girls," as the group's young men called them. Sylvia was the only child of doting older parents. Her father was deputy director of Israel's research institute for chemical and biological warfare; Sylvia called him a war criminal.

On May Day, Udi and Sylvia joined the small Matzpen contingent tagging along on the Communist Party march through the streets of Tel Aviv. The Communists carried red flags as well as blue-and-white Israeli flags; Matzpen members carried only red flags. Party members chased them away: Matzpen's presence embarrassed even fellow Communists. Matzpen members regrouped and marched in their own mini parade, carrying signs that read "Down with Zionism." Outraged passersby surrounded them. Udi, punched and kicked, was extricated from the mob by a policeman.

EVENING IN THE Gan Shmuel dining room. Udi and a friend sat at one of the Formica tables and mocked the "bourgeois revolutionaries" of the kibbutz. Even among the hundreds of diners who filled the hall, Udi's voice resonated. "Cherkas," he said, referring to the destroyed Arab village near the kibbutz, "that's Gan Shmuel's idea of socialist fraternity!"

A kibbutznik named Gabi, who'd been wounded in the thigh in the battle for Jerusalem, limped over to Udi's table. "Why don't you learn some history before making big statements?" Gabi said. "You talk about the Palestinians, but not a word about the expulsion of Jews from Arab countries."

Udi smiled.

"You know, Udi," Gabi continued, "we don't have firing squads in the state of Israel. But the way you're heading, you're going to end up before the equivalent of a firing squad."

ANOTHER NEIGHBOR EAVESDROPPING on Udi's table was Shimon Ilan, whose brother, Uri, was the martyr of Gan Shmuel. In 1955 the nineteen-year-old Uri Ilan had been sent with his unit on a mission into Syria, to replace a battery at an IDF listening post. The group of five soldiers was captured and imprisoned in Damascus. Isolated from his friends, fearing he wouldn't keep silent under torture, Ilan tore a strip from his mattress, tied it to his cell window, and hanged himself. When his body was returned to Israel, a note was discovered in his clothes, punctured holes forming the words "I didn't betray." Uri's family and that of Udi Adiv were neighbors and close friends. Before Uri went off on his final mission, he'd come to say good-bye to Udi's parents.

Udi was nine when Uri Ilan's body was returned to the kibbutz for burial. Moshe Dayan eulogized his "determined will," poets extolled his sacrifice. Gan Shmuel became known as "the kibbutz that didn't betray." And Uri Ilan became a powerful symbol for Gan Shmuel's young people.

But not for Udi Adiv. In his parents' home, he'd heard criticism of Uri as a fantasist who committed suicide out of fear, not strength. "Moshe Dayan knows very well how to send boys to their deaths," said Udi's mother, Tova. She dismissed the paeans to Uri's courage as "patriotic schmaltz."

Listening now to Udi's mockery of Zionism in the kibbutz dining room, Uri Ilan's brother, Shimon, wondered how far Udi was ready to go. Would he confine his anti-Zionism to Matzpen protests? Or was he planning more drastic action?

Shimon contacted the Shin Bet, Israel's internal security service. Keep an eye on him, Shimon was told. And let us know what he's up to.

MR. TAMBOURINE MAN

"MEIR, WHAT ARE YOU DOING? Are you *crazy*?"

"I'm not moving dis car," Meir said in accented English, "until everybody be quiet."

Meir had been driving on the highway in his secondhand Chevy station wagon, teenagers piled on each other's laps. And then he'd simply stopped in the middle of the lane. Honking cars speeded by, drivers shouting. But Meir refused to move until his passengers quieted. "Anything, Meir, just drive!" Calmly, as though starting the car from a driveway, Meir stepped on the gas.

The teenagers of the Detroit branch of Habonim, the socialist Zionist youth movement, entertained each other with stories about their beloved and wacky Israeli emissary. Like the time he was sitting in his car in a supermarket parking lot and an untended shopping cart began rolling toward him and Meir honked at it. Or how he infuriated the parents of his teenagers by driving them to picket lines in solidarity with migrant grape pickers at local businesses owned by members of the Jewish community.

In the windowless basement that was headquarters for Detroit Habonim, with torn couches and spray-painted graffiti denouncing the war in Vietnam and supporting Israel, Meir taught his young people Zionist history and Israeli music. He spoke about Israel as the place where Jews dared take responsibility for their fate, and the kibbutz as a society where idealists dared turn the vision of equality into messy reality. Meir was so successful that parents complained to the Habonim leadership that the new emissary was enticing their children with the dream of living on a kibbutz—which was, after all, the goal of Habonim.

Tirza stayed at home with the children—there was now a baby boy as well as a girl—and watched America on television. TV had been introduced in Israel just as the Ariels were leaving for America. Having your own TV, said Tirza, felt like having a private helicopter.

America bewildered, dazzled. How was it possible, wondered Meir, to drive for days and still be in the same country? Tirza couldn't grasp why no one seemed to understand her English. "Because," said Meir, "you're speaking in German," the other language Tirza almost knew.

IT WAS THE late 1960s, and Detroit was burning and rocking. Racial riots had destroyed large parts of the city's downtown. But at Motown headquarters you could walk in off the street and listen to a recording session of Smokey Robinson and the Miracles. Just a few years earlier, the Supremes had been playing local bar mitzvahs. Meir's teenagers took him to hear the great rock bands and blues singers passing through. Meir was drawn to protest folk singers like Phil Ochs and Peter, Paul and Mary—

though Pete Seeger's sing-along earnestness, he said, reminded him of a revivalist meeting.

Most of all there was Dylan. Mr. Dylan, Meir called him with reverence.

Dylan seemed to catch every mood, break every boundary. And how he kept reinventing himself: from folk singer to rocker to country musician. It was worth struggling with English just for "Visions of Johanna."

Listening to Dylan, Meir knew he had to write songs, ballads that told a story.

Though Meir's voice was thin, Dylan's was worse, and he'd become the voice of the generation. Go ahead, Dylan seemed to urge, your vulnerability is your strength.

MAGINOT LINE AT THE SUEZ CANAL

MOISHELEH STEMPEL-PELES, Motta's deputy commander and Arik's partner in tending to the brigade's widows, was killed in a firefight with terrorists in the Jordan Valley. Just before he died, as the helicopter evacuated him, he smiled and waved to his men.

Tough, coarse, empathic, Moisheleh had taught Arik how to help the widows in practical ways. Arik maintained regular contact with the families he and Moisheleh had adopted—and those families now included Moisheleh's wife, Daliah, and her two young sons. They had planned to reach many more war widows. But without his partner, Arik felt overwhelmed by study, work, family, reserve duty. Arik thought of the long list of widows waiting to be contacted, and guilt, an alien emotion, gave him no peace.

THE RUBBER DINGHIES crossing the Kishon River near Haifa Bay swayed in the fierce wind and rain. As the boats reached the opposite shore, men in helmets and drenched green coats rushed out and established the beachhead.

The 55th Brigade was conducting a three-day exercise, simulating a crossing of the Suez Canal. If Egyptian forces invaded the Israeli-held Sinai Desert, the paratroopers would cross the canal and take the battle into Egypt. That scenario was obviously far-fetched. How would the Egyptian army, whose soldiers had fled in the Six-Day War and left behind trails of boots in the desert, manage to cross the canal, let alone create a foothold on the Israeli side? Still, Israel needed to be prepared for any eventuality, however improbable.

In the evening, Motta summoned Arik and the officers from the scouts unit that had fought on the Kidron bridge in Jerusalem. The men laid their Uzis on the ground and sat around a table in the long tent that served as dining room. Rain hit hard against the undulating roof; a single lightbulb, illumined by a generator, flickered.

We are here, Motta explained, to discuss the scouts' ill-fated mission during the battle for Jerusalem, when you missed the turnoff to the Mount of Olives and ended up, disastrously, under the Old City walls. According to the scouts' version, repeated by the books beginning to appear about the war, the tank crews had been to blame for missing the turn. And then the scouts had tried to clean up the mistake, fighting against overwhelming odds.

Arik, who had participated in the rescue of the scouts and had later investigated the incident, knew the truth. There had been no battle against overwhelming odds. And the scouts had missed the turn, just like the tank crews before them.

Motta asked the men to recount that night's events. After each had dutifully confirmed the unit's official version, Motta said, "You know and I know that what you've said isn't accurate. *Hevreh*, you made one mistake after another. I'm not blaming anyone. You fought bravely. I want you all to look me in the eye and tell me whether what I've said is true or not."

"True," said Kapusta, the unit commander, a squat man with a thick mustache whose body carried four battle wounds.

Motta asked each man in turn: "True?" "True," each confirmed.

"Arik, give me the protocols," said Motta.

Arik handed over the notes he'd been taking. Motta put the papers in his pocket.

"I have no interest in destroying your myth," he said. "What was discussed here stays here. But we needed to establish the truth for ourselves."

THE 55TH BRIGADE was called up for reserve duty along the Suez Canal. It was June 1969, and a war of attrition had been going on along the canal for nearly a year. Hundreds of Israelis and Egyptians had been killed or wounded. Combatants burrowed in bunkers beneath sand embankments along the roughly two-hundred-meters-wide waterway. With the onset of summer, temperatures during the day went over a hundred degrees. Sandstorms choked the bunkers, but stepping outside meant risking sniper attack. Tanks and artillery exchanged fire, while commandos crossed and attacked each other's fortifications.

The IDF divided the canal into two sectors. Motta's deputy, who was to command the reservists in the southern sector, was abroad, so Motta asked Arik to take his place. "You're volunteering, right?" said Motta. "Right," said Arik.

An officer took Arik on a tour of the front. The bunkers reminded him of the Maginot Line, the French defense that had collapsed with the Nazi invasion. Where was the daring, the ingenuity of the IDF?

They came to an outpost known as the Pier. Wearing aviator sunglasses, hands on hips and legs spread on the sand, Arik surveyed the area and frowned. A five-meter-high sand embankment faced the canal; a trench surrounded the entrance to the underground bunker. Several hundred meters away, within easy reach of the enemy, three Israeli tanks were parked. Sitting ducks, thought Arik.

"Why are the tanks so close to enemy positions?" he asked.

"They see our tanks and they're scared away."

"So keep the tanks there during the day. But bring them back at night. And place paratroopers at the entrance to the outpost in case Egyptian commandos cross."

"They won't dare approach," the officer said.

One night Arik was patrolling on a half-track. He heard shots coming from the direction of the Pier. By the time he got there, the Egyptians were gone. They'd left behind three dead Israelis and a burning tank.

RIDING A JEEP through artillery bombardments, Arik spent his days among the outposts. Nights, he led his men in shooting at Egyptian positions across the water. "Why should they sleep well when we don't?" he said.

The enemy positions were so close that the paratroopers could fire within range without crossing the canal. Arik would target an Egyptian bunker, move his men to the edge of the water, and direct machine gun and mortar fire against the position. Arik calculated that it took the Egyptians inside the bunkers five minutes to emerge and return fire; in that time, his soldiers could easily sprint to another position, out of enemy range.

One night, as Arik's men opened fire, Egyptian soldiers immediately shot back. The Israelis were pinned down on the sand without cover. A soldier lying beside Arik raised his head and fell backward, a bullet in his forehead. "Run!" Arik shouted. He lifted the body onto a stretcher and ran with it, boots struggling against the sand.

Another night Arik received an intelligence report that Egyptian commandos would be crossing at the point where the canal meets the Great Bitter Lake. Around 9:00 p.m., Arik and a half dozen men entered the marshes along the bank, hiding in the papyrus reeds. The paratroopers took turns napping, four men alert, three asleep. Arik didn't sleep. Despite a cool wind, his shirt was damp with sweat.

A full moon rose. Voices from an Egyptian position just across merged with the slowly moving water.

No commandos appeared. Preparing to decamp as the first light broke, Arik looked up at the sky and suddenly remembered: *Apollo 11* was approaching the moon. In the coming hours, a human being would take his first steps on its surface. The whole world was watching the future on television, and here he was, lying in the mud of the Middle East.

FORTY-FIVE DAYS AFTER arriving at the canal, Arik returned to Tel Aviv. He had refused to take leave. The fighting along the canal—a war without a name—had penetrated his being: he had arrived at the canal overweight, and left ten kilos lighter. He was edgier than he'd ever felt. How could the army that astonished the world only two years earlier be acting so stupidly now?

Arik went to see Motta. "The bunkers are a rat trap," he said. "We're thinking tactically, not strategically." Motta promised to raise the issue, but he was about to assume command of the northern front, and Arik sensed that his mind was elsewhere.

From the time when he'd served as runner in the trenches of Givat Brenner during the War of Independence, Arik had taken for granted the entwinement of the battlefront and the home front. But the victory of the

Six-Day War had separated the two. Now, walking the oblivious streets of Tel Aviv, watching the young men with sideburns and flowered shirts and the young women in miniskirts laughing in cafés, he felt estranged. *How can they be sitting here like this while we're going through hell?*

REJOICING IN THE HILLS OF JUDEA

HANAN PORAT FELT a mystical relationship with Mother Rachel, whom the prophet Jeremiah had imagined weeping for the exiles of Israel. In leading the return to Kfar Etzion, he felt that he had comforted Mother Rachel.

And so when Hanan announced his forthcoming marriage to Rachel Hovav, one of the young women of Kfar Etzion, his friends jokingly told each other, Of course he would marry a woman named Rachel.

Two weeks after the children had first returned to Kfar Etzion in 1967, Rachel showed up alone and declared her intention to remain. Rachel's parents had been members of one of the fallen kibbutzim in the Etzion Bloc; her father had been a prisoner of war in Jordan during the 1948 war. And so even though she hadn't been one of the children of Kfar Etzion, she felt she belonged among them. The commune decided that she was suited to run the office, and though she found the work stifling, she agreed without complaint.

Hanan spoke of "ascents and descents" in the redemption process, and that is how Rachel described their courtship. Sometimes they did late-night guard duty together, and Hanan would recite poems written by the poet of the pioneers, the young woman known simply as Rachel. But those were rare and precious moments of being alone together; mostly they found themselves absorbed by the commune. And then Hanan would disappear for days at a time, traveling the country on some important mission. Worse, Hanan was wavering in his commitment to her. Many young women were in love with Hanan, the prince of religious Zionism; was Rachel really the one?

Despairing, Rachel considered leaving the kibbutz. Finally he asked her, matter-of-factly, to marry him. Hanan was a romantic, but also shy; his romance was most easily expressed about the land of Israel.

They married two days after Yom Kippur 1969. Hundreds of celebrants came from all over the country. The modest wedding was held outdoors. Under the canopy one of the rabbis summoned to bless the couple lamented that Hanan himself could have been a great rabbi—implying that he was wasting his time as a mere activist.

The newlyweds spent the coming days visiting relatives and touring in Jerusalem. And then Hanan returned to work. He didn't have time for a proper honeymoon.

KFAR ETZION'S YESHIVA for soldiers had outgrown its quarters and needed a new home. From an enrollment of some thirty students, the yeshiva was now attracting hundreds. The plan called for building a study hall and dormitory on a hill not far from Kfar Etzion. And around the yeshiva would form a new settlement, attracting those not interested in life on the kibbutz—like Yoel Bin-Nun, who intended to move in as soon as the first houses were ready.

Through the spring of 1970, tractors cleared land for the yeshiva. Prefabs were erected, along with a row of small one-family houses intended for the yeshiva staff and married students. Yoel was hoping the yeshiva would move to its new quarters before the holiday of Shavuot, Pentecost, which celebrates the giving of the Torah to Israel. What more appropriate way to dedicate a place of Torah study than on Shavuot?

But the work was going far too slowly. Impatient, Yoel organized a group of students and friends to complete the infrastructure, installing electricity and plumbing.

They completed the work just after Shavuot. On their first night on the hill, they nailed a mezuzah to the study hall. Then Yoel organized the students into shifts for night patrol. There were rumors of terrorists in the area, and Yoel feared an attack.

The students moved into the dormitory, and Yoel and Esther became the first couple to move into one of the houses, in effect the community's first permanent residents. There were no paved roads yet, but the settlement had a name: Alon Shvut—return to the oak tree, the lone oak that had been the marker of longing for the children of Kfar Etzion during their years of exile. To be a founding father of a new community in the land of Israel: What more could Yoel Bin-Nun have hoped for?

Toward the end of the week the IDF appeared, and distributed Uzis and bullet clips to the students.

THE KIBBUTZ BECKONS

ARIK COMPLETED HIS degree in economics. Yehudit was working as a psychologist. The decision to take up permanent residency in the city could no longer be deferred.

Arik assured Yehudit that her father would accept her decision to quit the kibbutz and remain with her husband. Yaakov Hazan was the beloved leader of Hashomer Hatzair—the *admor*, or Hasidic master, they called him only half jokingly, as much a spiritual as a political authority. Comrades consulted him about their personal problems; thousands of kibbutzniks, like Avital Geva's parents, considered him a friend. He never let himself forget, he said, that he represented the men and women who rose every morning before sunrise to work in the fields and the communal kitchens. While he criticized his rivals in the fiercest ideological terms, accusing them of distorting and subverting and destroying, he never gossiped about them. He was kind, passionate, self-righteous. Once, after an argument with Yehudit, he told her, "I was thinking all night about what you said, and I came to the conclusion that I was right."

Hazan's great love was his kibbutz, Mishmar Ha'Emek, "Guardian of the Valley." Photographs of the kibbutz from its early years in the 1920s showed a row of tents in a valley surrounded by bare hills; from one of those tents young Hazan had run the world movement of Hashomer Hatzair. During the War of Independence Mishmar Ha'Emek had withstood siege and blocked Arab forces advancing toward Haifa. Now it was one of the most prosperous kibbutzim.

Though he spent weekdays in Tel Aviv, where the movement's headquarters was based, Hazan insisted on returning every weekend to Mishmar Ha'Emek. Yehudit's two sisters had left Mishmar Ha'Emek and settled on their husbands' kibbutzim. That left Yehudit to maintain the family connection to the kibbutz. Every Friday she would prepare her parents' little apartment for their arrival. Before setting out to study in Tel Aviv, she had assured her father she would return when her studies ended.

"If I don't go back," she told Arik now, "it will destroy him."

"I'll take care of everything," Arik said.

ARIK WENT TO SEE Hazan in his Tel Aviv apartment and was struck once again by the modest lifestyle of one of Israel's most powerful men: two rooms, bed, couch, bookcase, a kibbutz apartment in the city. The only indulgence was a profusion of works by kibbutz artists, including a bust of Hazan as a young man.

There was respect—love—between Hazan and Arik. Hazan was proud of his son-in-law and shared with him the government's security deliberations. And though Arik insisted he didn't care about proximity to power, he enjoyed his proximity to Hazan.

Impatient with small talk, Arik got to the point. "Yehudit and I are staying in Tel Aviv," he said.

For the first time Arik heard contempt in Hazan's voice. "A person with your background, your values—*you* betrayed the kibbutz. But we won't allow Yehudit to betray it too."

Returning home, Arik said to Yehudit, "If you leave now, he won't survive it."

Arik would have to gradually wean Hazan's daughter away. He offered a compromise: Yehudit would move back to Mishmar Ha'Emek, while Arik continued living and working in Tel Aviv but spent weekends on the kibbutz. Not as a member, he emphasized. And sometime within the next few years, he added, this arrangement would end, and they would build their home in Tel Aviv.

THE SIX-DAY WAR incited dreams. Yoel Bin-Nun and Hanan Porat envisioned an expanded Israel with Jewish towns and villages in the hills of Judea and Samaria. And for Arik Achmon, the vision was a prosperous and efficient Israel centered on Tel Aviv. Not that Arik was drawn to the city. In his preference for simple food, in his routine of rising with the first light of day, in his ethic of service, he remained a kibbutznik.

Arik was proud of the kibbutz movement for setting the borders of Israel and creating a class of selfless servers. But his economic studies had confirmed what he knew from experience: that a centralized economy stifles initiative and rewards laziness. It was absurd. In the Middle East's military superpower there was a two-year waiting list for a telephone—unless, of course, you had the right connections.

Why was Israel so efficient during war and so incompetent in peacetime? A modern nation was waiting to be born here, freed of the outmoded fantasy of an agrarian collectivist utopia. Yes, Arik readily agreed, the old ideology had been necessary to create a state from nothing. But now utopian nostalgia was preventing Israel from becoming the great nation Arik believed it could be.

CHIMAVIR WAS A small aviation company of light planes that specialized in crop dusting. Owned by the same kibbutz federation to which Arik's former kibbutz, Netzer Sereni, belonged, ChimAvir intended to create a division of Piper Cubs for domestic travel. The director-general happened to be a friend of Arik's from Netzer, and he offered Arik a job. "Come help run the company," he said. "We'll create a revolution in domestic aviation."

Israel's new expansive borders offered opportunities. ChimAvir could thrive just by transporting soldiers back and forth to the Suez Canal. Still, Arik hesitated: What did he know about airplanes besides jumping out of them? But when he visited the company's hangar, inhaled the gasoline fumes, and watched the planes taking off, he said yes.

Arik wanted to adapt the management principles he'd learned at university to ChimAvir. But he quickly discovered that the company was run like a kibbutz. Initiative wasn't rewarded, and incompetence wasn't penalized. It was almost impossible to fire anyone. No longer a kibbutznik, Arik would never be appointed CEO, no matter how good he was.

He had thought he'd escaped the kibbutz, but here he was, being pulled back in. Weekdays he worked with the kibbutzniks of ChimAvir, weekends he spent with Yehudit on Mishmar Ha'Emek. He even agreed to occasionally work in its cowshed, in exchange for room and board. It was familiar, comforting, and smothering.

Arik tried to convince Hazan that the kibbutz needed to grow. Like the children's house: maybe it made sense to raise children collectively during a period of austerity. But why raise children away from their parents now?

"Did you or Yehudit suffer in the children's house?" demanded Hazan.

"No," Arik conceded, "but those were different times."

Hazan laughed dismissively. "There is no kibbutz without the children's house," he said. And there could be no Israel, of course, without the kibbutz.

THE HEAD OF ChimAvir was replaced, and the new director-general wasn't interested in domestic travel. "Our purpose is to provide service to farmers," he said.

"So keep doing that," Arik said, and quit.

Though he didn't know it then, a far better job was waiting. A group of entrepreneurs was forming a private domestic airline, and Arik was offered the position of CEO, along with 7 percent of the company's stock. "We'll take on the government and open Israel's skies," an investor said. For Arik, it was like receiving a battle order.

The company, Kanaf, had four light planes; its leading competitor had seven. Kanaf was headquartered in a Tel Aviv apartment. Every available space, including the porch, was turned into an office. Files were stored in the bathroom. No one wore ties, and everyone called each other by their first names and felt free to criticize Arik's decisions. Arik's salary was scarcely higher than those of the company's technicians.

Arik planned to set up a line between Tel Aviv and the Suez Canal, create a flight school, and teach skydiving. But every initiative required government approval. When Arik wanted to buy a plane, he needed the finance ministry's permission first to buy foreign currency. And to get that permission he had to explain to a skeptical bureaucrat how another plane for Kanaf would benefit the state of Israel.

Arik let slip to a ministry official that one of his partners happened to be the finance minister's son-in-law. (He'd been given 5 percent ownership of the company for precisely that connection.) Arik got permission to purchase dollars.

But even Kanaf's connections weren't enough when it came up against its competitor, Ya'af, one of whose owners was a close friend of transportation minister Shimon Peres. Arik was bidding against Ya'af for a franchise to test navigational aids for flight paths. Though Kanaf offered a more attractive bid, Ya'af won.

Arik appealed to the Supreme Court. Arik's partners were astonished. No one could recall a private company challenging the government's decision on a bid. Arik's lawyer phoned Peres and said, You're going to lose.

Peres, more perplexed than indignant, responded, But it's a government decision!

The hearing was scheduled for just after Passover.

On Passover Eve, Arik put on a white shirt and khakis and attended the seder in the dining room of Mishmar Ha'Emek. There weren't enough chairs to go around for the hundreds of participants, so Arik and Yehudit, along with the other young people, sat on benches on one side of the long table while Yehudit's parents and the other veterans sat on chairs across from them. As the kibbutzniks sang songs about the season's final rain and the coming harvest, Arik's mind was on the impending court case, his challenge to socialist Israel.

Kanaf won. Buoyed, Arik decided to launch a skydiving school. But he needed the approval of the IDF. The army replied: The only parachuting in the skies of Israel will be under our supervision.

This wasn't working. Kanaf could, at great cost, win isolated battles, but government control would continue to thwart initiative. There had to be a better approach, some way to manipulate the system against itself.

CHAPTER 12

THE INVENTION OF YISRAEL HAREL

ARIK ACHMON MEETS AN ADMIRER

SEVERAL HUNDRED OFFICERS from the 55th Brigade were gathered in a Tel Aviv movie theater for a day of briefings about "the situation," as Israelis called their permanent security crisis.

Though only a sergeant, Yisrael Harel, a newspaper editor in civilian life, sat among the officers. As the brigade's "culture officer," in charge of educational activities, he was invited to officers' meetings, but didn't quite belong among them. With his knitted *kippah*, Yisrael felt all the more an outsider. Religious Zionists were now thoroughly integrated into the brigade, but the officers' corps remained overwhelmingly secular, still heavily kibbutznik. Yisrael wished he could represent the religious Zionist community as an equal among the fighters and heroes of the 55th.

All his life Yisrael Harel had wanted to be part of the elite of sacrifice. He regarded himself and the Jewish state as extensions of each other; he even carried its name, "Yisrael," Israel.

Now Yisrael had a plan that could increase his scope of service among the paratroopers.

As culture officer charged with promoting the brigade's values, Yisrael knew of the work that Arik and Moisheleh Stempel-Peles had begun with the widows. That work, he believed, needed to be revived in an organized framework. And the man who would help Yisrael do that, he concluded, was Arik. Yisrael, diligent journalist, had researched Arik's past, learned that he had once been considered a promising young leader in the kibbutz movement, had raised the Israeli flag over the Dome of the Rock, was one of the brigade's most respected officers—everything Yisrael Harel, a noncombat soldier, had wished he could be.

When the briefings ended, Yisrael approached Arik, accompanied by the brigade's chief physician, Jackie King.

"Do you have a moment?" asked Yisrael.

Arik looked without curiosity at the young man in the *kippah* and the thick-framed glasses. The *tarbutnik*, the culture guy. *Not one of us—*

Jackie, though, was one of them. The religious doctor had performed heroically under fire in Jerusalem. And Jackie had done for medicine what Arik was trying to do for aviation: defying the socialist establishment, he had opened one of the country's first private clinics.

The three men took seats in the back of the emptying theater. Yisrael explained that he and Jackie had been visiting widows from the brigade, just as Arik and Moisheleh had done. But many families weren't being helped.

"We understand spirit," Yisrael said, "and you understand organization. Why not join forces?"

Yisrael was offering Arik the chance to renew his commitment to their fallen friends, to Moisheleh.

"I'm with you," Arik said.

REFUGEE BOY, NATIVE SON

YISRAEL HAREL WAS born Yisrael Hasenfratz, in the worst place and time for a Jew: Central Europe, fall 1939. Two years later, the Hasenfratzes, together with tens of thousands of other Romanian Jews, were deported by the fascist Iron Guard to an area of the Ukraine called Transnistria, beyond the Dniester River. Lacking the Final Solution's thoroughness, the Romanians placed some Jews in camps, shot others, and allowed still others to die of hunger and cold. Yisrael's father, a lumber merchant, was dispatched to a forced labor brigade; Yisrael's mother bribed a Ukrainian peasant family and found shelter for herself and her two small sons. Yisrael's younger brother died of hunger, but Yisrael and his parents survived.

After the war, they boarded a refugee ship running the British blockade of the land of Israel. Seven-year-old Yisrael would leave the hold, with its iron bunks from floor to ceiling laid so close together that survivors said it reminded them of the camps, and wander up to the deck, just to watch the kibbutznik sailors and listen to their songs.

Then two British speedboats appeared. Loudspeakers demanded the surrender of the crew. In the brief battle, refugees threw iron bars at the British soldiers boarding the ship. When the British took control of the ship, Yisrael stood with the grown-ups and sang "Hatikvah," the Zionist anthem of hope.

The Hasenfratzes were sent to a detention camp on Cyprus for illegal immigrants, and eventually landed in Haifa, where they remained, collapsing into the first embrace of home.

Growing up in Haifa in the early 1950s, in a two-room apartment that his family shared with another family of survivors, Yisrael dreamed of becoming a kibbutznik—the ultimate Israeli. As an Orthodox boy and a member of the Bnei Akiva youth movement, he would join one of the handful of religious kibbutzim. Yisrael would be like the plowman in the photograph hanging in the Bnei Akiva clubhouse: shirtless and in khaki shorts but wearing a cap, honoring Jewish tradition.

Until then, Yisrael did all he could to uproot the traces of exile from his being. When his parents spoke to him in Yiddish or German, he answered in Hebrew. His father, Yaakov, a gentle man who walked about singing cantorial snippets, was nearly deaf, the result of a beating in Transnistria; and deafness wasn't just a physical but a cultural condition. Every morning, Yaakov, who worked as a lumber inspector, set off for his office on the Haifa docks in jacket and tie—in a country where even the prime minister wore an open-necked shirt. Yisrael wore khaki shorts and sandals until the winter rains.

For all his efforts, sabra children still regarded him as not quite one of them. They delighted in devising new ways to mispronounce the name Hasenfratz. Yisrael persisted in the reinvention of himself, partly stoic, partly obtuse. Each time he was invited to a sabra classmate's home—one family in an apartment!—he marked another small victory of homecoming.

Yisrael was not only a refugee among sabras but a religious boy in "Red Haifa." Sometimes the kids from the secular youth movement affiliated with the ruling social democratic party, Mapai, and whose headquarters was located on the hill above the Bnei Akiva clubhouse—how symbolic, thought Yisrael—threw rocks at the religious kids below.

Yisrael detested Mapai. Entrenched in bureaucratic power, arrogant with entitlement, Mapai was particularly corrupt in Haifa, whose mayor even maintained his own private militia. When demonstrators to the right or left of Mapai took to the streets, members of Plugot Hapoel—longshoremen and sportsmen affiliated with the Histadrut union's soccer and boxing clubs—violently dispersed them.

IN HIGH SCHOOL Yisrael became a counselor in Bnei Akiva, assigned a group of children to mold into future kibbutzniks.

Every Shabbat afternoon, he walked hundreds of steps up to the Bnei Akiva branch in the Carmel, the middle-class neighborhood at the top of the mountain. Few Orthodox Jews lived there, and its tiny Bnei Akiva branch was confined to a room in a synagogue. Yisrael led a group of ten-year-olds, teaching them songs and playing games that served his real purpose: imbuing them with a love for kibbutz.

One especially mischievous member of Yisrael's group was the young Yoel Bin-Nun. Yoel had little patience for organized singing and dancing, and hovered outside the circle. He seemed to disdain as mere child's play the games that Yisrael organized, like Find the Flag, and refused to commit himself to regular attendance.

Still, Yisrael sensed that this clever boy, articulate beyond his years, could with proper guidance become a true Bnei Akivanik. It was hard work transforming a Yoel Bin-Nun from individualist into productive member of the *shevet*—the tribe, as a Bnei Akiva age group was called. But no one was better suited to meet that challenge than Yisrael, who submerged his own personality into the collective.

MEANWHILE SCHOOL WAS becoming a distraction from Yisrael's real life. There were hikes and campfires to plan, new children to recruit. Yisrael and his friends debated the merits of starting their own kibbutz or joining an already existing one. They had no intention of completing their matriculation exams; of what use was a high school diploma for a pioneer? One of Yisrael's friends broke up with his girlfriend because she refused to commit to life on kibbutz.

In his junior year, Yisrael dropped out of high school and apprenticed himself to a metalworker.

His school guidance counselor cautioned: "You're a smart boy, don't throw your life away."

"But who will build the land?" said Yisrael.

ON A SHABBAT morning in spring 1956, thousands of religious Jews began leaving their synagogues in the middle of prayers and walked together through the streets of Haifa. Many men still wore their black-striped prayer shawls. Yisrael and other members of Bnei Akiva were up front, singing songs extolling the day of rest.

They were protesting the municipality's decision to open an industrial trade exhibit on Shabbat. Though they carried no protest signs—this was, after all, Shabbat—there was anger and determination in the crowd. Even for Haifa, felt Yisrael and his friends, this public violation of Shabbat went too far.

Secular youth shouted taunts at the demonstrators. Some threw stones. From an apartment above, someone poured out a bucket of water.

The marchers turned a corner. Straight into an ambush.

Men with clubs rushed the crowd. They wore dark blue work shirts and khaki shorts. The mayor's militia.

Yisrael fell, bleeding from his head.

When the police finally intervened, it was to disperse the demonstrators. Yisrael was dragged into a police car. He was taken to be stitched—not to a hospital, where doctors would have filed a report, but to a first aid station affiliated with Mapai's labor union, whose doctors could be trusted to cooperate.

Afterward Yisrael was shoved back into the car and, despite his objections to violating the Sabbath, driven to a police station and charged with disorderly conduct. When Shabbat ended, an Orthodox politician intervened and Yisrael was released, charges dropped.

The wound that lingered was betrayal. To be beaten on Shabbat by Jewish thugs protected by Jewish police in a sovereign Jewish state—this was a violation of the most basic requirements of peoplehood. Some of Yisrael's friends were taking off their *kippot*, and Yisrael too had considered that possibility. But not now. He had seen the true face of secular enlightened Israel. He would remain loyal to his tribe.

LEADER, OUTCAST

IN NOVEMBER 1956, just after the war in Sinai ended, Yisrael was drafted. He and his friends from Bnei Akiva went to Nahal, the unit combining military training with agricultural work. They formed a *garin*, a pioneering group bound for kibbutz—eighty members strong, including women, drawn from Bnei Akiva branches around the country.

Following basic training, the group was dispatched to a religious kibbutz called Sde Eliyahu (Field of Elijah), in the Jordan Valley. In summer the Jordan Valley was virtually uninhabitable; even in the scant shade, temperatures were routinely 110 degrees. Just beyond the kibbutz's wheat fields and date palm groves rose the hills of Jordan and Syria.

Bnei Akiva had other plans for Yisrael. The army permitted each *garin* to exempt several of its most promising members from agricultural work and appoint them to the position of *kommunar*, a leader of one of the movement's branches, instilling pioneering values among urban youth. Yisrael was chosen. That meant missing those crucial formative months when the *garin* would be transformed into a collective. But like the young Arik Achmon, Yisrael wouldn't have imagined defying his movement's decision. He was appointed *kommunar* in Haifa, back where he began.

Yisrael worked eighteen-hour days, sleeping on the floor of the Bnei Akiva clubhouse. On Shabbat afternoons, he stood like a drill sergeant, surveying the lines of young scouts in their white shirts and blue scarves. Yisrael loved his community, its idealism and social solidarity and charitable instincts. But he was frustrated by its limitations. So long as religious Zionists continued to produce more lawyers and accountants than pioneers and commandos, they would remain an appendage to the Zionist saga.

There was something hard in Yisrael that both commanded respect and repelled. He could be hectoring, even abusive, responding to flagging ideological fervor as though to a personal affront: You don't deserve to call yourself a member of Bnei Akiva, you aren't worthy to be one of us. When he was merely Yisrael Hasenfratz, he'd felt diminished by irritations, unworthy ambitions. But as Yisrael the *kommunar* he was Israel itself.

ON KIBBUTZ SDE ELIYAHU, the *garin* was fraying.

Sde Eliyahu was founded in the 1930s by refugees from Germany, barely out of their teens. *Yekkes*: diligent, thrifty, stiff. The *garin* members, who had come expecting a familial embrace, were treated as outsiders. While other kibbutzim routinely sent visitors and food packages to their Nahal groups when they left for military exercises, the secretariat of Sde Eliyahu had to be embarrassed into those gestures. In other kibbutzim, Nahal soldiers were allowed to drive tractors, the most fun job on kibbutz; but Sde Eliyahu didn't trust the *garin* members behind the wheel.

Whenever he could take a break from his duties in Haifa, Yisrael hitched to Sde Eliyahu. He was appalled to discover that some of his friends wanted to dismantle the *garin* when their military service ended.

What about our ideology? Yisrael demanded. What about settling the land?

Forget those big words, friends advised. It's every man for himself.

Yisrael keenly felt his distance from the group. In an article for the page in Sde Eliyahu's mimeographed newsletter devoted to the *garin*, he sulked about its failure to maintain contact with its members outside the kibbutz. His aggrieved and sarcastic tone grated on his friends. "You think you're such a big shot," one said to him in the presence of other *garin* members, "but you're just a refugee from Halisa," the poor neighborhood near the Haifa docks where Yisrael grew up. "You were never one of us."

No one defended him.

YISRAEL HASENFRATZ CHANGED his name to Yisrael Harel.

He chose the name Harel after the legendary Harel Brigade, the Palmach commando force commanded by Yitzhak Rabin during the 1948 war. Yisrael Harel: curt, to the point. A name with which to make one's mark.

THE *GARIN*'S MEMBERS voted to disband. The childhood dreams, the teenage plans, the endless hours of argument and song—how had they abandoned it all so effortlessly?

Many of the *garin*'s members were now studying for the matriculation exams they had once dismissed, planning to attend university. Yisrael's parents were pressuring him to do the same.

In summer 1959 Yisrael moved to Sde Eliyahu for the last phase of the *garin*'s kibbutz service. By then, most *garin* members were already gone. Yisrael left just before the High Holidays. He walked out the gate and stood on the side of the road. Behind him the mountains of Jordan and Syria faded into mist. He extended his hand and pointed to the ground, to summon a ride from a passing car, and realized he was crying.

HUNT FOR THE HIDDEN PRINCESS

WITH THE END of his dream of life on kibbutz, Yisrael Harel was studying political science at Bar-Ilan University. It was at the wedding of a fellow student, Yosifa, in early winter 1962, that he met Sarah Weisfish.

Yisrael noticed Sarah, who was Yosifa's cousin, sitting at a table with her ultra-Orthodox family. Skirt to ankles, sleeves to wrist. The message: Keep away.

Yisrael was intrigued. Sarah's modesty only seemed to deepen her beauty—long, dark hair, alert dark eyes. Yisrael did what he had never done before: he walked over to a strange young woman and introduced himself. "My name is Yisrael," he began. "I'm a friend of Yosifa's."

"That's fine," said Sarah, and turned away.

Yisrael ignored the rebuke and the stares around the table and continued making small talk. Sarah looked straight ahead.

During a break in the dancing, Yisrael told Yosifa about his encounter with Sarah. "You don't know what you're dealing with," Yosifa said. "She comes from the heart of that world. Eleven generations in Jerusalem."

"Tell her I want to escort her to the bus stop after the wedding," Yisrael persisted.

"In her world there are no escorts," Yosifa replied.

Yisrael couldn't stop thinking of Sarah Weisfish. Yosifa tried to discourage him. Invite her to your home, Yisrael insisted; I'll just happen to be there.

If Sarah was surprised to see Yisrael, she didn't let on. He did his best to impress her with his propriety. Though he usually wore khaki shorts, he appeared in long pants. "He dressed up for you," Yosifa said dryly to Sarah.

Surprisingly, Sarah agreed to walk with him. She listened without comment to his monologue about Bnei Akiva and army and kibbutz. Then she said, "There's no chance. When I marry, it will be to a Torah scholar."

He waited outside her parents' home in one of Jerusalem's venerable ultra-Orthodox neighborhoods, long stone buildings built around courtyards with wells. When she emerged, he escorted her through the narrow alleys. "It's not appropriate," she said to him, but she didn't walk away.

Finally, Sarah's father hid her in a relative's home. Yisrael organized friends on a stakeout, following family members until the trail led to Sarah.

Address in hand, Yisrael set out for Jerusalem. It was snowing. Yisrael waited outside the house until Sarah appeared. They walked through the deepening snow, in secular neighborhoods where her father and brothers wouldn't likely search.

At last Sarah began speaking about herself. She told of growing up in a family so poor that ten people shared one and a half rooms; when her brothers returned home from yeshiva boarding school, Sarah and her sisters would move into her grandmother's cellar. Yet the Weisfishes, devoted to Torah study, considered themselves a kind of royalty. Remarkably, her father had also allowed her to cautiously explore the world beyond her ultra-Orthodox neighborhood. She had joined a library as a teenager, and the librarians, eager to open her mind, had plied her with novels. She was now studying biology in a junior college.

Yisrael asked if she could envision them together. She hesitated, and then repeated what she had told him before: I must marry a Torah scholar. But in Sarah's hesitation, Yisrael sensed the beginning of a yes.

The next time they went for an illicit walk, Sarah's father followed. When he caught up with them, he offered Yisrael a choice: marry Sarah or never see her again. "I want to marry her," said Yisrael.

Even Sarah's father had to concede that she had fallen in love. In his months of unrequited monologues, Yisrael had managed to convey his love for Israel and the Jewish people. Though he would never be a Torah scholar, Sarah respected his idealism.

They married that summer. Her family danced, more from obligation than joy. His friends raised bride and groom on chairs high over spinning circles. Yisrael rejoiced in his impossible victory. With enough chutzpah and determination, any border could be crossed.

THE HARELS LIVED in a small apartment in Petach Tikva, one of the indistinct towns around Tel Aviv. Yisrael had opened a small business importing electronic goods.

He still hoped to make his mark on Israel. He joined the young rebels of the National Religious Party (NRP), the political wing of religious Zionism. The NRP was run by an older generation of European-born Jews who accepted the party's role of junior partner to Mapai and who dealt mostly with religious issues, like Sabbath observance in the public space. Why, demanded the young rebels, don't we formulate our own policies on issues of national importance like defense? The partnership between the NRP and Mapai, said Yisrael bitterly, was like the relationship between a horse and its rider.

But Yisrael's path into politics was blocked by his fellow NRP rebels, who regarded him as an opportunist, and he reciprocated their contempt.

MAY 1967. WHEN Yisrael got his call-up notice to join the 55th Brigade in the orchards, his first concern was leaving Sarah. She was in her eighth month with their second child. Her due date was June 5. Sarah's parents suggested she move into their house in Jerusalem. Yisrael thought that made sense: If war breaks out, he reassured Sarah, it will be fought in Sinai and perhaps on the Syrian front, but certainly not in the capital. Jordan's King Hussein would be crazy to start a war in Jerusalem, with all its holy places.

And so they agreed Sarah would seek safety in her parents' home, near the border that divided Israeli from Jordanian Jerusalem.

THE NIGHT OF JUNE 6. Yisrael's shirt was stained with the blood of the wounded he'd helped evacuate from the medics' station. Where was Sarah now? The hospitals were filling up with wounded; would there even be a bed for her?

Yisrael entered a jeep taking a wounded man to the Bikur Cholim hospital. Yisrael explained his situation to the driver, who after the hospital stop-off took him to the Weisfishes' home. Perhaps two dozen family members were crammed into the small apartment. "He's alive!" someone shouted. Sarah was there; she hadn't yet given birth. "We heard rumors that all the paratroopers had been killed," she said calmly.

Yisrael glanced around the room. Among the children and old people were young, healthy men his age. Almost every kind of Jew was represented among the paratroopers—except the ultra-Orthodox. And here they were, preparing lamentations for the next holocaust.

Yisrael offered some words of encouragement to Sarah and fled.

THE ELITE SUMMONS YISRAEL HAREL

YISRAEL HAD MUCH to be grateful for in the summer of 1967. Sarah had given birth to a daughter. And he was writing—essays for religious Zionist publications warning against squandering the opportunities that the war had opened for Israel. Yisrael despised the national euphoria, the notion that Israel had just fought its last war. Precisely when the Jews lowered their guard was the time of greatest danger.

Yisrael wrote an essay about the need to encourage American Jews to immigrate to Israel. He noted that Arab intransigence might compel Israel to retain the new territories. And that, he conceded, would confront Israel with a severe demographic challenge. Massive American immigration, though, could save the Jewish state.

Yisrael mailed the article to *Ha'aretz*, the country's preeminent newspaper. For several weeks he heard nothing. Then, one Friday morning, he opened the paper and saw an essay with the headline, "The Defeat in the War for the Jews." And just below it, his byline.

No one from the newspaper had bothered to contact him, but what did it matter? The article took up nearly an entire precious *Ha'aretz* page. At that very moment, Yisrael Harel was being read by the nation's leaders!

A letter arrived from Eliezer Livneh, one of the Labor movement's preeminent intellectuals. He had read Yisrael's article with interest, Livneh wrote, and would like to meet, to discuss a matter of national importance.

Livneh informed Yisrael that a new organization was being founded to pressure the government into settling Judea and Samaria, the liberated territories. The group included Israel's two greatest living poets, Natan Alterman and Uri Zvi Greenberg, its leading novelists, Shai Agnon and Haim Hazaz and Moshe Shamir, and leading figures from the kibbutz movement. We would like you to join us, said Livneh.

Yisrael had read those writers since he was a boy, knew whole parts of their work from memory. And now the elite of the Hebrew renaissance was opening up to Yisrael Harel. It was his own Six Days miracle.

Livneh spoke of settling the land in terms of history and security and pioneering, the secular Zionist language Yisrael understood. Mercaz's messianism was alien to him; Yisrael's survivor instincts mistrusted utopian dreams.

Of course Yisrael would join. To go back to the old vulnerable borders was madness. And what nation would turn its back on its ancestral heartland, won in a defensive war against attempted genocide?

AS FANS STRUGGLED against the Tel Aviv humidity, the greats of Hebrew letters took seats around tables joined together in the café of the Writers' House. They were left-wing Zionists and right-wing Zionists, nurturing old grievances that bored a new generation of Israelis. Until the Six-Day War it would have been difficult to bring these writers and activists together in the same room. Yet as men of history, they understood the moment. Poet Uri Zvi Greenberg had even told a reporter who spotted him at the Western Wall that he had stopped writing: No poetry, he said, could be as compelling as the vision of Jewish paratroopers on the Temple Mount.

Presiding over this luminous gathering was Natan Alterman, the nation's most beloved poet. The great Israeli romantic, bard of the Jewish homecoming: "A man, a lover retrieved from the dust / Approaches a stall or two in the market / Buys amber earrings / For his wife retrieved from water." Alterman wrote his weekly newspaper columns in rhyme, as if only poetry were adequate to the Israeli story. His love for the land of Israel was inseparable from his famous love for women: "There are those more beautiful than her / but none as beautiful in the way she is."

Alterman looked around the table at the men who had answered his call to action. The Movement for the Complete Land of Israel, they were calling it. Here were the spiritual custodians of the nation's rebirth, carriers of the secular Hebrew ethos. And their voices needed urgently to be heard. A young novelist named Amos Oz had published an article in the Labor Party daily, *Davar*, warning against the corrupting consequences of occupation. As if the Jewish people could be an occupier in its own land! The debate among Israel's writers was linguistic: occupied territories versus liberated territories.

Yisrael sat silently, intimidated by reverence. Not only was he the youngest person around the table, and one of the very few with a *kippah*; he was the only unknown figure.

The movement, said Alterman, would be launched with a manifesto, proclaiming the irreversible return of the nation to Judea and Samaria. He urged those present to solicit signatures from their friends, fellow writers and intellectuals.

Hesitantly, Yisrael offered a suggestion. Why not expand the range of signatories to include other parts of the Israeli public—religious Zionists, for example? "There are many young people within my community who have been waiting for this moment," he said. "I'm sure we can find support among them."

Aside from the Mercaz yeshiva, brought to national attention by the Six-Day War, the religious Zionist community was hardly known for political daring. Its aging leaders preferred pragmatic politics to grand visions. In the "waiting period" before the war, they had been among the most dovish members of the cabinet, skeptical of a preemptive strike against Egypt and even initially hesitating over the conquest of the Old City.

Yet here was a young man suggesting a shift within one of Zionism's most moderate communities. Religious Zionists and West Bank settlement? Perhaps it was worth a try.

Yisrael, emboldened, offered one more suggestion: Why not reach out to younger writers? The only names Alterman and his friends were suggesting for their manifesto were authors of their generation. What about Amos Oz? "I'll be happy to contact him," Yisrael offered.

At the mention of Oz, there was silence around the table. For Alterman, Oz's offense was not only political but literary: he was part of a generational revolt against the writers of 1948, against the mythic Zionist themes of destruction and rebirth. Oz and his fellow young novelists wrote in a spare Hebrew about the Palestinian tragedy and the decline of kibbutz idealism. For Alterman it was no surprise that they opposed annexing Judea and Samaria: their Zionism, like their prose, was anemic.

Alterman, red-faced, pounded the table: a wordless veto.

Afterward novelist Moshe Shamir approached Yisrael and slapped both his cheeks, at once playful and rebuking. "What did you do?" he said. No one was allowed to upset Alterman.

"I think we can win over Amos Oz," Yisrael persisted. "If he were to get an invitation to join Alterman, he would be so flattered he wouldn't be able to resist. That's human nature."

CAFÉ CASIT

THE BLESSINGS OF the Six-Day War didn't cease for Yisrael Harel. Not only had he been courted by the elite, but now an old dream of becoming a journalist—nurtured as a child when he would stand at his neighborhood kiosk and read competing party newspapers—had become fulfilled.

The Movement for the Complete Land of Israel needed an editor for its newspaper, *This Is the Land*, and Yisrael was given the job. "But I've never been an editor," he protested. Don't worry, the movement's elders assured him, you'll learn.

The premier issue appeared in April 1968. The newspaper argued the need to annex the new territories on security and economic and, most of all, historical grounds. Yisrael wrote about Hebron's just-reborn Jewish community. He described men in prayer shawls walking through the market past sullen Arab merchants and half-ruined stone buildings, some with indentations marking where mezuzahs had been ripped out. After a long day of domestic chores, exhausted young women sat together and studied Torah. One of the founders of the kibbutz movement, Yisrael noted, once said that a sign of authentic settlement was the presence of children. And among the Jews of Hebron, there were many children.

According to Yisrael, even the Arab owner of the Park Hotel, where the settlers had held the seder, was happy that the Jews were returning: "'Building is cheap,' he said, smiling."

YISRAEL TURNED OUT to be a talented journalist. Working without an assistant, he published the twelve-page biweekly alone. The pay was symbolic, the hours open-ended, the pressure of editing the greats of Hebrew literature immense. But Yisrael had never been happier. He would have gladly served this cause and these men for no pay. There, on the masthead, was his name beside Alterman's.

Along with editing the paper, he helped coordinate movement events. When a decision needed to be made about the next conference or newspaper ad, Yisrael would go to Alterman's table in Café Casit on Dizengoff Street in Tel Aviv.

In Café Casit writers celebrated their book launchings and theater directors their opening night. The owner, Hatzkel Ish-Casit ("man of Casit"), a former pioneer who'd come to Tel Aviv to recuperate from malaria and was now a chain-smoking fat man, routinely extended credit he knew wouldn't be repaid to artists and renowned wild men cherished for their indulgences by an austere society longing for normalcy. The food was Eastern European, *cholent* and kishke and gefilte fish, which Hatzkel would distribute gratis when the mood struck him. He adopted struggling artists who received their mail at the café, sometimes addressed only "c/o Casit, Tel Aviv." Even as the city closed down well before midnight, Casit continued, smoky and boisterous. Sometimes a group would begin a Hebrew song and everyone would join in; on Independence Day people danced on the tables.

Alterman's table was a place of national pilgrimage. Politicians came to consult him about how to deal with rivals, generals confided military strategy, kibbutzniks shared their commune's dilemmas, young poets their work. After a few drinks he became expansive; after a few more, occasionally abusive. He once ended a friend's book-launching at Casit by pulling off a tablecloth, crashing dishes to the floor.

Yisrael sat in awed silence at Alterman's table, observing the writers as they drank shot glasses of brandy and argued about politics and gossiped about each other's infidelities. Yisrael was the lone man in Casit with a *kippah*, but he'd gotten used to being the exception.

Alterman and his friends in the movement appreciated Yisrael. Here was a young man who, in his total devotion to Zionism, seemed to belong more to their generation than to his own. Perhaps too, they sensed that, aside from his *kippah*, there was nothing particularly religious about Yisrael. Or rather, that what was religious about Yisrael was what was religious about them: awe at the nation's improbable survival and even more improbable return home, and a commitment to protect it at any cost.

YISRAEL WAS OFFERED a job as an editor at the Friday magazine supplement of *Ma'ariv*, one of the country's major newspapers. *Ma'ariv* allowed Yisrael to write as well as edit, and he turned out to be a talented investigative reporter. A series he wrote on corruption in local rabbinical councils drew national attention. Clearly Yisrael didn't fit the stereotype of the nice religious Jew.

MOTTA GUR HEARD about the rising young journalist in the brigade and offered Yisrael the position of chief education officer. The position included coordinating efforts to record the battle of Jerusalem for posterity—or what the brigade's cynics called Motta's PR campaign to become the IDF's chief of staff.

The Movement for the Complete Land of Israel had connected Yisrael to the literary and political elite; *Ma'ariv* had connected him to the media elite. And now this: a role that could gain him entry into the paratrooper elite. What more could Yisrael Harel have hoped for?

A PARTNERSHIP OF SERVICE

THE FOUNDATION FOR the Families of the Fallen of the 55th Brigade held its first meeting in the apartment of Moisheleh's widow, Daliah. On Arik's suggestion, Yisrael was elected chairman. Arik sensed that the position was important to Yisrael. We can put his ambition to good use, thought Arik.

The foundation's first decision was to assign friends of the fallen soldiers to their families. The volunteers—"Friends of Dad"—were instructed to visit the families at least once a month, assist the widows with practical problems, and attend family events like children's birthday parties. Arik and Yisrael each took responsibility for four families.

Meanwhile Yisrael was editing a narrative history of the battle for Jerusalem. A team of volunteers had assembled hundreds of interviews, diary entries, and letters to wives and girlfriends from among the fighters. When Yisrael had a question about the accuracy of a detail, he consulted with Arik. Also on ethical questions, like whether to write that one of the officers had been killed by friendly fire. "We can't write lies," Arik said, "but we don't have to reveal the whole truth."

Arik liked the diligent culture officer. He appreciated professionalism, and Yisrael was a fine editor. As for Yisrael's right-wing politics, Arik dismissed that as harmless delusion. Let him and his friends imagine they can determine the future borders of the state; meanwhile, the Labor Party will continue to rein in the utopian fantasies of the Jews.

"Srulik," Arik called him, a Yiddish endearment for Yisrael. The nickname seemed to Yisrael a subtle put-down, reminder of his outsider status as a religious Jew. But he kept his resentment to himself.

NATAN ALTERMAN DIED in 1970 at age fifty-nine. Some said the poet died of heartbreak. Only a mass immigration of Western Jews, he had argued, would allow Israel to absorb the West Bank without risking a Palestinian majority, but the Jews weren't coming.

Café Casit closed for the funeral. Yisrael Harel was assigned the role of escorting the poet's mistress behind the casket.

CHAPTER 13

UTOPIAS LOST AND FOUND

AVITAL GEVA, PROVOCATEUR

THE FARMERS HEADING toward the fields of Ein Shemer weren't sure they were seeing right. The trunks of the cypress trees had been painted purple and gold, gleaming in the first light of the day.

"What do you think you're doing?" demanded Haggai, Avital's neighbor and his commander in the reserves.

"Life has to flow," Avital said enigmatically. "It can't be confined into neat little categories."

Perhaps he wanted to remind his friends of the beauty of trees, not to take nature for granted. Perhaps he was trying to shock them out of their routine. Order was smothering the kibbutz, he said. At the weekly meeting, Avital suggested growing potatoes on the lawn.

Economically at least, Ein Shemer was thriving. The kibbutz inaugurated its first factory, a rubber-producing plant. At the weekly meetings the comrades debated the need to hire outside labor, a violation of their socialist ethos. But there was really no choice: Ein Shemer's several hundred members couldn't manage its expanding economy alone.

Every night after dinner the kibbutzniks gathered in the social room to watch television. The country finally had its first TV station—government-run, in black and white, with mostly news programs and sports. The Labor government insisted that programming end before midnight, to ensure a good night's sleep for the workers of Israel.

Ein Shemer's debate over May Day continued, more wistful than strident. On the first May Day after the Six-Day War, comrades were so disoriented that the kibbutz forgot to hoist a red flag, until someone climbed up the water tower and hung it himself. A year later, May Day was declared a half work day, compromise between those who still cherished the holiday and those who wanted to abolish it altogether. They still served borscht in the dining room in honor of May Day and held the military-style lineup, though attendance was sparse. Finally, the following year, the weekly kibbutz assembly voted to cancel May Day as a day of rest—though comrades who opposed the decision would be allowed to take the day off and work as compensation on Shabbat.

Who cares one way or another about the damned red flag? demanded Avital. Why are we wasting our time arguing about nonsense when our passion for the kibbutz is slipping away?

Part educator, part prankster, Avital proceeded to turn Ein Shemer into an art project. He connected the kibbutz houses with pink cloth, a reminder of interconnectedness. (And pink as faded red?) On Passover, for the communal seder, he turned the dining room into the Yellow Submarine, with psychedelic Beatles and Blue Meanies. Why? Perhaps because a kibbutz was evocative of the intimacy and claustrophobia of a submarine. Or perhaps just because.

Despite themselves, the kibbutzniks were intrigued. What was he going to do next?

He invited Ein Shemer's members to donate books they no longer needed. The growing pile on his lawn included works by Lenin and Stalin, agriculture manuals in German, a book by an early Zionist theoretician about the dignity of labor. Here was the collection of Ein Shemer's dreams, the once-holy books that had inspired Avital's parents and their friends to plant their garden in the wilderness. What would guide them now, when their dreams had been fulfilled?

Avital laid the books in rows, as if on shelves, and left them out in the sun and the wind to wither into the land.

He expanded the happenings to his Arab neighbors. He collected hundreds of books in Hebrew and Arabic, piled them on a hilltop, and distributed leaflets inviting people to help themselves, a coexistence of words. He helped a friend from art school fill a truck with dirt from the Israeli Arab village of Meiser and dump it into the neighboring kibbutz of Meitzar, then did the reverse. Literally sharing the land.

Just before the fall holiday of Sukkoth, when Jews build huts covered with palm fronds to recall their desert wanderings, Avital announced a competition for the most beautiful sukkah in Ein Shemer. The kibbutz had a communal sukkah, but the holiday celebration had become routinized. And so he was calling for "privatizing" the holiday, each family taking responsibility for its own sukkah.

Avital cut palm branches, piled them on the road, and invited families to take what they needed to cover their huts. At the entrance to the kibbutz, beneath the canopy of ficus trees, families built shacks made of board and cloth and decorated them with paintings and rugs. Avital and Ada brought cots into their sukkah and slept there through the week-long holiday.

TOGETHER WITH TWO FRIENDS from art school, Moshe Gershuni and Micha Ullman, Avital was exhibiting at Israel's leading galleries and museums. He assembled two kilometers of irrigation pipes that wound through the Israel Museum in Jerusalem; through the pipes played classical music. He rode a tractor over eighteen meters of rubber from Ein Shemer's factory and exhibited the tire imprints. The Israeli art world was charmed by his use of kibbutz motifs to mock and affirm.

But Avital's greatest satisfaction was in working with teenagers. He volunteered as a counselor at the Hashomer Hatzair seminar center, Givat Haviva, named for one of the young women who had parachuted to her death with Enzo Sereni. Young people responded to Avital because he was that rare adult who kept the exuberance of youth. Avital's goal was to convey the joy of communal life, not through lectures and seminars but through experience.

"Okay, *hevreh*, listen up," Avital called to the dozen teenagers standing in a clearing in the orchard. It was a summer morning, and the earth, deprived of rain since late spring, smelled of dry heat and pine needles.

"Every morning for the next week, you are going to plow this field," he explained. "Your mission will be to pull together while hitched to this plow." He pointed to a long block of wood, affixed with metal wheels. "This is soft earth, like butter," he continued. "Without rocks. But pulling the plow is still hard work. Before tractors, horses used to do it. You're going to test the strength of humans."

The young people stood with folded arms. The girls among them wore tight shorts, like city girls. Despite themselves, they were curious. They were from Mishmar Ha'Emek, Yehudit Achmon's kibbutz. Among them was

Arik's daughter, Tsafra, from his first marriage. "I think you know my father," she said to Avital.

"Arik Achmon's daughter! *Ya Allah*!"

They brought poles and connected those with steel wire, forming four rows, like galleys. Five to a row, they began pulling the plow. "Together!" called Avital. They inched forward.

Six dunams, one dunam a day. The hardest part was to keep from collapsing in laughter. When the team finished a morning of plowing, Avital built a fire at the edge of the field and they drank Turkish coffee. Together.

CAPITALIST PIONEER

ARIK ACHMON CAME upon a circle of reservists in faded green uniforms. The brigade had been drafted for a parachute drop over the sand dunes south of Tel Aviv. Avital Geva was standing in the middle of the circle, and everyone was laughing. Arik moved in closer and heard that he was talking about Arik's daughter, Tsafra.

"You should have seen her," Avital was saying, "hitched to a plow like a mule."

Arik joined the laughter. But he didn't really find the story funny, and he suspected that Avital was getting back at him for telling the guys about how Avital had wept in the hospital about the Soviet Union.

EVEN AS AVITAL GEVA was trying to revive the communal spirit of the kibbutz among its young, Arik Achmon was searching for a way to break the hold of socialism and turn an almost successful company into a model of rational capitalism.

There is only one way, he concluded, that his domestic airline, Kanaf, would thrive as a private company in a statist economy: subvert the system by joining it.

He had a plan. Israel's national airline, El Al, had founded a subsidiary for domestic travel, called Arkia, and Arik proposed to his partners that they offer it 50 percent of Kanaf. By creating a partnership with a government company, they would ensure access to government officials; by maintaining partial private status, they would keep their management professional, freed of party hacks.

Arik and his partners met with the finance minister, Pinchas Sapir, a big bald man who ran the centralized economy out of a small black notebook.

"State your case," said Sapir.

"We want Arkia to buy half our company," Arik said. "You have to allow private companies to exist."

Arik was offering a new model for an Israeli company. Besides, Arkia was failing; perhaps this arrangement would help revive it. Nor was Kanaf's case harmed by the presence at the meeting of Sapir's son-in-law, one of Kanaf's shareholders.

On Sapir's instructions, Arkia bought 50 percent of Kanaf. Now Arik had the access he needed: Kanaf-Arkia went into business with the army, ferrying soldiers between Tel Aviv and the Suez Canal.

"I CAN'T KEEP THIS UP ANYMORE," Arik said to Yehudit, "running back and forth between two homes. We'll visit the kibbutz every Shabbat. But our home is Tel Aviv."

When Yehudit finally told Hazan, he said nothing. Afterward he confided to an associate, "This is the blackest day of my life."

ARIK MOVED HIS family—there was now nine-month-old Yael, his first child with Yehudit—into an apartment in North Tel Aviv. When Yehudit saw the apartment, she wept. "From now on, these four walls are going to be our whole life," she said. She was exchanging the solidarity of the kibbutz for apartment buildings built on sand dunes. And how was she to raise her daughter alone, without the children's house?

The kibbutz awarded Yehudit a parting grant of 6,000 lira for her years of work, just enough to buy the Achmons' first washing machine.

FAREWELL TO KIBBUTZ GAN SHMUEL

LATE AT NIGHT on May Day, Udi Adiv entered Gan Shmuel's dining room and hung a banner with the Matzpen slogan "Down with Occupation." By morning the banner was gone.

At the next weekly kibbutz meeting Udi was denounced as a saboteur. "If the kibbutz won't accept ideological diversity," he countered, "I'll have to leave."

UDI TOOK A SABBATICAL from the kibbutz and moved to Tel Aviv. He worked as a caretaker for a handicapped man and devoted his free time to Matzpen.

One Thursday night, the Matzpenniks were sitting at an outside table at Café Casit, arguing and flirting. An activist tried to sell copies of the Matzpen newspaper to passersby. An angry crowd gathered. "Traitors!" "Our soldiers are fighting at the canal, and you're stabbing them in the back!" Someone pushed Udi, and he pushed back.

Hatzkel Ish-Casit, who rarely threw anyone out of his cafe, told the Matzpenniks to leave.

UDI'S YEAR IN TEL AVIV ENDED, but he didn't return to Gan Shmuel. Instead he enrolled in the University of Haifa, where a new program was preparing kibbutzniks, whose high school education didn't bother with matriculation exams, for university. One more sign of the changing kibbutz: increasingly young people were being allowed to choose professions, instead of being sent to study "useful" subjects like agriculture and education. Udi intended to study political science and economics, useful subjects for the revolution.

Udi informed Gan Shmuel's secretariat that he was quitting the kibbutz. No one tried to talk him into staying.

WELCOME HOME, MEIR ARIEL

MEIR AND TIRZA stood at the entrance to their house in Kibbutz Mishmarot, beside a wood crate containing their new American acquisitions, including a stereo and a collection of rock albums. It was late summer 1970. After two years in America, the Ariels were back. Meir looked around at the little red-roofed houses and dirt paths and clusters of cacti and lit a cigarette. Home.

The kibbutz provided the Ariels with a two-room house, double the size of their last abode. In the old house there was a hand shower with cold water, and no kitchen. Now they had a kitchenette and hot water. The two children shared a bedroom, while Meir and Tirza slept on a folding cot in the salon.

They're different, the kibbutzniks said. It wasn't just Tirza's tight jeans and denim shirt and the disposable diapers, a luxury in Israel. *They've stepped out, they don't quite belong to us anymore.* Beatniks, some called them.

Yet Mishmarot was different too. Volunteers from America and Europe, who worked the fields in exchange for room and board and Hebrew lessons, had brought something of the 1960s into the kibbutz. There were weekend dance parties to rock music, affairs between kibbutzniks and volunteers, rumors of drugs.

The sensible kibbutzniks of Mishmarot realized they couldn't simply dispatch Meir back to the fields and Tirza back to the nursery. And so the Ariels were given the job of supervising the foreign volunteers. Perhaps that would satisfy the couple's restlessness.

"TIRZA, I HAVE something to tell you."

Meir tried to sound matter-of-fact.

"In America, in the summer camp—I slept with one of the girls."

Tirza fell on the bed, weeping.

"I love you more than anyone," he said. "Don't leave me. I can't live without you."

"While I was cooking a whole day for the campers, that's what you were doing?"

"A man can love more than one woman at a time," he insisted. "I can't confine my love to only one woman."

Meir had a practical suggestion. "Why don't *you* find someone? There's an American volunteer who's making eyes at you. Do you want me to speak to him?"

"I want to die," said Tirza.

A few days later, she approached the American.

"Whatever is permitted to you," Tirza told Meir afterward, "will be permitted to me."

ISRAEL HAD FORGOTTEN the "singing paratrooper," just as Meir had hoped.

Yet anonymity too was oppressive. In his absence had emerged an exuberant Hebrew rock music that joined the Beatles with the Russian and Hasidic folk melodies of the pioneers, rock in minor key. Its creators had been influenced by the rebellious music filtering in from the West; and yet most of them emerged from the army entertainment troupes, which sang patriotic songs to raise soldiers' morale. The result of those conflicting influences were antiwar songs more wistful than angry, at once mocking and rooted, an opposition from deep within the national self.

Hebrew rock's great composer was Meir's childhood friend and musical collaborator from Mishmarot, Shalom Hanoch. Shalom, bone-thin and hawk-faced, had left the kibbutz at age sixteen to study in acting school and never returned. His songs were instant classics, taking the three-minute rock song to its melodic and poetic limits. One Shalom song, "Avshalom," with its plaintive refrain wondering why peace couldn't come now, became an anthem.

Meir had written some lyrics in Detroit and sent them to Shalom, who put them to music and recorded them. And Meir had sold some songs to other leading singers. Yet he remained unknown to the public.

He tried to suppress his envy of Shalom. But Shalom's success was a constant rebuke.

Why wasn't Meir out there, instead of being stuck on the kibbutz?

EVERY AFTERNOON, RETURNING from the cotton fields, Meir snipped a few leaves from a marijuana plant that reached the red-shingled roof of his house. Speaking tenderly to the leaves, he dried them in a frying pan on the kitchenette burner and rolled them into a joint.

Meir's father, retired as principal and now the kibbutz gardener, was perplexed. "What kind of plant is that, Meirkeh?" he asked.

"Japanese tomato," Meir replied.

Meir was on reserve duty when the kibbutz manager knocked on the Ariels' door. "I know what that plant is, Tirza," she said. "If you don't uproot it in twenty-four hours, I'm calling the police."

"It's Meir's, not mine," said Tirza. "Can't you wait until he comes back from reserve duty?"

When Meir returned home, the Japanese tomato plant was gone.

THE MISHMAROT DINING room, 8:00 a.m. Kibbutzniks in dark blue work clothes wandered in from the fields and chicken coops. They took any available seat and drank Turkish coffee and cut up vegetables on plastic plates with hard-boiled eggs and olives, tossing shells and pits into a metal bowl in the center of the table.

Into this morning celebration of diligence and frugality entered Tirza, sleepless with dilated pupils. Her neighbor, a young woman nicknamed Jo Jo, said, "This time you went too far, Tirza. Music until three a.m. I was up the whole night."

Tirza giggled. "We took LSD."

"Tirza, it can't go on like this. I have to get up to work. What's going to be here?"

Tirza didn't seem to hear. "I felt like I'm walking on the ceiling," she said.

"And what about the children in all of this?"

"They woke up and went back to sleep."

Mireleh, an old girlfriend of Meir's who had lost him to Tirza, joined in. "Don't tell Sasha," she pleaded, referring to Meir's father. "Whatever you do, don't tell Sasha."

MEIR ASKED THE KIBBUTZ for another leave. He needed to test himself in Tel Aviv, where the new Hebrew music was being created. He wanted to write songs—not as a "hobby," as some on the kibbutz suggested, but full-time.

Tirza was supportive: maybe this was her way out of Mishmarot. "Grow up and see if you can earn a living," she said to Meir. "Bring me one month's salary—that's all, just earn enough to support the family for one month—and we'll come and join you."

At the end of 1971 Meir moved to Tel Aviv. Tirza found him a one-room shack on a rooftop, built as a storage room, with an adjacent outhouse. She installed a cot, a small fridge, a radio, and a desk. Meir brought his guitar and accordion. He had a view of the sea. "Who needs anything more?" he told a visitor from Mishmarot.

Through a friend from the paratroopers, Meir got a part-time job as driver and schlepper for a film company. Meir had long considered becoming a filmmaker or an actor—he and Tirza had met in a theater workshop—but no one seemed to notice his potential.

Shalom, meanwhile, had left Tel Aviv for London. He was working with a leading British producer on an English-language album, writing songs with the help of a dictionary. Israel had been too confining. Shalom insisted on his right to define himself simply as a human being, to restrict his love to individuals, not collectives.

Meir was introduced to the Tel Aviv music scene as Shalom's friend. Producers considered Meir interesting and amusing but hopelessly noncommercial. His songs went on too long, and told stories rather than expressing accessible emotions. One well-known singer tried to be helpful. You've got talent, Meir, he said, but you need to write songs that can be played on the radio.

MEIR WANDERED THE STREETS of Tel Aviv. Thirty years earlier, it had been known as the White City. With its Bauhaus buildings and boulevards of sandy walkways shaded by eucalyptus trees, Tel Aviv had been the center of the Hebrew renaissance. But the White City had turned prematurely gray, as if overcome with the sorrows of the refugees from all the shattered diasporas who had since crowded into it. Languid in the long summer, once-chic buildings with rounded balconies peeled in the sun. Cheap hotels faced the sea; the central bus station, an outdoor strip of smoking buses, drew beggars and peddlers selling cigarette lighters and sewing needles.

Yet Tel Aviv was infinitely malleable. Here was the center of Israel's emerging film industry, of music and theater. For Arik Achmon it was the launching place for Israel's market economy; for Udi Adiv, headquarters of the coming revolution. Here Avital Geva was exhibiting with his friends, disrupting the propriety of the Israeli art world. And here Meir Ariel might somehow become Meir Ariel.

Meanwhile, though, he was broke. A friend visiting from Mishmarot worried that he was going hungry. Meir's life had come to resemble a song he'd written in Detroit, about wandering the streets with torn shoelaces and no responsibilities, trying to write a good line to whisper in a woman's ear.

His love life, at least, was thriving. He seemed to care most about baring a woman's soul, treating conversation as potential revelation. He went on into the night about the deadening effect of the kibbutz on creativity and of the army on the emotional life of Israeli men, and about the Bible's message about power in setting prophets against kings. Meir's lovers had never met an Israeli man, let alone a kibbutznik, quite like him. He was, they said, introspective, emotional. Almost feminine.

THE SABBATICAL ENDED. Meir returned to the kibbutz, to the cotton fields. He had failed to meet Tirza's challenge: he hadn't earned a single month's salary.

THE MOUNTAIN AND THE COAST

IN THE MOUNT ETZION military yeshiva, Yoel Bin-Nun was creating an educational revolution.

Teaching Bible, Yoel dared to bring into the study hall the findings of historians and researchers about the cultures of the ancient Near East. He compared the Ten Commandments to the Code of Hammurabi—to prove the moral superiority of Judaism over paganism, of course, but also linking ancient Israel with its neighbors, and insisting that faith must be tested by history. He cited biblical criticism to refute its claims, but in the process exposed his students to heresies like the multiple authorships of the Bible.

Yoel got away with it because his goal was not to provoke orthodox sensibilities but to restore the Bible as a living force. For Yoel Bible stories were not mere moralistic parables but a precise roadmap for his generation's experience, for a nation struggling to overcome its longings for normalcy and become a holy people in a holy land. Precisely the opposite vision to Arik Achmon's.

Yoel appeared taller than he was, perhaps because he was sturdy and broad-shouldered, perhaps because he projected great ideas. Often he appeared lost in thought, nibbling at the edges of his beard. He would look out to the distance with a slightly quizzical look, as if trying to focus on an image he could intuit but not yet see.

On a hike along the mountain ridge of Samaria, overlooking the sprawl of greater Tel Aviv on the Mediterranean, Yoel told his students about the tribes of the mountain and the tribes of the coast. Those who had settled on the mountain ridges, he noted, were the most faithfully monotheistic. For that reason, the Tabernacle, containing the Divine Presence, was brought to the mountain ridge. The final resting place of the Divine Presence, the Temple, had been built in Jerusalem, the Judean Hills.

But the tribes who settled on the coast, continued Yoel, were traders and idol-worshipping backsliders. "The tension exists in Israel today," he said. "Jerusalem and Tel Aviv: enough said? In the classic planning of most cities in the world, streets are straight, and at ninety-degree angles. They are intended to lead people to the commercial center. That is Tel Aviv. Where is the commercial center of Jerusalem? Jaffa Road—a long street that leads to the Old City, right? In ancient times, it was a long street leading to the Temple.

"The coast, the valley, creates a civilization that is entirely material. The person places himself at the center, seats himself on the throne, and calls himself a god. That is the fate of all materialist civilizations that don't have God in their midst."

AMONG YOEL'S MOST devoted students was an intense redheaded young man named Yehudah Etzion. Listening to Yoel speak about the mountains and the coast, Yehudah was galvanized. That is our real purpose in being in Kfar Etzion, Yehudah realized; resettling the mountains will spiritually renew the coast. Yehudah came to identify so deeply with the vision of the mountain that he changed his family name from Mintz to Etzion. His regret was that he'd been born too late to fight, like Yoel, in the Six-Day War. History had passed Yehudah by once, but he was determined not to let that happen again.

Yehudah, friends said, was a pure soul. Often he hiked alone through Arab villages, drinking coffee with the old men.

But there was a ruthless side to Yehudah. One Friday night, before entering the dining room, the yeshiva students danced in a circle. A young Arab man working in the kitchen came out and, laughing, joined them. No one seemed to mind his presence—except Yehudah, who pushed him away. Yehudah didn't see a human being but a gentile intrusion in the circle of purity.

Though only four years separated the two, Yoel was clearly the teacher, Yehudah the disciple. Yoel—scholar, soldier, visionary, iconoclast—was, for Yehudah, the ideal Jew. Once a week Yehudah came to Yoel's room for private study. Yoel sat with a newborn son on his lap and taught the writings of Rabbi Kook. In Yehudah, with his anarchic spirit and his craving for self-sacrifice, Yoel thought he had found a partner for the work of redemption.

They talked about the Temple Mount. To fulfill its mission of mediating between spirit and matter, Judaism required a sacred geography: concentric circles of divine emanation, from the unbearable intensity of the Holy of Holies, to the courtyards of the Temple, to the city of Jerusalem, to the land of Israel. When the Messiah came, the whole world would radiate holiness.

Our generation has been blessed, said Yoel, to be the instrument for the return of the Mount to the people of Israel. Yet Motta Gur had spoken too soon: the Temple Mount was not quite in their hands. Inconceivably, the Israeli government had ceded control of the Mount to the Muslim Waqf. What conquerors had ever behaved with such generosity toward an enemy that had sought their destruction and denied them access to their holiest site?

The goal of the generation of redemption, then, was to complete the conquest of the mountain—the ultimate mountain. Yoel, of course, wasn't advocating the destruction of the Dome of the Rock. That was the Messiah's prerogative alone.

We need an image to awaken devotion to the Temple, Yoel said, remind the nation of its destiny. No one knew, of course, what form a future third temple might assume; according to legend, it would descend whole from heaven. But based on rabbinic sources, Yoel noted, they did have a good idea of what the Second Temple looked like. A detailed stone model was even on display in the courtyard of one of Jerusalem's hotels.

Yehudah and several friends went to the model and, standing on each other's shoulders, took a photograph that simulated an aerial shot of the Temple's main pillared building, surrounded by courtyard and crenellated walls. That image was then superimposed on an aerial photo of the Temple Mount, from which the Dome of the Rock had been airbrushed. In the resulting photomontage, biblical and modern time converged.

The photomontage was turned into a poster. Yoel hung it in his one-room apartment. The poster spread among young religious Zionists, a tantalizing reminder of just how close their generation was to fulfilling centuries of longing.

THE FAMILY OF BEREAVEMENT

TWO DOZEN YOUNG WOMEN and children, each family accompanied by a reservist paratrooper, boarded the tour bus on a cold December morning in Tel Aviv. They seemed to be typical Israeli families on an outing: anxious mothers and indulgent "fathers" and boisterous children eating peanut-flavored snacks. The adults, though, were acutely self-conscious. A reservist entrusted with photographing the event was so flustered that he forgot to take out his camera.

It was Hanukkah 1971, and the Foundation for the Families of the Fallen of the 55th Brigade—the Friends of Dad—was holding its first outing, a bus trip to Mount Hermon on the Golan Heights. Arik Achmon had managed to acquire a free bus through his contacts. Yisrael Harel, reverting to his role as Bnei Akiva counselor, stood up front on the bus and led everyone in Hanukkah songs.

They came to a base of the armored corps just below the Hermon. The snow-covered peak was concealed in mist. The children in woolen caps climbed up tanks, while soldiers distributed jelly-filled doughnuts. As night fell, everyone gathered before an imposing makeshift menorah, bins filled with kerosene. A soldier dipped a burning torch into each bin. Flames rose against the fierce wind. "O Rock of Refuge, my salvation," sang the mothers and children and friends of Dad.

WITH EACH OUTING, the numbers of participating families grew. The IDF opened its secret installations to the foundation. "Civilians can't even dream of getting into these places," Arik said. The children were admitted into the cockpits of the latest Phantom jets, taken out to sea on rubber dinghies in an exercise with frogmen, shown weapons in the laboratories of the military industry that combat units hadn't yet seen. The children felt special, precisely as Arik and Yisrael intended.

In the summer, the two friends organized a four-day camp for the families of the fallen in a youth village located in the forest of Mount Carmel. During the year, the village was a school for young immigrants and children with difficulties at home. At Yisrael's request, the group chose a site with a kosher kitchen: religious children, he argued, should feel like equals at our events, and Arik readily agreed.

Arik of course was in charge of logistics, while Yisrael ran activities, which he modeled after a Zionist scouting camp. The children lived in tents and learned how to tie knots and chop wood. Along with soccer and volleyball they played a game called Escape from Atlit, simulating the British detention center for Holocaust survivors who were trying to slip into the land of Israel. Yisrael didn't tell the children that he himself had been one of those detainees in a British camp on Cyprus. Not even Arik knew he was a survivor.

CHAPTER 14

ACROSS THE BORDER

UDI ADIV FINDS A MENTOR

UDI WALKED THE cobbled streets of Wadi Nisnass, Haifa's Arab neighborhood near the docks. Burlap sacks with dried chili peppers and fava beans lined the sidewalks. Workmen's restaurants served hummus for breakfast. Udi was charmed. He belonged here, he felt, more than among the Jews.

Udi was leading a schizophrenic existence. He was enjoying student life at the University of Haifa, Israel's most integrated Arab-Jewish campus, and he felt as comfortable there as he could in any Israeli institution. He joined the university basketball team and was rarely without at least one girlfriend.

But his political life was drawing him farther toward the fringe. Even Matzpen seemed tame to him now. When Naif Hawatmeh, leader of a Marxist faction of the PLO, called for incorporating "Israeli progressives" into the Palestinian war against Israel, Udi was elated.

One of Udi's regular stops in Wadi Nisnass was a Marxist bookshop run by Daoud Turki, an Arab Israeli who had been expelled from Israel's Communist Party for supporting terrorism. The corner bookshop was so small, there was scarcely room for a table and chairs.

In his early forties, Daoud was a self-taught political theorist. He told Udi about the humiliation of growing up under Israeli military rule, which Arab Israelis had been subjected to until the government abolished it in 1966. To travel from Haifa to Nazareth had required a military pass. He spoke about how his father had almost been killed by a Jewish terrorist bomb in 1948. Terrorism, said Daoud, was simply a political tactic, the way wars were fought in the Middle East.

Udi confided to Daoud his frustrations with Matzpen. "The intellectuals lecture the petit bourgeois youth about trade unions," he said, mockingly.

Worse, Matzpen had endorsed a two-state solution, rather than the single binational state advocated by the PLO. "Israel is a colonialist state," Udi said. "Jews and Arabs are one nation."

"You and I agree about everything," Daoud said.

In fact there was a big disagreement between them, which Daoud kept to himself. Udi opposed all forms of nationalism and supported the Palestinian national movement only for tactical reasons, as catalyst for revolution in the Middle East. Daoud, though, was a nationalist, a pan-Arabist. He was willing to make room in Arab Palestine for a Jewish minority—as a religion, not a people. Just as there were Arab Muslims and Arab Christians, so too Arab Jews.

Daoud had one more secret. He had begun recruiting fellow Arab Israelis to bomb government and military installations. Udi's enthusiasm for Hawatmeh's vision of a joint Arab-Jewish "armed struggle" against Zionism intrigued Daoud. Why not broaden the underground to include radical Jews? For now, though, Daoud said nothing to Udi, and waited for an opening.

THE FORTY MEMBERS of Matzpen divided into two rival Trotskyite factions and a third pro-Mao faction called the Struggle. Udi joined the Maoists. One of the group' members advocated a Chinese-style cultural revolution, whose first act would be the destruction of pianos.

One evening in Daoud's bookstore, Udi provided the opening Daoud had been waiting for. "All around the world, the revolution is winning," Udi said. "The Vietnamese are about to defeat America. Communism is spreading in Latin America. It's just a matter of time before the Palestinians defeat Zionism. And what are we doing? Talking."

"I have a group I think you will be interested in," Daoud said.

"I want to meet someone from the Palestinian national movement," Udi said.

"It can be arranged," replied Daoud.

THE ISRAELI CHE GUEVARA

DAOUD ESTABLISHED SEPARATE CELLS for Arabs and Jews and placed Udi in charge of the Jewish cell. Daoud reassured him: We won't target civilians, only symbols of the Zionist power structure, like government offices and army bases. And an occasional assassination of political leaders like the archcriminal defense minister, Moshe Dayan. That made sense to Udi. True, civilians would be at risk with a bomb in a government office, but collateral damage was unavoidable in any war. As for killing soldiers, that was what war was about. Udi didn't think of the actual soldiers that he knew, like his friends in Gan Shmuel or the men with whom he'd fought in Jerusalem.

Udi's first recruit was Dan Vered, the Maoist who wanted to destroy pianos. Vered was a math teacher who had been radicalized by the New Left when he'd studied in Florida.

Daoud discussed scouting out the Haifa port and electric company facilities. And he assigned Udi the job of hiding stolen weapons.

But no weapons appeared.

AT 4:30 IN THE MORNING of September 5, 1972, Palestinian terrorists wearing ski masks invaded the Olympic village in Munich, shot to death two members of the Israeli national team, and kidnapped nine others. The terrorists—claiming to represent a previously unknown group, Black September, but in fact part of the PLO—demanded to be flown to Cairo with their hostages. When they boarded a helicopter provided by the German government, police sharpshooters opened fire. One of the terrorists detonated a grenade, killing the sportsmen.

For Israelis, the image of their athletes lying bound and helpless—in Germany—was unbearable. The Munich massacre seemed to prove that even when Jews became Olympic sportsmen, they were still somehow different from everyone else.

Yet Udi could no longer even grieve together with his fellow Israelis. The Palestinian resistance, he argued, had the right to take hostages.

At Daoud's behest, Udi was planning a trip to Athens, to meet a PLO operative. Udi's new girlfiend, Leah Leshem, a kibbutznik without a radical background whom he had met at university, was suspicious. "Are you going to meet with Black September?" she asked, anxious.

"I'll send you a postcard," Udi replied.

IN ATHENS, UDI WAS MET by a short, heavy man in his late forties who called himself Abu Kammal. Daoud had been vague about Abu Kammal's organizational affiliation. Udi assumed he was an operative for one of the PLO's factions, hopefully Hawatmeh's.

Abu Kammal kept his real identity hidden: he was an Arab Israeli from the Galilee named Habib Kawaji, who had been exiled for leading a pro-Nasserist movement. These days, Kawaji was working for Syrian intelligence, and Daoud's underground was being run by Syria's Ba'athist regime, but Kawaji didn't tell Udi that either. If Udi needed to believe that Kawaji was an independent PLO operative, what was the harm?

Kawaji spoke decent English. He didn't let on that he also spoke fluent Hebrew. In struggling English, Udi explained that his reason for supporting the PLO was to encourage a socialist revolution in the Middle East.

Yes, agreed Kawaji, revolution against corrupt Arab regimes was his goal too.

Kawaji revealed their final destination: We're going to Damascus.

Finally, thought Udi. No more games—

Udi posed for passport photos, and Kawaji took those to the Syrian Embassy. Udi's Syrian passport was issued under the name of George Houri, a Syrian-born expatriate, Kawaji explained, who spoke no Arabic because his family had moved to Argentina when he was a child. Udi was uneasy. "What's with you and Syria?" he asked. Was Kawaji working for the Syrian government rather than the PLO? The moral distinction, which would have been lost on most of his fellow Israelis, was crucial to Udi. The PLO was a revolutionary movement, the Syrian Ba'athist government reactionary and nationalist.

Kawaji reassured him. "We have friends in the Syrian regime," he said.

On the brief flight from Athens to Beirut, Udi felt afraid for the first time. There was no turning back. Beirut was the capital of Palestinian terrorism. Just recently an Israeli commando team had landed in Beirut and assassinated Palestinian terrorist leaders; one of the commandos killed in the operation was the son of a leader of Hashomer Hatzair whom Udi knew.

Udi approached passport control. "What do I say?" he anxiously asked Kawaji. "Why don't I speak Arabic?"

"Don't say a word," Kawaji replied. "Leave it to me."

No one asked Udi any questions.

Beirut, with its tall buildings and stylish boardwalk, astonished Udi.

An Arab city, and it's nicer than Tel Aviv— He caught himself: even he had internalized Israeli contempt for the Arabs.

Kawaji took Udi to a relative's home, where he'd parked his car. Before getting in, he checked under the chassis. "We have many enemies," he explained.

They crossed the border into Syria. Streams, grapevines, lush valleys. But Damascus disappointed: faded shops, uniform dress of gray suits and housecoats, life-size posters of Hafez al-Assad. Nationalists, thought Udi with distaste.

They drove to a house on the edge of the city. Aside from a refrigerator and cots, the villa was empty.

Kawaji took Udi to see the sights, the ancient covered market and the grave of Saladin, who defeated the Crusaders.

They visited the Jewish quarter. Only a few thousand terrorized Jews remained of a once-thriving ancient community. Forbidden to emigrate, they were under constant surveillance, subjected to periodic arrests.

In the quarter's police station, Kawaji introduced Udi to the commander as an American journalist. Udi nodded and smiled, trying to say as little as possible in his Israeli-accented English.

The commander explained to Udi that the job of the police was to protect the Jews from provocateurs. We aren't against the Jews, he said, only the Zionists.

"He's one of us," Kawaji said to Udi.

At the synagogue, they met the community's young rabbi. Udi approvingly noted his trimmed beard. *A modern man, not like Shlomo Goren and the other fanatical rabbis in Israel with their wild beards—* Speaking in the presence of policemen, the rabbi assured the American journalist of the Syrian government's benevolence. The government, he said, protects us.

What a cultured man, thought Udi, what a model Jewish community. Here was an alternative to the Judaism of power and conquest, proof that the Jews didn't need a state to be safe.

IN THE VILLA on the edge of Damascus, Kawaji presented Udi with an empty notebook and instructed: Write about your life, especially your military service.

"What's interesting about my military service?" asked Udi. "I was a corporal, I don't know any secrets."

Kawaji insisted. Udi relented. What could he reveal that wasn't available in any Israeli newspaper?

He wrote about basic training in the Nahal base near Kibbutz Gan Shmuel, about parachute drops in Tel Nof, about the antiquated Belgian FN rifle on which he'd learned to shoot.

Write the location of air force bases, Kawaji instructed.

Udi complied. *Who doesn't know that Tel Nof is near Givat Brenner?*

Kawaji requested an assessment of Motta Gur. A warmonger, wrote Udi.

As Udi filled the notebook, he might have thought about Uri Ilan, the other member of Gan Shmuel to reach Damascus, who committed suicide rather than betray military secrets under torture. Yet as Udi wrote in the notebook, he didn't think of Uri Ilan. Not as reproach, not even as irony. He simply forgot about him.

Udi was driven to an army camp in the mountains. He was given a Kalashnikov and taken to a firing range. What was this childish game? wondered Udi. As if he didn't know how to shoot. Still, there was something charming about training in the hills. *Just like Che Guevara—*

The only time he balked was when Kawaji asked him to photograph Israeli military installations. To attack installations was a legitimate act; to photograph them was an act of espionage. "I'm a revolutionary," said Udi, "not a spy."

AFTER EIGHT DAYS in Damascus Udi flew back to Athens, and then Tel Aviv.

Shin Bet agents detained him at the airport. But no mention was made of Beirut or Damascus, and he was released.

Udi told Daoud about the airport interrogation. "Even if they cut me to pieces," Daoud said, "they will get nothing out of me."

THE MOST HATED MAN IN ISRAEL

THE KNOCK ON THE DOOR came at one in the morning. A dozen Shin Bet agents and policemen broke into the tiny Haifa apartment that Udi shared with his girlfriend, Leah. "Face against the wall!" someone shouted at her. Udi was blindfolded, hands bound.

It was December 6, 1972. That same night, Turki, Vered, and dozens of other suspects were arrested.

Udi was driven to a police station, escorted into an interrogation room. Two men confronted him. "We know all about Daoud's group and your visit to Damascus," one said. "Daoud has told us everything." *So much for the big revolutionary—*

Yet even without Daoud's confession, the Shin Bet had known about Udi and his friends. The secret service had first been alerted to Udi by his neighbor in Gan Shmuel, the brother of the martyred soldier Uri Ilan. Shin Bet agents had been watching Udi along every step of his descent underground.

One interrogator told Udi that "Abu Kammal" was really Habib Kawaji, an agent for Syrian intelligence. "You're naive, Udi, they were using you," he said.

For two days Udi said nothing. Then, on the third night, an interrogator threatened to arrest Udi's parents if he didn't cooperate. For the first time, Udi seemed frightened.

Finally his interrogators brought in Vered, who confirmed that he and Daoud had talked.

Udi was given a notebook and wrote. He described his trip to Syria and readily acknowledged the information he'd provided. Surely, thought Udi, that would prove he hadn't revealed any secrets.

BANNER HEADLINES ANNOUNCED the unthinkable: a joint Arab Israeli–Jewish Israeli terrorist underground against the Jewish state. Until now, Jews had feared subversion from Arab citizens. No one had imagined *this*.

"The Syrian spy ring," as the media was calling it, had caused "major damage" to the country's security, according to one report. The minister of police declared that the group had in fact been apprehended before it could do real harm, but the public wasn't calmed.

The shock and revulsion focused on Udi—kibbutznik, paratrooper, liberator of Jerusalem.

The right-wing opposition, headed by Menachem Begin, blamed the

Israeli left generally, for doubting Israel's historic right to the territories won in 1967 and calling them "occupied" instead of "liberated." Hashomer Hatzair leader Yaakov Hazan countered that for the last fifty years, his movement had stood on the front line of Zionism and the state of Israel.

One defender of Hashomer Hatzair was Yisrael Harel. We can't discredit a great pioneering movement because of a radical fringe, he argued with friends. Udi Adiv, he added, was nothing more than an *esev soteh*, an errant weed.

UDI'S PARENTS, Tova and Uri, sat in the police station, spared at least the humiliation of speaking to their son through a barred window.

"What were you thinking?" demanded Uri.

"Daoud misled me," Udi replied. "I thought I was connecting to the Palestinians, not the Syrians."

I've dragged them into something that will change their lives forever—

But self-recrimination quickly passed. Udi had no reason to regret anything. Uri and Tova, after all, were part of the colonialist system. For all their progressive pretenses, they too were hypocrites.

They parted without an embrace.

ON GAN SHMUEL, the rhythm of daily life continued. But the intactness was gone. Though Udi hadn't managed to actually commit any terrorist act, Gan Shmuel's members felt as if he had blown up the foundations of the kibbutz. Udi wasn't only the son of Tova and Uri, he was everyone's son. Shortly after Udi's arrest, one of the veterans died of a heart attack, and his family blamed Udi.

Once known as the kibbutz of the soldier who didn't betray, Gan Shmuel now became known as the kibbutz of the traitor. Gan Shmuel members were thrown out of stores; bus drivers refused to stop near the kibbutz.

At the weekly meeting, Gan Shmuel's secretary general, Ran Cohen, suggested that the kibbutz pay for Udi's lawyer.

Shimon Ilan, brother of the martyred soldier Uri, was outraged. Did Ran Cohen really expect the family of Uri Ilan to help subsidize a traitor?

"I'm as outraged as anyone by what Udi has done," replied Cohen, an officer in the paratrooper reserves and leader of a small faction that combined New Left politics with Zionism. Cohen detested Matzpen for compromising the patriotism of Israel's radical left, and he especially detested Udi.

Still, he continued, Udi's parents, Tova and Uri, were their comrades. "Uri was the first son born on the kibbutz. He is like one of the eucalyptus trees here. How is he supposed to raise money for a lawyer?"

The members voted overwhelmingly to subsidize Udi's legal defense.

URI AND TOVA made the rounds of trial lawyers and searched for character witnesses. Uri tried to meet with Hazan, but the leader of Hashomer Hatzair, whose door was always open to any comrade, refused to see him.

On Ein Shemer, the kibbutzniks maintained a discreet public silence. The newsletter didn't so much as mention Udi's arrest and Gan Shmuel's trauma—which was shared by the entire Hashomer Hatzair movement. Founded in pre-Holocaust Europe, Hashomer Hatzair had seen itself as a dignified alternative to the thousands of young Jews who were becoming Communists and abandoning their people at its most desperate time. Hashomer Hatzair despised Jewish revolutionaries who fought for all oppressed peoples but their own. How, then, could Hashomer Hatzair have produced an Udi Adiv?

Avital Geva took Udi's actions as a personal offense. Udi was guilty of what Avital considered the worst possible sin: ingratitude. Ingratitude toward the kibbutz that had raised and cherished him, toward the movement that had taught him his passion for social justice. Avital felt proud of having initiated Udi's expulsion from the paratroopers. "I had that honor," he said.

EARLY ON THE MORNING OF February 11, 1973, several hours before the doors opened, the crowds were already gathering outside the Haifa district courtroom. When Udi and five fellow defendants appeared shortly before nine o'clock, they were greeted with shouts, "Death to the traitors!" The defendants, handcuffed to each other, marched into the courtroom, singing, in Hebrew, an old Soviet song: "Off they went / the guys of the Red Army / off they went to work."

Of the thirty-two alleged members of the ring, six defendants, including Daoud and Udi and Dan Vered, were identified as leaders and tried separately. Udi and Daoud were each charged with espionage, treason, and transferring military secrets to the enemy. The maximum sentence was life in prison.

Head raised in defiance, Udi's demeanor conveyed the message to his three judges: You have no authority to try me; my very presence in the dock is an indictment against the Jewish state.

Sylvia Klingberg, Udi's old girlfriend from Matzpen, had been studying in England but flew back for the trial. Sylvia approached the defendants' bench. "I didn't spy for Syria," Udi said urgently. "I was trying to contact Palestinian revolutionaries." That was what passed for their reunion after a two-year absence.

Udi's younger brother, Asaf, came to the trial. Asaf had never been drawn to radical politics. But Israeli society had criminalized his family, and Asaf felt solidarity with Udi and his friends.

UDI TOOK THE STAND. His pose of contemptuous calm was gone. Red-faced, agitated, he seemed to finally realize the seriousness of his situation. He put aside the revolutionary rhetoric and tried instead to convince the court that he was no spy or terrorist, that he hadn't intended to kill his fellow citizens, that all he had intended was to bring peace and justice.

"Did you serve in the Six-Day War?" Udi's lawyer asked him.

"I was in the paratroopers' brigade that fought in Jerusalem," he replied. "The mission of my company was to reach the Rockefeller Museum. At a very early stage of the breakthrough the Jordanians began to shell us. . . . My job afterward in the war was to evacuate the wounded and the dead."

"Did this influence your worldview?"

"Definitely. . . . People died, and for what? For some holy places? I thought, This war is being fought at my expense. This isn't what I intended. I hardly even saw the enemy. My impression was that my friends and I need to listen to our inner voices and sacrifice our lives not for this but for some higher goal."

"The indictment against you includes charges of harming the state's security," noted his lawyer.

"All I wanted was to bring a revolution for the peoples who live here, the Jews and the Arabs. I didn't intend any harm to the security of the state. I wanted to do something positive and good."

Udi said he regretted going to Damascus. He had hoped to meet like-minded revolutionaries, but now realized he had been duped by Syrian intelligence.

JUDGE: You told [Kawaji] everything you knew about the army?
UDI: He asked what weapons I knew, and I told him.
JUDGE: You gave information on army bases?
UDI: Yes . . . [But] I didn't think I was revealing anything . . . I didn't imagine that what I know they don't know.

The prosecutor handed Udi a copy of the loyalty pledge recited by recruits to the IDF. Did you violate this pledge? he asked.

"I am loyal to my principles," replied Udi.

THE GHOST OF CHERKAS, the destroyed Arab village near Gan Shmuel, intruded. One of Udi's fellow defendants, Mahmoud Masarwa, was a son of Cherkas. His brother, Rashid, had once applied, together with his Jewish wife, for membership in Gan Shmuel; the kibbutz had turned them down.

Mahmoud told the court how in 1948 his father, along with other villagers, was expelled from his land. On the site, he said, a kibbutz factory was built.

ONE MORNING, JUST BEFORE the hearing resumed, a man approached the defendants' bench. "Do you know what people say at the end of every argument about you?" he said quietly to Udi. "They say: 'Adiv simply wanted to kill me.' The indictment claims that you wanted to blow up factories and attack military camps. Any one of us could have been killed in those places."

"No one would have been killed," replied Udi, defensive.

Another man joined in: "If you, Vered and Adiv, had devoted even a small part of your time to studying Jewish history, just an eighth of the time you devoted to Marxism, maybe you would have been less skeptical of the right of this state to exist."

"Yes," added a third man, "if you would have shown any interest in Jewish history, you would have realized that this state is the last stop in the journey of suffering of the Jewish people."

UDI AND DAOUD were found guilty on all counts.

In his statement to the court before sentencing, Udi said, "I feel I'm going to prison for many years. I didn't think that I would pay such a high price for my acts. I have no choice but to accept it." Then he added, "There was some amateurishness here. Any great historical change happens through the masses"—not through ideological elites. That was Udi's way of explaining that the creation of a terrorist group had been a mistake.

Udi and Daoud were each sentenced to seventeen years. Dan Vered, who expressed regret and called himself a fool, was sentenced to ten years.

Udi tried to think clearly: in seventeen years he would be—forty-four years old. He was beginning his sentence as a young man, an athlete, a ladies' man. He felt like someone who had just been informed of a fatal illness.

ISRAEL, SUMMER OF '73

THE BORDERS WERE QUIET. The war of attrition along the Suez Canal had ended. King Hussein had expelled the PLO from Jordan, and terrorists no longer crossed the Jordan River. The euphoria of the summer of '67 was long gone, but what lingered was a self-confidence—a cockiness—in the country's ability to defend itself against any threat. Palestinian terrorism had gone international, with airplane hijackings and a shooting spree by Japanese terrorists in Israel's Lod Airport. But the IDF was well prepared to cope. Israeli commandos had performed stunning feats, regaining control of a hijacked plane at Lod Airport and airlifting an intact Soviet radar station from Egyptian territory.

As existential fears eased, suppressed social tensions emerged. The most acute was the status of Israel's Sephardim, Jews from Muslim countries who formed over half the country's population. Many still lived in substandard housing projects built by an impoverished Israel in the 1950s. Sephardim were vastly underrepresented in the Labor-dominated political system, and their culture was largely excluded from mainstream Israel. The history of Sephardic communities was scarcely taught in schools, Sephardi music virtually absent from the airwaves.

A group of angry young men calling themselves the Black Panthers—a takeoff on the radical American group—initiated a mass protest movement. Ashkenazi Israel, they noted, has turned us into second-class Israelis.

Where are the Sephardi government ministers? Why are new immigrants being given decent apartments while we are still living in shabby projects? Why isn't Maimonides, the great medieval Sephardi philosopher, taught in schools? Why are the prisons filled with young Sephardim? We didn't return to Zion to be turned into urban waste but to be Jews in the land of Israel.

The Ashkenazi Labor establishment reacted with defensiveness and contempt. Golda Meir—who took over as prime minister following Levi Eshkol's death in 1969—dismissed the Panthers as "not nice." Jerusalem mayor Teddy Kollek told a group of Panther demonstrators outside the municipality to get off the grass.

FOR ALL THE FISSURES, the ingathering of the exiles back to the land of Israel was intensifying. Tens of thousands of Jews from the Soviet Union, the most sealed nation in the world, were being given exit visas. Young men in ill-fitting gray suits, old men with gold teeth and peddlers' caps, and old bent women in kerchiefs disembarked at Lod Airport with bound boxes for suitcases and squinted into the Israeli sun. It was, Israelis said, a miracle. Until the Six-Day War, Soviet Jews, subjected by the Kremlin to a policy of enforced assimilation, appeared lost to the Jewish people. But inspired by Israel's victory, Soviet Jews were now demanding the right to return to their ancestral homeland. "We will wait months and years, all our lives if necessary," wrote eighteen Jewish families from remote Soviet Georgia, "but we will never renounce our hopes and our dreams."

The borders of the Jewish national home were still unresolved. Most Israelis were convinced that a return to the pre–Six-Day War borders would only tempt the Arab world to once again try to destroy the Jewish state. Even in the left-wing Hashomer Hatzair the argument was where, not whether, to settle.

But the Labor government resisted right-wing pressure to open the territories to unlimited Jewish settlement. Instead, Labor confined its modest settlement building to areas with sparse Arab populations, like the Jordan Valley and the Sinai Desert. To the frustration of Yisrael Harel and Hanan Porat and Yoel Bin-Nun, government policy was to prevent Jewish settlement in most of the West Bank, in the hope of an eventual land-for-peace agreement with Jordan. No more than a few thousand Jews had been settled in all of the territories, including Sinai and the Golan Heights. Right-wingers bitterly accused the government of turning Judea and Samaria, the Jewish heartland, into *Judenrein*—"emptied of Jews," a Nazi term—territory.

Still, for most Israelis, ambiguity over the territories was hardly an acute problem. Israelis traveled without fear in the West Bank, and Palestinians traveled freely in Israel. Palestinian workers filled the country's construction sites and restaurant kitchens. It seemed, in the summer of 1973, that the status quo could go on forever.

PART THREE

ATONEMENT (1973–1982)

CHAPTER 15

BRAVE-HEARTED MEN

AN ORDINARY DAY

On the eve of Yom Kippur 1973, Arik and Yehudit Achmon drove to Kibbutz Mishmar Ha'Emek to spend the holiday with Yehudit's parents. On Yom Kippur, Arik complained, Tel Aviv turned into a ghost town. Yom Kippur was the one day a year that edgy, garrulous Israel withdrew into silence. There were no radio or TV broadcasts, no flights in and out of the small international airport, virtually no cars on the roads.

Israel's annual renunciation of the tumult of modernity left Arik unmoved. He connected deeply with historical holidays like Passover and Hanukkah, which marked the nation's liberation and which spoke directly to his own experience—and of course Independence Day, his favorite holiday, perhaps because of its simplicity, its celebration of existence itself. The holiday was immediately preceded by Memorial Day, and Arik would go from one military cemetery to the next, standing beside the graves of friends. Then, as evening set in and Memorial Day became Independence Day, Arik and Yehudit went to Mishmar Ha'Emek for the torch-lighting ceremony, followed by folk dancing in the dining room. Afterward they would join a small group of friends from the kibbutz and slip away to someone's modest house to sing the old songs and drink cognac, and Arik would boast about how well he held his liquor and then throw up. In the triumph of Independence Day over Memorial Day was the story of the Jewish people in the twentieth century and, for Arik, the greatness of Zionism. Death yields to life. No self-pity.

But of what relevance to Arik was a holiday asking forgiveness from a God in whom he didn't believe?

Yom Kippur confronted secular Zionism with the limits of its ability to desacralize Judaism and transform its holidays into celebrations of nation and nature. On Yom Kippur, there was no way to avoid how Jews had always understood their holidays: as moments of intimacy between God and His people. On Yom Kippur, the secular Zionist effort of re-creating the Jews as a nation like all other nations came undone.

IN THE EVENING, Hazan summoned Arik for a talk. Hazan had forgiven his son-in-law for taking Yehudit out of the kibbutz. In the end, family mattered more than ideology.

"What I'm telling you now is a secret," Hazan said grimly. "The prime minister just phoned. The situation is moving toward an explosion with the Arabs, and it's going to be very bad."

The call from the brigade came to Hazan's number. Whenever Arik slept even a night away from home, he made sure to call brigade headquarters and leave a number where he could be reached, just in case. Stay near the phone, Arik was instructed; an emergency call-up could be imminent.

Arik had recently been promoted to one of the brigade's two deputy commanders. And Motta Gur, now military attaché at the Israeli Embassy in Washington, had been replaced as commander of the brigade by Danny Matt, a veteran of the 1948 battle for the Etzion Bloc.

Two p.m., Yom Kippur day. Arik felt the ground shake: dozens of planes taking off from an air force base near the kibbutz. "That's it," he said to Yehudit; "it's begun." Shortly afterward, Hazan's phone rang: Arik was to report to the paratroopers' assembly point, a base near Tel Aviv.

Arik and Yehudit agreed she should remain on the kibbutz. Arik's daughter from his first marriage, Tsafra, and Yehudit's children from her first marriage, Gidi and Amira, were all in high school on Mishmar Ha'Emek. There was one complication: Arik's son, Ori, age nine, had come to stay with Arik and Yehudit, because Ori's mother, Rina, was in America with her husband. Now Arik was leaving Ori alone with Yehudit. How would the boy manage without his parents during war? "I have complete trust in your ability to cope," Arik told Yehudit.

SIRENS SOUNDED LIKE a premature blast of the shofar that ends the Yom Kippur fast. It was the fifth war in Israel's twenty-five years of existence. Israelis assumed it would end quickly, perhaps even more quickly than the Six-Day War. After all, the IDF was stronger now than it had been in 1967. Surely Israeli intelligence had detected the Egyptian and Syrian troop buildup and allowed them to enter a trap.

But there was no trap. There had been ample intelligence warning; the highly visible buildup had been reported by Israeli soldiers at the front. But military intelligence insisted that the Arab armies were merely engaged in autumn maneuvers, that the Arabs were too afraid of Israel to attack and could never win, and so there was no need to call up reserves.

The situation could hardly have been worse for Israel. Tens of thousands of Egyptian soldiers had crossed the 195-kilometer-long Suez Canal on rubber boats and makeshift bridges. Facing them were less than five hundred IDF soldiers spread out in sixteen underground forts that formed the Bar-Lev Line. One by one, those positions were falling. Barely 300 Israeli tanks in all of Sinai confronted 1,300 Egyptian tanks; after the first day of battle, less than a third of the Israeli tanks were still operative. On the northern front, the Syrians had penetrated the Golan Heights, and the odds against Israel were only a little less overwhelming than in the south.

Israeli planes trying to stop the invaders faced Soviet SAM missiles, whose electronic gear, unknown in the West, made them hard to detect. Israeli tanks were crippled by Saggers, handheld antitank missiles, another Soviet-supplied technology for which the IDF had no answers.

Israel could have lessened the disaster by launching a preemptive air strike on Yom Kippur morning, when Israeli leaders concluded that an attack was imminent. But Prime Minister Meir and Defense Minister Dayan had decided to absorb the first blow, to prevent Israel from being labeled the aggressor.

ARIK KNEW NONE OF THIS when he drove to his apartment in Tel Aviv to pack. Jeeps and cars sped through the empty streets. People gathered around transistor radios, listening to emergency news broadcasts that began with the solemn Yom Kippur greeting, "Gmar hatimah tovah," signifying the hope of being sealed in the book of life.

Arik retrieved uniform and boots from his closet. He debated whether to take the Kalashnikov. He'd acquired the Russian semiautomatic four years earlier, during the War of Attrition, given to him as spoil by one of his soldiers returning from a raid. The Kalashnikov—"Kalach" in IDF slang—was a far better weapon than the Uzi Arik would receive at the base, which lacked the Kalashnikov's accuracy and range. Fighting with an Uzi, he thought, was like taking a pistol into battle. Arik's Kalashnikov was especially fine, a lightweight commando-issue model whose handle folded for easy bearing. He hesitated: his men would be fighting with Uzis. He put the Kalashnikov back in the closet.

IN THE MOUNT Etzion yeshiva, the Yom Kippur tranquillity went undisturbed. Too isolated to hear the sirens, the yeshiva students spent the day in prayer. After leading the prayers, Yoel Bin-Nun felt ill and needed to rest. The sudden fatigue unsettled him. He'd never had a problem fasting before; why now?

Toward evening an emissary from the army reached the yeshiva. When the fast ended Yoel stood on a chair, and his students, in white shirts and white *kippot*, gathered around. "The Egyptians and the Syrians have attacked on both fronts," Yoel said, deliberately matter-of-fact. "Don't wait for a call-up notice. Start heading toward your collection points." He ended with the prayer: "May God protect your leaving and your returning, from now until eternity."

Rabbi Yehudah Amital, head of the yeshiva and a Holocaust survivor, said, "No doubt the army is already driving them back."

"The Bar-Lev Line has fallen," Yoel responded.

"How do you know that?" demanded Amital. "You don't know! Why are you demoralizing us?"

But Yoel was certain. He recalled a briefing his unit had been given from an intelligence officer, who had insisted that Israel would have a seventy-two-hour warning before an attack. And what if intelligence misread the signals, Yoel had asked, and there was no warning? Impossible, replied the officer. Yoel persisted: What if the impossible happened? It would be a disaster, said the officer.

The impossible had just happened. Somehow Israel had been taken by surprise.

Hanan Porat convened a meeting of the Kfar Etzion secretariat to delegate responsibilities, like organizing volunteers to help with the harvest in case the men remained in uniform for longer than a few days. They met in the home of Avinoam "Abu" Amichai, whose wife, Sandy, Kfar Etzion's American, was in a Jerusalem hospital recovering from the birth of their second child, a boy. Hanan mentioned to Abu that he didn't have a pair of army boots. Abu had an extra pair. The boots were a size smaller than Hanan's, but he took them anyway.

After the meeting, Hanan and Abu stopped by Yoel's house. All three young men were reservists in the 55th Brigade, though each belonged to a different battalion. Yoel packed his prayer shawl and phylacteries into the small bag he kept for reserve duty. Esther was pregnant with the Bin-Nuns' third child, but she wasn't due until January. Whatever happened, he would surely be out of uniform by then.

They drove to their base. Hanan said, "A war on Yom Kippur isn't just a war against the Jewish people but against God Himself."

Abu had more personal matters on his mind. "At least I know I can rely on the kibbutz to take care of the circumcision," he said.

THE WAITING TIME

THE RESERVISTS OF THE 55TH BRIGADE clustered under the shade of eucalyptus trees, exchanging rumors. Most of them were now in their late twenties and early thirties, married with children. Yisrael Harel, convinced that the IDF was on its way to imminent victory, told Abu, "You'll probably be home for the circumcision."

The men signed for equipment and discovered their first surprise: the stocks were so depleted that many were left without guns. Arik found a pair of binoculars, missing a strap. He affixed a piece of fraying string.

Why weren't the paratroopers being sent to the front? Not even the officers seemed aware of a plan. Don't worry, some reassured, we're being saved for the best assignment. Just like in 1967. Remember how we worried then that the war would pass us by?

By day two, the base began to smell like an outhouse. The toilets, meant for at most several hundred soldiers, had to accommodate over 2,000. Food supplies were running low.

MEIR ARIEL DIDN'T MIND the waiting. What was the rush to get to the front? He felt an exhaustion no sleep could ease. He'd barely recovered from the last war; perhaps a part of him had never recovered.

On Yom Kippur day he'd been sitting with a friend, a DJ for Army

Radio, working on a playlist for an album. At age thirty-one, Meir had finally put the trauma of *Jerusalem of Iron* behind him and was ready to try again. Then came the siren. "There goes the album," Meir had said.

Now, together with a friend, he left the base, walked up to a rooftop of a nearby apartment building, and smoked a joint.

INSIDE THE PIT, the IDF underground command post beneath the Defense Ministry compound in Tel Aviv, there was scarcely room to move. The low-ceilinged, cubicle-like rooms and narrow labyrinthine hallways were crowded with shouting officers, exhausted assistants sleeping on the floor, retired generals hoping to be useful. There was too much cigarette smoke. Like a nest of nervous ants, thought Arik. The main war room, meant to accommodate perhaps ten people, was filled with four times that number. Arik looked wordlessly at Danny Matt: *This* was the IDF at war?

They were searching for friends who could "give us work," as Arik put it, some assignment worthy of the paratroopers. But no one seemed to know what to do with them.

The chaos inside the Pit reflected the desperation at the front. By the second day of battle, the IDF hadn't yet managed to organize. Reservists were heading toward the two fronts, often without waiting for assigned units. In the fallen forts along the Suez Canal, there were rows of Israeli POWs, stunned and disheveled, with hands padlocked over their heads. On the Golan Heights, Syrian tanks were approaching the Galilee.

Danny and Arik found a friend, a senior commander. "You have twenty-five hundred paratroopers sitting on their asses," Arik said. "The army is wasting its greatest resource."

"You can't imagine what's happened here," the commander confided. "I can't even get to the chief of staff. He's surrounded by three circles of clowns."

"All we need is to get stuck in this mess," Danny said to Arik.

Arik felt grateful for Danny's presence. Tall, angular, red-bearded, Danny was a "*yekke*'s *yekke*," as soldiers called him, a stickler. But most of all Danny was calm under pressure. He had earned his reputation during the siege of the Etzion Bloc in 1948: as one of the soldiers sent to defend the kibbutzim, he found himself alone against dozens of Arab fighters; he fired his machine gun until the barrel bent from heat.

At a meeting later that night, Danny and Arik were presented with theoretical options. One plan was to dispatch the brigade into Syria, behind enemy lines, but the idea disappeared as abruptly as it had been raised. Another was to send the brigade across the Red Sea to attack the Egyptians from the south, but that too turned out to be baseless.

"They don't know what to do with us," Arik said to Danny. "They don't know what to do at all."

A SUKKAH IN THE DESERT

03:00, OCTOBER 9, day three of the war. Brigade officers roused the men curled beneath eucalyptus trees: We're moving south.

The soldiers boarded requisitioned tourist buses and were driven to the airport, where transport planes took them to Sinai.

Yisrael Harel tried to ignore the various pains in his body. There was a throbbing toothache. And a sprained back, result of an awkward fall during his last parachute jump, on assignment for his newspaper. He'd been writing a profile of a father and three sons, all paratroopers, who had jumped together as a family; Yisrael had joined them, and landed badly.

Yisrael prided himself on his realism, on not being taken by surprise, least of all by the world's enmity toward the Jews. Israel was fated to periodically fight for its life; that was just the reality of Jewish history. But unlike 1967, this time at least Israel was fighting from secure borders. Surely even the most fanatical leftists would now realize the danger of withdrawing from the territories.

THE PARATROOPERS ARRIVED in Refidim, the largest IDF base in Sinai, some fifty kilometers from the canal and outside the range of fighting. Dozens of bodies covered with blankets were lined on stretchers across the airfield, then loaded onto transport planes heading to Israel. Helicopters and requisitioned Arkia planes brought in the wounded.

Paratroopers were dispatched to patrol the desert hills above Refidim. There was talk of an attack by Egyptian commandos.

Yoel Bin-Nun's unit was sent to dig foxholes along the perimeter of the airfield. The men were incredulous: Why is the IDF turning us into guards?

With evening the desert chill set in, but the sand still retained the day's warmth. Yoel dug a foxhole about forty centimeters deep. How, he wondered, was he to fulfill the commandment to build a sukkah? It was the holiday of Sukkoth (Tabernacles). The sukkah was a reminder of the divine protection that accompanied the children of Israel in the Sinai Desert. The sukkah was also a reminder of fragility, a temporary structure recalling transience.

The laws for constructing a sukkah are precise: it must have at least two and a half walls and a roof covered with branches or other living material, not so dense that the stars are blocked. Where would Yoel get the material to build a sukkah? A religious Jew is obliged to eat all his meals in the sukkah; at home, Yoel even slept in it. And here he was in Sinai, where the children of Israel had built their sukkahs.

Yoel wandered the base, collecting material. He planted four sticks around his foxhole, and hung burlap as walls. But what to do for the roof? Since burlap came from flax, he reasoned, it could be considered living material and therefore suitable for the sukkah roof. He cut holes in the burlap so that stars could be seen, placed it over the poles, and recited: "Blessed are You, Lord our God, Master of the universe, Who sanctified us with his commandments and commanded us to dwell in the sukkah."

IN REFIDIM, YISRAEL HAREL met a photojournalist he knew, a foreigner working for one of the wire services. "Since when do journalists go to war?" the photographer said, surprised to see an editor in uniform. "This is the Israeli army," Yisrael explained. "Everyone serves."

"I've got a spare camera with me," the photographer said. "Why don't you take it and see what you shoot?"

Yisrael took the camera.

"If you survive, you can bring me the pictures after the war," the photographer said.

A GLIMMER OF A PLAN

DANNY AND ARIK drove to southern command headquarters, some forty kilometers from the canal. They were still far enough from the front to avoid Egyptian shelling.

At headquarters—a bunker built into the hillside—they found the same chaos that had prevailed in the Pit. Radio operators sitting at a long table shouted over each other to be heard. Officers crowded around a map of Sinai on the wall, trying to determine how far the Egyptians had penetrated and how many reservists had made it to the front. Papers were strewn on the floor. A friend of Arik's confided, "Dayan was here yesterday. You see these?" He pointed to the scattered papers. "His face was the same color."

The southern front commander, Shmuel Gorodish, who'd been appointed to the post shortly before the war, acted as if the IDF were facing the Egyptians of 1967 rather than an effective fighting force that had managed to launch a surprise attack. He said to Danny, "I have a job for you. You'll swat the Egyptians in 'Missouri' for me tomorrow night." Missouri was an Israeli position that had fallen to the Egyptians, and thousands of Egyptian soldiers were camped there. Gorodish's language of contempt for the Arabs seemed to Arik one more symptom of the IDF's confusion.

Gorodish called to an aide, "Get me Arik [Sharon] on the phone."

Rather than lift the receiver, he turned on the speakerphone, allowing everyone in the room to eavesdrop on what should have been a private conversation with Sharon, commander of one of the three IDF divisions in Sinai.

"Your friend with the beard has arrived," Gorodish said to Sharon, referring to Danny. Gorodish repeated his suggestion that Danny's paratroopers attack the Egyptian encampment in Missouri.

There was a long pause on Sharon's end. "Shmulik," Sharon said finally, using Gorodish's nickname, "the Egyptians have two hundred tanks there, and one thousand armored vehicles, and at least ten thousand soldiers. I don't think this is a job for my friend."

"Okay, we'll cancel," said Gorodish, with the same impulsiveness that had led him to suggest sending the paratroopers against overwhelming forces.

Sharon has just saved our lives, thought Arik Achmon.

DANNY AND ARIK rode in a propeller plane through the white wisps of a cold, foggy dawn. It was Friday, October 12, day seven of the war, and they had been urgently summoned back to Gorodish's bunker.

Sitting around the table were Sharon and his fellow division commanders. Danny and Arik took seats near the wall and listened.

There was good news. The government had approved a plan suggested by Sharon to cross the canal. Sharon's forces had discovered a breach between the second and third Egyptian armies camped in Sinai, through which the IDF might slip undetected and establish a beachhead on the other side of the canal. Once having crossed, the IDF would cut off the supply route to the Egyptian forces in Sinai and attack from behind.

The force that would lead the crossing, Gorodish said, would be the paratroopers of Danny Matt.

"Let Arik [Sharon] and the paratroopers do the dirty work," he told a commander skeptical of the plan. "You will cross with your tanks and reach Cairo."

Finally, thought Arik Achmon, a mission worthy of the paratroopers. Once again, they were being given the central task of the war.

A PRIVATE CONVOY

AVITAL GEVA FELT STRANDED. Wounded in 1967 before the paratroopers had even crossed no-man's-land, he'd missed the battle and vowed that would never happen to him again. But it was happening again. He was now commander of Company D, 28th Battalion—which just before Yom Kippur had been separated from the brigade and dispatched for reserve duty in Gaza. When war broke out, the company was told to remain there and enforce an IDF curfew.

Avital hated reserve duty in Gaza, its refugee camps with sewage running through the alleys and shacklike houses with corrugated roofs held down by cinder blocks. He managed the shift from kibbutznik and artist into occupier by consoling himself that the occupation was temporary, that when the right moment came, Israel would no doubt withdraw from Gaza. Until then, the IDF needed to be kept out of the political debate about the future of the territories.

But patrolling Gaza now? In the middle of a war? What were he and his men doing policing the shantytown alleys while the rest of the brigade was surely fighting at the front?

Avital convened his men for a talk. "It's a disgrace we're not under fire," one said, and others agreed. "Get us out of here, Avital. "

"I'll try to find a company to replace us," Avital promised.

He approached the military commander of Gaza. "I've got to get to my brigade," Avital said. When he saw he wasn't getting through, he added, "It's the *hevreh* that fought in Jerusalem."

"I'll take care of it," said the commander.

When Avital told his men the news, they embraced each other.

A replacement company arrived. The hundred men of Company D loaded three trucks with crates of ammunition and C-rations and crammed inside. Outside its radio range, Avital had no idea where the brigade might be. He assumed he would hear about their exploits along the road. He instructed his drivers to head west, toward the front.

ONLY TWO OF the sixteen Israeli forts near the canal remained under Israeli control: Budapest at the northern end, and the Pier at the southern end. Despite constant aerial bombardment and infantry assault, the two dozen men inside Budapest continued to hold out. But the Pier's defenders, out of ammunition, had decided to surrender. Either that, radioed the Pier's commander, or another Masada—a mass suicide.

Exhausted men emerged from the Pier carrying their wounded and dead on stretchers. A photograph of the surrender appeared in Israeli newspapers: it showed a bearded soldier bearing a Torah scroll, an image that recalled the helplessness of exile. The anti-image of the Six-Day War.

Yet for all the setbacks, the IDF was regaining momentum. On the Golan front, a few dozen Israeli tanks had stopped the Syrian advance and saved the Galilee. In the south, a vast reservist army had formed, much of it spontaneously, ready to take the offensive.

The songs on the radio were angry, determined, irreverent, reflecting the spirit in the field. It was Israel's first rock 'n' roll war. In the instant songs written for battle, the electric guitar displaced the accordion. "Don't worry, I'm being careful and wearing a sweater," a soldier writes his girlfriend in one song. "And between the shelling and the bombing there's even time to rest."

TO THE CANAL

BENT IN HOODED GREEN COATS against the cold desert night, Arik and a team of three dozen men gathered around maps in the prefab dining room of Sharon's headquarters. Danny had placed Arik in charge of planning the crossing, code-named Operation Brave-Hearted Men. It was set for 20:00, Monday, October 15.

Some of the men began nodding off. Arik, who himself hadn't slept more than four hours in the last two days, called a ten-minute break and told everyone to go to the faucet outside and wash their faces. "*Hevreh*, this is the moment," he said. "We're going to pull it off."

Everyone understood: the success of the war depended on this mission. If the fighting ended with substantial Egyptian troops on the Israeli side of the canal, and without an Israeli invasion on the Egyptian side of the canal, Egypt would have won. It would be Israel's first defeat, and the damage to Israeli deterrence and morale would be devastating. But if the paratroopers succeeded in establishing a beachhead that could be widened, the result would be an astonishing comeback, perhaps Israel's greatest victory.

So far, though, nothing was going according to plan. The two-hundred-meter roller bridge that was supposed to be stored near the canal and laid across it in time of war was twenty kilometers away and had broken down. Meanwhile another bridge was slowly making its way to the canal. This was a World War II–era bridge made of eight pontoons, each attached to massive cubes filled with polyethylene to keep it afloat. Each pontoon was laid on a flatbed trailer, pulled by a tank.

The plan now was for the paratroopers to assemble at a position along the Bar-Lev Line known as "the Yard," a stretch of sand at the point where the Great Bitter Lake fed into the Suez Canal and that had been flattened and protected by embankments for the eventuality of an Israeli crossing. The paratroopers would cross in rubber boats, then spread out and create a beachhead on the opposite shore. And then try to hold out until the pontoon bridge arrived.

Not quite a suicide mission, thought Arik, but better not to calculate the odds. To get to the canal the paratroopers would travel on an exposed road, within easy range of Egyptian fire. Even if the paratroopers made it safely to the Yard, Egyptians waiting on the other side could easily pick them off in the water. And even if they made it safely across and established a beachhead, the absence of a bridge to transport tanks and infantry reinforcements meant that the paratroopers would face an Egyptian counterattack alone.

Arik looked around the room. There was nowhere he would rather be than among these men. Civilians, but there were no more dependable sol-

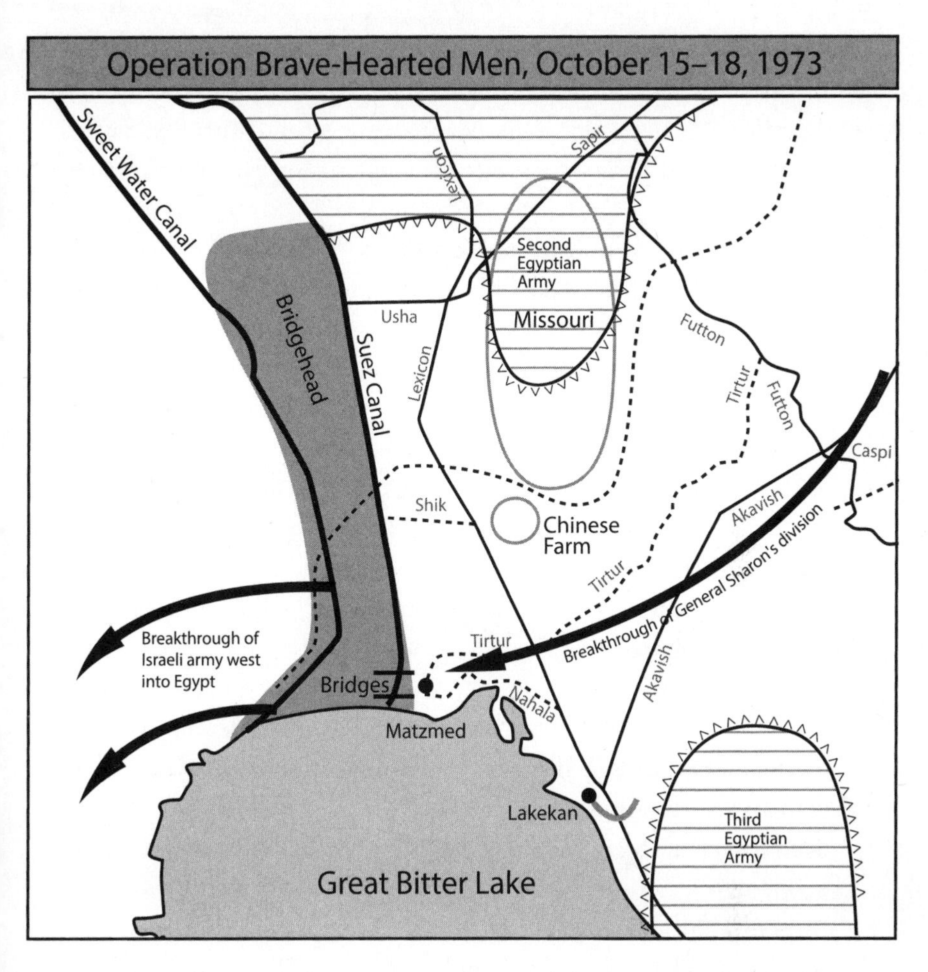

diers in any professional army. Men who didn't panic under fire, who charged without waiting for an order, who would risk their lives to evacuate a wounded friend. For all the screwups, the privilege of being one of them made it all worthwhile.

BUT HOW WOULD they get to the canal? When the brigade's quartermasters did an inventory they discovered only fifteen half-track personnel carriers, hardly adequate for even half a battalion.

The commander of the 71st Battalion, Dan Ziv, instructed one of his officers, Hanan Erez, to gather several dozen drivers, find half-tracks, and bring them back to the battalion's encampment on the sand dunes near the Refidim base. Ziv, a small man with great self-confidence, was a commander in the style of the old Unit 101. In the 1956 battle for the Mitla Pass, he had won a medal for driving into enemy fire and rescuing five wounded paratroopers.

"You have a single assignment," Ziv said to Erez, "and I couldn't care less where you find them. Above the ground, under the ground: find half-tracks."

"We're in the middle of the desert," Erez noted.

"If you don't have thirty-five half-tracks by fourteen hundred hours," said Ziv, "don't show your face in the battalion."

Erez found three dozen half-tracks parked in Refidim. The officer in charge refused to relinquish them without a signed order. Erez pointed his Uzi at the officer's chest. The half-tracks were released.

At 13:45, a caravan of thirty-five half-tracks led by Erez drove into the battalion's encampment.

DANNY GATHERED HIS OFFICERS. Israeli Phantoms flew fast and low.

"Whatever happens on the road," said Danny, "just keep moving toward the canal. Everything now depends on us."

Danny had one more request of Arik: that he join the first wave across the canal.

"I need you as my representative on the other shore," Danny said. He added, "I can't tell you to take this on."

"Of course," replied Arik.

YISRAEL HAREL, ASSIGNED to help direct traffic, approached Arik just as he was about to board a half-track. "I want to take your picture," Yisrael said. Both men understood the potential significance of the photograph.

Arik was forty years old, with thinning hair and sideburns. Binoculars hung around his neck on fraying rope. Squinting from exhaustion and single-minded focus, he tried to smile for Yisrael's camera. Instead, he managed only to open his mouth wide, as if there were something urgent he needed to say.

AT 16:30 THE MEN of the 71st Battalion, along with the brigade's command and an engineering company sent along for mine clearing, boarded the fifty half-tracks. All told, perhaps seven hundred men crammed into vehicles able to adequately accommodate half that number. Soldiers sat atop each other, to ensure their place in the crossing. "Can someone help me find my leg?" a young man called out.

Army chaplains distributed copies of the IDF's Prayer before Battle, and even many secularists quietly repeated the words: "Be with the soldiers of Israel, emissaries of Your people, who are going to war today with their enemies. Strengthen us and embolden us, fight our battles, hold the shield and rise up to help us."

Arik, accompanied by his radio operator and runner, boarded a half-track. Aside from his mini-entourage, he was, for the first time in many years, simply a soldier. For now he had no responsibilities; the brigade's other deputy commander was in charge of getting the convoy to the Yard.

The slow-moving half-tracks, led by a company of tanks, reached an intersection linking Sinai's two main roads. The entire IDF seemed stuck in the intersection: hundreds of flatbed trucks and buses and jeeps and ambulances and civilian vans drafted for the war effort, all seemingly honking at once and none of them moving. Unable to navigate sand dunes, the half-tracks were confined to the strip of asphalt.

Officers leaped from the half-tracks and pleaded, threatened, cursed. "We've got to get to the canal!" There were fistfights. One officer shot at the tires of a truck.

ARIK LOOKED AT his watch and fought despair: 20:00. They were supposed to be crossing the canal now. The convoy had finally cleared the intersection, but the traffic jam persisted. In the three hours since it had set out, the convoy had advanced barely four kilometers.

Arik sat beside the deputy commander of the 71st Battalion, a kibbutznik named Uzi Eilat. Legs pressed against his chest, Eilat told Arik, in a voice that suppressed emotion, "My brother was killed two days ago on the Golan." Arik listened in silence. "There's nothing to do but go on," Eilat added.

"You're right," Arik replied, wishing he had adequate words, "there's nothing to do but go on."

21:30. THE CONVOY reached the rendezvous point where the motorized rubber dinghies were waiting. The men loaded them onto the half-tracks, two on each vehicle. The boats were so heavy that a dozen men were required to lift each one. The soldiers crawled back into the half-tracks under the boats, which they held up as high as they could to deflect the sensation of smothering.

An empty road lay before them, expansive as the sands. Arik felt relief and foreboding: They'd reached the end of the Israeli line. From this point onward, they were on their own.

EXPLOSIONS SHATTERED THE SILENCE. The sky turned red and white. Just north of the road, barely two kilometers away, a terrible battle was under way. Dozens of tanks were burning.

The IDF's assault on the so-called Chinese Farm—an Egyptian agricultural station before 1967, where massive Egyptian forces had now concentrated—was intended to divert the enemy's attention from the paratrooper convoy and clear the road leading to the canal. Hundreds of Egyptian and Israeli tanks mingled blindly in the darkness, shooting at each other at point-blank range.

Several shells exploded near the half-tracks, but those appeared accidental. The convoy continued, undetected.

ARIK, LISTENING IN on the brigade's radio, heard the commander of the tank company leading the convoy, whose name was Yochi, request permission from Danny to join the battle. "My guys are fighting there," he said.

"Shalom," said Danny, releasing him. "Thank you."

Arik mentioned to Uzi, the deputy commander who had lost his brother, that Yochi the tank commander was heading toward the Chinese Farm. "Ah, that's Yochi?" said Uzi. "He's a friend of mine from the kibbutz."

Ten minutes later they heard massive explosions. The tank company had been ambushed. Among those killed was Yochi.

A PEACEFUL SHORE

ARIK INHALED THE SMELL of salt water. It was 01:00, five hours after the scheduled time for the crossing. The half-tracks entered into a large clearing fronted by high sand embankments: the Yard. Just beyond lay the dark, placid waters of the Suez Canal.

Soldiers rushed up the embankment, carefully raised their heads, and looked across the narrow waterway. In the light of a waning moon, they could discern reeds along the opposite shore, barely two hundred meters away. They opened fire, expecting a massive outburst in return. But from the other shore, only silence.

An explosion. "I'm hit!" someone cried.

Everyone fell to the ground. But there were no more explosions. A stray shell from the Chinese Farm. The paratroopers still hadn't been detected.

The injured soldier turned out to be Arik's runner, a kibbutznik named Amos. Arik checked his wound: shrapnel in the leg. "Nothing terrible," Arik reassured him.

"I'm afraid the war is over for me," said Amos.

Sweating despite the cold, the men unloaded the rubber boats. Arik joined a group dragging a boat filled with crates of ammunition up the steep embankment. The decline was even worse. The men continually slipped, and at any moment the boat seemed about to slide down and off into the water.

The first six boats were lowered into the canal. The men stood in the water, holding the boats steady to prevent them from drifting with the flow southward. The motors, covered with dust, failed to start. One boat began to sink. Engineers were summoned and within minutes all six boats, filled with paratroopers, were moving toward the western shore.

Arik, pressed against nine other men, watched the moonlight fragment in the gently flowing water. Though he wasn't wearing a jacket, he didn't feel the night's chill. He wished he could remove his ammunition belt, which he'd secured too tightly, and which was loaded with extra bullet clips that pressed into his stomach.

They can sink us now, no problem— But if there were Egyptians waiting, they were holding their fire.

The boats halted in a tangle of reeds.

A sapper laid explosives and blew a hole in the barbed wire fence. Engineers rushed through.

Paratroopers followed, firing as they ran. Still no return fire. They organized into two units and headed in opposite directions, to secure the immediate area. Two landing points, perhaps 150 meters apart, were marked with light reflectors mounted on stakes, to guide the next wave.

In the moonlight, Arik discerned mango and palm trees, reeds as tall as a man, a lushness stunning after the starkness of the desert. He felt almost welcomed.

Arik radioed Danny: The beachhead is secure.

THE RELAY OF rubber dinghies began, each crossing more efficient than the last. Within a few hours, some seven hundred paratroopers had crossed.

The paratroopers had slipped through undetected, but their luck was sure to end soon. Inevitably, the thousands of Egyptian soldiers on this side of the canal would find them. As the paratroopers widened their patrols, seeking to destroy bunkers and missile bases, they were inviting discovery. How long would they be able to hold out then, without a bridge in place to provide reinforcements?

Danny Matt and his staff crossed the canal. Arik greeted them. "Nothing can move us from here," he said.

THE BEACHHEAD WIDENS

05:30, OCTOBER 16, day one of the crossing.

Looking across toward the Yard, Arik saw bulldozers breaking through the embankment. Then, through the breach, plastic barges on wheels rolled into the water. Fastened together, they began ferrying tanks across the canal. The bridge hadn't yet arrived. But the army had found a temporary alternative: a dozen secondhand French-made amphibious rafts, able to hold a small number of tanks.

Arik guided the tanks to shore. All told, twenty-eight tanks were brought across—hardly the massive armored force envisioned in prewar scenarios of a crossing. Still, a beginning.

Danny dispatched three tanks to secure a nearby airfield that the Egyptians had turned into a logistics base. "Arik will go with you, he has a map," Danny said to the tank commander, Giora. Arik climbed atop Giora's tank and acted as guide, his body outside the hatch. "Don't fire randomly," he told Giora. "Our guys are patrolling."

Giora's tank led the way. Ten minutes later they came to a gate. The tanks turned onto the runway, firing at amphibious vehicles lined up alongside. The Egyptian soldiers seemed too stunned to return fire.

Arik ordered the tanks back toward the beachhead. "We'll send a unit to clean up later," he said.

As they tore through a thicket of reeds, Arik heard a gunshot behind him. Oil sprayed his back. A sniper had shot a jerry can affixed to the side of the tank.

A short distance later, Giora told Arik that he intended to rejoin his unit, which had meanwhile headed west, searching for missile bases. "I'll drop you off here," Giora said. "We're not far from the beachhead." In fact, they were a about a kilometer away, in an area where they had just been shot at. Arik wished Giora luck and began walking east.

AVITAL GEVA AND his mini-convoy had been on the road for two days and nights. They passed charred tanks and trucks, and dozens of sukkahs, some made of ammunition crates and covered with palm fronds.

Avital had heard of course about the crossing—everyone on the road was talking about it—and he was heading for the other side of the canal. But Company D's three trucks were stuck in a traffic jam that seemed without end. For long hours they simply stood still. Avital pleaded with drivers to let him pass: "We're trying to get to our brigade, the *hevreh* that crossed the canal." Brother, he was told, we're all trying to get somewhere.

The traffic jam was a purposeful surge, the anarchic expression of the IDF's remarkable comeback. Everyone was trying to go west, toward the front. The IDF's turnaround was due mostly to initiatives taken by field officers like Avital, who didn't wait for orders but did what they had been trained to do, what their instincts as IDF soldiers told them to do: seek out the Egyptians and push them as far back as possible from Israel's borders. Survivors of decimated tank units spontaneously created new units and returned to the inferno, waving from their turrets.

THE BATTLE OF GOG AND MAGOG

AT DAWN OF the second day of the crossing, a heavy fog covered both banks of the canal. Unlike the early-morning fog in Sinai, this fog lingered.

It cleared around 08:00. And then the shelling began. The paratroopers on the western coast of the canal had enjoyed thirty hours of relative quiet before the Egyptians realized they were facing a full-fledged invasion that threatened to cut off the supply route to their forces in Sinai. The Chinese Farm had still not been entirely cleared of Egyptian forces, and the bridge could not be safely brought to the Yard. Still, several thousand men, and several dozen more tanks, had managed to cross.

Arik was with Danny on his half-track, parked on a hill beneath the eucalyptus trees—"God's Little Corner," paratroopers were calling it. The sand erupted in explosions, and the two men leaped off the half-track into foxholes. When quiet returned, they lifted their heads and caught each other's eye. Wordlessly, they smiled and shrugged: Still alive.

PING-PING-PING OF STRAFING MIGS, whooshing streaks of Katyusha fire: thousands of explosives were fired at the four kilometers of the expanded beachhead.

As their men penetrated deeper into Egyptian territory, Danny and Arik confined themselves to the beachhead. There they faced a new danger. The Egyptians possessed a Soviet-made device that could detect the source of radio transmissions: within fifteen minutes of a broadcast from Danny's half-track, an Egyptian shell would crash at precisely the point where the half-track had stood. Danny and Arik were in regular communication with the paratrooper patrols. And so they needed to be in constant movement, day and night, driving in slow, repetitive circles. Like rabbits, thought Arik.

The brigade doctor ran with bloodied scissors from one foxhole to the other, oblivious to the shelling. One of the wounded was Arik's co–deputy commander of the brigade, Yehudah Bar, nicknamed "Yud-Bet."

Though a shell fragment had lodged in his arm, Yud-Bet insisted on remaining at the front.

Arik and Danny turned their instinctive reaction to their first shelling into a code: after a bombardment, they would look at each other, shrug, and smile.

THE EGYPTIANS TURNED their fire against the Yard, where thousands of soldiers and hundreds of tanks and supply trucks assembled, waiting to cross. Soldiers hid in craters formed by exploded shells and crawled under tanks. Trucks burned. The Death Yard, soldiers called it.

Two men were buried alive in foxholes. Danny ordered: From now on, foxholes must be no more than half a meter deep.

Hundreds of wounded were lined up on stretchers, waiting for long hours before half-tracks could risk transporting them to the rear. The bombardment was so intense that helicopters couldn't get close. The paratroopers in charge of the Yard barely slept. Their commander, Yossi Fradkin, kept himself awake by burning his arms with cigarettes.

A low-flying MiG appeared. Ariel Sharon, temporarily headquartered in the Yard, fired a machine gun at the plane. An explosion: Sharon's armored vehicle toppled into a crater. He emerged with a gash in his forehead. A medic bandaged him. A photographer caught the scene, and the picture of Sharon, bloodied bandanna around his head, became the iconic image of the war.

FOR TWO DAYS AND NIGHTS, Yoel Bin-Nun had been waiting with his unit on a sand dune for half-tracks to retrieve them and bring them to the canal. The men sat beneath a camouflage tent, listening to explosions in the distance and news updates from transistor radios. They were so close to the canal that Yoel could discern the blurred outlines of the Great Bitter Lake, just south of the Yard. But the war seemed to have forgotten them.

For the first time since the war began, Yoel had ample time to contemplate its meaning. Of course the war had meaning: It was, in essence, a spiritual war. He tried to piece together the pattern. The Jewish people attacked on its holiest day, devoted to purification and atonement. A total war, with the most massive tank battles since World War II. Two nuclear superpowers fighting by proxy. The entire world economy threatened by a new weapon—an Arab oil boycott against the West. What else could this be, if not the beginning of Gog and Magog, the final battle before redemption?

Yoel had received a postcard from his father, who expressed similar thoughts: Let's hope, wrote Yechiel Bin-Nun, that the prophecies concerning the woes of the end times have already been fulfilled in the Holocaust and that the Jewish people will be spared further suffering.

Gathered in a corner beneath the camouflage tent, a small group of religious soldiers prayed together. They repeated a Sukkoth hymn to the messianic era, "Kol Mevaser Mevaser V'omer": "The voice of the herald brings good tidings and proclaims: Your mighty salvation comes. My Beloved is coming."

ON ANOTHER SAND DUNE, Hanan Porat and his unit were also waiting to be moved west, to the canal.

It was the eve of Simchat Torah, the end of Sukkoth, celebrating the completion of the weekly reading of the annual Torah cycle. Hanan and the other religious soldiers finished their evening prayers. Though Simchat Torah is one of the happiest days of the Jewish calendar, marked by hours-long dancing with Torah scrolls, no one felt like forming a circle. How to dance in proximity to death?

A friend of Hanan's from his Mercaz days, Menachem Davidovich, called out, "*Hevreh*, it's Simchat Torah! Why are you sitting around like golems?" He grabbed Hanan by the hand and began dancing. Reluctantly, others joined and formed a circle, their heavy boots sinking in the sand. Hanan tried to ignore the pain in his feet, a result of the too-small boots he'd borrowed from Abu.

Menachem sang, "Behold, I am sending you Elijah the Prophet," herald of the Messiah. Hanan closed his eyes and tried to recall the majesty of Simchat Torah in Mercaz: the strong young men holding aloft silver-crowned scrolls as circles of dancers surrounded Rabbi Zvi Yehudah, whose vigorous clapping urged them on to more determined singing, repeating the same lyrics until they lost all sense of time, until Israel's ancient glory and modern resurrection merged like the beginning and the end of a circle.

AVINOAM "ABU" AMICHAI, Hanan's friend from Kfar Etzion, had been among those who had crossed the canal on the first night of Operation Brave-Hearted Men. He'd been on patrol ever since, helping to widen the beachhead. He hadn't made it back home for his son's circumcision after all.

On Simchat Torah he had helped secure a ramp—one of several long and high mounds of earth built by the Egyptians to overlook the canal. On Thursday evening, just after the holiday ended, Egyptian commandos attacked the ramp, firing RPGs and machine guns. They attacked the northern end; Abu, stationed on the other side, rushed toward the shooting. The Egyptians were pushed back. When the fighting ended, paratroopers found the bodies of four of their friends, among them Abu's, with a bullet in his forehead.

THE NEXT MORNING, Hanan Porat crossed the canal on a rubber float. He hadn't heard that Abu had fallen.

Almost as soon as Hanan and his friends stepped onto the opposite shore, they were hit by an artillery attack. Hanan looked up and saw a missile fell an Israeli Phantom jet.

Hanan's company turned north toward the city of Ismailia. They came to an abandoned village of mud huts. A mortar bombardment: it happened so suddenly that Hanan had no time to hit the ground. An 82-millimeter shell crashed into his right shoulder and then, astonishingly, bounced off. Hanan flew backward. Another shell exploded, filling his chest with shrapnel. His rib cage was shattered, his chest torn open.

Friends tried to stop the bleeding with bandages, but the flow was too strong. Someone ripped off Hanan's shirt and tied it tightly around his chest, and that stanched the wound. Hanan was lowered into an irrigation ditch. Explosions sprayed him with sand.

Gasping for air, he remained conscious. He didn't feel acute pain, only a sense of seeping away. *I'm going to die—* He said good-bye to his wife, Rachel, his three-year-old daughter, his one-year-old son. He thought he heard the soothing words of the Friday-evening prayer: "A Psalm for the Sabbath day. It is good to praise God and to sing to Your Name, to proclaim Your kindness in the morning and Your faithfulness in the night."

He was lifted onto a half-track. Through the shelling, Hanan made it across the canal on a raft. From the Yard he was flown by helicopter to the field hospital in the Refidim base. A medic spoke to him without letup, to keep him from losing consciousness. *Why is he driving me crazy with all this talk?*

Heaving, he was rushed off the helicopter. "We have to do it now," he heard a doctor say, and, without anesthesia, a catheter was jammed into his chest. Hanan went wild with pain. And then he began to breathe again.

MENACHEM DAVIDOVICH, who had led Hanan and the other soldiers in dancing on Simchat Torah, was killed by an artillery shell shortly after crossing the canal.

THE BEACHHEAD STANDS

AVITAL GEVA AND the men from Company D reached the Yard. They crossed the canal on rubber floats and found part of the 28th Battalion camped in a mango grove. Avital greeted his friends with hugs. "*Ya Allah*," said Avital, "you can't imagine how good it is to see you, you can't *imagine*."

The battalion, Avital was told, was about to head south toward Suez City, to cut off the supply lines of Egyptian troops in Sinai. The war was still before them. But for now, here he was, drinking Turkish coffee with the *hevreh* at a campfire in an orchard.

THE BRIDGE WAS pulled into the Yard and laid across the canal. Significant reinforcements began moving into Egypt. Paratroopers posted a handwritten sign on the western side of the canal: Welcome to Africa.

YOEL BIN-NUN and his friends reached the Yard on Shabbat morning, October 20.

They approached the bridge. Bolts of light exploded around them. Yoel burrowed into the shallow indentations left by tank treads. The sand exploded in another round of Katyushas. "Shema Yisrael," he silently recited the prayer before death, "Hear Israel, the Lord Our God, the Lord is One."

The explosions ceased. *Still alive—*

He crossed the bridge and entered Africa. Another barrage of exploding light. Yoel lay on the ground. A Katyusha hit a palm tree, and splinters flew around him. He repeated the Shema.

The unit proceeded northward, toward Ismailia.

They entered a village of mud huts. Roosters wandered the empty dirt road. Behind him, in the distance, Yoel heard the explosion of Katyushas.

TOGETHER WITH DANNY, Arik shuttled between either end of the beachhead along the western shore of the canal. He hadn't washed, shaved, or changed clothes in days. He slept only for a few minutes at a time, usually on the half-track.

Arik's tendency to suppress emotion, often a liability in civilian life, helped him cope now. He could ignore at will the carnage around him, focus on problems that required solutions. Like what to do with a friend who had been assigned to the Yard and who, Arik was convinced, was suffering from shell shock. Arik's friend complained that the commander of the Yard was persecuting him, denying him shelter during the shellings. Consulting with a doctor, Arik concluded that the best way to treat shell shock was to keep the soldier at the front until it passed and that sending him home prematurely would only deepen the trauma. Arik told his friend, "You're staying at the beachhead, but with me," and he brought him back to the Egyptian side of the canal.

TWO MIG-21S FLEW LOW over the beachhead, then shot straight up, somersaulted, and dived, firing rockets. Two Israeli Mirages brought them down.

Danny and Arik watched the dogfight from their half-track in the eucalyptus orchard. One of the Egyptian pilots parachuted and landed about a kilometer away. Limping and disoriented, he was captured and brought to Danny, who ordered the pilot checked by a doctor.

The pilot, a colonel, turned out to be the commander of an air base. When he realized that his side had lost the war, he explained, he'd decided to go down fighting. An enemy worthy of respect, thought Arik.

Afterward, Arik heard that one of the paratroopers had stolen the pilot's watch. Arik summoned the offender. "In my command, we don't take watches," he said, and ordered the watch returned. But Arik did take the pilot's handsome pistol as a memento.

THE FINAL BATTLE

ARMORED TROOP CARRIERS confiscated from the Egyptians transported Avital Geva's company to the southern outskirts of Suez City. The paratroopers had been dispatched there for "adjustments," a last attempt to take the city before a final cease-fire. It was an area of warehouses; burning containers released the smell of scorched oil. Just beyond rose sand-colored apartment buildings, many half built, in which Egyptian soldiers waited.

The battalion's company commanders met in a deserted apartment on the outskirts of town with the commander of the tank unit that would offer cover to the paratroopers as they conquered Suez City, house by house. The tank commander, Ehud Barak, had been one of Israel's leading commandos; dressed as a woman, he had been part of a unit that had assassinated PLO terrorists in Beirut. Avital, who knew Barak from reserve duty, greeted him with a hug.

The commanders sat on the floor, eating canned meat and corn. "There's no reason to rush," said Zviki Nur, commander of the paratroopers' 28th Battalion, "the city is surrounded. We're going to do this slowly but surely. First, Ehud's tanks will fire on enemy positions, and only then do we go in. No adventures."

Avital led his men, in groups of three, toward the first row of apartment houses. He had to be especially alert now. In a few hours, the rumor went, a cease-fire was going to be declared, and the last hours of a war, when soldiers lowered their guard, were the most dangerous of all.

A tank fired at a building. Avital ran through the smoke, shooting into the debris. But the building was empty; the Egyptians had fled. No one wanted to die in the last hours of a war.

The pattern was repeated. A tank fired, paratroopers entered, no resistance.

One bloc after another fell. The Egyptians regrouped in the center of town.

12:00. AVITAL HEARD THE ORDER on the radio: All forces cease fire. He and his men were in houses on one side of a wide, empty avenue. Egyptian soldiers were in houses across the street.

Tentatively, men on either side emerged. For a long moment, the Israelis in their olive green uniforms and the Egyptians in their khaki uniforms looked at each other. But no one fired a shot or aimed a weapon.

Spontaneously, soldiers from both sides ran into the street. They smiled and shook hands. An Israeli and an Egyptian embraced. There were shouts of joy.

Avital told himself: Be clearheaded! What if the cease-fire suddenly collapsed? What if an Egyptian opened fire?

He ran into the street. "*Hevreh*, have you all gone crazy?" he shouted. "Get back! Get back!" Reluctantly, his soldiers retreated. Egyptian officers were also shouting at their men to disengage. UN soldiers in blue helmets appeared and took up positions between the two forces.

CHAPTER 16

"OUR FORCES PASSED A QUIET NIGHT IN SUEZ"

THE WAR ENDS, AND CONTINUES

THE IDF HAD beaten back invaders on two fronts under the worst conditions it had faced since the War of Independence, brought the battle into enemy territory ten days after the invasion, and extended its reach to within ninety-five kilometers from Cairo and thirty-five kilometers from Damascus.

Yet the people of Israel felt defeated. The initial disarray had shattered Israeli self-confidence. For the first time since 1948, Arab armies had taken the initiative. In eighteen days of combat in Sinai and on the Golan, Israel lost over 2,500 men, a quarter of them officers, along with over 7,000 wounded—the largest number of casualties in any war since 1948. For a population of three million, the losses were devastating. Everyone seemed to know someone who had fallen. Once again, the toll was especially high on kibbutzim.

The 55th Brigade had led the most daring operation of the war and then endured sustained bombardment—more intense, said Danny Matt, than in any battle in World War II. Yet the brigade survived relatively intact, losing fifty-seven men (along with three hundred wounded)—half the number of its fatalities in the battle for Jerusalem.

Along with grief came rage. The Labor Zionist leadership had led the Jewish people through the twentieth century, remained steady through war and siege and terrorism, through waves of mass immigration and economic devastation. Until now. How had the pioneer statesmen and their hero generals become so complacent, so arrogant, that they had failed to notice the growing strength of Arab armies and the prewar buildup on the borders?

The world had never seemed to Israelis a more hostile place than it did in late October 1973. The Arab oil boycott, which punished pro-Israel countries with a suspension of oil deliveries, pressured Third World countries to sever relations with the Jewish state, while panicked European governments suddenly discovered the Palestinian cause. Only two countries—the United States and Holland—stood with Israel. And who knew for how much longer? The whole world is against us, Israelis told each other. This fatalism about "the world" was a negation of Zionism, which had aimed to restore the Jews not only to Zion but to the community of nations. Gone now was the Zionist challenge to outwit the curse of Jewish history. The war that began on Yom Kippur threatened the secular Zionist dream of a normal Jewish state, a nation among nations, and seemed to return Israel back to Jewish fate.

ARIK ACHMON STOOD with folded arms and shook his head in disbelief as UN supply trucks drove through Israeli lines on their way to the besieged Egyptian soldiers of the Third Army. Another few days, he thought, and we would have forced the Egyptians to surrender.

The Israeli government had yielded to American pressure to prevent another humiliating Egyptian defeat. The Americans were hoping that if a stalemate were created, peace talks might result. Yet many of the men of the 55th Brigade felt betrayed. They had turned the war on the southern front in Israel's favor. But the government that had failed to prepare for war and ignored warnings of the surprise attack, that had delayed a reservist call-up and vetoed a preemptive strike, had now committed its final folly.

Despite the cease-fire, sporadic shooting continued along the Egyptian and Syrian fronts. Reservists had been demobilized immediately after the fighting ended in the Six-Day War, but this time they were kept at the front. No one knew for how long. The men set up tent encampments in the agricultural belt on the "African" side of the canal, took over abandoned houses in Suez City, and prepared for a long winter.

Arik moved into Danny's headquarters in an Egyptian army bunker. It was cold and damp and infested with gnats. "The Holocaust cellar," they called it, after a museum of that same name on Mount Zion in Jerusalem.

THE MIRACLE MAN

HANAN PORAT AWOKE, delirious, from a ten-hour operation. "I just saw Abu," he told his wife, Rachel, standing by his bedside. "We danced together on Simchat Torah." In fact he hadn't seen his fallen friend since the first days of the war.

Part of Hanan's shoulder, where the missile had hurled into him, was gone. His surgeon showed him a fist full of metal. "This came from your chest," he said. There was more shrapnel that hadn't been extracted. Hanan's shattered ribs were tightly bandaged, and he could hardly move. Volunteers working the wards placed phylacteries on his arm and head.

As he regained focus, Hanan felt a sense of wonder. His survival, doctors agreed, had been miraculous. No one could remember a story quite like it. A shell bouncing off his shoulder? By thrusting him in the air, away from the blast, that initial crash of the shell had saved his life.

Leaders of the religious Zionist camp came to visit. Rabbi Shlomo Goren, the former IDF chief chaplain and now the country's chief rabbi, told Hanan that he was privileged to be wounded in the service of Israel. Hanan replied, "You, rabbi, were more privileged than even the Macabees. It took them a year to announce the miracle of Hanukkah. But when you blew shofar at the wall, you were announcing the miracle the same day." Goren laughed appreciatively.

Asked what he'd thought about in those moments just after his injury, Hanan replied, "I thought, 'So another one is being added to those who gave their lives for the Jewish people.' "

THE BARD OF SUEZ CITY

MEIR ARIEL'S UNIT was patrolling along the shore of Suez City when it came upon a bunker. Booted feet protruded from the aperture.

Meir and a friend crouched and entered. Inside, five Egyptian soldiers were asleep. *"Brah!"*—Out!—shouted Meir in Arabic. The dazed Egyptians lined up. Meir ordered them to empty their pockets. One produced a tag from an Israeli uniform. Meir and his friend looked at each other: he'd obviously taken it from a soldier's body, probably in one of the outposts of the Bar-Lev Line. Meir pointed his gun, finger on the trigger.

His friend was surprised to see him acting so decisively, so *military*. Any sudden move from the Egyptian, it seemed, and Meir would have fired.

IN MID-NOVEMBER ANOTHER CEASE-FIRE was negotiated, this time directly between Egyptian and Israeli officers. It was a hopeful moment: the first face-to-face negotiations between the two adversaries since the 1949 armistice.

But for Meir and his friends, living in an abandoned youth hostel in Suez City, the cease-fire simply meant a reduction in the level of fighting. Every so often, the Egyptians would remember the Israelis across the way and fire a single mortar, and Meir's crew would fire a single shell back.

Life in Suez City settled into routine. There was guard duty and hunting expeditions for sheep and calves to roast at the campfires where the stubble-faced men in woolen caps chain-smoked and argued into the night about the government's failures and sang the old songs, already nostalgic for a fading Israel.

Meir taught the men his songs. They sang "Legend of the Lawn," about teenage love in the midst of the entangled collective: "There's a pile of *hevreh* on the grass . . ." Someone suggested a post–Yom Kippur version: "There's a pile of grass on the *hevreh* . . ."

The men loved "our Meir," this pure soul who never argued or gossiped or raised his voice, who listened to their woes and was always ready with a kind word or, when words seemed inadequate, a sad empathic smile. *"Az mah, hevreh? b'sach hakol . . ."* (So what, guys? After all, it's only . . .), he said after a shelling, not bothering to complete the sentence. One of the men lost his home leave and was inconsolable; Meir held him until he calmed.

But as the weeks went on, Meir became withdrawn. Let him be, the men said to each other.

Meir was brooding over Tirza. As soon as he returned home from the war, she intended to leave for America to try her luck as an actress. She was beautiful, she had learned English in Detroit, and while doing some modeling in Tel Aviv, she'd met an American movie producer who offered to be her patron. Meir was devastated. He loved Tirza madly, which was the only way to love Tirza, the only way Meir could love. She said she'd be gone for a year. But who knew what could happen in a year?

It wasn't only Tirza. His life moved between army and kibbutz, communal impositions. He showed no anger, only what one friend described as a sad stillness.

The strap of his gun tore, and Meir didn't bother replacing it. He gripped the gun by its barrel, carrying it as an afterthought. One day, on patrol with his jeep, Meir suddenly called out, "I need to go back, I forgot something." The jeep pulled up in front of the hostel, and Meir ran inside and reemerged with his gun.

A friend from home sent Meir marijuana, along with seeds, and he planted those beside the hostel. When he stepped outside "for a smoke," even his commander didn't interfere.

One of the men confided to Meir that he feared he was going to die in Suez City. Wordlessly Meir produced a joint, the only comfort he could manage.

MORNING LINEUP IN the courtyard of the hostel. Thirty helmeted men stood at ease in a ragged row, reservist style. The daily inspection: Were the guns oiled? Bullet clips filled?

Strap hanging from his helmet, bootlaces open, Meir dragged his gun on the ground behind him and joined the line.

"Meir," said the commander sympathetically, "I have a suggestion. Why don't you bring your guitar for inspection?"

The next morning Meir showed up with gun and guitar. "Are the strings properly tuned?" the commander asked.

"Everything is in order," replied Meir.

AVITAL GEVA ENCOUNTERS YOEL BIN-NUN

EVEN IN SUEZ CITY, joked Avital's men, our commander can't resist doing an art project. Avital's "art project" consisted of laying strips of camouflage across the facade of the abandoned school where the hundred men of Company D had camped. He extended the cloth to the facades of nearby buildings occupied by other units. Then his men broke down the side walls, allowing soldiers and jeeps and even tanks to pass between the buildings, out of sniper sight.

With the new cease-fire, tensions eased. For the first time Avital could begin to think about the war. The sin of arrogance: Israel had really thought it was invincible. Golda and Dayan had assured that the new borders would keep Israel safe. But those borders had induced the very smugness that almost destroyed Israel on Yom Kippur. Why hadn't Israel's leaders aggressively pursued peace, checked every rumor of Sadat's readiness for negotiations, instead of dismissing and suspecting—waiting, as Dayan had put it, for a phone call from Arab leaders?

Peace, Avital now knew, was possible. Egyptians and Israelis had greeted each other, embraced, on the streets of Suez City. Avital had acted then as a responsible officer, protecting his soldiers from danger. But there had been no danger, only exhausted men celebrating their common humanity. How could enemy soldiers turn in an instant into friends? Apparently the Middle East could yield surprises that weren't only destructive but redemptive. Avital had seen a miracle. A vision of the end of days.

ONE SHABBAT MORNING, while visiting friends in the hostel, Avital heard a bearded young man with a knitted *kippah* speaking to a group of soldiers, evidently teaching some kind of class. The young man swayed slightly as he spoke, pulling the edges of his beard. Avital wasn't sure what he was talking about, something about the Torah reading of the week. But it wasn't the words that attracted him, but rather the bearded man's evident empathy. When someone argued a point, he tilted his head, listening with the same intensity, it seemed to Avital, with which he'd spoken. Someone who could take another's arguments as seriously as he took his own seemed to Avital worth knowing.

When the class ended, Avital approached Yoel Bin-Nun. "Listen, my *hevreh* are going crazy with boredom," Avital said. "Why don't you come by Company D and teach something about, you know, the Torah?"

And so the next Shabbat, after completing his morning prayers, Yoel went to the school. Avital greeted him with a hug; Yoel allowed himself to be embraced.

A dozen men sat on cots. Avital joined them. He felt like a child, ignorant of Judaism and eager to learn.

The Torah reading, Yoel explained in his deep voice, was about Joseph and his brothers. "*Hevreh*, look how beautiful this is," he enthused, and read a few verses from his pocket-size Bible. The descent of the children of Israel into Egypt had begun through an act of hatred: Joseph being sold into slavery by his brothers. That triggered a process in which the tribes of Israel were eventually enslaved. The redemption of the Jews would come, Yoel said, when they learned to love each other. And now we are back in the land of Egypt, secular and religious, correcting the sin of our last sojourn here. When we are united, redemption is possible.

Avital didn't know if the Jews had been chosen for some special destiny, if the Torah contained clues to understanding Israel's situation, if there was a God at all. But in Yoel's presence Avital felt, if not quite faith, then peace.

Avital's men confronted Yoel with their questions about God and their resentment toward the rabbinical establishment.

"I'll make you a deal," a kibbutznik said. "If you succeed in convincing me that God exists and that there is a divine hand guiding the world, I'm ready to become religious. But if I succeed in convincing you that it's all nonsense, then you'll become secular."

"You're asking me to give up my deepest beliefs," Yoel replied, smiling. "Let each person observe and interpret in his way, but the Torah belongs to every Jew. Shabbat belongs as much to you as it does to me."

"Listening to you," Avital said to Yoel afterward, "I feel half religious."

LATE AT NIGHT, Yoel and Avital sat on the upper floor of the abandoned school where Company D was camped and, wearing coats against the bitter wind that seeped into the unheated building, argued about the future of Israel. It didn't matter that Yoel was a corporal and Avital a captain, or for that matter, that Yoel was a scholar and Avital didn't know the most basic prayers. Somehow it didn't even matter that Yoel was a settler for whom annexing the territories was part of the redemption process, while Avital was a kibbutznik for whom withdrawing from the territories was the hope for peace.

They agreed about this: Israel's survival required moral renewal. "What I love about you, Yoel," said Avital, "is that you don't speak about rolling heads like the others here. 'Golda has to go, Dayan has to go, Gorodish has to go.' You're speaking about moral transformation."

"We need the moral vision of the kibbutz," Yoel said.

"Yoel, *habibi*, you should be prime minister."

YISRAEL HAREL UNDER FIRE

DANNY MATT ASKED Arik Achmon to prepare a report of the brigade's actions in the Yom Kippur War, as Israelis were calling it, just as Arik had done in the summer of 1967 about the battle for Jerusalem.

The assignment meant interviewing dozens of officers and soldiers. Arik asked Yisrael Harel to be his assistant. Not that Arik expected much help from him. *He's not a real fighter, he doesn't understand war—* Still, Arik liked Yisrael, his partner in helping bereaved families, and he'd enjoy the company.

Yisrael was thrilled. On home leave, he bought, for interviews, the latest model of tape recorder with his own money. Yisrael referred to himself as Arik's partner. When Yisrael wasn't around, Arik referred to him as "the tape carrier."

Danny moved headquarters from the "Holocaust cellar" to an abandoned Egyptian army base in the agricultural belt. Arik, who knew how important it was for Yisrael to be among the powerful, invited him to sleep in the officers' quarters, though Yisrael only held the rank of sergeant.

"Get him out of here," demanded a friend of Arik's, repeating a common sentiment among the officers. "He doesn't belong among us."

Arik refused. "He's the chief education officer, he's working with me, and he will have the status of an officer," he said.

ARIK AND YISRAEL traveled to the brigade's outposts along the patchwork front, interviewing reservists.

In Suez City Arik went to see a friend in the youth hostel. There he found Meir Ariel lying on a mattress on the floor, strumming his guitar. Arik expected Meir's usual effusive greeting. But Meir seemed withdrawn.

"What's with Meir?" Arik asked Meir's commander.

"He just misses home, like everyone," the commander replied. "He'll be okay."

Arik knew that Meir wasn't like everyone. And he wasn't at all sure that Meir would be okay.

ARIK AND YISRAEL sat on a rooftop in Suez City, drinking coffee with officers who had secured the Yard on the night of the crossing. They could clearly see Egyptian positions barely a hundred meters away. But the front had quieted, and no one felt the need to sit behind sandbags.

After the interview, Arik and Yisrael walked down the stairwell, back toward their jeep. Just as Yisrael was passing a window, a mortar shell, and then two more, exploded in the courtyard. The window shattered. Yisrael cried out. Arik, a few meters behind him, rushed down the stairs.

Yisrael leaned against the wall. Arik checked his head and torso: clean.

A medic ran up the stairs. He pulled down Yisrael's pants: a few metal and glass fragments in his thighs. You don't die from this, thought Arik.

There was a flow of blood. Flesh wounds, reassured the medic.

Yisrael was quiet, and Arik appreciated his restraint. "*Yihyeh b'seder,* Yisrael"—It will be okay—Arik reassured him, putting his hand on his friend's shoulder.

Arik and the medic carried Yisrael to the jeep and rode with him to a field hospital. "In a few weeks you'll forget it," the doctor told Yisrael.

When Arik returned to officers' quarters, he announced to his friends, laughing, "*Hevreh*, you won't believe it, but Yisrael Harel has just earned his Purple Heart."

FAR FROM HOME

A TRAUMATIZED ISRAEL resumed the motions of normal life. Universities opened two months late; a third of the students were still mobilized. With the scarcity of gasoline, drivers had to leave their cars idle for one day a week. Businesses were failing, kibbutzim had lost large parts of their harvests.

The men of the 55th had been called up in early autumn; it was now early winter. Sporadic shooting continued on both fronts. No one could say when this reserve stint, already the longest in the country's history, would end.

A truck mounted with a bank of phones circulated among the IDF positions, and the men lined up to call their families. Leaves were given grudgingly, usually for forty-eight hours. Problems accumulated on the home front, and reservists were demanding longer leaves.

Zviki Nur, commander of the 28th Battalion, decided to appoint an ombudsman to advise him on the most pressing cases. He looked for someone whose judgment would be trusted by his fellow reservists. He chose Yoel Bin-Nun.

Yoel took the assignment as a religious duty. All other armies, he said, march on their stomachs, but the IDF marches on its home leaves. Few armies fought in conditions of such intimacy between the home front and the actual front as did the IDF. Leaves raised motivation, reminding soldiers they were fighting to protect their families.

Past midnight, following Zviki's nightly briefings of the battalion's commanders, Yoel began what he called his office hours. He weighed need against need—a business going bankrupt, a pregnant wife confined to bed. When he felt overwhelmed, he asked for God's guidance. Avital saw it as a sign of Yoel's modesty that he made a point of returning afterward to his unit, rather than sleeping in the officers' quarters.

One afternoon, during a staff meeting, Yoel excused himself to pray. As Yoel headed toward the door, Avital called out, "You don't have to leave." Yoel found a corner to recite the afternoon service. Avital watched him slowly swaying: Avital wanted to offer himself the way Yoel was now, confessing his smallness before the enormity of existence. Unable to pray, Avital felt happy in proximity to Yoel's prayer.

YOEL WAS SENT for a three-day trip to the home front, to assess the most pressing cases. He flew to Israel in a Hercules transport plane, which hovered low to evade Egyptian radar.

Yoel informed the disappointed driver assigned to him that they would be spending no more than a few hours with their own families. "What did you think," said Yoel, "that we would live it up?" Yoel didn't even visit Hanan in the hospital; that would be stealing time from the men who depended on him.

Yoel's wife, Esther, in her ninth month with their third child, was furious. "You're taking care of everyone else's needs but your own," she said when he came home for a brief visit. "Your children haven't seen you in months, and I need you. Why don't you put yourself on your list?"

"I can't exploit my position for my own benefit," Yoel replied.

What's the point of arguing? thought Esther. He'll always do exactly as he thinks, regardless of the consequences.

ARIK ACHMON RETURNED home on leave to a desperate Yehudit. He had never known her so angry, so hurt. Since Yom Kippur, she had been alone with Arik's nine-year-old son, Ori. "He cries when he wakes up and doesn't stop crying until he gets to school," Yehudit said. "Then he waits for school to be over and starts crying again."

Most of all she was furious at Arik. Other reservists had pleaded special circumstances and been discharged. "Arik, just tell them what's happening here and I'm sure they'll understand. You're trying to build a second family, not easy under the best circumstances."

"Danny needs me at his side," Arik replied.

"What about me? What about your son? You're not eighteen anymore, Arik. It's time to stop defending the homeland and take care of your family."

Yehudit should know—this is the price people like us pay for having the right values and education.

"I'll see what I can do," he said, noncommittal.

"Arik, I can't go on."

"I know I can depend on you, Yehudit. I know you'll be strong."

Damn it, he's right—

MEIR ARIEL SINGS THE BLUES

ON GUARD DUTY around late-night campfires, the reservists in Suez City dissected the war. Who was responsible for the depleted stockpiles of weapons they had found on Yom Kippur? For the intelligence failure to read the most blatant signs of impending invasion? For the doctrine of Israel's invulnerability and the contempt for the fighting capability of the other side? For the strategic stupidity of the Bar-Lev Line? Someone had to answer for this.

The radio played a song that seemed to have been written for the men of the 55th: "We liberated the Wall for you and we drained swamps / We stood watch over you in difficult times / We gave you everything, we asked for nothing in return / . . . We knew that soon, soon, a day would come / But now there are those who are not so sure."

LATE AT NIGHT, on a hilltop overlooking the empty harbor, Meir Ariel sat on a chair stripped to its metal frame and strummed his guitar. He was supposed to be keeping watch for Egyptian commandos landing from the sea. But he'd sat here night after night, and no commandos appeared.

Meir and three other men, now sleeping in the adjacent tent, took turns on guard duty. They tried to make life comfortable. They'd hooked up a small generator to a jeep and brought a hot plate into the tent. Though it was against regulations, they'd installed a lightbulb, which they covered with a blanket.

Soon Meir's watch would end and he would drink a cup of tea steeped with apple slices and read a bit of Hemingway's *Islands in the Stream* and drift into World War II–era Cuba. He imagined a brightly lit casino boat from Havana appearing in the harbor and taking him far from here.

Strumming, he half spoke, half sang the words of a new song: "Reading *Islands in the Stream* by Ernest Hemingway / translated nicely by Aharon Amir / Soon he's going to amuse her on his wide bed / And he's one of the saddest men in the city."

He continued: "Maybe tomorrow I'll finally go on leave / I'm bound to the binoculars, just not to think / Light and tea with sliced apple await me in the tent / and a cigarette and a story, good and strong / . . . And then another gaze at the moon, at the city and the sea / And then a friend comes and says, Your time has passed."

Meir wasn't writing a protest song, just the forlorn cry of a soldier watching his life slip away. A lament for all the vitality consumed by the country's security needs.

Back in the tent, comfort eluded him. "Downed two sliced-apple teas, another four, five cigarettes / The song got stuck here / But now he'll amuse her on his wide bed / . . . Our forces passed a quiet night in Suez."

"A GENERATION IS ABOUT TO BE REPLACED"

HANAN PORAT LAY in a crowded ward for soldiers recovering from lung injuries. He thanked God that he wasn't in the burn unit, where the wounds were so unspeakable they were referred to among the hospital staff with the euphemism *Hashem yishmor*—"God protect us." He was healing, doctors said, remarkably well.

And then he read an article in a kibbutz newspaper, and the next phase of his life's mission was revealed. The article, written by a kibbutznik named Arnon Lapid, was called "An Invitation to Weeping." "I want to send you all an invitation to weeping," Lapid wrote. "We'll weep for hours, together, because I can't do it alone. . . . I will weep over my dead. . . . And you will weep over yours. . . . We'll weep . . . for the illusions that were shattered, for the assumptions that were proven to be baseless, the truths that were exposed as lies. . . . And we will pity ourselves, for we are worthy of pity. A lost generation . . . in a land that devours its inhabitants."

Hanan felt as if his wounds were being torn open. He would have shouted if he had the voice. Pity the generation privileged to restore Jewish sovereignty to the land of Israel? What small-mindedness, what weakness of character! Where would the Jews be now if, in 1945, they had thought like this Arnon Lapid? Israelis would do now what Jews always did: grieve for their dead and go on, with faith and hope.

A plan was forming in Hanan's mind. A response to despair. A new settlement movement, modeled on the pioneering movements that had built the state.

But this time the movement would be led by *religious* Jews. There was no choice but to step into the void left by the depleted kibbutzniks like Arnon Lapid. A movement of the faithful. All those who understood that Zionism was about not refuge but destiny, redemption.

The word would come forth from Hanan's hospital room, from his shattered body holding the unbroken spirit of Israel.

IN SUEZ CITY, Yoel Bin-Nun was reaching a similar conclusion. Why were Israelis, even some of his fellow paratroopers, speaking in such apocalyptic terms, as if this were the beginning of the end of the Jewish state, God forbid? Why were Avital and his friends speaking about the collapse of the *conceptzia*, the security concept of holding on to the territories that had guided Israel since 1967?

"*Hevreh*, what are you talking about?" Yoel berated. "Exactly what 'conceptzia' has collapsed? The government is responsible for the operational failures, and it has to pay the price, but why was the war such a surprise to you? It was the most expected thing that the Arabs would attack again! We recovered much faster than other countries would have in our place. All of France collapsed before the Germans in three weeks. It took *five years* to liberate it. We revived in less than three weeks and won. We should declare a day of thanksgiving!"

A great change, Yoel predicted, was coming. "The Israel that will emerge from this war will be a different Israel," he told Avital late one night. "A generation is about to be replaced."

"Okay, Yoel," said Avital, "so the right comes to power. I accept that my camp has to pay a price for what's happened. Okay. But what then? We build settlements all over the map. Fine, it's our land, the heart of the land of Israel. But what about the Arabs there? Do we annex them? Give them the vote? Or not? And then what? Another war? How does it end?"

THREE MONTHS AFTER THE WAR, Hanan Porat returned home. Though his shoulder and ribs throbbed, and it was sometimes hard to walk or even breathe, he dispensed with a cane and then stopped going to physiotherapy. He dismissed his wife's pleas to continue treatments. There were more urgent matters at hand.

Hanan had no name for his new settlement group, no funds, no roster of activists. But he did have the blessing of Rabbi Zvi Yehudah. Ignoring his pain, Hanan began a round of meetings with rabbis and politicians, similar to the frenetic activity he'd undertaken to found Kfar Etzion in the summer of 1967. But this time he felt even greater urgency: redemption was at war with apocalypse.

Hanan was sitting in a parked car near the Mount Etzion yeshiva when he saw Yoel, still in uniform, approaching. It was the first time they'd met since the war. They had left an Israel still infused with the spirit of 1967, and had returned to a shattered nation.

Hanan remained in the car and rolled down the window. "Yoel, something must be done to rouse the people," he said, dispensing with greeting.

Yoel wanted to laugh with joy. Only Hanan could have survived a direct hit by a shell and then so quickly return to his old self—optimistic, obtuse, one-pointed, unstoppable. "I'm with you completely," Yoel said.

ESTHER GAVE BIRTH to the Bin-Nuns' third child, a boy, and Yoel allowed himself a proper leave to attend the circumcision.

He arrived in Jerusalem during a snowstorm. A rabbi who taught at the Mount Etzion yeshiva and who lived in Jerusalem offered to drive Yoel, along with the mohel, the circumciser. Ordinarily the drive from Jerusalem, on a narrow road that wound through Bethlehem, took half an hour. But now, under blinding conditions, they drove so slowly that Yoel wondered whether they would arrive at all.

Just past Bethlehem, the car began to skid. Sunset was approaching. "I'm afraid there won't be a circumcision today," the rabbi said.

Yoel stepped out of the car. Standing in the blizzard, he prayed. "I raise my eyes toward the mountains, from whence will my help come. My help comes from the Lord, creator of heaven and earth."

A snowplow appeared. The car followed the plow up the inclining road, and reached the Bin-Nun home ten minutes before sundown. The circumcision, including the blessings, was completed within five minutes—"a Guinness record," Yoel joked. The baby was named Odeyah, "I give thanks to God." Yoel explained to celebrants that he'd chosen the name as a response to the war. "I give thanks to God," said Yoel, "because we were saved by a miracle."

The next day, he was back in Suez City.

AFTER A MONTH of convalescing at home, Yisrael Harel returned to Africa. Though shrapnel remained in his left leg, he was no longer limping.

The injury only confirmed for him his place in the brigade's inner circle. He felt closer than ever to Arik, literally his brother in arms, the man who had carried him, bleeding, down the stairwell in Suez City. Just like the song that was playing on the radio: "Be a friend to me, be a brother / extend a hand in troubled times / I'm your brother, don't forget." Arik was the antidote to the Haifa kids who had taunted him and thrown rocks at the Bnei Akiva clubhouse, to the Mapai goons who had split his head open during the demonstration against Shabbat desecration. What else had Yisrael Harel ever wanted but that Jews in a hostile world should treat each other as brothers?

THE FAITHFUL STEP INTO THE BREACH

A WINTER NIGHT in Kfar Etzion. Pine trees swayed in the fierce wind, and the thin windows of the concrete houses shook. Inside the kibbutz dining room, inadequately warmed by kerosene heaters, some seventy young men sat on benches around long tables. Most were recently demobilized soldiers. Yoel, on leave, didn't wear his uniform: the IDF had to be kept out of politics.

It was January 30, 1974, and the young men had gathered to found a group that would inspire Israel in its crisis of confidence—a rescue mission for the endangered spirit of 1967. It's up to us now, thought Hanan. He looked around the room: most participants had grown up in Bnei Akiva. The presence of a few bareheaded men—settlers from the small Labor Party settlements on the Golan Heights and in the Jordan Valley—only confirmed that the pioneering momentum had shifted to the Orthodox.

Hanan, the wounded hero, the first settler, called the meeting to order. Shirt untucked, knitted *kippah* pinned to unruly hair, he conveyed indifference to his appearance, a man devoted wholly to the nation. Whatever doubts had once tormented him about subsuming his spiritual needs to his public persona had vanished. What could possibly be more ennobling than the convergence of Israel's destiny with his own?

Speaking rapidly, Hanan denounced the government for its weakness. What had Israel gained by refusing to launch a preemptive strike on Yom Kippur morning and then surrendering to American pressure to save the Egyptians from defeat? Only the world's contempt. And now the government was preventing settlement in the land of Israel.

Hanan's audience understood that he was not speaking merely politically but theologically. God acted in history through the people of Israel; when they were strong, as in the Six Days, God's glory was augmented. But when Israel acted in fear toward the gentiles, God's Name was desecrated.

Yoel passed a note to Hanan, suggesting that the group choose a name. Hanan ignored him. Yoel wrote another note, and Hanan ignored that too. *He always does that to me—*

Yoel passed a third note: "We've been meeting for years, and nothing has happened. If we don't choose a name nothing will come out of here either." He added a Talmudic phrase: "The name determines."

This time Hanan responded. "A suggestion has been made that we choose a name," he announced. "Any suggestions?"

"Without question, Emunim," called out a young rabbi. The Faithful. The name was adopted unanimously.

The next day one of the papers reported that a *gush*, or bloc, of pro-settlement activists had formed. Hanan adopted the term: Gush Emunim—Bloc of the Faithful.

A MERGING OF ELITES

ON A FREEZING windy morning in early February 1974, a man smoking a pipe stood alone on a muddy slope overlooking the prime minister's office in Jerusalem and declared a hunger strike. He intended to continue until Defense Minister Dayan resigned for his failure to prepare the country for war. He tried to drive the wooden poles of his protest signs into the ground, but it was too rocky. Instead he gathered piles of stones to balance the signs. One was directed at Golda Meir: "Grandma + 3000 Dead = Failure."

His name was Motti Ashkenazi, and he had commanded Budapest, the only outpost on the Bar-Lev Line that hadn't fallen to the Egyptians. With shell fragments in his back, he and his men had held out for five days against constant bombardment that turned most of Budapest to rubble. And now Ashkenazi was demanding a reckoning. Why had he, as commander of a frontline position, received a mere half-hour warning before the Egyptians launched their attack on Yom Kippur? How could we go back to business as usual when that very mentality had led to the disaster?

Only one newspaper reported, briefly, on the hunger strike. It was hard to take Motti Ashkenazi seriously. Protest movements scarcely made a difference in Israel. The Labor Party, entwined with the state, seemed impervious to public pressure.

On day two of the hunger strike, a soldier on a single crutch appeared. He'd read about the protest, he explained, and left his hospital room to join. He said nothing more. Ashkenazi assumed he was suffering from shell shock. The two young men sat together in silence.

On day five, Ashkenazi felt close to collapse. He checked himself into the hospital, and doctors rushed him into surgery, removing the shrapnel in his back. The next day he signed himself out and resumed his hunger strike. Several dozen demobilized reservists joined him. By the end of the week the media was reporting the beginning of a movement.

YISRAEL HAREL WAS organizing a "university" in Africa for reservists whose studies had been interrupted by the war. Yisrael enlisted a hundred volunteer lecturers and planned over two hundred courses—in physics, classical languages, Jewish philosophy. Bar-Ilan, the Orthodox-sponsored university, agreed to serve as supervisor. An abandoned Egyptian army base was turned into the "university of the brigade," as the men called it, and a catalogue was printed.

But before classes could begin, the order came to decamp. Henry Kissinger, the American secretary of state, had negotiated a separation of forces between Egypt and Israel. Nearly five months after Yom Kippur, the last IDF units were leaving Africa.

THE NIGHT BEFORE demobilization, Yisrael invited a group of friends for a talk.

"*Hevreh*," he said, "what are we prepared to do to make this a state worth living in?"

"What are you suggesting?" someone asked.

"That we help Motti Ashkenazi."

"We're still in uniform, Yisrael," someone countered. "This isn't the place for this discussion."

"Srulik is right," said Arik, using his nickname for Yisrael. "This disaster has a father and a mother. There has to be accountability."

Yisrael was thrilled. He, a son of religious Zionism, and Arik, a son of Labor Zionism, would join together to help bring down the corrupt regime of Mapai.

Arik was unsparing in his critique of the political culture created by his party. "When you are in power for too long," he said, "political considerations became more important than national considerations. All the institutions and leaders I grew up believing in have failed. The system that I was sure was foolproof has failed in every way. We can't depend on anyone but ourselves."

THE NEXT DAY, February 21, 1974, the men of the 55th Brigade gathered along the Egyptian shore of the Suez Canal, near the spot where the paratroopers had first crossed. The farewell ceremony had almost been canceled: a tank brigade had been given the honor of being the last Israeli unit out of Africa, and the paratroopers revolted. We were the first ones into Africa, Danny Matt insisted, and we won't leave unless we are the last ones out. The IDF relented.

In June 1967 the paratroopers had ended their war by lining up, parade style, on the Temple Mount. Now they simply gathered around as Danny addressed them. "We, the paratroopers' brigade," he said, "were entrusted with being the lead unit in the force that brought about the turning point in the war and returned the initiative to the IDF. . . . You stood day and night beneath a murderous bombardment . . . deployed against us with a strength we hadn't known in previous wars. Thanks to our ability to hold the bridgehead, the IDF succeeded in transferring the necessary forces and establishing its great foothold on Egyptian soil.

"I was privileged to command you—veterans of the retaliation raids [of the 1950s], liberators of Jerusalem and trailblazers in the Yom Kippur War. . . . Let us hope that the [prophet's] vision will be fulfilled in us, that 'nation won't lift sword against nation and won't learn war anymore.' "

The Israeli flag was lowered from a pole mounted near the bridge. Then the men released balloons and colored smoke grenades.

Kibbutzniks and religious Zionists, Ashkenazim and Sephardim, university students and workers: they had created an intimate society. Now they were returning to their separate lives in a wounded and divided Israel. Someone scrawled a farewell message onto the side of an armored car: "From the wars of Egypt back to the wars of the Jews."

Arik walked slowly across the bridge toward the Israeli-held side of the canal. He had always managed to slip, seemingly without effort, from soldier back to civilian. But now he felt overwhelmed by a confusion of emotions: pride, anger, heartbreak. One more mission accomplished. But how many more times could they keep giving their all, compensating for the failures of their leaders?

CHAPTER 17

THE HOME FRONT

THE RESERVE DUTY THAT DIDN'T END

ARIK ACHMON RETURNED home, but only formally. By day he resumed his job as CEO of Kanaf-Arkia. Most of the employees had long since been demobilized, and Arik found a company recovering from the economic crisis of the war and its protracted aftermath. Nights he spent with Yisrael Harel, helping organize Motti Ashkenazi's campaign.

At a meeting of Ashkenazi's supporters in the Kanaf-Arkia office, Arik tried to focus on planning parlor meetings and lobbying politicians. But the activists seemed more interested in debating ideology. What should their position be on settlements, the social gap? "*Hevreh*, we're here to work, not to talk Zionism," Arik pleaded.

The activists agreed about this: the country's most senior political and military leadership, and especially Defense Minister Moshe Dayan, had to go. It was, as Arik put it, a matter of accountability.

But there was something deeper at work in the rage so many Israelis felt that spring toward Dayan. Nothing more clearly marked the reversal of the Six-Day War into the Yom Kippur War, elation and pride into depression and self-recrimination, than the transformation of Dayan from hero to villain. Dayan's self-confidence, his trademark eye patch, became now a symbol of self-willed blindness. The charming rascal, indulged when he pilfered archaeological sites for his private collection and whose adultery Ben-Gurion once excused by comparing him to King David, had now become a philanderer and a thief, symbol of the reckless sabra who lived above the law. Israel was devouring its favorite son, archetype of Jewish power. The savior, whose face had appeared on magazine covers and posters and key chains in the summer of '67, had become the destroyer.

The fate of Dayan, in good times and bad, was a measure of the manic depression of a nation on the edge of salvation or destruction.

ON A COLD AFTERNOON in late March, thousands of demonstrators crowded the slope overlooking the prime minister's office in Jerusalem. The earth was muddy after a rain, and people pressed close against the wind.

The lone demonstration begun by Motti Ashkenazi had become a mass movement. Teenagers in the blue work shirts of the Zionist youth movements called out to each other and hugged. Bereaved parents with impenetrable expressions and war widows wearing black dresses stood in silence. Demobilized reservists, still wearing their woolen hats from the long winter, clustered spontaneously by unit. Some men came in the simple olive green uniform of the IDF, flaunting army regulations against mixing the army with politics. Children sat on the shoulders of fathers. An Israeli gathering, festive and grieving.

One hand-painted protest sign read, "There Is No Justice as Long as There's Dayan" (*dayan* means "judge" in Hebrew). Another, held by two children, read, "Daddy Was Killed. Why?"

The hundreds of policemen, many on horseback, had little to do: this was a crowd that preferred singing to rioting.

Avital Geva was there. So was Yoel Bin-Nun. And Yisrael Harel. But not Arik Achmon. He felt uneasy at mass gatherings; ever since he'd left Givat Brenner as a teenager, he mistrusted the mobilized collective. For all his work for the cause, he never visited Motti Ashkenazi's vigil.

THE END OF NORMALIZATION

AT THE WEEKLY MEETING of Kfar Etzion, Hanan requested a leave of absence from his kibbutz duties, to devote himself full-time to organizing for Gush Emunim. "What will you do if we don't agree?" asked a member. "What God wants me to do," replied Hanan.

In a car borrowed from the kibbutz, he drove across the country, recruiting activists. He rarely slept at home, collapsing for a few hours' rest on the couches of friends. When asked about Motti Ashkenazi, Hanan was dismissive. "So you bring down the government, then what? The goal is to build a new Israel."

What was remarkable about Hanan Porat in the spring of 1974 was the absence of any visible mark of trauma, any indication that only months before he had been gasping for air through shattered lungs. At age thirty-one, Hanan retained a teenager's enthusiasm and certainties. His impersonal smile conveyed the promise of intimacy to those willing to share his vision.

Hanan spent a night in the apartment of an old friend from Mercaz, Yochanan Fried. It was here, in the summer of '67, that the failed dialogue between Mercaz students and kibbutzniks had occurred, where the breach between the two utopian streams first became apparent. And it was here that Hanan was now inspired to write his manifesto for Gush Emunim, proclaiming the passing of secular Zionism and heralding the Zionism of redemption.

He awoke before dawn and began to write. He quickly lost sense of time. The sun rose, the time for morning prayers came, and still he continued writing. "The aim: to bring about a great movement of reawakening among the people of Israel for the fulfillment of the Zionist vision in its fullness," he wrote. "Its purpose is the redemption of the people of Israel and the entire world."

Why, wrote Hanan, were young Israelis becoming increasingly individualistic, alienated from pioneering Zionism? The reason, he explained, was the inevitable failure of secular Zionism to fulfill its promise of normalizing Jewish fate. "The people of Israel had expected that, after the struggle for establishing the state, their right to exist would eventually be accepted by the nations, including the Arab nations, and that they would be allowed to live normal quiet lives like all other nations." But now, a generation after the founding of the state, it was clear that the struggle for survival and legitimacy would continue. The result was a growing disillusionment among Israelis regarding "the basic premises of the simplistic form of classical Zionism which saw in the land of Israel 'a safe refuge' and a solution to anti-Semitism."

The solution, wrote Hanan, was a return to the classical Jewish thought banished by secular Zionism and which "contains the key to understanding the uniqueness and the destiny of the people of Israel and the land of Israel. The process of the return of the nation to its land is an essential stage in the redemption process foreseen by the prophets of Israel and which the nation longed for through its exile."

The manifesto called for the immediate annexation of the territories won in the Six-Day War and for resisting—with *mesirut nefesh*, self-sacrifice, a phrase weighted with Jewish martyrdom—any pressure, military or diplomatic, to force Israel to withdraw.

As for the fate of the Arabs living in the West Bank and Gaza, Hanan offered a solution that was partly democratic, partly coercive. Any Arab willing to accept Israel's sovereignty and assume the responsibilities of citizenship—including military or alternative service—should be granted full legal rights. Any Arab who refused to accept Israeli citizenship for nationalist reasons should be encouraged, "by persuasion and financial incentives," to emigrate.

THE STUDENTS OF the Mount Etzion yeshiva leaned into wooden stands holding volumes of Talmud and resumed their arguments with the ancient rabbis. But the return to routine was anguished. Of the yeshiva's 150 young men who'd gone off to war, eight hadn't returned. In the study hall sat students missing an arm or a leg, and bandaged from burns.

Rabbi Amital, head of the yeshiva, walked bent like a mourner. A heavyset man with thick black beard, he spoke frankly about his struggles with faith and told his students that not every question has an answer. Before Yom Kippur he had given up smoking; now he started again. His daughter married, but he couldn't dance at the wedding. He spent weeks speaking with families and friends of each of his fallen students, to ensure that he knew them intimately, that they could continue, as he put it, to live in his memory. "Eight princes of men," he called them, quoting a verse from the book of Micah about eight protectors of the land of Israel.

Many of the students had come to this yeshiva because they believed that from here would go forth the vision of redemption. Now they were a shattered community. Beyond personal trauma was an urgent theological question: What was the meaning of a war on Yom Kippur? The Six Days had established the trajectory of the redemption; was this war, which left only demoralization, a setback to the plan for redemption, God forbid?

No, it couldn't be, said Rabbi Amital, trying to reassure himself as much as his students. A war in the defense of Israel was itself redemptive. Yes, war was a tragedy; but compared to the powerlessness of exile? The rabbi recalled how, when he was in the "pit of the Holocaust" in Hungary, he prayed that if he were fated to die, it should be as a soldier in the land of Israel.

A collection of Amital's talks on the war was published by the yeshiva. The book insisted that despite the war, the very existence of Israel proved that the Jews had transcended ordinary history and entered redemptive time. If a nuclear war were to happen, Amital wrote, and archaeologists in the future attempted to piece together the events of our time, they would no doubt assume that the creation of Israel happened decades, even centuries, after the Holocaust; for what people could possibly create a thriving state immediately after *that*?

Hanan was ecstatic. Rabbi Amital, he told friends, had written the textbook of Gush Emunim.

But when he tried to recruit Amital to the movement, he was rebuffed. Amital had written not a political manifesto but a response to a crisis of faith—not slogans but prayers, a cry from the depths. And that is what he called his book: *HaMa'alot MiMa'amakim,* Ascent from the Depths.

YOEL BIN-NUN RESUMED teaching Bible and the writings of Rabbi Kook. He too was in mourning: Mount Etzion's fallen soldiers were his students. One student, named Benny, had consulted with Yoel just before the war: he'd been asked to lead Yom Kippur prayers at one of the outposts on the canal but didn't want to miss the holiday in the yeshiva. What did Yoel think he should do? Yoel told him, "You'll have to decide for yourself," knowing exactly what he would decide. Benny went to the canal and fell there.

Still, Yoel resisted gloom. "In the Six Days I didn't share the euphoria," he told his students. "Now I don't share the despair."

Yoel arranged his shifts of nighttime guard duty to coincide with those of his students who needed to talk. He was especially concerned about the emotional state of one student, Moshe, who had lost a hand in battle. Moshe had leaned back inside his tank at precisely the moment it was hit by a shell, killing the other crew members. Now he was tormented by doubts: Why had God spared him? Why the randomness of death?

One afternoon teacher and student walked together on a hill of boulders. Wildflowers covered the moist earth. In the valley below, one of the fateful battles of the Macabees was said to have been fought.

"We speak of God as a righteous judge," Moshe said. "But where is the righteousness of judgment in war?"

"I also had those feelings coming out of the Six Days and Yom Kippur," Yoel said slowly. "Why him and not someone else? It seems so random. But you have to look at the problem in a broader way. In ordinary times God judges each person by his merits. But in time of war, judgment becomes collective."

"What does that mean?"

"Everyone who falls in battle is a messenger of the nation. True, the burden isn't divided equally. The families of the fallen suffer more. But we're all in the same place. The whole people of Israel fought. And those who were killed—they belong to all of us."

They walked for a while in silence.

"Each of us needs to find our own way to contribute to the collective," Yoel said. "Those of us who came back feel a need to justify our survival."

THE LAST INDEPENDENCE DAY

ARIEL SHARON SAT in Arik Achmon's living room. The hefty general nearly filled the small kibbutz-made couch that the Achmons had brought with them from Mishmar Ha'Emek.

"Listen, Arik," Sharon began, "you and I know each other. We can talk straight. Does your movement have political plans?"

Since being demobilized, Sharon had returned to politics, as a leader of the new right-wing bloc, the Likud, whose founding he had initiated. Now he wanted to know whether Motti Ashkenazi's movement could be a political asset.

"Our only goal is that those who failed should pay the price," replied Arik.

Sharon nodded. He himself had warned before the war that the Bar-Lev Line was untenable, only to be rebuffed. Sharon's performance during the war had confirmed Arik's opinion of him as the IDF's greatest field general.

But politically Arik had no sympathy for Sharon.

"As a movement we are neither right nor left," said Arik. "But I have been a lifelong member of the Labor camp. Despite everything, it is still my camp. The culture of the right has always been alien to me."

Afterward, when Arik told his father-in-law about his meeting with Sharon, Hazan warned him, "You're going to bring the right to power."

"If it doesn't purify itself," Arik countered, "Labor will bring the right to power."

BARELY A MONTH after demobilization from a six-month reserve stint, Arik was back in uniform. A cease-fire had just ended a war of attrition on the Syrian front and a battalion of paratroopers had been drafted to restore order in the IDF's northernmost positions, and Arik was asked to take command. "All right," he said, "but not for more than three weeks." He packed his bag, took his gun—now an M16, courtesy of the American arms airlift to Israel during the war—and headed up north.

He found chaos. Inside the army's most important electronic spying installation—located on the top of snow-covered Mount Hermon and captured by the Syrians at the beginning of the war, then recaptured by the IDF—there were no working telephones, no barbed wire fence, no water. That's how it is, he thought. When there's a mess that needs to be fixed, you call the paratroopers.

Three weeks later, the outpost restored, Arik was again a temporary civilian.

The Agranat Commission, appointed by the government to investigate the failures of the war, released its findings, and placed the blame entirely on the generals, in effect absolving the politicians. The chief of staff, David Elazar, was replaced by Motta Gur.

Demonstrators outside the prime minister's office cried shame. The Agranat Commission had exonerated Golda Meir, but the nation held her accountable. A week later, a broken Golda announced her resignation. She remained in office several weeks longer as a caretaker leader. Dayan refused to follow her lead. The protests intensified, and finally Dayan too was forced to resign.

"That's it, *hevreh*," Arik told his friends, "mission accomplished." They had helped lead the most successful protest movement in Israel's history. With the end of Golda's government, the era of the founders had ended too. What more could they hope to achieve?

We can't stop now, Yisrael Harel insisted. The protest movement was an unprecedented opportunity to deal with political cronyism and the waning of pioneering idealism.

Arik was dismissive. Did Yisrael really think he could manipulate Arik into helping him bring down Labor and replace it with the right?

"Do what you want," Arik said. "Just leave me out of it."

INDEPENDENCE DAY WAS APPROACHING. For Arik, the notion of celebrating this year—the torch-lighting ceremony on Mishmar Ha'Emek, the communal singing in the dining room—was unbearable. "For me," he told Yehudit, "there is no Independence Day anymore, only Memorial Day."

"We don't have to go to the kibbutz," she said.

"I need to get out. I can arrange a business trip to New York. It's not essential for work—"

"Go in peace, Arik."

ARIK FLEW TO NEW YORK shortly before Independence Day.

There he bought his first-ever pair of jeans. He felt a little self-conscious—he was almost forty-one—but still it felt right. Kibbutzniks of Arik's time had despised jeans as a symbol of Americanization, of bourgeois life. Which is one reason he wanted to wear them now: jeans were the uniform of the globalizing world that Arik hoped Israel would join.

On the evening of Israel's twenty-sixth Independence Day, Arik sat alone on the edge of the bed in a Manhattan hotel room. He thought of all those who had died on Yom Kippur for the mistakes of others, all those who had fallen in all the wars. He thought of how he had once believed the stirring rhetoric of politicians and generals. He wished he could weep.

INDEPENDENCE DAY ON MISHMAROT

A FEW DAYS after Meir returned home from Suez City, Tirza flew to America. The American movie producer she'd met while modeling in Tel Aviv had sent her a ticket. She was going to try to break into film.

Meir drove her to the airport. She assured him there was no "monkey business," as she put it in English, between her and the producer. Not that it mattered: Meir confided to her that there was this young Dutch woman, a volunteer on Mishmarot, whom he had his eye on.

As they parted, Meir said, "You have my blessing to fulfill your dream. I'll wait for you for five years. The door is open."

He didn't waste time grieving. A few days after Tirza left, the Dutch volunteer moved into the Ariel home.

MEIR WAS LEFT with two small children. Though there was no longer a children's house on the kibbutz, there were neighbors—and most of all Meir's parents. They silently endured the collapse of Meir's life in full view of the community. And they stepped in to help raise the children.

Being normal, just like everyone else, had always been so important for Meir. But now it was hard even to pretend. After a wild night, he'd show up late to work in the cotton fields. There were days he didn't come to the dining room.

Meir's friend, Moisheleh, invited him to an orgy in Haifa. Afterward, driving home late at night, the two kibbutzniks were so drunk they had to steer together to keep from crashing into oncoming traffic.

On the eve of Independence Day, the whole kibbutz gathered around a bonfire on the main lawn to sing the old songs. Meir slipped away with a young woman, a volunteer from France. They returned to the campfire a half hour later. The young woman, limping, was missing a sandal.

RABBI ZVI YEHUDAH COURTS MARTYRDOM

YITZHAK RABIN FORMED a new Labor government. Chain-smoking, curt, direct to the point of dismissive, Rabin, the IDF's commander in the Six-Day War, was Israel's first native-born prime minister. At age fifty-two, he wasn't prepared for the job. Though he'd served as ambassador to Washington, his only cabinet position had been minister of labor, a post he'd held for barely two months before being appointed prime minister.

Like other Labor leaders, Rabin's map for settlement included the Sinai Desert, the Golan Heights, and the Jordan Valley, which separates the West Bank from Jordan. What those areas had in common was that they contained little Arab population. The worst of all options for Rabin was settling precisely where Gush Emunim intended to—Samaria, the northern

West Bank, home to hundreds of thousands of Palestinians. Gush Emunim countered that Samaria was the most strategically significant of all the post–'67 territories, because its mountain ridge overlooked the coastal plain around Tel Aviv, where the vast majority of Israel's population and infrastructure were concentrated.

Gush activists spoke of Rabin with condescension. A weak man, they said, vulnerable to American pressure. They dismissed Rabin as Israel's first dejudaized leader, lacking the Jewish roots of the Labor leaders born in Eastern Europe. Rabin couldn't joke in Yiddish like Eshkol, had no memory of childhood pogroms in Russia like Golda. He was, they sensed in Gush Emunim, someone whose Jewish instincts couldn't be trusted.

Yoel Bin-Nun resented his friends' contempt for the commander of the Six Days, God's instrument in the redemption of Israel. Mocking Rabin for his supposed lack of Jewish rootedness was just another way of mocking his Israeliness. The native-born Rabin was the first fully Israeli prime minister. Yoel felt himself Israeli in every part of his being; his religious identity was most deeply expressed in his Israeliness.

Rabin presented his government to parliament on June 3, 1974. Two days later Gush Emunim confronted the government with its first crisis.

THE CARAVAN OF twenty cars and trucks drove over stony hills without roads, avoiding army roadblocks intended to thwart the would-be settlers. The activists had sent a letter to the government announcing their intention to build the first settlement in Samaria, near the West Bank city of Nablus. They were forfeiting the element of surprise, they said, because Jews should settle the land of Israel without subterfuge. Still, that didn't mean they needed to meekly appear before the army's roadblocks.

They came to a field of grass yellowing in the early summer sun. Nearby was an army base and an Arab village, Hawara. Young men unloaded a generator, a Torah scroll, a children's slide. They erected a dozen tents, hoisted an Israeli flag on a pole. Kerchiefed young women turned one tent into a kitchen, with gas burners and army-size pots. The young men began laying barbed wire around the camp.

Only a few hours later did the army discover that a hundred settlers had eluded the roadblocks. Soldiers surrounded the area.

The date was June 5, 1974—the seventh anniversary of the Six-Day War. It hadn't been planned that way: for the religious activists of Gush Emunim, the "secular" calendar held little meaning. Still, it was a curious coincidence for a movement aimed at resurrecting the spirit of '67. Activists saw that seeming coincidence as one more confirmation of their rightness in history.

Ariel Sharon appeared, along with Rabbi Zvi Yehudah Kook. Together, the big general in a short-sleeved shirt and the elderly rabbi in black fedora and long black jacket planted a sapling.

YOEL BIN-NUN ARRIVED LATE, as usual. He came late to his classes, late to prayer services—inevitable perhaps for someone who lived between normative and messianic time. Yoel didn't know how to drive—he didn't have time to waste on trivialities—and so had gotten a lift to the encampment with students, riding on dirt roads and skirting Arab villages to avoid roadblocks.

Esther had tried to convince him not to go. "What is this," she said, "a struggle against the British Mandate? Why are you building a settlement against the wishes of a sovereign Jewish government?" Yoel tried to reason with her: "The whole world is applying pressure on the government of Israel—America, the Europeans, the UN, the media, the left—but only our counterpressure is extreme? All we are trying to do is help the government stand strong. As long as the government is the final arbiter and can remove us if it chooses, then what we are doing is legitimate."

"Just don't drag me into it," said Esther.

Sharon, friends with Rabin from their army days, spoke to the prime minister on an IDF line. Sharon offered a compromise: let the settlers move to an army base, and the cabinet would decide their request. Rabin agreed.

The proposed base was near the Jordan Valley, and that would offer the Labor government a face-saving way out. The settlers, the government could claim, had agreed to resettle in a part of the West Bank included in Labor's map of settlement. Gush Emunim could claim victory too, the beginning of cooperation with the new government.

Yoel was elated. "This is our chance to transform settlement from a partisan issue into a national consensus," he told Hanan. Exactly as Kookians believed: the land of Israel would unite the people of Israel, not, God forbid, divide them.

Hanan agreed. “It’s the best of bad options,” he said.

He approached Rabbi Zvi Yehudah. The elderly rabbi was standing rigid, holding on to the barbed wire fence with both hands.

Hanan tried to remove his rabbi’s hands from the barbed wire. “It must be painful,” he said.

“No, no,” Rabbi Zvi Yehudah replied, seeming distracted, “leave it.”

Hanan told him that the group was prepared to accept the government’s offer and relocate. He was sure the rabbi would agree. Rabbi Zvi Yehudah, after all, had worried about a confrontation between settlers and soldiers, had even met two days earlier with the new defense minister, Shimon Peres, to try to convince him to approve the settlement.

But now the rabbi suddenly turned implacable.

“What is wrong with this place?” he asked. “Isn’t this Samaria?”

Yoel was horrified. Blood could be spilled here. *And we have an alternative!* But who was he to contradict Rabbi Zvi Yehudah?

General Yona Efrat, gray-haired and mustached, approached Rabbi Zvi Yehudah. The rabbi released the barbed wire he was still holding. He opened wide his long black coat and said, “If you want, take a machine gun and shoot me.”

“Honored rabbi,” replied Efrat, “we don’t shoot Jews.”

Hanan gazed with wonder at his teacher. Could there be a more exalted example of love of the land of Israel?

Yoel wept.

ONE BY ONE the squatters were lifted by their hands and feet to waiting buses. Some held tight to tent stakes, to the flagpole, to the land itself. Some men kicked soldiers; some women beat them with their fists. Yehudah Etzion, Yoel’s student, threw himself onto the earth, and was dragged away by a dozen soldiers.

Hanan lay on the ground. Sharon rushed over, pushing aside soldiers, and shouted, “He was wounded in the war!”

Yoel was revolted by Sharon’s behavior. An Israeli general attacking Israeli soldiers: Was there no shame?

Yoel was carried away without resistance.

THE HEAVENS ARE HIS KIPPAH

AVITAL GEVA RETURNED to the orchards. Weekends, his circle of conceptual artists resumed meeting in Ein Shemer, planning new provocations. Everything was the same, but nothing felt right. "There's no challenge left for me in the orchards," he told his wife, Ada. But in his forays into the art world, he longed for the purity of the fields.

"*Hevreh?* Everything is stuck," he said to friends around the breakfast table in the orchards. "And this is *our* failure. Our camp, the enlightened left—*we're* the corrupt establishment. So we brought down Golda and Dayan, so what?"

The only new ideas seemed to be coming from Yoel Bin-Nun and his friends. But how could Yoel, of all people, not realize that Gush Emunim, with its vision of unrestrained power and occupation, was repeating the very sin of arrogance that had led to Yom Kippur? "But really, *hevreh*, at least Gush Emunim is *doing*. All we do anymore is talk."

Avital bought a cow's tongue from a slaughterhouse, preserved it in formaldehyde, and installed the work in the Artists' House in Jerusalem.

FRIDAY EVENING, in the dining room of Ma'agan Michael, a kibbutz not far from Ein Shemer. Avital, surrounded by bales of hay, stood before the skeptical members. He had intended to bring piles of earth into the dining room, remind the kibbutzniks of their attachment to the land, but the culture committee said no and so he'd compromised on hay. What did they expect, a slide show?

Avital spoke about his art projects, the tongue in formaldehyde, the books he'd left to rot in his front yard, a piano he'd filled with sugar. He wasn't getting through.

"What's with the hay?" someone called out.

Avital looked down, laughed, started to explain, laughed again, and finally said, "Some artists work with wood, some with stone, so why not hay? For me, art is giving meaning to material. A farmer plowing his piece of land—he's also creating art."

Avital turned to the state of the country. "Yom Kippur was a big blow to the Israeli ego. But even after that blow it's still business as usual. Who is dealing with our real problems? Look, *hevreh*, just consider that in fifteen years there may not be water in Israel. But who is even talking about it? Look at the kibbutz. All the kibbutzim resemble English parks. One day we'll be growing potatoes instead of lawns."

"Who are you to come here and insult us?" someone called out.

Several members walked out.

"If we build greenhouses," Avital persisted, "we can reach harvests that are eight times as great as today."

"What is it you want?" a kibbutznik called out.

"My dream is to build a greenhouse that will create new technologies for Israel," he said.

"What does that have to do with art?"

"Everything is art. Also building a greenhouse."

It was an idea he'd long nurtured. But now, abruptly, he'd announced it and made a fool of himself.

A few days later he received a letter from the culture committee of Ma'agan Michael. Inside was a check for 2,100 liras. A note explained that twenty-one kibbutzniks had each contributed 100 liras, "to help you fulfill your dream."

What do I do now?

FRIDAY AFTERNOON, a tent camp in the desert. The 28th Battalion had been called up for a training exercise, and Zviki, the battalion commander, was briefing his officers. Meanwhile, sundown was approaching.

The religious officers asked to be excused to prepare for Shabbat. Zviki readily agreed.

"What about the rest of us?" demanded Avital. "Shabbat isn't only for the religious. Don't I deserve a Shabbat?"

"You're right," said Zviki, and ended the meeting.

When Yoel heard about the incident, he laughed with joy. *What a precious soul! Avital doesn't wear a* kippah*? The heavens are his* kippah.

CHAPTER 18

"END OF THE ORANGE SEASON"

THE LONELIEST MAN IN ISRAEL

FROM HIS CELL in Ramle's maximum-security prison, Udi Adiv tried to follow the momentous changes occurring outside. The self-confident, seemingly invincible Israel he had known before entering prison had been shattered. But the new Israel, traumatized and divided, felt too elusive to grasp.

The distancing was mutual. Udi Adiv had faded from public memory. The trial that had scandalized Israelis less than two years earlier seemed, in the aftermath of the Yom Kippur War, like history. Still, in Israel, no trauma was ever really forgotten, only displaced by new trauma, so that the country's emotional life resembled one of its archaeological sites, an accumulation of disrupted layers.

Udi had been in prison for nearly a year when the war began. In a letter to a childhood friend from Gan Shmuel, he had called the war an inevitable outcome of Israel's refusal to make peace—that is, dismantle itself as a Jewish state. But he confessed to feeling unease at being excluded from the Israeli collective at its most desperate time.

Still, those moments of emotional solidarity with his fellow Israelis were fleeting. At his insistence, he'd been moved to a cell of Arab security prisoners. A Shin Bet agent who came to check up on him urged Udi to express regret for his actions. "You think your Palestinian friends see you as one of them?" he said. "For them you're just another Jew." Udi replied, "My people are the revolutionaries of all nations."

The prison authorities took their revenge by denying Udi his most basic requests, like allowing his parents to bring him extra underwear. He was sent, for no apparent reason, to the X's, a punishment cell divided into three cages, each so small there was no room for a mattress. Sitting on the bare floor, he assessed his prospects for surviving prison as an intact person. You can do this, he told himself. Other revolutionaries came out of prison stronger.

He set himself a list of rules. First, forget your previous existence. Hope for nothing and expect nothing. Don't anticipate visits from relatives and friends, don't mark the wall of your cell with a calendar counting down the time, don't hang family photographs over your bunk. Approach prison with the same curiosity you would apply to any society; become a student of its ways. Accept the petty humiliations, like eating with a spoon. Be intellectually engaged and emotionally detached.

He settled into a monastic discipline. Following 5:00 a.m. wakeup and body count, he jogged for an hour in the courtyard. After breakfast in the dining room, where he ignored the taunts of "traitor" from Jewish criminals, he did an hour of calisthenics. Then he worked on his Arabic, reading the bland Arabic edition of the Histadrut labor federation newspaper, the only paper allowed into the security cells. He read—Lenin, Rosa Luxemburg, Sartre, Kant. Often, after the 11:00 p.m. curfew, he continued reading by the dim light of the corridor.

The warden—"that racist Romanian," Udi called him—ordered all Marxist books confiscated. From then on, he said, prisoners would read only what was available in the prison library. One of the prisoners appealed to the Supreme Court and won.

Udi had rarely been without at least one girlfriend since his teen years. Yet he accepted the absence of women with an equanimity he once would have believed impossible. Shortly before his arrest, he met a Frenchman who had spent time in a monastery. Udi had asked him how he'd survived without sex. The Frenchman replied, "My pleasure came from wisdom." If he could sacrifice for a religious delusion, Udi now reasoned, then I can do no less for the sake of truth.

Udi wrote Leah, who had been with him the night of his arrest: it's over between us. Leah had never been a real revolutionary. As a political prisoner, he explained to her, he needed a partner who was as committed as he was.

Leah left to study in Paris. Udi's old girlfriend, the elegant Matzpen activist Sylvia Klingberg, began visiting Ramle Prison.

UDI SHARED A six-square-meter cell with thirteen inmates, in a section of the prison whose cells faced an inner courtyard. The cells alternately housed Jewish criminals and Arab security offenders. Each cell had its own bathroom, with a hole in the floor and a cold-water shower. Three times a week prisoners were taken to a communal shower, with hot water. Udi felt grateful to be among the Arab security prisoners, whose code forbade molestation.

Udi was accepted by his Arab cellmates; he was almost one of them. Most were Palestinian citizens of Israel with whom he could speak Hebrew. Several were Marxists, and together they studied political texts. Even the devout Muslims, whom Udi regarded as simpletons, were civil. Udi befriended three young men from the Galilee who had planted a bomb on a beach, wounding a woman; they were, thought Udi, naive. He tried to educate them. "Violence should be directed only against the institutions of the state, not against the people," he said. "Our task as revolutionaries is to bring Jewish and Arab workers together." They nodded and smiled, but Udi suspected he wasn't getting through.

Udi was troubled by some of the talk of his fellow security prisoners, like the Palestinian who assured him that Israel would be destroyed by "our secret weapon, the Arab womb." "Human beings shouldn't be reduced to statistics," Udi admonished.

"Hey, Udi, look at this," called out a cellmate named Abu Tawfik, pointing to an article in the paper about a fatal car crash. "Three more Jews who are looking up at the flowers." He smiled.

Udi was perplexed. Abu Tawfik wasn't one of those primitive religious Muslims, but a Marxist like Udi. How could he be happy about the deaths of people just because they were Jews?

TO THE MOUNTAINTOP

THE SIEGE AGAINST ISRAEL DEEPENED. PLO terrorists crossing from Lebanon invaded an Israeli apartment building and killed eleven residents. Another PLO group seized hostages in a high school, and twenty-one teenagers were killed during an IDF rescue operation. The PLO formally adopted the "stages plan," declaring that any territory evacuated by Israel would be used as a base from which to destroy it.

To the dismay of Israelis, the legitimacy of the PLO only grew. In November 1974 PLO leader Yasser Arafat addressed the UN General

Assembly, where he denied the right of the "Zionist entity" to exist. Many delegates gave him a standing ovation.

GUSH EMUNIM BECAME a mass movement, impelled by faith in Israel's redemption and by fear of Israel's unraveling. Even for many secular Israelis, the group offered a way to fight back against the siege. Israel's leading satirist, Ephraim Kishon, urged that the young people of Gush Emunim—the "knitted *kippot*" generation—receive the Israel Prize, the nation's highest award. Even Yehudit Achmon's father, Yaakov Hazan, a fierce opponent of Gush Emunim, confessed that he wished Hashomer Hatzair were still able to produce such dedicated youth.

One autumn night several thousand young people, carrying backpacks and sleeping bags, crossed the invisible 1967 border. Their destination was two sites in the West Bank, marked by Gush Emunim for future settlement. One group, led by Hanan Porat, walked along the cliffs of Wadi Kelt in the Judean Desert, heading toward Jericho.

Through the night and into the next day, the protesters evaded army roadblocks and pursuing soldiers. They slipped into a cave and then out the other side. Finally they were surrounded, and the IDF carried Hanan and his friends down the cliff on stretchers.

SEVERAL NIGHTS A WEEK, Yoel Bin-Nun went to the Gush Emunim office for meetings. The office—small, crowded rooms with overflowing ashtrays and mattresses on the floor—was located in an apartment building a block away from what had once been no-man's-land separating Jordanian and Israeli parts of Jerusalem. The building's narrow windows had been built as protection against Jordanian snipers, a reminder of the fragility of the old borders the Gush was determined to permanently erase.

After one late-night meeting, Yoel was driving home with Hanan Porat when Hanan admitted to feeling exhausted. Yoel, who didn't have a license, couldn't help with the driving. He persuaded Hanan, who recently had driven into a ditch and been briefly hospitalized, to stop at the side of the road. They were just past Bethlehem, near Solomon's Pools, which had been a reservoir for ancient Jerusalem.

Hanan napped, and Yoel kept watch.

Hanan abruptly awoke and, as if resuming a conversation, said, "So let's say it's 1948, and the Arabs have accepted the [UN] partition plan. The Etzion Bloc is under Arab rule. Do you stay or not stay?"

"Hanan," Yoel replied slowly, "I didn't go through two thousand years of exile just to raise my children in exile in the Holy Land, when there is a Jewish state half an hour away."

"What, are you crazy?" said Hanan. "No matter what, we don't move from Kfar Etzion. Why is there even a question?"

PRIME MINISTER RABIN accused Gush Emunim of trying to topple his government, threatening Israeli democracy. Yoel wrote an op-ed appealing to Labor leaders to remember their roots. He invoked not the Torah but secular Zionism: there is nothing more sacred in the Zionist ethos, he wrote, than settling the land of Israel.

A kibbutznik with gray stubble and a woolen cap showed up at Yoel's door with a warning. His name was Yehoshua Cohen. As a young man, he had been an assassin for the anti-British underground the Stern Group (known to the British as the Stern Gang); later he became bodyguard and confidant to Ben-Gurion on the desert kibbutz Sde Boker, where both men had lived. A sympathizer of the settlers, Cohen had helped found the field school at Kfar Etzion.

"Yoel," Cohen said grimly, "your camp is going too far. You're trying to bring down Mapai, and it can't be done. The left will do anything to stay in power. They'll stage a coup here. They'll take over the radio and the TV."

"What are you talking about?" said Yoel.

"You don't know them like I do."

"You know the left of the old generation, Yehoshua. But I serve with their sons. Maybe some of the older people would want to do that. But the *hevreh* from the paratroopers? No way."

THE NEARLY-NINETY-YEAR-OLD WOMAN sitting beside Hanan in the front seat of the car keenly watched the landscape of terraced hills passing outside her window. Rachel Yanaít Ben-Zvi had an eye for the potential of empty space. One of the legendary figures of Labor Zionism, she had as a young woman founded a female workers' collective to train pioneers for agricultural labor rather than traditional women's roles and, as she later wrote, to "satisfy their passion for a partnership with mother earth."

For Hanan, the support of Ben-Zvi, who also happened to be the widow of Israel's second president, was a gift. Op-eds in the Israeli press were deriding the Gush as a distortion of Zionism, which had intended to replace the messianic fantasies of exile with the responsibilities of the real world. Opponents noted the contradiction at the heart of the Gush, a strange hybrid of Zionist activism and messianic passivity: Since redemption was imminent, why worry about problems like the demographic threat to the Jewish state of annexing two million Palestinians? Some on the left went so far as to condemn Hanan and his friends as anti-Zionist.

Yet here was Rachel Yanaít Ben-Zvi, confirming the Gush's claim to pioneering legitimacy.

They drove through the West Bank. Few Israeli soldiers were visible, their presence unnecessary in the pastoral calm. Just beyond the Arab village of Ein Yabroud, near Ramallah, rose Mount Ba'al Hatzor. Bulldozers were clearing the top of the hill. Hanan explained that this was the highest spot in southern Samaria, and that the army was building a radar station.

"Why don't you establish a work camp there?" suggested Ben-Zvi. Hanan grasped the historic reference: in the pre-state era, the pioneers had built roads and cleared land as prelude to creating towns and kibbutzim. Maybe Gush Emunim activists should help build this army base, continued Ben-Zvi. And then forget to leave.

Hanan brought the idea to the Gush Emunim executive. We'll ask the contractor building the base to hire our people, he said.

Nonsense, countered Rabbi Moshe Levinger, head of Hebron's settlers. As soon as the work is done, your construction workers will be sent packing.

But Yehudah Etzion, Yoel's devoted student and a member of the executive, was enthusiastic. He offered to organize a work group.

Yoel backed Yehudah: here was a way of bypassing the Rabin government's opposition, infiltrating rather than storming the territories. "We need to walk a thin line," said Yoel. "Create facts on the ground, and if possible without going head-to-head with the government."

Yehudah brought together ten friends willing to work on the base. Hanan convinced the contractor to hire them and secured a work permit from the defense ministry, granted on condition that the group not stay overnight in the West Bank and create a de facto settlement.

The group set out from Gush Emunim headquarters in a Land Rover that had once belonged to the Jordanian army. Yehudah, curly red hair protruding from a floppy kibbutz hat, rode atop the jeep, one foot propped on the spare tire attached to the hood. One of the young men was a doctor who took leave from work to join the construction crew.

Working against a fierce wind, they drove poles into the hard earth, constructing a four-kilometer fence on Mount Ba'al Hatzor. Evenings they returned to Jerusalem. Yehudah slept in the Gush office.

As the weeks passed without change, group members concluded that no settlement was going to come from their efforts. One by one, they dropped out.

Demoralized, Yehudah consulted with his teacher. "Yoel, we can't continue like this. Either we become a settlement or we will dismantle."

Yoel recruited several volunteers to help Yehudah. One morning they took a taxi from the Damascus Gate in Jerusalem to downtown Ramallah. From there they took a taxi to Mount Ba'al Hatzor. Yoel told the Palestinian driver to take them near El Yabroud, the village closest to the radar base, whose existence was a military secret. "Ah, to the radar," replied the driver in Hebrew.

That night Yoel returned to a disapproving Esther. "The land of Israel cannot be settled by trickery," she said.

THE ASCENT OF MEIR ARIEL

TIRZA ARIEL RETURNED home from America. She hadn't succeeded there as an actress. But, working as a makeup artist, she had managed to save some money. And she opened a private bank account.

"Everyone here has grandparents in the city, except for us," she told Meir, justifying her refusal to turn over her earnings to the kibbutz. "So only our children shouldn't have bicycles?"

Meir objected feebly. "We have everything we need," he said. Tirza was adamant. Some on the kibbutz suspected her of sinning against the collective, but this was Mishmarot, and no one made it an issue.

The Ariels resumed life as if nothing had changed. Tirza got a job marketing for Mishmarot's factory, which made frames for sunglasses. Soon she was pregnant with the Ariels' third child.

But for Meir nothing felt normal. He was sleeping with the wife of a neighbor, with teenage girls half his age. Though he didn't ask—that was the agreement between them—he assumed that Tirza was likewise having affairs. The house was a wreck—dirty clothes on the floor, dishes in the sink, broken toys in the yard.

"We have to stop this charade," he said to Tirza. "Whatever you want—separation, divorce. It's not your fault. It's my problem."

"Don't ever talk to me about divorce again," said Tirza.

ON PASSOVER EVE, Meir and Tirza and the children celebrated the seder with Tirza's parents in the dining room of Kfar Szold, their kibbutz in the north.

Meir sat glum, unable to join in the singing. What was the point of this ritual of pretend devotion? Every year, like dutiful children, the secular kibbutzniks recited passages from the Haggadah, extolling the God of Israel for ancient miracles. If there was a God, we shouldn't be making a mockery of the seder by eating nonkosher food. And if there wasn't a God, then why bother with the seder at all?

Meir stepped outside, into the Galilee silence. The singing in the dining room receded.

Meir gazed upward. The stars seemed fierce. Alive. He continued staring into the illumined void, as though he were expanding, merging into vastness.

And then he knew: Nothing was random. Of course there was a God. He had asked a question and the universe had responded. How could he have ever doubted the obvious?

THE BIRTH OF OFRA

ON APRIL 20, 1975, after a day of work on the fence, Yehudah and a dozen friends broke their daily routine. Instead of returning to Jerusalem they drove to Ein Yabroud, below Mount Ba'al Hatzor. They turned across the road into a valley without trees. Between the boulders, sage was in purple bloom.

They came to a row of abandoned barracks, partly stone-faced, without doors or glass in the windows. In 1967 the Jordanian army had begun building this base, but the Six-Day War had intervened. Yehudah's group intended to spend the night here and simply stay on.

A dozen supporters arrived from Jerusalem, with sleeping bags and gas burners and canned food. One young man missed his ride and hitched, part of the way on a donkey cart. Yehudah and his friends swept the concrete floors and laid plastic sheets over gaping windows and blankets across doorways. "If only the war had happened a little later," joked one young woman, "we would have gotten better housing."

Meanwhile, in a coordinated move, Hanan Porat was meeting with Defense Minister Peres in Tel Aviv to convince him to allow Yehudah's work detail to remain in the abandoned camp. "Look, Shimon," said Hanan, "you can't deny the spirit behind our repeated attempts to settle in Samaria. You have to allow this spirit some outlet, some positive expression. Otherwise there will be a very hard confrontation. Allowing the creation of a work camp could bring a certain calm. And what are we talking about? Some people working at an army base and then sleeping over."

Hanan of course wasn't threatening. All he was saying was that unless Peres conceded, matters could get out of hand.

Peres said, "If you say that you want a work camp and it isn't recognized as a settlement, I'm ready to issue instructions not to remove you. But we won't subsidize this, and we aren't committing ourselves to anything aside from basic security."

Peres must have understood the subterfuge, that what began as a daily work detail was now about to become permanent. Was Peres allowing himself to be duped because he supported settling the site? Or was he acting cynically, to embarrass his political rival, Rabin? Cynicism would not have been out of character for Shimon Peres. Unlike Rabin and Dayan and other leading Labor politicians of his generation, Peres was not a war hero but a bureaucrat. Though responsible for some of Israel's greatest military achievements—arming the IDF in 1948 and negotiating Israel's nuclear reactor with the French in the early 1960s—he hadn't served in the army. Rabin despised him as a schemer.

Hanan agreed to Peres's conditions. Without government deliberation, without word reaching the media, the first settlement in Samaria had just been established.

"THE BA'AL HATZOR Work Camp," read the sign. Twenty-five kilometers north of Jerusalem, eight kilometers northeast of Ramallah. Two dozen young people, three of them women, settled in. Hanan temporarily joined them, to supervise the transformation of an abandoned military camp into a settlement, just as he had done in Kfar Etzion.

Hanan objected to calling the embryonic settlement Ba'al Hatzor, after a Canaanite deity. Instead he suggested Ofra, after an ancient Israelite town in the area cited in the book of Joshua.

Supporters appeared with spring beds and chemical toilets and a small generator that kept breaking down. Teenagers from Bnei Akiva painted the barracks and plastered holes where pipes had been ripped out by pillagers. A truck arrived with cement blocks. A farmer on his tractor appeared every afternoon to help clear fields. When settlers offered to reimburse him for gasoline, he replied, "*Hevreh*, don't embarrass me."

Ofra's first family, a couple and a baby, arrived toward the end of the first week, close to midnight. They were given their own barracks. Two dozen young people crowded into the room, lit by kerosene lamp. Accompanied by a guitar, young men danced in a circle, their shadows on the newly painted walls.

Supporters came from around the country to celebrate the first Shabbat in Ofra.

Barely an hour before the beginning of Shabbat, Yoel told Esther, "I can't keep away." Esther and Yoel had long ago resolved never to spend Shabbat apart, and aside from Yoel's reserve duty, they'd maintained their vow. Reluctantly, Esther agreed to join him.

The Bin-Nuns packed up their three children and got a ride with a student of Yoel's. They reached Ofra with sundown.

The young people, mostly singles, crowded around long tables for the Friday-night meal, kibbutz-style. The singing went on for hours. Despite herself, Esther was charmed: here was the authentic face of Zionism, a youth movement atmosphere of purity, truth. These young people weren't singing for the television cameras, but to celebrate being together in the land of Israel. This is how it must have been, she thought, when her parents settled the Etzion Bloc in the 1940s, singing against the darkness.

"If the government agrees to turn this into a settlement," she told Yoel, "I could see living here."

Yoel Bin-Nun *(center, smiling)* hiking with friends from Bnei Akiva, early 1960s.
(Courtesy of Hannah Grajouer)

Yisrael and Sarah Harel on their wedding day, August 15, 1962.
(Courtesy of Ronny and Esti Columbus)

Avital Geva,
Kibbutz Ein Shemer, 1964.
(Courtesy of Amir Tomer)

Yisrael Harel *(in kibbutz cap)* with Sarah and two Israeli friends, Grand Canyon, 1965.
(Courtesy of Vardit Zik)

Ada and Avital Geva, Kibbutz Ein Shemer, 1965. *(Courtesy of Amir Tomer)*

Arik Achmon on the eve of the Six-Day War. *(Courtesy of Arik Achmon)*

Paratroopers pose with the Jordanian flag in the Rockefeller Museum, June 6, 1967; Meir Ariel is on the far right. *(Eli Landau)*

Motta Gur *(sitting in the center, turning left)* on the Mount of Olives, about to enter the Old City, June 7, 1967; Arik Achmon is sitting in foreground, with his sleeve rolled up. Moisheleh Stempel-Peles is standing in the foreground. *(Government Press Office)*

Counterclockwise from left:

Hanan Porat *(left)* at Rachel's Tomb, at the end of the Six-Day War. *(Courtesy of Rachel Porat)*

Meir and Tirza Ariel, Kibbutz Mishmarot, shortly after the Six-Day War. *(Courtesy of Tirza Ariel)*

Wedding of Yoel and Esther Bin-Nun, with Rabbi Zvi Yehudah Kook *(right)*, March 17, 1968. *(Courtesy of the Bin-Nun family)*

Wedding of Hanan and Rachel Porat, September 24, 1969. *(Courtesy of Rachel Porat)*

Udi Adiv, before his arrest, early 1970s. *(Courtesy of Udi Adiv)*

Arik Achmon poses for Yisrael Harel's camera, just before the crossing of the Suez Canal, October 15, 1973. *(Courtesy of Arik Achmon)*

Paratroopers in "Africa," 1974: Arik Achmon *(second from left)* and Yisrael Harel *(second from right)*. *(Courtesy of Arik Achmon)*

Hanan Porat in Sebastia, December 8, 1975. *(Moshe Milner, Government Press Office)*

Avital Geva, Kibbutz Ein Shemer, 1975. *(Courtesy of Amir Tomer)*

Hanan Porat *(left)* with Prime Minister Yitzhak Rabin during the latter's visit to Kfar Etzion, September 29, 1976. *(Moshe Milner, Government Press Office)*

Ofra, 1979. *(Moshe Milner, Government Press Office)*

Israeli soldier evacuates child from Yamit, April 22, 1982. *(Miki Tzarfati, Government Press Office)*

Clockwise from top:

Ofra, 1983.
(Herard Reogorodetzki, Government Press Office)

Meir Ariel on leave from Lebanon, 1983.
(Courtesy of Tirza Ariel)

Yisrael Harel, with megaphone, at a settlers' demonstration at Joseph's Tomb in Nablus, November 1983.
(Shmuel Rahmani)

Udi Adiv, released from prison, May 14, 1985; Udi's mother, Tova, is on the left.
(Reuven Castro, Ma'ariv*)*

Counterclockwise from left:

Meeting of Gush Emunim settlement leaders, July 1987: Hanan Porat is on the far left, with Yoel Bin-Nun beside him. *(Shmuel Rahmani)*

Meir Ariel on accordion, with Shalom Hanoch on guitar. *(Courtesy of Tirza Ariel)*

Arik and Yehudit Achmon on a visit to Nepal, 1998. *(Courtesy of Arik and Yehudit Achmon)*

Avital Geva *(left)* and Yoel Bin-Nun at memorial for paratroopers who fell in the Six-Day War, May 2007. *(Ricky Rosen)*

Udi Adiv, 2013.
(Frédéric Brenner)

Arik Achmon on the
Mount of Olives, 2013.
(Frédéric Brenner)

Yoel Bin-Nun, 2013.
(Frédéric Brenner)

A WEDDING IN RAMLE PRISON

"LET'S GET MARRIED," said Sylvia Klingberg, sitting across the metal grille from Udi Adiv.

"Married?" said Udi, trying to hide his surprise.

"It makes sense," insisted Sylvia. "It will be easier for me to get permission to visit. And for you to ask for a pardon."

"If you're ready to do it," said Udi, "then okay."

AS HE APPROACHED Ramle Prison, Dr. Marcus Klingberg, Sylvia's father, was horrified to encounter a crowd of journalists, including a TV news crew filming guests arriving for the wedding. Klingberg was the deputy director of Israel's top-secret biological weapons facility; what would his colleagues think when they saw him on the news? They might even suspect him of being a traitor like his new son-in-law.

Twenty awkward celebrants gathered. Among them was a Matzpen activist who had once been a student in the Mercaz yeshiva. There were, it seemed, almost as many prison guards as guests. The warden came by to offer good wishes. Udi's parents brought cookies and soft drinks from the kibbutz dining room. Sylvia's father brought cognac.

They were a handsome couple: Sylvia, with long black hair and a stylish dress; Udi, tall and slender, with close-cropped hair. He'd been allowed to exchange his brown prison uniform for a white shirt and jeans, his first civilian clothes since his arrest. He tried to smile for the camera.

Udi's father and younger brother, Asaf, held up a prayer shawl over the couple, while the prison rabbi, in black fedora and long gray beard, rushed through the blessings. Udi smiled, bemused or perhaps embarrassed. Then he smashed a glass, in mourning for the destruction of Jerusalem.

There would be no consummation. Udi had appealed to the courts for a furlough, but the judge had turned him down. It was dangerous to release Udi Adiv for even one minute, he'd said.

Udi and Sylvia were given exactly two minutes alone.

"I'm sorry," he said, and hugged her.

ZIONISM AVENUE

OFRA QUIETLY TOOK ROOT. Meanwhile Gush Emunim's public campaign to settle in Samaria, the northern West Bank, focused on a valley near Nablus known as Sebastia, the name of a Roman-era city and now of a nearby Arab village.

Gush Emunim was drawn to the area because it had been home to the capital of the northern Israelite kingdom, destroyed by Assyria in the eighth century BCE. There, around an abandoned Ottoman-era railway station, Gush activists repeatedly pitched their tents, only to be forcibly evacuated by the army. Each thwarted attempt brought a stronger one. Thousands hiked toward Sebastia. A couple was married there. During one evacuation a bearded protester was photographed carrying a Torah scroll as soldiers led him away. Israelis shuddered at that image: the young man was the soldier who had been photographed during the Yom Kippur War at the Suez Canal, carrying a Torah scroll as he was led into captivity.

So far the Rabin government had managed to block Gush Emunim's attempt to turn Sebastia into the breakthrough point for settlement in the northern West Bank. Frustration among Gush activists was growing. If we don't achieve a more tangible victory than a fictitious work camp in Ofra, they said, the movement will lose its momentum, its chance to change history.

AND THEN, UNEXPECTEDLY, Gush Emunim received a gift.

On November 10, 1975, the UN General Assembly voted, 72 to 35, with 32 abstentions, to declare Zionism a form of racism. The resolution, initiated by Arab nations and endorsed by the Soviet and Muslim blocs, was the culminating moment of the growing Arab success, impelled by the oil boycott, to isolate Israel. Sitting in solemn assembly, the UN in effect declared that, of all the world's national movements, only Zionism—whose factions ranged from Marxist to capitalist, expansionist to conciliatory, clericalist to ultrasecular—was by its very nature evil. The state of the Jews, the Israeli political philosopher J. L. Talmon noted bitterly, had become the Jew of the states.

Addressing the General Assembly, Israel's UN ambassador, Chaim Herzog, noted that the resolution had been passed on the anniversary of

Kristallnacht, the night of broken glass, the Nazi pogrom that in effect began the Holocaust. The attempt to destroy the Jews, said Herzog, was always preceded by the attempt to delegitimize them. Then he ripped up a copy of the resolution.

For all Herzog's resoluteness, the secular Zionism he represented was mortally threatened by the UN resolution. Zionism had promised to cure anti-Semitism by demythologizing the Jews, transforming them into a nation like all other nations. The reason for anti-Semitism, wrote one nineteenth-century Zionist theoretician, was that the Jews, a disembodied people without a land, were "haunting" the nations; anti-Semitism, he concluded, was a fear of ghosts. Give the Jews a state—a flag and postage stamps and marching bands—and they would become concretized, demystified. Normal. Zionism had been the Jews' last desperate strategy for collective acceptance among the nations. And now that strategy had failed. Zionism had been turned against itself: the very means for freeing the Jews from the ghetto had become the pretext for their renewed ghettoization.

Only Gush Emunim had a ready explanation for why this was happening. It was an old Jewish answer, and it first appeared in the Bible: "Lo it is a nation that shall dwell alone and not be reckoned among the nations." Not that Hanan and Yoel and their friends welcomed Israel's isolation. But it hardly fazed them. *Goyim* were acting like *goyim*; now Jews needed to act like Jews, embrace their unavoidable uniqueness and fulfill their redemptive destiny, the world be damned. Increased settlement in all parts of the land is the only answer to the UN resolution, Gush Emunim declared. And many Israelis now agreed.

Gush Emunim announced plans for yet another gathering in Sebastia, this time on Hanukkah, at the end of November. It quoted the book of the Macabees: "We have neither taken other men's land, nor possessed that which belongs to others, but the inheritance of our fathers."

TEN DAYS AFTER THE UN VOTE, on the night of November 20, terrorists crossed from Syria into the Golan Heights and entered a yeshiva in the settlement of Ramat Magshimim. The terrorists were drawn to a light in a dorm room. They broke in and opened fire, killing three students. Two of them were from the Mount Etzion yeshiva—students of Yoel Bin-Nun—who happened to be visiting friends.

Yoel was a teacher of soldiers; burying students was part of the job. But these boys had been gunned down, helpless. No way for Jewish soldiers to die in the land of Israel.

The people of Israel, thought Yoel, needed an infusion of strength. And Hanukkah was an auspicious time. The upcoming protest in Sebastia would be the eighth attempt to settle in Samaria since Hawara, and that too was auspicious: Hanukkah commemorates the small vial of oil that defied natural law and burned in the Temple for eight nights. Eight was a number for miracles.

THE MORNING OF NOVEMBER 30, the second day of Hanukkah, was bright and cold. Despite forecasts of heavy rain, several thousand people met at rendezvous points near the old West Bank border. They were Orthodox families with young children, Bnei Akiva girls in long skirts, and Bnei Akiva boys with white ritual fringes hanging down their jeans. They carried sleeping bags and knapsacks, filled with a change of clothes and sandwiches and menorahs to light the hills of Samaria.

They set out in cars and vans and buses. The slow procession came to an army roadblock. Protesters left their vehicles. Led by guides, they began walking east toward Sebastia, a day's distance by foot.

In the sun and wind marchers sang Hanukkah songs celebrating the courage of the few against the many. The UN, the media, the left, their own government, everyone was against them—but what did that matter? They were the children of the Macabees.

Walking at the head of the line was Naomi Shemer, composer of "Jerusalem of Gold."

Shortly after nightfall, the first trekkers reached a valley near the Palestinian village of Ramin. Four kilometers and one final hill separated them from the valley of Sebastia. Guides decided not to risk the slippery slopes in the darkness. Marchers unrolled sleeping bags beneath a cloudy sky and prepared to spend the night. They laid menorahs on rocks and lit candles in the strong wind, trying to protect the flames with their bodies. "We kindle these lights," they sang, "to recall the redemptive acts, miracles and wonders which You performed for our forefathers, in those days, at this time."

Then came the rain. Thundering, flashing. Hikers huddled beneath spread sleeping bags, but the rain penetrated. Nothing to do but wait out the night.

The government rejected a request from Gush leaders to open the roadblocks and allow them to bring food to the valley. They sent a taunting telegram to the cabinet: "Were your hearts moved more by the [Egyptian] Third Army than by your own citizens?"—referring to the previous government's acquiescence to American pressure to allow supplies to reach trapped Egyptian soldiers.

In the uncertain dawn, drenched protesters began arriving in Sebastia. The valley had turned to mud. Each new group was greeted by singing and dancing. The unstoppable force of those who felt as if they had personally waited through two thousand years of exile for this moment.

The rain continued, and most protesters soon left by buses provided by the army. But several hundred remained. And though Sebastia was declared a closed military zone, hundreds more continued to come.

The abandoned railway station was transformed into a kitchen, dispensing soup and sandwiches. Activists driving on the old train tracks smuggled in tents, and a camp rose around the small lake the rains had formed in the center of the valley. Zionism Avenue, read a makeshift sign, a response to the UN.

Though it had acted resolutely against previous attempts to settle Sebastia, this time the government hesitated. Jewish leaders from around the world were gathering in Jerusalem for a solidarity conference in response to the Zionism = racism resolution, and the government didn't want to mar the event with an ugly confrontation. By the third day of the protest, government officials were telling the press that the evacuation would be deferred until the following week. "The hand of God," said Yoel Bin-Nun.

In the freshly painted basement of the railway station, Gush leaders sat around a table, arguing strategy. The low-roofed, windowless room, barely two by four meters and dimly lit by a generator, was heavy with the dust of a half century of neglect. Under no circumstances do we voluntarily leave, said Rabbi Levinger. To Yoel, Levinger's words sounded like a threat of blood.

Fearing civil war, Yoel circulated among the soldiers, wishing them a joyful Hanukkah. He approached General Yona Efrat, commander of the central front, who had assured Rabbi Zvi Yehudah during the Hawara evacuation that the IDF didn't shoot Jews. "You're making a big mistake," Efrat told Yoel. "Instead of fighting the government over Samaria, you should be settling those areas like the Jordan Valley where there is consensus."

THE RAINS STOPPED. All through the week protesters came and went. Some hiked through fields of Palestinian farmers, trampling crops that got in their way.

Young people toured the nearby ruins of ancient Samaria, remnants of the eighth-century BCE palace of the kings of Israel and a kilometer-long avenue of pillars from Herodian times. Here is your past and your future, Sebastia seemed to say; the time has come to turn these ruins back into thriving communities.

Sympathetic kibbutzniks brought an oak sapling to plant in the makeshift settlement. "If heaven forbid they evacuate you," one said, "take the oak with you so that it won't be left here alone."

Several thousand demonstrators spent Shabbat in Sebastia. General Efrat brought his family. He blessed the wine, and soldiers and squatters shared a meal. Yoel calmed; there would be no fratricide here.

YISRAEL HAREL WAS in bed with a sprained back.

He tried to be helpful by phoning his friend, the IDF chief of staff, Motta Gur. "You know us, Motta," he said. "You know we're serious and responsible. But we can't control everyone in the field. Tell Rabin not to involve the army in an evacuation. Don't let it become violent."

In fact Motta had already told an outraged Rabin that the IDF shouldn't be employed for political ends like evacuating protesters. Nor did Motta conceal his sympathy for the would-be settlers. "My soldiers," he called them. He meant Yisrael, Hanan, and Yoel.

SUNDAY AFTERNOON, DECEMBER 7. A helicopter landed in Sebastia, and out stepped Defense Minister Peres.

Young people danced in welcome, convinced he'd come to announce the government's capitulation. But Peres didn't come with an offer. Instead, he told the Gush leaders in the basement that if the squatters didn't leave Sebastia within twenty-four hours, they would be forcibly removed.

Levinger tore his shirt in mourning. What a showman, thought Yoel with disgust. Levinger ran out of the room. Hundreds of protesters gathered around him. *"Hurban!"*—Destruction!—he shouted. "Tear your clothes! This is a day of mourning!"

Hanan followed Levinger outside. Among the angry young men in *kippot* and hooded coats, Hanan spotted a middle-aged, bareheaded man holding an unlit pipe—the poet Haim Gouri, who was writing a series of reports on Sebastia for the Labor Party daily, *Davar.*

Gouri was both moved and frightened by Sebastia. The schism between left and right, he said, was being fought in his soul. He had been a founder of the Movement for the Complete Land of Israel and loved the purity and self-sacrifice of these young religious people. But he feared their contempt for government authority, their willingness to tempt civil war. He believed that the land of Israel belonged in its small entirety to the people of Israel, that the Jewish claim to Judea and Samaria—the root of Jewish being, won in a defensive war—was as powerful as any people's claim to any land. But he was tormented by the Palestinian villagers watching the would-be settlers move toward Sebastia, felt the immovable force of their competing claim.

"Why don't you come inside and see what you can do?" Hanan said to him.

Gouri followed Hanan into the station. No one thought it odd that Israel's most intense political struggle was about to be mediated by a poet. Gouri suggested that a small group of squatters relocate onto a nearby army base, while the government then debated the next step—similar to the compromise that Rabin had suggested at Hawara. Peres didn't reject the proposal. The Gush leaders said they would consider it.

As Hanan and his friends debated in the basement, their followers gathered around bonfires against a bitter wind, awaiting a decision.

What was the point, insisted Levinger, of accepting a compromise that we rejected at Hawara and which Rabbi Zvi Yehudah had so adamantly opposed? "We must resist with full force," he said.

"Reb Moishe," said Hanan, affectionately addressing Levinger, "if we don't accept the compromise, the government will use all its force against us. God forbid, God forbid, there can be a disaster here. And we won't achieve anything."

"Don't push the government into a corner," pleaded Yoel. "We can't risk another *Altalena*"—the Irgun munitions ship that Ben-Gurion ordered sunk off the coast of Tel Aviv in 1948, as close to civil war as the Zionist movement ever got. "If our struggle is defeated, there will be no chance of resurrecting it."

As for the compromise, added Hanan, "we will turn it into a victory in the perception of the public. And once we're settled in the area, we'll know how to expand our presence."

A majority of the executive voted to accept the compromise.

The next morning a four-man delegation drove to Peres's office in Tel Aviv. One of the Gush leaders came barefoot.

Peres suggested moving thirty settlers to the army base. "Make it thirty families," said Hanan. Peres agreed; why nitpick? He has no idea, thought Hanan, what a difference there is between thirty Orthodox individuals and thirty Orthodox families.

Peres left the office, phoned Rabin, and finalized the deal. When he returned, he cautioned the delegation that this was an interim agreement, that the cabinet would reevaluate its status in three months and decide the settlers' fate. Then an aide brought brandy and shot glasses.

Until that moment, the Rabin government had managed to resist the pressures of Gush Emunim. But something in the government's resolve had been broken. The UN had conspired with Gush Emunim to defeat the Zionism of normalization. Symbolically if not intentionally, the Labor government was yielding to Hanan's Zionism of destiny.

Back in the car Hanan told his friends, "We have to present this as a great victory, to raise morale. We have to declare before the world that the government has permitted a Jewish settlement in Samaria." In fact, the government had agreed only to allow thirty families to move to an army base near Sebastia. But that was not how the compromise would be announced.

Unknown to Hanan, an emissary of Rabbi Zvi Yehudah had meanwhile appeared in Sebastia, with a message from the rabbi: No compromise. Yoel, who hadn't joined the delegation to Peres, was horrified. Would Rabbi Zvi Yehudah sabotage the agreement, just as he had at Hawara? And at what price?

Back in Sebastia, Hanan rejected the ultimatum. "It's too late," he said. Even Levinger agreed, warning against humiliating "the Kingdom," as Kookians referred to the government of Israel. The nine-day confrontation was over.

Levinger announced through a megaphone: the government of Israel has agreed to establish a settlement in Samaria.

Holding each other's shoulders, the young men danced. Yoel stood to the side and watched. He didn't like crowds. And he mistrusted ecstasy. He felt relief—they had avoided another *Altalena*. But no joy. This outcome could have been achieved at Hawara, without the confrontations of the last year and a half. And all because of Rabbi Zvi Yehudah. How could the man who once spoke prophecy be so wrong now?

Hanan was raised above the crowds. *"Am Yisrael chai!"*—The people of Israel live!—the young men sang. Hanan closed his eyes, smiled. Jacket open against the wind, arms spread wide, embracing the land.

THE LAW OF EXILE

A MONTH AFTER the terrorist attack on the Golan Heights, the Mount Etzion yeshiva held a memorial for its two fallen students. Several hundred mourners filled the dining room, the largest space in the yeshiva. Rabbi Yehudah Amital eulogized one of the young men: "His long day began with prayers at dawn and continued [with Torah study] into the late hours of the night."

Afterward, the young men returned to the study hall. One student, Yitzhak Lavi, approached Yoel and suggested a drill. If terrorists could strike in a yeshiva in the Golan, then why not here? Only recently there had been an army alert.

Yoel was head of the yeshiva's security detail, Yitzhak a member. But the group functioned more by consensus than hierarchy; this was, after all, a yeshiva, not an army unit.

Optimistic, dependable, Yitzhak Lavi was regarded as a leader among the students. He was the first *hesder* yeshiva student to become an IDF officer. Yitzhak, friends said admiringly, wouldn't think twice about charging into enemy fire.

Yitzhak and Yoel agreed to play the role of guards, and Adi Mintz, another student, the role of terrorist.

Yitzhak and Adi had their Uzis with them, Yoel his pistol; in these tense days, they carried their weapons at all times.

Adi removed the bullet clip from his Uzi. He kept the safety latch off, ready to shoot in simulation.

Yitzhak and Yoel waited near the back entrance to the dining room for the "terrorist" to appear.

Adi rushed toward them. Yitzhak overpowered him and grabbed the Uzi.

Adi retrieved his gun and instinctively inserted the bullet clip. He forgot to turn on the safety latch.

One more time, Yitzhak suggested.

Adi rushed toward Yitzhak again. Too soon: he wasn't ready. Adi aimed at his chest and fired.

Yitzhak fell.

Students hearing the gunshot rushed out of the study hall. A student, an army medic, removed Yitzhak's shirt and tried to stanch the bleeding. Yitzhak stopped breathing. Yoel placed his mouth against his, trying to revive him. Without success.

YOEL STOOD AT THE EDGE of the cemetery, watching the flag-draped coffin being lowered into the ground, but dared not approach the mourners. During the shiva, he stood outside the building where the Lavi family lived, walked around the block, stood again outside the building, and finally left.

His nights were torments. How could this have happened? During an exercise intended to prevent the death of students? Was it his fault? He should have checked Adi's gun. But this wasn't the army; everyone was responsible for himself. Still, technically he was in charge. However inadvertently, he had exposed his students to a fatal recklessness.

The police investigation absolved him of wrongdoing. When some yeshiva students wondered aloud about the sin that had caused the tragedy, Rabbi Amital denounced such talk as primitive, and the speculation ceased.

Still, Yoel knew what he must do: if no one would punish him, he had to punish himself. While the Torah didn't regard an accidental killer as a murderer, he was to be confined to a "city of refuge"—at once to protect him from the avenging family of the victim but also to punish him. *Din golah*: the law of exile.

Adi briefly left the yeshiva. Yoel stopped teaching, but then returned. He considered leaving his home in Alon Shvut. Though he wasn't an accidental murderer, he still felt bound, he confided to a student, by the law of exile.

A STRANGER IN THE MIRROR

ALL HIS LIFE Meir Ariel had wanted to be like everyone else. The only way to be normal was to accept the great pretense—to live as if death were illusory, as if this life would last forever. But he couldn't stop the voice taunting him with his own mortality. When he looked in the mirror, a stranger seemed to stare back.

Meir wrote a song in which he imagines being released from a psychiatric ward and told by doctors to visit the airport every month. It will help calm you, they say. Meir wanders the airport, disoriented by his kibbutznik provincialness, eyeing the beautiful women and humiliated by desire. The airport is the place of escape; but Meir isn't going anywhere. He watches the planes land and depart, like souls being born and dying. A Swissair Boeing takes off in an explosion of light. Orgasm, madness, birth, death: airport as world.

MEIR DISAPPEARED. At first Tirza pretended not to notice. But by the third day she began to worry. Where was the boy? In the hospital, the morgue? Had the earth swallowed him up?

In fact he was in a lockup in Tel Aviv. He'd been arrested while trying to buy hashish from an undercover cop in a park. He didn't have money to cover bail, and that was fine with him. Don't you want to call home? he was asked. Not necessary, he said.

Being in prison, Meir felt, was like visiting a foreign country. Who knew when he would have this chance again? He befriended the inmates and the jailers, who were fascinated with this strange and lovable kibbutznik. It wasn't every day, after all, that a kibbutznik ended up in jail. Meir spoke to his cellmates without patronizing them. He knew about human weakness and was no man's judge.

A week after his arrest, Meir finally phoned the kibbutz office. Tirza screamed. "I have to get you out of there," she said.

"It's no rush," said Meir. "I'm having an interesting time."

When Tirza arrived at the lockup, Meir greeted her without relief. "Who asked you to get me out?" he said.

"Autist, mefager, idiyot," said Tirza.

MEIR WAS READING PSALMS. The rich Hebrew stimulated him. And David's faith somehow soothed him. Meir had been raised on the Bible, but as history, not religious truth. As teenagers Meir and his songwriting partner, Shalom Hanoch, would joke about biblical characters, inverting the Bible's heroes and villains. Goliath was misunderstood, Meir would say, and then he and Shalom would go on about the upstart David who stole Saul's crown and how Ishmael and Esau were the good guys rather than their wimpy brothers, Isaac and Jacob. Meir would defiantly shout the ineffable name, Jehovah, daring God to defend His honor.

Meir loved the biblical heroes precisely for their flaws. That the Bible could be so brutally honest about the nation it was intended to celebrate seemed to attest to its credibility. Could its testimony, then, also be trusted about the God of Israel? Was the notion that there is a creator and a plan really more absurd than the notion that reality formed itself, and there was no plan?

Teach me Torah, Meir said to one of Mishmarot's founders, Yaakov Gur-Ari, a Talmud scholar in his youth. Yaakov had run the cowshed until the kibbutz shut it down, in part because members hated the smell. "The cow wants to nurse more than the calf wants to suckle," the old cowhand said to Meir, quoting the rabbis.

Yaakov suggested that, as a musician, Meir should learn how to read the Torah's musical notes, the way it is chanted in synagogue. And so, like a boy preparing for his bar mitzvah, Meir sat with Yaakov on Shabbat mornings, singing Torah.

IT'S ONLY ROCK 'N' ROLL

THE BIG ISRAELI rock band of 1976 was Tamouz, founded by Shalom Hanoch. Shalom had returned from London just before the Yom Kippur War. Though he'd managed to release an album in English, it was a bigger success in Israel than in England—no surprise, given Shalom's heavily accented English. It's cold in England, he said on his return home; one could die there and no one would notice.

But Shalom refused to feel at home in Israel. He sang of his alienation from collective identities in the elegant Hebrew of his kibbutz education. Yet Shalom's songs helped define a new generation's Israeli identity, at ease with itself and not requiring the constant self-reflection of the founders.

With its edgy keyboard, long drum solos, and bombastic guitar overtures, Tamouz was Israel's first great hard rock band—rock music that could have been created anywhere and just happened to be sung in Hebrew. No postwar angst or protest, no national emotions at all.

Despite itself, Tamouz reflected the new national mood, at least among many secular Israelis—a fierce insistence on normalcy, on getting on with life, pretending that Israel was anywhere.

Shalom brought several of Meir's songs into the group's repertoire, including the band's most emblematic hit, "End of the Orange Season." Shalom had composed the music, together with another band member, Ariel Zilber, who grew up on Udi Adiv's kibbutz, Gan Shmuel, and who left because, as he put it, playing rock 'n' roll seemed more interesting than picking cotton. "End of the Orange Season" was a paean to kibbutz romance, making love to the smell of orange blossoms, the next stage after the tenuous flirtations among the teenagers piled on the grass. Yet it became a metaphor for the end of the era of Zionist innocence, of the agricultural and egalitarian Israel, one of whose symbols was an orange.

Tamouz produced only one album before breaking up. Ariel Zilber, angry that the band wasn't playing his songs, appeared at concerts with a paper bag over his head.

For Shalom, working as part of a band, a collective, felt claustrophobic. It's starting to feel like a kibbutz, he said.

MEIR CONTINUED TO WORK in the cotton fields. Tamouz's popularity had no impact on his career. A friend produced a demo tape on which Meir sang "Our Forces Passed a Quiet Night in Suez," but the radio stations weren't interested.

Shalom went solo, revered as Israeli rock's greatest songwriter. But he knew the truth. "I'm good," he told a friend from Tamouz, "but there's someone who is better."

Yet outside the small circle of rock musicians, no one knew that Meir Ariel, adrift on a peripheral kibbutz, was writing his generation's greatest songs.

THE ART OF DECLINE

"THERE IS NO PLACE more conservative, more irrelevant, than this palace of polished marble," Avital Geva declared to a small crowd of the curious, about to enter the Tel Aviv Museum of Art. "It is a closed circle, a swamp without oxygen."

Avital stood beside a bookshelf filled with moldy books embedded in cement; worms crawled through the pages. He had submitted the work for inclusion in an exhibit of conceptual art, and this was opening night. But the museum director had refused to place the bookshelf within the museum for aesthetic reasons, and in the end compromised by installing it in the plaza.

Avital was obsessed with decay. In one exhibit he displayed bones and false teeth; in another, a plastic pond filled with fedoras and dead fish preserved in salt. How else to describe what was happening in the country? Leading members of the Labor Party were being accused of bribery and embezzlement. The kibbutz movement, once Israel's moral conscience, was paralyzed by inertia. The Zionist revolution was founded on Jewish labor; but now Arabs were working the fields and building the houses. And after its victory at Sebastia, Gush Emunim seemed immovable. "Just look at Hanan high on their shoulders," he told Ada, disgusted. "It's all power power power. They're destroying Judaism."

"You can't equate Gush Emunim with Judaism," argued Ada, who taught Bible in Ein Shemer's high school. "One of the major concerns of Judaism is the limits of power. The occupation is the problem, not Judaism."

"They're causing me to lose my love for Judaism," said Avital.

What was happening to him? He wasn't only protesting rot but creating it. Only his work with young people still evoked the joy of creation. He was teaching art—"teaching *life*," he said—at Ein Shemer's high school. And young people accepted him as one of their own, sharing their capacity for wonder.

Avital salvaged a discarded bus and turned it into a makeshift classroom. "What did you think, *hevreh*, that we're going to sit in little rows and copy the Mona Lisa? I'm here to teach you philosophy. To challenge basic assumptions. This cup of coffee—is it aesthetic or not? I want you not just to judge but to create. The only way to create something new is to see things in a new way. With the eyes of a child." Avital knew nothing of Zen Buddhism, but he was talking about beginners' mind.

"AND SO, AVITAL, our friend," began the interviewer from the regional newspaper, "you've come to a sad end. You've turned into a museum creature. Decadent . . . successful. They've given you a prize. How did you fall so low? By the way—how much?"

"Six thousand lira," Avital said, embarrassed.

The Israel Museum in Jerusalem had awarded Avital a prize for his work in collecting books about to be processed into pulp and distributing them in kibbutzim and Arab villages around Ein Shemer, a project he'd begun in 1972. "I began to realize that art isn't doing provocations in galleries in Tel Aviv," Avital told the interviewer. "That has no value compared to things that can be done here in the area."

"What was the response [to the project] in Ein Shemer?"

"In recent years they've become too sensitive to issues of cleanliness, and I was afraid they'd toss all these [worn books] in the garbage. . . . I put piles of books in Givat Haviva [the educational center of Hashomer Hatzair]. . . . The administrators were outraged. 'What's this, you're throwing books around like chicken feed?' The 'cultural avant-garde' of Hashomer Hatzair was concerned about aesthetics, that the books weren't arranged orderly like soldiers in a lineup. But no one there thought about salvaging thousands of books that were about to be turned into pulp. . . . This concern for beauty and perfection is making us empty."

TWO DUMP TRUCKS filled with compost appeared at Ein Shemer's high school. Avital guided them through the gate, past the single-story houses that served as dorms to a patch of lawn. "Here, here," he called out, "great!" The trucks proceeded to dump their loads onto the grass.

The principal ran out of his office. "Lunatic! What are you doing?"

Avital tried not to laugh. "It's an educational tool," he explained. "We're working on a project: Can garbage be aesthetic?"

"This time you've gone too far, Avital. I swear to you, you'll never teach here again. This gets cleared away right now!"

"Don't worry. I'll take care of it when the project ends. In two weeks."

They compromised on four days.

THE GREENING OF OFRA

JUST WAIT AND SEE how many leave when winter comes, warned the pessimists in the not-quite-legal settlement of Ofra. The winter of 1976 was especially bitter: snow covered the valley, and winds seemed intent on uprooting the settlers' barracks. But no one left.

Another three families joined, imparting a sense of permanence to the community. Families were allotted their own barracks, while singles lived in rooms lined with cots. Phone calls were made from the coffeehouse near the mosque in Ein Yabroud, the Arab village across the road. A van shuttled members between Ofra and Jerusalem, about half an hour away, driving through Ramallah.

Ofra was run as a kind of kibbutz, more by necessity than ideology. Though salaries weren't pooled, the dining room, bathrooms, and showers were all communal. Settlers rotated responsibility for kitchen and guard duty. At the weekly meetings they vehemently debated issues great and trivial. Should Ofra be a mixed secular-Orthodox community or entirely Orthodox? (Orthodox: several secular young people who joined soon left.) And if Orthodox, how open to modernity? (Open: they preferred university graduates to full-time yeshiva students.) Should the community hire a rabbi? (No, because he would likely disapprove of young women wearing pants instead of modest skirts and of married women not covering their hair.) Should they hire Arabs for building and gardening? (No, argued Yehudah Etzion: Jews must do their own physical work.) What should they serve for breakfast? (Yogurt.)

On Tu b'Shvat, the festival of trees, Defense Minister Peres visited Ofra and planted a sapling. It's time to end the fiction of Ofra as a work camp, Peres said. Ofra was hooked to the local electricity grid, and the army provided settlers with weapons for guard duty.

YISRAEL AND SARAH HAREL, with their four children, came often for Shabbat. Here in this hard beauty, in fields of boulders and wildflowers with terraces and wells and ancient ruins, the state of Israel could be reimagined, as if it were 1948 again and the country had not yet been disfigured by corrupt politics and pettiness and hasty housing projects. Here Yisrael's dream of a religious Zionist pioneering elite was coming to life.

He belonged among them. But it wasn't easy for a family man in his thirties to move to Ofra. Sarah had already made enough sacrifices for him, left her ultra-Orthodox family for Yisrael's world. Now Yisrael would be asking her to become a pioneer.

Sarah didn't understand Zionism, the pride of a Jewish flag and a Jewish uniform. But Jews settling the land of Israel: what could be more self-evident? Nor was she afraid of austerity: she had grown up in a house no less cramped that the Jordanian army barracks of Ofra.

"I like the people in Ofra," she said to Yisrael. "There is something pure about them."

A YEAR AFTER its ambiguous founding, Ofra was thriving. There were 140 residents, 80 of them children. There was a workshop for wooden toys and one for ladders ("Beit El Ladders," named for the nearby site of Jacob's dream). There was a chicken coop, and forty dunams were cleared for a cherry orchard. Around the concrete bunks were the beginnings of lawns and flower beds.

Hanan Porat spoke at the first-anniversary celebration: "They accuse us of being dreamers. That's true. Here Jacob dreamed his dream and his ladder reached the heavens, and he received the promise of Providence that this land would be his. Zionism is, in its essence, the fulfillment of the dream of generations."

The newspaper *Ma'ariv* offered this sympathetic report on Ofra's first anniversary: "Across from the entrance to Ofra is an Arab house. In the evening the *hevreh* go there to drink coffee, to improve their Arabic and to connect with the neighbors." The article quoted one of the young settlers: "If the Jews won't create ill will between us and the Arabs, we'll get along fine."

By "the Jews," he meant the left.

WHAT IS THIS, AMERICA?

THE FOUR-DAY CAMP for the fatherless children of the 55th Brigade resembled any Zionist youth camp in the summer of 1976. Tents in a forest clearing, hikes, campfires into the night.

Nearly two hundred children—far more than in previous summers—attended the four-day camp this year. Partly the increase was due to the Yom Kippur War, which made dozens of children eligible. Those included the three children of Avinoam "Abu" Amichai of Kfar Etzion. The increase in population was also because of a decision taken by Yisrael and Arik to open membership to families of fallen soldiers from the IDF's other two paratrooper brigades.

Arik served as camp director, Yisrael as activities director. Arik and a dozen fellow volunteers shared a room lined with cots. Yisrael slept in a tent.

When the camp ended, several members of the executive complained about the spartan conditions. Why don't we give the kids a good time instead of subjecting them to boot camp? Why not take them, say, to an amusement park?

Yisrael was outraged. What made the camp special was precisely its ability to impart the Zionist values that the children's fathers had sacrificed their lives to protect.

"We don't want to spoil them," Arik said, backing Yisrael. "They have to be prepared for life."

"They already know about life," someone countered. "What's wrong with giving them some fun?"

These bourgeois lawyers, Yisrael seethed afterward to Arik. What were they trying to do, turn Israel into America?

"I also prefer the way we've done things until now," Arik said. "But times are changing. Maybe it's not our job to be educators."

"That's *exactly* our job," countered Yisrael. "They're ruining everything we built."

"They're our comrades, Srulik. Don't treat them as enemies."

Yisrael, in the minority, quit.

WEEKENDS, ARIK SKYDIVED. To clear my head, he explained.

Arik had begun to skydive on a dare. One day in 1972, two young South African Jews on motorcycles showed up at his office. They had founded a skydiving club in Johannesburg, they explained, and wanted to do the same in Israel. But the IDF had vetoed the idea: the only parachutists in Israel's skies, said the IDF, would be in red boots.

Arik made the right calls, and together with his two investors, founded Israel's first skydiving club. "Of course *you're* too old to jump," one of the partners told him. "Oh, really?" said Arik, who since then had skydived over a hundred times.

One Friday afternoon, Yisrael accompanied Arik to the skydiving club, located near Kibbutz Ein Shemer, to photograph him for a newspaper essay. They went up together in a Piper Cherokee. Yisrael stood at the door and shot as Arik jumped. Arms spread wide, alert to the effect of the slightest move of a limb, a turn of the head, plunging at the speed of 260 kilometers an hour, he began to slowly count, savoring his discipline even as the world seemed to spin out of control. When he reached 35, he tugged open the chute.

Afterward Yisrael gave his friend a gift: a photo album with pictures of Arik conquering the skies.

OFRA, SUMMER 1976

"YOEL, WE NEED YOU," said Yehudah Etzion. He wanted a spiritual teacher for Ofra, someone who would make explicit the connection between the daily newspaper and the weekly Torah portion. Not an official rabbi—Ofra seemed adamant on that point—but a guide for the community's religious and moral and political dilemmas.

Ever since the shooting death of Yitzhak Lavi, Yoel had wanted to exile himself from his home. Now Yehudah was offering him the chance.

"We will need a bathtub for the children and a way to install a washing machine," said Yoel.

"I'll take care of it," said Yehudah.

FROM RELATIVES AND FRIENDS, Yisrael Harel faced incredulity. Yes, of course idealism is admirable, they said, but this time you've gone too far. "What are you looking for in the wilderness?" Sarah's father demanded.

Yisrael's editor at *Ma'ariv* summoned him. "We can't have one of our senior people living in an illegal settlement," the editor said. "It will reflect badly on the paper."

When Yisrael didn't respond, the editor continued, "You're going to have to choose between Ofra and your job."

Yisrael returned to his cubicle, phoned an editor he knew at a rival daily, and quit.

IN AUGUST 1976, shortly before the beginning of the school year, a dozen families, including the Harels and the Bin-Nuns, moved to Ofra. Each family was given a barracks, divided by a curtain into a parents' bedroom and a children's bedroom. The floors were rough concrete. But there were now indoor bathrooms and kitchen sinks.

Yoel and Yisrael's lives had converged at crucial moments—Bnei Akiva in Haifa of the 1950s, the paratroopers in the orchards of May 1967. But they had never been intimate. They had naturally gravitated to different parts of the settlement movement—Yoel to the messianists of Gush Emunim, Yisrael to the secularists of the Movement for the Complete Land of Israel. Yoel's knitted *kippah* covered most of his head; Yisrael's smaller knitted *kippah* was a badge of loyalty more than faith.

Now Yoel and Yisrael were neighbors; their children would grow up together. For both men, a shared goal was the only worthy reason for friendship. There was no place for trivial ambitions, for mere conversation. When matters of pride and hurt arose, those were given ideological justification. There would be no easy friendship between them.

On their first Shabbat in Ofra's prefab synagogue—the first building constructed by the settlers—Yoel and Yisrael were called up to bless the Torah. When each finished reciting his blessing, the congregation responded with the same joyful song, based on the words of Jeremiah, *"V'shavu banim l'gvulam"*—and the sons shall return to their borders.

AVITAL GEVA CELEBRATES A JUBILEE

IN KIBBUTZ EIN SHEMER they debated the delicate line between a growing restlessness among members and the need to preserve collectivist principles. Should parents be allowed to visit their babies and toddlers outside the allotted forty-five minutes a day? (Yes, provided they don't disturb the "educational order.") Should members be allowed to travel abroad if the ticket is a gift from a family member? (Yes, but then you forfeit your turn to a kibbutz-paid trip abroad for the next fifteen-year cycle.) Should the kibbutz pay the government television tax for televisions purchased privately by members? (No, but the kibbutz will buy fifty TVs.)

EIN SHEMER WAS preparing for its jubilee celebration. Avital joined the planning committee. The projects were predictable—a pageant, a sports day, a symposium on the future of the kibbutz. "Why don't we do something different?" Avital suggested.

"What do you have in mind?" someone asked warily.

"Building a greenhouse and growing tomatoes," he said.

The members were confused. "You've always been in the orchards," one noted. "What do you know about growing tomatoes?"

"Nothing! But I'll learn. This will be my gift to Ein Shemer for the jubilee. Every family will be given a plot, as big as they want, to grow tomatoes. It will bring the kibbutz together. What better way to celebrate the jubilee than by strengthening our togetherness?"

Avital approached Avishai Grossman, Ein Shemer's secretary general. There was a discarded chicken coop near the rubber factory, in the center of the kibbutz; why not let Avital turn it into a greenhouse?

Though Avishai wasn't much older than Avital, the kibbutz official regarded him as one would a mischievous child, with affection and exasperation. Avishai had never understood what Avital was trying to say with all his artistic provocations. What had been the point of painting the trees purple and dumping garbage on the high school lawn?

Still, Avishai could see nothing wrong with the project Avital was now proposing. Besides, it was just for a year, right? Not even Avital could turn this into a scandal.

EVENINGS, AVITAL'S FRIENDS helped him transform the chicken coop into a greenhouse. They removed the cages, spread plastic walls, and replaced the asbestos roof with plastic just before the first rains came. But how to make the dead earth, gray from two decades of neglect and compacted chicken droppings, come alive again? Avital took a sample of soil to a laboratory and was told: Impossible, you won't be able to grow anything in this.

Avital began intensively watering the ground. Then he ordered fresh soil—*hamra*, rich and red—and lay it over the ground. "Look at this delicious earth!" Avital said. "*Ya Allah*, you can eat it!"

Dozens of families signed up. "Each according to appetite," Avital said, encouraging families to claim as much space as they wanted within the one-dunam greenhouse. Kibbutzniks came straight from work, exchanging insights on their budding plants as rain and wind shook the plastic walls. For Avital, the tomatoes were just a pretext for a happening, a useful work of conceptual art—a reminder to his friends of the joy of communal life.

YISRAEL HAREL'S VINDICATION

SHORTLY AFTER THE HARELS moved to the wilderness, Arik and Yehudit Achmon drove to see them. "I can't help being interested in what's happening there," Arik told Yehudit. "You can't keep away," she said, though she too was curious to glimpse this unexpected turn in the saga of pioneering Zionism.

Smiling broadly, Yisrael introduced Arik to his neighbors as "my commander and friend." Then, still smiling, he brought his guests into his thirty meters of home. Yehudit thought of her father, living in a tent in Mishmar Ha'Emek.

In Arik's grading system, Yisrael had just moved up the scale from a mere *tarbutnik*, culture officer, to *magshim*, a pioneer who fulfills his highest ideals.

"Srulik?" said Arik, his intonation a slight questioning, as if seeing Yisrael for the first time. *"Kol hakavod"*—well done.

Yisrael had waited his whole life for this moment of vindication.

Deeply moved, he said, "You, Arik, are one of the people I most respect. I know how to recognize people of quality."

For the first time in their relationship, Arik regarded Yisrael as an equal. In one sense, more than an equal: even if Arik had agreed with the settlers ideologically, he wouldn't bring his family here. *In that respect, Srulik has surpassed me.*

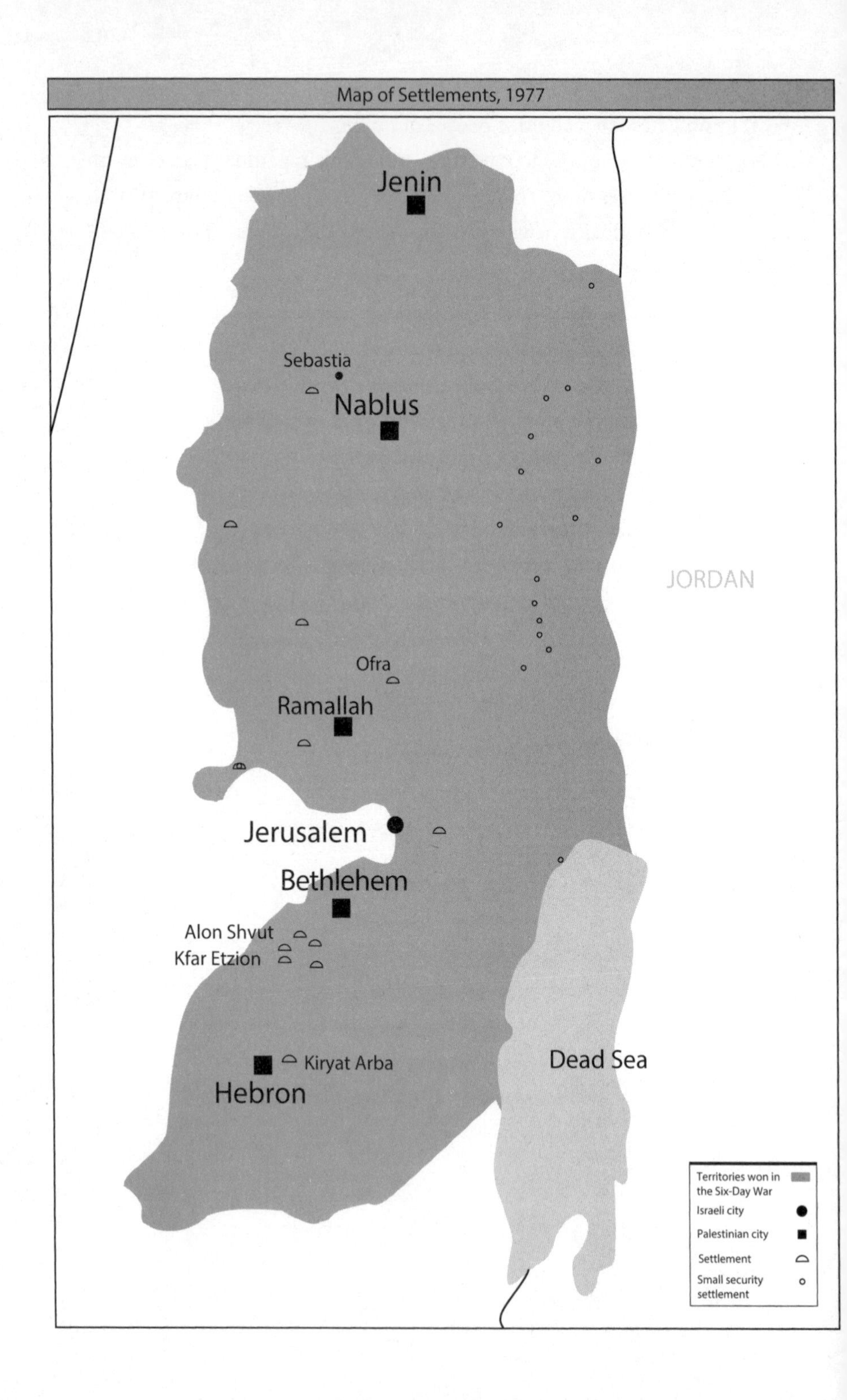
Map of Settlements, 1977
Jenin
Sebastia
Nablus
JORDAN
Ofra
Ramallah
Jerusalem
Bethlehem
Alon Shvut
Kfar Etzion
Kiryat Arba
Hebron
Dead Sea
Territories won in the Six-Day War
Israeli city
Palestinian city
Settlement
Small security settlement

CHAPTER 19

A NEW ISRAEL

REVOLT OF THE JEWS

AVITAL GEVA HAD a deep foreboding about this day. It was May 17, 1977, Israel's ninth national election day, and the Labor Party, which had never lost an election, was fighting its toughest contest. Corruption charges against leading party figures were accumulating; under suspicion, the housing minister, Avraham Ofer, committed suicide. Then, weeks before the election, Prime Minister Rabin abruptly resigned, following the revelation that his wife, Leah, maintained an illegal dollar account—all of $20,000—in the United States. Shimon Peres, the unloved technocrat, was hastily nominated to replace him. Meanwhile a new reformist party, the Democratic Movement for Change (DMC), was cutting into Labor's middle-class Ashkenazi base, strengthening the right-wing Likud. Even Arik Achmon, son of Labor Zionism, was planning to vote for the DMC.

On Kibbutz Ein Shemer, the old-timers reassured each other: Of course we've made mistakes, maybe we even deserve to lose some of our power; but the country won't commit suicide, the people of Israel know there is no Zionism without Labor at its head.

Avital spent the day with his young people, handing out Labor leaflets at polling stations. When the stations closed, he went to watch the election results with them at the high school dormitory, in the bomb shelter that also functioned as the TV room.

On the screen was Israel TV's news anchor Haim Yavin, who wore a tie in a country where even the prime minister often didn't. Israel Television, he announced, was making the following projection: the Likud—"not more and not less"—has won.

Impossible, thought Avital, though he'd anticipated precisely this result. Menachem Begin, that hysterical little man who despised socialism and spoke about the Holocaust as if it were still happening and who promised to fill the West Bank with Jews—prime minister of the state of Israel? Begin, Avital believed, would destroy Israeli democracy, drag the country into war.

The anxious young faces around Avital reflected his own fear. He tried to comfort them: "*Hevreh*, don't worry, eventually the wheel will turn again."

But to himself he said, *This is the destruction of the Temple—*

"THE COMMANDER OF HISTORY has spoken," Yoel Bin-Nun declared to Esther, invoking his most cherished description of God. They were watching Haim Yavin in their tiny salon, which also functioned as their bedroom and Yoel's study.

From outside Yoel heard cries of "*Mazal tov!*" Settlement building throughout Judea and Samaria would now become official policy. Labor, thought Yoel, deserved to be defeated, the arrogant humbled. This was historic justice for all those whose dignity Mapai had trampled.

But he felt no joy at Labor's defeat. If not for Labor, there would be no Jewish state. Though most Labor leaders opposed the settlement efforts of Yoel and his friends, Labor knew what it meant to settle and build. They understood the settlers' passion, even when they disagreed with them.

Yoel mistrusted the Likud. Begin had never been a pioneer, hadn't worked the land, regarded settlements as abstract points on a security map. However paradoxical it seemed, Yoel could imagine the Likud withdrawing from settlements sooner than Labor.

One of the veteran ideologues of the Labor Party, Yitzhak Ben-Aharon, appeared on screen. The majority has spoken, Mr. Ben-Aharon, the interviewer said. "If this is the people's decision," replied Ben-Aharon, "I'm not prepared to respect it." As if a law of nature had been violated.

So much for the left's democratic values, thought Yoel. Tonight Israel has finally become a real democracy.

WEARING A *KIPPAH*, Menachem Begin went to the Western Wall, placed a note in a crack, and recited a blessing of gratitude.

Finally, thought Yisrael Harel: an Israeli prime minister who honors Judaism. Who could imagine Rabin, or for that matter Ben-Gurion, praying at the Wall? Labor leaders were ingrates toward the very force that had preserved the Jews as a people and inspired their return to Zion. Now the Jewish state would make its peace with Judaism.

Begin, the first Holocaust survivor to become prime minister, had been brought to power by a new coalition—a revolt of all those who saw themselves as Jews first, Israelis second, like Sephardim and religious Zionists.

This coalition of outcasts from the Labor Zionist ideal of "real Israeliness" was presided over by Zionism's ultimate outcast. While most of the Labor movement had accepted the UN's 1947 plan partitioning the land into a Palestinian and a Jewish state, Begin's right-wing "Revisionists" had been bitterly opposed. As leader of the Irgun underground, Begin had been hunted not only by the British but by Labor Zionists, who feared that his anti-British violence would endanger the chances for a Jewish state.

In the most bitter accusation of all, Revisionists blamed Labor leaders for failing to seriously attempt to rescue the Jews of Europe. This much was unarguable: more than any Zionist leader, Begin's revered precursor, Zeev Jabotinsky, had tried to warn them. Flee the coming storm, he pleaded through the 1930s in Warsaw and Riga. And learn to shoot. Don't be the only people—you of all peoples!—that doesn't know how to protect itself.

Jabotinsky died in 1940, of heart failure, unable to save his people. But now his disciple, Menachem Begin, would protect the remnant, give the Jews the gift of secure and defensible borders. The most bitter schism in Zionist history was about to merge with the schism over the future of the territories.

Pressing a Torah scroll to his chest, Begin danced with settlers living in the army camp near Sebastia. There will be many more settlements, he promised.

Prime Minister Begin's first official act was to admit into Israel sixty-six Vietnamese boat people who had escaped the Communist regime and been denied entry across Asia. Their plight, he explained, reminded him of Jewish refugees from Nazism who had been turned away by every country, with only the sea to claim them.

THE ATMOSPHERE ON Ein Shemer seemed to Avital like a funeral—a funeral for the Israel they had helped create, and which, for all its flaws, had tried to keep faith with its highest aspirations. Some kibbutzniks could barely speak.

More than grief, more than fear, Avital felt anger—against his own camp, for ignoring the reasons for its electoral failure. He vented in Ein Shemer's newsletter: "Several weeks have passed since the elections . . . but we haven't heard one bit of self-criticism." To our shame, he continued, it was successive Labor governments that presided over the destruction of Zionist ideals, allowing the pursuit of wealth to become the new Israeli ideal. "The spirit of pioneering and volunteering has disappeared. We need to change this reality."

In the late afternoon, when his friends had finished work and patches of shade eased the late June sun, Avital paced in the orchards. Was he ready to detach from the art world and devote himself to renewing the kibbutz? Was he ready to help restore social justice to the Zionist dream? He had no clear vision, no plan, only the trust, almost religious, that his intuition would lead him to his place of truth.

HANAN PORAT INSTRUCTS THE PRIME MINISTER

FOR GUSH EMUNIM, it was the summer of extravagant dreams. Hanan presented Prime Minister Begin with a plan for the immediate creation of twelve new settlements, and spoke of settling the territories with a million, two million Jews. It felt to him like a kind of jubilee, a renewal of pioneering Zionism.

Begin declared Ofra a legal community, ending its limbo status. Several dozen families moved into mobile homes, and blueprints were drawn for permanent housing.

But as autumn approached, there was growing anxiety within Gush Emunim about Begin's resolve. Under pressure from the Americans, he hadn't actually founded any new settlements. What was he waiting for? "You can't trust the Likud," Yoel warned Hanan. "They would uproot settlements for a peace agreement."

A few days before Rosh Hashanah, Begin invited Hanan for a talk.

Speaking in his formal Hebrew, Begin acknowledged that American pressure was preventing him from founding new settlements. But, he continued, there was nothing stopping Hanan and his friends from acting without government permission. And then, Begin added, he would simply tell the Americans that he was outmaneuvered.

Hanan was appalled. Menachem Begin, the hero who expelled the British and carried the hope of restoring the wholeness of the land through decades in the opposition—acting like a ghetto Jew trying to appease the prince?

"As a man of honor," said Hanan, "you cannot agree to these kinds of tactics."

At their next meeting Begin acknowledged that Hanan had been right: there was no way to build settlements except under the auspices of the state. Given current political realities, Begin concluded, settlements would have to wait.

Redemption will not come from here, thought Hanan. The problem wasn't Labor Zionism but secular Zionism. Even Begin had lost his fire. It was now up to the camp of believers to lead the nation.

WHY NOT NOW?

BEN-GURION AIRPORT, 8:00 p.m., November 19, 1977.

The Boeing 737 landed, the door opened, and out stepped Egypt's president, Anwar Sadat. Slight, bald, mustached, he smiled and waved, pleased with the sensation he had caused. Prime Minister Begin stood at the foot of the stairs, erect as the soldiers in the honor guard. Behind him stood members of the Israeli cabinet.

How is this possible? wondered Avital Geva, watching the event live on TV. Begin—fascist, terrorist—had managed what no Labor leader had been able to do, bring an Arab leader to Israel on a public mission of peace. Did this mean that only the Likud, with its doctrine of strength, could reconcile with the Arab world? For the second time in recent months, Avital felt his most basic assumptions about Israel inverted.

Sadat passed the row of cabinet ministers and paused before Ariel Sharon. "Aha, here you are!" Sadat said in English. "I tried to chase you in the desert. If you try to cross my canal again I'll have to lock you up."

"No need for that," said Sharon, laughing. "I am glad to have you here. I'm minister of agriculture now."

So this is how it ends, thought Avital. He recalled that surreal moment when his men had mingled with Egyptian soldiers in Suez City, and enemies shook hands and even embraced. In this crazy Middle East, anything could happen, even a sudden outbreak of peace.

The next day, Sadat addressed a hushed Israeli parliament, its raucous debates deferred now to awe. He declared the words that Israelis had waited a generation to hear from an Arab leader: "In all sincerity I tell you: We welcome you among us with full security and safety."

Sadat proceeded to insist that Israel withdraw from all the territories it had won in 1967. Sadat understood: for all of Israel's power, the Arab world held the psychological advantage. To convince Israelis to yield territory, they had to first be convinced they would get real peace in return. The only pressure Israelis couldn't resist was an embrace.

Wherever Sadat went, he was met by welcoming crowds. Peace songs played on the radio. An artist mounted billboards bearing the words *Drishat shalom*—the colloquial term for "regards" but literally meaning, "demand for peace."

At a reception in the Knesset, former prime minister Golda Meir told Sadat in English, "It must go on, face-to-face between us and between you, so that even an old lady like I am will live to see the day—you always called me an old lady, Mr. President." Sadat and Golda laughed together. It didn't get any better than this: not merely a suspension of hostility but the embrace of enemies at the end of war.

HAVE THE JEWS GONE MAD? wondered Hanan Porat. Sadat attacks Israel on its holiest day, kills and wounds thousands of Jews, and the people of Israel treat his propaganda maneuver as if the Messiah has come. This was nothing more than an attempt to force Israel back to the 1967 borders so that the Arabs could try again to destroy it. What sane people would trade parts of its homeland like meat hanging in the market? And for what? Mere recognition of its right to exist, words that will evaporate when the last territories are evacuated.

"I warned you not to trust Begin," Yoel said to Hanan.

In fact, it was not yet clear what Begin had committed to offering in exchange for Sadat's visit. Some nine thousand Israelis lived in the farming communities of Sinai and in its new town, Yamit, built by the Rabin government. In Sinai's emptiness Labor had seen the way to fulfill its policy of resisting a return to the vulnerable 1967 borders without incorporating large numbers of Arabs. Would a right-wing government really uproot settlements built by the left?

Begin reciprocated Sadat's gesture with a visit to Ismailia, and an Egyptian honor guard welcomed the leader of the Israeli right. Israeli radio played a new hit song: "I was born into the dream / After thirty years I believe it's coming."

ARIK ACHMON HATED being taken for a fool. How could he have been so gullible? Everything the politicians and generals had claimed—that the Arabs only wanted to destroy Israel, that the conflict was insoluble: lies. Worse than lies: self-delusion. Even Arik had bought into the clichés. Sadat had reached out before the Yom Kippur War, there were hints of a truce that could have been expanded into negotiations, but Israeli leaders ignored his overtures. Now Sadat comes to Jerusalem, and the truth is exposed for all to see.

Arik's conclusions were being debated by Israelis. Some said that if only Israel had withdrawn from the banks of the Suez Canal before the war—as Dayan had wanted to do but Golda did not—Sadat might have begun a peace process rather than a war process. Yet even some on the left acknowledged that Sadat had needed a military victory to bolster his credibility among Egyptians before his journey to Jerusalem.

Meanwhile, the war continued to claim its victims. The IDF's chief of staff during the Yom Kippur War, David "Dado" Elazar, died of a heart attack at age fifty-one, broken by the commission of inquiry that had turned him into the scapegoat for the war's failures. Arik joined a memorial service at Tel Aviv University for Dado, whose calm under fire had helped win the war.

Arik ran into Yisrael Harel at the entrance to the hall. "Shalom, Arik," Yisrael said, reaching out his hand.

Arik shook it without enthusiasm. "Generations to come will weep over what you are doing in the territories," he said abruptly. "You will make peace impossible. You are bringing about the destruction of the Third Temple."

Yisrael was silent. Finally he said, "Arik, I ask only one thing: that whatever disagreements exist between us won't affect our friendship."

"Of course, Srulik," Arik replied, his tone softening. "What a question."

AFTER THE LAST of Ein Shemer's families had finished tending their tomato patches for the night, Avital Geva spread out a long strip of burlap and painted a slogan: "Peace Is Better Than the Complete Land of Israel."

"*Hevreh*?" Avital said to the high school students assisting him, "we're taking back the streets from Gush Emunim."

They were preparing for a demonstration of a new peace movement that didn't yet have a name. Avital was feeling desperate. The euphoria of the Sadat initiative had been replaced by mutual recrimination, prompted in part by renewed West Bank settlement building. Begin and Gush Emunim were working together again. However frustrated Hanan and his friends were by the slow pace of settlement—the settler population was growing by mere hundreds—embryonic communities were spreading. Some settlements were disguised as military outposts, implementing Begin's initial suggestion to Hanan of settlement by subterfuge.

Avital and his kids had driven around the countryside, writing graffiti on walls and signposts announcing the coming demonstration. Only when two of his boys were arrested for vandalism did Avital stop.

On Saturday afternoon, April 1, 1978, Avital filled a kibbutz van with young people and drove to Tel Aviv, to the Square of the Kings of Israel, a concrete expanse ending in the ugly monolith that housed the municipality. They hung their banner from two lampposts and went to eat hummus.

Toward sundown, the square began to fill. Young couples with babies and dogs, three generations of kibbutzniks, teenagers in the blue work shirts of Labor Zionist youth movements—a gathering of the secular left-wing Ashkenazi tribe. Until May 1977, they had never thought of themselves as a tribe. The rest of the country was divided into tribes—religious Zionists and Sephardim and ultra-Orthodox and Arabs—while they were simply Israelis, *the* Israelis. But Begin's rise had reduced them to one more tribe, reviled by other tribes as elitist and defeatist.

Now they were here to reclaim Zionism from the right. The slogans on their signs evoked the very elements championed by Gush Emunim—patriotism, security, resolve. "Zionist Values, Not Territory." "Security, Not Settlements." "Flexibility Requires Courage." Onstage a banner read "Peace Now," and that became the movement's name.

"Forty thousand people!" an astonished voice announced from the podium. They had lost their national preeminence; they were losing their socialist passion. But there was a new cause to galvanize them. The camp that had built the state would bring it peace.

An elderly man across a police barricade shouted, "What do you want, to give everything away? The Jews don't make war, the Arabs make war." Many Israelis felt the same way: Did the Arabs have a peace movement pressing their leaders to compromise? Now, in addition to all the pressure directed against Israel, there would be pressure from within.

"We want peace more than we want Shilo," a speaker said, referring to a new settlement near Ofra. A reservist in the army's most elite commando unit told the crowd that soldiers had the right to fight for peace. There was no peace movement like this anywhere—led by those who had fought the last war and would, if necessary, fight the next one. A speaker appealed to Begin: "We know that no one is more concerned with achieving peace than you. All we ask is that you heed our voice, the voice that until now has been the silent majority, and that you not be captive of an extremist minority." Who would have believed it, thought Avital. The left upholding Menachem Begin against the right.

Avital looked around and saw in this crowd his ideal Israel. Strangers smiled at each other's children, said "Excuse me" when they wanted to pass rather than elbow their way through. Where else could you bring together so many Israelis, that edgy people always on the verge of annihilation or redemption, and produce such an orderly and good-natured crowd? The sane Israel that wanted nothing more than to live, that knew that historical rights were not absolute and that only security needs, not biblical longings, could justify occupation, and that Israel's ability to win the next war depended on knowing it did everything it could to bring peace.

"SONG OF PAIN"

YOAV KUTNER, LATE-NIGHT DJ on Army Radio, was ecstatic. Finally: an Israeli album worthy of Dylan himself.

Meir Ariel's new album—his first since *Jerusalem of Iron* a decade earlier—was called *Shirei Hag u'Moed v'Nofel*, Songs of Holidays and Festivals and Falling. Holiday and festival songs evoked the kibbutz tradition of group singing. But the seemingly incongruous word *falling* suggested another, darker meaning, revealing a typical Meir wordplay: Songs of Spinning, Losing Balance, and Falling.

There was nothing like it in Israeli music. The album was poetic and discordant, tender and mocking. Meir's Hebrew combined the latest slang with rabbinic expressions, referenced the poems of Alterman and of the medieval Spanish Jewish poet Solomon ibn Gabirol, creating a language at once bawdy and exalted.

Kutner played the album incessantly for his small but devoted audience of insomniacs and soldiers on night duty. As DJ, Kutner was on a sacred mission: to educate the Israeli public in the intricacies of rock music. He did marathon sessions on Pink Floyd and Led Zeppelin and on such vexing questions as whether Paul McCartney was secretly dead. He saw this as his contribution to Zionism: bringing rock 'n' roll joy to the Jews. Kutner knew the healing power of music. As a teenager, he'd fallen off a cliff during a hike and awakened an amnesiac. One of his first recollections was prompted by hearing Simon and Garfunkel sing "The Sound of Silence."

Meir's album opened with "Song of Pain," perhaps the first Israeli song to frankly confront the Palestinian haunting of the Jewish return. "Song of Pain" tells a story—all the songs on the album tell stories—about a competition over a woman between Meir and a young man identified as an "educated Arab." Meir repeatedly invokes that phrase to mock his own liberal conceits. The Educated Arab woos the young woman away from Meir, and the song becomes a metaphor for the struggle between Arabs and Jews over the land.

"Song of Pain" was based in part on Meir's experiences among his neighbors in the Arab Israeli villages near Kibbutz Mishmarot. When tensions were unbearable at home, he would escape to friends there for days at a time.

Kutner felt no anxiety about playing "Song of Pain" and offending his superiors, because the IDF's official station was remarkably unmilitary; right-wing politicians repeatedly called for shutting it down, accusing it of being a bastion of the left. Kutner was no aberration but in some sense the soul of Army Radio. Besides, no one really cared what that lunatic did at two in the morning.

Reviewers loved the album. At age thirty-seven Meir seemed finally about to begin his musical career. In one newspaper interview, he was asked how he felt about being compared to Dylan. "I prefer to be called by my name," he replied, and if Dylan were Meir, he would have probably said the same. Asked about the "singing paratrooper" of the summer of '67, Meir noted, "I never saw myself as a paratrooper, in the full meaning of the word. And to this day I don't think I'm a great singer. The result was that I felt like a double fraud."

Despite the reviews, the album sold poorly. Meir occasionally played in a small club in Jaffa, and those concerts now attracted a few dozen passionate fans. He soon recognized their faces.

By the standards of Israeli music in 1978, the album was an eccentric work. The singer's voice, though compellingly earnest, was thin, the songs too long to be played on conventional radio, the lyrics so personal they were often incomprehensible, and the themes—infidelity, drugs, madness, the alienation of Arab Israelis—unsettling. The song that, musically at least, most approximated a conventional hit was "Terminal," Meir's fantasy about taking monthly trips to the airport to help him recover from mental collapse. But an ode to madness was hardly likely to find its way to the hit parade. Israelis wanted Hebrew song to remind them of what was best about themselves, a last repository of national innocence. Meir was trespassing on sacred ground.

Meir tried to accept his status with equanimity: he would never be Shalom Hanoch, revered by the crowds, but he would have a devoted audience, however small. The Meir Ariel of 1978 was less tormented, more self-confident. He was learning to regard his own flawed being with the same pity with which he regarded the inadequacies of others.

Meir mentioned to Tirza that his album had come out. But Tirza, afraid perhaps to discover in his songs a lover who wasn't her, appeared indifferent. Meir didn't mention the album again.

FACTS ON THE GROUND

EIN SHEMER'S JUBILEE YEAR ended. The greenhouse had succeeded beyond Avital's hopes. Kibbutzniks spent their leisure hours cultivating tomatoes, offering each other agricultural advice while Avital brewed Turkish coffee. The kibbutz allowed him to spend most of his workday in the greenhouse, and Avital hadn't felt so fulfilled since his early years in the orchards. He had no doubt that his life in the art world was over. He wanted to offer his creativity to the kibbutz. But what?

"You need to be silent for a few years," said Ada. "Do something that no one will know about."

The greenhouse: in its seething silence he could raise Ein Shemer's next generation of farmers, teach high school students cooperation and love of labor and the land, the values of the kibbutz.

Avishai, Ein Shemer's secretary general, was skeptical. Another year of the greenhouse? But we had agreed it would be a project for the jubilee, a way of bringing the kibbutz together. What was the point of extending it?

"Avishai, our young people know nothing about agriculture. It's unbelievable! On Ein Shemer! Let me take *hevreh* from the high school and work with them. We'll bring in the newest technology. It will be an amazing educational experience."

He can't say no to that, Avital thought. "Give me one more year."

Well, why not? thought Avishai. Everyone loves the greenhouse. And the young people love Avital. Maybe this will calm him down.

AVITAL BROUGHT IN rusted fans and a hot plate and discarded couches and turned the greenhouse into a teenage hangout. They came to talk with him about the future of the kibbutz and their imminent army service and their girlfriends. But most of all they came to work. "*Hevreh*," Avital exhorted, "let's do something interesting here. We have the space, we have the energy—*Yallah*!" The lights in the greenhouse were on at all hours; young people slept on the dirt floor and sometimes forgot to get up the next day for classes.

Avital had been given one more year, but in fact he regarded the greenhouse as permanent. *How did the* hevreh *from Gush Emunim call it? Establishing facts*— He had no plan for the greenhouse, only an intuition that the loves of his life converged in this cavernous space beneath a plastic roof that tore in the wind and where community seemed to grow as effortlessly as tomatoes.

An Ein Shemer member who did reserve duty with a scientist from the Volcani Institute of Agricultural Research brought the scientist to the greenhouse. He sat with Avital on a pile of sand. "You have the best ideas about agriculture in the world," Avital said. "We have the best young people. Tell us what to do."

The scientist suggested creating a hydro-solar greenhouse that would retain heat in pools of water, over which a spraying system, to be activated on cold nights, would create the effect of a tropical waterfall and generate heat. Avital drew a sketch, and his kids scavenged the kibbutz's garages and workshops for discarded pumps and motors. When the scientist returned the following week, he was amazed to see the system running.

The hydro-solar greenhouse was successful but, as it turned out, irrelevant. In Israel, with barely three months of winter, there was little need for a hothouse that would retain so much heat. Still, Avital considered the experiment a success because it had stimulated his young people.

The next project was growing vegetables on recycled water—the first hydroponic system in Israel. The greenhouse was also the first in Israel to grow vegetables in planters; for soil Avital used lava, culled from extinct volcanoes in the Golan Heights.

When teachers came looking for students cutting class, Avital helped them escape. "You're creating anarchy," the principal accused. "Listen," replied Avital, not unsympathetic, "we're giving students a chance to do things they couldn't do anywhere else. Of course they're going to want to come here."

The principal implicitly agreed: he paid Avital's water and electricity bills.

WHERE IS AVITAL GEVA?

The question was asked with increasing puzzlement in the Israeli art world. Was he suffering from artistic insecurity, a nervous breakdown? One newspaper critic wrote that Avital had gone off to the desert.

Old colleagues visited the greenhouse and left envious: Avital had managed to create a microcosm of his ideal world, the ultimate act of conceptual art.

"When are you returning to us?" one asked.

"Forget about me," said Avital. "Now I grow tomatoes."

SOME OF AVITAL'S friends on the kibbutz were leaving for the city. But the greenhouse—"my Garden of Eden," Avital called it—reminded him of why the kibbutz was so special. "Where else," he told a friend, "would a community give away its best real estate for free, in the central square, to a lunatic like me?"

Some kibbutzniks were beginning to ask that same question. When the second year of the greenhouse ended, without any sign that Avital intended to dismantle the big plastic structure in the middle of the kibbutz, the grumbling grew. *Kol hakavod*, it's all well and good that Avital is working with youth and the youth are our future, but what exactly is this about? When we ask him to explain the project, the answer constantly changes. One time it's about education, another time about new technology, yet another about renewing pioneering Zionism. *Nu*, really, we're not an anarchists' collective here. How much longer are we going to put up with this?

ON A HOT JULY AFTERNOON, with two gold-painted calves' heads strapped to the roof of his van, Avital drove to Hebron.

He entered the narrow streets of the West Bank city, crowded with slow open-backed trucks and donkey carts. Cavelike shops sold live chickens, clay pots, harnesses, glass-blown vases. Some of the stone buildings seemed little more than ruins. Avital felt adrift in a foreign place whose claim to being home only deepened his disorientation. For settlers, Hebron, burial place of Abraham and Sarah, was the wellspring of Israel's national life. But Avital felt the decrepit past trying, like a bitter old man, to stifle him. The anti-state of Israel.

He was on his way to Hadassah House, an abandoned building near the market that had been a Jewish-run clinic before the destruction of the Jewish community in 1929. A group of Jewish women and children had taken over the structure, demanding that the Likud government allow them to remain. After the initial settlement of Jews in Hebron in 1968, the government had moved them to a suburb of white stone apartment buildings called Kiryat Arba, on a hill overlooking the city. But the settlers had never abandoned their hope of returning to Hebron.

Avital's old group of artist provocateurs had organized a counterprotest. Though Avital had resolved to keep away from protest art, this wouldn't be some sterile exhibit in a museum. If Jews began moving into Palestinian neighborhoods, Avital felt, the result would be a bloodbath. Placing land before life seemed to him a kind of idolatry. A new golden calf. And so he'd bought two calves' heads in an Arab village near Ein Shemer, painted them gold, and was now transporting them through downtown Hebron.

He came to Hadassah House. Kerchiefed Jewish women peered from the grilled windows at the small crowd of protesters. One artist sat in a cage, perhaps mocking the squatters barricaded in Beit Hadassah, perhaps implying that all of Israel was being imprisoned by the settlers' vision of permanent siege. Avital was deeply moved by the presence of kibbutzniks in work clothes and muddy boots, who seemed to have come straight from the fields. *The real Zionists—*

Arab men in suit jackets over skirt-like pants and Arab women in gray housecoats and scarves tied under their chins stopped to watch.

Several men, settlers from nearby Kiryat Arba, approached the protesters. Nervous Israeli soldiers stood between the two groups. If Hebron doesn't belong to the people of Israel, a settler called out, then neither does Tel Aviv. By coming to demonstrate here, another settler shouted, you're telling the Arabs that it's permitted to spill our blood.

Avital and his friends ignored the settlers' taunts. Faith and memory versus art and peace: sacrament against sacrament. Avital laid his calves' heads on the street and set them on fire.

NEW JOURNALISM, OFRA STYLE

MORNINGS, YISRAEL HAREL drove from his home near Ramallah to the Tel Aviv offices of the newspaper *Yediot Aharonot*. Professionally, personally, he had every reason to feel satisfied. He had fulfilled his lifelong dream of becoming a pioneer, and had managed to preserve his journalism career despite moving to Ofra.

The Harels' cramped space was filled with the happy freneticism generated by four children and their friends, so unlike Yisrael's childhood home. Eldad, at fifteen the oldest of the Harel children, was a beloved counselor in Ofra's Bnei Akiva branch. Yisrael's wife, Sarah, was embraced by her fellow mothers, Ofra's strong young women, who appreciated her capacity for enduring hardship without complaint, though she sometimes offended them with her critical manner. Sarah still maintained certain ultra-Orthodox customs, like buying only meat slaughtered in an extra strict fashion. But in other ways she had broken with ultra-Orthodoxy. She had recently completed a master's degree and was working as a social worker.

Still, Yisrael felt restless. He had recently turned forty, and life offered few new challenges. He could remain at *Yediot Aharonot*, one more editor who would never reach the top—and he suspected that being Orthodox, not to mention a settler, ensured that he wouldn't. Or he could do what he really wanted: devote his life to settling Judea and Samaria, that urgent, fragile enterprise beset by enemies. He had none of the messianic certainty of Yoel Bin-Nun and Hanan Porat that settlement was irreversible. Yisrael was a Holocaust survivor; he knew that anything could happen.

Almost two years after the Likud upheaval, the settlement movement seemed stymied by a friendly but timid government, fearful of American opposition. For all the political and media tumult around the settlements, there were no more than 20,000 settlers in the West Bank, 500 in Gaza. Four years after its founding, Ofra barely numbered 400 residents.

Yisrael had a plan. First, create a magazine promoting the diversity of settler life and opinion to the Israeli public, break the media stereotype of settler as bearded fanatic.

Then create an umbrella council that would organize the settlers into a decision-making body, represent their needs to government ministries and their positions to the media, functioning at once as lobby, assembly and, when necessary, protest movement.

"Sarah, I've decided to quit *Yediot* and devote myself to public life."

She replied with a calmness that failed to conceal anxiety: "After all these years we finally have a secure financial base."

"I've been talking to heads of settlement councils," Yisrael said, "and they've promised to fund a representative council, with proper salaries."

"They won't keep their word," replied Sarah, and said no more.

In *Yediot Aharonot* they called it a leave of absence. But Yisrael knew as he cleared his desk that he was not coming back.

IN THE EMBRYONIC communities of Judea and Samaria, there was anguish and rage. On March 26, 1979, at a White House ceremony with Sadat and President Jimmy Carter, Menachem Begin committed Israel to full withdrawal from Sinai. For the first time, an Israeli government—the most right-wing in the nation's history—had agreed to uproot Jewish communities. And Begin had become the first Israeli prime minister to recognize the "legitimate rights of the Palestinian people." He didn't mean statehood in the West Bank and Gaza but a vaguely defined "autonomy." Still, settlers feared that Begin was opening the way to a terrorist state in the hills overlooking greater Tel Aviv.

Most Israelis, though, saw the peace with Egypt as a vindication of Zionism. In the coastal Sinai town of Rafiah, a ceremony was held transferring Israeli control back to the Egyptians, a stage in the phased withdrawal. Among those invited were handicapped Israeli and Egyptian war veterans; young men missing arms and legs embraced.

THE PREMIER ISSUE of *Nekudah*, the magazine of the settlements, appeared on December 28, 1979. Nekudah means "point" or "period"—and Yisrael Harel meant both a point on the map and an emphatic period at the end of a sentence. The cover of the first issue showed a crane moving a prefab house onto a West Bank hilltop, surrounded by emptiness. Building, transforming, defying, fulfilling: these were the themes of the articles crammed into the issue's eighteen nonglossy pages, hardly adequate to contain such passion.

The main feature was a profile of the new agricultural settlements in the Gaza Strip. It was titled "500 Against 350,000"—the ratio of Jews to Arabs in the area. In the next issue, Yisrael published the protocols of a Knesset debate over the future of Gaza's settlements. "The key to defending Ashkelon, Ashdod, Beersheba, is found in Gaza," declared agriculture minister Sharon. "I want to send a warm blessing from this podium to the settlers of the Katif Bloc [in Gaza]: Your efforts today are significant for future generations."

Left-wing Knesset member Meir Pa'il, a Palmach veteran and military historian, noted that since Sadat's visit to Israel, the fate of Israeli settlements in Sinai was now uncertain, and that residents there knew they were likely to soon be evacuated. "The disappointed residents of [Sinai settlements] Yamit and Sadot should be enough for us, before we add to their number the disappointed residents of Katif [the Gaza settlement bloc]. I agree that . . . they are very good people. Someone who goes to settle there is, I think, by nature a fine person. He is doing it out of deep faith and is certain that he's doing something positive. But those who send them—and it's them

I'm speaking about—in the end, they will have to look [the settlers] in the eye and explain to them how they will be evacuated and why they will be evacuated." Added Pa'il: "I told Arik Sharon a hundred times: I weep when he builds Katif, and I'll weep when he removes Katif."

NEKUDAH FUNCTIONED LIKE a movement bulletin board. In Ofra, the foundations were being laid for the first fifty permanent houses. A Japanese convert to Judaism, a descendant of samurai warriors, had moved to Kedumim. In Kfar Etzion the chickens seemed to have a disease, but still, twenty thousand eggs were being laid every week.

Nekudah conveyed, too, the community's resentments and fears. The Israeli media, *Nekudah* complained, routinely violated its own ethos of impartiality in covering the settlers. Reporting that government television Channel 1—still the sole TV channel—had broadcast an item about the settlements that quoted only opponents, *Nekudah* noted dryly: "Typical." At times *Nekudah* combined question marks and exclamation points to convey its ire.

Yet *Nekudah* encouraged self-criticism and even published opponents of the settlements. It ran poetry with mildly erotic imagery. The Orthodox community had never experienced anything quite like it. Some were grateful to Yisrael; others accused him of pandering to the left. Among *Nekudah*'s minuscule staff they joked that some readers took out subscriptions only to be able to cancel in protest.

Sarah was right: the community didn't ensure Yisrael's livelihood. There was never enough money to actually pay Yisrael a salary.

Yisrael set up office in a prefab building in Ofra, with two desks and one telephone. When visitors came, the secretary, an Ofra resident, went home to prepare coffee. On the wall hung a photograph of Shimon Peres planting a sapling in Ofra, shortly after the settlement's founding. Peres, now head of the Labor Party, had since become an opponent of the settlement movement, and the photograph expressed Ofra's longing to be part of the consensus.

Yisrael recruited smart young people with no journalistic experience and taught them how to become reporters, hoping to raise a generation of Orthodox journalists who would portray their community fairly in the mainstream media. He paid minimal salaries and demanded long hours that sometimes went through the night. He bullied, mocked, demanded, cajoled. He phoned a reporter at five in the morning to berate her for some obscure offense. Employees had to make do with sarcastic jibes instead of compliments. "A truck load of medals is on its way to reward you," he said to a staffer who had run the magazine in Yisrael's absence.

Even those who weren't intimidated by his insults submitted just the same. Yisrael wasn't asking you to help him, but the Jewish people. Even small requests became tests of commitment: Fail me, and you fail Jewish history. As much as they resented him, the young people stayed, at least for a while, because they knew that Yisrael, for all his flaws, was who he claimed to be: a Jew so totally committed to the well-being of his people that he had merged with it. If Yisrael didn't represent the highest aspirations of his people, he surely embodied their fears.

TO THE MOUNTAIN OF GOD

THE TEMPLE MOUNT gave Yoel Bin-Nun no peace. Its tantalizing proximity lured and accused: You liberated me and then abandoned me. The Mountain of God bereft of Jewish prayer—under Jewish sovereignty! As though the Exile, God forbid, hadn't ended. "Har habayit b'yadeinu"—the Temple Mount is in our hands—Motta had said in his deceptively simple manner on that morning in June 1967. But then, the war barely over, Moshe Dayan had removed his shoes at the entrance to the Al-Aqsa Mosque, sat cross-legged with Muslim authorities, and handed back exclusive authority on the Mount, surrendered the keys to the kingdom. As if he were the defeated party.

Yoel helped found an organization called El Har Hashem (To the Mountain of God), to lobby politicians and rabbis to change the ban on Jews praying on the Mount. Yoel understood the rabbis' fear of violating the inner core of sanctity. But he had studied the talmudic texts describing the Temple layout and determined that the Holy of Holies was situated in the area of the Dome of the Rock. Several leading rabbis, including Chief Rabbi Goren, had reached the same conclusion.

Most rabbis, though, weren't convinced—even Rabbi Zvi Yehudah opposed tampering with the Mount. El Har Hashem held a conference in Ofra to overturn the rabbinic ban; four hundred rabbis were invited, barely forty came.

Frustrated, Yoel said to a fellow activist, "We need to bring thousands of Jews to stand before the Temple Mount on the eve of Passover."

"And what will we do?" asked his friend.

"We have to show God that we are ready for redemption."

"If you have a realistic idea, Yoel, I'm ready to listen. But I'm not going to demonstrate against God."

LATE AT NIGHT, when Ofra was in total stillness, broken only by the footsteps of the two men on security patrol and the distant cry of a coyote, Yoel paced in his cramped living room. The floor-to-ceiling bookshelves were filled with the mystical writings of Rabbi Kook and Alterman's poems and accounts of archaeological excavations and well-worn sets of the Bible whose margins were marked with Yoel's notes—ancient and modern Israel absorbed into a seamless sacred canon.

Yoel was often joined by Ofra's founder, Yehudah Etzion. The two friends were preparing a manuscript about how to adapt the laws of the Torah to a modern state. The Torah was a blueprint for God's relationship with a holy nation living in a holy land. But in exile the Torah had lost its national dimension, and rabbis had dealt only with the needs of Jewish communities and individuals. Now the Torah had to be brought home, restored to itself.

For Yoel there was nothing theoretical about the relationship of the Torah to the collective. His most intense moments of prayer were requests for the nation, his moments of spiritual elevation and depression reflections of the nation's condition. Authentic Jewish religious experience happened through the collective. Yet Yoel was also an intensely private person, who preferred to pray at home rather than in a congregation, and whose political and religious instincts were contrarian.

Strained with lack of sleep, Yoel explained to Yehudah that it wasn't enough to long for the days of old, as a Shabbat hymn put it; the old needed to be renewed. Consider the biblical injunction to leave the land fallow every seven years. How to give those who work in a modern economy the experience of participating in a cycle of work and rest? "One part of the nation is involved in minute halachic questions, and the other part ignores it completely," Yoel said. "We need to take the concept of the sabbatical year in agriculture and extend it to other areas. Everyone should be entitled to a sabbatical."

"And how do we prevent the collapse of the economy?" asked Yehudah.

"A committee will decide which workers are needed to maintain essential services," said Yoel.

He could almost see it: just as Friday became Shabbat, so would the secular state of Israel evolve into the messianic Kingdom.

Evolve, Yoel emphasized: that was the crucial movement. Classic Kookian theology: the secular state as indispensable precursor, first flowering of redemption.

"Secular Zionism has outlived its usefulness," Yehudah retorted. "It performed an essential historical purpose, but it has lost its way. Now it is up to us create the next phase of Zionism and lead the people."

"There will be no redemption for Israel," said Yoel, "without working together with our secular partners."

YEHUDAH'S DESPAIR ABOUT secular Zionism was encouraged by a new mentor, an obscure far-right ideologue named Shabbtai Ben-Dov. A veteran of the most extreme anti-British underground, the Stern Group, Ben-Dov was a self-taught philosopher who knew thirteen languages. When Yehudah was in high school, Ben-Dov, a family friend, had given him a copy of his book *The Crisis of the State and Israel's Redemption*. With its too-long sentences and references to political philosophy, the book had meant little to Yehudah then. But he read it now with the intensity of someone encountering revelation.

The sin of secular Zionism, wrote Ben-Dov, was in trying to replace Jewish chosenness with the mediocrity of normalization. The secular state was stripping the Jews of the faith that had once sustained them. Ben-Dov proposed replacing the secular state with a theocracy governed by updated laws of the Torah—just as Yoel and Yehudah envisioned. But unlike Yoel, who felt gratitude for the state, Ben-Dov despised it. *This* is what Jews had dreamed of and suffered for, one more little nation-state with petty politicians and a second-rate copy of Western culture? Where was the grandeur that Jews had imagined would result from their return home?

Yehudah marveled at the ability of Ben-Dov, writing in the 1950s, to anticipate the current crisis of secular Zionism. It was as if Ben-Dov had written directly to him.

Yehudah showed Ben-Dov's book to Yoel. "If we follow his path," Yoel told his student, "we will be left with no state and no kingdom."

"He shows a way forward," countered Yehudah. "Rabbi Kook doesn't give us a program."

"There are no shortcuts, Yehudah. Even an avant-garde has to look backward and make sure the nation is following."

Yoel, thought Yehudah, has the emotional dependency on secular Zionism that an abused child has on his parents.

THE LEAN, RED-BEARDED young man in jeans and knitted *kippah* and work boots stood on a roof overlooking the Temple Mount. Peering through binoculars, he observed the changing of the guard of Israeli police at the Mughrabi Gate and the patrols of Muslim officials in the plaza around the Dome of the Rock. He jotted down their schedules.

Yehudah Etzion had a plan, the ultimate plan: to cleanse the Mount of the abomination of its spiritual occupier. And he had potential partners. A terrorist underground was forming to stop the withdrawal from Sinai. The group included two dozen settlers and their supporters, among them combat veterans with knowledge of explosives. The only way to stop the withdrawal, some concluded, was through an act so drastic that it would convulse the Middle East and make it impossible for Egypt to offer even its pretend-peace to the Jews. An act, say, like blowing up the Dome of the Rock.

For Yehudah, it wasn't a great conceptual leap from airbrushing the Dome of the Rock out of the photograph of the Temple Mount in the poster he and Yoel had conceived to the decision to actually remove the Dome. But the purpose of removing the Dome, he told his friends, shouldn't be merely to stop the withdrawal, but something far more grand: this would be the founding act for the redemption movement envisioned by Shabbtai Ben-Dov.

Underground members stole explosives from an army base, and Yehudah dug a pit for the cache in a friend's farm in the Golan Heights. They debated scenarios, including bombing the Dome of the Rock from the air. But an air force pilot who had joined the group refused to steal a plane from his base, and the group searched for an alternative plan.

In fact, most members were ambivalent about blowing up the Dome of the Rock. Won't Muslims attack Jews around the world in retaliation? What right do we have to endanger them? And what if we cause an Arab invasion of Israel?

"Our enemies are already doing everything they can to hurt us," Yehudah reassured them.

Yehudah didn't let on that he too had qualms. To bring dynamite into the Holy of Holies, center of divine peace—how dare they? He knew all the arguments Yoel was likely to make if he learned of Yehudah's plans: King David wasn't allowed to build the Temple because he was a warrior; the altar had to be made of stone uncut by blade, an implement of war. There was, Yehudah readily admitted, an element of sin in his plan.

Yehudah was soft-spoken, without hatred for Arabs. He admired their rootedness in the land, wished the Jews could be more like them. But someone had to take responsibility for this pivotal moment. And how to cut the umbilical cord of the new world being born without blood?

SEPARATIONS

WEARING HIS UNIFORM brown shirt and pants, Udi Adiv was led by a guard to the concrete table divided by a metal net. Sylvia, elegant as always, was waiting on the other side. She looks great, thought Udi ruefully. They pressed fingers through a hole in the net.

"Listen, Sylvia," Udi said, looking away. "This can't continue. I want a divorce."

Sylvia was silent.

"Don't you love me?" she said finally.

"Of course I love you."

"So why?"

"Why?" said Udi, suddenly angry. "I'm a *symbol.* You can't undermine me by taking a different political position."

Sylvia was part of a Trotskyite faction, and Udi was a disciple of Che Guevara. The Trotskyites believed in a revolutionary working class, the Guevarists in a Third World uprising against the West.

"But that's my belief," she said quietly. "We don't have to agree completely. I don't tell you what to think, and you can't tell me what to think."

It wasn't only the politics, Udi continued. She had let him down in other ways, like when she'd ignored his request to bring books and underwear for one of the prisoners. "You behaved selfishly," he said.

"I want to stay connected with you," Sylvia said.

"It's over."

Back in his cell, several hours passed before he restored himself to emotional equilibrium.

UDI PRIDED HIMSELF on being the good Jew, proving to Arab prisoners that not all Jews were racists. Yet the distance between Udi and his fellow prisoners only grew. Even the Marxists among them, he was shocked to realize, weren't entirely free of religious faith. Secular and fundamentalist alike dreamed of a return of the golden age of Arab rule. Udi tried to reason with them. "The revolution will be class-based, not ethnic-based," he said. "The workers of all nations will bring the revolution." To no avail. He didn't even bother trying to counter the Holocaust denial most of them took for granted.

Udi was friendly with all his fellow prisoners, even with the Muslim fundamentalists who in their long beards and white skullcaps repulsed him because they reminded him of Gush Emunim settlers. When a cellmate needed help in writing a Hebrew appeal to the Supreme Court, or tutoring in English, Udi didn't hesitate. But he was close to no one, and spent almost all of his time reading. Days would pass without a real conversation.

IN THE PRISON LIBRARY Udi found a collection of Freud's writings. He came to a conclusion that disturbed him: there were areas of reality that Marxism couldn't explain. Of course Marxism remained true in its understanding of history, the collective movement of humanity; but the individual had an inner life beyond the reach of ideology. It's not that Udi hadn't realized this before, but somehow its moral significance had eluded him. How much importance should a revolutionary give to individual needs? What happens when those needs conflict with the collective good?

Udi had a new visitor with whom to explore these ideas: Leah Leshem, who had been in his apartment the night of his arrest and who'd left after the trial to study in Paris. Leah had never stopped loving Udi. In Paris she would obsessively seek out political films about violence and torture, which gave her nightmares but which also linked her to Udi. When she felt lonely in a strange city, she thought of Udi, stoic in his cell, and resolved to be strong too.

Now that Udi had divorced Sylvia, Leah was hoping to take her place.

Though she shared Udi's radical politics, Leah was not an activist. In a letter to Leah after a visit, Udi warned, "The relationship between us cannot be compartmentalized: a warm, ideal, individualist relationship on the one hand and a practical political relationship on the other."

Still, Udi didn't reject Leah's overtures, and she became a regular visitor to Ramle Prison.

THE LETTUCE WAR

FROM THE EIN SHEMER NEWSLETTER: "A query: To whom? I don't know! Maybe to Avital? But I know he couldn't care less about anything that touches, bothers and worries [his fellow] comrade.... How much longer will we have to suffer the total freedom of [Avital's] donkeys, whether in our neighborhood, and in the gardens, but not in the greenhouse?"

Fair enough, thought Avital. His three donkeys—Ferdinand and Isabella, named for the Spanish monarchs who expelled the Jews in 1492, and Shulem, Yiddish for *shalom*—did on occasion trample the neighbors' flower beds. And sometimes his kids got a little rowdy, singing into the night around the campfires they built outside the greenhouse; and sometimes they got carried away and tossed plastic into the flames, and the smell wasn't so pleasant. And then there was that unfortunate incident when Avital loaded the donkeys into a new kibbutz van, and they'd chewed the upholstery and relieved themselves in the back. *Okay, sorry. But tell me,* hevreh*, are we going to become bourgeois farmers and worry about our rose beds?*

Avital had his supporters, including the editor of the newsletter: the letter complaining about the donkeys was accompanied by a drawing of three adorable donkeys smiling mischievously as they chew the neighbors' flowers.

Still the complaints were having an effect—especially since maintaining the greenhouse was expensive, and the economy was worsening. Inflation had hit triple digits, and agricultural exports were suffering. The situation had become so difficult that the kibbutz had reverted to the old practice of group weddings, to save on expenses (though reasonable requests for changes on the menu would be accommodated, the newsletter promised).

The kibbutz planning committee determined that a new sports center should be built on the prime spot where the greenhouse sat. As for the greenhouse, it would be either moved to a peripheral location or else dismantled. Avital was informed after the fact; he hadn't even been given a chance to defend himself.

"I see this as a *personal affront*," he wrote to the newsletter. "But I have objective arguments, which I will briefly cite." He went on for two pages, hitting at Ein Shemer's most sensitive point: its fear of losing its youth to the city. "We're not talking about buying a tractor," he wrote mockingly. "I believe that the goal of keeping connected with the boys and girls [of the kibbutz] and giving them challenges and opportunities to create—in our midst—is *the central problem and main goal* of the entire kibbutz movement, and of Ein Shemer especially, given the high percentage of young people who leave. . . . Have we completely lost our identity? Are boys who work in agriculture *and grow vegetables for our kitchen* and love this place and this land—is that less important than muscle-building?"

Avital's supporters forced the committee to bring its plan for a sports center to a vote among the comrades.

After dinner, when the kibbutzniks returned to the dining room for the weekly meeting, they found affixed to the walls lettuces grown in the greenhouse. Some were hanging from the rafters.

"It's not fair," complained an opponent of the greenhouse. "Avital is trying to manipulate us."

Avital knew his people: How could they oppose encouraging young people to grow such beautiful lettuce?

The kibbutzniks voted to retain the greenhouse. "For now," noted the resolution.

MEIR ARIEL ENCOUNTERS LIGHT

MEIR RETURNED HOME from the cotton fields, removed his muddied boots and the kaffiyeh wrapped around his head.

"Tirza," he began. "Something happened in the fields today."

"Nu?"

"I was crying out to the heavens. And I got an answer."

"What do you mean, you got an answer?"

"I encountered God."

"Are you on drugs, Meir?"

"No. Tirza, listen. I don't know what happened to me, but it was real."

What had he experienced? Fields transformed to light, all forms dissolving back into their common essence? Had the universe revealed to him that there is no death, only changing forms of oneness?

Meir didn't say. But whatever it was he'd experienced that day, Meir's faith in God was confirmed.

"TIRZA," SAID MEIR, "there's just one thing. Please, no more nonkosher meat in the house."

"What? What are you talking about?"

"I don't care what you eat outside the house. Eat, enjoy. But I want the house to be kosher."

Tirza was quiet. Then she said, "My father has just given us a pail of meat." Her father hunted wild boar. "What do you want me to do, just throw it out?"

"Finish the meat, but then no more."

"All right, Meir. We'll do it your way. All I ask is that you don't start surprising me with all that religious nonsense."

"I promise you," said Meir, "no surprises."

CHAPTER 20

BUILDING DIFFERENT ISRAELS

ARIK ACHMON, CEO OF PRIVATIZATION

KANAF-ARKIA WAS THRIVING. By contrast, the parent company, Arkia, was a disaster. In debt, with aging planes, some of them dating to the 1950s, with too many employees and an all-powerful workers committee that vetoed layoffs, Arkia symbolized all that was wrong with Israel's statist economy. How do you make a small fortune in Israel? went the joke. Invest a large one. No one even quite knew how much Arkia was worth; its managers could do no better than present books that were two years old.

As angry as Arik was with the Likud and its settlement policy, he found common ground with its stated commitment to a free market and privatization. And the first test case for privatization, the government decided, would be Arkia.

Arik and his partners placed a bid. Arik had big plans for Arkia: open new domestic routes, break El Al's monopoly on flights abroad, and fly charters to Europe. But most of all he intended to turn Arkia into a model of efficiency and worker-management relations. He would fire extraneous employees and offer those remaining shares in the company's profits. A humane capitalism, pursuing profit while protecting the worker. A capitalism worthy of a son of the kibbutz.

Not surprisingly, Arik happened to know the right person. The Likud's finance minister, Yigal Horowitz—nicknamed "Mr. I-Don't-Have" for his refusal to subsidize special interest groups—was an old friend of Arik's. They had met in 1955, when Horowitz, then an independent farmer, had bought twenty cows from Arik, then manager of Kibbutz Netzer Sereni's cowshed. With his keen eye Horowitz had noted that Arik delivered the same cows that Horowitz had chosen—an unusual act of good faith in a business where deception was widespread. And Horowitz never forgot it.

Over the years, when they met at farmers' conventions, Horowitz would refer to Arik as the most honest cowhand in Israel.

Arik's main competition for the bid was a group formed, as it happened, by Horowitz's two sons. Arik reassured his partners: If we make a convincing case, Horowitz will be fair. Horowitz, though, wasn't convinced. After all, a subsidiary company buying out the parent company would be unusual anywhere, let alone as Israel's first test case for privatization. Horowitz phoned Arik for reassurance. "We have real concerns about whether we can trust Arkia to your hands," he said. "Are you really serious, Arik?"

"Serious, ready, and clear about what we want."

They met in the finance minister's office, a small room with a plain table and wooden chairs without padding. "I'm giving you Arkia," Horowitz said. "Two things decided in your favor: your company's experience, and the integrity of your group. I already knew in 1955 that Arik Achmon is an honorable man."

There was one more obstacle to overcome. Arik needed the approval of the Histadrut labor union, which owned 50 percent of Arkia and was deeply suspicious of privatization. He would need inside help. And it so happened that one of Arik's closest childhood friends, Moisheleh Bankover, was now the Histadrut official in charge of negotiations. Arik and Moisheleh had studied together in kibbutz boarding school, they'd been drafted together, their military numbers were separated by a single digit, they had gone through officers training together.

Arik told Moisheleh he intended to give employees a 25 percent share of Arkia.

The deal was signed in December 1979. Kanaf-Arkia paid $1.5 million for 75 percent ownership of Arkia, along with assuming Arkia's $3.5 million debt. Employees were granted the remaining stock. Arik became CEO, and his partner, Dadi Borowitz, deputy. Horowitz raised a toast on shot glasses of brandy. What a country, thought Arik. Thanks to the sale of twenty cows, he was being given the chance to help modernize the Israeli economy.

"*SHALOM*, MY NAME IS ARIK and I'm the new CEO of Arkia."

Several hundred employees were assembled in a hall in Ben-Gurion Airport. Arik's appearance was meant to emphasize his direct style: unlike the previous CEO, who wore a jacket and tie, Arik wore jeans and a plaid shirt.

"My philosophy is simple," he explained. "A company has the right to earn a profit. Employees have the right to honorable wages and fair advancement in reward for productivity. I see two legitimate options for employees: one, to work by the book; two, to strike. Sanctions, slowdowns, are the cancer of the Israeli labor force. For me, sanctions are not legitimate, because you aren't fulfilling your responsibilities but you're still getting paid as if you were."

He stood feet apart, half smile anticipating the test of combat.

"Don't try to educate us," a woman called out.

Arik stared at her for what seemed like a very long time. *You people don't have a clue who you're dealing with—*

Finally he said, "You had better forget everything you think you knew until now. And whoever can't adjust should forget about working for me."

Arik approached his new mission just as he had planned his military missions: flexible in tactics, fixed on goal. Ruthless if necessary, generous when possible. He readily accepted the Histadrut's insistence on collective agreement with the ground workers, and granted longer vacations and salary increases to diligent employees.

"ARIK, YOU'RE GOING TOO FAR," complained one of his partners. "You're acting like a kibbutznik."

"Base salaries will be determined by what the company can afford," Arik replied. "But what matters to a worker isn't only how much money he makes but whether he feels he is treated fairly."

Arik exchanged his predecessor's big office for a small adjacent room, and in place of the CEO's Volvo continued to drive his old Fiat. He took a substantial pay cut, earning half the average Israeli CEO's salary. (He was compensated with shares: he owned 7 percent of the company.)

In case anyone in Arkia hadn't yet gotten the message that the era of status symbols was over, Arik moved the company from central Tel Aviv to modest quarters at Sde Dov, a small airfield near Tel Aviv. He bought several mobile homes from an evacuated Israeli base in Sinai and set those up as his headquarters, just like the mobile homes settlers were moving onto West Bank hilltops. For Arik, too, Israel was a kind of construction site, a work in progress.

Arik routinely left the office past 10:00 p.m. You stay as long as you need to, he told the managers. Some revered him, some detested him. In the end he knew there was only one group of people he could trust: the *hevreh* from the 55th Brigade. And so he brought in Fuchsy, the brigade's operations officer during the Yom Kippur War, to head Arkia's planning. And he appointed as company driver Papino, who'd been wounded in 1967 and adopted by Arik through his convalescence. And Yoske Balagan to head building maintenance. The paratroopers spoke about the Arkia staff as "the fighting family," and getting the job done as "fulfilling a mission."

In a flattering newspaper profile of the new Arkia, Yoske described the tensions between Arkia's old-timers and the boys from the 55th: "They ask me, 'Why do you work late at night when you don't get paid for extra hours?' The [work ethic] of 'this idiot' gets them angry. But what do they want? . . . I come from a different world, a world in which you have to give."

ONE BY ONE, Arik invited the pilots in for a chat. The most pampered among Arkia's employees, pilots evoked in Arik little of his sympathy for workers' rights. They had all the arrogance of the combat pilots they'd once been, expecting to be treated as a savior elite. Though the company had use for no more than fifty pilots, it was paying the salaries of seventy. They received three times their regular pay for overtime, got paid from the moment they left their homes for work, and were granted extravagant compensation for every minute of delay in takeoff, even when they were initiating sanctions and responsible for the delay.

Arik's goal was to dismantle that caste of privilege, replacing the pilots' collective contract with individual contracts. He needed to wait for the right moment, catch them off guard, look for the breach in their defenses.

His immediate goal was laying off twenty pilots. That turned out to be the easy part: the Histadrut agreed that Arkia would collapse without the layoffs. "The rules of the game are changing," Arik told a meeting with the pilots' representatives. "But we'll decide on the new rules together, through negotiations." Until the time came for confrontation.

TWICE A WEEK, Arik left work early for his other job. He stopped at home, exchanged jeans and sandals for IDF uniform and red boots, and drove an hour north to a base near Haifa. After two decades in the paratroopers, Arik had been entrusted with founding and commanding a logistics brigade, whose task during war would be to supply an armored division with shells and fuel and food, as well as create first-aid stations. Arik, now a colonel, commanded two thousand reservists—drivers, mechanics, doctors—maintaining hundreds of trucks and armored vehicles and storerooms with thousands of tons of ammunition.

As much as possible, Arik sought to integrate the units under his command. One unit, for example, was entrusted with removing bodies from destroyed tanks, a task that included not only retrieving body parts but also scraping pieces of skin from a tank's charred innards—because Jewish law, honored by the IDF, insists on the dignity of burial for any bodily remains. Arik paired the body-retrieval squad with the medical unit, so that the dead could be quickly identified.

Moving back and forth between Arkia and the IDF felt seamless to Arik. Both tasks required commanding large organizations that provided services—in one instance to airline passengers, in the other to combat soldiers. Both systems needed to be at their peak performance, meeting non-negotiable deadlines and ready for emergency.

Arik relished the daily test of his competence, his steadiness under pressure. His creativity was expressed by infusing cumbersome organizations with flexibility. He regarded the reservists under his command as "employees," and in a sense he regarded Arkia's employees as soldiers in an elite unit. If he often acted like an army commander in running Arkia, he often acted, too, like a CEO in running the brigade. Any soldier could approach him with a complaint or a suggestion. When someone addressed him as "commander," he corrected: "My name is Arik."

BETWEEN HIS WORK in Arkia and his enhanced responsibilities in the army, there were days that Yehudit didn't see Arik at all. Yehudit herself was working full-time—her therapy practice was thriving—and running the household. But Yehudit complained only when Arik spoke brusquely to the children.

The Achmons took out a large mortgage and built a house in North Tel Aviv. The area had become transformed from their student days into a center of the Israeli elite. The one-story house was modest, certainly compared to those of their neighbors, some of whom installed marble bathrooms. Arik owned a single suit, which he saved for travel abroad. He and Yehudit rarely vacationed; their children joked that, for all of Arik's access to free airline tickets, he was like a monkey without teeth, unable to eat peanuts.

The focus of admiring profiles in the business sections of the newspapers, Arik never felt more fulfilled. The newspaper photographs showed a handsome man in his late forties with thin lips and receding hairline exposing an implacable forehead. Yet his raised eyebrows exposed an involuntary tenderness, as though he were still capable of being surprised by the world, a naïveté disconcerting in a face so single-minded it could be mistaken for ruthlessness.

He would have laughed at the notion that he—of all people!—was capable of naïveté. He knew his strengths and weaknesses: not the most empathic person, but ready to go through fire for a friend. He wasn't nice, but he was good. True, he had a healthy opinion of himself. And why not? Everything he touched succeeded.

ARIK AND HIS PARTNER, Dadi, began turning a profit. Where Arik was precise, scrupulous, Dadi was reckless, grand. Dadi's expertise was buying and selling planes, and his sense of timing seemed impeccable.

Dadi had always wanted to be a paratrooper. And so Arik had brought him into the 55th Brigade as a quartermaster.

"You can't trust Dadi," Yehudit warned Arik. "He doesn't think twice about lying when it's useful to him. And the time will come when he will lie to you too."

"Dadi?" Arik said, laughing. "He idolizes me."

"Arik, be careful."

OPERATION SELF-SACRIFICE

ON A BITTER-COLD NIGHT in the Etzion Bloc, with the wind repeatedly knocking out the generator-powered electricity, Yisrael Harel stood before the leaders of the settlement movement gathered in emergency session and summoned all the gravitas his mournful face could manage.

There can be no settlement without land, Yisrael explained. Yet the settlements were being choked for lack of land on which to grow. Ofra had been allocated a ludicrous few hundred dunams—how could it hope to absorb the dozens of families on its waiting list? The Likud government wanted to create a law that would turn all non–privately owned land in the territories into state lands on which settlements could be expanded, but Begin feared the Americans. If the land issue wasn't resolved, and Palestinian autonomy declared, then a PLO state, God forbid, would emerge in Judea and Samaria.

Yisrael didn't mention the complexity of the state land issue. Many Arabs who couldn't produce a deed still claimed land their families had worked for generations. The Supreme Court had already uprooted one settlement rising on contested land. Yisrael believed in Arab-Jewish coexistence; yet settlement expansion would intensify Palestinian fears and resentments. Still, weighed against the threat of a PLO state, that risk was unavoidable.

Here, then, said Yisrael, was the plan: We will launch an open-ended hunger strike until the government agrees to turn much of the West Bank into state land.

There was unease in the room. Yisrael was asking them to protest against the most pro-settlement government since 1967. What would the public think?

"Everyone [in the government] agrees with us, everyone tells us how right we are, and nothing is being done," said a leader of the Gaza settlements. "That's why I plan to fast."

"I'm already hungry," said another Gaza settler. "But, seriously, I'm afraid it won't work. . . . We need to disrupt the public order. Tomorrow I can close the entire [Gaza] Strip. Five, six truckloads of tomatoes spilled on the road, and there's no construction work in Tel Aviv." Palestinian laborers would be blocked from reaching their jobs in Israel.

"At sixty liras a kilo?" someone said in mock horror at wasting expensive tomatoes.

"A hunger strike is the last resort before a violent struggle breaks out, and I'm afraid that will happen," said a representative from a settlement in Samaria.

Someone recalled that during a visit to the Etzion Bloc, Yitzhak Rabin had once expressed support for its return to Jordan: "Rabin said that he didn't mind visiting this place with a visa. How is it that he didn't leave on a stretcher?"

"Under no circumstances will we be dragged into acts of violence," said Yisrael.

YISRAEL AND FIVE other men set up a big tent across from the prime minister's office, laid mattresses on the ground, and declared a hunger strike. "Stop Strangling the Settlements," read one banner.

The strikers consumed only water, and on Shabbat, fruit juice. Operation Self-Sacrifice, they called it. A fellow faster said to Yisrael, "It may turn out to be a fast to the death." "It won't come to that," Yisrael reassured him. "They won't let us die outside Begin's door."

Begin sent his bureau chief to plead with the hunger strikers to end their fast and invited them to meet with the prime minister. Yisrael refused. "We're not interested in more promises," he said. His elderly parents also came to plead, but halfheartedly: they'd never had influence over him. Sarah tried another approach: "How will you be able to lead the struggle without strength?" "If I eat," Yisrael replied, "I won't be the leader of the struggle."

A week into the strike, the fasters agreed to meet with Begin. Yisrael insisted on entering the prime minister's office without assistance.

"Stop this hunger strike," Begin half demanded, half pleaded. "You're breaking my heart."

"You promised us there would be many more [settlements]," said Yisrael. "Why aren't you fulfilling this promise?"

"I gave my word to the Egyptians and to Carter," replied Begin.

"You keep your promises to the *goyim*. But not to your own voters."

"Until this man apologizes," Begin said to an aide, "I'm not continuing," and left the room.

"How can you speak that way to the prime minister?" a fellow striker berated Yisrael.

"I spoke the truth," Yisrael insisted. "I have nothing to apologize for."

Begin returned, and the meeting resumed. It ended without agreement.

The hunger strike continued into its second, then its third week. The big tent was surrounded by little tents: dozens joined the fast. Thousands came to show support.

On the fourth week, the hunger strikers permitted themselves soup.

Hanan Porat appeared and began making a speech about faith and redemption. Yisrael cut him off. "Hanan," he said, annoyed, "this group doesn't need ideological inspiration." Hanan offered to speak to Begin on the group's behalf; Yisrael told him his intervention wasn't necessary.

In fact Yisrael saw his fellow hunger strikers—most of them pragmatic young men who headed local settlement councils—as the nucleus for a new kind of settlement leadership, more mainstream, less mystical, than Gush Emunim. When this was over, he intended to form an umbrella council of settlements—expand the settlement leadership beyond Hanan and his friends.

As a result of the prolonged fasting, Yisrael experienced heightened clarity. He handled media, met with government representatives and well-wishers, and even continued editing *Nekudah* from the tent. Liberated from dependence on food, he felt exhilarated, seemed to intuit exactly the right response to every problem.

On the forty-fourth day, an emissary from Begin appeared with an offer: the government would set up a committee, to be chaired by Ariel Sharon, to find legal solutions to the land dilemma.

"It's a trick," a striker warned; "they'll bury us in committee." Yisrael disagreed: "It will be a committee with our supporters, most of all Sharon. Besides, you have to know when to stop. People are going to start giving out. This is the right moment."

The hunger strike ended the next day. It was the eve of Shabbat. On the door of the Harel home hung a sign prepared by Yisrael's children: "Welcome Home, Abba!" Yisrael, pale and gaunt, staggered into the bedroom and collapsed.

HE HAD BARELY SLEPT a few hours when he was awakened by an urgent knock on the door. Standing outside was a fellow hunger striker and one of the few secular Jews among the leaders of Gush Emunim. He had driven from his home in Kiryat Arba, near Hebron, with terrible news. Six settlers were dead, many more wounded, in a terrorist ambush on a group of Jewish worshippers in Hebron. They had left the Tomb of the Patriarchs after Friday-night prayers. The ambush occurred outside Hadassah House, where Avital Geva had burned the calves' heads a year earlier.

Nothing, Yisrael knew, would be harder for his community to tolerate than the murder of Jews in Hebron—a new Hebron massacre, evoking the victims of the 1929 pogrom.

The next morning, after restless prayers, the entire Ofra community crowded into the settlement's clubroom. On the wall hung a relief map of the land of Israel. Summoning all his strength just to stand before them,

Yisrael offered a military-style briefing. "It happened after prayers," he said, deliberately laconic. "Several terrorists stood on the roof, opposite Hadassah House, and fired into the *hevreh* with Kalashnikovs and grenades."

Despite our outrage, Yisrael continued, we must refrain from vigilante violence and allow the army to work. Those who want to do something constructive should work toward preventing the withdrawal from Sinai. "Every one of us will have to take some role in the public effort. At least something. Look, I've taken a leave without pay from my work in *Yediot Aharonot*."

Someone called out, "It seems to me that there are more than enough big shots circulating among us with official cars and walkie-talkies." Who did Yisrael think he was, presuming to be their leader?

There it was again, that old accusation Yisrael had heard as a young man. All his rage against those who had confused his passion for the Jewish people for self-aggrandizement focused now on this heckler. "So you found someone to blame," Yisrael said sarcastically. "Really, I don't have the strength to argue with you. I'm simply exhausted. . . . I'm amazed at how people who barely came to support us, people who continued going to work every morning, people who did nothing—how they dare at a time like this to criticize us. Chutzpah!"

A friend tried to calm him: "Congratulations for the hunger strike, but I don't think you know what every person here does for the community. I ask that every one of us engage in self-examination, not in examining his friend."

THE NEAR-SIMULTANEOUS EXPLOSIONS that wounded two Palestinian mayors and targeted a third happened on the thirtieth day following the massacre in Hebron, and that was the first clue that Jews were behind the attacks: thirty days marks the end of a phase of the Jewish mourning period. The attacks happened within half an hour of each other, and in the same way: bombs detonated when the mayors turned on the ignition of their cars. One man lost both legs, another a foot: whoever had done this knew exactly how much explosive was needed to maim rather than kill. A third mayor was spared when an Israel Police sapper tried to detonate a bomb attached to the garage of the mayor's home; the bomb blew up in the sapper's face, blinding him. The three mayors had apparently been targeted because they had supported attacks against settlers. The crippled mayors were to be a living warning.

The attacks were the work of Yehudah Etzion and his friends in the underground. Following the Hebron massacre, they'd decided to temporarily divert their attention from the Temple Mount. Yehudah, though, had been ambivalent: He helped coordinate the attacks but decided not to take part personally, fearful of getting arrested and destroying his plan.

The bombings were denounced by Prime Minister Begin, by Orthodox Knesset members, by the country's chief rabbis. Among settlers, though, there was little outrage; many supported the attacks outright. In Ofra some said with knowing smiles, It's the Shin Bet; who else could be so professional?

For Yoel, usurping the authority of the government of Israel was to challenge divine authority. Writing in his diary, he described the attackers as "Sabbateans," followers of a false messiah.

Yisrael Harel suspected that the attackers might be Arabs trying to discredit the settlement movement. "It isn't reasonable that Jewish hands committed these acts," he wrote in *Nekudah*. "And even less reasonable [to assume] that Jewish residents of this region were involved in the incident. All that [settlers] want is for these parts of the homeland, the heart of the land of Israel, to be under the laws of Israel and part of the state of Israel. If so, isn't it twisted to undermine the rule of law?"

On *Nekudah*'s cover was the headline "Who Harmed Coexistence?" Yisrael meant coexistence between Jews and Arabs. Along with that question appeared a photograph of an old Arab man wearing a kaffiyeh in animated conversation with a young Jewish man in sandals and knitted kippah. The young man was Yehudah Etzion.

YISRAEL HAREL, CEO OF JUDEA AND SAMARIA

EVERY FEW DAYS, Yisrael visited another settlement. He drove on dirt roads and on fresh asphalt to shaved patches of hill surrounded by ancient terraces. Some communities consisted wholly of rows of mobile homes; in others, rows of small houses with red roofs. Like a lost mythical land, Judea and Samaria was resurfacing. Yisrael was a practical man, concerned with organizational structures and political debates, but there were times when he felt overwhelmed by the beauty of the landscape and the poetry of the historical moment.

The purpose of his travels was to convince settlers to support an umbrella council of settlements. And the message he conveyed at meetings was as usual grim. True, he said, the hunger strike had been successful. The government was releasing more land, and settlements were being built again—there were now over three dozen in the West Bank and Gaza. But the permanence of those communities couldn't be taken for granted. What the government intended to do to the settlements in Sinai, it could one day decide to do to the settlements of Judea and Samaria.

The solution, concluded Yisrael, was unity: "We need an organization to represent us, just like the kibbutzim." Each kibbutz, he explained, sent delegates to its federation, entrusted with deciding the movement's practical and ideological direction.

Yisrael spoke of ensuring that the needs of settlers became part of the government bureaucracy, not granted as political largesse: "We pay national health insurance just like other citizens of the state of Israel, but we have to fight the bureaucracy to get benefits. Every year we have to fight the Education Ministry to build new classrooms. Our needs should be a natural part of the ministries' budgets."

It wasn't easy convincing the settlers to unify. There were austere kibbutzniks farming in the Jordan Valley desert and "quality of life" settlers living in West Bank suburbs, working-class Sephardim trying to move into the middle class and middle-class Ashkenazim trying to become pioneers. And each group had its own reservations about joining Yisrael's proposed council.

At a meeting in Kfar Etzion, the Orthodox kibbutz that was the first West Bank settlement, a member said to Yisrael, "There is a national consensus supporting [the existence of] Kfar Etzion. But if we join the council, and the government decides to dismantle Kedumim [a new settlement in Samaria], we would be forced to support Kedumim."

Yisrael could hardly restrain himself. "If there won't be Kedumim, there won't be Kfar Etzion," he said. "It pains me that I have to debate a pioneer in his own house. But I don't see how I can establish the council without the kibbutzim among us taking a leading role." Kfar Etzion voted to join the council.

In the Jordan Valley, Yisrael reassured the secular kibbutzniks that the council would not be a front for the messianists of Gush Emunim. In Kiryat Arba, the settlement near Hebron, he reassured the messianists that he had no intention of displacing Gush Emunim. "I'm not trying to fill the shoes of Rabbi Levinger and Hanan Porat," he said. "I don't have the charisma. But I can compensate with organizational skills."

Not that he wanted to exclude Gush Emunim, far from it: the messianists, with their capacity for self-sacrifice, were essential to the settlement movement. Moreover, Yisrael was a democrat: the council needed to contain all facets of the movement. Yisrael believed he could control the messianists, tame their excesses, and harness their fervor for the movement, just as utopian fantasies had helped the socialist pioneers overcome impossible obstacles. Far better those who erred in overzealousness than the bourgeois Orthodox Jews Yisrael had grown up with, decent people who would never change history.

THE STAGE WAS SET with a fan of Israeli flags, a harp, and photographs of Theodor Herzl and Rabbi Kook. The Samaria Girls' Choir sang an old pioneering song, extolling the spade and the hoe that together turn the land into "green flame." Aside from the photograph of Rabbi Kook, it could have been the setting for a convention of kibbutzim. A member of a veteran kibbutz who'd come to show solidarity told Yisrael, "Only here are these songs still sung."

In the end, most of the settlements sent representatives to the founding meeting of the settlers' council. The rules were determined by Yisrael. Decisions would be made by consensus. Along with official delegates he invited as nonvoting delegates "men of the spirit, who are essential for an ideological movement"—rabbis and intellectuals, including Yoel Bin-Nun.

Almost all the delegates were male and—despite Yisrael's hope for broader secular representation—Orthodox. They could have been divided into two categories: the "beards" and the "mustaches." The "beards" were Kookians, messianists. They wore big knitted *kippot* and white shirts and laced black shoes in winter and sandals with socks in summer. The "mustaches" tended to be more nationalist than devout, "religious" an adjective that described their Zionist identity, and redemption more self-generated than divinely imposed. They wore compact knitted *kippot* and jeans and kibbutz-style work shirts and work boots in winter and sandals without socks in summer. Yoel was closer to the beards, Yisrael to the mustaches (though he himself didn't have one).

Yisrael was unanimously elected chairman. No one was more capable of connecting the settlers to the political and military establishments than Yisrael Harel. Among settler leaders, he was the most worldly. The others knew how to organize settlement groups, evade army roadblocks; Yisrael knew how to make important contacts. His work in the media, in the Movement for the Complete Land of Israel, in the paratrooper association, had connected him with the secular elites in a way that few Orthodox Jews had achieved.

The council's closing proclamation reflected its desperate optimism, affirming the goal of annexing Judea and Samaria but warning that any other alternative—whether the Labor Party's vision of dividing the territories with Jordan or the Likud's vision of autonomy for Palestinians—would endanger Israel's survival. "Any foreign administration will necessarily lead to an independent Arab Palestinian state in the land of Israel, and threaten the existence of the people of Israel in its land."

The settlers called their new organization the Yesha Council. *Yesha* was the Hebrew acronym for Judea, Samaria, and Gaza. By happy coincidence, the word *yesha* also meant "salvation."

YISRAEL AND ARIK SURVEY THE LAND

YISRAEL HAREL STOOD on the empty hill and pointed to the hill across the valley, busy with bulldozers and cranes. Beside him stood Arik and Yehudit Achmon. Yisrael was taking his friends on a private tour of the landscape he was helping transform. On that hill, Yisrael said, an agricultural settlement is being built. Over there, an ultra-Orthodox town. And on that third hill, an upscale community of private homes. The land lay open, pristine and beckoning. "Look around you," continued Yisrael, "everything is empty. There is enough room to settle without dispossessing anyone."

Hands on hips, Arik slipped into the posture of a military briefing. Despite himself, he was impressed. Yisrael and his friends had figured out how to overcome the limited pool of religious Zionists and entice whole sectors of the Israeli public to the settlements. You want a big house with a garden for the price of an apartment on the coastal plain? Nofim is the place for you. You want to live in an ultra-Orthodox ghetto, complete with built-in sukkah on the porch? Come to Emanuel.

"As you can see, there are no Arab villages in sight," Yisrael said.

Nu, *really, Srulik: that's your answer to the demographic problem?*

You and I, Arik thought, represent opposite visions of Israel. With Arkia, Arik was trying to extract Israel from an outmoded socialist ideology and create a rational and efficient economy, connect Israel with the world through new air routes, create, in other words, a normal country—goals threatened by the settlements. Yisrael's outmoded pioneering ideology was building the anti-normal Israel, a Jewish ghetto that would be an outcast among the nations.

Arik detested the settlements as mimickry of the kibbutzim, the real expression of pioneering Zionism. When his parents and their friends built Givat Brenner, they had been on their own. But for the settlers, no amount of IDF protection was ever enough.

Here in this romantic landscape, thought Arik, was rising the greatest mistake in the history of Israel.

"Tell your father that I'm inviting him on a tour of the settlements," Yisrael said to Yehudit, referring to Hazan. "I promise to keep it discreet."

Sure, she thought. As if anything in this country was ever discreet.

They drove to the nearby settlement of Kedumim. Yisrael introduced Arik and Yehudit to one of the movement's rising stars, a woman in a tight kerchief and tight smile named Daniella Weiss. "We've won on every front," she told her Tel Aviv guests. "Except for one: We haven't yet managed to convince people like you. That will come, of course, the more everyone realizes we've reached the point of no return."

In the car on the way home, Yehudit said, "Did you notice that she didn't look us in the eye? She kept staring over our heads."

"Of course," said Arik; "she doesn't want to lose eye contact with God."

CHAPTER 21

HURBAN

"BEGIN, KING OF ISRAEL"

IT WAS AN early-summer evening in 1981, and Independence Park was filled with celebrants—old women in housecoats and slippers, workmen in undershirts with children on their shoulders. They were mostly Sephardi Jews, and they had come from Jerusalem's forgotten neighborhoods to celebrate their newfound assertiveness, and to give thanks to the man who had helped them find their voice, Menachem Begin.

Toward the front of the crowd young men held each other by the waist and sang "Begin, King of Israel," substituting the prime minister for King David in the old song. On a stage a banner proclaimed, "Peace, Security—Likud."

Prime Minister Begin appeared, and the crowd roared. Braced by aides, Begin slowly mounted the three small steps of the stage. "Say '*Shalom*' to Menachem Begin," a Yemenite Jew with side locks told his young son. "*Shalom*," said the child, laughing.

It was Israel's tenth and most traumatic national election campaign. With the economy in disarray, the Labor Party was leading in the polls. The prospect of a return to power of the party that symbolized Ashkenazi paternalism had roused a Sephardi revolt. It felt like the beginning of a civil war. Local Labor Party headquarters were vandalized; Likud supporters attacked Labor supporters on the street.

"Brothers and sisters," Begin began, and the the crowd cheered. Brothers and sisters! Labor leaders had rarely addressed them so intimately. They were the wrong kind of Israelis—their music ignored on the radio, their history not taught in schools, their guttural Hebrew mocked. The universities were filled with Ashkenazim, the prisons with Sephardim. In one sense it was a typical story of immigrant dislocation, but there was this unique anguish: the very religious faith that was the core of Sephardi identity and had inspired their return home had excluded them from Labor's Israel, from being truly welcomed home.

Labor had wanted, at least in principle, to absorb Sephardim into Israeli society. But Labor had been impeded by its dream of creating a new Jew, secular and socialist. By contrast, Begin's only expectation of Zionism's "new Jew" was that he learned how to defend himself. Sephardi, Ashkenazi, religious, secular—Begin couldn't care less. And so Sephardim loved this Polish Jew who kissed the hands of women and lectured foreign leaders about the Holocaust, because he loved Sephardim for who they were.

"Saddam Hussein calls on the world to help Iraq build atom bombs," Begin continued, referring to the Israeli air strike two weeks earlier that had destroyed the Iraqi nuclear reactor at Osirak. "We'll let Saddam Hussein build atom bombs—"

"Be-gin! Be-GIN!" Hands waved and teenage boys leaped, but most of all there was laughter, sheer pleasure in Begin's understated Jewish irony.

"When I was a prisoner in Siberia," said Begin, and he was again interrupted by chants. "Please, children—" He turned to the row of young men up front, and they instantly quieted to hear his memories of exile. In recounting these stories, Begin was telling the crowd that Israelis were not some new creature divorced from Jewish history. We were Jews first, Israelis second.

"LISTEN TO THEM," Arik Achmon said to Yehudit. "They can't even denounce us in proper Hebrew. *A-smol*"—duh left.

Even as a capitalist Arik remained a man of the left, by temperament, voting habit, commitment to social justice. But he was also an Israeli of the left in his sense of entitlement; and the Likud supporters were, as far as he was concerned, upstarts and ingrates. Who had built this country if not left-wing Ashkenazim? Who had suffered and fought and died so that the immigrants could have a home to come to?

However repulsive to Arik, the election campaign turned out to be good for Arkia. A new and reckless Likud finance minister, Yoram Aridor, had replaced the cautious Yigal Horowitz and sought to woo voters by reducing taxes on imported videos and color TVs (even though the country's only TV station was still in black and white). The Likud was interested in keeping down prices before elections—no simple matter, given the triple-digit inflation rate—and that included Arkia's flights to the southern town of Eilat, the most popular Israeli vacation destination.

A phone call to Arik from the transportation ministry: What will it take to keep you from raising prices?

A license for charters to Europe, Arik replied.

The ministry promptly granted Arkia charter flights to Paris, London, and Frankfurt, breaking El Al's monopoly on Israeli flights abroad. "Out-and-out election bribery," Arik called it, with the grim satisfaction of someone who was learning to master a game he despised.

AT A LABOR PARTY rally in Tel Aviv's municipality square, a comedian named Dudu Topaz mocked Likud voters as second-rate soldiers, "doing guard duty if they serve at all," while Labor voters served as pilots and commandos. He called Likudniks *chah-chahim*, greasers. Everyone knew which ethnic group he meant.

The next night, the Likud held a rally in the same square. Voice quivering, Begin cited the *chah-chahim* slur. "Until this morning I had never heard the word 'chah-chahim' and didn't know what it meant." In the underground struggle against the British, he continued, we made no distinctions between Jews. "When that—what's his name—Dudu *To*-paz—made his evil comments, the whole crowd that stood here yesterday cheered. Now let me tell Dudu *To*-paz about whom he [dared] speak. Our Sephardim were heroic fighters"—like the two captured underground members who blew themselves up with a smuggled grenade rather than allow the British to hang them. "Ashkenazis? Iraqis? Jews!"

Begin continued: "Yesterday, in this place, there were many red flags. Today there are many blue-and-white flags. That is the moral difference, the historic and ideological difference, between us and the socialist Labor Party. They still haven't learned what the red flag symbolizes in our time. . . . This is the flag of hatred of Israel and of arming the enemies of Israel who surround us. This is the flag of oppression of the [Soviet] Jews and suppression of Hebrew. This is the flag of the Gulag. . . . And this is the flag that was flown yesterday by those who were brought here from all the corners of the land by buses and by the trucks of the kibbutzim."

THROWN ON HEAVEN'S MERCY

MENACHEM BEGIN WAS narrowly reelected.

In a radio interview on the eve of Rosh Hashanah, the Jewish new year, Begin repeated his election-eve attack on the kibbutzim. Referring to a TV news clip that showed a kibbutznik beside a swimming pool, Begin contemptously compared him to "some American millionaire." "Millionaire kibbutzniks with swimming pools" entered the Israeli lexicon.

Avital Geva was beside himself. The most frugal, the most devoted workers in Israel: millionaires with swimming pools? Yes, Mr. Begin, Ein Shemer has a swimming pool, and let me tell you how it came to be built. The year was 1946. Our parents, who had left their homes in prewar Poland to build Ein Shemer, were grieving the destruction of the world they had left behind, cut adrift in the new world they were trying to create. Then someone had an idea: Let's do something that will give us and our children a sign of faith in the future. How about a swimming pool? It seems silly, I know: a swimming pool as their answer to destruction. But they were modest people, our parents, and a swimming pool offered a measure of comfort in this harsh land they were trying to tame.

But there was no money for a swimming pool, Mr. Begin. And so the kibbutzniks took jobs after a day's work in the fields, to pay for construction material. And they built the pool themselves, without hired labor.

And now, Mr. Begin, you want to destroy the kibbutzniks with ridicule, with demonization. What will be left in this country if you turn these good people into parasites?

ON POSTERS ALONG the Tel Aviv–Jerusalem highway, on banners hanging from porches, a nightmare image spread: a map of Israel and of the Sinai Desert covered with black diagonal lines, symbolizing the dismantling of the country by stages. First Yamit and the other settlements in Sinai, then the settlements in Gaza, then the settlements in Judea and Samaria, followed by the Galilee and the Negev. There would be no end to Arab territorial demands because the issue wasn't the borders of a Jewish state but its existence.

According to the timetable of the Egyptian-Israeli peace treaty, the Sinai peninsula was to be returned to Egypt in April 1982, in ten months' time. Begin appointed Ariel Sharon as minister of defense, and entrusted him with overseeing the evacuation, including the uprooting of Sinai's settlements.

Hurban, opponents of withdrawal were calling it. *Hurban* was the most dreaded word in the Hebrew language: literally "destruction," but more than physical ruin. *Hurban* meant the destruction of the Temple, the exile of the Divine Presence. And this *hurban* would be self-inflicted. It was a repudiation of the gift of the Six Days, a setback to the redemption process, a rebellion against the will of heaven. A spiritual tragedy that called for a spiritual response.

YOEL BIN-NUN WAS late as usual. It was just past dawn on Rosh Hashanah, and for the past hour Yehudah Etzion had been waiting for his friend in Ofra's prefab synagogue. Yehudah should have known: Yoel inhabited another time zone, perhaps another era. But how could he be late for *this*?

They were planning to tear open the gates of heaven, throw themselves on God's mercy, and appeal for a reprieve from the coming withdrawal. At Yehudah's urging, Yoel had agreed to revive an ancient tradition: blowing the shofar on Rosh Hashanah at sunrise, a practice halted during the Roman occupation because Jews feared the Romans would mistake it for a call to war. Sunrise had now passed. But if Yoel showed up soon they could still manage to preempt the morning worshippers and perform their desperate ritual.

Yoel appeared, without apology. The two young men covered their heads in prayer shawls and approached the Ark. The synagogue filled with early morning light.

They retrieved a Torah scroll and unrolled it to the story of the binding of Isaac, which is read on Rosh Hashanah morning and invokes a last-minute reprieve. Yoel sang the words in his deep voice. "And it came to pass, after these things, that God did test Abraham, and said to him, Abraham, and he said, Here I am."

Yehudah produced a shofar, a ram's horn, recalling the ram sacrificed in place of Isaac. He blew the shofar, thirty strong and distinct blasts, some staccato, some prolonged.

"The fate of the Sinai settlements hangs on the scale of judgment," Yoel said. "If there is a moment where they can be saved by heaven, it is now."

TWO DAYS AFTER Rosh Hashanah, on October 6, at the annual parade in Cairo celebrating the Egyptian attack on Israel on Yom Kippur, Islamic fundamentalists assassinated Anwar Sadat.

In Ofra, the news was greeted as miraculous: The Protector of Israel has saved us from ourselves. That night, in Ofra's synagogue, worshippers recited a psalm thanking God for destroying enemies: "God of Vengeance, repay the arrogant in kind."

Word of the Rosh Hashanah shofar blowing had gotten around, and some regarded Yoel with awe, as though he had manipulated heaven. "Here I am, trying to create a movement to stop the withdrawal," a neighbor said to him, "and you blow shofar and everything is reversed."

"It's not because we blew the shofar," insisted Yoel, perhaps fearing to take responsibility for an act of heaven.

That night Yoel walked in downtown Jerusalem. He looked at the faces around him and saw anxiety. What would happen to Israel now? Would the peace with Egypt hold?

The dissonance between Ofra and Jerusalem: here Sadat's death was seen not as reprieve but as threat. And if this was the attitude in right-wing Jerusalem, what must they be thinking in Tel Aviv?

Back in Ofra, Yoel said, "We're living in a fantasy world. The people want this peace. We're alone."

A FAREWELL TO SINAI

EARLY ONE MORNING in February 1982, Eldad Harel, almost eighteen, eldest son of Yisrael and Sarah, left the yeshiva where he was studying and hitched a ride south, toward Sinai. He carried a khaki knapsack, a sleeping bag, and a Kalashnikov, borrowed from Ofra's arsenal. Accompanying him was a friend named Dudi, who wore an Egyptian army coat his father had brought back from Sinai in the Six-Day War.

For both boys, this was a last fling before the army. It was also a farewell to Sinai, which Israel was scheduled to return to Egypt in two months, unless Eldad's father and his friends succeeded in preventing the government from withdrawing. Neither Eldad nor Dudi told their parents that they were leaving yeshiva without permission and planning to hike through Sinai in the middle of winter. Why worry the parents? We'll be back by the end of the week, the boys reassured each other; no one will even notice we were gone.

Short but powerful, Eldad would wander, alone, through the Arab villages around Ofra. He often visited a young man in Ein Yabroud, the village just across from his home (though, as Yisrael noted pointedly, those visits were never reciprocated); together they would catch poisonous snakes and sell them to a university laboratory. Eldad would disappear from school for days at a time to rock-climb in the Judean Desert, training to try out for the IDF's top commando unit. Once, climbing down a cliff, he found himself dangling over a fifty-meter drop without enough rope; friends pulled him back up, and Eldad calmly resumed the climb.

Near Eilat, Eldad and Dudi hitched a ride with an army truck that took them deep into Sinai's mountain range, near Santa Katerina, said to be the site of Mount Sinai. Where will we sleep? asked Dudi. Right here, said Eldad. It was so cold that Dudi thought they might die of exposure. They built a fire; when it died down, they buried coals in the sand beneath their sleeping bags.

By day, they hiked the remote hills. Aside from a few soldiers and Bedouin, they were alone.

On the last evening of their trek, they came to the southern tip of Sinai, near Sharm el-Sheikh. Total darkness set in. They stood on an unlit road, at an intersection, hoping to hitch a ride back to Eilat.

A semitrailer approached. Eldad stood at the edge of the road, extended his arm, and pointed toward the ground. Dudi stood a few meters behind. The driver, spotting Eldad, came to a stop. Eldad approached the cabin and asked whether he was heading toward Eilat. Sorry, said the driver.

Eldad closed the cabin door and walked toward Dudi. The semitrailer, slowly turning at the intersection, swerved and hit Eldad. The driver didn't notice that Eldad had fallen, and the massive tires rode over his body.

Dudi rushed toward him. Blood trickled from Eldad's mouth. "He ran me over," he managed to say before losing consciousness. Dudi ran after the truck. "Stop!" he shouted. But the driver didn't hear Dudi's cries and drove on.

Dudi grabbed Eldad's Kalashnikov and tried to fire in the air. But the gun jammed.

An army jeep appeared. An ambulance was summoned. Eldad's pulse weakened. By the time the ambulance arrived, he was dead.

YISRAEL WAS AWAKENED by knocking. It was past midnight, and Yoel was standing at the door.

Yisrael looked at Yoel's face. "Who?" he asked.

"Eldad."

"How?" Yisrael managed to ask.

Yoel told him.

"Should I stay?" Yoel asked.

"No need," said Yisrael.

"No!" Sarah screamed, and then went still.

Yisrael hugged her. They wept together, but quietly, so as not to awaken the other children.

NEIGHBORS FROM OFRA, Sarah's ultra-Orthodox relatives, paratrooper kibbutzniks wearing handkerchiefs for *kippot*, gathered together in the ancient Jewish cemetery on the Mount of Olives, just across the valley from the Temple Mount. Arik Achmon noted Yisrael's restraint: *Srulik is strong—*

Black-bordered ads appeared in *Nekudah*, signed by local settlement councils, repeating the words, "May you be comforted in the building of the land."

The seven days of mourning were observed at the Harel home. Motta Gur and Ariel Sharon came, along with Knesset members and journalists. Yisrael maintained composure by playing the host. The only time he broke down was before several paratrooper widows whom he had adopted.

Arik arrived with Danny Matt. Arik and Yisrael embraced.

"Tell me what happened, Srulik." In Arik's work with the widows, he had learned to avoid empty words of comfort, and focus instead on practicalities: What happened? What do you need?

Yisrael phoned Eldad's friend, Dudi. Come be with us, he urged. Yisrael wanted to reassure Dudi that the family didn't blame him.

When Dudi entered the Harels' crowded salon, Yisrael embraced him. When he left, Yisrael urged, "Keep in touch."

FROM SAVIOR TO DESTROYER

IN OFRA, IT WAS a year of tragedies. Two other residents were killed in accidents—devastating for an intimate community. Some suspected a flaw among the faithful that had weakened divine protection or even invited judgment. All of Israel was responsible for one another, the saying went—not only for taking care of each other's needs but literally responsible for each other's sins. Who, then, had brought disaster on them all?

Someone recalled that Yoel and Yehudah had blown the shofar on Rosh Hashanah morning. Whoever changes the order of shofar blowing, the rabbis had warned, invites disaster on Israel. By what authority had Yoel and Yehudah acted? At one of the funerals, a neighbor said to Yoel, "You and Yehudah blow shofar, and now we go to funerals."

"What do I know of God's calculations?" responded Yoel angrily. "I'm not responsible for Sadat's assassination, and I'm not responsible for this."

Yisrael Harel reassured him, "Don't worry, Yoel, I don't accept this nonsense."

But Yoel couldn't be calmed. *How dare they!* This was superstition of the worst kind. And what did it mean about the cohesiveness of the camp of the faithful if, in time of crisis, some of his neighbors could turn on him?

LEANING INTO A LECTERN, Yoel looked around at his students, the soldiers of the Mount Etzion yeshiva, and spoke about the binding of Isaac. According to most commentators, he noted, God's command to Abraham to sacrifice his son was a test of Abraham's faith. But one commentator, the Rashbam, had a different view. He saw the command as punishment—for Abraham ceding the land of the Philistines to Abimelech, king of Gerar. "'And God's anger was raised about this,'" Yoel quoted the commentator, "'because the land of the Philistines is included in the borders of Israel.'" Concluded Yoel: "You committed your son to a compromise on the land? Now return him to Me."

Yoel drew the inevitable connection. According to the book of Deuteronomy, he noted, the area of Yamit is included in the borders of Israel. "For the first time in the history of Israel, the government is violating its main purpose: protecting the people and the land." The government of Israel, the very power intended to fulfill God's will in history, was abusing its authority to undermine divine will.

A student said he wanted to join protesters planning to barricade themselves inside Yamit. "What does Rabbi Yoel think?" he asked.

"If it were possible to stop the withdrawal by bringing a hundred thousand demonstrators, who would physically prevent it with their bodies? It would be forbidden, my friends."

Yoel tilted his head and eyed with satisfaction the confused looks of his students. "Because," he continued, "that would mean violating the authority of the state of Israel. If the state cannot sign international agreements, it will be an empty shell." Preserving the authority of the state of Israel, even when it sinned, was a divine prerogative.

"Still, I do see value in protesting: to make clear that a part of the people of Israel has no share in this sin. A woman who is raped is permitted to her husband; a woman who acquiesced is forbidden to her husband. We need to say that this is a rape, and that we don't acquiesce. For the sake of history."

THOUSANDS OF MOURNERS were pressed together in the quiet side street before the Mercaz yeshiva, bent beneath a heavy rain. Rabbi Zvi Yehudah Kook's body, wrapped in a black-striped prayer shawl, was held aloft on a stretcher. Loudspeakers carried Psalms in broken voices. *"Abba"*—father—some mourners called out.

It was Purim, the holiday marking the victory of Israel over its enemies. No one more embodied the spirit of Purim, the promise of a happy ending for the Jews, than Rabbi Zvi Yehudah. Why was his soul being returned to heaven on this of all days? In a little over a month from now the withdrawal from Sinai would be completed. How would his followers endure the brokenness of the land without his militant optimism, his ferocious love for the land of Israel, for every Jew? Perhaps, some speculated, God has taken Rabbi Zvi Yehudah now to spare him from witnessing the imminent uprooting, the beginning of the unraveling of the Six Days. Perhaps, said others, he was taken to appeal in heaven against the *hurban*.

He was ninety-one years old, and he had suffered. A leg had been amputated—just as a part of the land of Israel was now being amputated. So it was for a *tsaddik*, a holy man: his being absorbs the travails of Israel.

Standing among the grieving students of Rabbeinu, "our rabbi," Yoel Bin-Nun felt gratitude and distance. He had learned the way of Jewish wholeness from Rabbi Zvi Yehudah. When the rabbi had grabbed his hand, long ago, at that ultra-Orthodox rally in Jerusalem, he'd transformed Yoel into an unconditional lover of the Jewish people, its sinners no less than its pious, perhaps more than its pious. And when Yoel heard him, on that awesome night in Mercaz, cry out for the severed parts of the land of Israel, the rabbi had bound him to its healing.

Yet in recent years Yoel's encounters with Rabbi Zvi Yehudah had become frustrating. Yoel had turned to him for guidance in dealing with unimagined complexities: How to act when the government of Israel is opposed to the wholeness of the land of Israel? How to relate to leftist brothers who in their unrealistic but understandable passion for peace were prepared for territorial concessions? Rabbi Zvi Yehudah had responded with the same insights Yoel could recite from memory. The rabbi hadn't tried to reach out to Yoel, understand how he had grown. *He wanted me to stay like the rest of his students, tape recorders quoting Our Rabbi—*

Yoel thought back to that night in Hawara, when Rabbi Zvi Yehudah had stood before an IDF officer, opened his coat jacket, and dared him to shoot. Yoel had wept then—upset, he thought, to see his rabbi so agitated. But perhaps he had realized that his trust in his teacher would never be the same, that he was now on his own. Perhaps, glimpsing his future loneliness, Yoel had wept for himself.

"THERE WILL BE NO WITHDRAWAL"

THE SIX-DAY WAR unleashed among Israelis paradoxical longings. Judea and Samaria promised a restored past; Sinai's vast emptiness promised a limitless future.

Nine thousand Israelis lived in Sinai's fourteen settlements. Labor governments had built these settlements, most of them farming villages, with national consensus. After all, Israel had fought four wars in Sinai, and the desert offered strategic depth. Unlike the West Bank, there was no demographic problem in Sinai. And the eucalyptus-shaded villages, built on sand, were small miracles, exporting dates and mangoes and roses.

The largest settlement in Sinai was the Mediterranean coastal town of Yamit. The sea was barely a kilometer away from the low, whitewashed houses rising from the dunes. At night, as the town fell silent, residents could hear the waves approaching.

Yamit was to be Israel's city of the future. Unlike so many Israeli towns, expanded under pressure of immigrant necessity and in seeming contempt of the landscape, Yamit was planned in harmony with its stunning surroundings. Most homes had a view of the sea. Electric wires and cables were underground. Parking was on the periphery; one could walk from one end of town to the other on tree-lined paths without crossing a street. Secular and relaxed, Yamit embodied the Sinai ethos: residents wore bathing suits and walked barefoot in the shopping center.

As the withdrawal date approached, Yamit began to empty. By spring 1982, most residents, along with farmers of the neighboring villages, had accepted government compensation and left. Refugees of peace, they called themselves bitterly. Their places were taken by political squatters, many of them West Bank settlers. Hundreds of Orthodox families moved into emptied apartments. Religious schools were established, along with separate afternoon study groups for men and for women. Yamit was transformed into a devout community, Sinai supplanted by Judea and Samaria.

ESTHER BIN-NUN DIDN'T want to go to Yamit. She was for positive action, not futile protest. But Yoel couldn't keep away, and Esther had long ago determined that no matter what, the family stays together. And so shortly before Passover, Yoel and Esther and their four children arrived in Yamit. They found an apartment stripped bare; even the light fixtures had been removed. They rolled out sleeping bags and settled in for the holiday.

Yisrael Harel, of course, intended to go to Yamit: the head of the Yesha Council belonged on the front line. But how could he bring the family? Expose their three surviving children—ages fifteen, ten, and seven—to yet another trauma so soon after Eldad's death?

Sarah was adamant: We are going to Yamit. "We're a family," she said. "Whatever we go through, the children will go through."

EVEN AMONG THE messianists of Gush Emunim, Yisrael Ariel, chief rabbi of Yamit, was regarded as an extravagant dreamer. Ariel saw the Six-Day War's new borders as merely the first step toward fulfilling the biblical promise of borders stretching from the Nile to the Euphrates. He was working on a multivolume atlas that would include all the important sites within that fantasy map.

A former Mercaz student, Ariel—then known as Yisrael Shtiglitz—had fought in Jerusalem with the 55th Brigade. On the morning of June 7, 1967, as the paratroopers were gathering at the Western Wall, he was assigned to help retrieve body parts of the scouts killed outside the Lions' Gate. Later that same afternoon, Ariel saw a column of prisoners of war. Moving toward him, single file, hands on head. Who were they? He felt a sudden panic: maybe they were Israeli POWs, and the Jordanians had won the war. How could he be sure? For all he knew, the war was lost and Radio Cairo had told the truth: Nasser's army had conquered Tel Aviv. He would not let them take him alive. He would die fighting, turn the Temple Mount into Masada . . .

Now, as Yamit began to empty and the Six-Day War's borders constricted, something in Rabbi Ariel broke again. As if his vision of destruction in the Six-Day War hadn't been hallucination but premonition.

YAMIT'S PROTEST LEADERS argued over tactics. How to stop the approaching withdrawal: With prayer and fasting? Civil disobedience? Violent resistance? Could they really raise a hand against Jewish soldiers?

Hanan Porat was ambiguous about the limits of protest. He spoke of creating a "balance of fear" to prevent withdrawal, but then warned of violence against soldiers. "We must not injure," he said, "but we are permitted to be injured."

Hanan was now a Knesset member, for a new right-wing party called Tehiya (Renaissance), founded to stop the withdrawal. But the party had won only three seats in the 1981 election. Yisrael Harel had warned Hanan: "Your strength as a leader is to be above politics. You'll lose your prestige and effectiveness." But Hanan was convinced that the new party, which united secular and religious in support of the post–'67 borders, was a spiritual achievement.

Hanan was also convinced that the withdrawal wouldn't happen. "In another few weeks, hundreds and thousands will come to the Yamit area, to strengthen us," he said. "With God's help there will be no withdrawal." Quoting the rabbis, he added, "'God's salvation comes in the blink of an eye.'"

Rabbi Levinger of Hebron delivered a Shabbat sermon in Yamit's synagogue, urging squatters to be prepared for *mesirut nefesh*, martyrdom, if necessary.

He's lost his mind, thought Yoel; he's telling Jews to commit suicide—

"I don't want to stay here," Yoel told Esther afterward. "There could be blood."

The Bin-Nuns left their bare apartment in Yamit and moved into an abandoned house in a nearby agricultural village.

THE ARMY SEALED the roads leading into Sinai. The thousands of protesters Hanan had promised were now effectively blocked. At most, mere hundreds would be able to slip through. The evacuation was scheduled for April 26, a week after Passover.

A crowd gathered at a roadblock outside Yamit. It was an early spring morning, though in the desert it felt like summer.

A teenager crawled under a police van and tried to puncture a tire; he was caught and dragged into the van. Protesters tried to push past police to retrieve him.

Buses and jeeps appeared, filled with paratroopers. They lined up on the sand.

Rabbi Ariel approached them. "Soldiers! Disobey orders!" he called out. "Don't allow Jews to be uprooted from their homes in the land of Israel. This is against the Torah."

The rabbi was arrested for inciting insubordination.

SONG OF THE SEA

MAIL SERVICE AND garbage collection in Yamit were suspended. All stores, except for one grocery, were ordered closed. Then the phone lines were cut.

A song by Naomi Shemer played on the radio, a plea against uprooting a sapling. The song became the anthem of a dying Yamit.

Settlers responded with acts of faith. Yoel wrote a report about a harvest in one of the agricultural settlements. He sent the report via courier to Yisrael Harel, who had briefly returned to Ofra: "Following the first day of Passover . . . the residents of Atzmona [a Sinai settlement], along with many guests, went out to harvest the first melons that were planted three months ago. The harvest will continue with God's help for another two months. . . . The event ended with singing and dancing. The 60-dunam area will produce, with God's help, around 250 tons."

STUDENTS FROM YAMIT'S military yeshiva, arms around each other's shoulders, led the crowd of religious Jews moving slowly from the center of town into the darkness, toward the sea. A young man bearing a torch, a pillar of fire, walked before them. There were high school students, old people, women with baby carriages. "Israel, trust in God," they sang.

It was midnight, the seventh day of Passover. The night, according to tradition, when the Red Sea split for the Israelites.

The crowd came to the shore, where the desert met the sea. As waves broke behind him, Rabbi Ariel addressed the faithful. He spoke of the biblical figure, Nachshon Ben-Aminadav, the first to leap into the Red Sea even before it parted: "[Nachshon] plunged into the water without making rational calculations, without considering the security situation. He offered his life, and in his merit the miracle occurred."

Yisrael Harel, back for Yamit's last stand, watched teenage girls looking expectantly toward heaven. What would happen to their faith, he wondered, when the bulldozers came?

THE LAST STAND

TALMEI YOSEF, A small agricultural settlement near Yamit, appeared deserted. Its lawns and vegetable gardens had withered; plastic from vanished greenhouses blew across the sand.

A month earlier, Talmei Yosef had been evacuated by the army; even its greenhouses had been dismantled. The families that had built Talmei Yosef had been too traumatized to resist, quietly boarding the IDF buses that drove them into sovereign Israel. There they were taunted by Israelis envious of the financial compensation offered them by the government. Millionaire extortionists, some called them.

As soon as the veterans left, Gush Emunim squatters took their place. And now the squatters were inside the red-roofed houses as the army returned.

The soldiers wore caps, not helmets, and carried no arms. Among the soldiers were young women, assigned to evacuate the female protesters. The soldiers divided into teams and began knocking on doors.

Yoel Bin-Nun had affixed a note to the front door of his borrowed house: "Officer/soldier, Shalom. . . . You are hereby warned that this act constitutes a crime against the people of Israel in its land."

Yoel's eight-year-old son, Odeyah—"Odi"—was troubled by the letter. "Abba," he said, "it's forbidden to tell soldiers not to do their job."

"Why, Odi?" asked Yoel. "Explain it to me."

"What if there's a war," said Odi, "and someone will say, I don't want to fight?"

Yoel stroked his son's head and said nothing.

When soldiers entered the house, Yoel sat on the floor like a mourner and was dragged away to a waiting bus.

YISRAEL HAREL DROVE to Atzmona, a Gush Emunim "protest" settlement of trailers and tents, near Yamit.

"I'm the head of the Yesha Council," Yisrael told soldiers at the roadblock. That Yisrael expected to be allowed through reflected the ambiguous identity of an organization at once quasi-official and oppositional. The soldiers let him pass.

Atzmona's several dozen residents, many of them Mercaz students, had made a theological decision: they would not resist the soldiers because that would violate the authority—the sanctity—of the Jewish state. Nor would they call on soldiers to disobey orders. Instead, they gathered together, reciting Psalms.

Several young men stood on a scaffold, pouring cement onto a skeletal structure: they were building Atzmona's synagogue.

Soldiers sat on the sand, waiting for the order to move in. Their commander, Amos, reminded them, "There aren't two sides here."

Yisrael approached Amos, who recognized the head of the Yesha Council. Pointing to the building crew, Yisrael said, "Look what faith these people have," and added, "Let them be evacuated last." Amos agreed.

A young woman, a settler from Hebron, asked Amos for permission to address his soldiers. Amos looked at Yisrael. Yes, Yisrael nodded. The kerchiefed woman spoke quietly about how the Jewish people had built a state from the wilderness, and now this good land would be returning to wilderness.

Amos said to her gently, "We have to finish."

She ignored him, her voice turning shrill.

Too bad, thought Yisrael, she doesn't know when to stop.

Settlers quietly accompanied soldiers to the buses. No one needed to be dragged. Several teenage girls collapsed, and were carried by female soldiers. The young men on the scaffold continued to pour cement.

When all the other settlers had been removed, soldiers approached the building site. The workers laid down their tools and slowly walked toward the buses.

All the hope destroyed in Sinai, all the youthful promise—

Yisrael returned to his car and wept.

TEN ACTIVISTS FROM a far-right fringe group, Kach (Thus), headed by an American-born rabbi, Meir Kahane, barricaded themselves in an underground bomb shelter in Yamit and vowed to commit suicide if the town were evacuated.

Chief Rabbi Shlomo Goren was flown down to Yamit and, shouting through a vent, tried to convince the protesters to emerge, but there was no response. One young man, a doctor named Baruch Goldstein who had recently immigrated from the United States and whose sister was barricaded within, stood outside, reciting Psalms.

"THE EVACUATION HAS BEGUN," announced loudspeakers mounted by protesters on Yamit's rooftops. "Everyone to your stations. Soldiers! We tell you today to disobey the order. . . . For the rest of your lives you will carry the knowledge that you uprooted a city in Israel."

Hundreds rushed to the rooftops. Helmeted soldiers laid ladders against the two-story buildings. Cranes lifted cages; from inside soldiers sprayed foam. Protesters threw stones and tried to topple the ladders with poles. Black smoke rose from burning tires. Loudspeakers played the staccato song "Ammunition Hill," conjuring the spirit of the Six-Day War:

"The sun rose in the east / over the fortified bunkers / over our heroic brothers / . . . on Ammunition Hill."

Young men in jeans and T-shirts, some in prayer shawls, were dragged into cages. "Shame!" cried the loudspeakers. The soldiers, warned by their officers against excessive force, didn't use their batons.

On one roof, high school girls in long skirts recited Psalms.

A shofar sounded. "Eretz Yisrael!"—Land of Israel!—a man shouted.

Yisrael stood on a rooftop with Sarah and the children. Protesters laid barbed wire down the middle of the roof. Somehow the Harels' seven-year-old son Itai found himself on the wrong side of the barrier. Sarah reached over and retrieved him.

"Utzu eitzah v'tufar!"—Their plans will come to naught!—the protestors around them sang. Yisrael didn't join in. Instead, he took photographs. Therapy, he told himself.

Soldiers reached the Harels' roof. "Disobey orders!" Sarah shouted at them. "Don't uproot settlements!" the Harel children chanted. Soldiers lifted them down the ladders.

GENERAL CHAIM EREZ, commander of the Sinai evacuation, entered the home of Rabbi Ariel. Leave us for a few minutes, Erez told his soldiers.

The rabbi said to the general, "After destruction comes renewal. Let's drink *l'chayim*." They raised shot glasses.

IT TOOK THE army two days to remove 1,500 protesters from the rooftops and from inside the houses. Few were wounded, none seriously. Thanks to the restraint of the army and the relative restraint of the settlers, the struggle for Yamit turned out to be a kind of theater, a play about civil war.

The last to be evacuated were the radicals in the bunker. After failed attempts to penetrate the steel door, a bulldozer crashed through a side wall. Protesters threw chairs; soldiers sprayed them with foam. "Let's see you hurt a rabbi!" shouted their leader, Meir Kahane, as he was dragged outside.

What could be salvaged—greenhouses, prefab structures, giant refrigerators in packing plants, five hundred dunams of trees, even bomb shelters extracted from the earth—was shipped back to Israel. The rest was bulldozed.

General Erez addressed his soldiers: "I believe that the sacrifice the state made was necessary. There was an opportunity [for peace] that couldn't be missed. . . . Those resisting the withdrawal aren't more Zionist than those who evacuated them, and they don't love Israel more than we do."

SEVERAL HUNDRED PEOPLE, among them Yoel and Hanan and Yisrael, managed to slip back into the ruined town.

They gathered at an IDF memorial for soldiers who had fallen in Sinai's battles. The memorial had been a series of concrete pillars, which now lay toppled and scattered. Sand blew in the hot wind. A singed smell rose from the ruins of the dynamited shopping center.

The ceremony began with the symbolic tearing of clothes of a mourner. The honor of being the first to "tear" was given to Avraham Bar-Ilan, Yamit's town planner. Immediately following the ceremony, Bar-Ilan intended to drive to Gaza, to become regional planner for its new settlements. What better response of a faithful Jew to *hurban* than to build in the land of Israel?

An army jeep appeared. "Don't start up again," a megaphone called. "Leave the area."

Yoel ignored the order and read aloud, from his pocket Bible, Ezekiel's vision of resurrection: "The hand of the Lord was upon me . . . and set me down in the midst of the valley, and it was full of bones . . . and, lo, they were very dry. . . . And He said unto me: Son of man, can these bones live? And I answered: O Lord God, Thou knowest. . . . Then He said unto me: 'Prophesy over these bones. Behold, I will cause breath to enter into you, and you shall live.' "

Yoel thought of the photographs taken in the death camps just after the war, the mounds of corpses that hadn't yet been burned. And of the state of Israel that arose three years later. A Jew couldn't help being an optimist. Even here, among the ruins.

Hanan read aloud a list of Sinai's destroyed settlements and vowed to return.

They sang "Hatikvah," the anthem of hope. They walked to the last intact building in Yamit, a synagogue. There they removed the round, wood-encased Torah scrolls. Slowly, silently, they walked toward the road out of town. Soldiers and police joined the procession.

PART FOUR

MIDDLE AGE

(1982–1992)

CHAPTER 22

THE FORTY-FIRST KILOMETER

ARIK ACHMON GETS CAUGHT IN A TRAFFIC JAM

ON FRIDAY AFTERNOON, June 4, 1982, as he was working in his garden, enjoying the beginning of the short Israeli weekend, Arik got the phone call he'd been expecting for months. "It's Operation Big Pines," his deputy commander said. "We need you at the base by tomorrow afternoon."

For months the army had been preparing an assault against the PLO infrastructure in Lebanon. Though an uneasy American-brokered cease-fire had been in place on the northern border, Arik believed it was just a matter of time before Israel was forced to protect its towns and kibbutzim from periodic Katyusha attacks. Now that time had come. The Israeli ambassador to London, Shlomo Argov, had just been wounded in an assassination attempt, Israeli planes had bombed PLO camps, and the Galilee, in turn, had been hit by Katyushas. The government had decided to send the IDF into southern Lebanon to uproot the PLO's "state within a state." Though the terrorist group that had shot the ambassador had in fact split from the PLO, Arik agreed that sooner or later the IDF would be forced to act, and it might as well be now.

The cease-fire had forbidden PLO attacks along the northern border; but PLO terrorism against targets elsewhere in Israel, and against Jewish communities in Western Europe, continued.

For many Israelis, the murderous intent of the PLO was embodied by the fate of the Haran family. Three years earlier, PLO terrorists crossing from Lebanon by sea broke into the home of Danny and Smadar Haran, in the northern coastal town of Nahariya. They caught Danny and the Harans' four-year-old daughter, Einat, took them to the shore, shot Danny, and smashed Einat's head against a rock. Meanwhile, Smadar had been hiding in a closet with her two-year-old daughter, Yael; to keep Yael from crying, Smadar had pressed her mouth shut and accidentally smothered her. It was a story that could have come from the Holocaust. Filth, Arik called the terrorists.

For the sixth time in its thirty-four years Israel was about to go to war. And one way or another, Arik Achmon had been involved in every one of those wars. In a normal country, a forty-nine-year-old CEO doesn't go off to battle. But you deal with the reality you've been given. Arik knew no better definition of Zionism than that.

Arik finished cutting the grass. Then he called his business partner, Dadi Borowitz. When Arik had left the 55th Brigade to form the 862nd Logistics Brigade, Dadi had insisted on joining him, so Arik put him in charge of field headquarters. Dadi, Arik liked to say, is connected to me by an umbilical cord.

On Saturday morning Arik said good-bye to Yehudit, who knew better than to ask useless questions like how long he would be gone, and drove his company car to his base in the north. For the last year he had spent increasing time there, preparing his brigade for its mission in a war in Lebanon: supplying the 90th Armored Division, which was to seize the Beirut–Damascus highway close to the Syrian border and prevent Syrian forces from assisting the PLO. In war games, in constant inspections of the brigade's supplies of tank and artillery shells and C-rations and medicines, Arik had worked his men until he felt they were ready.

As Arik entered the gate, dozens of trucks—*My trucks*—were pulling out. "Where to?" he asked. Requisitioned, he was told. He checked the orders; nothing to do. "Replace the missing vehicles," he told his staff. "Use whatever *proteksia* you can. But no 'borrowing' without permission."

The base filled with reservists and with civilian vehicles requisitioned for the war—vans, trailers, open-backed trucks from the Tnuva dairy cooperative, most of them unsuitable for moving tons of ammunition.

Arik was summoned to IDF field headquarters at Kibbutz Misgav Am. On the invisible map of terrorist attrocities that Israelis carried in their heads, Misgav Am was a landmark. Two years earlier, terrorists had invaded the kibbutz's children's house, seizing seven children as hostages; one child was killed in the IDF rescue mission.

Arik was told: a new division has just been formed, and you will have to supply them too. "Can you do this, Arik?"

Impossible—he barely had enough men to take care of the 90th. How could he provide logistics units for the whole eastern front? To say nothing of ammunition and fuel and food?

"We'll manage," Arik said.

THE TANKS BEGAN crossing the border on Sunday morning. Soldiers waved V's from turrets and held Israeli flags. As they entered the villages of southern Lebanon, Shiites as well as Christians threw rice and candies, welcoming the IDF as liberators from the hated PLO, which had terrorized southern Lebanon.

Arik's force gathered in the ripening apple orchards of Kibbutz Ma'ayan Baruch, near the border. Men spread sleeping bags and tied blankets to trees for shade. Drivers slept under their trucks. There were explosions in the distance.

Day two. Still in the apple orchards. The most intense fighting was happening to the west, along the coast, where infantry and tank units were battling PLO forces in refugee camps. PLO members fired at the advancing Israelis from mosques, schools, hospitals. IDF loudspeakers warned residents to flee. Tens of thousands of civilians, in cars and trucks, on foot, crowded the roads heading north. In some camps PLO fighters allowed civilians to leave; in others, they held civilians as hostages.

Meanwhile, progress on the eastern front was maddeningly slow. The tanks of the 90th Division were to have reached the Beirut–Damascus highway by now; instead, they were barely halfway there.

The IDF's strategy puzzled Arik. Why a frontal invasion, clumsy and predictable, which would allow PLO fighters to escape northward and regroup? Far more logical to land in the north and then proceed south, trapping the PLO forces. Why didn't defense minister Ariel Sharon understand what was so obvious to Arik?

Day three. Hundreds of trucks, loaded with tons of supplies assembled by Arik's men over the last days, slowly moved through an opening in the border fence into Lebanon. Green hills, villages, apple orchards: a familiar Galilee landscape. Arik set up base near the village of Marj Ayun, just north of the border, and waited for instructions.

Day five. Arik received an urgent message: Israeli tanks were trapped by Syrian forces near the village of Sultan Yakub, thirty kilometers north of Arik's position. IDF artillery batteries had moved in, to provide cover for the tanks to escape. But the artillery units were running out of ammunition.

Arik ordered 150 trucks, loaded with shells, to assemble. "I'm taking the convoy in," he told his deputy, and left him in charge of the camp.

With Arik's jeep in the lead, the trucks headed into the mountains, toward Sultan Yakub. They rode on a narrow two-lane road with cracked asphalt, flanked by pine forests and steep declines. There were no railings.

The convoy came to a halt: a traffic jam of hundreds of tanks and armored personnel carriers. Arik tried leading his trucks onto the opposite lane, but jeeps and personnel carriers transporting the dead and wounded were heading south toward the border. Why hadn't anyone thought about the logistical consequences of moving two divisions on one narrow road?

He would have to force his way through.

Several tanks blocked the road. Arik shouted, "Pull to the side! I'm bringing ammunition to the front!"

No response.

"Get the hell off the road!"

Arik jumped out of the jeep, ran toward the tanks. His three "falafels"—the circles of his colonel's insignia—were noted: the road opened.

Early afternoon. Arik's convoy had barely moved a kilometer.

Up ahead, a cluster of tanks blocked the road. The crews were taking a cigarette break. "*Hevreh*, move to the side," Arik said. No response.

He approached the commander. "I don't have orders to let you through," the commander said. "Get me your officer," Arik demanded. He was handed a radio. "Arik, is that you?" said the voice on the other end. The tanks let him pass.

A few hundred meters ahead, a lone tank stalled. Arik climbed on top, opened the turret. "Move!" he shouted below. "You're holding up the war!"

A groggy soldier emerged.

"Get out of here! Now!"

All through the day: shouting, pleading, directing traffic. Another hundred meters, another two hundred meters.

TOWARD EVENING, ARIK led his convoy off the congested road. They came to a hilltop. Israeli artillery were shelling Syrian positions. In the valley below, Israeli tanks were burning.

As the crates of shells were being unloaded, Arik received a call on his radio: the commander of the 90th Division, Brigadier General Giora Lev. An old friend: Lev had commanded the first tank unit to cross the canal in the Yom Kippur War, and Arik had stood on the shore to welcome him.

"We've had a rough time, Arik," said Lev. "There are many dead and wounded. You will have lots of tanks to repair."

Arik tried to respond but was unable to speak above a whisper. He had lost his voice on the road. He never fully recovered: his voice had become permanently hoarse.

AVITAL GEVA GLIMPSES THE ABYSS

BEGIN AND SHARON had promised the cabinet and the public a limited operation, creating a forty-kilometer cordon that would put the Galilee beyond Katyusha range. But Sharon, intending to expel the PLO from Lebanon and bring the Christian Phalangists to power, ordered the IDF to press on, and by the fourth day of the war, Israeli soldiers reached the edge of Beirut. There they lay siege to Muslim neighborhoods in the western part of the city, where thousands of PLO fighters were barricaded. If the PLO didn't quit Beirut, Sharon announced, the IDF would invade.

Now Arik Achmon understood why the IDF had largely opted for a frontal assault. As the siege went on into July, it became increasingly clear that the war had political, not just military, goals. In sending the 90th Division to seize the Beirut–Damascus highway and the Israeli air force to bomb Syrian targets, Sharon intended to expel the Syrians, too, from Lebanon. Only by expelling both the Syrians and the PLO, Sharon believed, would the Galilee be secure.

Yet the IDF had never before fought a war intended to transform the political reality of a neighboring country. Sharon knew that the cabinet, and the Israeli public, would not likely support such a far-reaching war. And so he bluffed his real goal. In doing so, Sharon risked the trust and unity of a people's army.

The national consensus supporting the invasion collapsed. For the first time, war didn't unite Israelis but actively divided them. There had never been antiwar demonstrations while soldiers were at the front; now protesters, many of them demobilized reservists, gathered outside the prime minister's house in Jerusalem. "We Don't Want to Die in Beirut," read one sign. "You are leading the Jews to the ovens!" an elderly man shouted at the protesters. Doves accused hawks of risking Israel's most precious strategic asset, the willingness of its people to fight. Hawks accused doves of eroding the country's will with a Western naïveté fatal in the Middle East. Hawks and doves, though, agreed about this: the greatest danger to Israel was now internal, and the danger was coming from the rival camp.

AVITAL GEVA STOOD on the edge of the cliff and looked down into the besieged city. Smoke rose from an Israeli air raid. Beirut, with its dozens of multistory buildings, made Tel Aviv seem provincial. *What the hell are we doing here?* Never had the IDF been sent to conquer an Arab capital. Even in victory, Israel always knew its limits. But with this government there appeared to be no limits. And soon the reservists of the 55th Brigade would have the honor of being among the first to go into Beirut. In Suez City the paratroopers had fought in four-story buildings. How did you take over a city with twenty-story buildings?

It was early August, and Avital and his friends were camped in the olive orchards of Kafr Sil, a village just above Beirut's airport. This was the second call-up for the 55th Brigade in less than two months. The brigade had been been mobilized at the beginning of the war but experienced little fighting. Now it had been drafted again. In briefings, commanders showed aerial photographs pinpointing the buildings their units were to seize, but the men didn't need aerial maps: the buildings were clearly visible.

Meanwhile, the Israeli air force was bombing PLO positions in West Beirut, trying to force Arafat to evacuate. Water and electricity were cut. It was Israel's first full-scale asymmetrical war against terrorists embedded in a civilian population. And civilian casualties were increasing.

The veterans of the 55th Brigade were approaching middle age, and this would likely be their last war. But there was little of the old feeling of purpose. At night, they sat around campfires, but no one sang.

"Okay," said Avital, "so we cleared the PLO *hevreh* out of the south. We did what we had to do. We all know who Mr. Arafat is. Okay. But what's next? So we'll go into Beirut. And change the government in Lebanon. And if the Syrians don't agree, then what? Damascus? *Hevreh*, where does it end?"

Yisrael Harel was one of the few to defend Sharon. "*Hevreh*," he said, "I can't help wondering what's happening here. In the War of Attrition, didn't we bomb cities along the canal? But then there was no protest movement, no Peace Now. Ah, but then the Labor Party was in power. Now, suddenly, we hear that 'this isn't our war.' Why, because now the Likud is in power?"

"Yisrael," said Avital, smiling, "why don't you plant a flag here and build a settlement?"

HANAN PORAT ISSUED a statement congratulating the IDF and the government for "restoring" southern Lebanon—the lands of the biblical tribes of Naftali and Asher—to the people of Israel. In an interview with the settlement magazine *Nekudah*, Hanan explained that he wasn't demanding that the government build settlements in southern Lebanon, only reminding Israelis of their birthright.

But that was the public Hanan; privately, he was grieving. His daughter, Tirza, had lost her fiancée, Nadav, in Lebanon. Hanan had loved Nadav for his modesty, his devotion to Israel; he felt as if he'd lost a son. Hanan wrote this poem: "My God / bless me to be like Nadav / Pure in heart and deed / he walked in Your ways / and loved You so / until he went to the cedars of Lebanon / went, and didn't return."

YOEL BIN-NUN APPEARED, in civilian clothes, in Kafr Sil. He had been discharged from the reserves several years earlier, following a hiking accident on the Golan Heights in which he broke a leg. But with the *hevreh* at the front, he couldn't keep away, and so he'd hitched his way north.

Avital greeted Yoel with a hug. "Here's the man!" Avital exclaimed.

The latest argument around the campfire was about Colonel Eli Geva, commander of an armored brigade who had announced he would refuse an order to invade Beirut, and who had been dismissed for insubordination. That was a first for the IDF. Some of the men were angry at Eli Geva: a *yefei nefesh*, a delicate soul—not a compliment.

"Eli Geva is trying to stop something terrible from happening," countered Avital. "I wish I had his courage."

"Let me tell you what I learned from my eight-year-old son, Odi," said Yoel. "We were in Sinai, just before the evacuation. Odi said to me, '*Abba*, it's forbidden to speak against the soldiers, only against the government. And it's forbidden to tell soldiers not to obey an order.'"

"'Why, Odi?' I asked him. 'Explain it to me.'"

"'What will happen,' said Odi'"—and now Yoel's voice was a talmudic singsong—"'what will happen if there is a war and someone will say 'I don't want to fight'? Odi said it in Sinai. After the destruction of the Temple, prophecy wasn't only given to fools but also to children."

ARAFAT REFUSED TO evacuate West Beirut. If Israel invaded, he warned, he would ignite hundreds of PLO arms caches buried under apartment buildings and schools and mosques. On August 12, Sharon ordered saturation bombing of West Beirut. There were hundreds of casualties, many of them civilians.

Under pressure from his Lebanese allies, Arafat broke. On August 21 thousands of PLO men began boarding ships in Beirut harbor, bound for Tunisia and Libya and Iraq. Arafat boarded a ship for Athens.

The men of the 55th Brigade were sent home.

DAYS OF PENITENCE

ISRAEL WON, AND THEN LOST. On September 14, Bashir Gemayel, the pro-Israel head of the Christian Phalangist militias and newly designated president of Lebanon, was assassinated by Syrian agents. The IDF moved into West Beirut to prevent PLO units left behind from regrouping. On September 16, Phalangist fighters moved into Sabra and Shatila, two refugee camps in West Beirut, and massacred hundreds of Palestinians. One Phalangist in spiked shoes stomped a baby to death.

Though no Israelis were involved in the slaughter, the IDF had allowed the Phalangists to enter the camps, assuming their mission was to fight the remaining PLO forces there. And the IDF had provided flares to help the Phalangists to identify PLO fighters. World outrage was directed against Israel. "*Goyim* kill *goyim*," Begin was reputed to have said bitterly, "and they blame the Jews."

This time, many Israelis shared the world's outrage. Even if Sharon and IDF commanders hadn't known what the Phalange intended to do, they should have suspected: in Lebanon, massacre was the preferred method of retaliation. Israelis shouted at each other on street corners: You've disgraced the Jewish people! You're encouraging our enemies! One Israeli woman, a Holocaust survivor, refused to let her son in the front door when he returned home on leave from Lebanon until he assured her that he hadn't been near the camps. When Begin emerged from a synagogue in Jerusalem on Rosh Hashanah, demonstrators shouted, "Murderer!"

Peace Now announced a protest rally in Tel Aviv to demand a commission of inquiry. In the greenhouse in Ein Shemer, Avital and his kids prepared banners.

"I'm not going," said Avital's wife, Ada. "Why do we always have to blame ourselves? Arabs massacred Arabs. Let's hear some self-criticism from our Arab neighbors for a change."

"You're right," said Avital. "But this whole war is rotten, and this is a chance to bring down the government."

Ada relented, but on this condition: she would bring a poster demanding that Arabs also demonstrate for peace. "And stay close to me," she said.

Hours before the rally began, the Square of the Kings of Israel in Tel Aviv was already filling with Israelis desperate to be cleansed from the shame. There were hand-written signs: "What Else Has to Happen?" "If I Forget Sabra and Shatila, May I Forget Jerusalem." "Why Did My Son Die?" And many Israeli flags.

The MC, actress Hannah Meron, stood on an artificial leg: she had lost a leg in a terrorist attack. "I refuse to live in shame," she told the crowd of hundreds of thousands, referring to Sabra and Shatila.

In the density of bodies, Ada got separated from Avital. Acutely nearsighted, she perceived the crowds as a devouring blur.

Ada held up her dissenting sign: "Where Are the Peace Protests in Umm al-Fahm?"—an Arab Israeli town near Ein Shemer. Protesters mistook her for a right-wing provocateur. What is she doing here? someone demanded. You don't belong here, someone else said. Ada wanted to say: I'm from your camp! But why do we all have to think the same way, just like the right?

But her voice caught, and she couldn't get out the words.

YISRAEL HAREL LED a delegation of settler leaders to Ariel Sharon. After Yamit, Yisrael had vowed to cut off all relations with Sharon. But now he told the defense minister, "Whatever there was between us I'm putting aside."

It was the time between Rosh Hashanah and Yom Kippur, known as the Ten Days of Penitence. And in the religious Zionist community anguished voices were demanding a national self-reckoning. Rabbi Yehudah Amital, head of the Mount Etzion yeshiva, invoked rabbinic Judaism's most damning language: the government, he said, had desecrated God's name, a sin that not even Yom Kippur can cleanse.

Amital condemned those of his fellow rabbis who had called for an invasion of Beirut. And he ridiculed Hanan Porat for calling south Lebanon part of Israel. Was the state of Israel obliged to conquer every part of the land promised to Abraham? In placing settlement in Judea and Samaria as its highest value, he accused, religious Zionism was distorting the Torah. Judaism's hierarchy of values put the well-being of the people of Israel before the wholeness of the land of Israel. Israel should sacrifice that precious posession for the sake of genuine peace, if that ever became possible.

This, from the rabbi whose book about the spiritual meaning of the Yom Kippur War, *Ascent from the Depths*, had been promoted by Hanan as the spiritual textbook of Gush Emunim.

The redemption movement now had its first heretic.

ARIK ACHMON DECLARES WAR

ARIK RETURNED FROM Lebanon to a company in crisis. The war had devastated Arkia. Israelis stopped vacationing abroad, and Arkia's charters to Europe were canceled. Only recently the company had bought its first jet, which now sat idle. Arik's partner, Dadi, had bought another two jets that were scheduled to be delivered in a few months. What were they going to do with them? And how would they pay for them?

Even worse for Arkia, President Ronald Reagan's deregulation of the American aviation industry was overwhelming the market with used planes—and selling used planes was a major source of Arkia's profits. The collapse of the Israeli tourism industry was temporary, a result of the war;

but the devaluation of the market for used aircraft was long-term. Arkia was facing the prospect of multimillion-dollar debt.

Arik announced a freeze in raises and canceled a course for Arkia pilots to learn how to fly a jet plane. The next day, pilots showed up late for work.

Arik suspended them. He told the pilots' work committee that he was canceling their collective contract and would agree to their return only on the basis of individual contracts.

The transportation ministry backed Arik. His board of directors backed him too. "We're the test case for privatization," he told the board. He "wet-leased" planes (along with pilots) from a rival company—"They're robbing us blind, but I don't care"—and continued flying to Eilat.

To Yehudit he said, "I've entered the battle of my life."

ARIK'S CONFLICT WITH the pilots was into its second month when he was invited to meet with the head of the Histadrut's work committees, Yisrael Kaisar.

The gray building with little windows that was headquarters of the Histadrut mega-union was known to Israelis as "The Kremlin." With its bureaucrats who could never be fired and the old lady pushing the tea cart, this was the fortress of socialist Israel. There was no labor union like it anywhere: not only did it represent the workers, but it also owned many of the factories.

Kaisar's office, Arik noted, was perhaps three times as large as that of the finance minister. The Yemenite-born Kaisar was one of the few Sephardim in the Labor hierarchy; he wore a white shirt with its collar spread open over his jacket collar, in the old style of Labor politicians.

"Who are you to go against the Histadrut?" he demanded.

Arik smiled. "Yisrael, leave the theatrics aside. Unlike you, I don't have big factories where no one knows what's happening. At the end of the month, I have to face the banks."

"Where is your shame, Arik? A kibbutznik, son-in-law of Hazan—how can you behave like a greedy capitalist?"

"I'm ready to do whatever you want, Yisrael. Just one thing: you write the checks for the extra pilots that the company can't carry."

"All right, all right, I'm familiar with your clever answers."

How to explain to Kaisar that all this began at a ceremony one summer evening in Kibbutz Givat Brenner, when eighteen-year-old Arik Achmon stood alone against the commune?

"I'm prepared to offer generous benefits," said Arik. "What's fair is fair. But the rules of the game have to change."

Kaisar instructed the pilots to return to work. For now, he said, give that lunatic what he wants; we'll force him to back down in court.

THE PILOTS' CASE against Arkia went to labor court. Arik knew he didn't have a chance: the court would force him to fulfill the pilots' collective contract. But he was prepared to shut down Arkia rather than give in.

"Is there a way out?" Arik asked his lawyer.

"There is a possible way out, if you have the courage. But no one has ever done it before."

"Speak," said Arik.

According to Israel's labor laws, the lawyer explained, if you fire a worker, the case moves from labor court to civil court. There the issue is defined as a contract violation, and the employer must pay the worker 200 percent compensation. But the firing stands. Crucially, if the worker suspects he is about to be fired, he can apply to the labor court for a staying order. And in labor court it is nearly impossible to fire an employee. The key, then, was to get the dismissal letter into the employee's hands and move into civil court.

"The pilots won't bear it," Arik said, catching on. If they were fired from Arkia, they would never fly again in Israel; the market was simply too small. "They'll back down and negotiate."

They devised a plan: as soon as the labor court issued its ruling forcing Arik to honor the pilots' collective contract, Arik would dispatch letters to every pilot, informing him he'd been fired. Timing was crucial. If the letters weren't sent simultaneously, pilots could warn each other and seek an injunction against the firing, keeping the case in labor court. But once they received the dismissal letters, the case would move to civil court.

The morning of the verdict, Arik waited in his office—the "war room," he called it. His personnel manager, Chaim Becker, a battalion commander in the paratrooper reserves, phoned from court: Now.

Arik sent word to messengers waiting in taxis, each equipped with a letter and the address of a pilot. The one-line letter read: "In another 24 hours, you are fired."

That evening, a delegation of pilots appeared in Arik's office.

After all-night negotiations, they reached an agreement. The company had the right to fire pilots, and the collective agreement would be replaced with individual contracts. In return, Arik agreed to benefits like extra pay for flights on Shabbat and holidays.

For the first time, the Histadrut acknowledged that privatization required new rules. And Arik Achmon seemed destined for one success after another.

FOR THE SAKE OF HEAVEN

IT WAS SATURDAY night, shortly after the end of Shabbat, and the earnest, short-haired young men crowding the study hall of the Mount Etzion yeshiva were still wearing their Shabbat white shirts and dark slacks and white knitted *kippot*. Many of the students had recently returned from the front, only to find their beloved rabbi, Yehudah Amital, under vehement attack from within the Orthodox community. Students had asked him to explain his recent pronouncements, and so he had summoned this unusual meeting—not a political talk but a religious talk about politics.

Speaking in a formal and slightly archaic Hebrew, Amital asked forgiveness from his students: "I have made you uncomfortable by turning to the media. . . . [But] I am convinced that these matters must be expressed for the sake of Heaven, for the honor of the Torah and for the honor of the land of Israel."

During the siege of Beirut, Amital continued, "I had hoped to hear at least a hesitating voice [among the rabbis]. . . . But the most unequivocal voice in support for an invasion [of Beirut] was heard in fact from the representatives of religious Zionism. . . . The fact that these voices were accompanied with biblical verses, sayings from the rabbis and expressions in the style of Rabbi Kook, may the memory of the righteous be a blessing, fills me with horror.

"Nothing should worry us more than another war. Every fallen soldier wounds the soul of the Israeli public, and beyond that, every war weakens the attachment of many Jews to the land of Israel." If peace becomes possible, he concluded, he would prefer a smaller state that would attract large numbers of Jewish immigrants than a larger state without peace and with fewer Jews.

The young men listened in silence. The rabbi asked for questions.

Hanan Porat sat in the last pew, holding his head in his hands. Hanan loved Rabbi Amital, had regarded him as his teacher and partner in restoring Jewish life to the Etzion Bloc. It was on Hanan's initiative that Rabbi Amital had founded the Mount Etzion yeshiva after the Six-Day War. The rabbi had performed Hanan's marriage ceremony. In his presence Hanan felt the power of Jewish survival, that one can endure anything and still remain a faithful Jew.

But now the man of faith was faltering.

Hanan raised his hand. Amital smiled and beckoned with both hands: Come up.

As he approached the Torah Ark, Hanan silently prayed: God, guide my speech, may I not utter unworthy words about my teacher and friend, Rabbi Amital.

Amital gestured toward the lectern. For a moment they stood together. With his long graying beard, suit and tie, and old-fashioned black yarmulke, Amital conveyed the wisdom and caution of the centuries. Hanan, approaching the age of forty but with shirt untucked and knitted *kippah* jaunty on the side of his head, still conveyed the urgency of youth, the refusal to wait any longer for redemption. He remained the same young man who had founded the settlement movement in the summer of 1967: without pomposity, incapable of duplicity, known to everyone as simply Hanan though he too was an ordained rabbi.

Holding either side of the lectern, Hanan began with the Torah portion of the week: God commanding Abraham to leave his homeland and his family. The commandment to settle Canaan, Hanan noted, obliges Israel to conquer the land, even at the price of war. "Can the value of a piece of land be greater than the value of human life? Why are we obliged to go to war, to kill and be killed, for inert territory? . . . How can the expectation of *tikkun olam*, repairing the world—which is so Jewish—the longing to see all the nations spiritually elevated, be reconciled with going to war, with destruction and blood, with mourning and orphanhood?

"Rabbi Amital, we cannot avoid this question."

In fact, Hanan determined, there was no contradiction between conquering the land and creating peace, because the return of the holy people to the holy land was a precondition for world peace. "The message of peace will come only from the Mountain of the House of God"—from the rebuilt temple. "Only from the power of a world transformation in the hearts of people will internal values change and will the craving for power and pride, the source of all wars in the world, be defeated."

The land of Israel, then, wasn't real estate to be traded away for an ephemeral political peace, but a divine trust containing the hope for world peace.

"What do I ask of you, Rabbi Amital? Only that together we will merit . . . the blessing which you recited before me on the day of my wedding: 'Bring rejoicing to the barren one [the land of Israel] by ingathering her children with joy. Blessed are You, Lord our God, Who gladdens Zion through her children.'"

Rabbi Amital let Hanan have the last word.

YOEL BIN-NUN'S RESPONSE to Rabbi Amital appeared in *Nekudah*. I understand the rabbi's anguish about the extremists in our midst, wrote Yoel, but he is wrong to posit the unity and spiritual value of the Jewish people against that of the land of Israel. There is no hierarchy of values here, insisted Yoel: "People and land are entwined. As it is written in the book of Samuel II: 'Who is like Your people Israel, one nation in the land.' The [kabbalistic work] Zohar notes: It is one nation when it is in the land. And without the land there is no unity for the nation of Israel."

MEIR ARIEL GROWS A BEARD

THE FIRST SNOWS were falling in the mountains of Lebanon when Meir's unit was called back to the front. No longer with the 55th Brigade, Meir was serving in an antitank unit. His fellow reservists were mostly kibbutzniks, like him, approaching middle age.

They were stationed on a mountaintop overlooking the Christian town of Jezene, south of Beirut. Following the Sabra-Shatila massacre, the IDF had withdrawn from Beirut. The fantasy of a new Lebanon was over. The Shiites, who had initially welcomed Israel as a liberator, now turned against the new occupier.

Meir's platoon settled into an abandoned stone villa. With each war, the transformation from civilian into soldier became harder for Meir to manage. He seemed to move in slow motion as he padded his body before setting out on patrol: seven ammunition clips, two grenades, two canteens, bulletproof vest. His most cherished piece of equipment was a pocket notebook in which he wrote lines for songs.

Meir added a new last line to the song he'd written after the Yom Kippur War, "Our Forces Passed a Quiet Night in Suez": "Our forces are passing a quiet night in Sidon," the Lebanese port city.

WITH HIS BEARD and Hasidic sidelocks, Moshe Landau was a singular presence in the unit. Moshe was a newly observant Chabad Hasid who believed that redemption was imminent. The more commandments a Jew fulfilled, Chabad taught, the more he enhanced the accumulation of goodness that would break through the density of matter and fill the world with light.

Moshe sat on his mattress on the floor, studying a text about gematria, numerology, divining hidden meaning and patterns through the numerical equivalent of Hebrew words. Meir, uninvited, sat down beside him and peered into the pocket-size book.

"What are you reading?" Meir asked. Moshe was reluctant to say. How could he possibly explain a complicated text to someone without a religious background?

Meir persisted. Moshe, relenting, explained, "Every Hebrew letter has an equivalent number. *Alef* is one, *kuf* is a hundred. *HaKadosh Baruch Hu*, the Holy One Blessed Be He, gave us the written Torah, but the Torah has a soul. If we study gematria, we can better understand what He wanted to say to us."

Take the word Elohim, Moshe continued, one of God's names, whose numerical equivalent is identical with *hatevah*, the Hebrew word for nature. "The Holy One is showing us that He and nature are the same. Everything you see is God Himself. When I see a leaf or a stone, I don't see the thing itself but the Owner Who created it and the Power that sustains it. God is trying to say to us: It's not nature, it's Me."

"If God is infinite," asked Meir, "why did he create a finite world?"

God, Moshe explained, is both nature and beyond nature.

"Interesting," Meir said, got up, and left.

In fact Meir was fascinated. He loved the Hebrew language, the way one word formed another, creating a web of meaning, like *adam* (man) and *adama* (earth). The very structure of Hebrew reflected the faith of the Hebrews in a purposeful, interconnected universe. For Meir, discovering gematria only deepened the majesty of Hebrew. God created through letters and numbers, the building blocks of reality. Hebrew spoke the hidden order of the universe. In conveying the messy details of life in the language of meaning, Meir could perhaps redeem his chaotic world.

MEIR RETURNED HOME on leave. He had grown the beginnings of a beard. His long curly hair remained black, but the beard was white.

"What's this?" Tirza demanded, afraid that Meir was becoming devout.

"A protest," explained Meir. "I'm not shaving until we get out of Lebanon."

"Why are you waging war at my expense?" said Tirza. "If you don't shave, you won't have a wife. Choose."

Meir shaved.

CRASH

ARIK ACHMON HAD outmaneuvered the strongest workers' committee in Arkia, stared down the Histadrut, proven that privatization required new rules. But Arkia's financial situation was becoming desperate.

The two Boeing 737s Dadi had ordered were delivered in early 1983. Dadi had hoped to begin paying for them by selling planes he had bought two years earlier. The system had worked until now: Arkia sold its used planes for cash, and bought new planes on credit. But now there were no buyers for the used planes.

The division of labor between Arik and Dadi had been complete: Arik was responsible for operations, Dadi for buying and selling planes. But now Arkia's debt was growing by tens of millions of dollars.

Arik told the board: It's Dadi or me. "Kibbutznik fool," Dadi taunted him. "You don't understand anything."

Arik counted his supporters: a clear majority.

But when the board gathered, it voted to relieve both Arik and Dadi of their positions, while retaining them as advisers.

Arik quit.

A few days later, Dadi was reappointed deputy CEO.

"What was I thinking?" Arik told Yehudit. "That I could be straight with them? That there could be trust in business? You tried to warn me about Dadi—but as usual I knew better. Dadi promised something to somebody, I'm sure of it. I don't know how, but he screwed me."

Kibbutznik fool.

CHAPTER 23

CIVIL WARS

FRATRICIDE IN JERUSALEM

EMIL GRUENSWEIG, A thirty-five-year-old kibbutznik, peace activist, and reservist officer in the paratroopers, didn't want to go to the demonstration. "It's not going to make any difference," he said to a fellow activist in an uncharacteristic moment of despair. He had just returned from reserve duty in Lebanon, wanted to spend the evening working on his master's thesis, about the rights and limits of free speech. No, his friend insisted, this demonstration is important, you need to be there.

It was February 10, 1983. Under pressure from much of the Israeli public, the government had formed a commission of inquiry into the Sabra and Shatila massacre. On February 7 the commission, headed by Supreme Court chief justice Yitzhak Kahan, had submitted its findings: though Defense Minister Sharon had no advance warning of the massacre, he bore indirect responsibility for allowing the Phalangists into the camps and should resign. The cabinet was about to meet in emergency session, and Peace Now was planning a march to the prime minister's office in Jerusalem, to demand Sharon's dismissal.

Emil Gruensweig, son of Holocaust survivors, had wandered with his family through Europe and South America before immigrating, as a teenager, to Israel. Here, he felt, he had finally come home. He moved to Kibbutz Revivim in the Negev Desert, taught high school there, and helped found an Arab-Jewish summer camp. For Emil, peacemaking was the responsibility of ordinary people. The difference, he would say, between having an opinion and being committed to one's opinion was the willingness to pay a price for it.

Since the Lebanon War, his natural optimism had faded. Though he'd opposed the war, he went when his reserve unit was summoned. It was also a hard time for him personally. Recently divorced, he had left the kibbutz and moved to Jerusalem. With his receding hairline, he looked prematurely middle-aged.

Toward evening Emil joined the demonstrators gathering in Zion Square in downtown Jerusalem. There weren't many of them, perhaps a thousand. Far-right activists who had come to disrupt, along with passersby from the city's working-class and ultra-Orthodox neighborhoods, surrounded the protesters. "PLO!" some shouted. "Kibbutzniks!"—as if that too were now a disgrace.

Pushing, punching. Someone spat in Emil's face. "Traitor! I'll finish you off!"

They began marching toward the prime minister's office. Emil linked arms with other protesters, formed a line, and led the besieged procession. "Sharon, go home!" they chanted. Emil, wearing only a sweater in the cold Jerusalem evening, marched in the center.

Counterprotesters along the route became more violent, grabbing posters and kicking. Helmeted police appeared helpless. Water poured down from a balcony.

They reached the prime minister's office. Police finally separated the protesters and the taunters, some of whom had followed the marchers all the way. The rally ended with the singing of "Hatikvah."

Protesters began dispersing.

And then—an explosion. Smoke. Screams. "Why are you screaming? What happened?" "Grenade! They've thrown a grenade!"

Many of the protesters knew the smell of an exploded grenade. But in the middle of Jerusalem, near the prime minister's office?

Emil lay on the ground, silent, a piece of shrapnel in his neck.

Ambulances evacuated the wounded. Emil bled to death on the pavement.

INSIDE THE PRIME MINISTER'S OFFICE, the cabinet voted to endorse the Kahan Commission and dismiss Sharon.

Ever since he was a boy, Sharon had been an outsider. In his farming village, Kfar Malal, his parents were so estranged from their neighbors that he had grown up without knowing what the inside of his friends' homes looked like. In the army he'd been repeatedly denied promotions for which he was most qualified. He's reckless and untrustworthy, opponents said;

his military exploits leave behind too many bodies. Supporters, though, regarded him as a savior, the IDF's most brilliant commander, inspiring his men to victory. And when the country was in desperate need, whether to stop terrorist incursions in the 1950s or defeat the Egyptians in 1973, it invariably turned to Sharon. And then, invariably, rejected him.

And now he had been dealt the final humiliation. Don't worry, Begin tried to reassure him. Great deeds still await you.

YOEL BIN-NUN HEARD the name on the radio and held his head. *Emil—*

They had argued during reserve duty. Vehemently, affectionately. Yoel loved Emil's purity and determination. Every argument between them began in agreement: Israel's situation was precarious, and drastic measures were necessary. Then what? We need to be strong, said Yoel. We need to be flexible, said Emil. We must stake our claim to what is ours, said Yoel. We must share the land, said Emil. Thwart those intending to destroy us, said Yoel. Try to negotiate with them, said Emil.

And now he was dead. Killed by a Jew. For Yoel, that was the most devastating realization of all: though there had been no arrests yet, without doubt a Jewish hand had thrown that grenade.

To toss a grenade into a crowd of Israelis risked killing the soldier with whom you shared a tent in basic training, the officer who led you into battle. And it had happened because of the atmosphere of hatred against the left. Traitors! PLO! If Emil Gruensweig were a traitor, then so was Yoel Bin-Nun.

LATE AT NIGHT Yoel sat at his desk, rage overtaking grief. "Mourn and weep!!" he wrote in longhand. "For the unity of the people of Israel in its land, against which cursed hands have been raised. For the sin we have sinned—and yes, we too, on the fringes of our [settler] camp have sinned before God in the reckless and cowardly use of words with life and death implications—'traitors,' 'PLO lovers,' 'enemy agents'—against an entire community . . . that fought in the ranks of the IDF despite its qualms and its pain [over the government's policies]. . . .

"And above all: For the innocent blood that has been spilled in the land. For us the land of Israel is not simply a homeland like France is for the French. This land cannot tolerate innocent blood. A man of faith, who fears Heaven and loves the land, will not say [about the murderer]: 'He is an exception, a madman.' These are modern, psychological expressions, emptied of the language of Torah. We say: 'And innocent blood shall not be spilled in the midst of your land, which the Lord your God gives you as an inheritance.'"

The next morning, Yoel delivered the article to Yisrael Harel. Yisrael looked at the manuscript—words underlined, sentences followed by multiple exclamation marks—and shook his head. A speech, not an article. "Yoel," he said, trying to be patient, "this isn't a modern way of writing. You can't underline words. And all these exclamation marks. In the army they teach us, 'When you shout I hear, when you speak I listen.' When you write more calmly, people can listen."

But Yisrael was upset by more than the style. Yisrael understood as well as Yoel the implications of Jew murdering Jew—a paratrooper, no less. But why did Yoel have this need to exaggerate his own camp's flaws? "I'm no less pained by what happened than you," Yisrael said. "But you're setting yourself up as judge of your community. Criticize, but within limits. We are under attack from all sides. And now along comes one of our most important spiritual thinkers and justifies the demonization. Yoel, you can't only criticize your community, you also have to defend it. You want to show the left how pure you are? Don't do it at the expense of your friends and neighbors."

Nevertheless, Yisrael published Yoel's accusatory lament in the next issue of *Nekudah*, beside a black-bordered photograph of Emil and a notice of mourning signed by the Yesha Council.

MOUNTAIN OF BLESSING

YISRAEL HAREL HAD AN IDEA. Each Independence Day was devoted to a theme, like the ingathering of the exiles and the longing for peace. Why not devote the coming independence day—Israel's thirty-fifth—to the great pioneering effort of this generation, the movement from the narrow coastal plain to the mountains, the heartland? What better response to the campaign of hatred against the settlers?

Yisrael made the necessary calls. Israel's thirty-fifth anniversary would be officially celebrated by establishing a new settlement called Bracha, blessing, on Mount Gerizim, near Nablus, the biblical Shechem. When Joshua

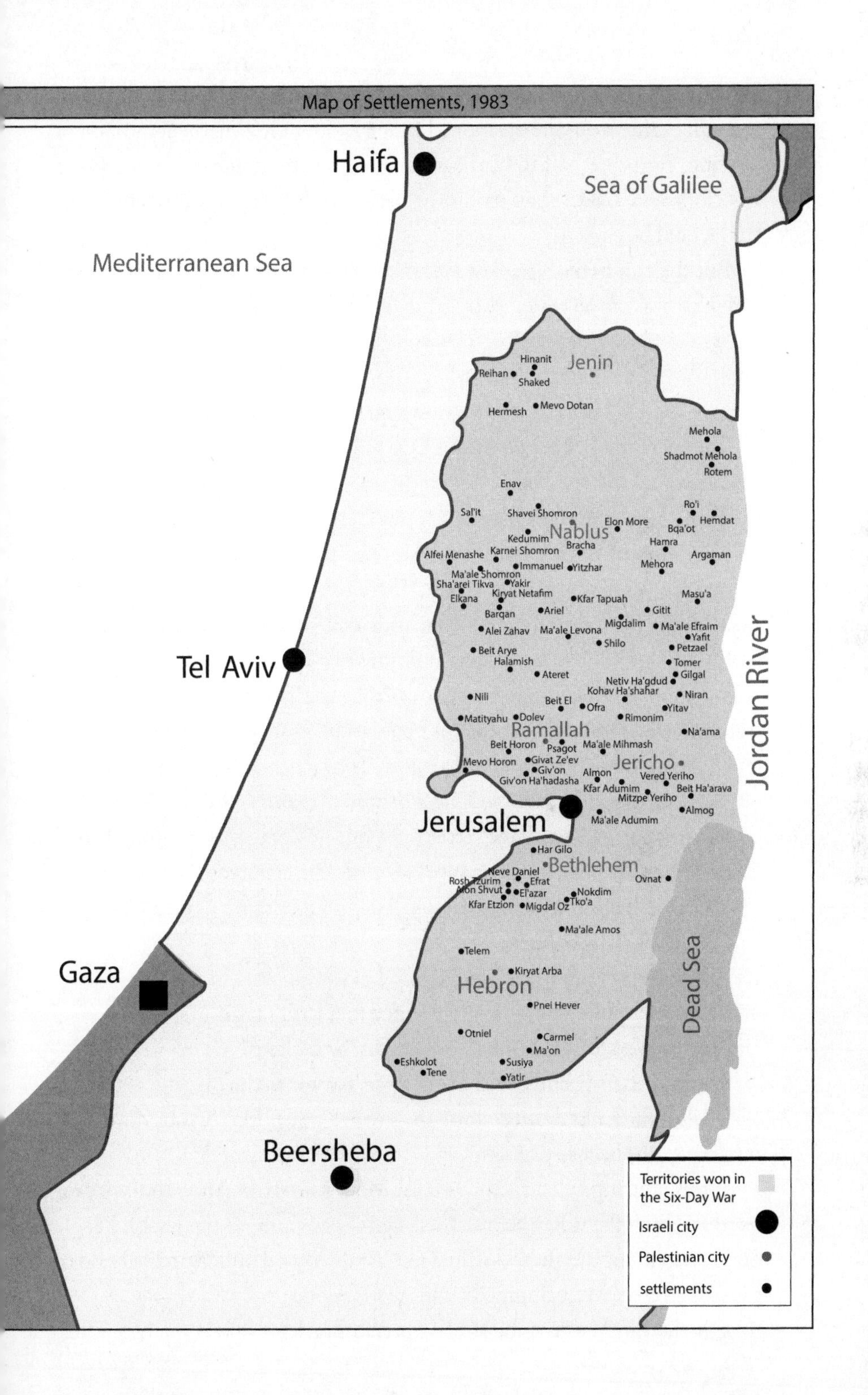

Map of Settlements, 1983

led the children of Israel into the land, he divided the tribes into two groups: one half of the people he positioned facing Mount Grizim, the mountain of blessing, the other half toward Mount Ebal, the mountain of curse. Those who followed God's ways would be blessed, while those who defiled the land would be cursed.

But the children of Israel could no longer agree about what was blessing and what was curse, which path led to life and which to death.

SO NOW THEY'RE TRYING to expropriate Independence Day, thought Avital Geva. What next, *hevreh*, the flag?

The morning of Independence Day 1983 was cloudy, with a forecast of heavy rain. Avital and friends set out in one of Ein Shemer's panel trucks to the Peace Now demonstration at Mount Gerizim.

They crossed the old border and stopped to take in the view. From this incline the coast was plainly visible. There were the giant chimneys of the electric company near Hadera that provided power to half the country; and farther south, the apartment buildings of Netanya and North Tel Aviv. Along the 160-mile-long coastal strip from the Lebanon border to Gaza were crowded most of the country's population, its major cities and industry and ports and lone international airport. The settlers had a point about the old borders, thought Avital. *It's not a defensible country—*

A car stopped, and three settlers got out. "What are you doing here?" asked a heavyset man, pistol on hip. His tone, Avital noted, was not curious.

"We're going to the demonstration," said a kibbutznik named Levi.

"Get the hell out of here."

"This is our country too," countered Levi.

The settler pulled his gun and pointed it at Levi's head.

"Whoa, *hevreh*," said Avital, "let's take a break here."

The gunman's friends pulled him aside, back into the car.

The kibbutzniks waited until they drove away. Levi wrote down the number of the license plate.

It was pouring when they arrived at Mount Gerizim. Thousands of protesters were in the valley below. Their signs—"A Curse to the Jewish People on the Mount of Blessing"—wilted in the rain. Avital pulled up the hood of his soaked coat. Mud clumped on his work boots.

On the mountain, cube-shaped prefab houses awaited their new residents, and a dais with wet flags awaited government dignitaries. A few thousand celebrants—far fewer than the number of demonstrators below—huddled under umbrellas.

Yisrael Harel noticed several Peace Now activists walking up the dirt road to the settlement and suspected mischief. He approached the IDF commander of the central front, General Ori Orr, and asked him to prevent disruptions. Orr dismissed the request. He's against us, Yisrael thought.

Yisrael wandered down to the valley. He saw a familiar hooded figure. "Avital!" he shouted. They embraced.

Yisrael confided, "I'm worried that if your *hevreh* try to disrupt the ceremony, there could be violence."

"I'll speak to the *hevreh*," Avital reassured.

There was no need after all for disruptions: the rain turned to hail, government officials abandoned the dais, and the ceremony was canceled.

PROSPERITY IN KIBBUTZ EIN SHEMER

EIN SHEMER RESEMBLED a construction site. The founders' courtyard was being transformed into a museum of Zionist pioneering. A new neighborhood was rising. And the long-debated sports center was finally being built—not on the ruins of the greenhouse, as some had hoped, but nearby.

The kibbutz was subsidizing its building projects by borrowing massively. And why not? With runaway inflation, interest rates were low. The right-wing government had removed some basic subsidies from the kibbutz movement. Water was more expensive, and there was debate within the kibbutzim about whether to stop growing water-intensive crops like cotton. But with the easy money flowing, that seemed like a relatively minor setback.

Ein Shemer was learning to live with the decline of socialist passion. When three families removed their children from the communal children's house and insisted on raising them at home, members voted against expelling the rebels. Some of Ein Shemer's women now wore perfume and modest jewelry. The *kova tembel*, beloved fool's cap, gave way to truckers' caps. On May Day, a lone half-empty bus, shared by Ein Shemer and Gan Shmuel, was dispatched to the workers' march in Tel Aviv.

Phones were installed in every apartment. No longer would members need to line up in the evening before the kibbutz's single pay phone.

Then the kibbutz secretariat decided to distribute color TVs to every apartment. Avital appealed to the secretariat to reconsider: in a year of 300 percent inflation, we should be cutting our budget, not overspending. Who, he asked, will be held responsible when the inevitable crash comes?

At the weekly kibbutz meeting, Avital's proposal to suspend distribution of color TVs was rejected. He and Ada were given a color TV too.

MEIR ARIEL GETS A NEW JOB

"WHAT'S THE PROBLEM?" Meir said to the secretary general of Mishmarot. "Ein Shemer lets its writers sit and work. Why not consider my work as a musician and composer as work for the kibbutz?"

"You don't earn enough from your music," the official noted. "The kibbutz can't afford to carry you."

Afterward Meir told Tirza, "They're not letting me breathe. Maybe we should leave for Tel Aviv."

"And wait for you to make a living? We'd starve first. I'd have to keep an eye on you every minute. The first week in the big city you'd get hit by a bus."

Meir laughed.

A PROFILE OF Meir appeared in the weekly *Koteret Rashit*; he had to be coaxed into doing the interview. "His songs are played mainly between 2 and 5 in the morning on Army Radio," wrote the reporter. "Meir Ariel. [The name] means very little to very many—and a great deal to a few. For them he's the greatest of songwriters, the Israeli Bob Dylan."

Question: "You and Shalom Hanoch began from the same place, Kibbutz Mishmarot. At least in terms of public status, he's gone much farther. Are you jealous of him?"

Answer: "I was jealous for a long time. I didn't have too many conceits, but I did think well of myself [as a musician]. My ego was inflated. It was hard for me to see him leap forward and overtake me."

Shalom was also interviewed: "Meir is a unique talent, and he has something to say. But he's not ambitious enough. . . . If he had to make his living from music he would try harder, he'd get somewhere. He doesn't go the conventional route, he allows himself to ignore the public. That's the advantage of a kibbutznik singer, but it's also a disadvantage."

In his low-key way, Meir was in fact trying to nurture a career. Once a week he sang in a small club in Jaffa. A good night drew a few dozen people. The audience—army age, heavily kibbutznik—rarely varied: hard-core fans, who knew all the words to the songs.

One night Tirza joined him. She was one of the few people in the room who couldn't sing along: she didn't know the words.

Afterward, Meir was given an envelope with cash, a percentage of the night's take.

"Aren't you going to open it?" Tirza asked.

"What for?" he replied. "It goes straight to the kibbutz."

"This is your money! You've already put in a full day's work. You're now doing an extra shift for the kibbutz. And how do you know no one is going to pocket it?"

Meir offered his sad, knowing smile.

ONE EVENING AFTER WORK, Meir said to Tirza, "You're speaking to the new secretary general of Kibbutz Mishmarot."

"That's the funniest thing I ever heard," said Tirza.

The secretary general—the *mazkir*—was elected by the kibbutz members and was a two-year position, combination ombudsman and representative to the kibbutz movement institutions. Meir was always available to listen to a kibbutznik's lament; now he would actually be in a position to help. And, as one of his musician friends put it, who if not Meir could assist the misfits and malcontents who took too many sick days and smoked too much hashish and wouldn't be able to survive anywhere else but on kibbutz?

On paper, Mishmarot was thriving. There were some 150 members, the largest number in the kibbutz's history. Its plywood factory was the biggest in Israel. But Meir knew the truth. Mishmarot was losing its reason for being. Many of its young people were leaving. The kibbutz was no ordinary society; unless nurtured, it would wither.

Meanwhile there were human needs that required attention—an old-timer who wanted better housing, a young person just out of the army who wanted to study literature. Meir tried to accommodate them all. *"Tembel!"* the treasurer shouted at him. "You're bankrupting the kibbutz!"

Meir's job, as he saw it, was to place people before institutions. At the weekly kibbutz meeting he addressed members not as "comrades" but with the bourgeois honorific "ladies and gentlemen." One of his friends, Yehudah, mentioned that he'd never had a bar mitzvah: Yehudah had been sent to Mishmarot as an immigrant child, and when his class had its collective bar mitzvah, only the children of Mishmarot members were included. A few days later Yehudah, now age fifty, received a book from Meir with this inscription: "To Yehudah, for whom they didn't make a bar mitzvah."

Meir sat in his office, bare feet on desk, doodling grotesque faces, which he then hung on the wall. He amused himself with little routines, like pretending to be a busy executive. When a friend phoned, Meir shouted to his empty office, "*Hevreh*, quiet! Can't you see I have an important call?"

IN THE NEIGHBORING KIBBUTZIM, the news that Meir Ariel had become *mazkir* only confirmed that Mishmarot wasn't a "serious" kibbutz. Its most successful crop, they joked in Ein Shemer, was musicians.

Avital Geva borrowed a kibbutz car and drove to Mishmarot to congratulate Meir. They lived mere minutes apart, but over the years had met only in reserve duty. Now Meir had become a spiritual partner for Avital, a fellow artist trying to reenergize the kibbutz.

Avital found Meir in his office, barely more than a cubicle, in a concrete row of little apartments.

"Wow, Meir!" said Avital, hugging him. "When I heard you were taking on the job I couldn't believe it. Meir Ariel? Unbelievable!"

"You'd be surprised," said Meir. "I'm actually enjoying it."

"And the endless meetings and all the nonsense?"

"This is my chance to give something back to the kibbutz. I've decided to take a break from performing—I want to focus on the job."

"Meir, I promise you: whatever sacrifice you make now will come back to you a hundredfold. You'll see, it will change your work. You'll be creating from a different place. Your music will thrive."

MISHMAROT HAD A small factory manufacturing eyeglass frames, and Tirza convinced the manager to let her try her luck as sales representative. Beautiful, charming when she wanted to be, she traveled to a trade fair abroad and returned with a year's worth of orders. A few months later she traveled abroad again and repeated her success.

She approached the manager of a failing kibbutz factory near the Lebanon border that produced sunglasses and offered to represent its line too. The manager agreed, and Tirza returned with more orders than the factory had ever received. Unkind neighbors speculated that she got her orders by sleeping with buyers. *They can't possibly hate me as much as I hate them—*

Success made her restless. Between sales trips she was treated like any other worker, running the machines and making frames. That seemed to her a waste of her talent. She had a better idea: Why not set up a sales company for all kibbutz factories, with her as head?

Her manager vetoed the plan.

Tirza confronted Meir. If they try to stop me from taking my next career step, she said, I'll quit the kibbutz and go into business for myself. "I don't expect you to quit, Meir. It's good for you here, you should stay. And don't worry, I won't move out, I'll just give up my kibbutz membership."

Meir said, "Here in this house I am your husband. If you want to speak to the *mazkir*, make an appointment with him during work hours."

At the next weekly meeting, Meir began, "Ladies and gentlemen, our comrade, Tirza, has a proposal to raise. Because of my personal involvement, I am asking your permission to excuse myself." He left the room.

The kibbutzniks voted against Tirza. "That's it," she said to Meir afterward. "I'm finished with them."

ARIK ACHMON DISCOVERS VULNERABILITY

"SO, ARIK," SAID HIS BOSS, the CEO of Hamashbir Hamerkazi, "what do you think of my managerial skills?" Hamashbir Hamerkazi was the purchasing company for the kibbutz movement, and for the last year Arik had headed one of its subsidiary companies.

"You really want to know?" replied Arik. "I think the way you run this company is a disgrace. You're burning the money of the kibbutzim. You would never be able to compete in a market economy."

Arik expected—hoped—to be fired. Instead his boss, mindful of Arik's connections with Yehudit's father, Hazan, let it be known through an intermediary that an apology would suffice. Arik responded, "It's time to part ways."

Since that encounter nearly a year had passed. And for the first time since the age of eleven, when he was assigned to work in the cowshed of

Kibbutz Givat Brenner, Arik was without a job. The word going around was that he'd been reckless with Arkia's money. Arik suspected that Dadi was spreading stories about him. Former associates didn't return his phone calls. Arik Achmon, who had always known exactly what to do in any situation, suddenly had no options.

Meanwhile, the Achmons' financial situation was deteriorating. With Arik unemployed, Yehudit was supporting the family, struggling with the mortgage.

Arik had left Arkia without compensation. Foolishly, during all his years in the company, he had waived the right to a contract. Arik had reasoned: I'm a stockowner; besides, if I ever leave the company, my friends on the board will take care of me.

The board did make him an offer: Return the 7 percent stock you own in exchange for $100,000—the same sum he would have received as compensation if he had a contract. Arik didn't know what the board knew: had he gone to labor court, he would have been awarded that sum even without a contract, because he was entitled to the same benefits that other managers received. And he wouldn't have had to return his stock.

During Arkia's good years, the board's offer would have been absurd. But Arkia appeared to be collapsing, and Arik was desperate. He signed.

In an interview with a financial magazine, Arik tried to make sense of why he had failed. I gave too much leeway to Dadi, he admitted; it was my responsibility as CEO to maintain closer supervision of his transactions.

A photographer from the magazine asked Arik to put on a tie. Arik, wearing shorts, went to change into long pants. No need, reassured the photographer; the photo will be from the waist up.

The next issue of the magazine featured a full-bodied cover photograph of the former CEO of Arkia, barefoot in a tie and shorts. Arik's severe, slightly bemused expression, intended to convey the impression of a powerful man still in control of his life, only made the humiliation worse.

JUST NOT THAT, Yehudit Achmon told herself every day as she came home from work. Just let me not find Arik in a state of depression. I couldn't bear to see this strong man break.

Arik reassured Yehudit: "I know what I'm worth. I couldn't care less what anyone says about me."

He kept himself busy, painting the house and working in the garden, reading history and military strategy and looking for work. And, as always, keeping in touch with the brigade's widows and helping with their problems, like employing a troubled teenage son in his skydiving club and then ensuring the boy got drafted into an elite combat unit.

As a psychologist Yehudit was devoted to helping people change, but she'd never had much hope for Arik's transformation. Usually for better, sometimes for worse, he was who he was. No one was more dependable and courageous, no one more ethical and trustworthy. And no one was more stubborn, more certain of his superior judgment and disdainful of human weakness. Perhaps in some way the good qualities were protected by the hard ones.

But lately Yehudit was noticing encouraging signs. When Arik spoke severely to the children, she chided, "You're using your commander's tone." Rather than dismiss her, Arik paused.

Arik's son, Ori, was drafted. Naturally Arik expected him to become a combat soldier, an officer. But after a brief stint in officers' school, Ori hurt his leg and had to leave the course. For Ori, the accident was fortuitous: he realized that his father's trajectory wasn't his. Arik called the commander of the school, an old paratrooper friend, and the commander offered to admit Ori back for the next course. Ori demurred; Arik pressed.

"Let him go his own way," Yehudit admonished. "You don't have to live through your son."

Arik never raised the matter again.

"EVOLUTION OR REVOLUTION?"

A NINETEEN-YEAR-OLD YESHIVA STUDENT named Aharon Gross was stabbed to death in a central square in Hebron, near the outdoor Arab market, in full view of hundreds of shoppers.

The "Jewish underground"—as the Israeli media was calling the elusive group that had blown off the legs of two Palestinian mayors—struck again, this time at Hebron's Islamic College. Three young men, faces wrapped in kaffiyehs, entered the courtyard of the school and opened fire, killing three students and wounding dozens more.

Yehudah Etzion opposed the attack. Not only was it immoral to deliberately kill innocents, he told underground members, but they were squandering their skills on acts of revenge rather than on the one act that could transform history.

Yet the destruction of the Dome of the Rock seemed more remote than ever. Yehudah had lost most of his fellow conspirators, and there seemed little to do but maintain the hidden stock of explosives for a more promising time.

One night Yehudah asked Yoel, "What do you think about removing the Dome of the Rock?"

Yoel was silent. When he finally spoke, his voice was quiet. "It would destroy one of the great miracles of our time—Jerusalem under Israeli sovereignty. Jerusalem would come under international control."

"That would only be the first stage," Yehudah replied.

"How do you know what will happen next?" Yoel said, his voice rising. "If you're not taking responsibility for the consequences of your actions, you're a Sabbatean," follower of a false messiah.

"You don't have the courage to take your ideas to their conclusion."

"Evolution or revolution?" demanded Yoel.

"The Messiah won't come through evolution," said Yehudah.

"Then you and I are finished," said Yoel.

THE LAST CASUALTY OF THE SIX-DAY WAR

UDI ADIV HAD reached his limit. The airless cell, the smell of too many bodies, the constant noise of transistor radios. The absence of green. Of Leah.

Perhaps for the first time in his life, Udi was in love. And he wasn't tormenting himself about betraying the revolution by yielding to personal needs. His own development, he noted in a letter to Leah, was the opposite of that of most people: where others move from self-centeredness to a measure of altruism, he needed to reclaim a sense of self. Udi allowed himself a warmth toward Leah that he had never shown Sylvia. "I await the time when you and I can be together," he wrote her. He signed his letters, "With love and embrace."

In Udi's letters to Leah appeared a recurring anxiety about his younger brother, Asaf, who had become a Trotskyite activist. Asaf had been radicalized during Udi's trial. Udi loathed Trotskyites: Sylvia's attraction to them was the reason he had divorced her. But Udi's concern for Asaf went deeper: Asaf, Udi wrote, was suppressing his inner life—precisely what Udi had learned to develop in prison.

In letters to Leah, Udi now referred to his revolutionary past as "my dark, dogmatic era." Responding to an interview he read with a former Matzpen activist who now called himself a Palestinian, Udi wrote that he too had once identified as a Palestinian. Now, though, "I consider myself a part of the Jewish society and people."

Yet however much Udi believed that his dogmatism was behind him, an old hardness persisted. He had abandoned the fantasy of revolution but remained a Marxist. In a letter to Leah he expressed regret for not having fasted on Yom Kippur—because that only alienated him from the traditionalist Sephardi inmates. "In order to raise the Jews to our level of secular democratic consciousness," wrote Udi, "we need to at least appear to descend to their primitive religious and nationalist beliefs."

TOGETHER WITH UDI'S PARENTS, Leah began a campaign for clemency. It was late 1983, and Udi had served nearly eleven years of a seventeen-year sentence. On the suggestion of his lawyer, Udi requested a transfer from the Arab security cell to a cell of ordinary criminals. It wouldn't help his cause for him to be identified with terrorists.

In the criminals' cell, Udi encountered little hostility, and none of it was political. Prisoners sensed his sympathy and confided in him. One young man told Udi he was planning to attend synagogue to prove he was a model prisoner. Udi chided him: faithfulness to the commandments should be without ulterior motive. Afterward the young man told Udi he was right, and would pray for its own sake.

Several op-eds noted the injustice of treating Udi as a dangerous traitor, rather than as a naive young man betrayed by ideology. Three of Udi's childhood friends from Gan Shmuel appeared outside the prison gates with a banner: "Free Udi!" It wasn't much, but Udi no longer felt alone.

Udi's father went to see Motta Gur. "Motta," said Uri Adiv, "I'm coming to you as the father of one of your soldiers. Udi came back shattered from Jerusalem. He wasn't the same boy."

Uri wasn't appealing to Motta only as a father but as one soldier to another. Leaving a wounded man on the battlefield was a crime in the IDF. And Udi was the last casualty of the Six-Day War.

"I'll see what I can do," said Motta.

FOR THE FIRST TIME Udi allowed himself to imagine life outside prison. During one of Leah's visits, he proposed marriage. Leah hesitated. She had always suppressed her needs for his, she explained. But Udi hadn't reciprocated. Didn't he realize how much she had suffered when he'd rejected her and married Sylvia? Leah could no longer deny her own needs. Marrying Udi when he could still be facing years of prison seemed to her one sacrifice too far.

Udi knew she was right. In a letter to Leah, he had noted that his father called her "the luck of your life." Wrote Udi: "He forgot to add that I am the misfortune of your life."

CHAPTER 24

IDOLATROUS FIRE

REVOLT AGAINST HEAVEN

IN THE JEWISH ENCLAVE in downtown Hebron, in the farming communities on the Golan Heights, a dozen young men, including leading activists in the settlement movement, were detained without explanation. It was Friday morning, April 27, 1984. Rumors and speculation spread among the settlements. Was it for the attack on the mayors? The Islamic College? Or something else, as yet unknown?

Yisrael Harel phoned contacts in the army, the government, the media. All we know, he was told, is that a disaster was averted at the last moment.

When Shabbat ended, Yisrael phoned prime minister Yitzhak Shamir at home. Menachem Begin had abruptly resigned as prime minister, broken by the ongoing casualties of the Lebanon War and by the death of his beloved wife, Aliza. And Shamir, like Begin a Polish Jew whose family had been killed in the Holocaust, had taken his place.

"I received very unpleasant information about actions that your people took," Shamir told Yisrael.

"What actions?" asked Yisrael.

"I can't say."

That same evening the news was released: members of the underground had been caught placing bombs under five Arab buses in East Jerusalem. If the bombs had gone off, hundreds might have been killed or wounded.

Impossible, thought Yisrael. These were sane people. They knew that if those bombs had gone off the settlement movement would have lost its moral high ground. Maybe the Shin Bet security service felt so frustrated by its inability to solve the other attacks that it had contrived an atrocity conveniently averted at the last moment.

In fact, the security service had been following the terrorists for months.

The plot to blow up the buses was the pretext the Shin Bet was waiting for to close in on the members of the underground.

An angry Yisrael appeared on the TV news. Our friends and neighbors have been arrested and not heard from since, he said. No phone calls to their families, no lawyers. Since when did people simply disappear in the state of Israel? What is this, Argentina?

On Sunday morning the police came for Yehudah Etzion.

WHAT MADNESS HAS taken hold of our camp? thought Yoel Bin-Nun. How could disciples of Rabbi Zvi Yehudah, who were taught to sanctify the state as the vessel of redemption and who celebrated Independence Day as a religious holiday—how could they take the law into their own hands and undermine Jewish sovereignty?

By midweek, the news was out: members of the underground had indeed confessed—to the attack on the mayors, the murder of the students in the Islamic College, even the attempt to sabotage the buses.

Yoel was interviewed by Israel Radio. "We have to face the enormity of this sin," he said. "They struck at the very existence of the state. Whoever usurps the role of the army and decides that he is fighting the war against Israel's enemies according to his own understanding has despaired of the very existence of a Jewish state. . . . There are no private wars. . . . They severely undermined the government's ability to maintain its sovereignty in the land of Israel. . . . And then of course there is the unbelievable moral degradation, particularly in the two most recent events [the Islamic College and the buses]. This is not only a matter of Jewish law but of natural law, of basic morality."

Didn't this slide into lawlessness begin with the mass squatting in Sebastia? the interviewer asked.

Yoel wasn't ready to go that far. "There is no comparison between a public struggle against an order or a law, with what happened here. This is not a case of people taking the law into their own hands but of challenging the essence of the state. . . . For me, a revolt against the state is a revolt against the Kingdom of Heaven."

In Israel's polarized debate, where talk shows consisted of opponents simultaneously shouting, here finally was a voice that couldn't be easily categorized. The nation began paying attention to Yoel Bin-Nun.

YISRAEL WAS OUTRAGED.

"I'm telling you as a friend," he said to Yoel, "you're going too far. You can't keep kicking your own community while it's lying bleeding in the road. You also have to offer some comfort, some solidarity. Otherwise, you're going to end up without a constituency. The left will never accept you, and your friends and neighbors will reject you."

"I heard what you have to say," Yoel responded testily. "But you can't always hide behind 'protecting the camp' and 'unifying our forces.'"

"I'm no less against what happened than you are. The difference between us, Yoel, is that I don't crave the approval of the left."

THE YOUNG MEN entered the office of the Yesha Council, nodded at each other, looked away. For years they had come together, planning demonstrations and settlements, arguing about how far to go in challenging a hostile Labor government and pressuring a sympathetic Likud government. They had envied each other's prominence and complained about each other's arrogance; but those were small disturbances among tempestuous personalities who had managed to stay focused on their shared vision. In the history of Israel, no group of activists had had a greater impact: they had transformed Israel's geography and politics and society. On the wall was proof of their victory, a map of the West Bank dense with dots marking settlements.

But now some of them were wondering: Did they still belong in the same camp? Could Moshe Levinger, the radical rabbi from Hebron, and Yoel Bin-Nun, the moderate rabbi from Ofra, continue to be comrades when they saw each other as betrayers of their camp's deepest values?

"Friends," began Yisrael Harel, "I know you're expecting me to give you information about the recent events. But I'm climbing the walls. No one is telling me anything."

"Who was authorized to issue a group indictment for all of us?" one delegate demanded. He meant Yoel.

Rabbi Levinger shouted, "At least these people [from the underground] did something for the Jewish people, while many here were sitting in cozy armchairs!"

Yisrael, who rarely raised his voice, shouted at Levinger: "*You're* the one who says the state is holy! I don't use such formulations. But then you go and support a group that undermines the authority of the state? What state can tolerate this?"

Yoel insisted on an unequivocal condemnation. "A call has to come from here for a general soul-searching in our community," he said.

Yisrael turned angrily to Yoel: "How can you go on the radio and make pronouncements? *I* don't know what happened, but you already pass judgment."

Like Kibbutz Gan Shmuel after Udi Adiv's arrest, the Yesha Council debated whether to fund the defendants' legal expenses. Only for those who express regret, said Yoel. The council voted to help defendants who didn't commit or intend to commit murder—in effect, those who had participated in the maiming of the West Bank mayors.

After the others left, Yisrael and Yoel lingered. They needed each other's company, especially now. They shared the same anxieties: How would they face their secular supporters who had trusted them to responsibly carry out the national mission? How would the settlement movement endure if it were no longer perceived as mainstream?

The phone rang. Yisrael listened silently to the voice on the other end. "God help us," he said. Yehudah Etzion had been implicated in a plot to blow up the Dome of the Rock.

LATE AT NIGHT, with only the call of the muezzin to break the stillness, Yoel wrote to Yehudah. "You have brought idolatrous fire into the holy dwelling place," Yoel accused. Judaism aimed at sanctifying the physical; Yehudah had attempted to coarsen the sacred. "You didn't blow up the Dome of the Rock, but you did blow to pieces the movement of the faithful that we founded.... Repent, Yehudah, for the sake of the true redemption you long for and tried to quicken (and thereby delayed), so that the idolatrous fire may be re-sanctified through a holiness arising from the courage of patience."

Was Yoel in any way responsible? There were nights he was convinced he was blameless. After all, he had taught Rabbi Kook's writings to hundreds of students, and none but Yehudah had so distorted those teachings. But there were also nights when he sensed he had unknowingly encouraged Yehudah's recklessness, as though he'd given his favorite disciple a weapon without checking whether it was loaded.

THE JEWISH UNDERGROUND was banner headlines for weeks. The revelation that religious Zionists—the dancing young men of Sebastia, some of them army officers—had planned to bomb crowded buses and destroy the Dome of the Rock, risking war with the Muslim world, strained even the Israeli capacity to endure the unexpected. Israel's president, Chaim Herzog, spoke of "poisoned fruit"; leading rabbis condemned the underground as madness. In the newspaper *Ma'ariv*, Srulik, a beloved cartoon figure in a kibbutznik's hat who embodied the scrappy Israeli, pointed a finger at himself with a stunned look that said, Who, me?

"I'm not surprised," Arik Achmon said to Yehudit. "The signs were there all along. Yisrael can talk all he wants about how they have the best youth. But they remind me of the Stalinists we grew up with, people who despised doubt and had answers to every question."

"It's interesting," replied Yehudit in her slow, thoughtful way, "that when the left turns extreme we produce traitors like Udi Adiv, and when the right turns extreme they produce murderers."

YISRAEL HAREL DROVE to the Israel Television studios in Jerusalem. After the confessions of the underground members and the report of Yehudah's Temple Mount plot, he could no longer avoid an unequivocal condemnation. They have harmed Jewish morality and most of all the settlements, he told the nation. Even if they are good people, I won't forgive them for this.

Driving back home, Yisrael felt again that moment of deep satisfaction when he returned to the cool mountain air and glimpsed Ofra's red-roofed houses rising with the hills. Against all odds, he and his friends had built a thriving community in the land of Israel.

Yisrael turned onto his street, lined with identical two-story houses, the bottom facade white stone, the top dark wood. He came to a sudden halt: his way was blocked by cars parked across the length of the road.

His neighbors were waiting for him.

Yisrael slowly got out of his car. "What's going on?" he asked.

"Who gave you the authority to speak in our name?" one man demanded.

Yisrael replied deliberately, controlling his anger. "If we are against the people of Israel, then the people of Israel will be against us. We've lost their support."

"We have a right to defend ourselves!"

"We have to live with the Arabs," Yisrael said. "We can't be a private army."

"All you want to do is appease the left!" someone shouted.

"You shut up," Yisrael said.

It was the same accusation he had made against Yoel.

TWENTY-SEVEN PRISONERS—knitted *kippot,* sandals, ritual fringes hanging from untucked shirts—entered the Jerusalem District Court, smiling and waving. Of course we're guilty, they seemed to be saying: guilty of love for our homeland, guilty of trying to protect our people. Family members, including a young woman in a white kerchief on which the word "Yamit" was embroidered, quietly read Psalms.

It was the largest trial of Jewish terrorist suspects in Israel's history. Six members were charged with murder at the Islamic College. Others were charged with attempted murder, or membership in an underground.

Defendants ignored the pleas of their guards and sat among their families, even left the courtroom at will, without permission or escort. One defendant blatantly ignored the procedings and studied Talmud.

Around the Friday-night family table, on Shabbat morning in synagogues, on Shabbat afternoon in Bnei Akiva meetings, the religious Zionist community confronted itself. In the pages of *Nekudah,* settlers and their supporters confessed and accused. Religious education was to blame for emphasizing ritual practice more than morality, wrote one. The government was to blame, wrote another, for not defending the settlers more vigorously against terrorist attacks. Whoever wants to fight the enemies of Israel, countered Hanan Porat, should join an elite unit of the IDF or the Shin Bet.

On the streets of Jerusalem teenage girls in long skirts and sandals collected money for the defense fund of the underground members—"the best of our young men," as supporters called them.

Rabbi Levinger was detained, suspected of providing halachic justification to underground members. At a demonstration outside Jerusalem police headquarters, Levinger's wife, Miriam, declared, "We always have to think about being moral! I've never heard anybody, any politician, Jew or Arab, say the Arabs must be moral." This, from an Orthodox Jew who routinely recited prayers affirming Jewish chosenness.

IN THE DESERT

ON JULY 22, 1985, fifteen months after the exposure of the underground, all twenty-seven defendants were sentenced to varying prison terms. Three defendants accused of murder were sentenced to life. Yehudah Etzion received seven years.

And now, Yisrael wrote in a *Nekudah* editorial, it was time for a pardon. The defendants had already served over a year in prison; all expressed degrees of regret. Yisrael noted a recent prisoner exchange in which over a thousand Palestinians, many of them convicted terrorists, had been released for three Israeli POWs held in Lebanon. "Failure to temper the verdict [against the underground members] will vindicate those who claim that the Israeli government acts cruelly toward its most faithful sons while revealing weakness toward its cruelest enemies."

Yisrael and Hanan and other settlement leaders visited the prisoners. Yoel, though, maintained an implacable distance. But his boycott didn't extend to the prisoners' families: every Friday night Yoel and Esther hosted the wife and children of an Ofra resident imprisoned with the underground; Yehudah's wife, Chaya, attended Yoel's Torah classes, even though he often used those as a platform to attack political zealotry.

Some neighbors accused Yoel of betraying his comrades. In the synagogue several refused to greet him. They had built Ofra together, shared guard duty, prayed and studied and mourned together. And now Yoel was regarded by a few of his neighbors as virtually a traitor. He could never know, when he set out to attend the wedding of a student or a meeting of rabbis, whether he would be welcomed or berated or shunned. Even in Mercaz, whose rabbis had passionately condemned the underground, Yoel was regarded warily. His opponents understood what he himself did not: that he had begun to look at his own community from a distance.

Under pressure, Yoel became even more vociferous—arrogant, some said. At meetings of the Yesha Council he shouted, pounded the table. Listen to him, opponents mocked, he's even begun quoting himself: "As

I said five years ago . . ." At a Yesha Council meeting, Yoel declared, "I'm ready to carry the people of Israel on my back for forty years." Who did he think he was, Moses?

Our kibbutznik friends in the brigade think of Yoel as a model of tolerance, Yisrael thought. They should see how he speaks to his own community.

"There is no longer a unified camp," Yoel told Esther. "I feel as if my own body is being torn apart."

"Maybe we should move," Esther suggested.

"Under no circumstances," said Yoel.

GRADUALLY, LIFE FOR Yisrael Harel appeared to return to normal. The media moved on to other scandals. New settlements were built. Yisrael continued to divide his time between his two offices, preparing the next issue of *Nekudah* while running the Yesha Council.

But, Yisrael knew, nothing would ever be the same again. The trust of many Israelis toward the settlers as the new pioneers was gone. Yisrael had devoted his life to turning religious Zionists from a defensive and peripheral community into the avant-garde of the Israeli ethos. But for all their attempts to appropriate the symbols of Zionist legitimacy, the settlers would likely remain an embattled group, damned by the cultural elite and confounded by their own limitations. There were moments when Yisrael suspected he had tied his life to a failed mission.

And everywhere there were reminders of his lost son, Eldad. In the young men in uniform returning on Shabbat leave to Ofra, in the Bnei Akiva kids going off to discover a well or an ancient ruin. Yisrael had rarely allowed himself to feel joy, but he had known satisfaction; now, without Eldad, carrier of his ethos, even that was denied him.

In a rare moment, he confided his despair to one of *Nekudah*'s young staff writers. "I'm finished," Yisrael said.

"WAITING FOR MASHIAH"

THE WAR IN LEBANON went on. A poster at the Peace Now vigil outside the prime minister's residence recorded the growing casualty rate—by 1985 nearly six hundred Israelis. The nation lost faith in the possibility of victory, or even in the ability to define victory. Israeli soldiers, targets of roadside bombs and suicide attacks, traveled through Lebanon in convoys. But how to withdraw without leaving the towns and kibbutzim in the north exposed again to Katyushas?

Inflation reached over 400 percent. Israelis rushed to spend their paychecks. The government printed a five-thousand-shekel note. Pickpockets, Israelis joked, kept the wallet and threw away the money. The Israeli tendency to improvise, expressed on the battlefield as daring, was exposed as mere recklessness in civilian life.

The radio played a song by Shalom Hanoch, mocking the Likud's Israel of instant money and messianic politics. The song was called "Waiting for Mashiah" —a Sephardi family name but also Hebrew for Messiah. There's a big deal in the offing, and a group of anxious investors are waiting in the offices of "Artzi-Eli"—Hebrew for "My land, my God"—for the wheeler-dealer Mashiah. But "Mashiah hasn't come, and Mashiah isn't calling." A policeman appears, informing the men that the stock market has crashed and that Mashiah has jumped off the roof. In a sneering voice, Shalom delivered the line that became the motto for this time: "Mashiah won't be coming, Mashiah won't be calling." It was an anthem that could have been written for Yehudah Etzion.

STILL, HOWEVER FITFULLY, the country was evolving. National elections brought a stalemate between Likud and Labor, and the two parties negotiated a national unity government, the first since May 1967. Shimon Peres, talented and vain, became prime minister for a two-year period, to be followed by the grim and unmovable Yitzhak Shamir.

The unity government withdrew from most of Lebanon, leaving a "security zone" in southern Lebanon along the Israeli border, to be defended by a pro-Israel Lebanese militia. Israeli casualties declined, and in northern Israel air-raid shelters were gradually turned into storerooms.

The unity government took on inflation too. The shekel was devalued, wages frozen, the budget cut, the public sector trimmed. Inflation declined from 400 percent to less than 20 percent. Once again the abyss needed to be in clear view to inspire the country's next miracle.

Look what we can achieve when the people of Israel are united, Yoel Bin-Nun told his students. He was speaking not just politically but theologically: Jewish unity—not the fantasies of a handful of fanatics—was the prerequisite for redemption.

ISRAEL'S IMMIGRANT ABSORPTION CENTERS filled with African Jews. They had left their thatched-hut villages in the Ethiopian highlands, partly in response to famine, partly to messianic expectation, and walked through jungle and desert toward refugee camps in the Sudan. There they kept their Jewishness hidden from the Muslim Sudanese soldiers, until Israeli agents smuggled them out and dispatched them to Israel by plane and boat. Thousands died on the road and in the camps; no Diaspora community had sacrificed so much on its way to Zion.

Yisrael Harel, emulating the kibbutz movement of an earlier era, mobilized the Yesha Council, and settlements welcomed Ethiopian immigrants. Dozens of Ethiopian families settled in Ofra. Immigrants became regular guests at the Shabbat table of the Harels and the Bin-Nuns and other Ofra families. Eventually, though, most of Ofra's Ethiopians left in search of jobs.

The arrival of the Ethiopian Jews, whose tradition identified them as the lost Israelite tribe of Dan, reminded Israelis of the country's essential purpose of ingathering the exiles. For all the problems facing premodern Africans entering a Western country, their arrival home was, for many immigrants, a sign that Mashiah had called.

CHAPTER 25

NEW BEGINNINGS

THE ELUSIVENESS OF HOME

WEARING AN ORANGE T-shirt and jeans, the tall, angular man with short black hair stepped out of the iron door in the prison wall and tried to smile at the small crowd of well-wishers and journalists. It was May 14, 1985, and Udi Adiv had served twelve and a half years of a seventeen-year sentence. The campaign to free him had succeeded.

"What are your plans?" called out a reporter.

"I can't," Udi pleaded, and raised his hands against his head as if in pain.

"Let him go to his father!" someone called out.

"Do you plan to start a family?" the reporter persisted.

"Yes," said Udi, "start a family, live my life—"

"What do you most long for?"

"Habayta habayta habayta"—Home home home—said Udi.

Leah put her arm around his waist and led him away.

First stop, his parents' home. Back to Gan Shmuel.

They arrived toward sunset. How the pecan trees have grown, thought Udi. And the lawns: Had they always been so lush? How could anyone who lived in such a place ever be unhappy?

Slowly, he walked the pathways of his childhood. Gan Shmuel's beloved son. And then its disgrace. *Will they curse me? So let them, I couldn't care less—*

Middle-aged people in shorts on rusty bicycles, old people in motorized carts. So bourgeois, he thought, but without malice. After all the upheavals of the century, what Gan Shmuel seemed to want most wasn't utopia but normalcy. And wasn't that what Udi now wanted too?

"Udi!" someone shouted and rushed toward him. Shlomit, a childhood friend, fell on his neck. "Come on," she said, "the *hevreh* are waiting for you inside." The *hevreh*: no matter what anyone else thought of him, for the *hevreh* from the children's house he would always remain Udi.

His parents' "room"—the kibbutzniks still called it that, even though it was now a two-room apartment—was crowded with childhood friends, with journalists and lawyers who had taken up his cause. His parents had written a "Welcome Home Udi" sign but decided not to hang it outside. Instead, it was stuck awkwardly between plates of cookies.

Hugs, kisses, but no tears. Udi had learned his restraint among these emotional ascetics. For the first time since his arrest, he was in a room filled with people who accepted him, even loved him, just as he was—not a monster, not a martyr, just Udi from Gan Shmuel.

The *hevreh* wanted to know: What was it like? How did you get along with the criminals? How did you keep your sanity? Udi smiled, embarrassed to speak about himself. "I don't consider the years in prison to be lost," he said. "I learned a lot about life."

The urgent questions went unasked. Could he really start again, find his place in an Israeli society that had transformed him into its symbol for treason? Would the "Udi Adiv affair" ever really end?

That night, Udi slept in his parents' apartment. The next morning they brought him breakfast from the dining room. Udi understood: he wasn't welcome there. *What do I care what those hypocrites think?*

But no, that is not how he wanted to return to Gan Shmuel. These people weren't his enemies. They were family.

Contacted by a reporter, Udi readily agreed to be interviewed. His parole agreement forbade political pronouncements, and so Udi tried, not always succesfully, to confine his remarks to the personal. It's important, he told the reporter, that I explain myself to the kibbutzniks who feel I betrayed them. Going to Damascus, he admitted, was "an act which can't be explained. A sane person wouldn't do such a thing."

Yes, I made a terrible mistake, he continued. But don't reject me, because I am your creation. After all, where did I learn my longing to perfect the world—my messianic politics—if not from Hashomer Hatzair?

UDI RECEIVED DOZENS of letters and postcards from well-wishers, some of whom he didn't know. One postcard had a single line: "Good luck in your future steps." It was signed Motta Gur.

There were also anonymous callers threatening to kill him. And every casual encounter contained the possibility of humiliation.

Leah accompanied Udi to buy a pair of glasses. "Name?" asked the clerk filling out the order. Udi hesitated. Leah broke the silence. "Ehud Adiv," she said, invoking Udi's formal name. No reaction: blessed anonymity.

Udi went from one friend's home to the other, trying to fill in the missing years, meeting spouses and children, hearing about careers. All that he would have once dismissed as bourgeois distractions: life.

Some sensed in him a deep confusion: Which of his old beliefs to repudiate, which to uphold?

Udi went to see a friend from the underground, Mahmoud Masarwa, who had been released as part of the terrorist prisoner exchange that Yisrael Harel had denounced in *Nekudah*.

Mahmoud asked Udi a favor: Would he accompany him on a pilgrimage to Cherkas, the village near Gan Shmuel destroyed after the War of Independence?

"There's nothing left of Cherkas," Udi said, "not even ruins."

Mahmoud persisted. And so they went to an orange grove across the road from Gan Shmuel, where the ruins of Cherkas had been. As a child Udi had imagined those ruins inhabited by ghosts.

Mahmoud walked through the grove, trying to remember where his house had been.

Every nation carries its legacy of injustice, thought Udi. To correct the injustices of the past meant imposing new injustices. But we need to remember what happened here. At least that.

"The past is gone, Mahmoud," said Udi. "This is Gan Shmuel now."

THREE MONTHS AFTER his release, Udi and Leah married. "I'm ready for a personal life," he told her.

They lived in a working-class Israeli Arab neighborhood in the town of Lod, near Tel Aviv. Leah was studying alternative nutrition. Udi cleaned stairwells, proud, he told Leah, not to have to rely on unemployment payments. "For years I've eaten three trays a day at the people's expense. Now I have to get used to getting my own tray." Every morning he ran four kilometers, past his former prison in nearby Ramle.

Udi enrolled at Tel Aviv University, studying history and political philosophy. He wrote a paper criticizing early Zionist pioneering from a Marxist perspective, and no one seemed scandalized. His teachers and fellow students didn't mention his past unless he did. The anonymous death threats faded. At age forty, normal life seemed possible for Udi Adiv.

LOSING THEIR RELIGION

ON KIBBUTZ EIN SHEMER, the good years abruptly ended. The government's austerity measures to curb inflation led to higher interest rates, and Ein Shemer's debt was growing at a rate of tens of thousands of dollars a month.

At the weekly meeting, anxious members debated whether to abandon the kibbutz's building projects midconstruction. Avital warned against taking out more loans to complete the building. Avital's father, Kuba, the architect who had planned the projects, glared at him from across the room but kept silent. Kuba let others make the case that Ein Shemer couldn't very well be left in its present state, disfigured with vast pits. The majority voted to continue building.

The kibbutz adopted a series of austerity moves, but the debt only grew. Trips abroad were canceled, meat served in the dining room sparingly. Members were told not to paint their apartments. Even travel by public transportation was discouraged; trips to the sea were via kibbutz truck alone. Hired workers were laid off; during the cotton harvest their places were taken by kibbutzniks volunteering extra hours. Avital went to work in the kibbutz's rubber factory.

Avital could have said, I told you so. Instead, he urged his friends to resist the temptation for mutual recrimination. If we waste our time accusing each other, he said, how will we heal?

Ein Shemer needed to find new ways to create and produce. And attract new members: the kibbutz, with a population of around three hundred members, not including children, was absorbing no more than three or four new families a year. Meanwhile the kibbutz was losing growing numbers of its own young people to the city.

But, Avital insisted, the crisis was an opportunity: "Leaving the kibbutz is not a new phenomenon. . . . The problem is—the faith of those who remain, their ability to change and influence. Our tragedy will be if young people stop believing that something can change here."

But instead of faith, the mood among Avital's friends was more ironic and sad. "We've lost our religion," one put it. Avital's generation—the children of the founders, as they still called themselves, well into middle age—were now running Ein Shemer. They honored the kibbutz as idea and loved Ein Shemer as home. But slowly they were realizing their untenable situation: they were socialists bound to a capitalist system. Some suspected they were caretakers of a beautiful idea that had almost worked, and that their task was to provide a dignified burial for the utopian dream.

IN THE GREENHOUSE, a team of high school students was working on improving the insulation of the new roof of the cowshed and examining why Ein Shemer's cows were more productive in winter than summer. Another team was growing roses for export to Holland. A third was creating computer programs for solar energy panels. The teenagers came after school hours and sometimes during school hours, and sometimes they worked through the night. Avital moved from team to team, offering coffee and soup, encouragement and hugs.

The greenhouse experimented with raising fish in water recycled from plants. Sooner or later Israel would face a water crisis, Avital explained, and raising fish in open ponds would no longer be practical. Irrigation pipes from the fish tanks dripped water onto rows of houseplants laid out on slanted trays. Excess water from the plants flowed down back into the fish tanks.

Late at night, when the last of the young people had gone, Avital would strip naked and swim with the fish.

ARIK ACHMON, DEFENSELESS

CLAUDE LANZMANN'S NINE-HOUR documentary film *Shoah* was being screened over two evenings at the Tel Aviv Museum, and Yehudit Achmon bought tickets. Arik went reluctantly. More than most sabras of his generation, he knew survivors intimately, had lived with them in Kibbutz Netzer Sereni, heard their stories in the cowshed. He had studied the mechanics of destruction. What could he learn about the Holocaust that he didn't already know?

But nothing prepared him for *Shoah*. Arik knew how to inure himself to the usual horrors. Lanzmann, though, told the story without historical footage, relying only on testimony by survivors, murderers, and bystanders. The film was excrutiating in its slowness: Lanzmann asks a question in French, the translator repeats it in Yiddish or German or Polish, then the answer by the interviewee, then the translation—in fact emphasizing the inadequacy of translation, from "there" to here. Meanwhile the camera lingers on the faces, records every twitch. Interviews take place in the fields and forest clearings where the killings happened, and the bucolic scenes become themselves part of the horror.

For the first time Arik felt as if he were there. Not trying to "understand" the system in his maddeningly dispassionate way, but one of them. Trapped. Helpless.

Arik had always assumed there was a way out of any situation. But of what use were courage and will and strategic planning against a state system wholly mobilized to gradually prepare you for extinction, while those who might help turned away in fear or indifference or hatred?

Arik, the resourceful sabra conceived by Jewish emergency, had intuitively understood: the only way to survive this knowledge and remain intact was to become an emotional Holocaust denier. But he could no longer feign detachment. He had reached the limits of the Zionist capacity to rescue, protect. *I know nothing—*

PRAYER FOR RAIN

WE'RE LEAVING FOR A YEAR, Meir Ariel told neighbors in Kibbutz Mishmarot. Just to try life in the city.

Few believed it. This time they're going for good, neighbors said. Tirza had been serious about quitting the kibbutz: she was now managing a private factory for producing eyeglass frames.

Meanwhile, Meir's career was stagnating: he had released a second album, another critical success and commercial failure. Perhaps he would have better luck in Tel Aviv.

But Meir's disappointment with kibbutz life was also spiritual. The kibbutz had been an experiment in human transcendence, yet it remained, in its way, material, concerned primarily with organizing the physical needs of its members. The kibbutz, Meir believed, had failed to recognize its own spiritual essence.

The Ariels found a big shabby house with a wild garden on a Tel Aviv street near the sea. Tirza spent most of the week away, at the eyeglass factory in the north. She paid the rent. Meir began recording a third album and promised to maintain the house. But when Tirza returned home on Thursday night, she would find the week's dishes in the sink, cigarette butts on the floor, dirty clothes left on unmade beds. *"Mefager, idiyot!"* she shouted. "I work all week to support you, and you leave the mess for Tirza to clean up?" Meir smiled, embarrassed, admitted she was right. "Without you I'm lost," he said, coaxing her close. Tirza knew she shouldn't give in, and knew she always would.

MEIR, NEARLY FORTY-FIVE, was reassigned to reserve duty in the IDF's entertainment division. Once a week he and Yehudah Eder, former guitarist for Tamouz, put on their old IDF uniforms and traveled to remote army bases. Meir's ideal reserve duty: instead of guns, they carried guitars.

One night, driving home from a base on the Golan Heights, Meir said to Yehudah, "You know what my dream is? To do a road show."

"A road show?" said Yehudah, laughing. "In Israel?" One could drive the length of the country, from the Lebanon border to Eilat, in eight hours, and cross the width of "greater Israel," from the Mediterranean to the Jordan River, in an hour and a half.

"Why not?" insisted Meir. "We'll be just like rock singers in America."

"We'll have groupies," said Yehudah.

Yehudah, founder of Israel's first academy for jazz, was one of the country's most sought-after guitarists. He could have played with anyone, but he chose to accompany Meir. Aside from Dylan, no one moved him more than Meir, and in precisely the same way, by combining irony and romanticism, in words that seemed to have been said for the first time. So Meir couldn't fill a club in Tel Aviv, couldn't afford to pay his musicians: the very lack of success meant singing for the song alone. Someday, Yehudah knew, Israel would regret the way it had treated its greatest balladeer.

They called it "Meir Ariel's Election Tour." Meir, claiming to be running for prime minister, would show up with a makeshift band in a forlorn town—they would only play the periphery, kibbutzim and impoverished towns in the Galilee and the Negev—set up in a public space, and play for whoever showed up. And if no one came, they would play anyway.

Meir rented a van. Tirza paid—"naturally," as she put it. Yoav Kutner, the DJ from Army Radio, brought congas. A film crew producing a documentary on the trip rode in a separate van.

They set out during the harvest holiday of Sukkoth, October 1987. The Wondrous Election Campaign, read a sign taped to Meir's van. A six-day tour, from north to south, sleeping in the clubrooms and empty children's houses of kibbutzim along the way.

The town of Kiryat Shmona, on the Lebanon border. The band set up in a concrete square with falafel stands and cafés where young men played backgammon in the middle of the day and old men in berets drank arak. Most of them ignored Meir as he spoke into a microphone: "Ladies and gentlemen! Happy holiday to the residents of Kiryat Shmona! We are Meir Ariel and the Charisma band. We're running for office and we want to seize the government and establish the time of the Messiah right now!"

A crowd gathered. A mother with a stroller, a barefoot boy, a Druse man with a great mustache. An old man in a straw fedora danced gracefully alone, holding high a beer bottle.

Back in the van, Meir talked about fame. "I wanted to be famous, period," he said, speaking of his youth. "I don't care how you make it happen, I just want to be famous. That was then, in those days. And then suddenly *Jerusalem of Iron* fell on me and spread my name among the public. . . . I was described everywhere as the singing paratrooper who participated in [the battle of] Jerusalem and wrote [the song] in the middle of the battle."

Meir raised his arms as if he were shooting a gun, then gestured as if throwing the gun aside, retrieved an imaginary pen from his pocket and scribbled furiously on his palm, then shot again. "In the middle of the battle, as we charged the enemy. . . . Not just writing, but writing with his blood. I'd stab myself with my pen, draw a drop of blood and write with it."

A WARM AUTUMN EVENING on the grass of Kibbutz Mishmarot, the lawn made famous by Meir and Shalom's song. But now, instead of a tangle of teenagers, there were rows of chairs. Almost the entire Mishmarot community turned out for the concert.

Meir's father, Sasha, had died three weeks earlier. Meir had written a kind of eulogy for him, a lament for Meir's failure to live up to his father's expectations. "The Snake's Shed Skin" opens with Meir lying under a bridge, chewing on the stem of a wildflower while cars are in constant movement above his head. Where were all those people going? And why couldn't Meir heed his father's advice and be more purposeful like them? Meir feared he would always be a kind of fool, brilliant, openhearted, hopelessly archaic. (He calls the cars "wagons.")

The language was exquisite, the melody haunting even in major key. But he didn't sing it here tonight.

Kutner screamed into the mike: "Where are the Rolling Stones? Where are the Doors? Everything's dead, everything's finished!"

The teenagers on the grass laughed. The old-timers looked at each other and smiled: *Nu*, Meirkeh and his friends.

IN BEERSHEBA, AT THE EDGE of the desert, Meir and the band approached the entrance to a prison, explained they wanted to play for the inmates. The guards told them to go away. Beersheba is a good place to put a prison, said Kutner; who would want to escape?

They drove on the desert road past Sde Boker, Ben-Gurion's kibbutz. They came to the Ramon Crater, vast and primal. Stop the car, said Meir. Retrieving a prayer book, he stepped outside and quietly read the Prayer for Rain, recited on Sukkoth, when the land of Israel prepares for the first rains of autumn, after months of sealed sky. "Remember the twelve tribes You led through the split waters," Meir recited. "Their descendants whose blood was spilled for You like water. Help us, for troubles surround our souls like water. For the sake of their righteousness, grant abundant water."

For days clouds had been gathering. But no rain had come.

Back in the car, Meir sensed his friends' unease. Could it be that Meir Ariel, bohemian kibbutznik, bard of Israeli angst, would become one of *them*—the black-hatted ghetto Jews darkening the land of the free Hebrews? The possibility was not inconceivable in 1980s Israel. After all, another great Israeli bohemian, the actor and wise guy Uri Zohar, producer of lascivious comedies and winner of the nation's highest honor, the Israel

Prize, for helping create the new secular Israeli culture, had vanished into the yeshiva world and reemerged as Rabbi Uri Zohar, preaching against secularism.

But no: Meir's friends knew he wouldn't betray himself. So what exactly did Meir's interest in Judaism mean? Was it a whim, one more Meir Ariel challenge to smugness? Or maybe, as Shalom Hanoch assumed, simply an expression of Meir's deep interest in the Hebrew language, which couldn't be fully understood without its religious origins?

Meir tried to explain: "One day I realized that I can't circumcise my son and marry [in a religious ceremony] and celebrate the holidays without understanding what it's all about." But his interest in Judaism was more than a search for identity: "I believe in God, I believe that the Torah is the true version of existence, to the formation of the world."

"So why don't you take it to the end?" asked one of the band members.

"I don't understand the concept of taking things to the end."

How to explain himself in a society that coped with its drastic human diversity by categorizing? "My faith in God is entirely personal and I don't feel any need to join any camp," Meir added. That included the secular camp. "I don't really feel at home in secular society. I feel we're missing something."

It began to rain. Pour.

"Wow," said Kutner.

Meir watched the rain in silence.

ARTICLES ON THE TOUR appeared in the press; the film *Meir Ariel's Election Campaign* was screened on Israel Television.

Meir wrote a letter to the Mishmarot community, explaining that he and Tirza had decided to remain in Tel Aviv. "I dare to say we have no real reason to leave the kibbutz," wrote Meir, "not as an ideal and not as a community of friends. Therefore we see our departure in technical terms only, for the sake of fulfilling our potential in the open market." Reassuring, he continued, "Needless to say this has nothing to do with any argument or resentment, or any feeling of ill-treatment. Ours is a departure with love for friends and place."

But then he abruptly changed tone. "True, there is disappointment, in particular with the way a lie has been accepted"—an apparent reference to the loss of Mishmarot's egalitarian ethos, especially the benefits, like private cars, accorded managers in the plywood factory, about which Meir had often complained.

Then Meir changed tone yet again. "We won't swear to this, but we have good reasons to return [to the kibbutz], if only to fulfill 45 years of investment in friendships and in assets, and the departing grant [we received from the kibbutz] scarcely compensates for all of that."

But, he concluded with oblique hostility, "Members don't only leave the kibbutz, the kibbutz also leaves its members."

A FAILURE OF EMPATHY

DAVID GROSSMAN, the Israeli novelist, stood before the Ofra residents crowded into Yoel and Esther Bin-Nun's salon. Slight, redheaded, Grossman looked even younger than his thirty-two years. But the appearance of innocence was misleading: Grossman was no less fierce in his ideological commitment than the settlers.

He had come to Ofra, he explained, as part of a journey through the West Bank that had already taken him to Palestinian towns and refugee camps. Now he had a simple request of the people in this room: that they suspend political argument and try to enter into the consciousness of their Palestinian neighbors. Can you imagine how they see the occupation, what its most hateful aspects would be?

"The situation isn't our fault!" someone called out. Others nodded.

That's not my question, insisted Grossman. Let's say you're right, and history will vindicate you. Still: How do you think your neighbors in Ein Yabroud experience your presence here?

Grossman was asking Ofra's settlers for empathy. But the response was more defensiveness.

Grossman tried again. I can't bear the thought, he said, that even a moment of my time would pass without meaning or enjoyment. The thought of being detained at a roadblock or locked at home under curfew is unbearable.

"At the intersection coming into Tel Aviv I also get held up an hour every morning," someone responded. Laughter.

Some did try to grapple with Grossman's challenge. One young woman spoke of her unease at the second-class status of Israel's Bedouin. A young man said he rebuked soldiers who mistreated Palestinians at a roadblock. But even those well-intentioned responses didn't answer Grossman's question. In the end, he noted, the settlers weren't able to step out of their worldview even for a moment and see themselves through Palestinian eyes. Grossman's experiment in empathy had failed.

GROSSMAN'S FURIOUS ACCOUNT of his journey through the territories appeared in May 1987, as a special issue of the magazine *Koteret Rashit*. A month later it was published as a book, *Hazman Hatzahov* (The Yellow Time), and then in English as *The Yellow Wind*. The territories, wrote Grossman, were seething—with humiliation, with rage, with dreams of revenge: "One day we will wake up to a bitter surprise."

Grossman's portrait of Ofra's settlers was devastating. Though warm and hospitable, he wrote, they were sealed in their own certainties, trapped by ideological clichés that diminished language and thought. "Their houses are almost bookless, with the exception of religious texts, and, in general, they have little use for culture." The settlers were "historical people, and historical people become—at certain moments—hollow, and allow history to stuff them, and then they are dangerous and deadly." And, warned Grossman, the next generation of Jewish terrorists, successors to the settlers' underground, was now being incubated in the settlements and yeshivas of religious Zionism.

As for Yoel Bin-Nun, Grossman acknowledged his stand against the settlers' underground, yet dismissed him as a faux moderate, noting that on his wall hung the photomontage of the Second Temple superimposed on the Mount—the image Yoel had created, Grossman wrote pointedly, together with the imprisoned underground leader Yehudah Etzion.

Yoel was outraged. Hollow historical beings? What was the Jewish people without historical consciousness? And how could he write that the settlers posssessed no secular books? He'd been in Yoel's home, he saw the library! No use for culture? Sitting in that room were journalists, an art critic, teachers, scientists. And how dare he imply that Yoel was somehow in the same camp as Yehudah Etzion because of an educational poster on the wall?

Grossman, Yoel concluded, had come not to engage the people of Ofra but to judge them. He would never allow himself to write about Palestinians with the same contemptuous stereotypes. Apparently empathy was meant for everyone but settlers.

Yoel began writing a rebuttal, which he intended to turn into a book, *The Blue and White Time.*

CHAPTER 26

UNDER SIEGE

A DIFFERENT KIND OF WAR

IT WAS EARLY EVENING, and Yisrael Harel was driving home from Jerusalem. Since the outbreak of riots in the West Bank and Gaza—what the Palestinians were calling the intifada, or uprising—that once-routine drive had become a gauntlet. One young man from a settlement near Ofra, whose car was hit by a Molotov cocktail, emerged with a melted face; a boy from Ofra was hit in the head with a rock and became an epileptic. Yisrael drove without a seat belt, in case he had to escape from a burning car. He wore a pistol, just in case.

Yisrael had been stoned several times, but there was no way to prepare for that moment of shattered glass. Like a car crash but worse, because the violence was intentional. Yisrael would often pick up a hitchhiking soldier or settler, and company helped ease the tension. But now he was alone.

Yisrael passed IDF jeeps, whose windshields—and even the rotating blue lights on their roofs—were covered with mesh wire against stones. For Yisrael that protectiveness conveyed an unbearable weakness: Since when did soldiers of Israel fear teenagers with rocks? Why was the IDF allowing itself to be humiliated?

The narrow road approached the village of Baytin. In the fading light, the white stone houses, some with antennae shaped like the Eiffel Tower, seemed to emerge from the hills. Several houses flew Palestinian flags—a defiant gesture, since the red, black, and green colors of the PLO were banned by Israel.

Yisrael turned a bend. Up ahead, a barrier of stones across the road. And behind it, teenagers and children, some with kaffiyehs wrapped around their faces.

Crash: splintered windshield.

Yisrael stepped out of the car. A rock hit him in the shoulder. In the leg.

He aimed his pistol at the crowd. A warning: he wouldn't shoot at anyone unless his life was threatened. Rocks fell around him. He pointed the gun straight up and fired. The young people ran.

Back in the car, Yisrael swerved around the stone barrier, accelerated, and resumed his journey home.

IT HAD BEGUN with an accident. On December 8, 1987, a truck driven by an Israeli hit a car near Gaza, killing four Palestinians. A baseless rumor spread that the attack had been deliberate, revenge for the stabbing murder of an Israeli two days earlier in the Gaza City market. Rioting spread through the Gaza refugee camps, and then into the West Bank. The army expected a quick end to the disturbances. But the violence only intensified into an organized revolt.

Israelis had prided themselves on maintaining a benign occupation. There was, after all, a degree of prosperity, at least in the West Bank; and the army's presence in the lives of Palestinians had been minimal. Arabs as well as Jews could travel in any part of the land between the Jordan River and the Mediterranean Sea. True, there was occasional terrorism and stone-throwing and IDF curfews; still, the territories had been relatively quiet.

But suppressed rage had been released, and the territories were now a low-level battlefield. Palestinians threw rocks and Molotov cocktails, Israeli soldiers fired rubber bullets. Black smoke rose from burning tires, white smoke from tear gas. Stone walls in Palestinian towns and villages were covered with graffiti, drawings of swords piercing the map of Israel dripping blood. The Palestinian teenager with a slingshot against Israeli soldiers with M16s shattered a cherished Israeli self-image: Who was David, who Goliath?

The army didn't know how to cope. Yitzhak Rabin, defense minister in an uneasy unity government of Likud and Labor, told soldiers to "break the bones" of rioters. One commander ordered Palestinian detainees to lie facedown on the ground, then ordered his soldiers to beat them with clubs.

How to control the violence? Some settlers who shot at rioters, or even fired in the air, were detained by Israeli police. A settler was wounded in a stabbing attack in Hebron and managed to shoot his assailant; police seized his weapon, returning it only after a public outcry. "We are prevented from exercising our right to self-defense," noted a leaflet distributed in Ofra.

"Those who rise to kill us are protected by the Israeli government, and we are required to flee."

Yet for leftists, the problem wasn't Israeli restraint but brutality. Left and right no longer seemed capable of even perceiving the same reality.

OFRA WAS UNDER SIEGE. School buses were accompanied by armed guards and fitted with plastic windows. On especially bad days on the roads, the army insisted that cars leaving the settlement travel in convoys. A company of soldiers moved in: for Ofra, civilian and military life, always intimate, became inseparable.

To be a settler now meant risking one's family's safety on a daily basis. Yet settlers continued to travel the roads; large families crowded into Subaru station wagons, flying Israeli flags as though every day were Independence Day. They continued to hike to biblical sites. The land of Israel is won through suffering, Ofra's residents quoted the rabbis, strengthening each other's resolve.

Yisrael and Sarah Harel didn't try to restrain the movements of their three remaining children. Yisrael was moved by Sarah's courage: she would stand outside Ofra's gate and hitch a ride to Jerusalem. We waited two thousand years to come home, she seemed to be saying; do they think they can deter us with stones? Yisrael recalled how, after the death of their son Eldad, he couldn't bring himself to attend Ofra's Purim party; but Sarah went, dressed in a lion's costume.

Not only did almost none of Ofra's five hundred residents leave; but more families were moving in. The settlement population generally—around seventy thousand at the beginning of the intifada—was expanding.

Still, settlers were feeling increasingly isolated. The Ofra newsletter noted the absence of visitors—relatives from the other side of the old border who were afraid to come to the settlement for bar mitzvahs, the mailman who refused to come without armed guard. Only beggars, the newsletter added sardonically, continue to come here. In Ofra they spoke with contempt for the fearful Jews of Tel Aviv, compared to their own children, fearlessly walking the land.

Media hostility intensified the sense of siege. A sticker denouncing left-wing Israeli journalists appeared on settler cars: "The people oppose a hostile media," with a drawing of a snake wrapped around a microphone. Yoel

Bin-Nun argued with his neighbors. It's our media too, he reminded. If we make our case convincingly, we will be heard.

A JEWISH ARGUMENT OVER LAND

WORKING AT NIGHT, the young men uprooted a part of the fence separating Ofra from several hundred acres of unworked, Arab-owned land. The fence was extended eastward, and the settlement instantly expanded. This was no partisan act: Ofra's leaders had decided to seize the land for a building extension. After all, they reasoned, the land was all but abandoned; and without expansion, Ofra would not survive.

No compensation was offered the Arab owner, no explanation given to the Israeli authorities. A fait accompli, passed without incident.

Over the years Ofra's left-wing opponents had accused the settlers of seizing Arab land, but those charges appeared nebulous. The first settlers, after all, had moved into an abandoned Jordanian army camp. The Jordanians had expropriated private land to build the camp and, it turned out, hadn't observed their own legal requirements. Still, the army camp had remained empty, unclaimed, for nearly a decade after the Six-Day War.

Yoel Bin-Nun tried to convince himself that this new expropriation was legitimate. Necessary. And anyway the land was neglected. No one's livelihood was threatened. *But there are some fig trees—*

THE DISTORTION OPENING Meir Ariel's third album, *Yerukot* (Yellow Blue), was the first jarring note. Then came Meir's voice, angry and taunting. The song, "Midrash Yonati"—literally, "Commentary on My Dove," a rabbinic metaphor for the Jewish people—was a vehement attack on the settlers, who seize land "like a thief in the night." Invoking a saying of Rabbi Zvi Yehudah Kook about the Western Wall—"There are people with hearts of stone and stones with hearts of people"—Meir lamented, "Stones in the heart of Jerusalem / . . . She doesn't pursue justice, doesn't want peace / because there is no peace without justice"—a play on two biblical verses.

Meir's critique was no mere left-wing polemic but a religious disputation. Meir was insisting that settlers had distorted the Torah he had come to love. He drew on the Exodus from Egypt, the apocalyptic prophecy of Ezekiel, the love between God and Israel in the Song of Songs. Meir's protest was so layered with biblical and rabbinic references that almost every line required commentary.

"Midrash Yonati" was a philosophical argument for how Judaism understands the holiness of the land of Israel. Just as a Jew relinquishes mastery over the world every seventh day, he surrenders control over his land every seventh year. The laws of *shmitta*, of leaving the land fallow on the sabbatical year, apply only to the land of Israel, a reminder that one cannot entirely possess holy land.

Meir didn't minimize the enmity of Israel's neighbors. The modern exodus of the Jews resembled the first exodus, when the Israelites stood on the shore of the Red Sea, with Pharoah behind them and the unparted waters before them: it was, sang Meir, the same dangerous procession "on the way to the sea."

But existential threat didn't absolve Israel from moral responsibility. The generation of Jews privileged to return home must be especially worthy, because they are the repository of the dreams of the Jews in exile: "The lands beyond the sea are behind us / We are their longing."

THE MOUNTAIN AND THE COAST, REVISITED

GUARD DUTY WAS mandatory for men in Ofra. But not everyone took the responsibility seriously. Ofra's "security committee" decided to impose fines and publicize the names of shirkers. The protocol of a meeting of the security committee from May 20, 1988, listed the names of four Ofra residents who didn't appear for their shifts. They included Yoel Bin-Nun, who, the minutes noted, was fined with a double shift. "We apologize about the fines and the publicizing of names—but we have no choice. . . . *Shabbat shalom*, a peaceful Sabbath to all."

Yoel was no shirker; he was simply overwhelmed with other responsibilities. Along with teaching at the Mount Etzion military yeshiva and leading hikes from the Ofra field school and training teachers in Bible studies, he was founder and principal of a progressive religious girls' high school in Ofra. The premise of the Ofra Ulpana was that religious girls should be exposed to no less a rigorous education than boys. If we keep our young women in the nineteenth century, Yoel argued, we will lose the brightest among them. The girls were taught cooking but also how to change a tire. When some girls said they wanted to study Talmud, just as the boys did, Yoel organized a class in his home.

Yoel spoke of "the living Torah," relevant not only to religious ritual but to all of life. Mathematics was the code of God's creation, history the unfolding of God's plan. Most of all, Yoel stressed love for the people of Israel in all its diversity. On Memorial Day, the girls went to ceremonies on secular kibbutzim; then they spent a Shabbat with ultra-Orthodox families.

Yoel emphasized a religious education based on trust, not fear. A key was left hanging outside the school canteen, and any student could help herself to snacks and be expected to leave the proper payment. Yoel tried, without success, to convince the Ministry of Education to allow matriculation tests in the Ulpana without supervision. He trusted, too, his students' religious and political maturity. He taught not only Jewish but Greek philosophy. And he invited dovish politicians who explained why they opposed annexing the territories, and a prominent journalist who explained why he didn't believe in God.

Yoel worked out a compromise with Ofra's security committee: he fulfilled his guarding responsibilities in the summer. For a full week he sat in the booth at Ofra's front gate. There he held his meetings—with a journalist seeking out the settlement movement's most outspoken moderate, with a student confessing a crisis of faith.

A FRIEND WAS driving Yoel home from Jerusalem. As the car entered the town of El Bireh, past Ramallah on the way to Ofra, a rock smashed the windshield. Yoel saw several teenagers running into a school building. One of them, a big young man, was wearing a red sweater.

Yoel entered the school. Meanwhile his friend contacted the army—many settler cars were now equipped with two-way radios—and waited for the soldiers.

Yoel found the principal in his office. "Some young people broke the windshield of my car," Yoel said, deliberately calm, "and they escaped into this building."

The principal, an older man with a gray mustache, examined the bearded settler with the large knitted *kippah*. Yoel's soft-spoken demeanor reassured him.

"Can you identify them?" asked the principal in Hebrew.

They went from classroom to classroom. The big young man had removed his red sweater, but Yoel easily spotted him. He made no attempt to escape. "Come with us," the principal ordered, and the offender passively complied. "He's not one of our students," the principal told Yoel, as if in apology.

They waited together until soldiers came. Yoel felt appreciation toward the principal, a fellow educator trying to protect his community from the consequences of its rage.

IN HIS LATE-NIGHT PACING, Yoel was reaching heretical conclusions about the future of Judea and Samaria. The intifada, he knew, was a turning point. The settlement movement, Yoel was now saying, had succeeded in settling on the ground, but it had failed to settle in the hearts of the Israeli people. Peace Now, Yoel conceded, was partly right: the settlers had never seriously thought about the Arabs living in the land. The Yesha Council had opposed every peace plan, but never offered a realistic plan of its own.

Desperate plans were being promoted by the settlers' radical fringe—the mass expulsion of Palestinians from the territories, even creating a "state of Judea" that would secede from the state of Israel. Since the withdrawal from Sinai, and especially since the outbreak of the intifada, it was no longer unusual to hear some religious Zionists proclaim their alienation from the secular state they once revered. If the secular state, heralded by Kookians as the carrier of redemption, was now betraying the messianic process, then religious Zionists needed to present an alternative to the state.

Yoel was rethinking one of his most cherished metaphors, the relationship between the mountain and the coast. He had taught a generation of young religious Zionists that the responsibility of those who lived on the mountain—in Judea and Samaria—was to bring spirituality to those who lived on the coast—greater Tel Aviv. In ancient Israel, he'd noted, prophecy had come from the people of the mountain, aimed at the mercantile people near the sea.

But even as the Israelis of the coast were drifting away from their Jewish roots, the Israelis of the mountain were retreating into a self-enclosed provinciality. Religious Zionism had been founded as a mediation between modernity and tradition, but parts of the religious Zionist community were adopting ultra-Orthodox ghettoization. And they were replacing the messy engagement with reality—the essence of the Judaic approach to life—with a purist ideology that bypassed historical process. If the alienation between the mountain and the coast continued, Yoel now taught, Israel would, God forbid, face *hurban*, destruction. "The body pulls to excessive materialism, and the soul to detached spirituality," he told a journalist. "For the people of Israel, there are always two trends competing: holiness, and an openness to the world. The question is: What is the relationship between the two?" The coast needed the mountain to remind it of Israel's spiritual destiny; but the mountain also needed the coast, to remind it that redemption must happen in the real world. Judaism could work only through balance between reality and dream.

Yoel stopped writing his rebuttal to *The Yellow Wind*. Though he still believed that David Grossman had wronged the settlers, Grossman had anticipated the intifada while Yoel, who prided himself on his farsightedness, had not. Yoel's grievance toward Grossman now felt to him petty. *I can't write propaganda—*

"[WE MUST] REDEEM the Mount from its shame," Yehudah Etzion told a small group of followers, and pointed toward the golden Dome of the Rock rising across the valley. He was standing on the Mount of Olives, near the spot from which Motta Gur had surveyed the Old City walls just before ordering the paratroopers to move toward the Lions' Gate.

It was January 1989, and Yehudah had just been released from Tel Mond Prison, after serving five years for plotting to destroy the Dome of the Rock and for participating in the terrorist attack against West Bank mayors. Instead of going directly home to Ofra, though, he had walked seventy kilometers from the prison gate to the Mount of Olives, carrying a silver-rimmed flag embroidered with the verse from Isaiah, "For Zion's sake I won't be silent." At thirty-seven, his curly red hair was thinning, his beard turning gray.

The people aren't ready for the Temple, Yehudah told his supporters. And so he was founding a new "redemption movement" to educate the people about the need to re-create the Jewish state, freed from westernization and run according to the laws of Torah, updated to the conditions of modern sovereignty, and with a rebuilt Temple at its heart.

In Ofra, Yehudah's neighbors greeted him with the traditional welcome of bread and salt. Not that they agreed with Yehudah's politics; they were simply embracing a friend who had made a mistake, paid for it, and returned home. Only Yoel, who lived at the other end of the street, kept away. When the two former friends happened to meet, Yoel greeted him perfunctorily and quickly moved on. And Yoel removed from his living room wall the photomontage of the Second Temple imposed on the Dome of the Rock.

SURROUNDED BY HIS Ulpana girls in sandals and denim skirts and yoga-style pants, Yoel read from the small, heavily annotated Bible that had accompanied him on treks across the land. It was a bright spring afternoon in the Arab village of Silwan, just outside Jerusalem's Old City walls. Rising in the near distance were the domes of the Temple Mount. The group stood on a hilltop overlooking Hezekiah's Tunnel, built by the Judean king Hezekiah in 701 BCE to provide water for Jerusalem in preparation of an anticipated siege by the Assyrian king Sennacherib. Since the intifada, few Jews ventured into Silwan. But Yoel was adamant: We are not abandoning Hezekiah's Tunnel.

"[Hezekiah] appointed battle officers over the people," Yoel read aloud. "Then, gathering them to him in the square of the city gate, he rallied them, saying, 'Be strong and of good courage, do not be frightened or dismayed by the king of Assyria or by the horde that is with him, for . . . with him is an arm of flesh, but with us is the Lord our God.' "

And then Yoel saw them: a half dozen young Arab men, pointing at him and the girls and whispering. "Stay here," he told his students.

Slowly, he walked toward the young men. A pistol was tucked in the back of his pants, concealed by overhanging shirt.

Yoel noted that one young man appeared to be the leader. "Salaam alaikum"—Peace be with you—Yoel said in Arabic. "Alaikum salaam," the young man responded, then added in Hebrew, "Aren't you afraid?"

"La, min Allah bas," replied Yoel in Arabic: I only fear God.

"Ah, good," the young man said.

Yoel didn't know much more Arabic, and the conversation turned to Hebrew.

"It's good you came without a weapon," the young man said. "Otherwise there would have been a *balagan* here."

"Why should we fight each other?" said Yoel. "Muslims, Jews, we all believe in God."

They parted with a handshake.

THE INTIFADA WAS radicalizing not only part of the right but also part of the left. Peace Now was now advocating a Palestinian state—another Jewish fantasy, said Yoel, as if Yasser Arafat and the PLO were prepared to live in peace beside a Jewish state in any borders. The Jews, so long without the responsibilities of sovereignty, were reverting to the temptation of magical politics. Instead of tearing the nation apart between two unrealistic visions—annexation and land-for-peace—Israelis needed to reestablish a politics of realism, of consensus.

Writing in *Nekudah*, Yoel suggested some elements of that elusive consensus: no annexation and no withdrawal, while conditioning any major initiative in peace or war on a solid majority. Yoel called for dividing the territories into Jewish and Arab cantons: Jews would vote in Israeli elections, Arabs in Jordanian elections. Yoel acknowledged that there was in his plan a measure of injustice for Palestinians, who would be denied national sovereignty, but there was no perfect justice in this world—especially given Palestinian rejection of Israeli sovereignty.

The search for a politics of realism and consensus was, for Yoel, a theological imperative. That was the audacity of Yoel's new theology: political pragmatism as precondition for redemption. In lectures to students he repeatedly returned to June 7, 1967, when he had stood on the Temple Mount with atheist kibbutzniks. That is how redemption comes: through unity, not through the purist separatism of Yehudah Etzion.

Yoel discerned one leader capable of re-creating a national consensus: Defense Minister Rabin. True, relations between Rabin and the settlers were often strained. Rabin had outraged settlers by calling them a "burden" on the IDF—to which Yisrael Harel had responded in *Nekudah* that the state of Israel is also a burden on the IDF.

But Yoel sensed that Rabin, unlike fellow Labor leader Shimon Peres, understood that a peace agreement with the Palestinians was impossible, and that only interim arrangements aimed at daily coexistence could work.

Yoel noted that in 1975, when Rabin was prime minister, he had concluded an interim agreement with Egypt, in which Israel withdrew from part of the Sinai Desert without uprooting settlements. Gush Emunim, and Yoel too, had bitterly opposed Rabin then. But, Yoel now argued, we had failed to understand Rabin's intentions. Unlike the Likud, Rabin had no illusions about genuine peace with the Egyptians, and so he'd preferred a nonbelligerency arrangement that was less than formal peace and wouldn't require total Israeli withdrawal. And nonbelligerency, after all, was all that remained for Israel of its cold peace with Egypt.

If we continued to demand Israeli sovereignty over all of Judea and Samaria, Yoel warned, we will end up with nothing, just like in Sinai. But if we separate settlement building from annexation, we might find Rabin our most effective ally.

YITZHAK RABIN OFFERED his usual limp handshake to the two men in knitted *kippot* who had come to his office at the Defense Ministry in Tel Aviv. The message of that perfunctory handshake was, Let's dispense with protocol and get straight to business.

Rabin gestured to the two settlers to sit and prepared himself for an unpleasant conversation about the IDF's lack of resolve toward the intifada.

"We're here to encourage you to run for prime minister," Yisrael began.

Rabin raised his eyes from the desk. His long and dour face showed surprise. "I assumed," he said slowly, in his deep monotone, "that you were here to talk about settlement issues."

For all his anger at Rabin, Yisrael sensed that the greatest danger to the settlements came, paradoxically, from the right—that only a right-wing leader would have the credibility among the public to withdraw.

What prompted their private initiative, Yoel explained to Rabin, was the nation's demoralization. The intifada showed no signs of easing, a no-win war with the Shiite Hezbollah militia was dragging on in the "security zone" in southern Lebanon, and the unity government was faltering. We need a leader truly committed to national unity, said Yoel. "All of Zionism's historic accomplishments were achieved when the nation was united. Like the Six Days. And our failures happened when we were divided. If we tilt too far right or too far left, the ship will be destabilized."

Despite himself, Rabin was intrigued. He had surely never expected to hear any of this from settler leaders. Still, Rabin was careful not to reveal his political ambitions, and shifted the conversation to the security situation.

Later, Yisrael would say that they had wasted their time, that Rabin was no different from other Labor politicians blinded by the illusions of the left. But Yoel disagreed. The abrupt and strangely shy defense minister, he insisted, represented the best of the historic Labor Party. Yoel didn't know it then, but the respect he felt toward Rabin was mutual.

WHAT'S WITH THE ADIV FAMILY?

AT 9:00 A.M., on September 9, 1988, two men and two women were led handcuffed into the Jerusalem District Court. The defendants, Jewish members of a Trotskyite faction called Derekh Hanitzotz, Way of the Spark, were accused of belonging to a Palestinian terrorist organization. Among them was a thirty-four-year-old with graying hair named Asaf Adiv. His older brother, Udi, sat among the defendants' relatives and friends.

More than any other family member, Asaf had been traumatized by Udi's trial and imprisonment. Asaf joined a Trotskyite faction that even others on the Israeli far left regarded as a cult; he worked in factories to rouse the workers to revolution. Udi had tried to reason with him: Yes, socialism, but *scientific* socialism, not the Trotskyite fantasy of a workers' revolution—let alone in Israel, where workers tended to vote Likud. Asaf had responded angrily when Udi, as precondition for release from prison, had repudiated his underground activities, and finally stopped speaking to him altogether. Asaf hadn't even come to his parents' house to welcome Udi back from prison.

On a visit to London, Asaf and his friends had contacted a representative of the Marxist PLO faction, the Democratic Front for the Liberation of Palestine (DFLP)—the group responsible for one of the worst terrorist attacks, the Ma'alot massacre in a high school in northern Israel in 1974. (Udi, before his arrest, had hoped to contact the DFLP.) The Israeli Trotskyites were given underground aliases: Asaf was "Nasser."

Back in Israel, though, their activities hadn't gone further than publishing an anti-Zionist newspaper. Unlike Udi before his arrest, Asaf and his friends had no intention of supporting the Palestinians with violence.

Yet shortly after his arrest Asaf pleaded guilty to charges of subversion. That was because his interrogators, he explained in court, had threatened to arrest Udi if he didn't cooperate. But now he was rescinding that guilty plea. Udi was touched by Asaf's loyalty.

Udi got a call from a radio interviewer. So what's with the Adiv family? the interviewer asked.

We're very political, Udi replied.

Udi was relieved that there was one detail of the family's politics that the media didn't know. For the last five years, Sylvia's father and Udi's former father-in-law had been held incommunicado in an Israeli prison for spying for the Soviet Union. Dr. Marcus Klingberg, former deputy director of the Institute for Biological Research, Israel's top-secret research center for non-conventional warfare, had handed over Israel's most sensitive data to the patron of Israel's Arab enemies. Israel's security establishment regarded Klingberg as the most dangerous spy in the country's history—so dangerous that even his warders weren't told his true identity.

Sooner or later the public would learn about Klingberg, and then, Udi knew, the phone calls would come. His one consolation was that he was no longer married to Sylvia. *Imagine what the media would do to me if I hadn't divorced her—*

THE TRIAL OF ASAF and his friends ended with a plea bargain. The defendants confessed to membership in a terrorist organization and received relatively lenient sentences. Asaf was sentenced to eighteen months in prison.

In contrast to the rage and fear around Udi's trial, the atmosphere this time was relatively subdued. No taunting crowds outside the courtroom, no hysterical headlines. The circumstances were different, but so was Israel. The country seemed to want to exonerate its wayward children. We accept the plea bargain, a Shin Bet official told a reporter: "These are people who were innocently manipulated by a terrorist organization."

UDI'S WIFE, LEAH, was frustrated. Udi preferred privacy to intimacy, seemed more interested in reading than in talking. As if he were still in prison, holding off the outside world. She tried to give him space, not rebuke him when he abruptly walked away mid-conversation. She told herself to be patient, that old prison habits would eventually pass.

They tried to adopt a child. But the authorities turned them down. The couple sued, and the judge declared: Udi Adiv is unfit to be the father of an Israeli child.

We need to get out of here, Udi said to Leah. Go somewhere where no one knows the name Udi Adiv.

In June 1989 he received a BA in philosophy and Middle Eastern studies from Tel Aviv University. He was accepted by the University of London for a doctoral program in political science.

At Ben-Gurion Airport Udi was called aside. He was frisked, his suitcase searched. An agent opened a tube of toothpaste and squeezed. Toothpaste dripped. Udi laughed.

ARIK ACHMON REINVENTS HIMSELF AGAIN

ARIK WAS MANAGING a subsidiary company for one of Israel's wealthiest men, shepherding packages from abroad through customs, and he'd had enough. He had helped found Israel's domestic aviation industry, commanded a brigade, overseen the country's first experiment in privatization. What was he doing trapped in a dead-end job, a cog in someone else's ambitions?

On January 1, 1990, Arik made a new year's resolution: he would quit his job and become a management consultant. He assumed he needed no formal education in management. He had, after all, spent most of his life trying to make systems more efficient, from the Netzer Sereni cowshed to his logistics brigade in the IDF.

And so, at age fifty-seven, Arik Achmon was starting again. He put out word that he was available for consultations. Weeks passed, then months, and no one called. Arik was patient. "I'm halfway there," he joked with Yehudit; "the consultant is ready, he just doesn't have any clients." She bought him a computer. "Meanwhile, learn how to use this," she said.

THE FIRST CALL came from the director of the industry department of the national kibbutz federation. "Arik, we have a problem on Ein Gev," the director, an old friend, said.

Kibbutz Ein Gev was on the shore of the Sea of Galilee. Until the Six-Day War, its farmers and fishermen had lived under Syrian guns on the Golan Heights just above. Now the kibbutz was trying to cope with growing debt. One kibbutznik had an idea for an improved electric blanket, Arik's friend explained, and he'd convinced the kibbutz to set up a factory. But the factory was faltering, and the inventor, who was also the CEO, refused to step aside. "He comes from a powerful family on the kibbutz and no one can stand up to him. He thinks he can conquer the world with his electric blanket. Meanwhile the kibbutz is pouring money into a black hole. You're a kibbutznik, Arik, you understand the sensitivities. Plus he's a fighter pilot, a war hero."

"Kibbutz politics don't worry me," said Arik. "And taming pilots is my second profession."

"I want you to become the company's chairman. Do what you can to control him."

After a month with Arik, the CEO resigned. For the next two months Arik ran the factory alone. Then he hired a new CEO. Soon afterward the factory shut down and the pilot left the kibbutz.

OTHER JOBS SOON FOLLOWED.

One night, after listening to Arik on the phone with a client, Yehudit said, "All you did was tell him what's wrong with his company. You didn't ask him what he thinks."

"He's not paying me to hear his own ideas," Arik said.

"Arik, you have to learn to listen to people. You act like you know better than anyone."

"But it so happens that in this case I do know better." He was genuinely perplexed.

"Arik, how do I put up with you? You're dealing with human beings, not abstract systems."

Listen to the client, she says. What am I, a psychologist? Who knows: maybe it's worth a try—

TEL AVIV UNDER SIEGE

THE SIREN, RISING AND FALLING, came at 2:00 a.m. Arik and Yehudit slept through it.

But the explosion, which sounded as if it were coming from down the block and shook the windows of their house, did wake them. "Yehudit," Arik said laconically, "it seems that something is happening."

It was January 18, 1991. The Americans were bombing Iraq, and Iraqi leader Saddam Hussein, who had vowed to burn half of Israel, had just fired the first Scud missile at Tel Aviv, which fell about a kilometer away from the Achmons' home. In the weeks leading up to war, every Israeli citizen had been given a survival kit for nonconventional warfare, including gas mask and atropine injection against nerve gas; families with small children were given plastic cribs to encase them. Arik had dismissed the preparations as a kind of hysteria. "Saddam won't dare attack us with chemical weapons," he'd said to Yehudit. And even if he did attack, Arik continued, his warheads held barely enough chemicals to affect a few buildings in the vicinity of a fallen missile—a fact that failed to calm his wife.

"Arik, what do we do?" Yehudit, nervous, asked now.

"Let's set up the sealed room," he said. *It will help calm her—*

Yehudit retrieved the supplies she'd bought for a "sealed room" as precaution against nonconventional attack—plastic sheets to cover windows, first aid kit, canned food and bottled water, wet towel to place under the door against chemical penetration.

More explosions.

Eight missiles—all with conventional warheads—fell that night on the Tel Aviv area. A few people were lightly wounded from the blasts, but four died from their gas masks, including two elderly women who suffocated because they forgot to remove its seals and a three-year-old girl who was strangled when her panicked father pulled the straps on her mask too tightly.

The next day Yehudit's daughter, Amira, and her two small children moved in. When the siren sounded, they rushed into the sealed room and put on gas masks. Arik, though, refused to wear his. "I'll join you in the sealed room, but there are limits," he said.

"You're undermining the family's morale," Yehudit complained. "If you're joining us you should wear a mask."

"I'll solve the problem for you," he said.

When the next siren sounded, he sat in the living room, watching TV.

FOR THE FIRST TIME in his life, Arik found himself useless during war. Retired as commander of the logistics brigade, he had asked to continue serving in some capacity and been assigned to a unit attached to the general staff, whose mission was to plan logistics in real time if an unexpected front—say, against Egypt—opened during war. But there was nothing for the unit to do now: this was a missile war, and there was no tangible front.

Instead this turned out to be Yehudit's war. She joined a team of psychologists treating Tel Aviv residents—like the man who'd left his armchair when he heard a siren, and seconds later the tail of a Scud crashed through the ceiling, sending fragments into the chair.

The Scud attacks were a reversal of the wars Israel had known. The home front was now the battlefield. This was also Israel's first war that wasn't a communal experience. Each family was on its own, in its sealed room: an atomized war for a postcollectivist Israel.

And for the first time in its history Israel was under attack and wasn't hitting back. The government acceded to American requests for Israeli restraint, to maintain Arab support for the war against Saddam. But the government lacked an adequate missile shield and couldn't even protect its people. The Americans delivered Patriot missiles against the Scuds, but those were experimental and often inaccurate.

With every siren Israelis repeated their ritual of confinement, waiting in sealed rooms for the soothing voice on the radio to tell them when they could remove their gas masks. They listened skeptically to the reassurances of their leaders and to military experts who had insisted before the war that Saddam wouldn't dare attack.

Every afternoon there was an enormous traffic jam on the Tel Aviv highway heading south. Scud attacks usually happened at night, and Tel Aviv residents were abandoning the city.

Many of the Achmons' neighbors fled. Arik and Yehudit stayed. After each missile attack, Arik went to the scene to survey the devastation—partly out of curisiosity, partly out of instinct.

Some Tel Aviv residents temporarily relocated to settlements in the West Bank and even Gaza. The territories were the safest place in the land: clearly Saddam wasn't going to risk killing Palestinians. The Yesha Council instructed settlements to turn schools into shelters for the Tel Aviv "refugees." Yisrael Harel noted a certain grim satisfaction among his neighbors: after three years of intifada, Tel Aviv was seeking refuge in Ofra.

THE GULF WAR ended on February 28, 1991, six weeks after it began. Believing Jews noted portentously that that date coincided with Purim, the holiday of Jewish triumph over attempted annihilation. Dozens had been wounded, hundreds treated for trauma. But while thirty-nine Scuds had been fired, mostly at population centers, only one Israeli was killed by a missile. Even secular Israelis spoke of divine protection for Israel.

As the Scuds fell, planes filled with Soviet immigrants were landing at Ben-Gurion Airport. The Iron Curtain had parted and hundreds of thousands were coming home. For nearly three decades Jews around the world had campaigned to "let my people go." In the 1970s, the Iron Curtain had partly opened, only to be shut again with the Soviet invasion of Afghanistan in 1979 and the crisis in Soviet-American relations. But now, with the unraveling of the Soviet Union, that final miracle of a terrible and awesome century, the Jews were free to leave.

Israel was facing chaos. The housing shortage was acute. Tent camps were rising in public parks, and there was talk of opening army barracks for temporary shelter. Israel inherited the elite of a failed superpower, but the economy wasn't absorbing the gift. Classical violinists and cellists filled the streets, playing for coins. Scientists and engineers worked as night watchmen.

Even as straightforward a matter as processing immigrant belongings was overwelming the system. Port warehouses were crowded with crates marked with Cyrillic letters and filled with heavy dark furniture, samovars, pianos (every Russian family seemed to have one). Astonishingly, immigrants had no way of retrieving their crates, which officials had neglected to number or catalog. Outraged immigrants were reporting back to family and friends in Russia that Israel was dysfunctional, that perhaps it was better to wait or even reconsider emigrating altogether.

Arik was hired by the Jewish Agency, the quasi-governmental organization charged with bringing immigrants to Israel, to advise it on how to streamline the process. Arik was appalled to discover that there was no contact among the half-dozen government ministries involved in processing immigrants. The agency in charge of bringing in immigrants by plane had no relationship with the agency bringing in their crates by ship. No one was dealing with customs.

Arik formed a team that created an interagency computer link, and a one-stop clearing center where the immigrants met representatives from all the relevant ministries. The system began to work. For immigrants it meant the ability to quickly identify and reclaim their crates. For Arik, it was another victory in his war for a rational Israel.

"ISRAEL IS WAITING FOR RABIN"

THE COLLAPSE OF the Soviet Union was one of the great blessings in Israel's history. The entire former Soviet bloc, whose countries had severed relations with Israel under Kremlin pressure, reopened embassies in Tel Aviv. So did many African countries that had cut relations with Israel under pressure of the Arab oil boycott two decades earlier. China and India established diplomatic relations with the Jewish state. The UN formally repealed its "Zionism-racism" resolution, passed in 1975 as a Soviet initiative and the most bitter symbol for Israelis of the renewed pariah status of the Jews. The Zionist goal, so long deferred, of restoring the Jewish people to the international community seemed finally vindicated.

Yet a solution to the Palestinian problem seemed more remote than ever. During the Gulf War many Palestinians had stood on their rooftops cheering as Scuds fell on Tel Aviv, alienating even Israeli leftists. The intifada of mass riots gave way to an intifada of stabbing sprees. A Gazan ran through the streets of Jaffa with a sword, attacking passersby; he was wrestled to the ground by an Arab Israeli garage worker named Abd al-Karim Abd al-Ghani, who was stabbed to death. Another Palestinian stabbed a fifteen-year-old Jewish girl named Helena Rapp so many times that her heart was exposed. An Israeli reservist named Amnon Pomerantz made a wrong turn into a Gaza refugee camp; his car was surrounded and he was burned alive.

Elections were held that spring. In the gap between Israel's growing acceptance around the world and the ongoing conflict with the Palestinians, the Labor Party—headed once again by Yitzhak Rabin, to the delight of Yoel Bin-Nun—tried to present voters with a new vision. Let's take Tel Aviv out of Gaza and Gaza out of Tel Aviv, Rabin demanded. The implicit message was Israeli withdrawal from Gaza, and many Israelis were ready to hear it. "Israel Is Waiting for Rabin," the Labor slogan went, a takeoff on the morale-boosting song from the weeks before the Six-Day War, "Nasser Is Waiting for Rabin."

Though the IDF had largely defeated the intifada, in fact the intifada won. Many Israelis now understood that the price of maintaining the whole land of Israel was permanent occupation of a hostile people. Decades of war and terrorism had failed to break Israel; but in face of defiant women and children, Israelis felt helpless.

On June 23, 1992, the Labor Party returned to power. It was almost exactly twenty-five years since General Rabin had led the IDF in the Six-Day War. And now Rabin had returned as elder statesman to try to extricate the nation from the consequences of that victory. Watching Rabin's election-night speech on TV—"I will navigate . . . I will determine"—Yoel thought about how the Commander of History was again about to make His presence known in Israel.

PART FIVE

END OF THE SIX-DAY WAR

(1992–2004)

CHAPTER 27

A NEW ISRAEL, AGAIN

YOEL BIN-NUN IS WAITING FOR RABIN

July 13, 1992

The Prime Minister of Israel
Yitzhak Rabin

Shlomot, peace upon you!
All leaders of nations are appointed with God's will, and especially a leader chosen by the people of Israel in its land. And so [I offer] this blessing: May God give you and your government wisdom and strength and wise counsel, to stand upright and represent the entire people of Israel.

That said, Yoel Bin-Nun proceeded to berate the newly elected prime minister for violating the very hopes expressed in his blessing. Rabin had deeply disappointed him: instead of forming a national unity government, drawing together the people of Israel, Rabin had created a narrow left-wing coalition, with the added insult of backing from the ultra-Orthodox party Shas. The National Religious Party (NRP), representing religious Zionism, had been willing, Yoel noted, to enter Rabin's coalition and compromise on settlement building. Knesset member Hanan Porat, too, Yoel added, had been reasonable.

The religious Zionist community felt its two deepest values, education and settlement—"which are your values too"—under assault by the new government. Rabin had handed the education ministry, long the domain of the NRP, to the antireligious and far left party Meretz. And no less dangerous, he had appointed as deputy education minister a Knesset member from Shas, as if that were a reasonable balance—one ultra against another.

As for settlements, continued Yoel, one could negotiate political arrangements with our Arab neighbors and still protect the right of Jews to live in the land of Israel. Yet Rabin had declared a partial but far-reaching freeze on settlement building. If settlers felt "pushed into a corner," they would fight back—"with respect, with observance of the law, but with determination, for our very existence."

Hopefully, though, there was still a chance for dialogue, "to explore ways of cooperating to prevent confrontation, despite the deep disagreements between us."

Respectful but firm: precisely the tone, Yoel believed, that a straight talker like Rabin would appreciate.

Yoel wrote his letter in longhand. It was easier for him to concentrate that way. Besides, he reasoned, everything Rabin read was printed; this way would be more memorable.

Yoel faxed his three-page letter to the prime minister's office.

A few weeks later he received by mail a one-line note, in Rabin's hand: "I am deeply grateful."

The brevity was no surprise; the warmth was. Yoel saved the note and took it as encouragement to continue the connection.

THE ART WORLD REDISCOVERS AVITAL GEVA

GIDEON OFRAT, PREEMINENT CURATOR and art historian, walked through the plastic flaps of the Ein Shemer greenhouse, certain that Avital Geva would reject his proposal out of hand. It was a Shabbat afternoon in August 1992, and the humidity inside the greenhouse was stifling. Avital, wearing a tank top and shorts, greeted his guest, in round wire glasses and pressed white pants, with a hug. Twenty years earlier Ofrat had championed Avital's artistic provocations, had considered him one of Israel's most vital artists. When Avital withdrew to the greenhouse, Ofrat, distraught, had come to see him. You've rejected the art world but not art, Ofrat had said to him then. And the greenhouse, he'd insisted, was itself a work of art. Avital laughed: Who cares if it's art or not?

Now Avital took Ofrat on a tour of the greenhouse. Barefoot teenagers were tending rows of giant cucumbers laid in plant pots on slanted trays, so that excess water from the pots drained down into pools below, providing nutrients to fish. And plastic tubes fed water from the pools back into the plants. It was, explained Avital, an experiment in conservation: trying to raise fish without changing the water. In a corner was an old bus, transformed into the greenhouse's computer center. There were sculptures formed from discarded agricultural and industrial materials. A seamless flow, noted Ofrat, of nature-technology-humanity-art.

Over Turkish coffee, Ofrat explained why he was here. He had just been appointed curator for the Israeli exhibit at the Venice Biennale, the international art event. Each country selected an artist to represent it. And Ofrat wanted Avital and the greenhouse to represent the state of Israel.

Avital closed his eyes and said nothing. Ofrat waited for the rejection. "Amazing idea," Avital finally said.

Then came the conditions. First of all, no artistic representation of the greenhouse, only the greenhouse itself. That meant shipping the whole structure and everything in it, from cucumbers to fish. "We're not an exhibit," said Avital.

"No metaphor," agreed Ofrat. Art for life, not life for art.

"And we'll need a dunam of land. And a team of ten young people to set up the greenhouse and run it."

Ofrat nodded. But was any of this feasible? Would the Italians agree to expanding the Israeli pavilion to a dunam? How would Ofrat raise the money—for shipping, for expenses for a whole team?

"And it's not about me, Avital Geva. The greenhouse is about group cooperation."

Ofrat respected Avital's emphasis on the collective, the opposite of the Western notion of the lone artist. Still, Ofrat explained, he would need to present an artist to the art world.

"Give me a week to decide," Avital said. They compromised on three days.

"WHAT DO I NEED THIS FOR?" Avital said to his wife, Ada. He had managed to extricate himself from the media exposure, the marketing hype, the egos and the jealousies. Why subject himself to all that again?

"Do it," urged Ada. Avital, she argued, was trying to save the spirit of the kibbutz movement; this was a chance to spread his message.

Ofrat was half hoping that Avital would say no. Who needed his wavering, his demands? Any normal person would have grabbed the opportunity. But Avital was responding as if Ofrat were suggesting a complicated medical procedure.

"Nu?" asked Ofrat.

"I need another twenty-four hours," said Avital. "And another dunam."

When Ofrat phoned the next night, Avital said, "I suggest you find someone else. Because the terms are tough." He proceeded to read a list of seven demands—including bringing over not ten but twenty young people. And at the end of the Biennale the entire greenhouse would be shipped back to Israel. "Nothing remains there but the grass."

Ofrat calmed himself: There's still time to find someone else.

In a fax to the director of the Biennale, Ofrat tried to explain his choice of an artist who no longer saw himself as an artist and an art project that many would no doubt deny was art. Avital, wrote Ofrat, had quit the art world because he saw museums and galleries as "a barrier to achieving a bridge between art values and life values." The greenhouse, Ofrat argued, would challenge art's isolation from reality. "We are showing a life-work both realistic and utopian, rather than an aesthetic object."

There was no answer. Ofrat flew to Venice. Before meeting the director, he surveyed the grounds of the Biennale. The only possible space to accommodate Avital's demands was at the fair ground's very center. Israeli chutzpah: How dare he ask for it?

"There is no other place," agreed the director.

Back in Israel, Ofrat excitedly reported to Avital: All your conditions will be met.

Avital listened grimly. "I need another forty-eight hours before giving you my final okay," he said.

"If you withdraw now," Ofrat replied, "my health will be on your conscience."

Avital phoned Ofrat the next night. "I'm in," he said. "But no media interviews."

IN THE ISRAELI ART WORLD, some celebrated Ofrat's choice as a sign of the establishment's vitality. "You've brought Avital back to us," a leading curator told Ofrat. Others, though, responded with contempt. One critic compared the greenhouse to a kindergarten. Another insisted that

Avital owed the art world an explanation: Why did you leave, and why have you suddenly returned? Retorted Ofrat: Avital owes no explanation to anyone.

Ofrat brought a potential donor to Ein Shemer. They found Avital in the dining room, serving lunch: it was his turn for kitchen duty. They helped him clear the tables and then went across the dirt road to the greenhouse.

Ofrat offered his latest thoughts. The greenhouse, he said, was formed of "concentric circles"—the inner circle a space for meeting and conceptualizing, then a circle with computers and worktables, and finally an outer circle of plant and fish cultivation. "A Platonic construct, leading from pure idea to material and nature."

"Too grandiose," dismissed Avital. "I don't want anything more in Venice than cultivation, maybe a computer."

Ofrat was horrified. A shack with cucumbers? The whole point was to elevate the greenhouse from pure nature to culture, the interplay between science and society and art! The Israeli dream, Ofrat was calling it.

In barely ten months from now, in June 1993, the Biennale was to begin. Would Avital pull out over some unimagined pique, some violation of his ethos that even Ofrat hadn't anticipated? Maybe I won't be able to raise the money, Ofrat thought hopefully.

ARIK ACHMON RETURNS TO THE SKIES

THE PHONE CALL Arik had been expecting, in one form or another, came a few months after the elections of 1992.

Arik had volunteered for Rabin's campaign, organizing a national network of parlor meetings. And now that Labor was finally back in power, he assumed there would be some expression of appreciation. Not that he was looking for a job: he was in increasing demand as a consultant, advising some of Israel's biggest companies. What he was hoping for was another opportunity to serve, especially now that he was no longer on active reserve duty.

The phone call was from an official in the transportation ministry. The government was embarking on the largest building project in Israel's history—a new international airport terminal, with a budget of close to $2 billion. Would Arik join the board of the Airports Authority? It was a public position, without salary. And it would take up at least one day a week of his time.

"You are returning me to aviation, my first love," he said.

Then, warily, he asked, "Yisrael is okay with this?"

He meant the new transportation minister, Yisrael Kaisar—former Histadrut labor union leader and Arik's nemesis from his Arkia days.

"He wasn't enthusiastic," the official acknowledged, "but I'll get this through."

The two old rivals met at a luncheon celebrating the launching of "Ben-Gurion [Airport] 2000."

"Here is the kibbutznik who turned into an enemy of organized labor," Kaisar greeted Arik with a small smile.

"Yisrael, I'm not certain that that's what you really think of me," Arik replied, smiling widely in return. "I remember you as a worthy adversary."

"You saved Arkia," said Kaisar.

Ben-Gurion Airport, near Tel Aviv, was the country's only international airport. Small and overcrowded, it was a holdover from an earlier, improvised Israel. Arriving passengers gathered on the tarmac and were driven by bus to the terminal; those waiting to greet them had to stand outside the building.

Arik was appointed head of the development committee for the new terminal. The terminal, the committee decided, must have easy access for planes, incorporate the most modern systems, and be more than a big hangar. "It needs to be inspirational," Arik said. "Not bombastic, but worthy of the state of Israel."

Backed by Airports Authority head Motti Debby, Arik and his colleagues resisted government pressure to hire retired air force officers as project managers. But that's how it's always done, Arik was told. Not this time, he retorted. This project would be run by professionals. That, after all, was the symbolic message of the new terminal: Israel was joining the globalizing world.

Arik wanted to hire architectural and consulting firms from abroad; Kaisar wanted only Israelis. "You're screwing with me again?" he said.

"Yisrael, we don't have the expertise. This is a chance to do things the right way, not the way we usually do."

They compromised: for every firm hired from abroad, an Israeli firm would be hired to work with it.

They argued about location. Kaisar wanted to move the airport to the Negev desert, to encourage development of Israel's most neglected region.

"Why drag everyone to the south?" said Arik. "You can't impose ideology on practical need."

Kaisar yielded to the vision of a new, normal Israel.

URI BEN-NOON, CEO of the Dead Sea Works, was an unlikely friend for Arik Achmon. Paunchy, gray bearded, with an extra-large knitted *kippah*, Uri was a devout Jew who liked to quote the Talmud and his father, a Chabad Hasid who had been exiled by the Communists to Siberia. Uri offered Arik insights into the weekly Torah portion; Arik didn't know what he was talking about.

They had met in the early 1960s, when Uri joined Company A, 28th Battalion, then under Arik's command. Uri, Arik quickly realized, wasn't the kind of soldier likely to charge into machine gun fire; Uri, who didn't like to run at all, once claimed to be a radio operator to avoid a training exercise. But Uri had social skills, so Arik appointed him company clerk, in charge of manpower. Uri never forgot that it was Arik who had insisted the unit's kitchen become kosher, allowing religious soldiers to feel at home.

Years later, when Arik resigned from Arkia, Uri had been one of the very few in the business community to stand by him, finding him a job. After Arkia, Arik liked to say, I learned that I could fit all my real friends into one taxi and still have room. Uri Ben-Noon was one of those friends.

And now, having recently become CEO of the Dead Sea Works—one of Israel's most profitable companies, producing fertilizer from the Dead Sea—Uri hired Arik as his consultant.

In Uri the CEO, Arik recognized a soul mate. They shared a fierce commitment to truth: if Arik found anything wrong with my conduct, Uri said appreciatively, he wouldn't cover for me. And they shared a respect for employees: Uri came to work at 6:00 a.m., to greet the morning shift.

Uri intended a major company expansion. The Dead Sea was rich in magnesium, the lightest metal in industrial use; yet the company was only producing potash. "My managers don't think big," Uri explained to Arik. "Each of them is in his own separate world. I need you to get them to act like a team."

Arik met with each of the two dozen managers separately. He began by introducing himself, though that was hardly necessary: everyone knew that Arik had been Uri's commander.

"Tell me about yourself," Arik said, and proceeded to listen. Just as Yehudit had admonished him: Pay attention to people. It wasn't easy. *How can I sit here for two hours listening to this nudnik?* But slowly he began to understand: a company isn't an abstract system, it's a living organism. People like to talk about themselves; if you appear interested, it helps build trust. Sometimes Arik found himself genuinely interested. What the managers revealed about their lives and thoughts helped him understand the company's weaknesses and strengths. He had always focused on accomplishing the mission, even if that meant ignoring the emotional needs of others. Now the mission required paying attention to those needs.

The managers suspected him of being a spy for Uri. Some shared sensitive information with Arik, to see whether it leaked. "You don't know me yet," Arik said, "but you'll learn that what you say to me in confidence stays with me." Gradually he won their trust and became a channel of communication between Uri and his staff.

Even as he protected confidences, Arik tried to protect Uri. When a manager whom Arik felt was disloyal to Uri was up for promotion, Arik protested. "Don't be so hard, Arik," Uri admonished. "Sometimes even you have to learn to forgive and forget."

IN MAY 1993, Arik turned sixty. He gave himself a present: a renewed subscription for skydiving. Leaping from the plane, stretched out toward earth, he felt an old vigor and self-confidence, a man astride his world.

FIRST FRUITS IN VENICE

THE METAL OUTLINES of a greenhouse were already visible when Avital, laughing and running toward his friends, appeared in the Venice fair grounds. In three weeks, the Biennale would open, and with it a fully functioning replica of the Ein Shemer greenhouse. An advance team of kibbutzniks had been working for nearly a week, clearing and measuring and fastening. "You're amazing, *amazing*!" Avital exclaimed, grabbing his friends and kissing them.

And then Avital got to work. Kneeling, he screwed metal arches together. Someone in a cherry picker sawed off branches extending into the greenhouse space. Wooden planks were hammered into chairs. Avital had agreed in the end to build a new greenhouse rather than dismantle the one in Ein Shemer, and that meant more work against a pressing deadline.

They were middle-aged men in blue work shirts, young people in T-shirts. There was no boss; the collective trusted itself.

ON THE EVE OF SHAVUOT, the harvest holiday of first fruits, they completed the basic structure. As they unrolled the plastic roof, church bells were ringing.

Exhausted and energized, Avital's team gathered around a long wood table for a celebratory meal of vegetables and white cheese. Rafi baked *pitot* in a small clay oven. On a gas burner, Turkish coffee was brewing in a blackened tin pot, just like in Ein Shemer.

Rafi offered a kibbutznik's version of blessing: "Okay, so let's bless the fruit of the vine, of the field." He quoted the Bible: "'A holiday of Shavuot shall you make for yourself.' A time to plant, a time to sow . . . and to eat." Laughter. "At this hour, as the final preparations on the kibbutz are being made for the ceremony of the first fruits, as Comrade Hankeh has made her peace with the Yemenite dance for the ceremony—" Laughter. "At this very hour we are eating a dairy holiday meal with bread the work of our hands. Happy holiday!"

Gideon Ofrat appeared, as relieved as he was joyful. "*Hevreh*, really, what amazing work," he said. "In whatever name I speak for—art, the state of Israel, whatever—thank you."

THE FORTY-FIFTH BIENNALE opened on June 9, 1993. There were acrobats on stilts trailing streamers, women with shaved heads wearing wings. An empty frame hanging from a tree turned passersby into momentary portraits. In the Russian pavilion, conceptual artist Andrei Monastyrsky celebrated Soviet kitsch. In the German pavilion, Hans Haacke tore up the floor; a sign on the wall read "Germania," Hitler's name for Berlin.

The American pavilion exhibited new works by the eighty-one-year-old sculptress Louise Bourgeois; her name was engraved over the Greek-pillared entrance.

In the midst of this celebration of the artist, of pure art, Avital and the *hevreh* grew cucumbers. There was much curiosity about the Israeli exhibit. It was undeniably beautiful: a three-meter-high domed plastic structure overflowing with greenery, at its center a long fish tank with sheets of water pouring from showers above and turning the air into mist; at once moist with new life and ethereal, shimmering and transparent. But what exactly was it doing here?

The very presence of the greenhouse challenged the other exhibits, just as Ofrat had hoped: is there a purpose for art beyond its own expression? It was, in its way, an echo of the ancient argument between Athens and Jerusalem: was the highest human achievement aesthetics or divine service?

Avital, of course, would not have put it that way. And yet as the greenhouse evolved into a holistic model, Avital's idea of existence had become holistic too. Nothing was extraneous. It was a vision of a purposeful universe.

Avital loathed being turned into the center of attention, becoming part of the show. When an Israeli TV crew filmed him watering plants, he said testily, "Leave me alone."

Unfazed, the reporter turned to the camera: "The message here is that the greenhouse is the work of a team."

Finally Avital relented and gave a brief interview to the Israeli crew, but only to emphasize the centrality of the *hevreh*: "This is what defines us: a group of young people, all of them army graduates, all of them serious— And the fact that we can work together for years— And we're not alone. In Israel there are hundreds of places where *hevreh* work together, doing great things. Thanks to"—he clasped his hands—"being together."

Avital Geva, age fifty-two. The camera showed a man with bright blue eyes, short graying hair, spare long face, stubborn chin, bashful yet mischievous smile. In his tank top and baggy blue kibbutz pants, he looked like one more worker in the greenhouse, just as he intended.

Yet Avital was acutely aware that, for many Israelis, his egalitarian vision wasn't the future but the past. At the Biennale, the state of Israel was celebrating its collectivist heritage just as the kibbutz was beginning to concede defeat. Even Ein Shemer had recently shut down its children's house, returning its young people to the nuclear family. And most kibbutzim were deeply in debt to the banks. Ein Shemer had avoided bankruptcy only by selling ninety dunams of orchards to a developer, who was building a shopping mall on land that Avital and his friends had cultivated.

BACK HOME, AVITAL received an invitation to participate in an art exhibition in Japan. He wrote, "If you want to see me, come to Ein Shemer. I'm busy working on the roof of the greenhouse with the children."

Government officials, potential donors, and old friends came to congratulate him. One of them was Arik Achmon.

"Avital, I'm deeply impressed by what you've accomplished," said Arik. "You've come a long way from harnessing my daughter to a plow."

Avital laughed and gave Arik a pot of mint.

A PRECIOUS INHERITANCE

MEIR ARIEL WAS walking past a synagogue in Tel Aviv early one evening when a man standing at the entrance waved him over. We need a tenth man to complete the *minyan*, the prayer quorum, he said. Meir readily agreed. After prayers—too fast for Meir, who lingered over the words—he was invited to return for the synagogue's afternoon Talmud class.

The next day Meir joined the men around a long table, listening to them argue with the ancient rabbis. Meir had long since become expert in Bible, quoting from memory long passages from the Prophets and the Song of Songs. But here was Jewish knowledge that had been denied him on the kibbutz.

Meir became a regular in the synagogue's study circle. His parents' generation of Jews had been the first in three thousand years to sever the continuity of religious faith, a necessary rebellion, perhaps, to create a new life in the land of Israel. But now the son was restoring the Jewish millennia to the Israeli decades.

Every morning he withdrew to his study and prayed in phylacteries. Sometimes he would spend as long as two hours reading from the prayer book, savoring the sacred Hebrew, talking to God in his own lyrical Hebrew. Then he would work on a song.

Tirza couldn't understand why Meir was wasting his time in prayer. When a friend called, asking for Meir, Tirza said, "He can't talk now, he's swaying."

Prayer calms me, Meir explained to her. To a friend, he said, "If not for the Torah, I'd be in an institution."

ON FRIDAY AFTERNOON, in the hours before sunset, Meir swept the yard of his house near the sea, paid his tab at the grocer so as not to carry debt into Shabbat, then took an especially long shower, purifying the body and washing away the week. As a favor to him, Tirza lit Shabbat candles. Meir stopped smoking for twenty-four hours and tried not to violate Shabbat by driving. He preferred to perform, he said, during the "six days of creation." But when he had a performance on Friday evening that he felt compelled to play, he would circle his car in a ritual of his own making and declare the vehicle his temporary home—honoring the spirit of Shabbat if not quite its strict observance. Then, with Tirza driving, he would fill a silver goblet with wine and bless it. If his Judaism was to be authentic, it had to be an expression of his being, not an imposed set of rules.

Word got around that Meir Ariel—of all people!—was becoming an observant Jew, and a journalist for the newspaper *Ma'ariv* came by to interview him.

Her questions were about the technicalities of observance, which she read off like a shopping list. Do you light a fire on Shabbat? Separate meat and milk dishes? How much time do you spend studying Torah? The questions revealed her anxiety: Was Meir Ariel, the bohemian whose songs broke all the taboos of Hebrew music and who championed marijuana and spoke openly of his open marriage, about to be lost to secular Israel?

Meir answered patiently, trying to expand the conversation to ideas, avoid being labeled.

"So that's it?" asked the journalist. "Now you're Orthodox?"

"I'm not exactly secular and not exactly Orthodox," Meir replied. "I'm pareve. . . . [I haven't] gone all the way in observing the commandments."

He felt, he said, like someone who'd been given a precious inheritance and was now assessing its worth.

"How can you as a religious person perform in a pub?"

"It is an honorable place where people gather, like a synagogue. . . . We are in the land of Israel, in clubs where people allow themselves to be happy."

And why didn't he wear a *kippah*?

"I'm waiting for the moment of love. One should take that on with love and feeling. Maybe I'm postponing many [other observances] so as not to frighten my environment."

CHAPTER 28

ALMOST NORMAL

THE HANDSHAKE

IT WAS SATURDAY NIGHT, August 28, 1993, and Ofra had just experienced the most depressed Shabbat in its history. Its residents had known many traumatic moments—terrorist attacks and the Sinai uprooting and the Jewish underground and the intifada. But nothing like this. The day before, the media had reported on a deal, concluded during secret negotiations in Oslo, between the Rabin government and the PLO. The details were still unclear, only that Israel and the PLO had agreed to recognize each other and enter into formal negotiations. And as a show of goodwill, Israel would turn over most of the Gaza Strip and the West Bank town of Jericho to Arafat. In Ofra the news was greeted like a death sentence.

Yisrael Harel was waiting outside his house when the black government car, accompanied by a jeep with border police, appeared. The call had come from Motta Gur just as Shabbat ended: at a time like this, explained Motta, he wanted to be with his friend Yisrael. Motta felt a debt to Yisrael. As chief education officer of the 55th Brigade, and then as head of the paratroopers' commemoration efforts, Yisrael had helped preserve the legacy of the battle for Jerusalem.

"How is everyone?" Motta asked, resting his hand on Yisrael's shoulder, just as he had when he last visited Yisrael's home, during the mourning for his son Eldad. "Lousy," said Yisrael, managing a half smile.

Yoel Bin-Nun saw the vehicles parked outside Yisrael's home and hurried over. Others did too, until Yisrael's living room was crowded with neighbors.

Motta listened silently to their rage and grief. Had the government lost its mind? Did Motta really think we could make peace with an archmurderer whose life's purpose was to destroy the Jewish state? How could you, liberator of Jerusalem, be part of a government that endangered Israel's hold on Jerusalem, to say nothing of the lives of thousands of Israelis in Judea and Samaria and Gaza? In the end the PLO wasn't interested in Ofra, it wanted Tel Aviv. Nothing would come out of this pretend peace except blood.

"Friends," said Yisrael, seeking calm, "Motta has come on a private visit."

Motta, now deputy defense minister, was pale and very thin. Yisrael knew Motta's secret: he was fighting a rare cancer known as carcinoid, which spreads with agonizing slowness. Motta asked Yisrael to take him and his secretary to an inner room. There, she gave him a shot of morphine.

Motta returned to the salon. Looking around at the angry, anxious faces, he said, "I'm here as a friend. I know you are in pain. But I want to be clear: I support the agreement. I think this is a good strategic move for Israel. This can save the state from demographic disaster and raise our status around the world."

Yoel could hardly control himself. How could Rabin, of all people, have legitimized Arafat? Had he been wrong about Rabin all along? For months Yoel had been trying to get settler leaders and Rabin to reach a compromise over building in the territories. In a meeting with Rabin, Yoel had warned him that there would be no peace between Arabs and Jews without peace among Jews.

And Motta: just recently Yoel had gone to see him and pleaded, Don't surprise us. At the very least give us, the settler leaders, some warning if you are about to radically change the status quo. Work with us; we can help control emotions among our people.

Yoel said now, "You promised me, Motta: no surprises. Instead you've left us with the phone dangling in the air and you've cut the cord. What am I supposed to say now to my community?"

"Look, Yoel, I'm here," Motta replied. In fact Motta too had been taken by surprise by the Oslo agreement. "Whatever problems come up, I will be your address," he promised the settlers.

Yoel of course had his own address. However heartbroken, he resolved not to give up on Rabin just yet. Perhaps that connection could help contain the damage.

ARIK ACHMON WATCHED the TV broadcast from the White House as President Clinton nudged a reluctant Yitzhak Rabin to shake the hand of

Yasser Arafat, and thought, We can do business with him. Of course Arafat is detestable, but he's no fool. He understands that America is the only superpower and that he has no choice. If we compromise, so will Arafat.

Arik had met Rabin on several brief occasions, in the army and then in Labor Party circles, and each time confirmed the same impression: Rabin is the best of us. Modest, awkward in the spotlight, he placed the nation's interests before his own. Like the best army officers, he was open to change, curious about opposing opinions. When elected prime minister in his first term, in 1974, he'd been the first sabra—native-born Israeli—to lead the country; now, nearly twenty years later, he was still Israel's only sabra prime minister. Unlike the prime ministers born in Eastern Europe, Rabin wasn't haunted by anti-Semitism, and rarely spoke of the Holocaust. He took the ability of the Jews to defend themselves as a given. Only a leader with that kind of self-confidence, believed Arik, could make peace.

In his inaugural speech as prime minister, Rabin presented a vision of the Jewish state integrated into the family of nations, fulfillment of the Zionist dream of normalization. The old order was changing, Rabin had said then, and Israelis had to stop believing that the whole world was against them. Challenging the biblical saying of Balaam, Rabin declared that the Jews were not fated to forever dwell alone. If Israel was to find its place in the new world, it had to abandon its psychological ghetto.

Seeing Rabin and Arafat together at the White House ceremony signing the Oslo Accords, Arik felt that vision was about to be fulfilled.

YISRAEL HAREL WATCHED Rabin shake Arafat's hand and thought, They've lost it. Israel's ruling elite, the children and grandchildren of the pioneers, had lost their socialism, and now they were losing their Zionism too. All that remained for Israel's elite was an ideology of peace. A false peace. A peace of fools.

Normalization, Yisrael feared, was happening prematurely, before the Jewish state had been accepted as normal. How would this people continue to make sacrifices for survival, retain its alertness? Rabin himself had said in a candid moment that he feared an exhaustion among his people. But exhaustion was no basis for policy, not for a people confronting existential threat.

Yisrael was writing a weekly column for *Ha'aretz*, the left-wing newspaper, as a token right-wing voice. In his columns he bemoaned the loss of pioneering ideals. If leftists opposed settlement in Judea and Samaria, he asked, then why weren't they settling in the Galilee and the Negev, areas within the borders of pre–'67 Israel that were at risk of losing their Jewish majority?

Yisrael had loved the kibbutzniks from the moment he first encountered them as sailors on the illegal boat that transported his family and other Holocaust refugees trying to reach the land of Israel. The kibbutzniks had carried a broken people on their backs. But now they were depleted, their revolutionary passions spent. *Like my friend, Arik Achmon, the kibbutznik of North Tel Aviv—*

Yisrael was tormented by a heretical thought: Could it be that the ultra-Orthodox were right? That the secular Zionists were doomed to fail because they had excised the soul of the Jewish people, its religious faith, creating an identity too thin to transmit?

He confided to a journalist: "I used to say that if I had to be confined to a desert island, I would prefer to be with my kibbutznik friends from the paratroopers. But I can't trust them with the Jewish future anymore."

Urgent—Personal!

September 29,1993

The Prime Minister
Mr. Yitzhak Rabin

Mr. Prime Minister!
As you know, I have been trying these last years, and investing mighty efforts, to attempt to prevent a dangerous schism in Israeli society, in particular over Jewish settlement.

But how could Yoel continue in that role after Rabin had done the unthinkable and legitimized Arafat?

Soon, *if there will not be a drastic change*, I will no longer be able to influence [settlers] in a moderate direction.

The letter was replete with exclamation marks, combined exclamation and question marks, underlined words—the sputtering style that Yisrael Harel had tried to erase from Yoel's writings for *Nekudah* but which, in his current agitation, Yoel couldn't suppress.

Yoel took some comfort from the fact that the Oslo Accords didn't explicitly call for a Palestinian state or the redivision of Jerusalem—both of which, Rabin told the Knesset, he opposed. The only way to prevent the Oslo Accords from leading to a Palestinian state, Yoel insisted, was to recognize the Yesha Council as an official parallel body to the new Palestinian Authority, with control over the settlements. But if Rabin continued on his present course, wrote Yoel, "I fear a great explosion."

YOEL WAS SHOWN into the prime minister's office and left alone with Rabin. No aides or note-taker, Yoel noted appreciatively. *A gesture of trust—*

Yoel had resolved to avoid emotion: his relationship with Rabin, he understood, was based on an exchange of analyses of Israel's situation. And discretion: aside from his wife, Esther, he told no one about their deepening connection.

"The premise of the peace process is wrong," Yoel said to Rabin. "Fatah is not more moderate than Hamas. They share the same goal. There is a division of labor between them: Hamas continues with terrorist attacks while Fatah pushes for diplomatic gains. Strategically they are working together."

"Nonsense," retorted Rabin. "They are divided by an abyss of hatred."

Yoel mentioned a slogan he had recently seen on a wall near Ramallah: "Fatah and Hamas Together until Victory."

"It's just a slogan," said Rabin, waving his hand in dismissal.

Then he said, "We're not here to convince each other about the things we don't agree on, but to find those things that we do agree on."

They agreed on this: no withdrawal to the 1967 borders, an undivided Jerusalem, a security border along the Jordan Valley. No settlements, said Rabin, would be moved in the interim stages of an agreement.

If Rabin remains committed to an interim rather than a comprehensive approach, thought Yoel, we can work together.

"I will continue writing to you," said Yoel, "but I absolve you of any responsibility to reply. You are the prime minister, you will make the decisions. I only ask that you read what I write."

Rabin nodded and offered his limp handshake.

THE TRAITOR AND THE PROPELLERS

THOUGH THE CRUCIAL details had yet to be negotiated, many Israelis reacted as if the war was over. At a progovernment rally in Kings of Israel Square in Tel Aviv, young people released balloons and danced with giant Israeli flags and leaped ecstatically into a pool of water. State schools were instructed to offer education for peace. Army Radio played peace songs.

With rare exceptions, the Israeli media uncritically embraced the Oslo process. Newspapers assured readers that they would financially benefit from peace; on the cover of the financial section of *Yediot Aharonot* appeared a drawing of a dove with a hundred-dollar bill in its beak. A *Yediot* reporter was dispatched to Tunis to write about Mr. and Mrs. Arafat at home; Yasser, the reporter noted, personally served his guests soup.

A majority of Israelis supported the Oslo Accords. Partly the changing mood was a result of the intifada: a growing number of Israelis had concluded that the price for absorbing the territories was too high, that occupation undermined Israel's Jewish and democratic values, that the Jewish people hadn't returned home to deprive another people of its sense of home. And so if the right's policies had led to the intifada, then the left's policies ought to be given a try. The 1970s and '80s had been the decades of Greater Israel, and the '90s seemed about to become the decade of Peace Now.

There was also, as Rabin noted, the changing international atmosphere. During the Sebastia showdown of 1975, much of the public had supported Gush Emunim as an expression of its contempt for the UN's Zionism-racism resolution. But Israel was no longer being instantly demonized, and Israelis responded with a readiness to take risks for peace.

Israel was once again reinventing itself. For the first time in almost twenty-five years, inflation dropped below 10 percent. Thanks largely to Russian immigration, the economy was expanding by about 6 percent a year. Though the population had grown by 10 percent in four years, the threat of mass homelessness passed. Instead, Russian families doubled up in small apartments, worked at two or more jobs, and quickly entered the middle class. It was Israel's most "normal" immigration: most Soviet immigrants had come to be part of not a Jewish state but a western state; Israel was simply as far west as they could reach. Yet they were also becoming Israeli. In Russia, families tended to have a single child, an expression of uncertainty about the future; now hopeful immigrant parents were risking a second.

Foreign investors, Michelin-star chefs, California winemakers—all were discovering this new Israel. Israelis were traveling the world and returning with a longing for the civility of abroad. There was less pushing in lines at the bank and at bus stops. The claustrophobic sensation of too many survivors from too many traumas pressing against each other in too little space was easing. Once, when the six beeps announced the hourly radio news, bus drivers would turn up the volume and passengers fall into communal silence; now, on days when there were no terrorist attacks, drivers and passengers ignored the news.

Privatization of government companies, first tested by Arik Achmon a decade earlier, was on the agenda. The miracles of capitalism: instead of the two-year wait for a telephone under the old system, the wait was now a matter of days and dropping. Even the notorious government bureaucracy wasn't immune to the new spirit: one could now get an Israeli passport in one day, delivered to your door. A new commercial TV channel easily overtook the government channel. Then came cable: twenty channels, two hundred channels! Products from around the world appeared on supermarket shelves—Italian pasta replaced the local noodles made bright with yellow dye. McDonald's opened with celebratory media coverage: Israel was truly becoming part of the world.

THE SETTLERS AND their supporters reacted to Oslo just as Yoel had feared. The end of Zionism, they were calling it. One protest poster read: "For sale: Used State, 1948 Model, in Good Condition." In opening the way to an Israeli withdrawal, Rabin, some said, was leading the Jews to another holocaust: after all, even Labor Party dove Abba Eban had once called the pre-'67 lines "Auschwitz borders."

The attacks against Rabin turned brutal. Posters of his face wrapped in a kaffiyeh appeared on the streets of Jerusalem. Graffiti declared him a traitor. Stickers demanded, Oslo Criminals to Justice. In the magazine *Nekudah*, a settler leader compared Rabin to Philippe Pétain, the French general who collaborated with the Nazis. In an editorial, Yisrael Harel denounced "the government of evil."

Rabin reciprocated the contempt. He compared antigovernment protesters to "propellers," spinning pointlessly. "They don't affect me," he said dismissively, using a Hebrew phrase which could also be interpreted as "I couldn't care less about them"—which is exactly how the right understood it. He compared the Likud to Hamas and labeled both the enemies of peace, outraging his opponents by implying that the chief democratic opposition was no better than a murderous fundamentalist group committed to Israel's destruction.

How were Israelis to argue with restraint when both right and left were convinced that if their opponents prevailed, the state would be not merely diminished but destroyed?

Terrorism intensified. The stabbing sprees in Israeli cities continued; dozens of Israelis were killed and wounded after the signing of the Oslo Accords, more than in the year before the peace process began. Rabin noted that the attacks were initiated by Hamas, which opposed the agreement, and called the new terrorism victims "victims of peace"—a phrase that further outraged his opponents. Arafat, Rabin insisted, would control Hamas more effectively than Israel ever could because he would be operating without the constraints of the rule of law—"without the Supreme Court and B'tselem," an Israeli human rights NGO, as he cynically put it.

Yoel watched with horror as his community and the leader he loved turned against each other. How could students of Rabbi Zvi Yehudah, the camp that had consecrated Jewish unity and the Jewish state, speak with such contempt for the government of Israel—for the man who brought the victory of the Six Days?

But Rabin too, Yoel believed, was hardly blameless. How could the man who had given the people of Israel its moment of greatest unity initiate a process that was leading to its unraveling?

Every few weeks Yoel would sit up late at night and write another letter in longhand to Rabin. The prime minister's bureau chief, Eitan Haber, would include Yoel's latest fax in Rabin's weekend reading package. In one letter Yoel pleaded with Rabin to reach out to the settlers: "Most settlers are not personally hostile to you, the relationship can still be salvaged." He urged Rabin to be firm in negotations with the Palestinians, berated him when Yoel sensed weakness, praised him—grudgingly—when Yoel sensed strength. "Congratulations (for now?) on your firm stand," he wrote Rabin. He offered the prime minister political advice: the Israeli public doesn't want a leader perceived as desperate for peace at any price. He signed one letter "with respect and anxiety," another, "with pain."

The letters contained urgent requests. Ofra needed a bypass road around Ramallah. The Gaza settlements needed access to the Mediterranean shore. Settlements needed land on which to expand, otherwise they would become isolated islands. Only the IDF, and not Palestinian police, must be responsible for security on roads leading to settlements. Yoel challenged Rabin: If we share the same goal of preventing a PLO state and an Israeli withdrawal to the '67 borders, then you have no choice but to strengthen the settlements.

Rabin treated Yoel's requests seriously. Yoel wrote Rabin about ensuring Israeli control over an ancient synagogue in Jericho, where settlers were praying and studying. "As far as I know there were no provocations there," Yoel wrote. "And if there were—let's deal with it together." Rabin's office wrote back, saying that religious life in the synagogue would remain under Israeli control. Construction began on a bypass road between Ofra and Jerusalem. And the Gaza settlements were given access to part of the coast.

Yoel had no official standing among the settlers; many considered him an irritant or worse, a virtual sellout. Yet Rabin devoted hours to conversations with him. The requests were all one-way; Rabin never asked Yoel to convey a message to settler leaders, never urged him to try to temper settler opposition. For Rabin the meetings were an end in themselves. He needed to know how his policies were perceived by a worthy opponent.

Yoel tried explaining the settlers to Rabin: "You must understand our situation," he wrote. "On the one hand Hamas has declared open war on us. . . . On the other hand, the PLO is fighting against Jewish settlement in Yesha on the diplomatic front. . . . Even angels would be hard-pressed to remain steady under such pressure."

And Yoel tried explaining Rabin to the settlers: He isn't our enemy! When the Yesha Council invited a pyschologist to suggest ways of unnerving Rabin, Yoel was outraged: We are pouring oil on the fire! Yoel reminded settler leaders that, as prime minister during his first term, Rabin had withdrawn from parts of Sinai but, unlike Begin and Sharon, hadn't uprooted a single settlement there. So who was left, who right?

Yoel had resolved not to divulge his meetings with Rabin to settler leaders. But he did confide in Yisrael Harel.

"You're naive," said Yisrael. To himself he added: Rabin gets thousands of faxes, and Yoel thinks he has a personal relationship with him. Yoel always has to imagine himself at the center. Now he's adopted Rabin as a father figure.

A SETTLER NAMED Chaim Mizrahi was murdered while buying eggs in a Palestinian village. The killers turned out to be members of Arafat's Fatah. Only after intense pressure from the White House did Arafat condemn the killing—by fax.

"During our [last] meeting," Yoel wrote Rabin, "you repeated two or three times the sentence: 'As long as the Shin Bet tells me that it is Hamas [that is behind the terrorist attacks]—it's Hamas!' Two days later it was revealed that the murder of Chaim Mizrahi, may God avenge him, was carried out by Fatah!"

Rabin, warned Yoel, "was trapped in a conceptual failure"—a charged term that evoked the behavior of Israeli leaders who, in the days before the Yom Kippur War, ignored approaching danger because they believed the Arabs were incapable of attacking. Like Golda Meir, Yoel was implying, Rabin was ignoring reality.

And yet, continued Yoel, astonished, Rabin was intent on transferring guns to Fatah—weapons that would sooner or later be turned against Israel. "Until now I thought I knew where you want to go, and I knew we disagreed. Now, though, I don't know where you are leading us! Do you know??"

Yoel was warning of two approaching disasters. The first was external: after winning territorial concessions from Israel, Arafat would betray the peace process and return to terrorism. The other threat, though, would come from within. Growing despair among the settlers and their supporters would lead to "acts of desperation." The result, he wrote Rabin, would be a tragedy for them all.

DESECRATION OF GOD'S NAME

SHORTLY BEFORE DAWN on February 25, 1994, Baruch Goldstein, a physician in the town of Kiryat Arba near Hebron, put on his reservist uniform, though he was not on reserve duty, loaded the Galil assault rifle he kept in the closet, and put another four bullet clips in his pockets. He moved quietly, so as not to awaken his wife and children. Then he walked toward the Tomb of the Patriarchs, burial place of Abraham and Sarah, Isaac and Rebecca, Jacob and Leah.

It was the holiday of Purim, which celebrates the undoing of Haman's plan to destroy the Jews of ancient Persia. And the thirty-five-year-old physician was on his way to write the next chapter of Jewish triumph over their enemies.

Tall, soft-spoken, with long beard and sidelocks, the Brooklyn-born Dr. Goldstein was noted for his piety. Every morning he immersed himself in a *mikveh*, a ritual bath. Often, when his busy schedule permitted, he would join the dawn prayers at the Tomb of the Patriarchs. His neighbors could call the doctor at any hour, and he made house calls. He had treated hundreds of Israelis wounded in terrorist attacks; whenever an attack occurred in the Hebron area, the army immediately beeped him.

Even in hard-line Kiryat Arba, Baruch Goldstein was considered extreme. He was a disciple of the far-right rabbi Meir Kahane, who had been assassinated by an Arab terrorist in New York in 1990. Kahane created a Jewish theology of vengeance and rage. The purpose of the Jewish people, he had preached, was to defeat Amalek—the biblical tribe that attacked the Israelites in the desert and whose evil essence passes, in every generation, into another nation seeking to destroy the Jews. When Jews erase Amalek, God's name will be glorified and the Messiah will come.

The ultimate Kahanist holiday was Purim. Haman, as the Scroll of Esther pointedly notes, was a direct descendant of the king of Amalek. The holiday is the story of triumph over Amalek.

Kahane's minuscule movement, Kach, was banned from the Knesset for racism. And Kahanism was marginal among the settlers. But not in Kiryat Arba. Its town council even had a Kahanist member—Dr. Goldstein. Kahane had loved his doctor disciple: "There is no one like Baruch," he'd said, no one so willing to sacrifice.

Lately Goldstein was in despair. He'd been treating too many terrorist victims; a close friend had died in his arms. Goldstein blamed the government and the IDF for weakness, for desecrating God's name in its war with the new Amalek, the "Arab Nazis," as he called them. Interviewed by a journalist, the doctor had said, "There is a time to kill and a time to heal."

Baruch Goldstein approached the entrance to the Tomb of the Patriarchs.

"Purim same'ah"—happy Purim—he greeted the Israeli guards. They assumed that Dr. Goldstein was on his way to morning prayers.

As he walked the worn stone steps that led up to the sand-colored, fortresslike building, Goldstein carried with him the accumulated humiliations of Hebron. The Jewish pilgrims confined by Muslim rulers to the seventh step of this building. The massacre of Jews in 1929. The terrorist attacks that embittered the Jewish return after 1967.

He entered a small room with a high domed ceiling, the shrine of Abraham and Sarah. Two stone cenotaphs behind bronze gates marked the graves in the cave below. Jewish prayer books and Bibles crowded the shelves: this was the building's synagogue. An adjacent hall, marking the graves of Isaac and Rebecca, was the mosque. A green metal door separated the two rooms. Goldstein opened the door. From the hall came chanting: *"Allahu akbar,"* God is great.

He entered the hall and hid behind a pillar. Men were bent on embroidered prayer rugs. Kerchiefed women were grouped along a wall. The hall was especially crowded: it was the Muslim fast of Ramadan.

He fired.

Panicked men ran for the door, directly into the line of fire, trampling those still prone on prayer rugs. "They're killing the men!" a woman screamed.

He ran out of bullets. Reloaded. Emptied the second clip and loaded a third. A fourth. He was firing not at men in prayer but at Haman and Hitler and Arafat, at Amalek.

As he paused to load his fifth bullet clip, he was overpowered. By the time soldiers arrived, twenty-nine worshippers were dead, dozens more wounded. There was blood on the prayer rugs, on the stone floor and walls. The murderer, beaten to death, lay in his own blood.

AS SOON AS the morning reading of the Scroll of Esther ended in Kfar Etzion, Hanan Porat headed toward Hebron. Hanan was a father figure to the settlers, and today his place was among his people in Kiryat Arba. Reporters would soon be descending on the town; left-wing politicians would be demanding a government crackdown on all the settlers, not just on their extremist minority. Hanan intended to strengthen the settlers' spirits, and urge them, too, to condemn the massacre, not to allow the left to taint a whole community with the act of a renegade.

Before leaving home Hanan assembled a plate of *hamantaschen* and other sweets, a symbolic offering for the holiday. He put on a peddler's cap, a kind of joke: on Purim it was customary to dress up, enhance the merriment. All the more important, given the gloom of this day, to push back with the spirit of Purim.

Hanan loved Purim. For Jewish mystics it was a day to transcend this world of duality and taste the world to come, where there is no evil, only good. According to one tradition, a Jew was supposed to get so drunk on Purim that he couldn't distinguish between Haman and Mordechai—Amalek and Israel. Evil as illusion, a foil to invigorate the good, as Rabbi Kook taught.

Purim was a time of wildness, of rupture in mundane reality. And now Hanan had to deal with the consequences of a madman who had distorted the holiday's redemptive meaning.

Hanan wasn't surprised to learn that the murderer had been a follower of Meir Kahane. Hanan had long regarded Kahane and his misfits with an almost aesthetic distaste. *Outsiders. Not part of us*— In Brooklyn Kahane had organized vigilante patrols to protect Jews in urban neighborhoods, and he had tried to do the same in Judea and Samaria, as if the Jews were a besieged minority in their own country. Hanan despised Kahane's thuggish style, his apocalyptic messianism, so unlike the optimistic messianism of the Kookians. Hanan had always dismissed Kahane's followers as mere nuisance, best ignored.

A crew from Israel's Channel 2 TV was waiting at the entrance to the Kiryat Arba town council. Hanan ignored the crew and greeted friends standing inside the doorway. "Happy Purim!" he called out, smiling. "Happy Purim, *hevreh*!"

"Are you happy, Hanan Porat?" the reporter asked.

"We're happy because today is Purim," Hanan replied. "On Purim you must be happy even if there are crises. I came to strengthen the people here. But I consider what was done terrible."

He entered the office and forgot about the interview.

That night Channel 2 news showed Hanan, in peddler's cap, smiling and wishing his friends happy Purim. "We're happy because today is Purim," he told the camera. "On Purim you must be happy even if there are crises."

And that was it. Without his condemnation of the massacre. As though he were indifferent. Happy.

For many Israelis, the enduring image of the Hebron massacre became a grinning Hanan wishing Baruch Goldstein's neighbors a happy Purim.

THE SHOCK AND REVULSION among Israelis toward the massacre were profound. Dozens of rabbis, among them those from settlements, signed a letter stating that "there can be . . . no forgiveness for the murder of people at prayer before the Creator of the world." Speaking to the Knesset, Yitzhak Rabin excommunicated the mass murderer from the community of Israel.

In Kiryat Arba, opinions were divided. Some residents hailed Goldstein as a savior. Rumors spread that the Palestinians had been planning a massacre of Jews and that Goldstein had preempted them—a Purim miracle. A thousand mourners walked in a muddy field in a drenching rain to bury Dr. Goldstein, beside a park dedicated by the town council to Meir Kahane. Yisrael Ariel, the former rabbi of the destroyed town of Yamit, eulogized Goldstein and compared him to Rabbi Akiva and other martyrs.

In his lead editorial in *Nekudah*, Yisrael Harel denounced the massacre as a "repulsive act . . . that should shake the soul of every person created in God's image. . . . We are not part of the same camp [with those who support the massacre]. . . . Our camp . . . will continue to be built with holiness and purity."

Then, in a second editorial appearing just below the first, he abruptly changed tone: "The attacks against us have been so relentless, so hateful, that we were tempted to wonder whether the tragedy that happened in Hebron—and it was great, but fateful especially for us, the settlers—was greater than the Holocaust." The two sides of Yisrael Harel: Humane and empathic, mocking and self-pitying.

Hanan Porat had feared that the settler mainstream would be blamed for Goldstein, and that was precisely what happened. The symbol of that convergence was Hanan himself.

Columnists accused Hanan of rejoicing despite the massacre, and wondered whether he would have shown any less enthusiasm for celebrating Purim had there been Jewish victims. "*Haman* Porat," taunted Labor Knesset member Haggai Merom. The beautiful boy of religious Zionism, leader of the orphans of Kfar Etzion, wounded paratrooper, hero of Sebastia: the gloating face of the Hebron massacre.

It's a lie! Hanan told friends, journalists, colleagues in the Knesset. They edited out my condemnation! They're trying to destroy me, and through me, the settlement movement! I, Hanan Porat, a supporter of mass murder? I, who denounced the Jewish underground, including some of my closest friends? Who insisted on coexistence with our Arab neighbors in Kfar Etzion and sought no revenge for the murder of our parents? When a friend was killed by terrorists a few years ago before Purim, I still said, "Happy Purim," because that is what a Jew affirms!

The denials scarcely helped. Israelis recalled not only Hanan's "Happy Purim" but the smile that went with it.

Yoel Bin-Nun was furious with Hanan. He had desecrated God's name: Yoel knew of no more damning indictment. So what if they edited his condemnation? That was no excuse! Who knew better how to manipulate the media than Hanan Porat? He should have known how his comments, his demeanor, would emerge on TV.

For Yoel, the incident was an expression of Hanan's long pattern of denial. Like reassuring protesters in Yamit that the evacuation wouldn't happen because, according to the logic of redemption, it couldn't happen. Or refusing to offer a realistic plan for the Palestinian problem. Of course Hanan hadn't celebrated the massacre. He was only trying to do what he always did, encourage the people, impart a bit of light. But his behavior revealed that he hadn't absorbed the severity of the moment. Hanan's inexhaustible optimism, his faith in imminent redemption, were both strength and fatal weakness. Redemption was an opportunity, not an excuse to deny reality.

Yoel decided there was no point in arguing with Hanan. And that decision, he knew, marked an ending between them.

Personal Only!

March 25, 1994

Prime Minister
Yitzhak Rabin

Shlomot!
There is a vast and worrying gap between you and the public at large. . . . *The public doesn't trust the PLO, and rightly so*, and continues to see it, and ongoing Palestinian terrorism, as an existential threat. . . . *There is wide popular support for Jewish terrorism!* . . . If you won't understand this, and if you won't insist on an end to [Palestinian] terrorism as an absolute pre-condition for negotiations [with Arafat], you are likely to forfeit both the peace process and the prime ministership. . . . The key is in your hands!

Even as he warned Rabin of the consequences of his ill-conceived policy, Yoel warned the settlers of the consequences of Jewish terrorism.

The next victim of right-wing violence, Yoel predicted in *Nekudah*, would be a Jew. "The murder of gentiles [by Jews] ends with the murder of Jews. . . . The threats are already being heard, the justifications are already being written. . . . Words that are spoken don't remain in the air. There are those who absorb the message and rise up and act."

DESPITE THE OSLO ACCORDS—*because* of them, said critics—Palestinian terrorism reached its highest level in years. Hamas sent suicide bombers into markets and onto buses. Left-wingers blamed Baruch Goldstein for provoking Palestinian revenge; right-wingers countered that Hamas needed no pretext to kill Jews. Rabin declared that the best answer to Hamas terrorism was to strengthen the peace process with Arafat. But many Israelis now blamed Arafat himself for encouraging terrorism. Rabin's assurance that Arafat would suppress terrorism wasn't happening. Arafat speaks about the "peace of the brave" on CNN, Israelis noted bitterly, but preaches holy war in Gaza.

Ariel Sharon compared the left's faith in peace with Arafat to its old infatuation with Stalin—a fatal inability to distinguish enemy from friend, mass murderer from peacemaker. And he warned that handing over control of most of Gaza to Arafat would lead to Katyushas on neighboring Israeli towns like Ashkelon and Ashdod.

Arik Achmon laughed when he heard that one. Katyushas on Ashkelon! The right knew only how to frighten. What did they think, that the government would allow Katyushas to fall on Israeli cities? That the IDF was incapable of dealing with a few rockets?

In a speech in a Johannesburg mosque intended to be off-limits to the press, Arafat argued that his peace overtures were merely tactical. He recalled that the prophet Muhammad declared a cease-fire with an Arabian Jewish tribe and then, when he became strong enough, broke the cease-fire and destroyed the tribe. A reporter smuggled out a tape recording, and the speech made headlines in Israel. Even many Israelis who had supported the Oslo process concluded, We're being played for fools.

Yoel Bin-Nun's articles in *Nekudah* were increasingly anguished. Two approaches divided Zionism, he wrote. The first was total: "Everything! . . . This approach swept us all up after the Six Days to the peaks of euphoria—the 'complete' land of Israel in our hands—and from there, with prophetic urgency, to sounding the great shofar of total redemption." The second approach, he added, was that of classical Labor Zionism—gradually building the land and accepting the limits of reality.

"In the storms of my heart I am close to the first approach. . . . And so my criticism and my feelings of pain and rage are directed at myself. But since Camp David and Yamit, I have understood that we need to return in penitence to classical Zionism. That approach, partial and pragmatic, aspires for all [of the land] but builds in small steps. Another settlement, another house and another road. The building of the people of Israel in its land—not as a means of ruling over the Arabs, not as a basis for sovereignty [over Judea and Samaria] and the prevention of withdrawal . . . but as a liberating act of the resurrection of the nation returning to its land."

As usual, *Nekudah* was inundated with outraged letters against Yoel. In the magazine's satirical section appeared this notice: "We regret to inform readers that we can no longer publish any more responses to Yoel

Bin-Nun's article from issue #23"—which had appeared over a decade earlier and was still presumably aggravating *Nekudah* readers.

Yoel's own bitter response revealed his sensitivity. "There are some who sit in the safety of Tel Aviv and cancel their subscriptions to *Nekudah* because of the 'hostile' ideas of the man from Ofra," he wrote. "And they preach . . . love of the land of Israel to those who are sitting in Judea and Samaria for 25 years."

ILLICIT ENCOUNTERS

FOR A MAN violating one of the deepest taboos of his community, Yisrael Harel seemed surprisingly at ease. Gracious, even smiling, he sat in the garden of a suburban home near Tel Aviv and exchanged small talk with Yezid Sayigh, an Oxford political scientist with a trim beard and a slight English accent who also happened to be part of the PLO's negotiating team with Israel.

They were meeting to test the possibility of a dialogue between the Yesha Council and the PLO. No less. Not that either man recognized the legitimacy of the other's political movement. But the Oslo process had forced the PLO and the settlements into a new proximity. Was it now possible to get to know the demonic other as neighbor?

The idea had come from Yossi Alpher, a former senior official of the Mossad who headed a think tank for strategic studies. Until Oslo your Palestinian neighbors were "locals," without political power, Alpher had said to Yisrael. But now they were represented by the Palestinian Authority. "Since you wish to remain in the territories, you should be interested in seeking some sort of common language with your new neighbor," said Alpher.

Alpher noted that Yisrael didn't seem disturbed by the proposal. Though Yisrael wrote editorials in *Nekudah* insisting that Oslo could be defeated, he sensed that the dream of a complete land of Israel from the river to the sea was over. Perhaps it was easier for him to reach that conclusion because he had never been a messianic determinist. Based on Jewish history, he knew that destruction was as possible as redemption.

Alpher proposed, as a first step, a meeting with a Palestinian academic from abroad. Not a good idea, thought Alpher, to begin with a Palestinian leader from the West Bank whose son may have thrown rocks at Yisrael's car. Meeting a PLO academic rather than someone with Jewish blood on his hands, as Israelis put it, might also ease settler criticism of Yisrael should the encounter be prematurely exposed. For now Yisrael needed to keep the meeting from his colleagues at the Yesha Council, who would almost certainly respond with outrage, perhaps even demand Yisrael's resignation. In meeting with a member of the PLO—even a soft-spoken professor from Oxford—Yisrael would be labeled a defeatist, precisely the accusation he routinely raised against Rabin and the left.

"I'm thinking of meeting someone from the PLO," Yisrael told his wife, Sarah. "I feel responsibility as a leader to deal with the new situation."

"Is it responsibility or curosity?" asked Sarah.

"You're right," said Yisrael, "I am curious."

Now here he was, on this warm June afternoon, under a lemon tree in Yossi Alpher's garden, with a gentleman from the PLO.

Yisrael had intended to open with a lecture, asserting that the return to Judea and Samaria was an inevitable consequence of Jewish history. Instead, he found himself talking with Sayigh about their families and professional lives. Sayigh told him that he'd been born in Lebanon, to a Palestinian family that had fled the town of Tiberias in the Galilee during the 1948 war. It was hard to identify the professor with the murder of Israeli civilians.

Alpher suggested that each man present his vision of a final status agreement. Sayigh proposed a confederation of two states without borders between them. Yisrael proposed Jordan as a Palestinian state—after all, a majority of its people were Palestinians, and Jordan was historically part of the land of Israel—with West Bank Palestinians voting in Jordanian elections.

Their differences were unbridgeable. Still, when the meeting ended two hours later, both men said they wanted to meet again.

THE ABYSS DEEPENS

SUNDAY MORNING, JANUARY 22, 1995. The IDF soldiers, many of them paratroopers with red berets in their epaulets, gathered, as they did every week after their Shabbat furlough, at the intersection of Beit Lid near the coastal town of Netanya. There they waited for buses that would take them back to their bases. Many were recent recruits; some had been dropped off by their parents.

A young man dressed in an IDF uniform and carrying a briefcase approached a group of soldiers gathered at a kiosk. He moved into the crowd. The suitcase exploded.

Soldiers and passersby rushed to help the wounded. Three minutes later, another suicide bomber exploded.

Twenty-two dead, sixty-six wounded, almost all of them soldiers.

Israelis don't regard fallen soldiers as martyrs but as children. And so Israelis went into deep mourning for the children of Beit Lid. Prime Minister Rabin addressed the nation, promising to pursue terrorists despite the peace process—"no border will deter us"—and to pursue peace despite the terrorists. Israel, he declared, would not withdraw to the 1967 borders, would preserve a united Jerusalem "forever" and maintain its security border on the Jordan River. "In this bitter hour there is not right or left, no religious or secular," he said. "We are all the people of Israel."

And then he slipped. Explaining why peace was the best guarantee to prevent terrorism, he said, "We don't want the majority of the Jewish population . . . of whom 98 percent live within sovereign Israel [outside the territories], including united Jerusalem, to be vulnerable to terrorism."

Was Rabin really making a distinction between a terrorist attack in Beit Lid and a terrorist attack in Ofra? Was the prime minister of Israel telling the settlers that their lives, the lives of their children, mattered less to him than the lives of the "98 percent" who lived in sovereign Israel?

That is certainly how the settlers and their supporters heard those words. Rabin, they accused, was signaling to the terrorists that killing settlers was a lesser offense.

Yoel faxed Rabin: "Is your intention to break our spirit? It won't succeed!" Then, softening, he added, "There is a deep crisis of faith between a majority of settlers and the government, much more than is warranted, not so much because of your deeds but primarily because of the style of your pronouncements."

They met soon afterward. Yoel said, "When you speak about 98 percent, how can one expect reactions other than rage and despair?"

"Do you expect me to be attacked and not respond?" demanded Rabin.

"The settlers hear this as abandoning them in the field of battle." Yoel chose that last phrase carefully: abandoning a wounded soldier was a violation of the IDF's deepest ethos, which Rabin himself had nurtured.

"I didn't mean it to be understood that way," Rabin said.

"I know you, and I know you didn't mean it. But that is how it is being understood."

"I won't apologize," Rabin said. "But I won't repeat it."

RABIN'S OFFICE INVITED Yoel to an Independence Day reception, in the Defense Ministry in Tel Aviv.

Yoel approached Rabin to wish him a happy holiday. Standing beside the prime minister was Israel's chief rabbi, Yisrael Meir Lau, in gray beard and black fedora.

"If Yoel were the leader of the settlers," said Lau to Rabin, "it would be possible to reach an agreement with them."

"I'm not so sure," Rabin said dryly. "I'm the recipient of some of his love letters."

Yoel took it as a compliment.

A FRAGILE EMPATHY

IN AN OLD COUNTRY HOUSE in a village near Oxford, three prominent Palestinians and three prominent settlers sat facing each other beside a fireplace. The Palestinians and the Israelis were a long way from home.

Yossi Alpher asked Yisrael Harel to open.

Yisrael spoke with a frankness that impressed the Palestinians. "How do I listen to the other side without weakening my cause?" he asked. "It's easier to know your neighbor as a stone thrower."

It was June 1995. The dialogue was still a secret. Yisrael was waiting for the right moment to tell his colleagues in the Yesha Council, but the right moment never seemed to come. And so Alpher had organized a two-day meeting far from the conflict and the danger of exposure.

Yisrael brought with him two partners, both secular academics who lived in settlements and whose Zionism was tough but pragmatic, without messianism. There was Yosef Ben-Shlomo, professor of Jewish philosophy, and Ozer Schild, former president of the University of Haifa.

On the Palestinian side there were also two academics—Yezid Sayigh was joined by his friend Walid Khalidi, editor of the *Journal of Palestine Studies*. And there was a Fatah activist named Sufian Abu Zaida, popular with the Israeli media because he spoke a fluent Hebrew learned in Israeli prison.

Yezid Sayigh spoke next. "Like Yisrael Harel I have learned that an examination of other people's views must lead me to look at my own views too," he said.

Yosef Ben-Shlomo told of being brought as a child to the land of Israel from Poland just before the Holocaust. As a teenager he had been an admirer of Gandhi; after the Six-Day War he signed a petition against Jewish settlement in Hebron. But Arab rejection of Israel's existence convinced him that Israel had to settle the territories. Though secular, he joined Gush Emunim's squatting attempts and was evacuated seven times. "They needed eight soldiers to carry me." But now, he added enigmatically, "I may be on the brink of a third change of heart."

Walid Khalidi spoke of his family, who had lived in Jerusalem's Old City for six centuries and had produced judges, scholars, and the last Arab mayor of Jerusalem. "This has always been part of my daily consciousness. This may have in a sense stunted my own growth, since it allowed me little flexibility for alternative development."

One way or another, they were all admitting that the conflict had not only energized and defined them but also depleted them. They shared a kind of relief: they could see themselves in each other, men whose people's historical claim totally claimed them, whose people's suffering denied them peace. But could they really allow themselves empathy, or would the other side exploit that as weakness?

Sufian Abu Zaida insisted on telling his story in Hebrew. He was born in the Jabalya refugee camp in Gaza and dreamed of taking vengeance on the Jews. In Beirut he joined Fatah, then returned to Gaza as an operative. Intending to "clean up" the camp, he shot a drug dealer, was caught, and spent twelve years in prison. There he studied Hebrew by reading the Israeli dailies. In getting to vicariously know Israeli society, he found he could no longer hate Israelis. "Yisrael Harel's articles were the hardest to understand, due to the rich vocabulary he used."

Abu Zaida spoke about his experiences lecturing to Israeli high school students.

"When will Israelis be invited to appear before Palestinian schoolchildren?" demanded Ben-Shlomo.

"There is no chance today, but it will come," Abu Zaida replied.

AFTER LUNCH—there was a mix-up with Yisrael's kosher meals, and he stoically ate salad—the conversation resumed in the salon. They argued, intensely but without rancor, about competing claims and colonialism and morality, even considered keeping settlements intact under Palestinian sovereignty.

Turning to Abu Zaida, Ben-Shlomo asked, "When you say that Palestinians are willing to compromise, does this mean they will acknowledge the Jews' moral right to a homeland in Palestine, just as the Israeli left recognizes the Palestinians' moral right to a homeland in Palestine?"

Abu Zaida: "Jews whose grandparents were born thousands of miles away while my brothers in exile have no right to return—we don't recognize it."

Yisrael Harel, sarcastic: "When we recognize the Palestinian's right of return, he will be able to recognize our moral right." In other words: the right of return will mean the destruction of the Jewish state, and then its right to exist won't matter.

There was a third option: Palestinians would exercise their right of return in a Palestinian state, not in the state of Israel. That would mean the end of Israeli control over Judea and Samaria, and the end of Palestinian claims over lands that were now the state of Israel. Yet no one mentioned that option.

THE NEXT MORNING at breakfast, Alpher was gratified to see settlers and Palestinians mingling. Yisrael invited Sufian Abu Zaida to address meetings at settlements, as a way of preparing his community for the new reality. Abu Zaida readily agreed.

At the final session the Israelis continued to press for Palestinian recognition of their national legitimacy, and the Palestinians continued to resist.

KHALIDI: We can coexist with a deep moral-ideological abyss. Let's distinguish between daily life and the political superstructure. . . . This can at least end the bloodshed, and this is the most important moral imperative.

YISRAEL: This isn't enough. You can't separate us from our history.

The Jews wanted to talk principles, the Palestinians practical details.

KHALIDI: For nineteen years, prior to '67, you survived without Bet El [a settlement near Ofra].

YISRAEL: To give up Bet El today is to declare that it was never important to us to return to the land of Israel. It was easier when we never had it. Our real message must be to find a new formula that doesn't constitute a betrayal of either side.

They were all keen on continuing.

A JEW IN TEL AVIV

YAIR LAPID, the young talk show host who was always ready with a clever rejoinder, seemed perplexed. Why, he asked his guest, Meir Ariel, haven't you promoted your new album? No media appearances until now, no marketing. You've even confined sales to a single music store in Tel Aviv. "It's as if you've said, 'I'm releasing an album but I'm imposing a blackout.'"

"You're right," said Meir, smiling nervously and clutching his guitar. "I tried very hard not to release [the album], but in the end it weighed so heavily on me that I put it out and that's it. But that doesn't mean that anyone has to hear it. In all seriousness I say that anyone who wants to do his soul any good shouldn't listen to this album. It's a hard album, with hard material."

The audience laughed.

The album was called *Rishumei Pecham* (Charcoal Sketches), and Meir was right: these were not songs one listened to for pleasure. One was an apocalyptic vision based on the book of Daniel and sung partly in Aramaic; another was about an old kibbutznik so frustrated by economic failure that he beats his wife and children; another was based on the Talmud's musings on the varied forms of divine justice inflicted on Titus, the Roman general who burned the Temple, and which Meir turned into an allergory for the fate of material-driven empires. Meir had sent the songs to his friend, Shalom Hanoch, hoping he would produce the album. But Shalom refused: even for Meir, this was pushing the limits of obscurity.

Two years earlier Shalom had produced Meir's fourth album, *Zirei Kayitz* (Seeds of Summer), which contained some of his most accessible love songs. Yet the album sold poorly. Meir had long since accepted his place on the respected periphery of Israeli music. But he was tormented by his inability to provide for his family. Defiantly anticommercial, *Rishumei Pecham* seemed a taunt against the music industry.

Meir produced the album on his own new label, Ariel Productions. The minimalist songs, backed by a plaintive accordion that had lost its Zionist vigor, were all recorded in a single day. Meir's son, Shachar, a musician in his mid-twenties, was producer, while Tirza ran what business there was. Initially Meir refused to promote the album. Only on Tirza's insistence did he agree to appear on Yair Lapid's show.

Rishumei Pecham was Meir's favorite among his own albums. His only concept album, it was at once a protest against a devouring modernity and a eulogy for the Israel of communal values. Like Avital Geva, he was raising a kibbutznik's last cry against the new Israeli culture of McDonald's and cable TV, against the banks to which the kibbutzim were mortgaged and the real estate developers uprooting orange groves for shopping centers.

More than in any previous work, Meir was exposing something of his growing devotion to Judaism and the God of Israel. Much of the language and imagery of *Rishumei Pecham* was drawn not only from the Bible—a common source of inspiration for Israeli artists—but also from the Talmud and rabbinic commentaries and kabbalah, mostly absent from secular Israeli culture.

Meir understood God's existence partly through language. There are no words for things that don't exist, he told a friend. And so if there is a name for God, He must exist. Meir found amusing the notion that the world evolved without a creator and that a human being was a material construct without a soul. "The human being is nothing more / than a piece of sophisticated mud," he sang. "And he has a certain personality / and a perfect shape. And that's / sophisticated—for mud." He continued: "Mud that dries up—disintegrates . . . / And a human being who dries up—he too disintegrates / Except that / . . . He has a tombstone, and an address / and that's—sophisticated." The proof for Meir of the existence of a soul was its ability to give its incarnation a name.

MEIR WAS INTERVIEWED on Army Radio by his old friend Yoav Kutner. What, wondered Kutner aloud, was *Rishumei Pecham* actually about?

KUTNER: I'm thinking of your career. . . . You get wonderful reviews, you produce wonderful albums. . . . And yet you still haven't made it. Not one of your albums has sold.

MEIR: Of course I'd be happy if—

KUTNER: You do everything backwards. Your previous album, *Seeds of Summer* . . . was, quote, "commercial." Meaning that it was a less difficult album. . . . With Shalom Hanoch's help it flowed and was pleasant to listen to. . . . And it didn't succeed. . . . And instead of trying even harder to do something light, you go and do your least accessible album . . .

MEIR (switching to English): Man, I'm telling you, I'm gonna make it. Not only nationwide, but also— That's why I'm speaking English! International wild!

Reverting to Hebrew, Meir explained that Israel was such a small market, why not sing in a foreign language?

KUTNER: Chinese is big these days.

MEIR: Chinese, exactly. . . . We need to create in every language. Folk songs in Romanian—in Israel!

"SHALOM ALEICHEM"—PEACE BE WITH YOU—Meir said in archaic Hebrew, and bowed his head in chivalrous greeting. Covering his long graying curls was a beaten black fedora.

"Aleichem shalom," replied his friend Menachem Regev: And peace be with you.

Every Wednesday evening Meir came to Menachem's Tel Aviv

apartment, where friends gathered to study the Torah reading of the week. Menachem, a graphic artist, had grown up secular, become ultra-Orthodox, left that community, and was now, like Meir, in transit between worlds. Menachem, whose hobby was inventing Hebrew fonts, shared with Meir a love of the resurrected language, a sense of awe simply to be speaking it. On Menachem's walls were framed album covers he had designed, including some of Meir's.

The living room filled with a dozen men. There were musicians, former kibbutzniks, a psychiatrist. Someone rolled a joint. A newcomer appeared. "Baruch habah"—Blessed be the one who comes—people greeted him. No one asked how he knew to come; if you found your way here, you belonged.

"*Yallah,* Meirkeh," said Menachem, using the Yiddish endearment for Meir's name, "let's begin." Meir read from the book of Numbers, the portion about Balaam the magician, who intended to curse Israel but instead blessed it. Meir read the text like poetry, cherishing every word. Several men put on *kippot*; others remained bareheaded.

Then the discussion began.

Did Balaam bless or curse Israel when he proclaimed it a nation that would dwell alone? What did it mean to be a chosen people?

The Jews, said Meir, aren't any better than anyone else; the heart isn't more important than the brain. But every nation has a unique role. Our role, said Meir, is to remind the world of God's oneness.

How do we know there is only one God? someone demanded.

Because that's what's written, someone replied.

Everyone laughed.

The conversation turned, inevitably, to modern Israel. Could the Jewish state find its place in the Middle East, or was it destined to remain apart, as Balaam seemed to predict? Could Israel trust the Palestinians to make peace? Was Arafat partner or nemesis? Was the return of the Jews home fulfillment of ancient prophecy? And what about the rabbinic establishment and its monopolization of Judaism?

More than the arguments, the gathering itself was the message: Judaism doesn't only belong to the Orthodox, we too are custodians of the Torah, we too have the right to struggle with the tradition.

Finally, around 3:00 a.m., Menachem turned to his friends and said, "You don't have anywhere to sleep?"

"Good night, *hevreh*," said Meir. And though Friday evening was still two days away, he added, "Shabbat shalom"—Sabbath of peace.

A SOLDIER'S DEATH

SHORTLY BEFORE DAWN on July 17, 1995, Motta Gur, pistol in hand, entered the walled garden of his house in North Tel Aviv. The garden was the place he loved most. Standing near the loquat tree, he pointed the gun at his temple and fired. A preemptive strike: the rare cancer that had been spreading slowly and excruciatingly in his body for nearly ten years was about to reach the brain. In a note of farewell, he told his family that he hadn't wanted to be a burden.

Arik Achmon got the call shortly after Rita Gur found her husband in the garden. If I'm ever in a similar situation, thought Arik, I hope I'll have the courage to do what Motta did.

In the last years, as Motta became increasingly ill, Arik would meet him every few weeks in his office at the Defense Ministry, and Motta, one of the strongest men Arik knew, would confide how unbearable the pain was, how humiliating the loss of bodily control.

At the house, Arik found Rita and their four children quietly grieving. Rita said she was at peace with Motta's choice. "Motta restored his dignity in his own eyes," she said.

Arik focused as always on the practical questions. What does Rita need, what about the funeral arrangements? Rita asked Arik to be among the eulogizers, representing the family of fighters.

For a brief moment, Israelis united in grief. Motta represented the nobility of the old Israel, its readiness to take responsibility without seeking reward. Commentators recalled how Motta, appointed commander in chief of the IDF after the Yom Kippur War, restored the army's faith in itself; how he commanded the astonishing rescue of Israeli hostages in Entebbe Airport in Uganda in 1976, after terrorists had hijacked an Air France flight from Tel Aviv. An elderly woman told a journalist how, during a paratrooper raid against terrorists in Gaza in 1955, Motta had carried the dead body of her son for kilometers under fire. Motta had kept in regular touch with her, inviting her to family events. "Today I lost my second son," she said.

Journalists described Motta as a first-rate military man but a failed politician, ending his career as mere deputy defense minister. Yet Arik knew another story: Motta had confided that Rabin had offered him the defense ministry, but because of his illness Motta had to decline. Perhaps that was not only Motta's tragedy but the nation's: after serving as defense minister, Arik believed, Motta would have become Rabin's successor as prime minister. And Motta, with his commitment to the peace process and his love of the settlers, could have been a healer.

Thousands gathered in the military section of the Kiryat Shaul cemetery near Tel Aviv. The rows of identical flat white stones, generals buried beside privates, were a last repository of egalitarian Israel. It was a hot July day; pine trees provided patches of shade. The mourners were secular and religious, young paratroopers in red berets and veterans who had fought with Motta in Jerusalem. There were Yisrael Harel and Yoel Bin-Nun and Hanan Porat. Yitzhak Rabin, barely protected, walked among the crowds.

"Motta was our Kotel," our Wailing Wall, Hanan told a journalist, the one man in this government to whom settlers could confide their trauma. Hanan noted that it was the seventeenth of Tammuz, the fast day marking the Roman breach of the walls of Jerusalem and the countdown to the destruction of the Temple. What does it mean, he wondered aloud, that the commander who proclaimed "The Temple Mount is in our hands" has been taken from us on this day?

The eulogies began with Arik. "Motta's path in life was to be the first, as a fighter and a commander," he said in his hoarse soldier's voice, a permanent reminder of his time in Lebanon. "He was a statesman, a family man, a man of the book. And he was first in almost all those areas." Motta entered politics without becoming a politician, said Arik, just as he had devoted his life to the military "without taking on military poses."

Arik recalled how, after the battle for Jerusalem, Motta had wept inconsolably as Arik told him the names of their fallen friends. "That was the real Motta," he said.

"His family and friends and all of Israel have lost a good and honest man, who loved and was loved. The heart weeps."

THE PARTNERSHIP

THE RABIN GOVERNMENT was negotiating with the Palestinians over the next stage of withdrawal from the territories, and Yoel Bin-Nun was feeling desperate. The first withdrawal had included most of Gaza but only a symbolic concession in the West Bank, the town of Jericho. The next withdrawal, though, would be more substantive: the IDF would be pulled out of West Bank cities, leaving the settlers far more vulnerable.

Inevitably, Yoel knew, there would be dozens of mistakes in the government map that would jeopardize settlers' security and other Israeli interests and which a discerning settler eye could easily detect. But there was almost no communication between the Yesha Council and the government; Motta had been Yisrael Harel's channel. And so, though he held no official position in the settlement movement and no one had appointed him intermediary, Yoel concluded that it was now up to him.

Rabin had come to love Yoel. That was the impression of Rabin's bureau chief, Eitan Haber. These days, when Yoel faxed Rabin his latest handwritten complaints, Haber would bring the letter directly to Rabin's attention; Rabin would read carefully, writing notes in the margins. And when Yoel called for a meeting, he was quickly admitted. Now Yoel phoned Haber with a request that, even for Yoel, was impertinent. "I want one of our people to look at the government's maps" for the next phase of withdrawal, he said. Haber balked: not even the Palestinians had seen the maps yet.

Yoel pressed. "There are problems that can be quietly settled. We have enough disagreements between us as it is. I'm asking for one person from our side to look at the maps before they go to the Palestinians."

Haber phoned back. "Whom do you suggest?"

Yoel offered the name of a settler leader who was an expert on topography. "Nothing will be leaked," he promised.

Through the summer of 1995, Yoel pressed Rabin to deal with the corrections Yoel's colleague had suggested. The isolated settlement of Tekoa needed to be connected to the Etzion Bloc. And what about the centuries-old Jewish cemetery in Hebron? And why wasn't the Ofra bypass road being built more quickly?

HANAN PORAT WAS INCONSOLABLE. How could Rabin be doing this to Mother Rachel? The mother of the Jewish people! Where was his Jewish soul?

As part of the next phase of the Oslo process, the government of Israel was negotiating the transfer to Palestinian rule of Rachel's Tomb, on the border between Bethlehem and Jerusalem. Rachel's Tomb was among the most beloved places of Jewish pilgrimage, especially for single young women seeking husbands. Jewish women marched in protest from Jerusalem to Bethlehem. Right-wing politicians denounced Rabin's insensitivity as a form of madness.

Sensing a threat to the tomb, Hanan organized a group of Mercaz students to establish a yeshiva in the small domed building. The government body in charge of holy places forbade the group from bringing in books and furniture. But after each visit the yeshiva students "forgot" religious books and thereby created a small library. And then one night students brought in tables and chairs via a back entrance through the adjacent Muslim cemetery. Classic Hanan: create facts on the ground and force the government to live with it.

The growing public protests forced the government to modify its plan: Rachel's Tomb would remain under Israeli military protection, but Palestinian police would patrol the road leading to the tomb. That arrangement, said Hanan bitterly, was reminiscent of the time of exile, when Jews visited Mother Rachel under foreign rule.

Hanan went to see Rabin. The two men had a complicated relationship. Rabin hadn't forgiven Hanan for the mass squatting at Sebastia, which Rabin blamed for undermining the stability of his first government. But then, during the 1992 elections, when the Likud made a campaign issue of Rabin's temporary breakdown on the eve of the Six-Day War, Hanan publicly defended the prime minister, and Rabin's door was open to him.

While waiting to enter the prime minister's office, Hanan encountered Rabbi Menachem Porush, a venerable ultra-Orthodox politician with a long white beard. Hanan told Porush that he'd come to plead for Mother Rachel. Porush asked if he could join the meeting. By all means, said Hanan.

Hanan opened by spreading out a large aerial photograph of the area around Rachel's Tomb. Hanan sensed that the way to reach Rabin was through security rather than historical arguments. Hanan noted the close proximity between Rachel's Tomb and the Jerusalem neighborhood of Gilo. If Palestinian police controlled the road to the tomb, he argued, they would be within shooting distance of Gilo's Jewish homes.

Suddenly Porush approached Rabin, embraced him, and began weeping. "This is Mama Ruchel!" he cried out, using the Yiddish for Mother Rachel. "How can you give away her grave?"

Rabin, embarrassed, asked Porush to calm himself. "How can I calm myself?" cried Porush. "The Jewish people won't forgive you if you abandon our mother's grave."

In the presence of the two men, Rabin phoned Foreign Minister Shimon Peres. Renegotiate the arrangements for Rachel's Tomb, said Rabin.

The road to the holy site remained under Israeli rule.

OSLO II—THE WITHDRAWAL of the IDF from West Bank cities—passed in the Knesset, but just barely, 61–59. On this, the most sensitive Israeli issue, Rabin relied on a majority achieved by a political bribe: wooing a right-wing Knesset member, Alex Goldfarb (a former paratrooper, as it happened) with a government position. "Goldfarb's Mitsubishi," right-wingers contemptuously referred to the deal and its perks. They were especially outraged by Rabin's reliance on anti-Zionist Arab parties for his bare majority. On an issue of such fateful importance to the Jewish people, how could Rabin violate the sensibilities of so many Israelis?

Rabin retorted: I will make peace with whatever majority is available.

It was Yoel Bin-Nun's nightmare: the collapse of the most minimal Israeli cohesion. The passing of Oslo II without a Jewish majority in the Knesset, Yoel wrote Rabin, "is not morally and historically binding on the whole of the people of Israel and surely not on Jewish history." Still, Yoel pledged to continue to oppose any attempt to undermine the rule of law and to prevent civil war.

But that was not the mood on the streets. On October 5, 1995, tens of thousands of protesters filled Zion Square in downtown Jerusalem. Young men in knitted *kippot* leaped up and down shouting, "Rabin traitor!" "Rabin Nazi!" One young man burned a poster of Rabin in a kaffiyeh. "Because of this man the state is going to be destroyed!" he shouted.

Benjamin Netanyahu, Ariel Sharon, and other leaders of the Likud opposition stood on a balcony several stories above the crowds. A banner across the balcony's facade read, "Death to the Arch-Murderer," a reference to Arafat. But many in the crowd weren't interested tonight in Arafat. "Death to Rabin!" hundreds chanted.

A burning torch was propped up on the sidewalk. Beside the torch was a handwritten sign: "A memorial candle for Rabin."

YOEL WENT TO SEE RABIN.

The rabbi challenged the prime minister over the impending withdrawal. "If this is what you're giving away now," demanded Yoel, "what will you have left to offer in a final-status agreement?"

The two were alone.

"Yoel," said Rabin, looking at him steadily, "there will be no final-status agreement. It is impossible to reach an agreement on Jerusalem. We will continue to manage the interim agreement and to proceed in stages."

"What does that mean?"

"To expand the Palestinian areas, give them more authority."

No withdrawal to the 1967 borders; no redivision of Jerusalem. Had Rabin come to regret legitimizing Arafat as a peace partner? Or had Rabin realized all along that only an interim agreement was possible?

"You have unleashed forces you won't be able to control," said Yoel.

"I can't rule out that danger," acknowledged Rabin. "But we'll do our best."

If only the settlers could know that the man they reviled as a traitor was doing all he could to protect them, thought Yoel. But of course they couldn't know. Yoel's partnership with Rabin—for that is what it had become—depended on discretion. In the streets they were chanting, "Death to Rabin!" *Death to the commander of the Six Days!* Yoel's inability to reveal the truth, to stop the campaign of hate, tormented him.

The greatest threat, Yoel knew, came from within. Only the Jews could defeat the Jews. Yoel had learned, through repeated trauma, that the Jews needed to accommodate each other's conflicting dreams and fears. Right, left, Orthodox, secular: all would have to live together again as a people in its land.

Yoel got up to leave. "Thank you," he said.

Rabin tilted his head, as if puzzled by the gratitude. He didn't need Yoel's thanks, just as Yoel didn't need his. They had a job to do together, and they were doing it. For all the differences between them, they belonged to the same elite: those who took responsibility for the fate of the Jewish return home.

Rabin offered his perfunctory handshake. Yoel took leave of his prime minister, his commander. He faced yet another late night of worry for his people and exasperation at their failures, pacing his study until he collapsed into restless sleep.

CHAPTER 29

CAREENING TOWARD THE CENTER

A BLOW TO THE HEART

AS SOON AS YOEL heard the news, he knew: a Jewish hand had done this.

It was Saturday night, November 4, 1995. Yitzhak Rabin had just left the stage of a peace rally in a Tel Aviv square when a young man waiting in the VIP parking lot rushed from behind and fired twice into his back. The news said only that Rabin was badly wounded. Yoel retreated to his study to pray. Inexplicably, he felt a great calm. Rabin will be okay, he thought. So bound did Yoel feel to Rabin that afterward, when he heard that Rabin had died even as he was praying for him, Yoel wondered whether the calm he'd felt then was the departure of Rabin's soul.

WHEN SHABBAT ENDED, Hanan Porat set out toward Bethlehem, to Rachel's Tomb. According to tradition, this night was the anniversary of the death of Mother Rachel, and Hanan intended to join the thousands of pilgrims gathering at her grave.

He turned on the radio and heard the news. Unable to continue, he pulled over to the side of the road. To keep from crying out, he bit his lip—so hard he drew blood. He thought of his last meeting with Rabin, how the prime minister of Israel couldn't resist the grief of an elderly Jew for Mother Rachel. *And now Mother Rachel is weeping for her son, Yitzhak—*

THE ASSASSIN, YIGAL AMIR, was an Orthodox Jew, a law student at Bar-Ilan University, one of the major institutions of religious Zionism. Though not a settler, Amir had been active in the pro-settlement movement.

In all the years of war and terrorism, Israel had never experienced such open grief. Thousands of teenagers spontaneously gathered in the square where Rabin had been murdered, lighting candles and singing the old Zionist songs. The radio repeatedly played "Song for Peace," anthem of the Israeli peace movement, which Rabin had sung with others on the stage just before his murder and whose bloodstained lyrics sheet had been found in his breast pocket. Trauma hotlines were overwhelmed with callers. A sticker appeared on Israeli cars, *"Shalom, Haver"*—Farewell, friend—quoting President Clinton.

Yoel joined the seemingly endless line passing before Rabin's casket outside the parliament building in Jerusalem. Some held handwritten signs that read, "Thank You." A bearded man in a *kippah* held a sign: "I Am Ashamed."

Yoel paused before the flag-covered coffin and tore his shirt collar, like a mourner for a close family member.

But he didn't weep. Grief would come later. First must come the reckoning.

Three young men from West Bank settlements appeared at Yoel's door. They came separately, yet offered variations of the same story: each had heard a rabbi declare that, under Jewish law, Rabin deserved the death penalty. None of the young men knew Yoel personally, but they came to him because they didn't know whom else to trust.

Yoel knew that several rabbis had discussed whether, under Jewish law, Rabin deserved the death penalty as a *moser*, someone who hands over a fellow Jew for persecution or death, or even as a *rodef*, who actively seeks to kill a fellow Jew. A letter had circulated among rabbis inquiring about the halachic relationship to the Rabin government, and hinted at the possibility of *moser*. Had the assassin—Yoel refused to say his name, calling him only "the evil one"—received a rabbi's blessing? And even if he hadn't, would he have been wrong, given the prevailing atmosphere, to assume that his act would have religious legitimacy? And most terrifying of all: How many more potential assassins were wandering among them?

THE RELIGIOUS ZIONIST COMMUNITY was under siege. Government ministers blamed the entire right, and especially religious Zionists, for creating an atmosphere of incitement that had led to the assassination, as if anyone who had opposed the Oslo process was an accomplice with

Yigal Amir. A Tel Aviv bus driver called a young man in a *kippah* "murderer" and threw him off the bus. At army hitchhiking stations, religious soldiers returning from frontline service in Lebanon were denied lifts. A new sticker appeared: "We Won't Forgive, We Won't Forget."

The emergency meeting of religious Zionist leaders—"Assembly of Self-Reckoning"—began with a minute of silence. Then, facing the packed Jerusalem hall, Rabbi Yehudah Amital of the Mount Etzion yeshiva declared: "We cannot say, 'Our hands have not shed this blood.'" Another speaker, a professor of Jewish thought, wondered whether a return to exile might not be preferable to civil war among Jews.

Others, though, were concerned less with self-reflection than with self-protection.

Yisrael Harel confided to the audience that he had approached left-wing leaders and proposed a joint left-right rally against violence. But the left, he said bitterly, wouldn't allow the right "to ruin [its] pleasure" in implicating its ideological rival. "Those sitting here—everyone, including Rabbi Amital . . . all sat together this week in the defendant's dock."

Yes, he conceded, "we should beat our breasts in remorse." Not for the murder, but for failing to have the courage to control the "fringe extremists." But, he concluded, "not only has our way of life not failed, but it is *the* way. The royal road of Zionism and Judaism."

Yoel sat in the audience, seething. Even now, with the nation torn and bleeding, Yisrael's impulse was to protect his camp.

Yoel approached the podium and demanded the right to speak. "If there will be, God forbid, another political murder in the state of Israel, it may not continue to exist," he said, voice shaking. "At this very moment, while we are sitting here, there are still people speaking about *rodef* against certain [political] figures. . . . I agree wholeheartedly with all that has been said here about the beauty of the religious community and of religious Zionism and of religious education. . . . But all this depends on one thing: that all those who spoke about *rodef*, who ruled *rodef*—and I know that there are, that there were those in the last half-year who spoke about *rodef*—not fools, not fringe characters, [but] Torah authorities— If they will not resign from all their rabbinic positions until the end of the shivah [the seven-day mourning period]—until the end of the shivah—this is an ultimatum—then I will fight them before the whole people of Israel."

"Give us names," Yisrael demanded. "If you have proof, I will go with you to the police."

"I'll provide names after the shivah," said Yoel, and left the hall.

FOR DAYS AFTERWARD, Yoel's pronouncements made headlines. Journalists waited outside his home. The law of *rodef*—for most Israelis an obscure halachic concept—entered the national lexicon.

Yoel approached the two chief rabbis—one Ashkenazi, one Sephardi—and confided two names to them. Both were leading rabbis within the settlement movement. Yoel asked the chief rabbis to create an investigative committee. And he asked that they keep the names private. Naively, Yoel hoped that the rabbinic community would purge itself, without police involvement. Yoel, after all, had no hard evidence against anyone.

But one of the chief rabbis leaked the names to the media. When Yoel heard the news, he thought, They've buried me—

Now the police felt impelled to act. Humiliatingly, leading rabbis were summoned for police interrogation. An emergency meeting of hundreds of rabbis condemned what it called the "incitement" against the rabbinic community, and everyone understood whom the rabbis meant. The Yesha Council denounced Yoel by name.

Yoel received death threats and began wearing a bulletproof vest. Several young men, reservists from an elite combat unit, volunteered to serve as his bodyguards. On Shabbat they accompanied him to the Ofra synagogue. An outraged Yisrael told Yoel: Now you are turning your neighbors into potential murderers. Yisrael stopped speaking to him.

When no indictments resulted, Yoel publicly apologized to "all those innocents who were hurt." Still, Yoel insisted that, for all his tactical missteps, he had achieved his goal. As a result of his public challenge, even extremist rabbis had been forced to disavow the political relevance of *rodef*. Yoel was convinced he had prevented the next assassination.

In turning himself, a rabbi from Ofra, into a symbol of the nation's grief and rage, Yoel helped religious Zionism return to the mainstream. Israel's healing began with Yoel's torment.

"IS CIVIL WAR POSSIBLE?" read the banner hanging in the auditorium of the high school on Kibbutz Ein Shemer. The several hundred students who had gathered to hear Yoel Bin-Nun address that question all wore the uniform of Hashomer Hatzair—blue work shirt with white shoelace crisscrossing at the neck. But the austere socialism of Hashomer Hatzair was gone. Instead there were boys with shaved heads and earrings, girls with jeans torn at the knee.

Yoel stood before them: long graying beard and paunch, white knitted *kippah*, long fringes of *tzitzit* extending beneath bulky gray sweater. Deep lines marked his forehead, and his eyes were wide with sleeplessness.

"No enemy from without can endanger us more than the split from within," he began. "The first and second temples were destroyed because of internal conflict. Our responsibility is to emphasize the commonality of the people of Israel and to push the fanatics of all sides beyond the pale. I don't want to belong to a camp but to the [whole] people of Israel."

Suddenly Yoel paused. Smiling widely, he gestured to a middle-aged man sitting among the young people. "My comrade in arms!" exclaimed Yoel.

Avital Geva looked away, embarrassed by the attention.

Over a decade had passed since they'd seen each other last, in a Lebanese village on the edge of besieged Beirut. Now Yoel told the audience how during reserve duty shortly after the Yom Kippur War, Avital had demanded that Shabbat rest be granted to secular soldiers too. "Don't think that Avital and I don't have arguments," he said. "But there is friendship. We'll argue forever, but democratically."

"How does democracy go with annexing the territories?" a teacher called out.

"Good," Yoel replied, like an officer speaking to a new recruit. "I don't believe we can or should rule over the Palestinians, even though I think that the people of Israel has an exclusive right to the land of Israel. After Oslo, settlement no longer means ruling over the Palestinians. They now have self-rule. But settlements will prevent a Palestinian state, which would endanger Israel's existence."

"So what status will Palestinians have?" pressed the teacher.

"The solution is cantons—Jewish and Arab areas. It's not the ideal solution, but since the Palestinians aren't ready to accept our existence, it's the only solution."

Yoel returned to the question of Jewish identity. "You aren't new creatures called Israelis but a continuation of the Jewish people," he said pointedly to the students. "You don't have to be religious to know the Jewish tradition. I talk with Maimonides; he's alive for me."

"If I don't study Torah, then I'm responsible for the schism?" a girl called out.

"The sad answer is yes," replied Yoel.

"Come here and eat pork and there won't be a schism," a boy called out.

Yoel smiled, tried to be patient.

Avital said, "Yoel, you've done more to bring us together than anyone else in this country. You've stood against your own camp. What do we need to do from our side?"

"Break the stigma that Judaism belongs only to a certain kind of people," replied Yoel.

Afterward they embraced. Avital held Yoel's shoulder and didn't let go, as if to give him strength. "*Ya Allah*, Avital Geva!" said Yoel, sounding like Avital. For the first time since the assassination, Yoel seemed happy.

They walked around the kibbutz, the earth moist with the winter rains. Avital spoke about his sons. One was a combat pilot, another an infantry officer.

"I have three Golanis at home," Yoel said, referring to an infantry unit. "They tell me that the paratroopers philosophize, while Golani does the real work."

They laughed.

ELECTIONS WERE CALLED for May 1996. Yoel endorsed Labor Party leader Shimon Peres, despised on the right as initiator of the Oslo process.

At a meeting in a synagogue in a town near Tel Aviv, Yoel declared that the peace process was the will of God. "Who appointed you a prophet?" one man demanded. "How do you know the will of God?"

"Just as I knew when I went up to Ofra twenty years ago," said Yoel.

A young man asked quietly, "What went wrong?" Yoel replied, "We didn't listen to the moral arguments of the left."

Shortly before the elections, as the country was still grieving for its fallen leader, for itself, Hamas terrorists resumed suicide bombings. Israeli intelligence determined that Arafat was secretly encouraging Hamas—and then presenting himself as the moderate alternative whom Israel needed to strengthen with additional concessions. On car bumpers appeared a new sticker, "*Shalom, Haverim*" (Farewell, Friends)—all those killed as a result of the Oslo process promoted by Rabin.

Both the right-wing dream of greater Israel, and the left-wing dream of Peace Now, Yoel concluded, were delusions. Instead, Israel needed to seek consensus, source of its spiritual strength, and from that political center manage an insoluble conflict. Just as Rabin would have done.

The suicide bombings destroyed the vast lead the Labor Party had held in polls after the assassination, and the Likud, headed by Benjamin Netanyahu, returned to power. For some on the left, it was the final betrayal.

The Likud government ended the partial freeze on settlement building that Labor had imposed, and resumed large-scale construction in the territories. But a majority of Israelis continued to support the Oslo process. Netanyahu's mandate from the public was to negotiate more toughly than Labor, but to continue negotiating. More and more Israelis, including many Likud voters, were concluding that there was no alternative to a two-state solution.

THE DISAPPOINTMENTS OF YISRAEL HAREL

YISRAEL'S CLANDESTINE MEETINGS with members of the PLO continued. He even succeeded in involving several hard-liners from the settlement community.

Inevitably, though, in an intimate country with few secrets, the Israeli media discovered the improbable dialogue. When the story appeared, the Yesha Council convened in an emergency session. Yisrael was accused of betraying the trust of his colleagues, of legitimizing terrorists. "This is one of the most important steps I've taken as head of the Yesha Council," he countered.

The council condemned those of its members who had met with Palestinians without its approval. But despite calls for Yisrael's resignation, a majority backed him.

Still, when his term as head of the Yesha Council ended, Yisrael didn't seek reelection. He needed change, sought a wider scope of influence. His ambitions had always been greater than the religious Zionist community.

Yisrael had an idea: to bring together leading figures from across the political and cultural spectrum to devise solutions to Israel's internal conflicts. Boldly, the former head of the Yesha Council approached the Rabin Center—founded to preserve the legacy of Yitzhak Rabin—and suggested that it sponsor his initiative. The center promptly hired Yisrael to establish the Forum for National Responsibility.

After a yearlong deliberation, members of the forum released the Kinneret Covenant, which offered a shared vision for a Jewish and democratic Israel. But when the final document was released, Yisrael's name wasn't among the impressive list of signatories. He had resigned, following a personal dispute.

Yisrael's weekly column in *Ha'aretz* brought him a measure of satisfaction. As the token right-winger, he enjoyed scandalizing the leftist elite. Yisrael's columns bemoaned the decline of secular Zionism, and especially the kibbutzim. The children's houses were all closed; even kibbutz dining rooms, center of communal life, were being abandoned. Since childhood Yisrael had venerated the kibbutz. Yet he also resented kibbutzniks for opposing the settlers, for mocking their pioneering credentials. In his mourning and longing for the vanishing kibbutz was also a taunt: Look at the vitality of my camp, and look what's become of you.

Yisrael found his vindication in the growing influence of religious Zionist youth in the IDF. In Yisrael's generation, few paratrooper officers had been religious; now, though, Orthodox recruits were forming a new sacrificial elite. On Shabbat mornings in Ofra, young men in small knitted *kippot* precariously pinned to military haircuts gathered outside the synagogue exchanging army stories, while their younger brothers eavesdropped.

Still, the settlements also threatened the place of religious Zionists in the IDF. If a future government gave the order to evacuate settlements, would Orthodox soldiers obey? And if many refused, how would the army be able to trust its religious recruits? Yisrael understood: the settlements that had empowered a generation of religious Zionists could also destroy them.

A HOLISTIC UNIVERSE

THE GREENHOUSE WAS THRIVING. The young people who came here to learn how to raise fish with minimal water and how to grow lettuce without soil now included girls in kerchiefs from neighboring Arab Israeli villages, Russian immigrant boys from a drug rehabilitation center, shy Ethiopians with few words. The whole people of Israel, as Avital put it. For Avital, everyone was *hevreh*, even the donkeys and the fish. Two dogs were squabbling in the greenhouse; Avital chided them, "*Hevreh*, calm down."

But how much longer could he maintain this vision of a pluralistic Israel imbued with the old kibbutz values of work and improvisation and cooperative effort?

So far Ein Shemer remained true to its egalitarian essence. But even in this strong kibbutz, some were saying they were tired of being an idealistic elite: we're normal people, just like other Israelis, we don't wake up in the morning thinking of the big issues anymore, just of how to get through the day. The direction was clear. Other kibbutzim were moving toward private ownership and differential salaries. Privatization: how Avital detested that word! *Hurban habayit*, he called it, literally destruction of the home, but with a historical resonance recalling the destruction of the Temple. The god of money was penetrating even here. The temple of the kibbutz was falling.

The settlement movement had tried to inherit the kibbutzim as the pioneering avant-garde, but it had only divided the nation. Where, then, would the next vision come from?

Hevreh, this isn't America, Avital admonished his young people. This land of light and stone would yield blessing only if it was cherished, nurtured. Materialism was as much an existential threat—more!—than all the wars and terrorism. If the Jews lost their narrative, forgot the dreams that had brought them home, how would they survive in the Middle East?

Late at night, kept awake by anxieties, Avital sought comfort in the greenhouse. He sat there with eyes closed, listened to the drip and flow, the sprinklers forming mist across the lotus-covered pool, the rusty fans swaying thickets of reeds. And Avital one more organism in a mutually sustaining whole.

FAREWELL TO OFRA

WITH NEARLY THREE THOUSAND RESIDENTS, Ofra was thriving. There were three elementary schools, three synagogues, the girls' high school founded by Yoel Bin-Nun, a field school and even a center for cave studies, an art gallery, a library, a supermarket.

But for Yoel and Esther, Ofra no longer felt like home. Yoel's neighbor Yisrael Harel had resumed speaking to him, but some others continued to shun him. Yehudah Etzion, Yoel noted bitterly, had long since been forgiven, even though his mad plot to blow up the Dome of the Rock would have endangered the very existence of Israel; yet Yoel was despised as a heretic.

Three years after the assassination, the Bin-Nuns left Ofra. They moved back to Alon Shvut, the settlement in the Etzion Bloc that Yoel and Esther had helped found nearly three decades earlier. Back to the national consensus: even left-wingers acknowledged that the Etzion Bloc, close to Jerusalem, would remain part of Israel in any future agreement with the Palestinians.

The Bin-Nuns settled in a modest white stone house, the end of a row of attached single-family homes, with a strip of yard in the back. Hundreds of families now lived in Alon Shvut; thousands filled the neighboring Jewish towns and villages spread among the Etzion hills. Here at least, in its birthplace, the settlement movement had won. Yoel was grateful for what his generation had achieved. Wisdom, he said, required knowing what to leave for future generations to complete.

True, Yoel hadn't imagined, as a student in Mercaz, being confronted with the unbearable choice between preserving the intactness of the people of Israel and the intactness of the land of Israel. The cruelty of the dilemma: to be the generation entrusted with the wholeness of the land, only to be forced by circumstance to leave it again. But in the hierarchy of Jewish values—people, Torah, land—peoplehood came first. After all, Yoel argued, the Jews had been a people before they received the Torah and possessed the land.

In the patch of garden at the entrance to his home, Yoel planted a willow tree. Long ago he had learned from Rabbi Zvi Yehudah to love the willow, which lacked flavor or scent and symbolized the Jew without redeeming qualities—no less than the fragrant and tasty citron, symbol of the saintly Jew. Every autumn, before the holiday of Sukkoth, when blessings were recited over the four species—palm branch, citron, myrtle, and willow, evoking the unity of Israel—Yoel hung a sign outside his door, urging passersby to help themselves to branches of the willow tree. It was his way of spreading love among Jews.

HOMECOMING

UDI ADIV COMPLETED his doctorate at the University of London. His subject was how Israeli historiography turned Jewish trauma into Zionist myth.

He moved back to Israel. England was cold, he said, its people distant. Udi missed the Israeli landscape, even the intense Israeli temperament. "I'm married to this place," Udi told a friend. "A Catholic marriage."

Leah had returned to Israel six months before. The Adivs had adopted a two-year-old boy from São Paulo, and Leah had gone there without Udi, who'd stayed in London to finish the doctorate. Alone, Leah had brought their son back to Israel.

Leah had tried to understand Udi's need to withdraw, had hoped he would change. But Udi remained distant. Evenings he would leave the house without explanation and return late at night. They shouted at each other more than they spoke. Finally, Leah filed for divorce.

Udi got a job teaching political theory at the Open University in Haifa. He was a popular lecturer, encouraging students to call him with problems. One student was shocked to discover his past. "But he's so nice," she said.

He moved into a small apartment in a working-class block near the Haifa shore. Perhaps for nostalgia, he kept his old revolutionary books, like a collection of Castro's speeches. On the wall hung a satirical poster of Karl Marx as a construction worker, leaning against a rail and smoking a cigarette. The kitchen table was crowded with piles of books, Arabic newspapers, and Palestinian nationalist memorabilia, like a key chain with the Palestinian flag.

Udi regarded the Oslo process as a personal vindication. Not for his radical excesses—he had long ago repudiated the trip to Damascus—but for his insistence that Israel accept Palestinian nationalism. That view was hardly peripheral anymore. Growing numbers of Israelis were accepting the once-daring notion that the conflict with the Palestinians was between two legitimate national narratives. Even Udi's critical approach to Israeli historiography was becoming mainstream. A new generation of Israeli historians was examining the most basic premises of the nation's identity; after all, in the era of peace, it was now safe to dismantle myths that had sustained the nation under siege.

Even Udi's anti-Zionism was no longer taboo. Though the radical group Matzpen had long since dissolved, its antipathy to Zionism was embraced by some Israeli intellectuals. In falling out of love with the Israeli story, Udi had been a kind of harbinger.

On a trip to London, while waiting in Heathrow Airport for a return flight to Israel, Udi was approached by a stranger. "Do you remember me?" the man asked. Udi didn't. "I was one of your interrogators," he said. "So where are you in life?"

Udi gave him a terse summary of life since prison.

"Listen, Udi," the man said, "all of us are for an agreement with the Palestinians." By "all of us" he meant the Shin Bet.

Udi took it as a kind of apology.

ARIK ACHMON REBUKES MEIR ARIEL

IN MAY 1997, in honor of the thirtieth anniversary of the Reunification of Jerusalem, Channel 1 TV filmed Meir Ariel returning to the scene of the 1967 battle. Meir was accompanied by an army buddy, Yechiel Cohen, a cameraman for Channel 1 who had since become bitterly anti-military. The two men turned the segment into a cynical critique of the consequences of the Six-Day War and of the Israeli ethos.

Channel 1 invited Yisrael Harel to respond. Yisrael was head of the Association of Paratroopers Who Liberated Jerusalem and Crossed the Canal, custodian of the legacy of the 55th Brigade, charged with organizing the annual commemoration of the battle for Jerusalem and ensuring that the brigade's ethos was taught to a new generation of soldiers. But Channel 1 intended to screen the segment on a Friday evening, and Yisrael, an observant Jew, couldn't come to the studio. And so he asked his friend Arik Achmon to appear in his place.

Sitting in the Jerusalem studio of Channel 1, Arik watched the film segment with growing outrage. In one scene Meir and Yechiel wander the Arab market of the Old City. Meir says: "We returned and reunited and liberated. It's all a lie. For a lie of words people are dying."

Referring to the waiting period in the orchards before the Six-Day War, Yechiel says, "They brainwashed us. 'Jerusalem, the Wall—*Hevreh*, three thousand years, the land of our fathers! In another two weeks, *hevreh*, you're going to bring salvation to the people of Israel.' What salvation?"

Meir demurs. "There was a feeling of a war of survival, no?"

In another scene Meir sits under an olive tree, plays the guitar, and sings, "Jerusalem of iron, of lead and of blackness." Yechiel, overcome, covers his eyes.

The interviewer asks Meir if he ever brought his children to the Old City. "Never," Meir says emphatically. "To educate my children that I was part of the battle and to force Jerusalem on them when I myself didn't know what to do with this? . . . I didn't liberate anything."

Arik loved Meir, felt himself at least partly responsible for Meir having become a paratrooper in the first place. But this time, Meir had gone too far. *He and Yechiel are desecrating the memory of our fallen friends—*

Mustering his self-control, Arik said in a measured voice: "I'm not sure that they represent what they thought then. . . . Meir's song expresses totally different feelings. . . . They don't, at least, represent me.

"What the fighters of Jerusalem all share in common is pain. We had many, many casualties; the price was very high. Ninety-seven dead . . . four hundred wounded. Some are still severely handicapped. [But] I also feel deep satisfaction. Under nearly impossible conditions . . . we fulfilled a mission—a mission of rescue. . . . We didn't set out to restore the sacred sites of the nation. Central command didn't order us to liberate the land of our fathers." Instead, the paratroopers had been sent to Jerusalem to stop the Jordanian attack on West Jerusalem. Quoting a famous Hebrew phrase, Arik said, "'If someone comes to kill you, rise up and kill him first.'"

Arik concluded: "Maybe it's not popular, but I feel honored to be part of a group—in which Meir and Yechiel are also very respected members—that is the true elite of the people of Israel."

"I GIVE THANKS"

ON SUKKOTH, MEIR ARIEL built a big wood shack in his yard near the Tel Aviv beach. He covered the roof with palm branches, from which hung tinsel and colored glass balls. Musicians, kibbutzniks, religious penitents, dropped in at all hours, singing around long, white-cloth-covered tables to Meir's accordion. Meir offered each guest a pomegranate that, in his chivalrous way, he peeled himself. One Sukkoth he sat through the night arguing with a friend about the words in Ecclesiastes, "vanity of vanities."

Meir stopped performing on Friday nights. His Torah learning deepened. He kept a detailed journal of his daily studies—mostly Talmud but interspersed with Zionist history and Greek philosophy and Israeli literature—written in tiny script, two sentences squeezed into a single line. Meir often dedicated the day's learning to a friend who needed healing or the uplift of a departed soul. "To the loving memory of Hussein ibn Abdallah, King of Jordan, who went to the world of his fathers today." "For the souls of the three IDF soldiers killed yesterday." "For the success of the children of Israel in the European soccer championship." He argued with the rabbis: Why shouldn't a non-Jew be allowed to become a *nazir*, an ascetic? He compared Jewish thought, which he called time-dynamic, to spatial thought: the latter, he wrote, fears death and so battles the concept of time. But Jewish thought accepts death as natural.

The wild years were ending. Meir craved home, stability. He was writing some of his most beautiful love songs, and they were about Tirza. Every morning he woke her with coffee and cake in bed. Afternoons they took beach chairs and went to the sea. Fridays, he brought her flowers.

Still, hurts lingered. Meir wrote a song called "Get Into the Car Already," which depicts a weeping Tirza and an impatient Meir, who has exhausted his capacity for apology.

In an interview, Meir admitted a psychological addiction to drugs. "I need hashish to exist and be a pleasant person," he said.

Meir earned his first gold album: a collection of greatest hits. A poster of the album hung, along with strips of Indian cloth, in his living room. Life was better than he ever could have imagined. He was beloved by almost everyone who knew him, from the country's leading singers, for whom he wrote hits, to Zion the owner of the fast food place across the street from Meir's house and whom he celebrated in a song. Meir, said a friend, was the happiest sad person he knew.

AND THEN CAME THE INTERVIEW.

Meir hated giving interviews to the media. He hated the simplistic questions and even more his answers, which seemed to him either too glib or too emphatic. Still, interviews were part of the music business. And now that he had his own independent label, as Tirza reminded him, he couldn't afford to pass on the publicity.

"Meir Ariel Goes Wild," read the headline of the interview that appeared in the newspaper *Yediot Aharonot* on August 12, 1998. Russian immigrants, declared Meir, should be denied the vote until they've learned Israeli reality. The host of the Israeli version of the *Candid Camera* TV show was a "human monster." West Bank settlers were the "Chippendales" of Zionist pioneering. And homosexuality was deviant, and gays responsible for spreading AIDS.

Most of those barbs went unnoticed. But the outrage—and hurt—among gays was profound. Meir Ariel, of all people? The humane kibbutznik, troubadour of bohemian Israel? Columnists denounced him as a bigot; passersby spat at him on the street. Gay activists poured water on him as he emerged from a concert. "Meir Kahane, Meir Ariel!" they chanted, comparing him to the far-right rabbi.

A friend from the paratroopers said, "Meirkeh, let's get the *hevreh* together and we'll stop the harassment."

"God forbid," said Meir.

Meir and Tirza fled Tel Aviv. They moved to Pardes Hanna, the village bordering Kibbutz Mishmarot. They rented a stucco house with a red roof and a dirt yard, a larger version of a kibbutz house.

Meir stopped performing. I've been silenced, he told a reporter.

Shalom Hanoch, Meir's childhood friend and musical collaborator, pleaded with him to apologize. You're a poet, not a man of proclamations, Shalom argued. They should apologize to me, Meir countered, with unusual vehemence.

But then, on the eve of Yom Kippur, Meir wrote a letter to the gay newspaper in Tel Aviv, *Hazman Havarod* (The Pink Time), apologizing for what he called his ignorance, and affirming his abhorrence of stereotypes. He asked forgiveness "for hurting you, dear homosexuals and lesbians." He added: "Don't be surprised if I call you 'dear,' because you are dear to me as human beings." The association of gays and lesbians accepted the apology.

But when Meir began appearing again in clubs, few came. One night

Tirza drove him to a performance in a pub in Jerusalem; four people were inside. Tirza forbade Meir to play.

Meir's smile turned sad, weary. One friend detected in him an exhaustion with life. Mornings, Meir sat in prayer shawl and phylacteries, praying and writing songs. Sometimes he spent a whole morning that way, bound in devotion.

The songs he was writing were now openly, unapologetically, spiritual. One song was based on the prayer Modeh Ani (I Give Thanks), with which a traditional Jew begins the day. Meir's version is a modern Israeli's attempt to claim the tradition on his own terms. "I give thanks before Thee," he wrote, quoting the prayer, and then added his own words, "and to You." Even as he respected the formal language of the prayer, Meir needed to speak to God the way he spoke to everyone: intimately, as a friend.

Meir further expanded the prayer, giving thanks for "all the good and the bad and the good" that God has done for him, his family, his people, his land, and all of humanity—a circle of blessing that emanated from the particular to the universal.

Welcoming a new day also brought an awareness of mortality: "Slowly, silently / the future creeps toward us." But anxiety gave way to gratitude as he noticed Tirza beside him in bed. "It will be good, better than good, very good / It's starting this morning, this morning / You laugh toward me / from your sleep."

Meir had always seen the skull behind the face; now he was also glimpsing the soul.

IT BEGAN WITH what seemed like the flu. Take aspirin, said the doctor. But Meir's fever only rose.

When rashes appeared on his back and stomach, Tirza took him, against his will, to the hospital. After examining Meir, the doctor asked Tirza, Do you have children? They're abroad, she said. Tell them to come home, he said.

The illness was called Mediterranean spotted fever, caused by a tick and easily cured with antibiotics. But Meir had been diagnosed too late.

Tirza, dazed, accompanied Meir into intensive care. Meir smiled at her and said, "I'm under *hashgaha*," a Hebrew word that could imply medical care or divine protection.

Meir was connected to a respirator, a dialysis machine, a catheter, three IVs, four monitors. He lost consciousness.

Meir died shortly before dawn. It was July 18, 1999. He was fifty-seven years old.

Tirza held his face, swollen and blackened from cortisone. What have they done to you, Meirkeh, she repeated over and over, what have they done to my beautiful boy.

MEIR WAS BURIED in the little cemetery of Kibbutz Mishmarot, shaded by pine trees, near the cotton fields where he had spent much of his life. The greats of Israeli music gathered; Shalom Hanoch appeared stunned.

A kibbutznik eulogized: "Meir lived, suffered, and sang his loves. . . . One was Tirza, the one and only . . . to whom he dedicated his songs, whom he longed for and returned to from his wanderings. . . . She was the source of inspiration, the model for all the women he loved—and he loved all the women in the world. . . . His second love was . . . Mishmarot . . . whose lawns were planted by his father . . . Meir lived for many years outside of Mishmarot, but he never left the kibbutz and the kibbutz never left him. On holidays and on days of mourning a place of honor was reserved for him, the place of the tribe's storyteller."

Then everyone sang: "There's a pile of *hevreh* on the grass . . ."

A newspaper eulogy celebrated Meir as the greatest Hebrew poet since Alterman. A leading entertainer said that Meir's largely ignored album, *Charcoal Sketches*, should be included among the books of the Prophets. A gay music producer who had bitterly attacked Meir now urged Israelis to remember his "wonderful writing," rather than "a few words in the newspaper." Meir, wrote one critic, was the link between the rock music of Shalom Hanoch and the poignant songs of old Israel.

In death Meir became something more. Many young Israelis saw in his spiritual path a role model for a new Israeli Judaism, rooted in tradition but open to change. The kibbutznik bohemian turned religious Jew became a beloved and unifying figure, embraced by secular and religious alike, as if Meir had intuited a future healing of Israel's cultural divide.

TIRZA CHOSE a large, rough stone for Meir's grave, unique among the flat white stones that surround it. The epitaph is a line from one of Meir's songs: "I stepped out to breathe some wind." Meir inhaled not merely air but wind. Like so much of his work, the line is also a wordplay: the Hebrew word *ruah* means both "wind" and "spirit."

THE OPTIMIST

FOR ARIK ACHMON, life had never been better. He was doing what he loved best, advising leading companies and government ministries on strategy and reoganization, helping Israel become more efficient, more rational.

He was still stubborn, insulting on occasion, maddeningly self-confident. (Was it his fault if his opinions were almost always right?) But Yehudit knew how much he had grown. Arik learned how to say, "I love you," and came close to tears when he spoke of her. They took trips abroad together. On a cruise in Russia, a band played Soviet songs from World War II—"Cossack horsemen galloping to battle!"—and Arik and Yehudit happily sang along in the Hebrew translations of the Red Army anthems on which they'd been raised. (When they came upon a statue of Stalin in a village square, Yehudit felt an involuntary warmth, then immediate horror. How, she mentally berated her father, could you have taught us to venerate a monster?)

Yehudit's own career was thriving: she was recognized as one of Israel's leading experts on ethics in psychology. Between Yehudit and Arik there were five children, eight grandchildren.

The wounds of the past, though, remained. Arkia Airlines had become a major company, thanks in large part to the changes Arik had brought as CEO, for which he had gotten no credit. And he could have been a millionaire. When he'd left Arkia, he'd sold back his stocks—7 percent of the company. Now those stocks were worth millions.

"I have only myself to blame," he told Yehudit.

"Losing Arkia was the best thing that ever happened to you, Arik," she said. "You were so arrogant."

"I thought I could do anything,"Arik agreed.

"And then you came down to earth. You learned to tolerate weakness."

"I wouldn't have forfeited that experience for anything. True, I lost millions of dollars."

"It's only money," said Yehudit.

"And what I got in return was priceless."

IT WAS EARLY JULY 2000, and President Bill Clinton had just invited Israeli prime minister Ehud Barak and Palestinian Authority chairman Yasser Arafat to negotiate a peace agreement at Camp David. According to Israeli press reports, Barak intended to offer a Palestinian state on most of the West Bank and Gaza, with East Jerusalem as its capital. For the first time, an Israeli prime minister was committing to Palestinian statehood. Perhaps for the first time in history, a nation was voluntarily offering to share sovereignty over its capital city.

And Arik Achmon, a liberator of Jerusalem, was ready for the deal. He would celebrate the peace of Jerusalem, not mourn its redivision. He of all people wouldn't allow emotion to confound Israel's good. Israel would do what it had to do, in peace as in war. That, for Arik, was the meaning of Zionism: to take responsibility for one's fate in the circumstances that fate presented.

No, Arik knew, it would not be an easy or a happy peace, but a Middle East peace. Israel of course would have to remain vigilant. Arafat had disappointed, hadn't stopped the terrorism and the hate. Still, Barak was about to offer the Palestinians a state, just as they had demanded. Surely Arafat would agree. In exchange he would have to abandon the dream of destroying the Jewish state demographically by overwhelming it with the descendants of refugees from 1948. But what choice did he have? To go to war against Israel? That was laughable. Even Arafat no doubt realized that the Palestinians couldn't afford to reject another offer of statehood, as they had in 1947 to disastrous results. Say what you wanted about Arafat; he wouldn't subject his people to another catastrophe when the alternative was a Palestinian state with East Jerusalem as its capital.

Arik's greatest anxiety for the future of Israel was focused not on external threats—Israel, he was convinced, could defend itself against any enemy—but on what Israel was doing to itself by building settlements in the West Bank. In his systematic fashion, Arik listed the ways in which settlements threatened Israel. Rather than contributing to Israeli security, as settlers claimed, their communities were a burden on the IDF. Economically, the settlements were a black hole, devouring billions in government subsidies that should have gone to education and infrastructure. Socially, settlements were dividing Israeli society into two warring camps. Politically, settlements were undermining a two-state solution, which alone could save Israel from the demographic threat and an impossible choice between the two essential elements of its identity, as a Jewish and a democratic state. Diplomatically, settlements threatened to turn Israel into a pariah. And the occupation, which settlement building would make irreversible, was morally corrupting young Israelis, who were drafted into a system that gave them power over helpless civilians. If historian Barbara Tuchman were to add a chapter to her book *The March of Folly*, concluded Arik, it would focus on the settlements.

The depth of Israel's dilemma: for one part of the nation, remaining in the territories was an existential threat; for another part, the existential threat was withdrawing. How could Israel determine its relationship with the territories won in the Six-Day War without tearing itself apart?

But if the Palestinians accepted the historic compromise that Ehud Barak was about to offer, Israel, Arik was certain, would confront the settlers, uproot dozens of Jewish communities, and end the threat to itself.

Of course Arik was an optimist. To be an Israeli meant knowing that, with enough determination, any obstacle, any trauma, could be overcome. He didn't believe in God; Israel was a gift the Jews gave to themselves. Still—he felt a sense of awe at how much had been accomplished, in such short time, against such odds.

He had grown up with the state, had been present, one way or another, at every major moment in its history. He had seen Israel evolve from agrarian backwater to world-class economy, from a country fighting for its life with imported carbines to the military power of the Middle East. How many times had he been saved from death, had he and his friends helped save the state? The impossible victories, the self-inflicted defeats: How much history had been compressed into a single generation! If Arik were a religious man, he would have called his life a miracle.

WHO OWNS THE MEMORY?

JULY 11, 2000. President Clinton, Israeli prime minister Barak, and Palestinian leader Arafat secluded themselves at Camp David to negotiate a peace agreement.

Yisrael Harel initiated an ad in the newspaper *Ha'aretz* opposing the redevision of Jerusalem. The ad quoted a speech by Motta Gur to the veterans of the 55th Brigade: "And if someone will come who will try to take away Jerusalem, he will not, because you will not allow it. You will not allow it because it is ours by right. Because there is no justice in giving it away. . . . Jerusalem is ours—forever." The ad was signed by dozens of veterans of the 55th Brigade, including Yoel Bin-Nun. "We, paratroopers who fought in the battle for the liberation of Jerusalem, are committed to Motta's testament."

"By what right?" Arik Achmon demanded when a friend of Yisrael phoned, asking him to add his name to the ad. Motta, after all, had made that speech in 1995, shortly before his death; since then, nearly five years had passed, and the political situation had changed drastically. Who knew what Motta would say today?

Arik thought: Yisrael has used us all along, annexed the paratroopers' legacy to his settler agenda, to say nothing of advancing his own career. But this was one step too far.

When Yisrael heard Arik's reaction, he was unrepentant. He had used Motta's own words; what more did Arik want?

Yisrael thought: Arik presents his position as a matter of principle, but he's really just bitter because his camp has lost its preeminence to my camp.

Arik resigned from the board of the paratroopers' association headed by Yisrael. And he kept relations with Yisrael to a formal minimum.

A NEW CENTER

THE CAMP DAVID negotiations failed. Israel had endorsed a Palestinian state and offered to withdraw from about 91 percent of the West Bank; the Palestinians rejected the proposal but made no counteroffer. In September Ariel Sharon, leader of the Likud opposition, walked on the Temple Mount, accompanied by a large security contingent, to protest the construction work of the Muslim Waqf, which was destroying ancient Jewish artifacts on the holy site. Palestinian riots broke out in Gaza and the West Bank. Palestinian leaders cited the Sharon visit as the trigger for the second intifada, as it came to be called. Mere pretext, countered Israel; the violence had been planned long before, to coincide with the scheduled conclusion of the Oslo process in September 2000.

Two Israeli reservists who took a wrong turn on the way to their base and ended up in Ramallah were lynched by a mob—inside a Palestinian police station. The next day Israeli newspapers featured a large photograph of a young man holding his bloodied hands up in victory for the cameras. For the Israeli public, that was the moment when the peace process with Arafat died. A lynching inside a police station became the symbol, for Israelis, of Arafat's real intentions toward peace.

In December 2000 Clinton presented his vision of a final status agreement: almost all of the West Bank and all of Gaza would be Palestine, with land swaps between Israel and Palestine to compensate for "settlement blocs" that would remain under Israeli control; Jewish neighborhoods in Jerusalem would stay part of Israel, Arab neighborhoods would become part of Palestine. Prime Minister Barak said yes, Arafat effectively said no. President Clinton blamed Arafat.

Then came the suicide bombings. It was the worst wave of terrorism in Israel's history. The home front became the battlefield. The Palestinians, Israelis said bitterly, weren't interested in undoing the occupation of 1967 but the "occupation" of 1948—that is, the existence of a Jewish state in any borders. The Palestinian insistence on the return of refugees from the 1948 war and their descendants not to a Palestinian state but to the state of Israel convinced even many Israelis on the left that the real obstacle to peace wasn't West Bank settlements but Israel's very being.

Newspapers ran interviews with leading figures of the left who confessed to having been deceived by Palestinian leaders. Our world has collapsed, said journalist Amnon Dankner; the despair among my friends, he added, is similar to the shattering among Communists after Khrushchev's anti-Stalin speech in 1956. Yankeleh Rotblit, the lyricist who wrote "Song for Peace," which Rabin had sung onstage just before he was killed, told an interviewer that he was no longer sure peace was possible.

Yet even as they turned away in disillusionment from the peace camp, most Israelis didn't turn to the settlers' agenda. After three decades of vehement schism between left and right, a majority of Israelis now found themselves in an amorphous center. In principle, most Israelis accepted a two-state solution and were prepared to make almost any territorial compromise that would bring peace; in practice few believed that any territorial compromise could achieve that.

ARIK ACHMON HATED to be taken for a fool. And Arafat, Arik conceded, played us for fools. Maddeningly, the settlers had been right, at least about that. The choice, Arik concluded, had never been between land or peace. Israel's dilemma was far more cruel: it would have to abandon the territories—save itself from the occupation for its own long-term survival—but without getting peace in return.

Arik had a plan. If Israel couldn't occupy the Palestinians and also couldn't make peace with them, that left only one option. Israel needed to build a security barrier that would separate most of the West Bank and Gaza from Israel proper, prevent the unbearable ease with which suicide bombers simply walked across an open border into Israeli cities. And then Israel would unilaterally withdraw behind that barrier, and evacuate—forcibly if necessary—all settlers on the other side. Israel needed to stop waiting for the illusion of a negotiated agreement and determine its own security borders.

A Zionist had to believe in a way out, even if the solution was no solution at all.

A DOZEN SOMBER men and women, some of them leaders of the kibbutz movement, some former high-ranking army officers, gathered in the Ein Shemer greenhouse. Avital Geva had been holding weekly meetings among his friends—"the greenhouse parliament," they called it—to discuss Israel's future, and today Arik Achmon had been invited to address them about unilateral withdrawal.

The unilateralist idea, hardly Arik's alone, was gaining ground among desperate Israelis. Arik had helped found a group called Hetz (Arrow) to lobby politicians for unilateralism, and Labor Party leaders were debating it too. Avital had reached the same conclusion as Arik: the left had been correct about the dangers of occupation, but the right had been correct about the chances for peace.

On the plastic walls of the greenhouse were stickers from the left's old battles. One read: "The Seventh Day: Time to End the Six-Day War."

Avital, in dark blue work clothes, served chicken soup. "No one should speak," he said, "before the soup soothes your throats and warms your hearts."

The members of the greenhouse parliament sat in a circle on armchairs made of rough wood logs. Arik presented them with a map proposing the route of a security fence in the West Bank and Gaza, in effect an interim border. The implications of Arik's map were clear to these veterans of the left: the fence would be a marker ending the utopian dreams of both greater Israel and of Peace Now.

"Why not build the fence on the green line?"—the old 1967 border—one man demanded.

"That's a solution for a negotiated agreement," replied Arik. "The goal for now is to uproot the least number of settlers while keeping out of Israel's borders the maximum number of Palestinians."

Avital watched Arik with concern. Arik was red-faced, agitated. Avital had never seen him like this.

"We spent our entire lives defending the state," concluded Arik. "The danger now is coming from within. We have to separate ending the occupation from making peace."

Afterward Avital put his arm around Arik's shoulder and said, "Listen, man, you're not so young anymore, you have to watch your health. Don't take this so much to heart."

"There's no time for that," Arik replied. "We have to save the state."

PILGRIMAGE

IN A CLEARING in a pine grove on Ammunition Hill, near the trenches where paratroopers fought Jordanian soldiers in the toughest battle in Jerusalem, Yoel Bin-Nun, wearing a black suit and sandals, stood in the center of a circle of young people. It was close to midnight on the eve of Jerusalem Day 2004, the holiday celebrating Israel's reunification of the Holy City in 1967, and Yoel was leading his students, as he did every year on this anniversary, on an all-night walking tour of the battleground. In the footsteps of fighters, he called it.

This year, though, the group included participants from a pre-army leadership program for secular recruits who, like Yoel's students, were on a track for combat units and perhaps officer training. The young men had ponytails and shaved heads and earrings, and there were a few young women, too, in Indian skirts and kaffiyehs. One young man wore a sweatshirt with the words *Tikva LeYisrael*, hope for Israel. By bringing together Orthodox and secular, Yoel was honoring what was for him the spiritual essence of Jerusalem Day: the memory of Jewish unity in May 1967, which made the June victory possible.

Yet no date on the official Israeli calendar emphasized the divisions among Israelis as did Jerusalem Day, which was celebrated almost exclusively by religious Zionists. Most Israelis ignored the festivities, many skeptical of celebrating the unification of a city so deeply divided emotionally between its Arabs and Jews.

Hands on hips, as if leading a military briefing, Yoel described the vulnerable Israel of May 1967. "There was widespread unemployment," he said. "More people were emigrating than immigrating. The joke Israelis told was, 'Last one out of the airport, shut the lights.'"

Since then, Israel had changed almost beyond recognition. From a country of barely 3 million, Israel was now over 7 million strong, and growing. But in one way Israel had scarcely changed: its people still felt almost entirely alone in a hostile world. Israelis didn't merely debate the country's future but its chances for long-term survival. The Six-Day War had created a country caught in paradox: Goliath to the Palestinians but David to the Arab and Muslim worlds; the only democracy that was a long-term occupier, and the only country marked by neighbors for disappearance.

Yoel led his group toward the old 1967 border that had cut through Jerusalem. They came to an ultra-Orthodox neighborhood of graying stone apartment buildings and half-built yeshivas named for destroyed Jewish communities in Europe. Posters advertised pilgrimages to Hebron and to Rachel's Tomb and promised "protected buses," with bulletproof windows. A few men in black rushed through the quiet streets, avoiding eye contact with Yoel's group.

Yoel told of walking these streets on the night of the breakthrough into East Jerusalem. "I was twenty-one years old in 1967," he said. "I had just been released from the army, and this was my first reserve duty. I was given the assignment of finding the battalion that was going to break through the lines, and our battalion was to follow them. It was frightening to be running through empty streets and everything is totally black. And then the Jordanians began shelling us."

Wordlessly Yoel pointed to two stone markers, each with the name of a paratrooper killed on this spot.

"Why is Jerusalem important?" asked a young woman.

Yoel explained that Jerusalem had been chosen as the capital of ancient Israel because it was outside tribal borders. Each tribe was allotted its own territory, and Jerusalem united them all. "What unites the Jewish people isn't any holy place in Jerusalem but Jerusalem itself."

They came to an empty lot and a scattering of old red-roofed houses: the '67 border. They stood on the edge of a slope; below them was Road One, built where no-man's-land had been. Road One connected Jerusalem's northern and southern neighborhoods. But it also divided: on one side were Arab neighborhoods of East Jerusalem, on the other side, Jewish neighborhoods of West Jerusalem.

Yoel said, "It was a good idea to build a road in no-man's-land, where there were minefields and barbed-wire fences. To make this a living area. But you can look at this road in two ways. It depends on your point of view."

They crossed the road, into the silent streets of Sheikh Jarrah, a middle-class Palestinian neighborhood. From the garden of the American Colony Hotel came the scent of jasmine. "Be mindful that we're passing through a neighborhood," Yoel admonished. "We're not a conquering army. Please don't raise your voices."

They came to a fork in the road. "My battalion was supposed to go left, onto Salah a Din Street and from there to the Rockefeller Museum. If the battalion had gone that way, it would have encountered very little resistance. Instead our commander turned onto Nablus Road, which faced no-man's-land, and that is where the Jordanian fortifications were. The result of that mistake was very costly."

"How could he make such a mistake?" a young woman asked.

Yoel smiled. "I see some of you have trouble accepting human error. We had twelve hours to prepare for war. We were supposed to parachute into Sinai. At the last minute we were sent to Jerusalem. We went in without adequate maps. We didn't have guides who knew these streets. Mistakes happen all the time in war."

And what of the mistakes that followed the war? Yoel had come to regard both the peace movement and the movement for greater Israel—the two camps that had tried to determine the results of the Six-Day War—as utopian fantasists. Who more than Yoel had struggled with the illusions and failures of his own camp? And yet each camp had expressed something essential about Jewish aspirations.

Yoel paused before the entrance to an alley. The paratroopers, he explained, called this the Alley of Death. A Jordanian machine gun had been positioned at the opposite end, toward which the paratroopers charged. "Over and over. When one fell, another charged. For paratroopers there is no such thing as not fulfilling a mission."

They approached the hexagonal tower of the Rockefeller Museum, and entered the courtyard. Yoel pointed to a plaque commemorating three Israeli soldiers killed here by friendly fire.

The group walked toward the Old City walls.

They came to a sculpture of basalt stone, shaped like a massive uprooted tree trunk, a memorial for the Israeli scouts killed on the night before the breakthrough into the Old City. Yoel told the story of how the scouts, veterans of Unit 101 and the most elite commandos of the IDF, had missed the turn toward the Mount of Olives and found themselves exposed beneath the Old City walls. "It was one of the worst mistakes of the battle for Jerusalem," he said.

But, he continued, the disaster may well have saved hundreds of lives. The plan had been to block the escape route to Jericho; had the scouts succeeded, the Jordanian soldiers would have been trapped in the Old City and forced to fight. "The liberation of Jerusalem could have been a trauma for the people of Israel and for the world. Instead we entered the Old City with hardly a shot being fired."

Yoel had been careful all night not to preach faith, but now he couldn't resist. "This is how the Master of History arranges events," he said.

Rows of dancing teenage boys approached. They wore knitted *kippot* and white shirts and held each other by the shoulders. Some waved large Israeli flags. "May the Temple be rebuilt quickly in our time!" they sang. They were followed by police cars, army jeeps, and two ambulances. "I'm not so sure they understand what happened here," Yoel said of the dancing teenagers. "They take united Jerusalem for granted. It's not so simple."

Yoel watched them with unease, sadness. Suddenly he seemed aged. Once his place would have been among them. Everything had seemed so clear then, in the summer of '67, when Israel had abruptly emerged from the nightmare of annihilation into the dream of redemption. And when the settlers' opponents had raised moral and practical questions—What about the Arabs in the territories? What kind of Israel are you bequeathing us?—

Yoel and his friends had responded with faith. Of course it would work out in the end; what choice did we have? Reject God's gift of wholeness? Return to the terrible vulnerability of May 1967?

They came to the so-called Dung Gate, the entrance leading to the Western Wall. Above them was the Temple Mount.

"When I reached the Temple Mount that morning," Yoel told his group, "my commander said to me, '*Nu,* Yoel, what do you say?' I said to him, 'Two thousand years of exile are over.' That's what I felt at that moment. If the Israel Defense Forces are standing on the Temple Mount, it is the end of exile. I admit I was naive. Redemption is a process; it's complicated."

One day, he believed, Jews would celebrate the story of modern Israel as they now celebrated the exodus from Egypt. Perhaps with even greater awe: in the ancient Exodus, after all, Jews had left a single country, while in the modern exodus they'd returned home from a hundred countries. A people keeping faith with its lost homeland and returning after two thousand years: impossible. The farther away we moved from the founding of Israel, the more extraordinary the story would appear.

One day, Yoel knew, Jews would look back at this time and wonder: How had they done it? Reclaimed land, language, sovereignty, power? Reversed the destruction of the Jews back to their origin, their vigorous youth? Replaced skeleton heaps in death camps with paratroopers at the Wall as the enduring Jewish image of the century?

As a young man Yoel had wanted it all: redemption now. He had touched the Temple Mount, glimpsed the end of the story. The Jewish reverence for the Western Wall had seemed to him a retreat from the messianic opening back into exile. How to exchange the grandeur of the Temple Mount for a mere retaining wall without intrinsic holiness?

Of course Jews had returned home with vast dreams of redemption. That is who they were: a people set apart by God as a test case for divine intimacy with humanity. But in the tumultuous love story between God and His people, failure was no less instructive than success. And so the new dreams of Zion—socialist perfection, the wholeness of the land, even the seemingly modest dream of normalizing the Jews as a nation among nations—had each successively faltered. The messiah was still tarrying.

In their disappointment, some Jews had forgotten how to celebrate, how to be grateful. It was a recurring Jewish problem, as ancient as the first Exodus. But as Jews sang at the Passover seder, weren't the dreams that had been fulfilled in some sense enough?

The beginning of dawn appeared over the Mount of Olives. Yoel knew how to evoke drama: He had deliberately choreographed the night to end here, with the first light. The call of the muezzin came from green-lit minarets. Groups of Orthodox young men hurried past Yoel's mixed, anomalous group.

Yoel's religious students joined the crowds moving toward the Wall. Yoel took leave from the secular young people, shaking each one's hand. He retrieved prayer shawl and phylacteries from his backpack and headed toward the retaining wall of the Temple, grateful to be a Jew in this time.

ACKNOWLEDGMENTS

MY GRATITUDE FIRST of all belongs to the men of the 55th Brigade. I had the privilege of extensively interviewing all of the book's main protagonists, except for Meir Ariel, who died before I began this project.

No one contributed more time, energy, and wisdom to this book than Arik Achmon. I had the extraordinary good fortune to meet Arik as he was about to turn seventy and beginning to reflect on his life. There was no request that I made of him—and my requests became increasingly demanding over the years—that he didn't do his best to meet. Our working relationship became a close friendship. Arik tried mightily to protect me from errors in fact and judgment; the errors that remain are mine alone.

I am deeply grateful to my editor and friend, Claire Wachtel, who stuck by this book even when I violated every deadline.

Two institutions successively gave me a home and made it possible for me to write this book. The first was the Shalem Center, where I was a senior fellow from 2003 to 2010. Shalem's generosity and support gave me what every writer longs for, the gift of time. My gratitude to Shalem's Daniel Gordis, Yishai Haetzni, David Hazony, Yoram Hazony, Roger Hertog, Daniel Polisar, an especially devoted friend to this book. Natan Sharansky and Vera Golovensky, who were at Shalem during my time there, provided generous friendship and support.

The Shalom Hartman Institute, where I am currently a senior fellow, has provided the intellectual and spiritual environment in which I could complete this book and move to the next phase of my work. My gratitude to Rabbi Donniel Hartman, who has been at once mentor, colleague, and friend. And thanks to my colleagues and friends at Hartman who provided useful editorial feedback and other help: Alan Abbey, Tal Becker, Stuart Schoffman, Hana Gilat, Laura Galinski, Yehuda Kurtzer, Gil Troy, and Noam Zion.

The following friends provided generous financial support: Mark Gerson, Harold Grinspoon and Diane Troderman, Seth Klarman, Rabbi John

Moscowitz, Joe Nadler, Julie Sandorf and Nessa Rapoport of the Revson Foundation, Shoel Silver, Larry and Judy Tanenbaum, Phil Wachs. Thanks also to Michael and Laurie Davis, Michael Diamond, Wendy Eisen, Michael Granoff, Jim Moscowitz, Judy Nyman, and Orna Shulman.

I was blessed with a succession of superb research assistants. Rivki Rosner and Devora Liss saw the book through its final years; their devotion to and deep understanding of this project, along with their friendship and wonderful humor, helped me persevere. Rona Yona, Itiel Ben-Haim, and Avishai Ivri helped define and solidify the project in its earlier stages. I am profoundly grateful to them all.

As for my gratitude to my wife, Sarah, for all she put up with during these interminable years of "the book": *ein milim*.

Michael Oren encouraged me to write this book and continued encouraging me as I struggled to make sense of the material. I could not have seen this through without his love and friendship.

Sam Freedman and Jonathan Rosen provided the camaraderie of writers. They were devoted readers of repeated drafts and generously offered their wisdom.

Rabbi John Moscowitz, one of the most courageous Jewish leaders I know, helped nurture this project from the beginning.

David Suissa, for whom no favor is ever too much, has been a friend in all ways.

Julie Sandorf embraced me with her generous friendship and encouragement.

Carolyn Hessel of the Jewish Book Council has, once again, been a devoted friend.

And gratitude to: Esteban Alterman, for his help with the photographs but most of all for his courage and inspiration; Frédéric Brenner, for his great images; David Brumer, beloved friend who died too soon; Zev Chafets, for everything; Edoe Cohen, whose enthusiasm for this project helped get me going; Tim Cowles, who helped inspire me to write this book when, at a providential moment, he sent me as a gift his collection of *Life* magazines from the Six-Day War; Rabbi Yoel Glick, for his love and guidance and extraordinary friendship; Jonathan Kessler, Linda Frum, and J. J. Schneiderman, devoted friends of this project.

A succession of interns, working through the Shalem Center and the

Shalom Hartman Institute, provided valuable assistance: Rachel Adams, Benji Davis, Zach Fenster, Josh Freedman, Ariel Futter, Rachel Greenspan, Asaf Hadani, Elad Kimelman, Nicky Kolios, Candace Mittel, Valerie Oved, Nathaniel Rabkin, Adam Sadinsky, Clara Scheinmann, Davida Schiff, Maya Tapiero, Josh Wertheimer, and Jonathan Yudelman.

Yossi Alpher provided a copy of the English translation of his book on the Palestinian-settler dialogue, published in Hebrew as *Vegar Ze'ev Im Ze'ev* (And the Wolf Shall Dwell with the Wolf). Menachem Regev provided a copy of Meir Ariel's diary of his daily Torah study.

Nissim Calderon generously shared with me his research for a biography he is completing on Meir Ariel. The time we spent together sharing our love for Meir was one of the joys of this project.

The following graciously permitted me to quote from their songs, poems, books, articles, and films: Alut (the Association for Autistic Children), Uri Elitzur, Haim Gouri, Haim Hefer, Aviv Havron, the Hitman family, Arnon Lapid, Didi Manusi, Baruch Nevo and Nurit Ashkenazi, Gideon Ofrat, Talma Aligon-Roz, Yitzhak Rubin, Hemi Sal, Yisrael Shadiel, Hemdat Shani, Yoram Taharlev, Gidi Weitz, and Tamar Ze'evi.

Special thanks to Tirza Ariel for permission to quote from Meir's work, and for all she does to keep alive Meir's memory and spirit.

The following publishing companies graciously allowed me to quote from their works: Sifriyat Beit El, Hakibbutz Hameuhad, Keter, Ma'arakhot, and Yediot Aharonot.

Also thanks to Channel 1 Israel TV and Israel's Channel 2 for the use of archival material.

Along with interviews with the main protagonists, *Like Dreamers* is based on interviews with their family, friends, comrades-in-arms, and associates. My gratitude to the following interviewees:

VETERANS OF THE 55TH RESERVIST PARATROOPER BRIGADE

MOSHE AMIRAV, MEIR ARAD, Rabbi Yisrael Ariel, Yossi Asaf, David Atid, Menachem Amit Balu, Naftali Bar-Ilan, Yaakov "Vaksi" Barnea, Uri Ben-Noon, Amikam Berman, Shmuel Biran, Nadav Briner, Uzi Chaplin, Miki Cohen, Yechiel Cohen, Yitzhak Deri, Shlomo Dror, Ori Dvir, Haviv Elhanani, Eshed Eliezer, Yoel Elitzur, Hanan Erez, Haggai Erlichman, Yossi Fradkin, Yaakov Gafni, Gabi Garbiyeh, Matti Greenberg, Yiftah Gutman, Ran Hakim, David Harris, Amnon Horev, Yaakov Ingmar, Shimon "Kacha" Kahaner, Yehudah Kandel, Karni Kav, Menachem Kendelstein, Ofer Kolker, Moshe Natan Landau, Eran Levizon, Danny Matt, Reuven Michael, Zvi Mina, Itzik Nadan, Rabbi Gil Nativ, Meir Nitzan, Zviki Nur, Michael Odem, Shlomo Ofek, Yishai Peleg, Reuven Polechik, Noach Rabinovich, Moisheleh Rabinovitch, Yoram Ronen, Ido Rosen, Yosef "Yoske Balagan" Schwartz, Avraham Sela, Shmuel Shaked, Uri Shapira, Eliezer Shefer, Azriel Sorek, Nachman Syrkin, Danny Valeh, Yosef Vilchik, Aryeh Weiner, Itzik Yifat, Uzi Yitzhakov, Yoram Zamosh, and Dan Ziv.

SETTLERS AND RELIGIOUS ZIONISTS

SHIYA ALTMAN, Rabbi Yehudah Amital, Yehudit Amir, Vardina Bardugo, Avraham Bar-Ilan, Moni Ben-Ari, Michael Ben-Horin, Yohanan Ben-Yaakov, Shifra Blass, Eliaz Cohen, Rabbi Sha'ar Yashuv Cohen, Esti and Ronny Columbus, Yossi Faber, Uri Elitzur, Yehudah Etzion, Haim Falk, Avi Farhan, Ella Florsheim, Rabbi Yochanan Fried, Rabbi Menachem Froman, Haya Ganiram, Sima Gillis, Rabbi Avi Giser, Elchanan Glatt, Rabbi Shimon Golan, Hannah Grajouer, Rabbi Menahem Hacohen, Rabbi Alon Goshen-Gottstein, Elyakim Haetzni, Ze'ev "Zambish" Haver, Aliza Hart, Arieh Horowitz, Mira Kedar, Shalom Keinar, Yigal Kirshenfest, Benny Katsover, Rabbi Isser Klonsky, Miriam Levinger, Menachem Loberbaum, Tzipi Luria, Miri Maas, Baruch Marzel, Yisrael "Winki" Medad, Rabbi Yaakov Meidan, Gil Mezuman, Brigitte Milo, Moshe "Moshko" Moskowitz, Moshe Nahaloni, Yehudah Neuman, Rabbi Ze'ev Neuman, Yaakov Oppenheim, Henia Oppenheimer, Yochai Rodik, Motti Ronen, Varda Rosen, Amos Safrai, Dudi Bar-Selah, Bambi and Yair Sheleg, Sarah Shpitz, Haggai Segal, Hemdat Shani, Ze'ev Valk, Ruth Waldman, Pinchas Wallerstein, Rafi Yanai, Baruch Yefeh-Nof, and Vardit Zik.

KIBBUTZNIKS AND PEACE ACTIVISTS

ELI ALON, MANU ALON, Ruth Atzmon, Janet Aviad, Rivkaleh Avidor, Rina Ben-Nachshon, Yehudit Tidor Baumel, Lea Berenstein, Ilana

Carmi, Shlomit Canaan, Ran Cohen, Yuval Danieli, Shlomit Dekel, Ruth Eitzman, Avraham "Avremel" Frank, Lea Gilboa, Avishai Grossman, Batsheva Gurevitch, Uzi Hagi, Milca Har-Tal, Amos Kayatzky, Rachel Marder, Tami Mor, Ilana Neuman, Haggit Ofran, Amnon and Yael Peltin, Ilana Peltin, Dodik Por, Tamar Reiner, Tzali Reshef, Hemi Sal, Moishe Shachvitz, Yoav Shachvitz, Hedva Shain, Yehudah Sagi, Avraham "Pachi" Shapira, Rafi Shapira, Gidi Sivan, Doron Spector, Shlomo Svirsky, Avshalom "Abu" Vilan, Yehudit Zaidenberg, Adam Zartal, Haim Zeligman, and Miraleh Ziv.

FAMILY MEMBERS

OFRA AND MOSHE ACHMON, Yehudit Achmon, Tova and Uri Adiv, Tirza Ariel, Shahar Ariel, Shiraz Ariel, Udi Ariel, Aya Atid, Dror Bareket, Esther Bin-Nun, Enya Fast, Ada Geva, Rita Gur, Sarah Harel, Mona Hershkovitz, and Rachel Porat.

FRIENDS AND ASSOCIATES

EHUD BANAI, Ro'i Bar-Zakai, Dori Ben-Zeev, Naor Carmi, Gil Dor, Hanna Dvir, Yehudah Eder, Ari Elon, Eitan Haber, Issa Halaf, Lihi Hanoch, Shalom Hanoch, Haim Kessler, Yoav Kutner, Asher Levy, Mark Linton, Avihu Medina, Aharon Megged, Naomi Mizrahi, Yosifa Nachshon, Micha Odenheimer, Atara Ofek, Hava Pinhas-Cohen, Menachem Regev, Micha Shagrir, Miki Shaviv, Yizhar Shabi, Alona Turel, Micha Ullman, Meir Uziel, Hanan Yovel, and Ariel Zilber.

And thanks to the following for help in various ways:

Stefanie Pearson Argamon, Tikva Armon, Josh Block, Karen Brunwasser, Aaron Cohen, Ami Cohen, Florence Cohen, David Ehrlich, Leibel Fein, Jonathan Fong, Toby Perl Freilich, Ella Gadasi, Zach Gelman, Rabbi Steve Gutow, Maria Reis Habito, Alvin Hoffman, Toby Kahn, Michael Kotzin, Charley Levine, Jonathan Mark, Paul Michaels, Alicia Mog, Hava Na'eh, Lynn Pelkey, Martin Raffel, Asaf Rahmani, Nessa Rapoport, Matt Ronen, Rachel and Shlomo Rosner, Shmuel Rosner, Amos Sabah, Yehudah Shohat, Ruth Wheat, and Hannah Wood.

NOTES

CHAPTER 1: MAY DAY

5 "The Progressive World": *Al Hamishmar*, March 8, 1953.
13 "the beautiful and pure": Haim Gouri, "Hareut," http://www.izkor.gov.il/Song.aspx?id=19.
16"Once people were ready": *Alon Ein Shemer*, May 1, 1967.
17 "Comrades should know": *Alon Ein Shemer*, May 6, 1967.

CHAPTER 2: THE CENTER

25 keenly aware of their redemptive role: Shlomo Aviner, *Rabenu*, ed. Ze'ev Neuman (Jerusalem: Sifriyat Beit El, 2004), 229–32.
30 "A serious boy": Assessment by Yoske Ahituv, to Moshe Eyal and Lippa Aharoni, February 3, 1966.
32 "We must make more": www.meirtv.co.il/site/content_idx.asp?idx:5410&cat_id=3778.
33 "'They divided My land!'": Joel 4:3.

CHAPTER 3: BORN TO SERVE

38 Givat Brenner was torn: There were three main kibbutz movements. Meuhad, to which Givat Brenner belonged, was the largest (a majority of its members were pro-Soviet). The pro-Western minority within the Meuhad movement seceded and formed the Ichud kibbutz federation. Kibbutz Artzi, the federation of Hashomer Hatzair kibbutzim (to which Avital Geva's kibbutz, Ein Shemer, belonged), was entirely pro-Soviet. There was a fourth movement, far smaller than the others: Hakibbutz Hadati, the federation of Orthodox kibbutzim, a part of the religious Zionist movement.
39 On a Friday evening: *Yoman Hakibbutz—Givat Brenner*, July 26, 1951.
52 The 28th Battalion was absorbed: The Israel Defense Forces (IDF) is composed of a standing army of draftees and a reservist army. Young men enter the reserves following their three-year service as draftees. (Young women are drafted but are, for the most part, exempt from reserve duty.)

The paratrooper corps—which included the standing army's paratrooper brigade (the 35th) and, along with the 55th, another reservist paratrooper brigade (the 80th)—was Israel's elite combat force in the formative years of the state. Some two thousand men served in the 55th at any given time.

The brigade contains three combat battalions, each with about four hundred men. Those battalions are the 28th, the 66th, and the 71st.

CHAPTER 4: A TIME OF WAITING

55 On the streets of Cairo: Naftali Arbel and M. Mizrahi, eds., *The Six Day War* (Tel Aviv: Mizrahi, 1967), 25–26.

56 The reservists of the 55th Brigade left: Yisrael Harel, ed., *Sha'ar Ha'arayot* (The Lions' Gate; Tel Aviv: Ma'arakhot, 1972), 11–49; Motta Gur, *Har Habayit Beyadenu* (The Temple Mount Is in Our Hands; Tel Aviv: Ma'arakhot, 1973), 25–48.

58 "What's good about Arik": Gur, *Har Habayit Beyadenu*, 28.

59 One song promised: Yechiel Mohar (lyrics) and Moshe Vilansky (music), "Anahnu Na'avor" (We Will Pass), http://shironet.mako.co.il/artist?type=lyrics&lang=1&prfid=334&wrkid=8446.

59 "Nasser is waiting": Haim Hefer, "Natzer Mehakeh LeRabin" (Nasser Is Waiting for Rabin), http://shironet.mako.co.il/artist?type=lyrics&lang=1&prfid=168&wrkid=6342.

60 "The city that sits": Naomi Shemer, "Yerushalayim Shel Zahav" (Jerusalem of Gold), http://shironet.mako.co.il/artist?type=lyrics&lang=1&prfid=938&wrkid=1619.

61 On Shabbat afternoon, in the waning light: Harel, *Sha'ar Ha'arayot*, 26.

62 "It's clear to me": Ibid., 31.

65 Shabbat morning, June 3: Ibid., 36–37.

CHAPTER 5: NO-MAN'S-LAND

68 On Israel Radio: Chaim Herzog, Israel Radio, June 5, 1967.

70 Deeply tanned: Harel, *Sha'ar Ha'arayot*, 54–55.

71 The buses, slow and weighted: Ibid., 57–60, 160–61.

75 The battle hadn't even been engaged: Gur, *Har Habayit Beyadenu*, 194–95.

76 A medic, hearing the whistle: Harel, *Sha'ar Ha'arayot*, 83–84.

76 He was Yossi Yochai: Ibid., 37.

77 A paratrooper entered a courtyard: Avraham Shapira, ed., *Siah Lohamim: Pirkei Hakshavah Vehitbonenut* (Soldiers' Talk; Tel Aviv: Haverim Tze'irim Mehatnuah Hakibbutzit, 1967), 227.

77 From the back of an alley: Ibid., 117.

78 Their commander, Michael Odem: Ibid., 120–21; Gur, *Har Habayit Beyadenu*, 231–35.

81 "*Nu*, Motta, are we moving?": Gur, *Har Habayit Beyadenu*, 262.

83 Motta ordered tanks from another unit: Harel, *Sha'ar Ha'arayot*, 138; Gur, *Har Habayit Beyadenu*, 269–85.

CHAPTER 6: "THE TEMPLE MOUNT IS IN OUR HANDS"

87 Motta and Arik stood: Gur, *Har Habayit Beyadenu*, 288–92.

89 Motta took the radio: Ibid., 308–9.
90 "Cease fire," he ordered: Ibid., 316.
92 Rabbi Goren hurried: Ibid., 321.
93 Rabbi Goren sent his assistant: Simcha Raz, Hila Welberstein, and Rabbi Shalom Y. Klein, eds., *Mashmia' Yeshuah* (Mercaz Shapira: Or Etzion, 2010), 334. This is based on the version that Rabbi Zvi Yehudah told his students. According to another version (Harel, *Sha'ar Ha'arayot*), it was Captain Yoram Zamosh who sent the jeep.
96 "give me the shofar": Uzi Eilam, *Keshet Eilam* (Eilam's Arc; Tel Aviv: Yediot Aharonot, 2009), 93.
96 Motta watched the *nazir*: Gur, *Har Habayit Beyadenu*, 334.
98 Meir Ariel ran down the steps: Moshe Natan, *Hamilhamah Al Yerushalayim* (The Battle for Jerusalem; Tel Aviv: Otpaz, 1968), 334–35.

CHAPTER 7: "JERUSALEM OF IRON"

100 A doctor from the 55th Brigade: Harel, *Sha'ar Ha'arayot*, 172–73.
100 "People of Israel!": Ibid., 169.
101 Some Israelis came to loot: Ibid., 175–80.
104 Along the road were lines: Ibid., 190.
109 To Hanan Porat: Ibid., 192.
109 Accompanied by nurses, the wounded arrived: Ibid., 191.
109 "Many Jews risked their lives": Gur, *Har Habayit Beyadenu*, 335.

CHAPTER 8: THE SUMMER OF MERCAZ

113 As the crowds crossed: Jerusalem Post Staff, "200,000 at Western Wall in First Pilgrimage since Dispersion," *Jerusalem Post*, June 15, 1967; Amos Ben-Vered, "200,000 Bikru Bakotel Hama'aravi" (200,000 Visited the Western Wall), *Ha'aretz*, June 15, 1967; Yitzhak Shor, "200,000 Naharu El Kotel Hama'aravi" (200,000 Converged on the Western Wall), *Al Hamishmar*, June 15, 1967.
114 Despite intense pain: Aviner, *Rabenu*, 207.
114 Hanan Porat hitched a ride: Amia Lieblich, *Yaldei Kfar Etzion* (The Children of Kfar Etzion; Jerusalem: Keter, 2006), 375–94; Yochanan Ben-Yaakov, ed., *Gush Etzion: 50 Shnot Ma'avak Viytzirah* (Gush Etzion: 50 Years of Struggle and Creation; Kfar Etzion: Beit Sefer Sadeh Kfar Etzion, 1978), 307–13.
116 Every summer they attended: Lieblich, *Yaldei Kfar Etzion*, 261–68.
118 The symbol of that restoration: Haim Hefer, "Hatzanhanim Bokhim" (The Paratroopers Weep), *Bamahaneh*, June 12, 1967.
122 Hanan read a poetic account: Hanan Porat, *Et Ahai Anokhi Mevakesh* (I Seek My Brothers; Jerusalem: Sifriyat Beit-El, 1992), 13.
122 A dozen friends: Ben-Yaakov, *Gush Etzion*, 327.
125 "Before we speak about the moral questions": *Shdemot* 29 (Summer 1968): 15–27.

CHAPTER 9: THE KIBBUTZNIKS COME HOME

132 "the metals got switched": Tamar Ze'evi, "Shuli Nas'ah Tfila, Hatzanhan Ariel Higshimah" (Shuli Sent Forth a Prayer, the Paratrooper Ariel Answered It), *Ha'aretz*, June 25, 1967.
132 Her conversation with Meir: Ibid.
133 "We wish Meir success": *Niv Mishmarot* 428, July 7, 1967.
135 one, about a soldier returning: David Atid (lyrics) and Yair Rosenblum (music), "Hayiti Na'ar"(I Was a Boy), http://shironet.mako.co.il/artist?type=lyrics&lang=1&prfid=281&wrkid=1089.
135 "After urgent consultations with my wife": "Ha'ish Shehafakh Zahav Lebarzel" (The Man Who Turned Gold Into Iron), *La'ishah*, December 19, 1967.
136 "red Czars": *Alon Ein Shemer*, June 23, 1967.
139 Uri wanted to ask his son: Author's interview with Uri Adiv.

CHAPTER 10: THE CHILDREN RETURN TO THEIR BORDERS

143 "What do you want, *kinderlach*?": Author's interview with Hanan Porat. Slightly different versions of this meeting appear in several books: Lieblich, *Yaldei Kfar Etzion*, 388; Gershon Shafat, *Gush Emunim* (Jerusalem: Sifriyat Beit El, 1995), 27; Gershom Gorenberg, *The Accidental Empire* (New York: Henry Holt, 2006), 112–13; Haggai Huberman, *Keneged Kol Hasikuyim* (Against All Odds; n.p.: Sifriyat Netzarim, 2008), 28–29.
143 On September 27, 1967: Ben-Yaakov, *Gush Etzion*, 329–30; Lieblich, *Yaldei Kfar Etzion*, 392–93.
144 "Today we have removed the disgrace": *Hatzofeh*, September 28, 1967; Gorenberg, *The Accidental Empire*, 117.
145 One group of interviewees: The missing text was published by Shdemot, *Siah Lohamim Biyshivat HaRav Kook* (Soldiers' Talk in the Rav Kook Yeshiva), no. 29 (Spring 1968): 15–28.
147 The first rains: Ben-Yaakov, *Gush Etzion*, 330–32.
148 Letters of gratitude: Kfar Etzion archives.
150 "History is returning": Kfar Etzion archives.
151 "Is this where those crazy people came": Haggai Segal, *Ahim Yekarim* (Dear Brothers; Jerusalem: Keter, 1987), 21–22.
152 Novelist Moshe Shamir: Ibid., 22.
155 "Okay childhood": Meir Ariel, *Yerushalayim Shel Barzel*, record, Hed Artzi, 1967.

CHAPTER 11: ATTRITION

163 Another neighbor eavesdropping: Omri Asenheim, "Ad Hakatzeh" (To the Limit), *Ma'ariv*, December 24, 2004.

CHAPTER 12: THE INVENTION OF YISRAEL HAREL

186 Yisrael wrote an essay: Yisrael Harel, "Hatvusah Bamilhamah al Hayehudim," (The Defeat in the War for the Jews), *Ha'aretz*, September 5, 1967.

187 "A man, a lover": Natan Alterman, "Beod Erev Yored" (As Evening Falls), in *Arbaim Shirim* (Forty Poems; Bnei Brak: Hakibbutz Hameuhad, 1970), 65, translated by the author.

187 "There are those more beautiful": "Nishbati, Eynai" (I Swore, My Eyes), in Alterman, *Arbaim Shirim*, 5, translated by the author.

189 Yisrael wrote about: Yisrael Harel, "Banim Shavim Ligvulam" (Sons Return to Their Borders), *Zot Ha'aretz*, April 26, 1968.

189 In Café Casit: Batya Carmiel, *Batei Café Shel Tel Aviv, 1920–1980* (The Cafes of Tel Aviv, 1920–1980; Eretz Yisrael Museum and Yad Yitzhak Ben-Zvi, 2007), 231–56; Meir Suissa, director, *Kol Anshei Casit (Casit—Not Just a Cafe)*, 2010.

CHAPTER 14: ACROSS THE BORDER

208 Daoud was a self-taught political theorist: Yitzhak Rubin, director and producer, *Udi Adiv–Daoud Turki*, 2001.

209 Chinese-style cultural revolution: Eitan Haber and Yossi Melman, *Hameraglim* (The Spies; Tel Aviv: Yediot Aharonot, 2002), 169.

210 "Are you going to meet": Ibid., 176.

211 Udi's Syrian passport: Ibid., 177.

212 "We have many enemies": Ibid., 177.

212 In the quarter's police station: Ibid., 178.

212 Write about your life: Ibid., 178–79.

214 He described his trip to Syria: Ibid., 187.

215 Hashomer Hatzair leader Yaakov Hazan: *Al Hamishmar*, December 17, 1972.

216 Uri tried to meet with Hazan: Ze'ev Zahor, *Hazan—Tnuat Hayim* (Hazan—A Biography; Jerusalem: Yad Ben Zvi, 1997), 246.

216 "Off they went": Haber and Melman, *Hameraglim*, 188.

217 "Did you serve": David Zohar and Yosef Wachsman, "Hashofet LeDan Vered: 'Tireh Eikh She'ata Mistabekh' . . . Adiv: 'Hitkavanti Lemahapekhat Hamonim—Lo Leteror' " (The Judge to Dan Vered: "Look How Much Trouble You're Getting Into" . . . "Adiv: I Meant a Revolution of the Masses—Not Terrorism,' " *Ma'ariv*, March 6, 1973; Mordechai Ben-Tal, Meir Shoshani, and Aryeh Meir, " 'Yesh Lehapil Hamishtar Hatzioni' " ("The Zionist Regime Must Be Overthrown"), *Davar*, March 6, 1973.

218 "Do you know what people say": David Zohar and Yosef Wachsman, " 'Od Pesha Tzioni'—Hegivu Hane'eshamim al Hapalat Hamatos" ("One More Zionist Crime," Said the Defendants About the Downing of the Plane), *Ma'ariv*, February 27, 1973.

219 "I feel I'm going to prison": Meir Shoshani and Aryeh Meir, "Turki veAdiv Le' 17 Shnot Ma'asar" (Turki and Adiv Given 17 Years in Prison), *Davar*, March 27, 1973.

CHAPTER 15: BRAVE-HEARTED MEN

229 reservists in the 55th Brigade: the 55th Brigade was now known as the 247th Brigade. The brigade's battalions also changed their numbers: the 28th became the 416th, the 66th became the 564th, and the 71st became the 565th. For the sake of clarity in this narrative, the old numbers have been kept. (In 2010, the original numbers of the brigade and its battalions were reinstated.)

235 "Don't worry, I'm being careful": Talma Aligon-Roz (lyrics) and Kobi Oshrat (music), "Ein Lakh Mah Lidog" (You Have Nothing to Worry About), http://shironet.mako.co.il/artist?type=lyrics&lang=1&prfid=780&wrkid=4450.

237 But how would they get to the canal?: In 1970 Arik had founded a reconnaissance battalion, the first in the IDF, that concentrated the 55th Brigade's elite scouts units. The battalion, commanded by Arik, became a model for other IDF infantry brigades. The reconnaissance battalion was supposed to lead the crossing of the canal, but lacked sufficient vehicles to reach it.

237 commander of the 71st Battalion: Abraham Rabinovich, *The Yom Kippur War: The Epic Encounter That Transformed the Middle East* (New York: Schocken, 2004), 404; Yisrael Harel, ed., *Abirei Lev* (Brave-Hearted Men, Keren Hatzanhanim, n.p., n.d.), 42.

240 assault on the so-called Chinese Farm: In the first night of the operation in the Chinese Farm, the 14th Armored Brigade, under the command of Amnon Reshef, lost 120 soldiers. Another 62 were wounded. No IDF brigade had ever suffered such losses in so short a time. The following night, the 890th Brigade, the paratroopers' brigade of draftees, lost 41 soldiers and over 100 wounded.

240 "My guys are fighting there": Rabinovich, *The Yom Kippur War*, 362; unpublished account written by Hanan Erez.

241 The first six boats: Harel, *Abirei Lev* , 32.

242 Arik radioed Danny: Ibid., 32.

244 "God's Little Corner": Ibid, 36.

246 It was the eve of Simchat Torah: Harel, *Abirei Lev*, 45.

CHAPTER 16: "OUR FORCES PASSED A QUIET NIGHT IN SUEZ"

264 "An Invitation to Weeping": *Igeret*, November 20, 1973.

266 "Be a friend to me": Yoram Taharlev (lyrics) and Yair Rosenblum (music), "Heyeh Li Haver, Heyeh Li Ah" (Be My Friend, Be My Brother), http://www.taharlev.com/songs_selection_song.asp?id=77.

267 A winter night: Shafat, *Gush Emunim*, 27–33.

268 On a freezing windy morning: Motti Ashkenazi, with Baruch Nevo and Nurit Ashkenazi, *Ha'erev Beshesh Tifrotz Milhamah* (War Will Break Out This Evening at Six; Bnei Brak: Hakibbutz Hameuhad, 2003), 151–63.

269 Yisrael Harel was organizing a "university": Harel, *Abirei Lev*, 74.

270 The next day: Ibid., 74, 76.

270 "We, the paratroopers' brigade": Ibid., preface.

CHAPTER 17: THE HOME FRONT

272 thousands of demonstrators: Ashkenazi, *Ha'erev Beshesh Tifrotz Milhamah*, 194.

273 He awoke before dawn: text of manifesto in Shafat, *Gush Emunim*, appendix; Gorenberg, *Accidental Empire*, 267.

274 "Eight princes of men": Elyashiv Reichner, *Be'emunato: Sipuro Shel Harav Yehudah Amital* (In His Faith: The Story of Rabbi Yehudah Amital; Tel Aviv: Yediot Aharonot, 2008), 82.

275 If a nuclear war were to happen: Rabbi Yehudah Amital, *Hama'alot Mima'amakim* (Ascent from the Depths; Jerusalem-Alon Shvut: Agudat Yeshivat Har Etzion, 1974), 37.

280 The activists had sent: Shafat, *Gush Emunim*, 65.

280 They came to a field of grass: Ibid., 67.

281 Sharon, friends with Rabin: Gorenberg, *Accidental Empire*, 284.

282 He approached Rabbi Zvi Yehudah: Shafat, *Gush Emunim*, 68.

282 General Yona Efrat: Segal, *Ahim Yekarim*, 29.

282 One by one the squatters: Ibid., 29; Gorenberg, *Accidental Empire*, 285.

CHAPTER 18: "END OF THE ORANGE SEASON"

288 One autumn night: Shafat, *Gush Emunim*, 113.

289 "satisfy their passion": Rachel Katznelson Shazar, ed., *The Plough Woman: Memoirs of the Pioneer Women of Palestine*, trans. Maurice Samuel (New York: Herzl Press, 1975), 137–38.

290 "Why don't you establish": Shafat, *Gush Emunim*, 159; Segal, *Ahim Yekarim*, 34; Gorenberg, *The Accidental Empire*, 306.

292 On Passover eve: Liron Negler-Cohen, "Ve'abba Hozer Veomer: Meir Ariel Shelo Hikartem" (And Dad Says It Again: The Unknown Meir Ariel), Ynet, September 15, 2011.

293 "Look, Shimon": Shafat, *Gush Emunim*, 160; Segal, *Ahim Yekarim*, 34–35.

294 Supporters appeared with spring beds: Shafat, *Gush Emunim*, 160.

295 As he approached Ramle Prison: Marcus Klingberg with Michael Sfard, *Hameragel Ha'aharon* (The Last Spy; Tel Aviv: Sifriyat Ma'ariv, 2007), 241–42.

296 During one evacuation: Shafat, *Gush Emunim*, 153.

297 quoted the book of the Macabees: 1 Macabees, 15:34.

298 The morning of November 30: Shafat, *Gush Emunim*, 181–87.

300 Sympathetic kibbutzniks brought an oak: Ibid., 193.

300 Young people danced: Ibid., 199–200, 217–18; Segal, *Ahim Yekarim*, 33; Gorenberg, *The Accidental Empire*, 334–35.

306 Teach me Torah: Meir Ariel, *Brakhot Vehespedim* (Blessings and Eulogies; Pardes Hanna-Karkur: Ariel Hafakot, 2005), 66–67.

309 "And so, Avital": Eli Alon, "Avital Kemutzag Muzeoni" (Avital as a Museum Item), *Hashavuah Bakibbutz Ha'artzi*, May 23, 1975, 14–15.

311 Hanan Porat spoke: Yehoshu'a Bitsur, "'Ofra El Pritsat Derekh' Ne'emar Be-

hagigat Yom Hahuledet" ('Ofra Toward a Breakthrough,' It Was Said at Its Birthday Celebration), *Ma'ariv*, May 10, 1976.

311 "Across from the entrance to Ofra": Yigal Lev, "Hashorashim Shel Ofra" (The Roots of Ofra), *Ma'ariv*, May 21, 1976.

CHAPTER 19: A NEW ISRAEL

319 the Likud—"not more and not less": Israel Television, May 17, 1977.

320 "If this is the people's decision": Israel Television, May 18, 1977, interviewed by Yaakov Achimeir.

322 "Several weeks have passed": Avital Geva, "Le'an Lehafnot et Hatotahim?" (Where Should the Cannons Be Aimed?), *Alon Ein Shemer*, July 8, 1977.

322 Begin invited Hanan: Shafat, *Gush Emunim*, 318–19.

323 "Aha, here you are!": Yehuda Avner, "Bygone Days: The Night Sadat Came," *Jerusalem Post*, November 17, 2007.

324 "In all sincerity": Statement to the Knesset by President Sadat, November 20, 1977, Knesset website, www.knesset.gov.il/process/docs/sadatspeech_eng.htm.

324 "It must go on": Israel Television, November 21, 1977.

325 "I was born into the dream": Uzi Hitman, "Noladti Lashalom" (I Was Born for Peace), http://shironet.mako.co.il/artist?type=lyrics&lang=1&prfid=778&wrkid=2282.

326 On Saturday afternoon, April 1, 1978: Helga Dudman, "Politics and Manners," *Jerusalem Post*, April 5, 1978.

329 "I prefer to be called by my name": Smadar Shir, "Bob Dylan HaYisraeli" (The Israeli Bob Dylan), *Ma'ariv*, May 3, 1979, 40.

332 On a hot July afternoon: Yosef Tsuriel, "Mizbe'ah Verashei Egel Behafganat Omanim BeHevron" (An Altar and Calves' Heads at Artists' Demonstration in Hebron), *Ma'ariv*, July 11, 1979; "Hashalom Zakuk Lelohamim" (Peace Needs Fighters), *Alon Ein Shemer*, July 13, 1979; author's interview with Yuval Danieli.

335 "500 Against 350,000": Avi Rosenfeld, "500 Mul 350,000" (500 Against 350,0000), *Nekudah*, December 28, 1979.

335 "The key to defending Ashkelon": "Sharon: Nakim Kehilah Yehudit Hazakah Birtzu'at Aza" (Sharon: We'll Establish a Strong Jewish Community in the Gaza Strip), *Nekudah*, January 11, 1980.

339 Shabbtai Ben-Dov: Segal, *Ahim Yekarim*, 43–45.

340 Underground members stole explosives: Segal, *Ahim Yekarim*, 117–19; Etzion, interview.

343 "A query: To Whom?": Shlomo Burlass, "She'iltah" (A Query), *Alon Ein Shemer*, February 27, 1981.

344 "I see this as a *personal affront*": Avital Geva, "Ha'im Yukam Haheikhal Al Horvot Gan Hayerek" (Will the Sports Center Be Built on the Ruins of the Green Garden?), *Alon Ein Shemer*, January 9, 1981.

CHAPTER 20: BUILDING DIFFERENT ISRAELS

349 "They ask me, 'Why do you work late'": Avi Valentin, "Hagvul Hem Hashamayim" (The Limit Is the Sky), *Ha'aretz*, October 30, 1981.

351 There can be no settlement without land: "Glalei Izim Vehashe'elah Hayehudit (Goat Droppings and the Jewish Question), *Nekudah*, February 22, 1980; "Bimkom Ma'amar Rashi" (Instead of an Editorial), *Nekudah*, March 21, 1980; "Bimkom Ma'amar Rashi—Shvitat Hara'av" (Instead of an Editorial–The Hunger Strike), *Nekudah*, May 16, 1980.

353 "Stop this hunger strike": Harel, interview; Shafat, *Gush Emunim*, 352–53.

355 "It happened after prayers": Segal, *Ahim Yekarim*, 70–71.

356 "It isn't reasonable that Jewish hands": "Bimkom Ma'amar Rashi—Ha'ikvot Molikhim El Vaitzman" (Instead of an Editorial: The Trail Leads to Weizman), *Nekudah*, June 13, 1980.

356 "Who Harmed Coexistence?": *Nekudah*, June 13, 1980.

358 The stage was set: "Hahlatot Ve'idat Moetzet Hayishuv" (Decisions of the Conference of the Settlement Council), *Nekudah*, January 9,1980, 4.

359 "Any foreign administration will necessarily": Ibid.

CHAPTER 21: *HURBAN*

361 It was an early summer evening in 1981: Yossi Klein, "Journeys Into the New Israel," *Village Voice*, October 26, 1982, 22–26.

363 "I had never heard the word 'chah-chahim'": M. N. P. Michelson, "'Ish Lo Paga Be'edot Hamizrah Kmo Hama'arakh'" (No One Hurt the Mizrahim as Much as the Labor Party), *Yediot Aharonot*, June 29, 1981.

364 "some American millionaire": "Se'arah Be'ikvot Divrei Begin Al Hakibbutznik Hamitnaheg Kemillyoner" (Storm Over Begin's Comments About the Kibbutznik Acting Like a Millionaire), *Yediot Aharonot*, October 1, 1981.

364 Yes, Mr. Begin: No author cited, *Anashim Veshorashim—Sipuro Shel Kibbutz* (People and Roots—The Story of a Kibbutz; Tel Aviv: Photo Opest Omanim Meuchadim, n.d.).

370 Thousands of mourners: Aviner, *Rabenu*, 310–11.

373 "We must not injure": Segal, *Ahim Yekarim*, 127, 130.

373 "In another few weeks": Aliza Weisman, *Hapinui* (The Evacuation, Jerusalem: Sifriyat Beit El, 1990), 236.

374 A crowd gathered at a roadblock: Ibid., 267; Haggai Segal, *Yamit, Sof* (Yamit, The End; Jerusalem: Sifriyat Beit El, 1999), 249.

374 A song by Naomi Shemer: "Al Kol Eleh" (For All These), http://shironet.mako.co.il/artist?type=lyrics&lang=1&prfid=738&wrkid=4052.

375 "Following the first day of Passover": Segal, *Yamit, Sof*, 87.

375 Students from Yamit's military yeshiva: Ya'akov Ariel, "Yoman Yamit" (Yamit Diary), *Nekudah*, April 5, 1985.

377 Ten activists from a far-right fringe group: Weisman, *Hapinui*, 337; Segal, *Yamit, Sof*, 18, 113–14.

377 "The evacuation has begun": Weisman, *Hapinui*, 346.

378 General Chaim Erez: Ibid., 325.

378 The last to be evacuated: Segal, *Yamit, Sof*, 114.

379 "I believe that the sacrifice: Ibid., 234

379 "Don't start up again": Segal, *Ahim Yekarim*, 135.

379 Ezekiel's vision: Ezekiel, 37:1–14.

379 Hanan read aloud a list: Ibid., 135.

CHAPTER 22: THE FORTY-FIRST KILOMETER

388 "We Don't Want to Die in Beirut": Yehudah Kaveh, script and director, *Tkumah* (Resurrection) (16)—*Sedek Babayit* (Schism at Home), editor and producer of the series *Gideon Drori.*

390 One Phalangist in spiked shoes: Ze'ev Schiff and Ehud Ya'ari, *Israel's Lebanon War*, trans. Ina Friedman (New York: Simon and Schuster, 1984), 264.

391 Hours before the rally began: Michal Yudelman, "400,000 Rally to Denounce Gov't," *Jerusalem Post*, September 26, 1982; Yosef Valter and Yitzhak Ben-Horin, "Me'ot Alfei Mafginim Tavu Hakira Rishmit, Yetziat Tzahal Milvanon, Piturei Begin VeSharon" (Hundreds of Thousands of Demonstrators Demanded a Commission of Inquiry, the IDF's Withdrawal from Lebanon, the Resignation of Begin and Sharon), *Ma'ariv*, September 26, 1982.

392 Ten Days of Penitence: Reichner, *Be'emunato*, 154–55.

395 he had summoned this unusual meeting: Hanan Porat, "Hapulmus Im Harav Amital Al Eretz Yisrael" (The Debate with Rabbi Amital Over the Land of Israel), *Nekudah*, August 28, 1983; Yehudah Amital, "Bemilkud Hashlemut" (In the Trap of Wholeness), *Nekudah*, December 24, 1982; Yoel Bin-Nun, "E Efshar Lerabe'a et Hama'agal (It's Impossible to Square the Circle), *Nekudah*, January 14, 1983; Porat, *Et Ahai Anokhi Mevakesh*, 93–97; Reichner, *Be'emunato*, 158–59.

CHAPTER 23: CIVIL WARS

402 "PLO!" some shouted: Shlomit Hareven, *Yamim Rabim—Autobiographia* (Many Days—An Autobiography; Tel Aviv: Bavel, 2002), 127–32.

403 "Mourn and weep!!": Yoel Bin-Nun, "Velo Yishafekh Dam Naki Bekerev Artzekha" (And Innocent Blood Shall Not Be Shed in Your Land), *Nekudah*, February 27, 1983.

404 Yisrael published Yoel's accusatory lament: The murderer turned out to be a ne'er-do-well named Yonah Avrushmi, who had lived temporarily in Ofra. A settler, taking pity on Avrushmi, had offered him employment in his workshop. The media and the public didn't consider Avrushmi a settler, and the Ofra community wasn't held responsible for him.

408 A profile of Meir: Aviv Havron, "Zamar, Kmo Parpar" (A Singer, Like a Butterfly), *Koteret Rashit*, April 21, 1983, 32–33, 51.

412 A photographer from the magazine: *Ksafim*, July 4–10, 1983.
414 "What do you think about removing the Dome": Author's interviews with Bin-Nun and Yehudah Etzion (a different version appears in Segal, *Ahim Yekarim*, 112–13).
415 "my dark, dogmatic era": Udi Adiv to Leah Leshem, December 15, 1984.
415 "In order to raise the Jews": Adiv to Leshem, October 7, 1984.
416 "the luck of your life": Adiv to Leshem, February 27, 1983.

CHAPTER 24: IDOLATROUS FIRE

417 When Shabbat ended, Yisrael phoned: Harel, interview. A slightly different version of this conversation appears in Segal, *Ahim Yekarim*, 171.
418 An angry Yisrael: Yisrael confided to journalist Tom Segev his suspicion that the plot to blow up the buses may have been a Shin Bet provocation. Segev published Yisrael's speculation as part of a larger interview with him, in the weekly *Koteret Rashit*, on February 5, 1984. In a letter to the editor that appeared in the following week's edition of *Koteret Rashit*, Yisrael noted that he hadn't intended to accuse the Shin Bet and had been merely speculating with a colleague, and complained that Segev had in effect betrayed his trust.
418 "We have to face the enormity": Segal, *Ahim Yekarim*, 175.
420 The phone rang: Segal, *Ahim Yekarim*, 180–81.
420 "You have brought idolatrous fire": Ibid., 225–26.
421 Srulik, a beloved cartoon figure: Dosh, *Ma'ariv*, May 6, 1984.
422 "We always have to think about being moral!": Robert Rosenberg, "Levinger Remanded for Two More Days," *Jerusalem Post*, May 23, 1984, 1.
423 "Failure to temper the verdict": "Haninah, Bimkom Ma'amar Rashi" (Pardon, Instead of an Editorial), *Nekudah*, July 26, 1985.
425 "Waiting for Mashiah": Shalom Hanoch, "Mehakim Lamashiah," http://shironet.mako.co.il/artist?type=lyrics&lang=1&prfid=960&wrkid=2091.

CHAPTER 25: NEW BEGINNINGS

427 "What are your plans?": Yitzhak Rubin, director and producer, *Udi Adiv—Daoud Turki*, 2001.
428 "an act which can't be explained": Amiram Cohen, "Hakeleh Hakaful Shel Udi Adiv" (The Double Prison of Udi Adiv), *Al Hamishmar*, May 24, 1985.
434 They set out during the harvest holiday: Ido Sela, director, *Masa Habhirot Shel Meir Ariel* (Meir Ariel's Election Campaign) (Ariel Hotzaot, 1987).
436 "I dare to say we have no real reason": *Niv Mishmarot*, November 29, 1987.
437 David Grossman, the Israeli novelist: David Grossman, *The Yellow Wind*, trans. Haim Watzman (New York: Farrar, Straus and Giroux, 1988).

CHAPTER 26: UNDER SIEGE

441 "We are prevented": Ofra archives.

445 "Some young people": Gorenberg, *The Accidental Empire*, 333.

447 "[We must] redeem the Mount from its shame": Yossi Klein Halevi, "Coming Home—An Underground Leader Returns," *Long Island Jewish World*, March 31–April 6, 1989.

449 Writing in *Nekudah*: Yoel Bin-Nun, "Rak Haskamah Leumit Ta'atzor et Ha'hidarderut Lemilhamah Kolelet" (Only National Consensus Will Stop the Slide Toward Total War), *Nekudah*, February 26, 1988.

CHAPTER 27: A NEW ISRAEL, AGAIN

463 July 13, 1992: The letters written by Yoel Bin-Nun to Yitzhak Rabin that appear in chapters 27 and 28 are from Yoel's archives.

464 Gideon Ofrat, preeminent curator: Gideon Ofrat, "Yomanei Geva," in Gideon Ofrat, ed., *Avital Geva: Hamamah* (Avital Geva: Greenhouse) (1993): 15–29).

470 The metal outlines of a greenhouse: Itamar Shweika, director, Nechemia Sal, producer, *Melafefonim BeVenetziah II (Cucumbers in Venice II)* (Ulpanei Kibbutz Barkai, 1993).

472 "Leave me alone": Live broadcast from the opening of the Biennale, Israel TV, Channel 2, June 9,1993.

474 Do you light a fire on Shabbat?: Liora Hacohen, "Az Nathil Kol Yom Lehitpalel" (So We'll Start to Pray Every Day), *Ma'ariv*, March 18, 1994.

CHAPTER 28: ALMOST NORMAL

481 a drawing of a dove: *Yediot Aharonot* (Mamon section), September 15, 1993.

483 "the government of evil": "Bimkom Ma'amar Rashi, Hamahaneh Hu Tahor" (Instead of an Editorial, The Camp Is Pure), *Nekudah*, July 1994, 14.

489 "repulsive act": "Bimkom Ma'amar Rashi, Vehayah Mahanenu Tahor" (Instead of an Editorial, And Our Camp Shall Be Pure), *Nekudah*, March 1994, 14.

492 "Everything! . . . This approach": Yoel Bin-Nun, "Kol Hanotesh Beyamim Eleh Hu Arik" (Everyone Who Defects in This Time Is a Deserter), *Nekudah*, May 1994, 32–35.

493 For a man violating: Joseph Alpher, *And the Wolf Shall Dwell with the Wolf* (unpublished translation of the Hebrew work, *Vegar Ze'ev Im Ze'ev: Hamitnahalim Vehafalestinim*; Tel Aviv: Hakibbutz Hameuhad, 2001), no page cited.

496 In an old country house: Alpher, *And the Wolf Shall Dwell with the Wolf*, no page cited.

506 Sensing a threat: Haggai Huberman, *Hanan Porat—Sippur Hayav* (Hanan Porat—The Story of His Life; Tel Aviv: Yediot Aharonot, 2013), 260–62; Nadav Shragai, *Al Em Haderekh: Sippuro shel Kever Rahel* (At the Crossroads: The Story of Rachel's Tomb; Jerusalem: She'arim Leheker Yerushalayim, 2008), 198–99.

506 While waiting to enter: Huberman, *Hanan Porat*, 262–63; Shragai, *Al Em Haderekh*, 207.

CHAPTER 29: CAREENING TOWARD THE CENTER

512 The emergency meeting: "Mismakh: Kenes Heshbon Hanefesh" (Document: The Assembly of Self-Reckoning), *Nekudah*, December 1995, 58–65.

521 In May 1997: Eitan Oren, director, *Mabat Sheni*, June 6, 1997.

523 He kept a detailed journal: Meir Ariel's unpublished journal, courtesy of Menachem Regev.

523 "I need hashish to exist": Zvi Gilat, "Meir Ariel: Homer Meshubah" (Meir Ariel: Excellent Stuff), *Ma'ariv*, April 4, 1997.

524 "Meir Ariel Goes Wild": Tzachi Cohen, "Meir Ariel Mishtolel" (Meir Ariel Goes Wild), *Yediot Aharonot* (Zmanim Moderniyim), August 12, 1998.

524 "for hurting you, dear homosexuals": Meir's letter to *Hazman Havarod* quoted in Yuval Karni, "Hazamar Meir Ariel Mevakesh Slicha Mehahomosexualim" (The Singer Meir Ariel Asks Forgiveness from the Homosexuals), *Yediot Aharonot*, October 7, 1998.

526 "Meir lived, suffered, and sang his loves": David Atid, "Dvarim Al Kivro Shel Meir Ariel BeMishmarot" (Words Spoken at the Grave of Meir Ariel in Mishmarot), *Koreh Bamoshavah*, July 23, 1999.

530 an ad in the newspaper *Ha'aretz*: *Ha'aretz*, July 28, 2000.

BIBLIOGRAPHY

BOOKS IN ENGLISH

Alpher, Joseph. "And the Wolf Shall Dwell with the Wolf" (unpublished translation of the Hebrew work, *Vegar Ze'ev Im Ze'ev: Hamitnahalim Vehafalestinim*). Tel Aviv: Hakibbutz Hameuhad, 2001.

Arbel, Naftali, and M. Mizrahi, eds. *The Six-Day War*. Tel Aviv: M. Mizrahi, 1967.

Gorenberg, Gershom. *The Accidental Empire*. New York: Henry Holt, 2006.

Grossman, David. *The Yellow Wind*. Trans. by Haim Watzman. New York: Farrar, Straus and Giroux, 1988.

Katznelson Shazar, Rachel, ed. *The Plough Woman: Memoirs of the Pioneer Women of Palestine*. Trans. Maurice Samuel. New York: Herzl Press, 1975.

Kook, Abraham Isaac. *The Lights of Penitence, Lights of Holiness, the Moral Principles, Essays, Letters and Poems*. Trans. by Ben Zion Bokser. Mahwah, NJ: Paulist Press, 1977.

Moskin, J. Robert. *Among Lions*. New York: Ballantine, 1983.

Oren, Michael, *Six Days of War*. New York: Oxford University Press, 2002.

Rabinovich, Abraham. *The Yom Kippur War: The Epic Encounter That Transformed the Middle East*. New York: Schocken, 2004.

Schiff, Ze'ev, and Ehud Ya'ari. *Israel's Lebanon War*. Trans. by Ina Friedman. New York: Simon and Schuster, 1984.

Segal, Haggai. *Dear Brothers: The West Bank Jewish Underground*. Woodmere, NY: Beit-Shammai, 1988.

BOOKS IN HEBREW

Alpher, Yossi. *Vegar Ze'ev Im Ze'ev: Hamitnahalim Vehafalestinim*. Tel Aviv: Hakibbutz Hameuhad, 2001.

Alterman, Natan. *Arbaim Shirim*. Tel Aviv: Hakibbutz Hameuhad, 1970.

Amital, Yehudah. *Hama'alot Mima'amakim*. Jerusalem; Alon Shvut: Agudat Yeshivat Har Etzion, 1974.

Anashim veShorashim—Sipuro Shel Kibbutz. Tel Aviv: Photo Opest Omanim Meuchadim, n.d.

Ariel, Meir. *Brakhot Vehespedim*. Pardes Hanna-Karkur: Ariel Hafakot, 2005.

Ashkenazi, Motti, Nurit Ashkenazi, and Baruch Nevo. *Ha'erev Beshesh Tifrotz Milhamah*. Tel Aviv: Hakibbutz Hameuhad, 2003.

Avidor HaCohen, Shmuel. *Ha'ish Neged Hazerem*. Tel Aviv: Yediot Aharonot, 2002.

Aviner, Shlomo. *Rabenu*. Edited by Ze'ev Neuman. Jerusalem: Sifriyat Beit El , 2004.

Ben-Yaakov, Yochanan. *Gush Etzion: 50 Shnot Ma'avak Viyetzira*. Kfar Etzion: Beit Sefer Sadeh Kfar Etzion, 1978.

Carmiel, Batya. *Batei Café Shel Tel Aviv, 1920–1980*. Tel Aviv: Eretz Yisrael Museum and Yad Yitzhak Ben-Zvi, 2007.

Eilam, Uzi. *Keshet Eilam*. Tel Aviv: Yediot Aharonot, 2009.

Haber, Eitan, and Yossi Melman. *Hameraglim*. Tel Aviv: Yediot Aharonot, 2002.

Harel, Yisrael, ed. *Sha'ar Ha'arayot*. Tel Aviv: Ma'arakhot, 1972.

———, ed. *Abirei Lev*. N.p.: Keren Hatzanhanim, n.d.

Hareven, Shlomit. *Yamim Rabim—Autobiographia*. Tel Aviv: Bavel, 2002.

Huberman, Haggai. *Kneged Kol Hasikuyim*. N.p.: Sifriyat Netzarim, 2008.

———. *Hanan Porat: Sippur Hayav*. Tel Aviv: Yediot Aharonot, 2013.

Gur, Motta. *Har Habayit Beyadenu*. Tel Aviv: Ma'arakhot, 1973.

Klingberg, Marcus, and Michael Sfard. *Hameragel Ha'aharon*. Tel Aviv: Sifriyat Ma'ariv, 2007.

Kutner, Yoav, ed. *Meir Ariel—Atzma'i Bashetah*. N.p.: Kinneret, 2010.

Lieblich, Amia. *Yaldei Kfar Etzion*. Jerusalem: Keter, 2006.

Natan, Moshe. *Hamilhamah Al Yerushalayim*. Tel Aviv: Otpaz, 1968.

Ofrat, Gideon. *Avital Geva: Hamama*. N.p., 1993.

Porat, Hanan, *Et Ahai Anokhi Mevakesh*. Beit-El: Sifriyat Beit-El, 1992.

Raz, Simcha, Hila Velberstein, and Shalom Y. Klein. *Mashmia' Yeshuah*. Mercaz Shapira: Or Etzion, 2010.

Reichner, Elyashiv. *Be'emunato: Sipuro Shel Harav Yehudah Amital*. Tel Aviv: Yediot Aharonot, 2008.

Segal, Haggai. *Ahim Yekarim*. Jerusalem: Keter, 1987.

———. *Yamit, Sof*. Jerusalem: Sifriyat Beit El, 1999.

Shafat, Gershon. *Gush Emunim*. Jerusalem: Sifriyat Beit-El, 1995.

Shapira, Avraham, ed. *Siah Lohamim: Pirkei Hakshavah Vehitbonenut*. Tel Aviv: Kvutzat Haverim Tzeirim Mehatenuah Hakibbutzit, 1967.

Weisman, Aliza. *Hapinui*. Jerusalem: Sifriyat Beit El, 1990.

Zahor, Ze'ev. *Hazan—Tnuat Hayim: Hashomer Hatzair, Hakibbutz Ha'artsi, Mapam*. Jerusalem: Yad Ben Zvi, 1997.

FILMS

Kaveh, Yehudah, director. *Tkuma (16)—Sedek Babayit*, 1995. Editor and producer of the entire series: Gideon Drori.

Rubin, Yitzhak, director and producer. *Udi Adiv–Daoud Turki*, 2001.

Sela, Ido, director. *Masa Habhirot Shel Meir Ariel*, 1987. Producer: Ariel Hotzaot.

Shweika, Itamar, director. *Melafefonim BeVenetziah II*, 1993. Producer: Nechemia Sal; edited in Ulpanei Kibbutz Barkai.

Suissa, Meir, director. *Kol Anshei Casit*, 2010. Producer: Doron Eran.

NEWSPAPERS AND PERIODICALS

Al HaMishmar
Alon Ein Shemer
Alon Gan Shmuel
Alon Ofra
Bamahaneh
Davar
Ha'aretz
Hashavua Bakibutz Ha'artzi
Hatzofeh
Igeret
Jerusalem Post
Koreh Bamoshava
Koteret Rashit
La'isha
Ma'ariv
Nekudah
Niv Mishmarot
Shdemot
Yoman Hakibbutz—Givat Brenner
Yediot Aharonot
Zot Ha'aretz

LYRICS

Meir Ariel, "Agadat Deshe" (Legend of the Lawn). Music: Shalom Hanoch.
Meir Ariel, "Yerushalayim Shel Barzel" (Jerusalem of Iron). Music: Naomi Shemer.
Meir Ariel, "Laylah Shaket Avar Al Kohoteinu BeSuetz" (Our Forces Passed a Quiet Night in Suez). Music: Meir Ariel.
Meir Ariel, "Midrash Yonati" (My Dove's Midrash). Music: Meir Ariel.
Meir Ariel, "Neshel Hanahash" (The Snake's Shed Skin). Music: Meir Ariel.
Meir Ariel, "Haben Adam Eino Ela" (The Human Being Is Nothing But). Music: Meir Ariel
Meir Ariel, "Modeh Ani" (I Give Thanks). Music: Meir Ariel
Haim Gouri, "Hareut" (The Camaradie of Fighters). Music: Sasha Argov.
Shalom Hanoch, "Mehakim Lamashiah" (Waiting for Mashiah). Music: Shalom Hanoch.
Haim Hefer, "Natzer Mehake LeRabin" (Nasser Is Waiting for Rabin). Music: Traditional.
Uzi Hitman, "Noladti Lashalom" (I Was Born for Peace). Music: Uzi Hitman.
Yechiel Mohar, "Anahnu Na'avor" (We Will Pass). Music: Moshe Vilansky.
Naomi Shemer, "Yerushalayim Shel Zahav" (Jerusalem of Gold). Music: Naomi Shemer.
Talma Aligon-Roz, "Ein Lakh Ma Lidog" (You Have Nothing to Worry About). Music: Kobi Oshrat.
Yoram Taharlev, "Heyeh Li Haver, Heyeh Li Ah" (Be My Friend, Be My Brother). Music: Yair Rosenblum.

RADIO AND TELEVISION

Kol Israel
Channel 1
Channel 2

PRIVATE PAPERS

Bin-Nun, Yoel
Adiv, Udi
Ariel, Meir

INDEX

Page numbers in *italics* refer to map citations of locations.

ABOUT THE AUTHOR

YOSSI KLEIN HALEVI is a senior fellow at the Shalom Hartman Institute in Jerusalem and a contributing editor of the *New Republic.* An internationally respected commentator on Israeli and Middle Eastern affairs, he writes often for leading American publications, such as the *New York Times*, the *Wall Street Journal*, and *Foreign Affairs.* He is author of *At the Entrance to the Garden of Eden: A Jew's Search for God with Christians and Muslims in the Holy Land*, and *Memoirs of a Jewish Extremist.* He lives in Jerusalem with his wife, Sarah, a landscape designer; they have three children.